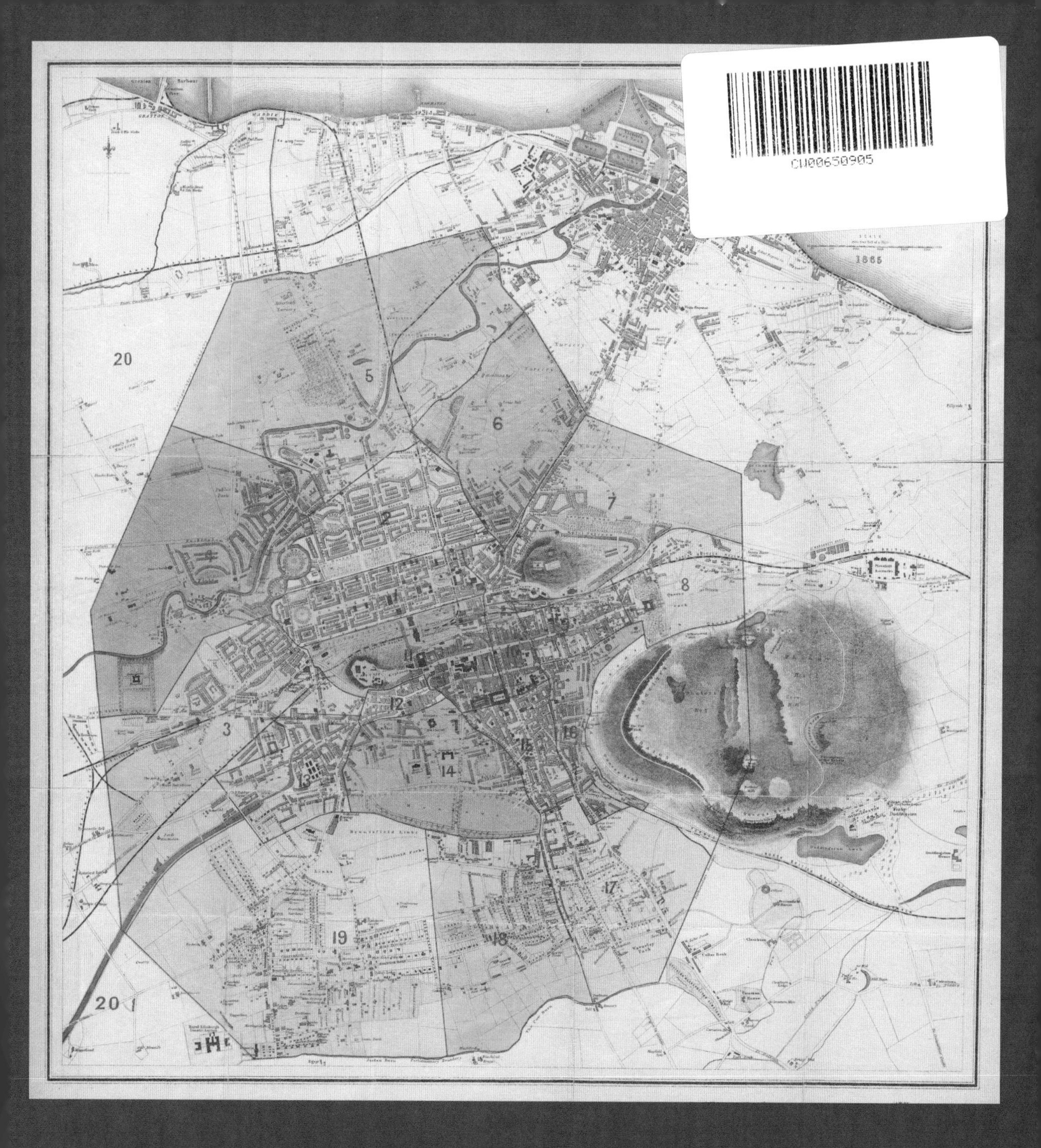

Map of sanitary districts in H.D. Littlejohn *Report on the Sanitary Condition of the City of Edinburgh* (1865).
Scale of original 5.2 inches to one mile.

INSANITARY CITY

Henry Duncan Littlejohn, 1859, aged 33
Photograph by John Moffat, 1819–94.

INSANITARY CITY

Henry Littlejohn and the Condition of Edinburgh

PAUL LAXTON and RICHARD RODGER

Insanitary City: Henry Littlejohn and the Condition of Edinburgh

First edition

First published in 2013 by
Carnegie Publishing Ltd
Chatsworth Road
Lancaster LA1 4SL
www.carnegiepublishing.com

British Library Cataloguing-in-Publication data
A catalogue record for this book is available from the British Library

ISBN 978-1-85936-220-4 *hardback*

Designed and typeset in Ehrhardt and Myriad by BBR, Sheffield
Printed and bound in China by 1010 Printing

Dedicated
to the memory of
Rachel Antoinette Hedderwick
1920 · 2008
last grandchild of Sir Henry Littlejohn

Contents

List of figures

Picture acknowledgements

Images and the permission to reproduce them have been obtained from a variety of institutions and individuals. Each of these is gratefully acknowledged, and identified in brief in the captions to figures. Where no attribution exists in the captions then the authors have produced these diagrams, images and maps and state here their copyright over them.

The sources for the figures are noted as follows:

City Art Centre, Edinburgh Museums and Galleries: 3.10; 3.19; 4.15
Edinburgh City Archives: 1.3; 1.9; 1.10; 1.11; 3.1; 3.7; 3.11; 3.12; 4.1; 4.2; 4.12; 4.14; 5.9; 6.2
Edinburgh Central Library: 2.4; 2.5; 4.7; 5.12
Liverpool University Special Collections: 3.15
Lothian Health Service Archives: 2.7
National Museums of Scotland: 6.5
National Library of Scotland, Map Library: end papers; 2.1; 3.9; 3.17; 4.4; 4.8; 4.13; 4.19; 4.20; 5.4; 5.5; 5.16.
National Registers of Scotland: 1.7
Royal Commission on Ancient and Historical Monuments of Scotland: 1.4; 2.8; 2.10; 2.11; 3.8; 5.2; 5.3
Royal College of Physicians, Edinburgh: Frontispiece; 2.6; 3.6; 3.13; 3.14; 4.18
Scottish National Portrait Gallery: 3.18; 6.7
Scottish Borders Council Museum and Gallery Service: 5.8
Wellcome Library, London: 1.5; 4.23
University of Edinburgh, Fine Art Collection: 4.9
University of Edinburgh, Special Collections: 1.6

List of tables

Abbreviations

CAC	City Art Centre, Edinburgh Museums and Galleries
ECA	Edinburgh City Archives
ECL	Edinburgh Central Library, Edinburgh Room
HC	House of Commons
HL	House of Lords
MOH	Medical Officer of Health
NLS	National Library of Scotland
NMS	National Museums of Scotland
NRS	National Registers of Scotland
ODNB	Oxford Dictionary of National Biography
OS	Ordnance Survey
PP	Parliamentary Papers
RCAHMS	Royal Commission on the Ancient and Historical Monuments of Scotland
RCPEd	Royal College of Physicians of Edinburgh
RCSEd	Royal College of Surgeons of Edinburgh
SNPG	Scottish National Portrait Gallery

Acknowledgements

Insanitary City was conceived a long time ago. Richard Rodger encountered Henry Littlejohn when completing a Ph.D. on Scottish housing at Edinburgh University; Paul Laxton met Littlejohn when supervising Liverpool University geography students on field courses in Edinburgh in the early 1990s. We have long viewed mid-Victorian Edinburgh through Henry's sharp eyes.

Friends, family and colleagues have often wearily asked, 'Aren't you finished the Littlejohn book, yet?' or quipped, 'will this be a posthumous publication?' In the lengthy process of acquiring our own significant archive of Littlejohn materials, we have been aided by many individuals who have been extremely generous with their time, and patient with our requests for yet more information. Their cheerful goodwill has made our work both easier and more meaningful. We are deeply in their debt. Foremost among these supporters has been the longstanding contributions made by Chris Fleet, Senior Map Curator at the National Library of Scotland, who over many years has directed the NLS' digitised mapping initiative, making it the leading institution in the UK in this field. Our recourse to Chris' knowledge and his generous assistance in providing access to digitised maps has been invaluable as a base for the many new maps presented in the book. These add immense value to our text, and to an understanding of spatial relations in cities generally, and in Edinburgh specifically.

Our long-accumulated debts are many and considerable. Curators of various collections have been immensely helpful, both in seeking out images and providing access to their resources. If they are named here in brief it is only because we neither wish to embarrass them nor do we wish to strain our readers' patience. However, it would be wrong not to mention Christian Algar (British Library, Colindale); Jill Forrest (University of Edinburgh Fine Art Collection); Neil Fraser (Royal Commission for Ancient and Historical Monuments of Scotland); Laura Gould (Lothian Health Services Archives); Rosemary Hannay (Scottish Borders Council Museum and Gallery Service); Jennifer Melville (Aberdeen Art Gallery); Iain Milne (Royal College of Physicians of Edinburgh Library); Reverend Sinclair Horne (Scottish Reformation Society); Sarah Jeffcott (Scottish National Portrait Gallery); Ian O'Riordan (City Art Centre, Edinburgh Museums and Galleries); Marianne Smith and Steven Kerr (Royal College of Surgeons of Edinburgh Library); Alison Stoddart, Kevin Maclean, Andrew Bethune and Jimmy Hogg (Edinburgh Central Library); and Margaret Wilson (National Museum of Scotland). Each of them has been very receptive to our efforts to produce relevant illustrative material, some even waiving charges in exchange for copies of our book. In the years spent in the National Library of Scotland we have enjoyed the expert service of many of the reading room staff; their faces are often more familiar than their names, but their cheerful service deserves acknowledgment. Other librarians completed our questionnaire about their copies of the *Report* or sent images of their holdings: Hiroe Nagano (Keio University Library, Tokyo); Valerie Hart (Guildhall Library); Valerie McLure (Royal College of Physicians and Surgeons, Glasgow); Nick White (London School of Economics Library); Adam Hart (University of Aberdeen Medical Library); Jack Eckert (Countway Medical Library, Harvard University); Bruce Bradley (Linda Hall Library, Kansas City); Elaine Challacombe and Jim Curley, (Wangensteen Historical Library, University of Minnesota); David Smith (General Research Division, New York Public Library). The generous assistance of the Carnegie Trust for the University of Scotland, Royal Society of Edinburgh, and Strathmartine Trust to finance the reproduction of images and to scan H.D. Littlejohn's *Report on the Sanitary Condition of Edinburgh* is also acknowledged here. It has been reproduced from a private copy.

We have had immense encouragement from friends and colleagues over many years – we dare not mention how long! Gerry Kearns and Graham Mooney, both specialists in Victorian public health, read the complete text and pronounced it publishable. Dawn Kemp, Director of Heritage at the Royal College of Surgeons of Edinburgh until 2009, gave invaluable support to the project, often over lunch, and also ensured that some Littlejohn papers and memorabilia were safely deposited with College. We have also had unstinting encouragement from Iain Macintyre, Rebecca Madgin, Genevieve Massard-Guilbaud, Bob Morris, the late David Reeder, Jen Scott (a serious and creative student of H.D. Littlejohn), and Nuala Zahedieh, not least for the use of her flat. We would also like to thank Peter Atkins, Susan Buckham, Ann Cameron, Marney Conley, Helen Dingwall, Duncan Forbes, Mark and Mary Hedderwick, Ian Levitt, James McCarthy, Iain Maclachlan, Peter Milne, Stuart Nicol, Lou Rosenburg, Greg Ross, Diana Webster, Brenda White, Charlie Withers and Minoru Yasumoto. Sandra Mather, skilled cartographer and colleague for 40 years, drew several of the maps and assisted Paul Laxton, amateur cartographer, in others. To all these, their consistent interest has meant much to us and we hope they will be pleased as well as relieved to see it in print.

In addition, we have benefited from commentators at seminars and conferences including London School of Hygiene and Tropical Medicine; European Urban History Association, Stockholm; École des Hautes Études en Sciences Sociales, Paris; Centre for the Social History of Health and Healthcare, Glasgow; and the Royal College of Surgeons of Edinburgh. Student participants from Leicester, Liverpool and Edinburgh universities and many others who have tramped the streets with us as part of field trips, urban walks, summer schools, and undergraduate courses have been party to the ideas and themes as they have been worked out and their forbearance with our enthusiasms is also appreciated.

A considerable part of the research for this book has taken place electronically, on Merseyside; thanks are due to the University of Edinburgh appointing Paul Laxton an Honorary Fellow, giving access to vital resources for research. He also wishes to thank Richard and Maki Stott for years of accommodation and breakfasts in Priestfield Road. Funding from the Royal Society of Edinburgh, Carnegie Trust for the Universities of Scotland, and the Strathmartine Trust is also gratefully acknowledged for the financial support that enabled the illustrations and facsimile to be produced.

Over many years both authors have enjoyed the friendship as well as the scholarship and professional advice of Richard Hunter, Edinburgh City Archivist. The camaraderie of the search room is an experience no historian should miss; provided the researcher has a sense of humour, he or she will always discover more about Edinburgh than can be learned simply from the documents. This accolade is also meant for the staff of the ECA past and present: Brenda, Pam, Stephanie, Jo, Vikki, and Peter. They, and researchers too, work under very difficult circumstances, and Edinburgh historians and local taxpayers deserve better archival facilities consistent with the city's status as a World Heritage site and capital city.

No authors should overlook the input from their publisher. Alistair Hodge of Carnegie Publishing has always supported our commitment to produce the best possible research to the highest possible standard, and at a competitive price. He has been painstaking with our text and patient in the face of two demanding authors. Chris Reed and Amanda Thompson at BBR have applied their skills and experience in book design, and we wish to acknowledge the efforts of all concerned in the production process. We hope that anxieties raised were ultimately worthwhile.

Finally, we also owe so much to our 'support team'. Jane Laxton and Susan Rodger have provided moral and practical support, and a great deal more. Their input cannot be under-estimated. B&B in Edinburgh and New Brighton have been provided over many years and kept us going in the long hours while trading versions of the text. Our children have also left home in the course of this project, though we think this is not a case of perfect correlation. They, too, have lived with the 'Littlejohn project', and for a higher percentage of their lives than we have.

The book is dedicated to the memory of Rachel Hedderwick, daughter of Henry Littlejohn's youngest child Dorothy and until her recent death the sole survivor of Dr Littlejohn's large family. Rachel deposited most of the family archive with Edinburgh City Library, later transferred to the City Archives, and welcomed Paul Laxton to her home in East Saltoun to examine papers, pictures and furniture, and tell of Littlejohn family lore – always confirmed when checked – over tea and cake or lunch. She was a Littlejohn: the determined jaw, robust unsentimental kindness, conservative in many ways, but with some deep liberal instincts. Her opening question was often 'How's the book?' It is a matter of great sadness that she has not lived to see it in print.

Preface

Insanitary City does two things: first, it provides an interpretive commentary on an extraordinary nineteenth-century account of Edinburgh, Henry Duncan Littlejohn's *Report on the Sanitary Condition of Edinburgh,* 1865; and, second, it reproduces a facsimile of the original document. Read together, they permit a better understanding of the dynamic internal structure of cities in general, and of Edinburgh in particular. Underlying Littlejohn's *Report* lies a paradox: why, in the epicentre of the Scottish enlightenment, where Edinburgh University and the Royal Colleges produced more medical graduates than anywhere else in the British Isles, was the urban environment so hostile to health?

Littlejohn's *Report* has been described as 'the most comprehensive and detailed report of the health and related circumstances of any town in Scotland, and possibly even in Great Britain … a model report, and one which has been approached in excellence at no time since' (Womersley 1987). Praise indeed set beside the well-known and often quoted reports of Edwin Chadwick and other 'sanitarians'. Perhaps because it was so 'comprehensive and detailed', researchers have been disinclined to explore its scope and significance. More likely, it occurred to us as we researched various aspects of the history of Edinburgh, it was the gaps in the social history of the nineteenth-century capital that were the deterrent to understanding the context of the *Report*. Whereas it is relatively easy to compile lengthy booklists of well-researched works on Birmingham, Leeds, Liverpool and Glasgow and, indeed, on many smaller towns, there is a dearth of such publications on Edinburgh's post-1750 history. The historical framework – the signposts – for those researching the larger urban places in Britain is more fully formed.

The underlying explanation for the long gestation of this work is that understanding Henry Duncan Littlejohn's *Report on the Sanitary Condition of Edinburgh* required a sound knowledge of how his own study had been conducted. How were new districts defined? What statistical calculations and adjustments were essential to understand the social contours of the city, and the health of the public? We dissected first the mechanics and methodologies that lay behind the *Report*. We had to understand the mentalities of medical men and the motives of vested interests; the management of the media was another perspective to be factored in to the study, and the maze of personalities in the political arena required forensic analysis. Digitising the *Report* and its many appendices enabled us to analyse in considerable detail Littlejohn's statistical evidence (all his arithmetic was checked) and the language he employed. A digital text also facilitated comparison with contemporary materials produced by the City

Council, public bodies, newspapers, professional organisations, and individuals as contained in official documents, pamphlets, census returns, and data. Maps, plans and photographs were scrutinised with the same care as text and data. As a matter of interest we subsequently constructed a Venn diagram of the areas we had traversed – housing, civil engineering, legal and parliamentary procedures, municipal administration and parish government, medical jurisprudence, poverty, policing, demography, topography, cartography, photography, migration, religion, and a variety of health related topics: community medicine, occupational health, epidemic disease, interment, food adulteration, and many more. With its pragmatic approach our methodology might not have impressed a Ph.D. supervisor, but our sustained and systematic approach would, we trust, have impressed Dr Littlejohn, especially as most of it was conducted in an era before *The Caledonian Mercury, The Scotsman*, the *Edinburgh and Leith Post Office Directories* and the marvellous maps of the National Library of Scotland were digitised.

Insanitary City reflects our research journey, not just in the footnotes, but in its *structure*. Littlejohn's *Report* was itself founded on exhaustive archival research, painstaking fieldwork, meticulous record-keeping and careful statistical analysis. It was also the product of its times, or rather, the inheritor of its times: divisive battles over the relief of poverty and the resulting rift in the Church of Scotland; the legacy of bitter disputes in the council chamber over the rescheduling of municipal debts, and over tax assessments; the absence of a unitary authority to govern the city until 1856; and the personality clashes among councillors. Each contributed to Littlejohn's inheritance and influenced the *Report*. These expansive historical landscapes, affected the management of public health prior to his appointment as Medical Officer of Health in 1862, and occupy the first three chapters. How Littlejohn's analysis and 'suggestions' were woven into the consciousness and consciences of different layers of authority in Edinburgh is discussed in the last three chapters. Omnipresent are the inter-relationships of poverty, work and health, coupled with Littlejohn's prime concern to reduce levels of morbidity and mortality.

How should you read the *Insanitary City*? From beginning to end is one approach! Exploring the many entirely new maps and previously unpublished illustrations is another. However, flicking back and forth between our text and the relevant sections of Littlejohn's *Report*, reproduced here as a facsimile, will, we believe, reveal more of the social, economic, and political dynamics of mid-nineteenth-century Edinburgh within which Littlejohn had to function. Ultimately *Insanitary City* explores the tensions inherent in the public sphere as the city sought to address the consequences of private actions upon the public's health. Such tensions offer insights on cities past and present.

Paul Laxton and Richard Rodger
October 2013

CHAPTER 1

Revealing the Insanitary City

On 9 August 1865 the *Edinburgh Evening Courant* reproduced a tabular report by Dr H.D. Littlejohn, headed 'Health of the City'.[1] It recorded – as had similar reports for more than two years – the mortality in the previous week in the five districts of Edinburgh, together with further data on births and illegitimacy. This particular weekly report differed from previous reports only in the detail of the statistics. Yet just one week later the entire basis of public health debate in Edinburgh would be transformed; on 16 August 1865, the Town Council received and debated Dr Henry D. Littlejohn's *Report on the Sanitary Condition of the City of Edinburgh*. Its publication was of such great significance that for the next twelve days the *Evening Courant* and *Caledonian Mercury* newspapers published *verbatim* the 120 pages of his *Report*.[2] Several thousand copies of Littlejohn's *Report* were printed, including a less expensive, more accessible 'People's Edition' in which the statistical appendices were omitted.[3]

Informed medical opinion in *The Lancet* subsequently described Littlejohn's research and his *Report* as 'monumental'.[4] This was no exaggeration. Instead of using the Registrar-General's five registration districts, Littlejohn had 're-districted' the city of Edinburgh, devising nineteen sanitary districts as the basis for a statistical analysis that was designed to avoid the distortions introduced by the aggregation of many diverse areas. This might seem neither difficult nor ambitious. Yet it was, in fact, a 'monumental' task. Even drawing up a complete list of Edinburgh's streets, Littlejohn explained, was 'a task of no little difficulty', since none existed.[5] The exercise, intended to identify much more precisely the cause of death within specific areas, involved the development of a new social geography of the city, by defining areas according to their topography,

1 *Evening Courant*, 9 August 1865, 9b. The first of such reports had been published on 24 June 1863, 2g.

2 *Evening Courant*, 16 August 1865. The remaining serialised sections were as follows: 18 August, 3a–e; 21 August, 21 5cd; 22 August, 3a–d; 23 August, 3a–d; 24 August, 2c–f; 24 August, 4ab; 25 August, 6a–d; 28 August, 2d–f; 31 August, 6f–7b; 1 September, 6f–7b; 2 September, 7b–d. The *Caledonian Mercury*, 16 August 1865, 2a, introduced the publication by stating 'this report possesses an interest which cannot fail to commend it to careful attention'.

3 Edinburgh City Archives (ECA), Edinburgh Police Accounts, 1865–66, Watching I/1/18/2, items 1–3, 'Expenses connected with Report on the Sanitary Condition of the City by the Medical Officer of Health'; and Edinburgh Police Accounts, 1866–67, I/(1)/17/2 'Further Expenses connected with the Report on the Sanitary Condition of the City by the Medical Officer of Health.' The 'People's Edition' was published in 1866.

4 *The Lancet*, 10 October 1914, 913–14.

5 *Report*, 5.

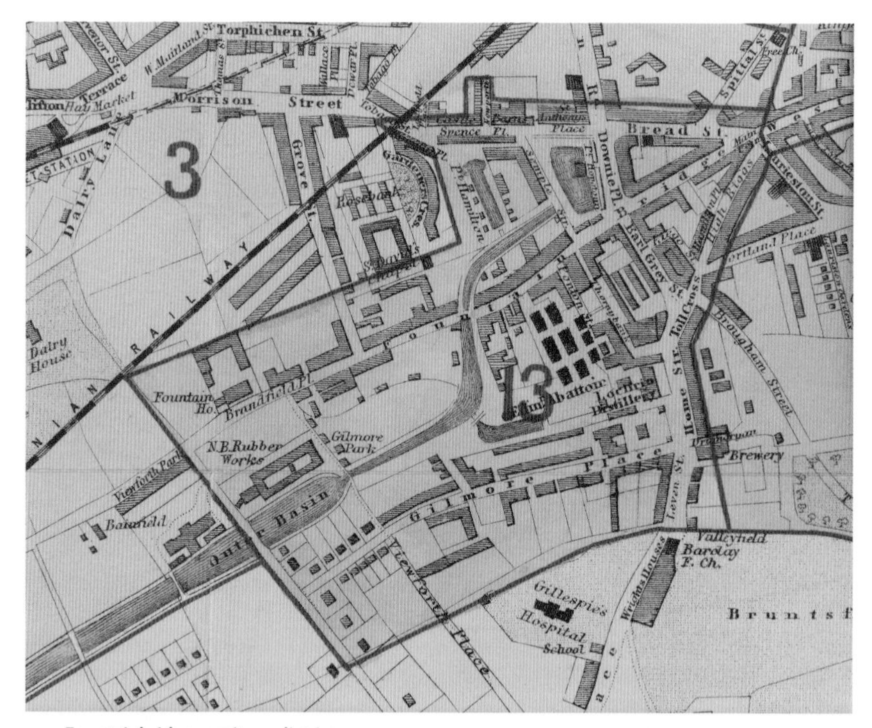

1.1 Fountainbridge: sanitary district 13
Detail from Littlejohn's map of new sanitary districts. The Registrar-General's five districts were too crude and Littlejohn's nineteen new districts provided more subtlety and corresponded closely to an understanding of local topography and social characteristics. [Source: *Report*, map]

drainage arrangements, social composition and economic activities. In fact, this project – involving the reassignment of the 170,444 Edinburgh residents in the 1861 census to newly defined districts – was only the first part of the exercise Littlejohn had set himself.[6] Aided by his part-time clerk, Littlejohn then had to reassign deaths and causes of death to the nineteen new districts.[7] The objective was simple enough: 'to test for the first time by reference to the mortality, the sanitary condition of the portions of the city inhabited by the richer and poorer classes.'[8] What this actually involved were frequent site inspections, close by close and court by court, to identify households and to clarify street addresses, and two years of arduous research, undertaking tens of thousands of calculations using only logarithms, a slide rule and mental arithmetic.

The *Report* consisted of 120 pages of text, tables, maps and diagrams, with a substantial statistical appendix presenting data on population, mortality by

6 Littlejohn discovered that in the possession of the City of Edinburgh there were census returns compiled at the level of individual streets, and so was required to obtain permission from the Registrar-General in order to make a copy.

7 Adjustments in the number of deaths had also to be made to take account of temporary visitors to each district, as well as by correcting the data for those who, though they died in an Edinburgh institution, were normally resident in another district of the city.

8 *Report*, 5.

cause, nuisances, and data on cholera deaths in 1848–49 and fever epidemics in 1847–48 and 1857–58.[9] The appendix is best envisaged by modern readers as a spreadsheet of 36 columns and 1,100 rows. This extraordinary geographical specificity distinguished 1,062 individual streets, wynds and closes, the latter carefully given their street numbers. In the process of writing the current work, Littlejohn's arithmetic (to two decimal places) has been checked using electronic calculators: only five minor errors were encountered, three of which were certainly the printer's!

In anticipation of the publication of his *Report* Littlejohn's public relations campaign ensured that public health in Scotland would never be the same again. The public, prepared by his weekly 'Health of the City' reports, found the evidence in his *Report on the Sanitary Condition of Edinburgh* impressive and the conclusions compelling. Littlejohn's analyses of environmental health were combined with exhaustive statistical calculations and methodological rigour to produce an authoritative document which drew extensively on more than a decade of expertise as city Police Surgeon, university lecturer, and public health expert for the Scottish Board of Supervision. Nor was Edinburgh itself the same again. An informed public meant that the Town Council could not bury Littlejohn's *Report* and, despite vigorous opposition from some quarters, it was the subject that dominated council elections in November 1865, just three months after the publication of Littlejohn's *Report*. The successful campaign by the publisher, William Chambers, focused exclusively on the *Report*, as the press report of his first speech to the Town Council as Lord Provost indicated:

> 'We have heard of various projects for embellishing the town, such as by a Town Hall, a West End Park, and so on; but it appears to me that all, or nearly all, of these designs must give place for a time to some distinct measures of sanitary improvement. (Applause.) On this subject, as you know, there has been a most valuable sanitary report made by Dr Littlejohn, an indefatigable public officer whom Edinburgh is very fortunate in possessing, and some of whose views, as respects opening up the Old Town by cross and diagonal streets through the more dense and confined masses, cannot be too soon carried out. (Applause.) It is, indeed, a most curious circumstance that, after all that has been done one way or another, a large part of Edinburgh still remains exactly what it was before Columbus discovered America, or James IV perished at Flodden. (Laughter.) There is scarcely anything like it in the world.' He continued with passion to speak in general terms of the need to combat 'deadly epidemics' and what he referred to as the 'monstrous crying evil'. 'Much is about to be done … in the metropolis and in Leeds; and Glasgow, to its great honour, has led the way in Scotland.' (Applause.)[10]

The newly elected Lord Provost of Edinburgh then promoted municipal interventions in the property and housing markets as part of a slum-clearance and rebuilding programme that swept away almost 30% of the houses in the

9 Much of this material pre-dated the collection of civil registration data in Scotland, which began only in 1855. Thus, Littlejohn used manuscript entries in the Royal Infirmary to identify and analyse cholera and fever deaths in the 1847–48 epidemic. See University of Edinburgh Archive, Lothian Health Board, Royal Infirmary Admission Ledgers.

10 *Evening Courant*, 11 November 1865, 5a–d.

medieval Old Town.[11] By 1884 death rates had fallen appreciably: by as much as 43% in the central Tron district, and across the whole of Edinburgh by 20%.[12]

Obituaries tend to exaggerate: strengths are recalled and failings forgiven. Criticism in death is unanswerable from the grave. And so, to present Henry Duncan Littlejohn through his obituaries as 'one of Edinburgh's and of Scotland's great men' and his life's work as 'enduring and fruitful everywhere' is to risk hyperbole.[13] Yet, without exception, Littlejohn was considered 'one of the greatest public health authorities of our time',[14] and was held in high esteem by his fellow practitioners who described his 'monumental report on the sanitary condition of the city' [of Edinburgh] as distinguished.[15] Within six months Littlejohn's *Report* had even attracted attention at the other ends of the earth.[16] The founder of the Wellcome Bureau of Scientific Research, Sir Andrew Balfour, described Littlejohn as Edinburgh's first 'and likely to be her greatest Medical Officer of Health'.[17]

In a pre-1914 world accustomed to understatement, superlatives such as 'greatest' and 'monumental' genuinely mark out Henry Littlejohn as exceptional.[18] There is, however, no need to rely on death-bed assessments. Judges extolled the clarity of the evidence he would be called upon to give from the witness box in high-profile murder cases, where Littlejohn's exemplary forensic skills were matched only by his exceptional exposition of events. University students recounted his inspirational teaching as a lecturer who combined intellectual rigour with wit and a deep reservoir of practical experience.[19] He held his students 'spellbound'.[20] Proof of this popularity and an indication of his impact on public health education generally was the memorial which 3,200 former students signed in 1897 when 'the Doctor' – as Littlejohn was known to generations of students – was appointed Professor of Forensic Medicine in the University of Edinburgh.[21] As for the *Report on the Sanitary Condition of the City of Edinburgh*

HEALTH OF THE CITY.

The following is the report of the medical officer of health for the week ending July 11:—

The mortality of the city continues to decline. 66 deaths have been registered as against 94, 90, and 73 of the preceding weeks. The following table shows the mortality of each district:—

	Males.	Females.	Total.
St George's	4	9	13
St Andrew's	5	3	8
Canongate	12	7	19
St Giles'	7	8	15
Newington	5	6	11
	33	33	66

Of these 73 deaths, only 1 occurred during the first week of life, 1 during the first month, 11 in the first year. From 1 to 5 years, 13; from 5 to 30, 14; from 30 to 60, 12; from 60 to 80, 14; and above 80 years, 2. Diseases of the brain proved fatal in 10 cases; diseases of the heart in 3; diseases of the chest (other than phthisis) in 9, and di·eases of the abdomen in 10. Only 4 deaths were attributed to debility. Of these, 1 is registered during the first mouth, 1 above 60, and two above 80 years. Consumption was fatal in 6 cases. Of these, 4 occurred below 30 years, and 2 beyond that age. The following table shows the prevalence of the zymotic diseases:—

	St Geo.	St And.	Canon.	St Giles'.	Newin.	Total
Fever,	...	1	1	...	1	3
Diphtheria,	1	...	...	2	...	3
Small-pox,	...	...	...	...	...	0
Scarlet Fever,	...	1	...	...	...	1
Measles,	...	...	2	1	1	4
Hooping-cough	...	...	...	...	...	0
Erysipelas,	...	...	1	1	...	2
Total,	1	2	4	4	2	13

The mortality from these diseases is the same as was recorded last week. Of the cases of fever, only 1 is registered as typhus—it occurred in the Royal Infirmary; the other 2 are reported as gastric, and occurred in Great King Street and Beaumont Place. Stockbridge, Grassmarket, and South College Street furnished each a case of diptheria. There was no death from small-pox or hooping-cough. The cases of erysipelas occurred in the south side of the town; both were above 56 years of age. Of the 8 deaths not tabulated under the preceding heads, 2 were the result of operations; 3 of falls from a height; 2 of cancer; and 1 of disease of the spine.

The following table shows the sex and the distribution of the births, which also show a marked diminution in number:—

	Males.	Females.	Total.	Legit.	Illegit.
St George's,	10	16	26	23	3
St Andrew's,	5	5	10	10	0
Canongate,	13	14	27	25	2
St Giles',	14	9	23	23	0
Newington,	5	9	14	14	0
Total,	47	53	100	95	5

Reported by HENRY D. LITTLEJOHN, M.D., Medical Officer of Health.

13th July 1863.

1.2 A typical weekly Health Report compiled by Littlejohn

Newspapers printed a report of this kind by the MOH every week from June 1863 to May 1941.
[Source: *Caledonian Mercury*, 15 July 1863]

11 *The Lord Provost's Statement to the Town Council, 5 Dec. 1865* (Edinburgh, 1865). For an account of the Edinburgh Improvement Act, 1867, see below, chapter 6.

12 PP (HC) 1884–85 [C. 4409], Royal Commission on the Housing of the Working Classes, Evidence of Dr Henry Littlejohn, Q. 18,996, Appendix B. See also Registrar-General for Scotland, *Annual Reports of Births, Deaths, and Marriage*, 1855–75.

13 *British Medical Journal*, 10 October 1914, 648–50.

14 *The Glasgow Herald*, 2 October 1914.

15 *The Lancet*, 10 October 1914, 913–14.

16 *The Mercury* (Hobart Tasmania), 'Improvement of Edinburgh', 26 February 1866, 3d.

17 Wellcome Library, Archives and Manuscripts, WA/BSR/BA/Pub/A1/11, memorandum on Sir Henry Littlejohn, 12 October 1914 by Andrew Balfour, CMG, MD.

18 *The Scotsman*, 2 October 1914, 5ab. *The Scotsman* simply stated: 'It is as a great Medical Officer of Health and medical jurist.'

19 *The Student* (Edinburgh University Student Magazine), New Series, I, no. 5, 7 June 1889, 65–6; and N.S., XI, no. 1, 22, 1–3, 302–3, and 307; J.D. Comrie, *History of Scottish Medicine* (London, 1932) notes that often there were 250 students in Littlejohn's classes. See also H.D. Littlejohn, 'Valedictory address to the Edinburgh medico-chirurgical society', *Edinburgh Medical Journal*, XXXI (1885–86), 601–12, for an indictment of university medical education and the lack of practical experience in medical jurisprudence.

20 *British Medical Journal*, 10 October 1914, 648. The *BMJ* provides a lucid account of Littlejohn's teaching style, his practical demonstrations, memorable stories, memorabilia and anecdotes, each designed to imprint a particular point of forensic science on the minds of his students.

21 *Edinburgh Evening News*, 1 October 1914, substantially republished in the *Glasgow Herald*, 2 October 1914. The *Australian Town and Country Journal*, 6 December 1890, 19a, recounted how

1865, with which Littlejohn's name and reputation are inextricably linked, this was described by a recent medical authority as 'the most comprehensive and detailed report of the health and related circumstances of any town in Scotland, and possibly even in Great Britain ... a model report, and one which has been approached in excellence at no time since.'[22] There seems little reason to depart from this assessment.

What follows is not a comprehensive evaluation of the life and work of Sir Henry Duncan Littlejohn, MD, FRCS. To undertake such a task, though worthwhile, would require greater ambition than is relevant to this assessment, confined as it is to the publication of the *Report*. But it is important to explore the social and political background that framed the *Report*. These were wider, national debates concerning health and poverty, and the role of Church and State in providing safety and security for all citizens. These topics were of a philosophical nature and related to the rights of man, civil liberties, and the sanctity of property. Consequently they engaged the foremost minds of the Scottish Enlightenment – itself centred on Edinburgh – and spanned issues that were explored and debated over several decades. To rationalise personal freedom and individual rights with public responsibility and state intervention was the puzzle that absorbed many churchmen, professors, scientists and doctors, as well as the educated public in salons and assemblies. For the cognoscenti, public health and poverty were issues of intellectual and philosophical significance; for the general public, decisions about disease and poverty could be matters of life and death.

Littlejohn's *Report* was also significant, therefore, because in 1865 it drew a line under such debates. The meticulous research and pain-staking, even forensic, analysis upon which the *Report* was based provided solid empirical foundations upon which to construct public policy in areas such as overcrowding, lodging-houses, drainage, burials, occupational health, animal keeping and slaughtering, diseased meat, bakeries and food quality, and the construction of new streets, and town planning. However, to have some sense of Littlejohn the man, the professional and the author of the *Report*, a short account of his career is highly informative.

Henry Duncan Littlejohn: a curriculum vitae

Henry Duncan Littlejohn was born in Leith Street, Edinburgh, on 8 May 1826, the seventh of nine children to Isabella Duncan (1787–1858) and Thomas Littlejohn (1780–1841), a baker and merchant.[23] He completed his education at the Royal High School, Edinburgh, in 1841 before studying medicine at Edinburgh University as an extra-mural student at the College of Surgeons.[24]

influential the 'celebrated' Littlejohn's teaching had been for Dr Devereux Gwynne-Hughes, the newly appointed Medical Officer of Health for Sydney.

22 J. Womersley, 'The evolution of health information service', in G. McLachlan (ed.), *Improving the Common Weal: Aspects of Scottish Health Services, 1900–1984* (Edinburgh, 1987), 556.

23 The Littlejohn family originated from Forgandenny, Dron parish, Perthshire. We are grateful to Greg Ross for this information.

24 ECA SL137/5/1 and SL137/15/6, Royal High School Matriculation Book 1827/28–1842/43, and Library Register 1838/39–1864/65. Littlejohn received the Geography prize in Mr Mackay's

1.3 Henry Duncan Littlejohn and his wife Isabella Duncan
The *carte de visite* of Isabella, mother of their 13 children, was taken in July 1879 at Ross and Thomson's studio in Princes Street. She was 45. Henry sat for this portrait in the 1850s when he was in his late 20s. For details of their children see notes 26 and 41. [Source: ECA, Littlejohn papers]

He graduated LRCS and MD in 1847.[25] Littlejohn married Isabella Jane Harvey (1833–86) on 6 May 1857. They had three sons and ten daughters.[26] He was awarded an honorary doctorate from Edinburgh in 1893, and a knighthood in 1895 'for services to sanitary science'.[27] Sir Henry Duncan Littlejohn died at Benreoch, Arrochar, on 30 September 1914 in his 89th year.

Aged just 16, Henry Duncan Littlejohn began his medical education in 1842. He studied under a galaxy of medical stars. In his first and second years he attended lectures given by Robert Graham, an eminent botanist

class of 1839 and other prizes in Greek and Latin in 1840 and 1841. Another prizewinner in 1839 was W.D. Maclagan, a member of a very distinguished Edinburgh medical family, *Caledonian Mercury*, 3 August 1839, 3cd; 8 August 1840, 2ef; 7 August 1841, 2fg. David Maclagan and his son Douglas have the rare distinction of the only father and son to have been presidents of both the Royal Colleges of Physicians and of Surgeons in Edinburgh. See I. McIntyre and I MacLaren (eds), *Surgeons' Lives* (Edinburgh, 2005) 82, 98.

25 Edinburgh University Archives, Da43 1847, Medical Examinations, 1847. Uncharacteristically late for one of his final examinations, which caused his answers to be rushed and inadequate, his skills as a both surgeon and physician were recognised as excellent across the medical curriculum.

26 The *Dictionary of National Biography* entry for Henry Duncan Littlejohn states that 'in addition to their son they had at least one daughter'. For details of their children and grandchildren see note 41. The family grave is in the Dean Cemetery, Edinburgh.

27 NRS, GD1/895/6, Personal papers of Littlejohn family, notification by Lord Rosebery to Henry Littlejohn of the award of a knighthood, 28 June 1898.

1.4 The Littlejohn bakery business: Leith Street, 1960s
[Source: RCAHMS]

whose classes could attract audiences of 200 students, and Professor (later Sir) Robert Christison (pharmacology). John Goodsir lectured on practical anatomy and cellular theory; James Miller (surgery), recently appointed as professor in succession to Sir Charles Bell and, in 1848, as surgeon to Queen Victoria, audaciously conducted a public trial of chloroform on 10 November 1847 only one week after Professor James Simpson, physician and obstetrician, and another of Littlejohn's teachers, had discovered it. James Syme (clinical surgery) instructed Littlejohn and his classmates in the operating theatre rather than the lecture theatre. Other distinguished lecturers included Thomas Traill (medical jurisprudence) who, with Christison and Syme, produced the standard work on post-mortem procedure. Traill lectured to Littlejohn and his cohort of final year students in 1846–47 on forensic pathology, which was central to his subsequent career.[28] Further practical knowledge was obtained in pharmacy during his first two years of medical studies in the New Town Dispensary, founded by Alison.

28 Thirteen of Littlejohn's sixteen lecturers appear in the *Dictionary of National Biography*: William Pulteney Alison; Sir Robert Christison; John Goodsir; Robert Graham; William Gregory; William Henderson; Robert Jamieson; James Miller; Alexander Monro (tertius); Sir James Young Simpson; James Syme; Allen Thomson; Thomas Stewart Traill. Lecturers not included were Drs Handyside, Glover, and Kemp.

1.5 Littlejohn's lecturers
Standing: James Miller (Surgery); John Hutton Balfour (Botany); John H. Bennett (Physiology); Seated: James Y. Simpson (Midwifery); Thomas S. Traill (Medical Jurisprudence); William P. Alison (Clinical Medicine); Robert Jamieson (Natural History). Louis Ghemar: artist *c.*1849.
[Source: Wellcome Library, London]

Remarkably, Henry Littlejohn held four posts concurrently. After a very short period as house surgeon and assistant pathologist at the Royal Infirmary, Edinburgh, and as a medical practitioner and obstetrician[29] in the Scottish border town of Selkirk, Littlejohn's successful admission to the Royal College of Surgeons in 1854 was quickly followed, aged 28, by an appointment as Police Surgeon[30] for Edinburgh, a post he held until 1862, when this post was combined with a second office, the newly created position of Medical Officer of Health, which he held for 46 years until his retirement in 1908.[31] As Police Surgeon Littlejohn also discharged the responsibilities of Medical Adviser to the Crown in Scotland in murder cases or those involving sudden deaths. Frequently called to give expert evidence in the Justiciary Courts, judge Lord Young clearly regarded his evidence very highly: 'There are four classes of witnesses – liars, damned liars, expert witnesses, and Sir Henry Littlejohn'.[32] Thirdly, Littlejohn obtained a lectureship in Medical Jurisprudence at the Royal College of Surgeons, Edinburgh, in 1855 and continued to teach there for forty-two years until

29 *The Medical Directory for Scotland 1852* (London, 1853).

30 For details concerning the appointment see below, chapter 3.

31 ECA SL, Police Accounts, 1862–63, notes that HDL was paid £155 p.a. as Surgeon of Police and then as 'Police Surgeon and Medical Officer of Health' from 1862 the annual salary of £500.

32 H. Sutherland, *A Time to Keep* (London, 1934), 71. We are grateful to Richard Hunter for bringing this quotation to our attention.

27

NAME. Henry Duncan Littlejohn

AGE.	BIRTH-PLACE.	PLACE OF RESIDENCE IN EDINBURGH.
22	Edinburgh	54 Albany Street

COURSE OF STUDY.

SESSIONAL YEAR.	CLASSES.	TEACHERS' NAMES.	UNIVERSITY OR SCHOOL.
1842-43	Natural Philosophy	Mr Glover	Edinburgh School
	Anatomy	Dr Handyside	" "
	Botany	" Graham	University Edinr
	Practical Pharmacy	N: T: Dispensary	
1843-44	Materia Medica	Dr Christison	" "
	Physiology	" Thomson	" "
	Practical Anatomy	" Handyside	School "
	" Pharmacy	N: T: Dispensary	"
1844-45	Chemistry	Dr Gregory	University "
	Natural History	Mr Jameson	" "
	Practical Anatomy	" Goodsir	" "
1845-46	Surgery	" Miller	" "
	Clinical Surgery	" Syme	" "
	Practice of Medicine	Dr Alison	" "
	Anatomy	" Monro	" "
	Practical Chemistry	Mr Kemp	" "
	Med: Jurisprudence	Dr Traill	" "
	Dispensary Practice	N: T: Dispensary	"
	Hospital		
1846-47	Surgery	Mr Miller	" "
	Midwifery	Dr Simpson	" "
	Clinical Medicine	Drs Alison & Christison	" "
	Practice of Do	Dr Alison	" "
	Pathology	" Henderson	" "

1.6 Henry Littlejohn's student record, 1842–47
[Source: University of Edinburgh Special Collections]

appointed to the Chair of Forensic Medicine in the University of Edinburgh in 1897, a position he held until 1905.[33] A former student, Halliday Sutherland, later revealed that 'Wee Hell', as the poor of Edinburgh called Littlejohn, was 'a dapper, little man' and that his 9 a.m. class 'was always crowded'.[34] To these positions Henry Littlejohn added, fourthly, significant further concurrent duties for the Board of Supervision as a medical adviser (from 1859) and commissioner (from 1873). This was the central agency of the Scottish Poor Law with overall responsibility for sanitary matters throughout Scotland and for whom he prepared over 700 reports and memoranda.[35]

To these four posts, any one of which 'would have taxed the sole energies of any ordinary man', 'the nimble, natty Dr Littlejohn' added a considerable amount of voluntary work.[36] This included nine years as director of the Royal Infirmary Board, and fifty years in various capacities associated with the Royal Hospital for Sick Children, of which he was one of the founding members of the medical committee.[37] Littlejohn was president of the Royal College of Surgeons (1875–76), president of the Medico-Chirurgical Society of Edinburgh (1883–85), president of the Institute of Public Health (1893)[38], active in various capacities within the British Medical Association and National Association for the Promotion of Social Science; vice-president of the Scottish Burial Reform and Cremation Society Limited and president of the Edinburgh Cremation Society.[39] Littlejohn was also a kirk elder, first at Lauriston Place United Presbyterian Church and, later, at St Giles' Cathedral.[40]

These onerous professional commitments, however, pale compared with those to his wife Isabella and their thirteen children, five of them born by the time

33 Littlejohn succeeded the eminent Professor Douglas Maclagan in the chair of Medical Jurisprudence. Henry Littlejohn, in turn, was succeeded in both the extra-mural lectureship at the Royal College of Surgeons and as professor in the university by his son, Dr Harvey Littlejohn.

34 H.G. Sutherland, *A Time to Keep* (London, 1934) 71.

35 PP (HC) 1861 XXVIII, Board of Supervision for the Relief of Poor in Scotland, 15th Annual Report (1860), xv–xvi. Significantly, Littlejohn was appointed a commissioner under the Poor Law Act, 1845, section 83, and not under the Nuisance Removal Act, 1856. The Board of Supervision became the Scottish Local Government Board in 1897. Littlejohn wrote five reports for the Board before 1873, the first on an outbreak of Asiatic cholera in Wick in 1859. See I. Levitt, 'Henry Littlejohn and Scottish health policy 1859–1908', *Scottish Archives*, 2 (1996), 63–77.

36 *The Scotsman*, 2 October 1914, 5ab; *Sydney Morning Herald*, 28 February 1925, 13g.

37 E. and S. Livingstone, *The Royal Edinburgh Hospital for Sick Children 1860–1960* (Edinburgh, 1960) opened on 15 February 1860 at 7 Lauriston Lane and moved to Sciennes Road in 1895. We are grateful to Anne Donnelly, librarian, Royal Hospital for Sick Children, Edinburgh for information on this point.

38 Edinburgh University Archives, Minutes of Senatus, X, 30 June 1893 records the approval of the motion 'to offer the Honorary Degree of LL.D. … on the special occasion of his presidency of the British Institute of Public Health'. Hard men to please, however, the Senate rejected the notion to award an honorary LL.D. to the Lord Mayor of London.

39 *The Scotsman*, 4 February 1910, 10c. Cremation was legalised by the Cremation Act 1902.

40 NRS, CH3/1152/3, /5, /14; /16; /21; /27–30, Lauriston Place United Presbyterian Church. The United Presbyterian Church was an evangelical variant of the Church of Scotland, and encouraged civic activism as a means of missionary outreach. See also W. MacKelvie, *Annals and Statistics of the United Presbyterian Church* (Edinburgh, 1873), 198. Despite its popular name as a cathedral, St Giles' was, and is, a Church of Scotland, that is Presbyterian, place of worship.

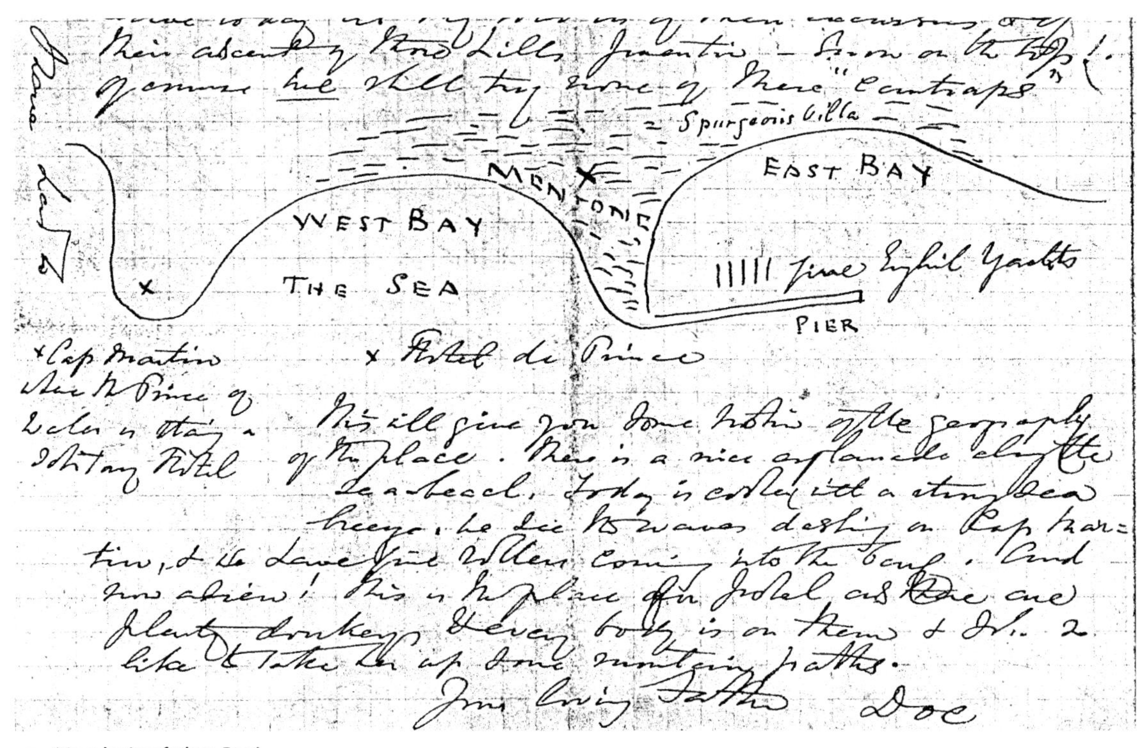

1.7 'Your loving father, Doc'
Letter from Littlejohn (in Mentone, near Nice) to his daughter, Rachel, 25 March 1892. [Source: NRS GD1/895/6]

the Report was published.[41] From his correspondence and family memorabilia it is evident that Henry Littlejohn enjoyed a strong emotional attachment to the eleven children who survived childhood. The personal correspondence that survives is warm and affectionate, and in its detailed accounts of events, visits, menus, hotel guests, journeys, the family dog, and the minutiae of daily life apart, was written with a precise yet informal language that confirms close relationships, especially with his daughters. On one occasion, Littlejohn wrote 1,800 words to Rachel from his hotel in Menton, near Nice, including a sketch map 'to give you some notion of the geography of the place'.[42] In his terms of address – 'My dear children' or 'Dearest children', and signed 'Love to all' and 'Ever yours', generally followed by the initials 'HDL' – the importance of family relationships is evident.[43] 'HDL' addressed Rachel and Dorothy in Brussels as 'My darling EXILES',[44] and in a Christmas letter to them wrote that he 'could not resist

41 Two of their children died in childhood (Mary Constance in 1870 aged 5, and William Arnold in 1871 aged 11 months) and three others (Helena 1900, Maud 1904 and Herbert 1905) before Henry passed away in 1914, leaving only eight surviving children, four of whom married. He had three grandchildren: Helena (daughter of Jessie and the Revd William Perry, an Episcopalian priest), and Ivar and Rachel Hedderwick, born after Littlejohn's death to his youngest daughter Dorothy.

42 NRS, GD1/895/6, HDL to Rachel Littlejohn, 25 March 1892.

43 NRS, GD1/895/6, letters, 25 March 1892; 30 March 1892; 2 April 1892; 14 April 1894; Summer 1894, n.d.; 30 September 194; 23 December 1894.

44 NRS, GD1/895/6, HDL to Rachel and Dorothy Littlejohn, winter 1894–95.

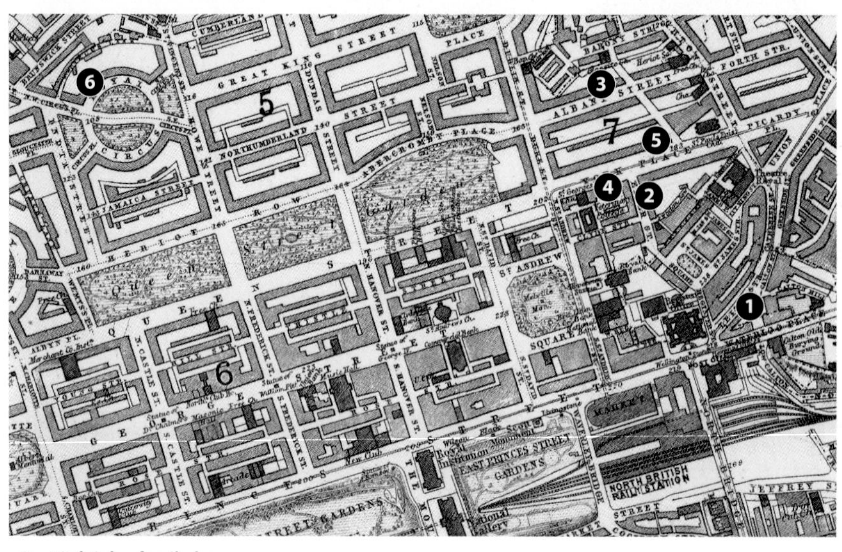

1 33 Leith Street (1826–40)
2 2 Elder Street (1840–45)
3 54 Albany Street (1845–47)
4 67 York Place (1847–60)
5 40 York Place (1860–66)
6 24 Royal Circus (1866–1912)

1.8 Littlejohn family homes

sending you £1 10/– [£1.50] the other day that you might have something to help your expenses at this festive season'.[45] 'HDL' also received expressions of gratitude and affection from his children. He commented favourably, 'Contents of Gladstone gave great satisfaction' in a letter to his children in the autumn of 1894, and annotated the flap of an envelope, 'Jessie full of thanks for NOVELL toothbrush'.[46]

As teacher, forensic surgeon, Medical Officer of Health, poor law medical adviser, and expert witness for the Crown, Littlejohn brought systematic analysis, 'keen attention to detail', statistical evidence, and standardised administrative procedures to bear on public health issues. In each capacity – as the educator of generations of Medical Officers of Health, as the author of influential reports to the central medical agency of the Scottish Poor Law, the Board of Supervision,

45 NRS, GD1/895/6, HDL to Rachel and Dorothy Littlejohn, 23 December 1894.
46 NRS, GD1/895/6, HDL to his children, 14 April 1894; 30 September 1894.

1.9 Ben Reoch house, *c*.1900
This postcard shows the family retreat in Arrochar, Loch Long, with Sir Henry, two of his daughters, and Tony, one of the family dogs. [Source: ECA Littlejohn archive]

1.10 Henry Harvey Littlejohn in 1874, aged 13
Henry Littlejohn's elder son, 'H.H.L.', was Medical Officer of Health for Sheffield, Chief Police Surgeon in Edinburgh and assistant to his father 1906–08, and Dean of Medicine and Professor of Forensic Medicine at Edinburgh University. The younger son, Thomas Herbert Littlejohn, was MOH for Scarborough and then Hampstead, 1901–05.
[Source: ECA, Littlejohn archive]

on topics ranging from hospital provision in Aberdeen to dry earth closets in Stranraer, and from the disposal of town refuse in Kilmarnock to lodging-houses in Ayr – Littlejohn occupied a pivotal position in the development of public health policy in Scotland. In the course of writing numerous sanitary reports he travelled the length and breadth of urban and rural Scotland.[47] He knew more about public health in nineteenth-century Scotland than anyone else.

Though knowledgeable and 'indefatigable', as Littlejohn was once described, these qualities themselves could achieve little if they were detached from practical steps to implement best practice. Thus, Littlejohn's significant contribution to the public health of Scotland was achieved by his preparation of standard procedures that were then sent out as circulars to all town clerks in Scotland by the Secretary of the Board of Supervision for the Poor Law in Scotland. For example, on 24 September 1892, Malcolm McNeill, Secretary to the Board of Supervision, wrote to the town clerks:

> I am directed by the Board of Supervision to transmit to you, in duplicate, the subjoined 'Memorandum as to the Treatment of Diarrhœa and Cholera' and 'Memorandum of Instructions for Disinfection', which have been prepared by their Medical Officer Dr. H. D. Littlejohn, for the information and guidance of Local Authorities and their Officers.[48]

47 Levitt, 'Henry Littlejohn', Appendix 2.
48 PP (HC) 1893–94 XLIV, 425, Board of Supervision for Relief of Poor in Scotland, 48th Annual Report, 1892, Appendix A, 74–5.

1.11 A Littlejohn family group at Ben Reoch House, *c.*1890
The picture was taken four years after Mrs Littlejohn died. In the window: Beatrice and Herbert; standing: Winnie, Jessie and Nellie; seated: Sir Henry, Dorothy, Isobel, Rachel, Maud and Mildred. Only Harvey was absent. [Source: ECA Littlejohn archive]

Littlejohn's recommendations were influential. His circulars were numerous and were distributed throughout Scotland. Not only was he reactive to outbreaks of disease, as his position required him to be, he was often prescriptive, evaluating risks in anticipation of public health problems. This was the case, for example, in 1889 when, in order to contain the risk of smallpox, procedures were proposed to disinfect the 84,000 tons of imported rags used in the manufacture of paper.[49] Littlejohn's visit to Elgin in 1866 encouraged an 'active' town clerk and an expanded cleaning[50] staff to address several public health nuisances, resulting in a town that was 'externally as clean as he could have wished' on his return

49 PP (HC) 1889 CCCVI, 907, Board of Supervision, 44th Annual Report, App. A, 26–7.

50 The terms 'cleaning' and 'cleansing' were used interchangeably and inconsistently by contemporaries, even in the titles of committees and officers. We have used cleaning but have allowed cleansing in titles and contexts which reflect the sources on which the text is based.

in 1877.[51] Locally, Henry Littlejohn often worked behind the scenes to promote public health and influence outcomes. This was the case at Methilhill (Fife) where, after making an interim assessment of a cholera outbreak in 1869, he made an appointment to meet the principal landed proprietor of the parish at Wemyss Castle to seek her compliance with his recommendations.[52] She acceded.

In Edinburgh, Littlejohn was instrumental in efforts to build the new Edinburgh City Hospital, described as 'the most up-to-date fever hospital in the kingdom'.[53] Important contributions were also made nationally in evidence to select committees and royal commissions on issues that included cattle plague (bovine tuberculosis), river pollution, noxious business, death certification, working-class housing conditions, and compulsory notification of disease.[54] It was, however, Littlejohn's research for and detailed preparation of *The Report on the Sanitary Condition of the City of Edinburgh* (1865) that forms the principal foundation upon which his reputation – in the city and beyond – was founded, and which is therefore the main subject of this study.

51 *Aberdeen Journal*, 23 October 1877, 4f; 27 November 1877, 3h; and 14 April 1880, 7d.

52 PP (HC) 1867–68 XXXIII, 625 [3957], Board of Supervision, 22nd Annual Report, App. A (11).

53 *The Glasgow Herald*, 2 October 1914.

54 PP (HC) 1873 X, 431 Select Committee on Noxious Businesses; PP (HC) 1893–94 XL, 195, Select Committee on Death Certification, Evidence, 140–47, digest of evidence, 332; PP (HC) 1875 LXIV, 249, Evidence to the General Board of Health, 4–15; PP (HC) 1884–85 [C. 4409], Royal Commission on the Housing of the Working Classes. Vol. 5 Scotland, Minutes of Evidence, Littlejohn, Q.18,939–19,058, and Appendices A–C; PP (HC) 1882 XXIX, 1, Royal Commission on Smallpox and Fever Hospitals in the Metropolis, 285; PP (HC) 1876 XXXVIII, 117, Local Government Board Committee Inquiring into Treating Town Sewage, 102–3; PP (HC) 1869–69 XI, 1, Select Committee on Operation of Poor Law in Scotland, 284; PP (HC) 1873 XXVII, 1, Royal Commission into Endowed Schools and Hospitals, First Report, 546, 553; PP (HC) 1872 XXXIV, 1, Royal Commission into Rivers Pollution, 4th Report, 49; PP (HC) 1864 VIII, 1, Select Committee on Cattle Disease Prevention, Report 6–7, Evidence 203–7; PP (HC) 1866 XXII, 323, Royal Commission on Cattle Plague.

CHAPTER 2

Public health and medical police before the 1850s

Why was an analysis of the state of public health in Edinburgh necessary in 1865? In a city renowned internationally for its medical education and enlightenment, and for training prominent sanitarians appointed to English boroughs in the 1840s and 1850s, it seems paradoxical that the state of public health in Edinburgh itself should be in disarray.[1]

Fundamental to the insanitary conditions that prevailed in Edinburgh was the growth of the city itself. The decades of the 1810s, 1820s and 1830s experienced the fastest rate of population growth during the entire nineteenth century, averaging almost 2.5% each year. As a result, the population of Edinburgh doubled, from almost 68,000 in 1801 to 136,000 in 1831 – equivalent to raising the current population of the city to over 1 million.[2] Most of this early nineteenth-century increase, two-thirds in fact, was the result of two significant migrations to Edinburgh: first, of Irish migrants, mainly from Leitrim, Monaghan, and Cavan;[3] and, second, of agricultural workers from the eastern and southern Scottish highlands.[4] In crude numbers, the Irish population in Edinburgh was the sixth largest in mainland Britain in 1851 (fig. 2.1).[5]

Impoverished Irish and Scottish rural workers generally lacked the specialist skills to obtain steady employment, and so congregated in precisely those ancient

1 A. Chitnis, *The Scottish Enlightenment and Early Victorian English Society* (London, 1986), 35. These sanitarians included William Henry Duncan (Liverpool Medical Officer of Health, appointed 1847); Andrew W. Barclay (Chelsea, 1855); Charles Clay (Ashton Under Lyne, n.d.).

2 R. Rodger, *The Transformation of Edinburgh: Land, Property and Trust in the Nineteenth Century* (Cambridge, 2001), 23, table 1.3.

3 PP (HC) 1852–53 LXXXVI, Census of Scotland, 1851, and Census Enumerators' Books show that where counties were identified 56.7% were from Leitrim, Monaghan, and Cavan.

4 The collapse of the kelp, wool and beef markets adversely affected the west highland economy and resulted in migrations to west-of-Scotland burghs. By contrast, the surplus labour on the extended and consolidated farms of the east of Scotland around the Moray Firth and to the east of the Highlands resulted in migrations principally to Edinburgh. These migrations were not simply the result of Highland clearances, therefore, but of more subtle variations in regional economies within the Highlands. See C.W.J. Withers, *Urban Highlanders: Highland–Lowland Migration and Urban Gaelic Culture, 1700–1900* (East Linton, 1998), 87–104. Only 2.7% of the Edinburgh population in 1851 were Highland-born (p.88). For an overview, see M. Lynch, *Scotland: A New History* (London, 1991), 67–77.

5 The crude numbers were: London 109,000; Liverpool 84,000; Glasgow 60,000; Manchester 53,000; Dundee 15,000; Edinburgh 12,514, with Birmingham 9,000 and Leeds 8,500. Outside northern and western English boroughs, the Irish in British cities was mostly 4–5% in 1851; in Edinburgh, with a total population of 160,511, it was 7.8%. The figure for Glasgow was 18.2%, and Dundee 19%. See PP (HC) 1852–53 LXXXVI, Census of Scotland, 1851.

and dilapidated areas of the Old Town increasingly vacated by the Edinburgh bourgeoisie as they migrated in the early nineteenth century to the northern New Town beyond Heriot Row.[6] Thus, in Edinburgh, more so than in any other Scottish burgh, the bourgeoisie abandoned the medieval core of the insanitary Old Town to the less well-off and to immigrants whose poverty levels and irregular incomes accelerated the subdivision or 'making-down' of one-room, or at best two-room, apartments. This was decades before municipal powers and sanitary engineering were capable of delivering an environmental counter-attack.[7] Effective demand for housing was weak, and the quality and quantity of accommodation was impaired further by the haemorrhaging of the supply of new house building for all but the very rich following the national financial crisis that affected Edinburgh particularly in 1825–26.[8] For twenty years or so, many Edinburgh building sites remained incomplete, and the developments of others, as in the Grange, arrested. Already by 1830, as the census returns clearly showed (fig. 2.2) Edinburgh was socially and residentially segregated: in the New Town 40% of residents were described as in the 'professional' or 'capitalist' classes. This compared to 20% in Leith and the parish of St Cuthbert's, and 5% in the Old Town parishes.[9]

At the heart of the deepening problem of housing in the Old Town and Canongate in the period 1800–50 was the issue of poverty.[10] There were 870 parishes in Scotland. In 1818, only 145 of these (16.7%) made an 'assessment', that is, levied a charge on residents of the parish to assist or 'relieve' the poor.[11] When a royal commission on the Scottish Poor Law was set up to investigate reform in 1844 – ten years after the introduction of a new Poor Law in England and six years after a new measure was adopted for Ireland – still only 230 parishes in Scotland (26.4%) made assessments to care for the poor.[12] Very few of these parishes were in the Highlands, and so the incentive for Scots to remain in their parish of birth or settlement was weaker than elsewhere in the United Kingdom. Lemming-like, they often made first for the towns and cities, and then for the Empire.[13] Impoverished, they were accommodated in what

6 R. Rodger, *Housing in Urban Britain, 1780–1914* (Cambridge, 1995), 38–43. For a convincing alternative account of the building of the Edinburgh New Town to that of A.J. Youngson, *The Making of Classical Edinburgh* (Edinburgh, 1966) see A. Lewis, 'The builders of Edinburgh's New Town 1767–1795', Edinburgh University, Ph.D. thesis, 2006.

7 See R. Rodger, 'The Victorian building industry and the housing of the Scottish working class', in M. Doughty (ed.), *Building the Industrial City* (Leicester, 1986), 151–206, for a general treatment of the form and nature of Scottish housing.

8 R. Rodger, *The Transformation of Edinburgh*, 76, 82.

9 PP (HC) 1833 XXXVII, Census of Great Britain, 1831, 970–2.

10 The jurisdictions of Edinburgh are themselves a complicated issue. For their evolution see R. Houston, *Social Change in the Age of Enlightenment: Edinburgh, 1660–1760* (Oxford, 1994), 105–21. The 'ancient royalty' refers to the Old Town and the 'Extended Royalty' relates to areas included by extending municipal jurisdictions into the northern New Town in 1832 and 1856.

11 J.H.F. Brotherstone, *Observations on the Early Public Health Movement in Scotland* (London, 1952), 68.

12 PP (HC) 1884 XX, 1, Royal Commission on the Administration and Practical Operation of the Poor Laws in Scotland, Minutes of Evidence and Appendices 1844 [544], [563], [597].

13 M. Fry, *The Scottish Empire* (Edinburgh, 2001); M. Anderson and D. Morse, 'The people' in W.H. Fraser and R.J. Morris (eds), *People and Society in Scotland, Vol. II, 1830–1914* (Edinburgh, 1990), 13–23.

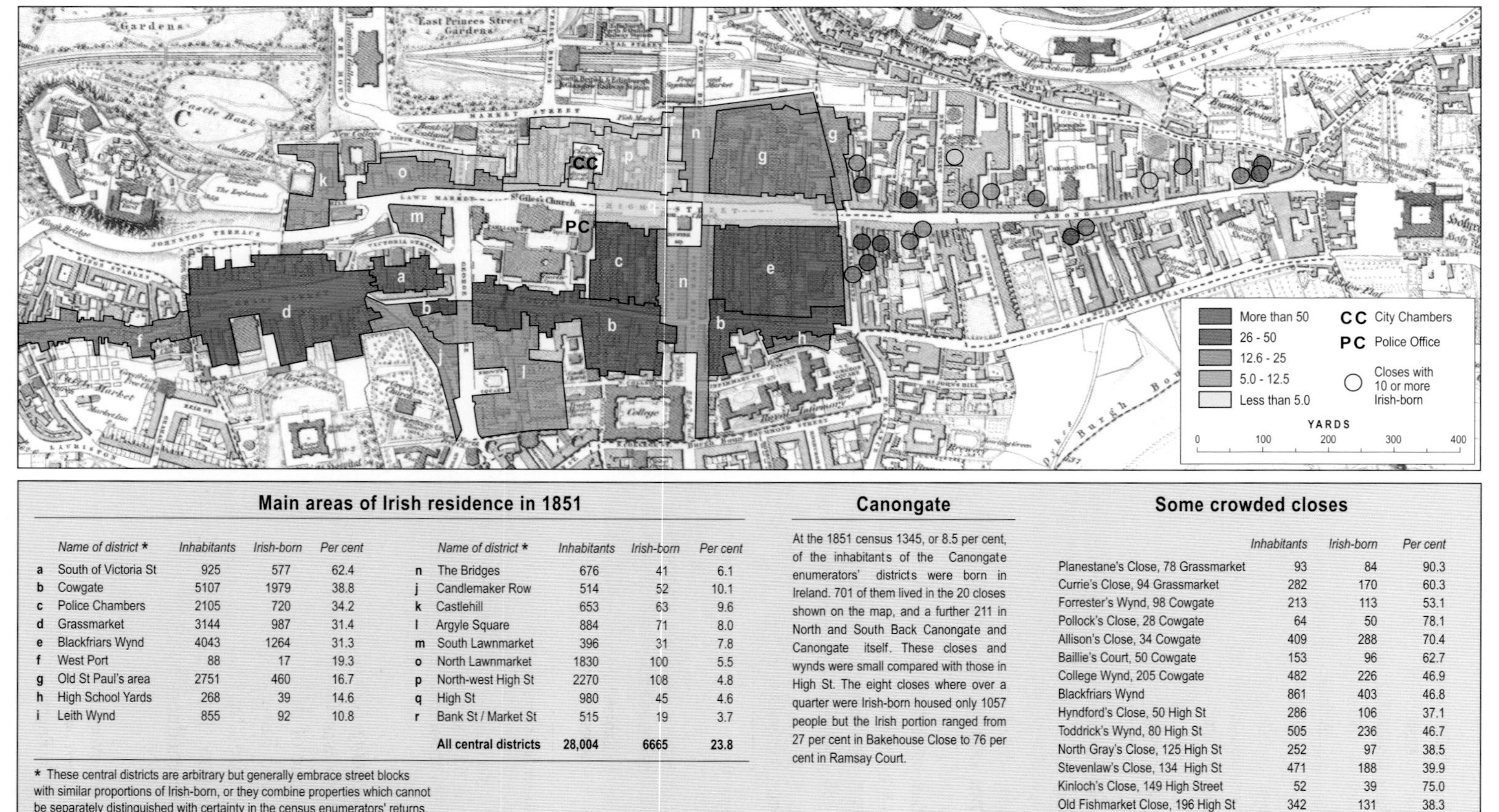

Main areas of Irish residence in 1851

	Name of district *	Inhabitants	Irish-born	Per cent
a	South of Victoria St	925	577	62.4
b	Cowgate	5107	1979	38.8
c	Police Chambers	2105	720	34.2
d	Grassmarket	3144	987	31.4
e	Blackfriars Wynd	4043	1264	31.3
f	West Port	88	17	19.3
g	Old St Paul's area	2751	460	16.7
h	High School Yards	268	39	14.6
i	Leith Wynd	855	92	10.8

	Name of district *	Inhabitants	Irish-born	Per cent
n	The Bridges	676	41	6.1
j	Candlemaker Row	514	52	10.1
k	Castlehill	653	63	9.6
l	Argyle Square	884	71	8.0
m	South Lawnmarket	396	31	7.8
o	North Lawnmarket	1830	100	5.5
p	North-west High St	2270	108	4.8
q	High St	980	45	4.6
r	Bank St / Market St	515	19	3.7
	All central districts	**28,004**	**6665**	**23.8**

* These central districts are arbitrary but generally embrace street blocks with similar proportions of Irish-born, or they combine properties which cannot be separately distinguished with certainty in the census enumerators' returns.

Canongate

At the 1851 census 1345, or 8.5 per cent, of the inhabitants of the Canongate enumerators' districts were born in Ireland. 701 of them lived in the 20 closes shown on the map, and a further 211 in North and South Back Canongate and Canongate itself. These closes and wynds were small compared with those in High St. The eight closes where over a quarter were Irish-born housed only 1057 people but the Irish portion ranged from 27 per cent in Bakehouse Close to 76 per cent in Ramsay Court.

Some crowded closes

	Inhabitants	Irish-born	Per cent
Planestane's Close, 78 Grassmarket	93	84	90.3
Currie's Close, 94 Grassmarket	282	170	60.3
Forrester's Wynd, 98 Cowgate	213	113	53.1
Pollock's Close, 28 Cowgate	64	50	78.1
Allison's Close, 34 Cowgate	409	288	70.4
Baillie's Court, 50 Cowgate	153	96	62.7
College Wynd, 205 Cowgate	482	226	46.9
Blackfriars Wynd	861	403	46.8
Hyndford's Close, 50 High St	286	106	37.1
Toddrick's Wynd, 80 High St	505	236	46.7
North Gray's Close, 125 High St	252	97	38.5
Stevenlaw's Close, 134 High St	471	188	39.9
Kinloch's Close, 149 High Street	52	39	75.0
Old Fishmarket Close, 196 High St	342	131	38.3

2.1 The Irish in the Old Town and Canongate, 1851
Closes in the Old Town recorded very high concentrations of Irish-born residents. Yet there were noticeable variations between neighbouring closes.
[Sources: OS 1852, and Census Enumerators' Books 1851]

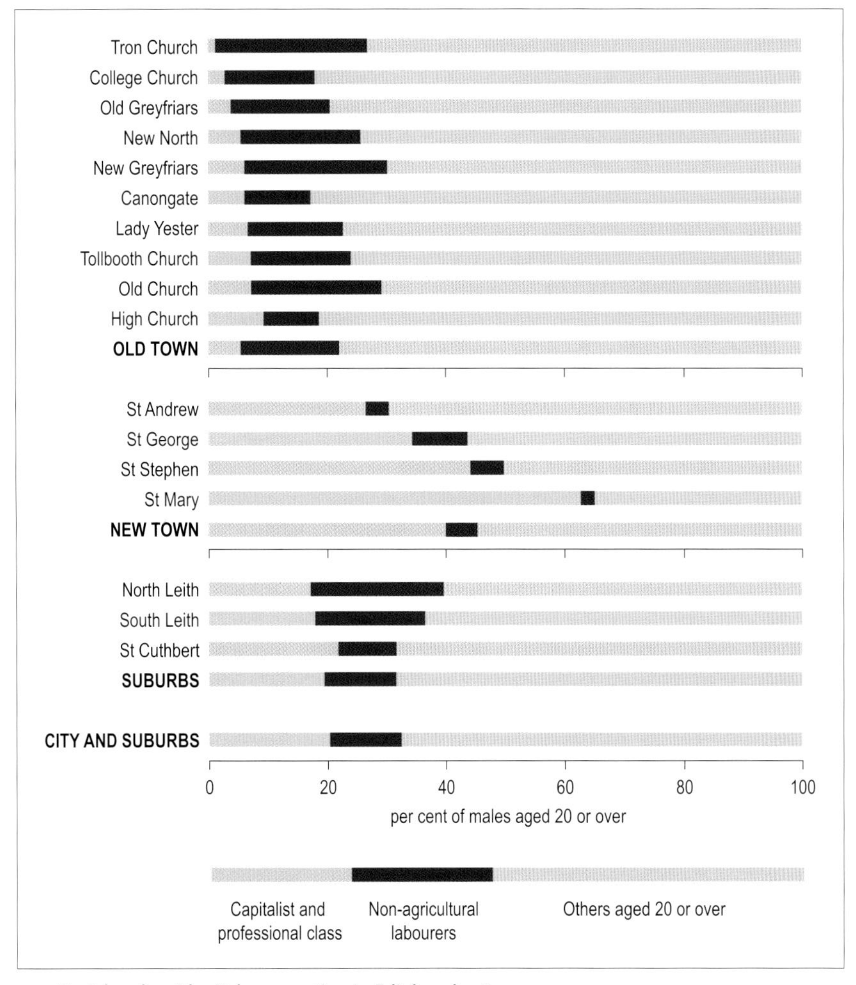

2.2 Social and residential segregation in Edinburgh, 1831
The data from the rudimentary classification of occupations for each parish have been arranged to show the sharp distinctions in the social character of the three divisions of the city and its suburbs, well established before the Victorian period.
[Source: *Abstract of the population returns of Great Britain*, 1831, 970–1]

the *Edinburgh Evening News* described as 'chambers of death'.[14] The publisher William Chambers was far from complimentary about the city in 1840, which he identified as 'one of the most uncleanly and badly ventilated' cities compared to other British and European cities; and Friedrich Engels, who knew European cities well, visited Edinburgh in 1844 and developed a class-based assessment of the housing situation: '[the] brilliant aristocratic quarter … contrast[ed] strongly with the foul wretchedness of the poor in the Old Town.'[15]

14 *Edinburgh Evening News*, 10 September 1853.
15 W. Chambers, *Report on the Sanitary State of the Residences of the Poorer Classes in the Old Town* (Edinburgh, 1840), 1; F. Engels, *The Condition of the Working Class in England in 1844* (London, 1936 edn), 34.

2.3 Multi-storey living: Leith Wynd, St Ninian's Row
The rear of number 33 Leith Street, the birthplace of Henry Littlejohn and the location of the family bakery business. Until the 1960s a large sign above the bricked-up windows advertised 'LITTLEJOHN'S CELEBRATED SHORTBREAD'.

The extent and nature of this 'foul wretchedness' is difficult to convey. Multi-storey tenements, commonly of six, eight or more storeys, dominated housing in the Old Town.[16] A few still survive. The built form, 'story piled on story [*sic*]',[17] conditioned life in urban Scotland, and as one Australian account explained: 'In the ground floors the dwellings were dark, even at noonday, and the inhabitants might literally be said to live in "the Valley of the Shadow of death".'[18] It was imperative to step cautiously through the insanitary Edinburgh streets, as Swift noted in 1794:

> a man that walks through Edinburgh streets in a morning, … is indeed as careful as he can to watch diligently and spy out the filth in his way; not that he is curious to observe the colour and complexion of the ordure or take its dimensions, much less to be paddling in or tasting it, but only with a design to come out as cleanly as he may.[19]

According to Defoe in 1725, 'there is none in the World where so many People live in so little room'.[20] The rhythms of cooking, cleaning, washing, sleeping, mourning, gossip and social interaction, including children's play and most routine activities, were each influenced by the physical features of tenement design, and in particular by the common stair. It was water supply and disposal that presented the greatest challenge to living conditions in Scottish burghs since to pipe water through an existing tenement was, and is, a fiendishly difficult and expensive activity; to introduce internal water-closets was a major construction project rarely undertaken in early nineteenth-century New Town houses let alone the tenements of the less well-off.[21] In his 1847 report on the Sanitary Condition on the Old Town of Edinburgh James Stark observed that '100,000 of the inhabitants of Edinburgh are strangers to the comforts of these conveniences [water-closets] … even Edinburgh itself stands more in need of sanitary improvements than most English towns.'[22] As late as 1915, three in ten of Edinburgh households still shared a water-closet.[23]

Blackened sandstone tenements discoloured by decades of sooty deposits were, with their ill-lit wynds and ill-paved narrow streets, 'no-go' areas to all

16 D. Defoe, *A Tour Thro' the whole Island of Great Britain, Divided into Circuits or Journies*, vol. III (London, 1727), 575–87, describes these as 'thronged buildings, from seven to ten or twelve story high'. By 1748, when the 4th edition was published, Defoe had revised this to 'six to ten stories high,' Vol. IV, 69. A few still survive as in Leith Street, Leith Wynd.

17 W. Chambers, *Report*, 1.

18 *The Mercury* (Hobart, Tasmania), 26 February 1866, 3d. See also R. Rodger, 'The Victorian building industry and the housing of the Scottish working class', 153–69.

19 J. Swift, *A Tale of a Tub* (London, 1704), section III.

20 D. Defoe, *Tour* (London, 4th edn, 1748), 69. Defoe's description of the tenements, of excrement and emptying chamber pots, and about the living arrangements, were substantially reproduced by nineteenth-century writers such as William Chambers and Alexander Wood.

21 A. Lewis, thesis, 7–22.

22 J. Sutherland (ed.), in *Journal of Public Health and Monthly Record of Sanitary Improvement*, 268–9. The estimate of 100,000, or two-thirds of the population of Edinburgh in 1847, probably reflects the tendency from the early nineteenth century to build New Town flats with toilets.

23 PP (HC) 1917–18 XIV, Royal Commission on the Housing of the Industrial Population of Scotland, Report, 77.

2.4 Blackfriars' Wynd, Cowgate, 1856
The photographer, Thomas Keith, was a pre-eminent gynaecological surgeon and a pioneer of photography. His pictures include numerous images of Edinburgh as social commentary. [Source: ECL]

2.5 Upper College Wynd, 1870
The photographer Archibald Burns took this and a series of related images prior to demolitions associated with the Edinburgh Improvement Act 1867. [Source: ECL]

except those who returned to these lofty Scottish rookeries each night.[24] Dr George Bell explained the debilitating nature of living conditions in Blackfriars' Wynd by recounting how ten consumptive Irish immigrants lived in a single room.[25] Dr Lee, the minister to the Old Church of Edinburgh, testified to the Royal Commission on Religious Instruction in 1836 that on one day he had visited seven flats in which there was not a single bed.[26] In another account of the

24 D.A. Symonds, *Notorious Murders, Black Lanterns, & Moveable Goods: The Transformation of Edinburgh's Underworld in the Early Nineteenth Century* (Akron, 2006), 52–73.

25 G. Bell, *Day and Night in the Wynds of Edinburgh* (Edinburgh, 1849); G. Bell *Blackfriars' Wynd Analyzed* (Edinburgh, 1850), 10, 12–25.

26 PP (HC) 1837 XXI, 31, Royal Commission on Religious Instruction in Scotland, *Report*. The commissioners investigated the opportunities for public worship, religious instruction and pastoral guidance in the Presbytery of Edinburgh in order to identify the parishes where such opportunities were inadequate. The numbers belonging to each denomination were established, and statistics gathered relating to attendance and to seat-rents. The commissioners were instructed to pay particular attention to the poor and working classes, but experienced some difficulties in defining these groups, leading to uncertainty about their findings. The Report concluded that the poorer classes were found to be the most neglectful of public worship, and that this was attributable to a lack of decent clothing, the need for rest after a working week, the high cost of seat-rents and, most commonly, the general indifference to religion.

condition in which the Edinburgh poor subsisted, evidence presented in 1842 to Edwin Chadwick's *Report on the Sanitary Condition of the Labouring Population of Great Britain* explained that chickens roosted on bed posts, and dogs and donkeys shared dwellings with humans so that there was a shocking stench and swarms of vermin in the tenements of central Edinburgh.[27]

The precarious and marginal nature of daily existence in Scotland's capital city was summed up by the extent of overcrowding in some closes of the Old Town, which was four times greater than in the cells of Edinburgh prison. Small wonder, then, that William Chambers concluded that, 'the construction of the town is radically unfavourable to health', and despaired of short-term efforts to address the situation, since 'the evil is too monstrous for cure by ... superficial means'.[28] Yet a solution was available. It was advanced from the best informed of sources: the 'active and intelligent' Inspector of Lighting and Cleansing, Alexander Ramsay, who, in his Report on the drainage and purification of the crowded parts of the city in 1843, 'strongly recommends an officer of health' to address environmental conditions.[29] Ramsay also costed the appointment of a Medical Officer of Health as adding a farthing (¼*d*. or about 30p in 2011 prices) to local taxes for duties which included sanitary inspection, removal of nuisances, lodging-house surveillance, lime-washing closes, and statistical analysis. These themes were taken up and promoted to packed audiences a few weeks later in a series of fifteen lectures by James Simpson, advocate and philanthropist.[30] In responding to 3,000 working-class signatories requesting him to address them on housing and living conditions, Simpson reflected on the need for a Medical Officer of Health:

> Customs and practices subversive of health, and productive of disease, could not prevail; fever could not break out and spread unheeded, or the stricken be deserted and left to die by frightened relatives and neighbours, all of which have again and again happened, if there were appointed a Medical Officer of Health, in every great town, whose sole duty it should be to visit at all times the whole town, but especially the places where disease is most likely to break out, and advise the means of relief and prevention.[31]

The debate over the appointment of a Medical Officer of Health – and even what constituted a Medical Officer of Health – haunted Edinburgh citizens for the next twenty years.

27 PP (HL) 1842 XXVI, Poor Law Commissioners' Report on the Sanitary Condition of the Labouring Population; J.E. Hanley, *The Irish in Scotland* (Cork, 1943), 102–3, describes pigs kept in attics that were so heavy that had to lowered from upper storeys in cradles when the practice was banned in 1831.

28 W. Chambers, *Report.*

29 *Caledonian Mercury*, 25 December 1843, 3f; *The Scotsman*, 30 December 1843, 3b.

30 J. Simpson's lectures were reported in the *Edinburgh Weekly Chronicle and Scottish Pilot*, 16 December 1843 to 13 April 1844. The lectures were subsequently published as *Brief Reports of Lectures Delivered to the Working Classes of Edinburgh: on the means in their own power of improving their character & condition* (Edinburgh, 1844), http://www.jstor.org/stable/60200647

31 Lecture 4 (6 January 1844, 15–16), 'Sanatory Improvement – Officers of Health', reported in *The Scotsman*, 6 January 1844, 3h.

Public health and the development of medical policing in Scotland

'The poor in Scotland, especially in Edinburgh and Glasgow,' stated Friedrich Engels in 1844, 'are worse off than in any other region of the three kingdoms,' and, as if to ensure the point were not missed and that the Irish were not unfairly blamed, reiterated that 'the poorest are not the Irish, but Scotch'.[32] Poverty, disease, and public health were inextricably linked in the debates of the 1820s, 1830s and 1840s, and Engels had been briefed on this during his travels through Britain. One of his sources was Dr William Pulteney Alison, an Edinburgh physician and long-time critic of the system of poor relief in Scotland.[33] Alison had calculated that in 1841 there were 23,000 persons, or 16.8% of the population of Edinburgh, who 'during at least part of the year "of necessity must live by alms"'.[34] Of this number, only 7,000 were entitled to 'legal relief', which meant that 11.6% of the population were destitute, had 'no lawful means of subsistence', and were a charge 'on the *industry* of the country'.[35] This was both 'more injurious and more unjust' than in England, where the costs of a lower level of pauperism (9%) were met by property owners through poor rates.[36] In Edinburgh, higher levels of pauperism and destitution contributed directly to an annual mortality rate of 1 in 27.4, or 10% above the highest recorded mortality rate recorded in England (in Liverpool, at 1 in 30.1). Alison linked life expectancy and the incidence of contagious disease in urban Scotland with public health and the living conditions associated with the prevalence of pauperism:

2.6 William Pulteney Alison (1790–1859), *c*.1850
Alison was Professor of the Practice of Medicine 1842–55 (physiology, pathology and therapeutics) and a member of the Aesculapian Club, a group of 11 distinguished Edinburgh surgeons and 11 distinguished physicians committed to 'the art of healing'. [Source: RCPEd]

> Let us look to the closes of Edinburgh, and the wynds of Glasgow, and thoroughly understand the character and habits, the diseases and mortality, of the unemployed poor, unprotected by the law, who gather there from all parts of the country; let us study the condition of the aged and disabled poor ... let us compare these things with the provisions for the poor, not only in England but in many other Christian countries; so far from priding ourselves on the smallness of the sums which are applied to this purpose in Scotland we must honestly and candidly confess, that our parsimony in this particular is equally injurious to the poor and discreditable to the rich in Scotland.[37]

In its wide-ranging approach to public health Littlejohn's *Report* followed in a tradition established in the eighteenth century as part of the Scottish Enlightenment,

32 F. Engels, *The Condition of the Working Class in England in 1844* (London 1936 edn), 67–8. Although Engels' work was not published in English until 1887, he knew of Dr W.P. Alison and may well have met him on his visit to Edinburgh.

33 S.M.K. Martin, 'William Pulteney Alison: activist, philanthropist and pioneer of social medicine', St Andrews University, Ph.D. thesis, 1997. For biographical details of Alison, see the entry by L.S. Jacyna, *Oxford Dictionary of National Biography* (subsequently *ODNB*) (Oxford, 2004), and Online.

34 W.P. Alison, paper read to the Statistical Section of the British Association, Manchester, 28 June 1842, published as 'On the destitution and mortality in some of the large towns in Scotland', *Journal of the Royal Statistical Society of London*, 5:3 (1842), 289–92. See also *JRSS*, 4 (1841), 288.

35 At the time of the publication of Littlejohn's *Report* in 1865 the three Edinburgh parishes spent the equivalent of over £4 million *per annum* on the relief of paupers. See *The Scotsman*, 19 April 1865, 2cd.

36 Alison, 'On the destitution and mortality', 290.

37 W.P. Alison, *Observations on the Management of the Poor in Scotland and its Effects on the Health of the Great Towns* (Edinburgh, 1840), 66.

centred in Edinburgh and with important links to continental Europe. The newly founded medical school (1726) introduced 'a flexible but rigorous curriculum' modelled on that at Leiden University which 'emphasized practical expertise at the bedside' and 'swiftly elevated the quality of Edinburgh's medical training above and beyond its older rival school at Cambridge and Oxford'.[38] The basis of this imported curriculum was 'teaching medicine as a practical skill and not as a theoretical subject' and, although attendance at the most extensive and distinguished medical lectures of any offered in Britain was not compulsory, clinical experience was. Indeed, for most of the eighteenth century Edinburgh University was exceptional in Britain in requiring students to have treated patients prior to their graduation.[39] 'Medicine in the Scottish Enlightenment was as concerned with teaching aspiring doctors as with caring and curing,' and so political economy and moral philosophy, known as 'Scotch Knowledge', were also as part of a 'professional approach to medical education'.[40] Indeed, Scottish national identity itself was constructed upon a basis of such a wide-ranging discourse.[41]

In addition to the Leiden connection, Scottish medical education was shaped by continental influences. The lectures of the German physician and hygienist, Johann Peter Frank published between 1779 and 1827, *A Complete System of Medical,* were intended, significantly, not for doctors but for rulers and their administrators.[42] Frank stressed that a country's greatest asset was its population, and in so doing forged a link between the welfare of the state and the state of the people's welfare. Similarly, in pre-revolutionary France, Jean-Jacques Rousseau claimed that degeneration and disease were inextricably associated with social inequality.[43] It followed that to protect people from the adverse effects of the environment in which they lived and worked involved 'policing' or monitoring their health, and making recommendations to ameliorate conditions. It was in this respect that continental European thinking was most advanced, particularly in France, where after a half-century of initiatives hygienists had established their position as 'leaders in public health until the late 1830s'.[44] During the Revolution

38 A. Budd, *John Armstrong's* The Art of Preserving Health: *Eighteenth-Century Sensibility in Practice* (Farnham, 2011), 9.

39 L. Rosner, *Medical Education in the Age of Improvement: Edinburgh Students and Apprentices, 1760–1826* (Edinburgh, 1991), 47; J.D. Comrie, *History of Scottish Medicine to 1860* (London, 1927), 197. On medical societies see J. Jenkinson, *Scottish Medical Societies, 1731–1939: Their History and Records* (Edinburgh, 1993), Appendix 1.

40 A. Chitnis, *The Scottish Enlightenment and Early Victorian English Society* (London, 1986), 7, quoted in Martin, thesis, 26.

41 R.B. Sher, *Church and University in the Scottish Enlightenment: the Moderate Literati of Edinburgh* (Edinburgh, 1985); R.H. Campbell and A.S. Skinner (eds), *The Origins and Nature of the Scottish Enlightenment* (Edinburgh, 1982); N.T. Phillipson, 'The Scottish Enlightenment' in R. Porter and M. Teich (eds), *The Enlightenment in National Context* (Cambridge, 1981), 19–40.

42 J.P. Frank, *System einer vollständigen medicinischen Polizey* (1779–1827). For selections from Frank's work see E. Lesky (ed.), *A System of Complete Medical Police: Selections from Johann Peter Frank* (Baltimore 1976), see especially the Introduction.

43 J.-J. Rousseau's *Discours sur les Sciences et les Arts* (1750) and *Discours sur l'origine et les fondements de l'inégalité parmi les hommes* (*Discourse on the Origin of Inequality*) (1755) claimed injustices were the result of controls applied to human behaviour by political authorities and the educated elite.

44 A.F. La Berge, *Mission and Method: the Early Nineteenth-Century French Public Health Movement* (Cambridge, 1992), 315.

two developments influenced French public health directly: first, there was a recognition that the poor were citizens, too, with health-care rights; second, an investigation in 1791 by the French Royal Medical Society reported on hospital conditions and proposed improvements to management, including the regulation of numbers admitted, private beds for each patient, specialist hospitals, and the separation of patients according to ailments. The approach in France aimed to decrease mortality and morbidity, improve quality of life, and go beyond the customary practice of controlling epidemic disease and nuisance to address the underlying causes of ill-health. It was a proactive rather than reactive approach.[45]

In both France and Germany 'medical policing' was adopted in the last quarter of the eighteenth century to address the fact that poverty and indigence were considered socio-economic problems, and not just moral ones.[46] Thus in a continental context, medical policing, like other forms of policing, had a defensive role in counteracting the disorder increasingly associated with the rapid growth of towns and cities.[47] What distinguished medicine in these countries was greater state involvement, whether by hospitals or dispensaries for outpatients, organised through municipal or departmental authorities. This approach was founded on the argument that patients could be treated promptly, locally, before their ailments became so acute that they were weakened physically and so debilitated that they could no longer work. 'Care in the community' was not a construct of the twentieth-century British state; it was part of community medicine two centuries previously. The health of the public was not a matter to be left to choice or chance. It was axiomatic that if there were a direct causal relationship between ill-health and indigence, then poverty was the central problem of public health and that medicine had a political dimension.[48]

In Scotland a line of distinguished sanitarians and hygienists promoted the cause of medical policing. Foremost among them, and almost contemporary with Frank, was John Roberton, author of the influential *Treatise on Medical Police*.[49]

45 A.F. La Berge, 'The Paris health council, 1801–1848', *Bulletin of the History of Medicine*, 49 (1975), 339–52; A.F. La Berge, 'The early nineteenth-century French public health movement: the disciplinary development and institutionalization of hygiene publique', *Bulletin of the History of Medicine*, 58 (1984), 363–79. For a useful annual list of developments in France, see E.H. Ackerknecht, 'Hygiene in France, 1815–1848', *Bulletin of the History of Medicine*, 22 (1948), 117–55.

46 Medical police was a term not unknown in England. It figured in the noted textbook by W. Buchan, *Domestic Medicine: A Treatise on the Prevention and Cure of Diseases by Regimen and Simple Medicines* (London, 1772), ix; J. Ireland, *Hogarth Illustrated* (London, 1791), 140, where it was recommended that 'strict attention to the medical police of a city so crowded with inhabitants was warranted'; T. Laycock, 'A treatise on medical police, and on diet regimen', *Westminster Review*, March 1846, EUL Special Collections, P.201/1; W. Nisbet, *First Lines of the Theory and Practice in Venereal Disease* (Edinburgh, 1787), 335, commented on the need for medical police.

47 S. Kaplan, *Bread, Politics and Political Economy in the Reign of Louis XV*, vol. 1 (The Hague 1976), 11; L. Jordanova, 'Policing public health in France 1780–1815', in T. Ogawa (ed.), *Public Health: Proceedings of the 5th International Symposium on the Comparative History of Medicine* (Tokyo, 1981), 12–32.

48 G. Rosen, 'Cameralism and the concept of medical police', *Bulletin of the History of Medicine* 27 (1952), 21–42; L. Jordanova, 'Medical police and public health: problems of practice and ideology', *Society for the Social History of Medicine*, 27 (1980), 15–19.

49 J. Roberton, *A Treatise on Medical Police, and on Diet, Regimen, &c: in which the permanent and regularly recurring causes of disease in general, and those of Edinburgh and London in particular, are described; with a general plan of medical police to obviate them, and a particular one adapted to the local*

Andrew Duncan, senior, defined medical policing as 'the application of the principles deduced from the different branches of medical knowledge, for the promotion, preservation and restoration of general health', and recommended in 1798 that physicians should advise town councillors as to the best means of preventing disease.[50] Indeed, police statutes were soon passed in Glasgow (1800) and Edinburgh (1805) (see chapter 3) and covered watching, lighting, street cleaning and water supply.[51] This engagement by civic authorities with general or public health issues in the early nineteenth century spread quickly to other burghs and was endorsed by William Alison, who as newly appointed Professor of Medical Jurisprudence and Medical Police in 1821 stated in his *Lectures on Medical Police* that medical knowledge applied and 'adopted by the legislature and Magistrates [councillors]' was the best 'means of preserving and improving the public health'.[52] Alison's views on medical policing significantly coloured Littlejohn's approach to public health.[53]

To 'police' was to watch or monitor; to engage with authorities who could act legitimately in the public interest involved 'jurisprudence'.[54] Medical policing, therefore, sought to reveal general principles through the systematic analysis of public health, and then to promote recommendations to the public authorities. Accordingly, doctors, scientists and social reformers in the early nineteenth

circumstances of these cities (Edinburgh, 1808–09), 2 vols, vol. II, 223–93, EUL, Special Collections, S.B. 613–4 Rob.

50 A. Duncan, *A Short View of the Extent and Importance of Medical Jurisprudence, Considered as a Branch of Education* (Edinburgh, 1798), 4. For an assessment of Duncan's role in the history of medical police see G. Rosen, '*From Medical Police to Social Medicine* (New York 1974), and B.M. White, 'Medical police. Politics and police: the fate of John Roberton', *Medical History*, 27 (1983), 407–22.

51 G.S. Pryde, *Central and Local Government in Scotland Since* 1707 (London, 1960), 12. Pryde notes (p. 15) how these Police Acts provided a model for other Scottish burghs, and this resulted in 'nearly uniform patterns of burgh government in Scotland' which in turn made subsequent municipal reform in Scotland easier than in England. See also D.G. Barrie, '"Epoch-Making" beginnings to lingering death: the struggle for control of the Glasgow Police Commission, 1833–46', *Scottish Historical Review*, 86 (2007), 256–7.

52 W.P. Alison, *Lectures on Medical Jurisprudence and Medical Police*, I, 2, quoted in Martin, thesis, 44.

53 Alison and many other influential figures in public health and social administration were influenced by Dugald Stewart, Professor of Moral Philosophy at Edinburgh University, whose lectures they attended. See M.W. Flinn, 'Introduction' to the *Report on the Sanitary Condition of the Labouring Population of Gt Britain* (Edinburgh, repr. edn 1965), introduction, 22–3, who identifies three categories of social reformers heavily influenced by Dugald Stewart: (i) aristocratic politicians; (ii) civil servants and inspectors; (iii) socio-medical reformers. Flinn comments that Stewart's disciples were his best work. See also D. Stewart, *Elements of the Philosophy of the Human Mind*, 3 vols (Edinburgh, 1792, 1814, 1827), vol. 1, 224, quoted in Jacyna, *Philosophic Whigs*, 39.

54 This interaction of medical police and jurisprudence was crucial and explains why university professors often combined them in the title of their post. M. Crowther and B. White, *On Soul and Conscience: The Medical Expert and Crime* (Aberdeen, 1988), 7–8, explain medical policing as 'the use of medicine in the service of the state, both to protect the health of its subjects and to keep them under control', though in 'Medicine, property and the law in Britain, 1800–1914', *Historical Journal*, 31 (1988), 855, they go further by saying that medical jurisprudence may be defined to be 'that science which teaches the application of every branch of medical knowledge to the purposes of the law'. The issue of advising civil authorities on practical policies, however, is not incorporated here, nor in contemporary definitions of medical jurisprudence or forensic medicine. See A.S. Taylor, *The Principles and Practice of Medical Jurisprudence* (London, 1865), xvii.

century increasingly conducted experiments to explore how, if at all, topography, humidity, seasonality, diet and food quality, drainage, education, the rate of decomposition of corpses, air quality and other variables influenced health.[55]

By the early nineteenth century, therefore, and certainly after the publication of Alison's *Lectures* in 1821, there was a greater willingness to see medical problems in a wider social context. Medical science sought to identify the causes of disease, rather than just the causes of the spread of disease, and was influenced by the teaching at Edinburgh University of Alison and his acolytes.[56] Their purpose was to identify what practical preventive measures could be taken to improve public health, and their efforts ensured that Scotland was pre-eminent in the realm of medical jurisprudence by virtue of the compulsory nature of the subject in the medical examinations at both Edinburgh and Glasgow universities.[57] Medical policing, therefore, was inextricably connected with medical jurisprudence. As their congested, overcrowded cities came under attack from cholera, urban officials – with legal powers that were enshrined in Police Acts after 1805 in Edinburgh – were increasingly concerned about courses of action designed to minimise epidemics.

Community medicine and the nature of poverty

The developing social and residential division of early nineteenth-century Edinburgh was, perhaps predictably, reflected in medical politics. Nowhere was this more marked than in the foundation in 1815 of the New Town Dispensary intended to provide relief to the sick and poor, to attend women in their own homes during and after childbirth, and to inoculate children. The New Town Dispensary was in direct competition both geographically with the Public Dispensary established in the Old Town in 1776 and, in terms of the medical reputations and incomes of the doctors involved.[58] A 'civic war' existed over the future governance of these dispensaries: should they be managed by either medical supervision, or by managers elected by subscribers to increase public participation – a proposal described by Lord Henry Cockburn as 'impracticable and

55 See also, J. Cleland, *The Annals of Glasgow* (Glasgow, 1816) for an account of the state of the poor, and who in 1819 undertook the most extensive and sophisticated local census on local conditions *The Rise and Progress of the City of Glasgow* (Glasgow, 1820).

56 D. Guthrie, *Scottish Influence on the Evolution of British Medicine* (London, 1960); H.M. Dingwall, *A History of Scottish Medicine* (Edinburgh, 2002).

57 M. Crowther and B. White, 'Medicine, property and the law', 857. For a comparison of the relationship between medical training and licensing in Glasgow and Edinburgh, and relations with the respective town councils see C.F. Lloyd, 'The search for legitimacy: universities, medical licensing bodies, and governance in Glasgow and Edinburgh from the late eighteenth to the late nineteenth centuries' in R.J. Morris and R.H. Trainor (eds), *Urban Governance: Britain and Beyond since 1750* (Aldershot, 2000), 198–210.

58 O. Checkland, *Philanthropy in Victorian Scotland: Social Welfare and the Voluntary Principle* (Edinburgh, 1980), 202–3, suggests this was a Whig–Tory divide, but L.S. Jacyna, *Philosophic Whigs*, 25–36, shows that this is too simplistic a view of the conflict over the Edinburgh dispensaries. This raises the question of whether, as C. Hamlin claims ('William Pulteney Alison, the Scottish philosophy, and the making of a political medicine,' *Journal of the History of Medicine and Allied Sciences*, 61 (2006), 144–86), medicine with its considerable call on resources could not be anything other than political, and a medical extension of Adam Smith and Dugald Stewart's political economy.

dangerously popular'?[59] Fragmented responsibility for public health management was a consistent feature of public health management until a single Public Health Committee assumed overall responsibility in 1872.

William Alison was one of the founders of the New Town Dispensary, and in the course of the next quarter of a century he and his colleagues treated over 190,000 medical and surgical cases – the equivalent of twenty per day – and made 84,000 home visits, or an average of nine per day.[60] This was social or community medicine in action. It was organised hierarchically by 1821 with three Extraordinary Medical Officers – Alison, as consulting physician and consulting surgeon advised nine Ordinary Medical Officers 'on all difficult and important cases'.[61] In turn, these nine doctors were assisted by clerks, normally advanced medical students, who paid a guinea (£1.05) each quarter to dispensary funds. James Kay, later Dr James Kay-Shuttleworth, was employed as an assistant in 1826 and accompanied Alison on his visits to the poor of the Canongate and Cowgate. He recalled the experience fifty years later:

> If there had been any tendency in the culture of the scientific spirit to extinguish compassionate sympathy, I had at my side constantly the example of Professor Alison, who combined both in equal proportion.[62]

The New Town Dispensary developed a pyramid structure or line-management model to administer the health of the city's sick poor. Medical officers undertook home visiting with follow-up visits, vaccination, prescriptions and surgical procedures; they provided a comprehensive community health service which, despite its name, was not confined to the New Town. Social inclusion was a core principle; Alison was insistent that need alone was qualification for treatment.

The experience gained in attending the sick poor was complemented by expertise obtained in dealing with epidemic disease, based on studies of three epidemics – measles, smallpox and fever – made by the New Town Dispensary between 1816 and 1818.[63] Most significant was the report on the fever epidemic of 1817–19 because this identified 'exciting' and 'predisposing' causes, that is, both epidemiological and environmental explanations.[64] Patients caught fever from a specific (exciting) contagion but were more susceptible to it when weakened and exposed to unhygienic living conditions (predisposing causes). In Alison's words:

> contagion ... acts most rapidly and most certainly on the human body when enfeebled by deficient nourishment, by insufficient protection against the cold,

59 The term 'civic war' was used by Henry Cockburn, *Memorials of His Time* (New York, 1856 edn), 268–69. See also L.S. Jacyna, *Philosophic Whigs*, 25.

60 Annual Report of the New Town Dispensary for 1841, 12–13, quoted in Martin, thesis, 65–6. Vaccinations and midwifery involved a further 13,000 consultations.

61 Annual Report of the New Town Dispensary for 1821, 14.

62 F. Smith, *Life of Sir James Kay-Shuttleworth* (London, 1974 edn) 12, quoted in Martin, thesis, 68.

63 Published in the *Edinburgh Medical and Surgical Journal*, 13 (1817), 400; 14, 1818, 123–24; and 15 (1819), 311.

64 For a further discussion of exciting and predisposing causes see C. Hamlin, 'Predisposing causes and public health in early nineteenth-century medical thought', *Social History of Medicine*, 5, 1992 5, 43–70; J.V. Pickstone, 'Dearth, dirt and fever epidemics: rewriting the history of British 'public health' 1780–1850', in T.O. Ranger and P. Slack (eds), *Epidemics and Ideas: Essays on the Historical Perception of Pestilence* (Cambridge, 1992) 125–48.

2.7 Canongate Fever Hospital
Littlejohn was concerned that there was insufficient capacity in the city to deal effectively with epidemic disease. His campaign for an isolation hospital was successful only in 1897, at Craiglockhart, where three new streets bear Littlejohn's name. [Source: Lothian Health Services Archives]

> by mental depression, by occasional intemperance, and by crowding in small, ill-aired rooms, all of which are constant concomitants of destitution in the poorer inhabitants of this and other great towns.[65]

Edinburgh was under attack in terms of epidemic disease precisely at that point in the nineteenth century when it was experiencing its fastest rate of growth, 3% p.a.[66] Alison devised an integrated, preventive approach which in a two-year period isolated more that 1,000 patients in a separate hospital, Queensberry House, and enabled doctors to recommend for fumigation the homes of fever victims. The New Town Dispensary was instrumental in demonstrating that destitution was a major factor in the spread of communicable disease, and consequently medical opinion, championed by Alison, became a central element in a thirty-year campaign to reform the Scottish Poor Law.

The New Town Dispensary studies were significant for four reasons. First, evidence indicated that the removal of the predisposing (unhygienic) causes would confine the fever. Though it was impossible to remove the overcrowding and insanitary conditions, it was possible to remove the patient from them by isolating them in a fever hospital. Second, it was logical to identify areas in the city where inhabitants would be most 'predisposed' to disease, epidemic or otherwise,

65 W.P. Alison, lecture to the statistical section of the British Association for the Advancement of Science, 18 September 1840, printed as *Illustrations of the Practical Operations of the Scottish System of Management of the Poor* (Edinburgh, 1840).
66 R. Rodger, *The Transformation of Edinburgh*, 23, table 1.3.

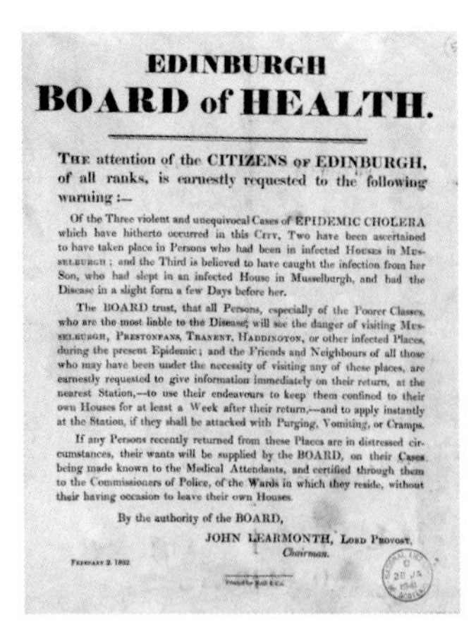

EDINBURGH
BOARD of HEALTH.

THE attention of the CITIZENS OF EDINBURGH, of all ranks, is earnestly requested to the following warning:—

Of the Three violent and unequivocal Cases of EPIDEMIC CHOLERA which have hitherto occurred in this CITY, Two have been ascertained to have taken place in Persons who had been in infected HOUSES in MUSSELBURGH; and the Third is believed to have caught the infection from her Son, who had slept in an infected House in Musselburgh, and had the Disease in a slight form a few Days before her.

The BOARD trust, that all Persons, especially of the Poorer Classes, who are the most liable to the Disease, will see the danger of visiting MUSSELBURGH, PRESTONPANS, TRANENT, HADDINGTON, or other infected Places, during the present Epidemic; and the Friends and Neighbours of all those who may have been under the necessity of visiting any of these places, are earnestly requested to give information immediately on their return, at the nearest Station,—to use their endeavours to keep them confined to their own Houses for at least a Week after their return,—and to apply instantly at the Station, if they shall be attacked with Purging, Vomiting, or Cramps.

If any Persons recently returned from these Places are in distressed circumstances, their wants will be supplied by the BOARD, on their Cases being made known to the Medical Attendants, and certified through them to the Commissioners of Police, of the Wards in which they reside, without their having occasion to leave their own Houses.

By the authority of the BOARD,

JOHN LEARMONTH, LORD PROVOST, *Chairman.*

FEBRUARY 2. 1832

2.8 Board of Health notice, 2 February 1832
Handbills publicised the existence of cholera and advocated a number of strategies to limit contagion. [Source: RCAHMS]

and this focused attention on a social medicine approach.[67] Thus medical police (observing where disease was most prevalent) and medical jurisprudence (identifying courses of action available to public authorities such as fumigation, isolation, and street cleaning) were fused through the observation, analysis and recommendations of medical experts.[68] In this sense Alison was 'ahead of his time in social ideas'.[69] Third, the New Town Dispensary quarterly reports and epidemic studies were the subject of extensive reporting, and considerable local interest, in the columns of *The Scotsman* newspaper, which commenced publication in 1817. In this respect, Littlejohn's 'Weekly Reports' in 1865 followed in a pattern that had been established almost half a century previously and which familiarised the reading public with sensitive issues associated with public health. Fourth, several agencies cooperated to deal with epidemic disease. A Fever Board[70] established in 1817 paid for in-patient care, burials, and the actual fumigation itself; the Public Dispensary paid for the fumigation materials; and the Destitute Sick and Clothing Society, organised on a district basis, supported the families. This geographical dimension was another element that figured prominently in Littlejohn's approach in the 1860s.

The Fever Board became permanent, and its organisational framework was recommended to the medical committee of the Edinburgh Board of Health when it met to draw up measures to combat cholera in 1831.[71] These included the powers assigned to the Police Commission concerning hospital isolation, fumigation and whitewashing of homes, and the removal of victims, much in keeping with those previously operated by the Fever Board. The Edinburgh Board of Health also had powers to remove nuisances such as pigs and dung-hills, restrict the movement of vagrants and beggars, and to establish facilities to clothe and feed the poor, for which purpose they set up nine soup kitchens and a clothing store. Organisationally the Edinburgh Board of Health divided the city into thirty areas, corresponding to the police wards; a 100-strong team of doctors, supported by a reserve list of a further 40–50 doctors, were assigned to specific districts and made daily visits.[72]

Before the cholera outbreak in 1832, municipal powers concerning epidemic disease in Edinburgh were anticipatory in character. This was a legacy of the

67 C. Hamlin, 'Pre-disposing causes', 52–3 argues that public health in Britain need not have taken the direction based largely on the Chadwick Report. See also C. Hamlin, *Public Health and Social Justice in the Age of Chadwick: Britain 1800–1854* (Cambridge, 1998), 84–97.

68 This approach was not unique since elements of it existed as a result of proposals by the London Fever Hospital 1801 which further underlines Hamlin's view that Chadwick's approach was not inevitable.

69 J. Brotherstone, *Early Public Health*, 65.

70 Modelled on the Manchester Board of Health. Other fever boards existed in Liverpool, Chester and London.

71 The medical committee was composed of members of both the Royal College of Physicians of Edinburgh, and of Surgeons. Alison was a member of the committee. For an account of the formation of the Edinburgh Board of Health, see R. Christison, 'Account of the arrangements made by the Edinburgh Board of Health', *Edinburgh Medical and Surgical Journal*, 37 (1832), cclv–cclvi; H.P. Tait, 'The Cholera Board of Health, 1831–34', *Medical Officer*, 98 (1957), 235; C.F. Brockington, 'The cholera, 1831', *Medical Officer*, 96 (1956), 75.

72 The initial model was the London Board of Health. See Martin, thesis, 88; D. Porter, *Health, Civilization and the State: A History of Public Health from Ancient to Modern Times* (London, 1999), 120.

outbreak in 1817 when the Edinburgh Fever Board was set up. Using these powers, it was easier – and cheaper too – to target pigs, beggars and the Irish than to deal with sewers and drains where nuisance powers were weak. On the positive side, from 1832 the medical police role could be funded from local taxation and was the obvious way to administer medical relief to the poor where poor rates were absent.[73] *The Scotsman* made the point in 1831:

> if the public are assessed for lighting and cleaning the streets, why should they not be assessed for the expense of checking contagious fever, and thereby protecting themselves and families from this malady ... this ought not to be left as a matter of *charity*. It is a matter of police.[74]

Despite this development in the management of fever, it remained a fractured responsibility into the 1850s.

The Edinburgh Police Bill 1832, one of a series of Local Acts of Parliament, consolidated and extended the authority of police commissioners (see chapter 3).[75] To these 'acts for regulating the Police' functions of watching, cleaning and lighting in Edinburgh further Local Acts specifically referred to environmental health issues such as drainage (1809), street improvements (1816, 1827, 1831, 1833), lighting (1818), gardens and green spaces (1809, 1822), slaughterhouses (1850), and slum clearance (1853).[76] In short, the concept of 'police' went far beyond watching property to watching a range of environmental health concerns, and so demonstrated that the term 'public health' was deeply rooted in a broad Scottish vision of civic responsibility.[77]

Poverty, public health and environmental inequalities

William Alison had over a quarter of century of first-hand experience of the health of the poor in Edinburgh. He had conducted studies of fever and analysed admissions to the Royal Infirmary, as did Henry Littlejohn a generation later. There were data on Edinburgh fever patients, the destitute sick, and admissions to the House of Refuge and those fed by the soup kitchen. The data were not strictly comparable over time, but in the absence of civil registration and data on the causes of death, the statistics were reasonably robust, and indicative in broad terms of an

73 The English approach of raising funds through Poor Law assessments was impossible in Scotland where patchy Poor Law provision existed.

74 *The Scotsman*, 9 November 1831.

75 45 Geo. 3, cap. 21; 52 Geo 3, cap. 41; 57 Geo. 3, cap. 33; 3 Geo. 4, cap. 78; 7 Geo. 4, cap. 115. Edinburgh Town Council extended the scope of their urban management with a further series of local Police Acts passed by Parliament in 1834, 1837, 1848, 1854 and 1856. See 4 and 5 Will. 4, cap. 76; 7 Will. 4, cap. 32; 11 and 12 Vict., cap. 114; 17 and 18 Vict. cap 118; 19 and 20 Vict., cap. 53.

76 M. Atkinson, *Local Government in Scotland* (Edinburgh, 1904), 69–72; I. Maver, 'The Scottish provost since 1800: tradition, continuity, and change in the leadership of local self government', in J. Garrard (ed.), *Heads of the Local State: Mayors, Provosts and Burgomaster since 1800* (Aldershot, 2007), 29–46.

77 P.E. Carroll, 'Medical police and the history of public health', *Medical History*, 46 (2002), 461–94, notes that medical policing covered seven areas: nuisances, sanitary engineering, food adulteration, dangerous materials, occupational hazards, pharmacy, communities (poor, prostitutes).

increase in poverty in Scotland.[78] It was against this background that Alison wrote a letter to the Lord Advocate about the relationship between fever and poverty:

> I have never been able to satisfy myself that the degree of diffusion in one place more than another depends on any other than two conditions, viz. the Crowding and the Destitution of the people.[79]

In his *Observations on the Management of the Poor*, published in January 1840, Alison argued convincingly that recurring epidemics were not just the 'occasion' of much suffering, but were inevitable or, as he put it, a 'foregone conclusion'. Epidemics were 'the indication and test of much previous misery and destitution'. Continuing with this theme, Alison delivered his key point:[80]

> It is not asserted that destitution is a cause adequate to the production of fever ... nor that it is the sole cause of its extension. What we are sure of is, that it is a cause of the rapid diffusion of contagious fever, and one of such peculiar power and efficacy, that its existence may always be presumed, when we see fever prevailing in a large community to an unusual extent.[81]

The relationship between poverty and public health was clearly stated. Fever originated from a specific source of contagion, but its spread was exacerbated by 'pre-disposing causes', principally malnourishment, overcrowding, insanitary conditions and, significantly, destitution.[82] Poverty weakened the constitution by 'pre-disposing' individuals to disease. A spiral of decline could easily be initiated: an incapacitated person might well lack the ability to work, and this incapacity would further intensify poverty. Overcrowding and the social distress of unemployment contributed further to the chances of infection. This also had a cyclical dimension, and statistical evidence from Dundee and Glasgow subsequently confirmed that economic depression in these cities was associated with higher levels of fever between 1836 and 1839.[83] By 1827, Alison's conviction of the link between destitution and unemployment led him and others in 1832 to found the House of Refuge for the Destitute in Morrison's Close off the High Street which, in an effort to prevent vagrants spreading cholera, provided shelter and food for 1,003 individuals in an eight-month period.[84] Eventually the House of Refuge, with semi-official recognition from the police and a £10 annual subscription from the Queen, incorporated other charities such as the Society for the Suppression of Begging (1813), and both the Night Refuge and

78 The statistical record accumulated after 1816 shows Alison and institutional managers engaging with an emerging British statistical movement and part of what has been termed a social science movement. See F. Driver, 'Moral geographies: social science and the urban environment in nineteenth-century England', *Transactions British Institute of British Geographers*, 13 (1988), 275–87.

79 NLS SNPG MS 583/581, Watson Autographs, Alison to the Lord Advocate, 10 December 1838.

80 W.P. Alison, *Observations on the Management of the Poor in Scotland, and its Effect on the Health of the Great Towns* (Edinburgh, 1840).

81 W.P. Alison, *Observations*, 10.

82 R. Christison, 'Account of the arrangements', cclxxxi.

83 This was probably due in part to the different industrial base in these cities. See R. Rodger, 'Wages, employment and poverty in the Scottish cities, 1841–1914', in G. Gordon (ed.), *Perspectives of the Scottish City* (Aberdeen, 1985), 25–63, and Appendix 1. Recessions in the building trades in 1817, 1826 and 1836 were partly responsible for the cyclical downturns.

84 Martin, thesis, 123.

Soup Kitchen (1832).[85] Almost a century later the diet of the Edinburgh poor 'compared unfavourably with the diet of public institutions'.[86]

Together with medical professors from Glasgow University and the Andersonian Institution, Alison argued for the isolation of patients in order to break the transmission of disease, and for the disinfection of homes to reduce the chances of catching fever. This Scottish approach was fundamentally different to that of Chadwick in England and Wales where medical authorities stressed that fever was preventable by passing legislation to improve the sanitary state of towns.[87] Whereas the medical training of many Scots identified work, wages and food as social priorities to address the problems of public health, in England the emphasis was on drains and sewers. Essentially an environmental-health measure, sanitary reform 'did not tamper with class relations'[88] in England whereas it expressly addressed them in Scotland. In England, the 'hydraulic' Chadwick sought to flush out the towns to rid them of foul smells, since, as Hamlin has noted, 'the sanitary initiative was so important to the [Poor Law] commission because it was an alternative to the claim that destitution caused disease. That claim was fundamentally incompatible with the New Poor Law.'[89]

Both English and Scottish approaches recognised the environmental and contagionist dimensions of public health. Both recognised that the human spirit was frail, and that the moral fibre of the poor could not always resist the attractions of the beershop or the reach of the pawnbroker. However, in Scotland, and particularly in Edinburgh, where Alison practised, lectured and published as Professor of Medical Jurisprudence and Medical Police from 1820 until 1855, the emphasis on the role of poverty and destitution as the cause of disease diminished the reliance on environmental factors which featured so strongly in Chadwick's *Report*.

The contrasting interpretations of public health in mid-nineteenth-century Scotland and England were based on different intellectual and medical perspectives. Present on both sides of the border, though, was a view that poor relief damaged an individual's sense of responsibility and independence. To this moral judgment, Thomas Malthus added an economic one in his *Essay on the Principle of Population* (1798).[90] By providing a contribution towards household income, Malthus argued, poor relief encouraged 'imprudent' marriage: a relief payment, he claimed, contributed to living expenses, and encouraged a couple to wed before financially they were able to maintain a family. Early marriages

85 R.J. Morris, 'Philanthropy and poor relief in nineteenth-century Edinburgh. The example of a capital city without a national State government', *Mélanges de l'Ecole française de Rome. Italie et Méditerranée*, 111:1 (1999), 373.

86 Edinburgh Royal Society, 'The feeding of the working classes', *British Medical Journal*, 2, no. 2080, 1900, 1390.

87 P. Laxton, 'Fighting for public health: Dr Duncan and his adversaries, 1847–63', in S. Sheard and H. Power (eds), *Body and City: Histories of Urban Public Health* (Aldershot, 2000), 78–9.

88 M.A. Crowther, review of C. Hamlin, *Public Health and Social Justice in the Age of Chadwick: Britain 1800–54*, in *American Historical Review*, 105 (2000), 280–1.

89 C. Hamlin, *Public Health and Social Justice*, 4, 90, brackets added. See also the excellent analysis in M.W. Flinn, 'Introduction', *Report on the Sanitary Condition*, 1–73, and conclusions, 421–5.

90 T. Malthus, *An Essay on the Principle of Population, as it Affects the Future Improvement of Society* (London, 1798).

enlarged family size, increasing the population and labour force, and thus, through the laws of supply and demand, forced down wages through surplus labour. This was an element in the reasoning that lay behind the Poor Law Amendment Act, 1834, in England and Wales which denied relief to the able-bodied unemployed but provided workhouse accommodation for paupers.

In Scotland, since poor rates were collected only in a minority of parishes, and in others were based on voluntary donations at the church door, the vagaries of church revenues rendered this a defective framework for poor relief.[91] Voluntary charity, as the accounts of some organisations in Edinburgh showed, could barely cope in non-epidemic years; and in crisis years it was hopelessly inadequate. If, as Alison and voluntary relief workers claimed, poverty was increasing in Scotland in the 1830s and 1840s as a result of the dislocation caused by industrialisation, then it was beyond the capabilities of medical charities, such as the Public Dispensary, House of Refuge, Society for the Suppression of Begging, New Town Dispensary, and the Destitute Sick and Clothing Society, and the limited poor law relief in Scotland to deal effectively with scale of the problem of poverty.[92]

Based on Alison's Edinburgh data, as relief payments declined so admissions to fever hospitals rose, as did burials, and all at public expense.[93] This fever–destitution–poor relief relationship was reinforced with the intriguing observation that inhabitants in the upper, windy storeys of high-rise Edinburgh tenements were more susceptible to fever than their neighbours in the lower floors where rents, and thus incomes, were appreciably higher. This observation showed that, of 47 inhabitants in the two uppermost storeys of a tenement, 37 people caught fever, and of 50 residents in the lower storeys, only 5 did so. Higher incidences of fever in hyper-ventilated upper tenement rooms cast serious doubts simultaneously on both the miasmatic and contagionist explanations of epidemic fever. The *London Medical Gazette* concluded that 'disease follows famine as the shadow follows the substance'.[94]

91 The Scottish Poor Law Act, 1579, 'For punischment of strang and Idle Beggars, and reliefe of the pure and impotent' and its successors in Acts of the Scottish Parliament, 1592 c.17; 1593 c,4; 1594 c.8; 1661 c.281; 1663 c.43 were designed both to suppress vagrancy and to support the impotent poor. As in England, those who as a result of their age, infirmity or mental incapacity could not work were maintained by the parish, but, unlike south of the border, the 'able-bodied' unemployed were denied a legal right to relief. Occasional, discretionary payments were made to the poor as an act of charity from voluntary funds and church collections, but not from an assessment levied upon the inhabitants of the parish. The result was a superior system, some claimed, because the poor relief was not a charge on the hard-working, because it did not demoralise or encourage idleness among the poor, and because it did not disrupt the labour market by maintaining wages artificially to the disadvantage of the employer.

92 For further details of some of these organisations see 'The medical charities of Edinburgh', *The British Medical Journal*, 2 (no. 761) (1875), 13,035; Anon., *The Aged Poor: Centenary of the House of Reform (Queensberry House), 1832–1932* (Edinburgh, 1932); Anon. *House of Refuge for the Destitute, and Asylum for their Children: Origin, Progress and Nature of the Institution* (Edinburgh, 1855).

93 'On the causes of epidemic fever' (by an editor), *London Medical Gazette: A Journal of Medicine and Collateral Sciences*, 5 July 1844, 449–55. The article clearly draws heavily on W.P. Alison's *On the Epidemic Fever of 1843 in Scotland and its Connection with the Destitute Condition of the Poor* (Edinburgh, 1844). For the statistically inclined, the correlation coefficient, though based on very few observations in 1840 but part of a much longer series of statistics produced by Alison, was –0.7.

94 *London Medical Gazette* (1844), 451.

Church, State, and the state of public health

Scottish thinking on the issue of poverty and public health was in turmoil in the 1830s and 1840s. Social policy was paralysed. What developed in these decades was 'a multi-dimensional controversy concerned with matters that reached far beyond institutional reform to Scottish national identity'.[95] Even the introduction of civil registration – at face value an uncontroversial measure to count the number of births, marriages and the causes of death at the district level and so provide quantitative indicators of population change – proved contentious. It was only approved in 1855, eighteen years after the system had been introduced in England and Wales.[96] It was an issue that cut across the interests of the Church, State, medicine, governance, and education. Physicians saw registration as a legitimate extension of medical policing; Church authorities feared that a change in parish registrations would deny a fee to the session clerk, often a school-teacher, and thus undermine the educational provision of the parish.[97] With the number of inhabitants living in parishes levying a poor law assessment rising in 1839 to 1.14 million or 45% of the Scottish population, then the transition to a system of state-organised poor relief was a real and threatening possibility for the Church of Scotland. To counter this, a proposal from a distinguished lawyer, David Monypenny, embodied the approach of the conservative wing of the Church of Scotland. By assigning full legal, as opposed to purely ecclesiastical, powers to those new churches developed as part of the Church Extension movement in the 1830s to minister to the urban poor, it would be possible to raise and administer poor rates and thus retain Church control of the poor relief system.[98]

Every issue – and certainly those of poverty, parish responsibilities, public health, and policing – produced antagonistic responses. The controversy was fuelled by the publication in 1840 of one of the most influential pamphlets of the nineteenth century, W.P. Alison's *Observations on the Management of the Poor in Scotland and its Effects on the Health of the Great Towns,* and by the publicity campaign generated in advance of publication.[99] Alison's pamphlet was a devastating indictment of the old Poor Law in Scotland.[100] Social conditions were reported to be far worse than in England: infectious disease was more prevalent;

95 C. Hamlin, 'William Pulteney Alison', 157.

96 Bills to register births, deaths and marriages in Scotland were introduced in 1834, 1835, 1837, 1847, 1848, and 1849 before, finally, that of 1854 was passed. That each successive measure was unable to command sufficient support indicates the extent to which opinion was divided and policy paralysed.

97 A. Cameron, 'The establishment of civil registration in Scotland', *Historical Journal*, 50 (2007), 378–95.

98 PP (HC) 1839 XX, 177, Report by a Committee of the General Assembly on the Management of the Poor in Scotland, Appendix 1, Table 1. The committee concluded that from the mid-eighteenth century until 1820 church collections and voluntary funds had been sufficient to provide for the poor, but thereafter had proved insufficient due in part to the slow growth of congregations. The particular parishes identified were called *quoad sacra* parishes because of their limited secular authority.

99 Though described as a pamphlet it was in fact 198 pages.

100 For further information on the Old Poor Law see R.A. Cage, *The Scottish Poor Law, 1745–1845* (Edinburgh, 1981); T. Devine, *The Scottish Nation, 1700–2000* (Harmondsworth, 1999), 100–2; R. Mitchison, 'The Poor Law' in T.M. Devine and R. Mitchison (eds), *People and Society in Scotland, vol. I, 1760–1830* (Edinburgh, 1988), 252–67.

and, while the mortality rate in 1837–38 in England and Wales was 1 in 45 and in London 1 in 32, in Edinburgh it was 1 in 22 and in Glasgow 1 in 24. A cycle of despair existed among the Scottish urban poor: they were mistreated, abandoned or orphaned in childhood; they reached adulthood without vocational skills or moral instruction; they turned to alcoholism, crime or violence; they mistreated their own children; and they passed on their vicious habits and despair to the next generation. High birth rates complemented high death rates. Prostitution was widespread. Destitution discouraged moral restraint, contrary to the views of Malthusian social reformers.[101]

A pamphlet war broke out as a result, stoked by commissions and official enquiries and supplemented by public debates and speeches.[102] Forceful arguments were deployed by Alison in his *Observations* to replace the Old Poor Law with a secular system of standardised state relief. In a thoroughly modern, pre-Keynesian under-consumptionist approach, Alison claimed that benefits cushioned the effects of economic downturn and so reduced exposure to fever and ill-health generally. The Alisonian view was countered by conservative churchmen who defended the existing system, and an alternative evangelical vision within the Church of Scotland, led by the charismatic Dr Thomas Chalmers.[103]

In 1816 and 1824 Chalmers conducted two experiments[104] designed to demonstrate how the Church of Scotland should reassert is waning spiritual and moral supervision over the crowded, unhealthy and increasingly irreligious populations of nineteenth-century working-class Scottish towns and cities.[105] His approach was based on the traditional character of the rural parochial ministry: regular household visits by elders and deacons, a system of day and Sunday schools, a ministry focused on small, well-defined parishes and their congregations, and parish-based poor relief financed exclusively by church-door collections and voluntary contributions.[106] The principle of atomised churches,

101 See, for example, J. Bruce, *Letters on Destitution and Vice in Edinburgh* (Edinburgh, 1850).

102 W.P. Alison alone contributed 20 pamphlets in 1840–41.

103 S.J. Brown, *Thomas Chalmers and the Godly Commonwealth in Scotland* (Oxford. 1982); A.C. Cheyne, *Studies in Scottish Church History* (Edinburgh, 1999), 79–106. See also S.J. Brown's excellent entry on Thomas Chalmers in the *Dictionary of National Biography*, and S.J. Brown, *The National Churches of England, Ireland and Scotland, 1801–46* (Oxford, 2001), especially 24–31 on the structure and governance of the Church of Scotland. For interpretations of the Disruption, see D.J. Withrington, 'The Disruption: a century and a half of historical interpretation,' *Records of the Scottish Church History Society*, 25 (1993), 118–53.

104 These were in the parishes of Tron (1816) and St John's (1819), both in Glasgow. See S.J. Brown, *Thomas Chalmers and the Godly Commonwealth*, 91–151; R.A. Cage and E.O.A. Checkland, 'Thomas Chalmers and urban poverty: the St John's experiment in Glasgow 1819–37', *Philosophical Journal*, 13 (1976), 39–52. For a later experiment designed to improved inter-denominational collaboration to address poverty, see S.J. Brown, 'The Disruption and urban poverty: Thomas Chalmers and the West Port Operation in Edinburgh 1844–47', *Records of the Scottish Church History Society*, 20 (1978), 65–89.

105 Active church-going as reflected in the number of seats per 1,000 population is considered to have been in decline between 1760 and 1840, and to have enjoyed a recovery after 1840, unlike in England and Wales where church-going in towns was higher than in rural areas. See H. McLeod, 'Religion' in J. Langton and R.J. Morris (eds), *Atlas of Industrialising Britain, 1780–1914* (London, 1986), 212–17; C. Brown, *The Social History of Religion in Scotland since 1730* (London, 1987), 72–86; C. Brown, 'Did urbanization secularize Britain', *Urban History Yearbook, 1988*, 1–14.

106 There were strong Malthusian overtones in this stance. Chalmers rejected utilitarianism on the grounds that material improvements would not bring happiness.

'the godly commonwealth', each with a congregation of about 2,000 souls, was considered to be the most effective territorial basis upon which to revive the social structure of closely knit Christian communities, to eliminate pauperism, and to integrate an increasingly disaffected working class into a communal spirit reminiscent of a pre-industrial era.[107] Parish-based, church-directed initiatives were promoted as a replacement for the culture of dependency and degradation that resulted from welfare payments under the Poor Law. These were the principles that Chalmers expounded as convener of the Church of Scotland's Committee on Church Extension in 1834 in the attempt to reach the unchurched poor, and which he advanced in opposition to efforts to reform the Poor Law.

'The godly commonwealth' did not go unchallenged by earthly authors. Alison in particular contested the findings of the parish mission at St John's, Glasgow. Massaged figures and unsupported claims for the Glasgow experiment were the basis of Alison's persistent critique, which was complemented by his brother's systematic demolition of Chalmers' parish-community ideal in a two-volume work which simultaneously ridiculed Malthusian views.[108] With his community approach described as a fraud and a failure, Chalmers deferred retirement and travelled to Glasgow in September 1840 for a showdown with Alison at the annual meeting of the British Association for the Advancement of Science. The gladiatorial nature of the contest was evident. Public interest latched on to the oppositional nature of the debate, which hijacked the business of the British Association.[109] A larger auditorium was booked, and the debate was conducted over a four-day period! Extensive press coverage reported the conflicting visions of social theory that juxtaposed an environmentalist or medical police approach with a moral approach. Social and environmental reform – Alison's view – was the exact mirror image of that held by Chalmers based on faith and the inherent strength of the human spirit. Urban and rural, past and present, tradition and modernity were the counterpoints in a highly public discourse that also touched the very core of personal faith and private conscience. Alison's approach was later captured by Glasgow's eminent Medical Officer of Health, W.T. Gairdner: 'he [Alison] did not talk about religion, he only acted it.'[110]

107 Chalmers' territorial approach was developed in 1838 and announced in a public lecture at St George's, Edinburgh, in January 1839. See *Scottish Guardian*, 25 January 1839, quoted in S.J. Brown, 'The Disruption and urban poverty', 66.

108 A. Alison, *The Principles of Population and their Connection with Human Happiness* (Edinburgh, 1840), 2 vols, quoted in S. Brown, *Thomas Chalmers*, 292.

109 The Revd William Whewell, President of the British Association for the Advancement of Science expressed his 'misgivings' in a letter to the Marquis of Northampton, past-president of the BAAS and president of the Royal Society, concerning 'the stormy questions which now agitates the Church of Scotland to its very foundation ... combined so closely with our assembly'. Whewell added, 'I cannot doubt this is an utter violation of all the principles we set out in our objects and maxims'. Quoted in J.B. Morell and A. Thackray (eds), *Gentlemen of Science*, Camden Fourth Series, vol. 30 (London, 1984), 345.

110 A.H. Douglas, 'The Harveian discourse: on the life and character of Dr Alison', *Edinburgh Medical Journal*, 11 (1866), 1075. See also A.H. Douglas, *Life and Character of Dr Alison: the Harveian Discourse for 1866* (Edinburgh, 1866), and M. Barfoot (ed.), *'To ask the suffrages of the patrons': Thomas Laycock and the Edinburgh Chair of Medicine, 1855* (London, 1995).

2.9 Statue of Revd Dr Thomas Chalmers (1780–1847) in George Street, Edinburgh
Chalmers was a leader in the Disruption and co-founder of the Free Church of Scotland, 1843. He urged greater involvement by the clergy in the lives of the poor as a means to address poverty and ill-health.

Several newspapers took an active role in the argument. *The Scotsman*, for example, commented on 'the unquestionable force' of Alison's arguments concerning destitution and disease, and stated that 'no sane person … will be found to deliberately deny the right of every human creature when disabled by infirmity or want of employment, to obtain the means of subsistence from the community in which he lives'.[111] The *Scottish Guardian*, *North British Review*, *Chambers' Edinburgh Journal*, and the *Edinburgh Magazine* were all supportive of this viewpoint. A quarter of a century before he became involved in the Improvement Scheme for the Old Town, William Chambers agreed in 1842 'with Dr Alison and many other physicians, in thinking that "deficient nourishment, want of employment, and privations of all kinds, and the consequent mental depression", if not themselves adequate to produce the continued fever of Edinburgh, are much more powerful than "any cause external to the human body itself" in diffusing it'.[112] The *Edinburgh Medical and Surgical Journal* also commented on the prevalence of the poor and indigent in the larger Scottish burghs, supported Alison's analysis, and criticised Church administrators for the inconsistent nature of poor relief.[113] It was a war of words conducted as much about political economy as it was about public health. In what might now be termed a 'score draw', Chalmers' oratorical eloquence eclipsed the evidential medical reports that formed the central basis of Alison's arguments.[114]

Importantly, both the Royal Colleges in Edinburgh were also involved in a public way. The Royal College of Physicians was deeply committed to improved sanitary conditions and public health in Scotland in the 1830s and 1840s, as their reports indicate, and appointed committees to consider the college's responses to police powers, registration and nuisances.[115] On the grounds that it was an extension of their long-held endorsement of medical policing, the Surgeons were strongly supportive of the need for civil registration and actively sought legislation for this in the 1840s, assisted by several Scottish town councils and the London Statistical Society.

By the following year, 1841, economic depression was widespread and poverty severe. Chalmers continued to denounce the English Poor Law as 'a

111 *The Scotsman*, 15 January 1840; 22 April 1840.

112 PP 1842 (8), Sanitary Enquiry. Scotland reports on the Sanitary Condition of the Labouring Population of Scotland. Appendices, 153–9, W. Chambers, 'On the Sanitary Condition of the Old Town of Edinburgh', 157.

113 *Edinburgh Medical and Surgical Journal*, 53 (1840), 505, 509, and the *London Medical Gazette*, 26 (1840), 759, 856 and *British and Foreign Medical Review*, 9 (1840), 544 also criticised the *status quo*.

114 Hamlin, 'William Pulteney Alison', 180 notes that, despite their intense opposition, relations between Chalmers and Alison were cordial since 'they recognised the other as having reached an opposite conclusion within a common framework'.

115 Alison was an omnipresent figure on sub-committees between 1834 and 1856, often writing as chair on behalf of the Royal College of Physicians of Edinburgh. Martin, thesis, 319–25, notes that the RCPE were also represented by Alison on the medical sub-committee of the British Association for the Advancement of Science, and on the Medico-Statistical Association, of which he was president in 1852. Advised by Alison, the RCPE opposed the English system of classifying the cause of death according to the part of the body and the duration of the disease. It was an important point on which to oppose William Farr, assistant registrar for England, and the campaign, though successful, inevitably deferred the introduction of civil registration.

moral gangrene', and workhouses as 'pauper bastilles'.[116] His own emphasis on community contributions, education, moral improvement and self-help through savings clubs and benefit societies foundered both because there was insufficient financial and administrative backing to build the necessary new schools and churches, and because his assumption that working-class communities could work cohesively was unrealistic. Significantly, Chalmers' platform had elicited support from an increasing number of Church of Scotland ministers, so that by 1833 this evangelical group formed a majority in the governing body, the General Assembly, which witnessed tumultuous scenes in the ensuing decade known as 'The Ten Years Conflict'. Though there was a division of opinion over how to deal with poor relief, the schism in the Church of Scotland occurred over the fundamental issue of patronage whereby the Crown, wealthy landowners, universities and town councils selected parish ministers in the Church of Scotland. The inability of the evangelical wing of the Church of Scotland in the years between 1833 and 1843 to persuade the courts, government or senior Church figures to abolish patronage and to withdraw State interference in appointments caused almost half the members of the General Assembly and 37% of ministers to walk out of the annual meeting on 18 May 1843, leave the Church of Scotland, abandon their parishes with the 'livings' that supported their families, and to found the Free Church of Scotland on 18 May 1843 with its own general assembly.[117]

'The Disruption', as it was euphemistically called, was 'by far the most spectacular … split in British church history'.[118] By 1851 the percentage of churchgoers attending a Church of Scotland Sunday service had fallen to just 16%, from 44% in 1835. Conversely, Free Church attendance rocketed to 37% of all churchgoers, with the result that, together with the United Presbyterians (27%), they outnumbered the established Church by almost four to one. Thus, by 1851 the Church of Scotland had become a minority sect.[119] Religious factionalism in Scotland was endemic, but from 1843 the political power of the church, previously a monopoly of the Church of Scotland, was shattered and replaced by an era of religious pluralism. The issue of patronage acted as a catalyst to unify opposition to the Church of Scotland that was class-based and both rural and urban.[120] The rift was permanent, and Scottish social policy was never the same again.

With the credibility of the Church of Scotland as an agent of social policy in tatters in 1843, and disenchantment over parish-based administration by kirk sessions that were dominated by large landowners and Church nominees, previous opposition to a review of the Poor Law evaporated. Even before the Disruption occurred, a royal commission had been appointed to address the contentious issue

116 S. Brown, *Thomas Chalmers*, 294.

117 W. Ewing (ed.), *Annals of the Free Church of Scotland, 1843–1900* (Edinburgh, 1914), vol. 1, reproduces the Act and Declaration of Disruption in 1843 and biographies of the ministers who formed the Free Church of Scotland.

118 C. Brown, 'Religion, class and church growth' in W.H. Fraser and R.J. Morris (eds), *People and Society in Scotland* (Edinburgh, 1990), 317.

119 C. Brown, *A Social History of Religion*, 61.

120 A.A. MacLaren, *Religion and Social Class: The Disruption Years in Aberdeen* (London, 1974).

2.10 Royal College of Surgeons of Edinburgh, Nicolson Street
W.H. Playfair, architect, 1829–32; Francis Caird Inglis, photographer. [Source: RCAHMS]

of poor relief in Scotland.[121] A year later the Poor Law Commission's *Report* was delivered containing sensational revelations of inadequate relief and the neglect of sick and lunatic paupers. The previously admired Scottish system of poor relief was shown in evidence to the Royal Commission and in parliamentary debates to be seriously defective, as the MP for Renfrewshire commented:

> nothing could be more disgraceful than the present state of the poor in Scotland. The poor law system of Scotland has been praised, but directly the light was let in upon it the sturdiest Scotchman felt ashamed of it.[122]

The Poor Law Amendment (Scotland) Act, 1845, followed from the Royal Commission *Report*.[123] It was something of a mongrel. The retention of the parish as the basic unit of poor-relief administration and the transfer of authority from

121 PP (HC) 1844 XX, 557, Report of the Royal Commission for Inquiring into the Administration and Practical Operation of the Poor Law in Scotland. Appointment was in January 1843 and approval given in the same month as the disruption, May 1843.

122 *Hansard*, 12 June 1845, 423–4, quoted in S. Blackden, 'The Board of Supervision and the Scottish Parochial Medical Service, 1845–95', *Medical History*, 30 (1986), 151.

123 Poor Law (Scotland) Act 8 and 9 Vict., cap. 83.

2.11 Royal College of Physicians of Edinburgh, Queen Street
Thomas Hamilton, architect, 1844; Alexander Adam Inglis, photographer. [Source: RCAHMS]

kirk session to parochial board composed of session elders and major property owners blurred the change.[124] Nor were the newborn parochial boards required to finance poor relief from property assessments since voluntary contributions continued to be an acceptable practice; by avoiding a confrontation over this issue, the legal draughtsmen enabled individual parishes to retain a degree of autonomy. In fact, most preferred to move to a system of property assessments, so that within six years of their foundation the Board of Supervision reported on 'the progress of the change from Voluntary Contributions to Assessment' to

124 Only with the passage of the Local Government (Scotland) Act, 1894, were all members of parish councils elected. The Act also replaced the Board of Supervision with the Local Government Board for Scotland.

finance parochial boards. Whereas 74% of the 880 Scottish parishes in 1845 were reliant on voluntary contributions, by 1851 74% were not.[125] Whatever the method of funding, the New Poor Law was dominated by a single fact: 'by 1890 it was assisting fewer than at any time since the 1830s.'[126]

Earlier decisions in the 1820s on eligibility for relief in the Scottish law courts were confirmed in 1845: only the disabled, not the able-bodied unemployed, were entitled to poor relief.[127] It was a fundamental distinction between Scottish and English poor-relief systems.[128] Despite features in common with English boroughs – unprecedented urban population growth in the 1820s and 1830s and an employment roller-coaster of severe distress in the early 1840s – Scottish burghs possessed none of the machinery of relief associated with the Poor Law Amendment Act, 1834, in England.[129] There were no Poor Law Unions, or Boards of Guardians; Scotland had poorhouses, not workhouses, to reflect the ineligibility of the unemployed. Though local Poor Law administrators were subject to the overall control by a central board, the Board of Supervision in Edinburgh was mainly a concession to anti-English sentiment opposed to poor-relief administration from the Board of Health in London.

Parochial boards assumed responsibility for poor relief and, until 1872, for education. They also assumed responsibility for civil functions, including public health and sanitary inspections. In 1845 when the Poor Law came into effect, fewer than half the parishes provided medical relief to paupers, and 'centralized authority was conspicuous by its absence'.[130] Under the 1845 Act all poorhouses had to provide medical aid to the sick and infirm, supervised by a medically qualified person; all parishes were obliged to use their funds to provide the sick poor with medicines and medical attendance, and parochial boards could subscribe to charitable institutions to obtain treatment for their sick and lunatic poor. Far from being 'feeble', as Best has claimed, the Board of Supervision was accused of exerting 'tyrannical power' in evidence to a select committee in 1869. No doubt the reality lay somewhere between these opposing views, with Board officials claiming some credit for having influenced parochial administration.[131]

125 PP (HC) 1867–68 XXXIII, 625 [3957], Board of Supervision, 22nd Annual Report, v–vi.

126 I. Levitt, *Poverty and Welfare in Scotland, 1890–1948* (Edinburgh, 1988), 7, quoting PP (HC) 1910 XLVI, Cd. 4978, Royal Commission on the Poor Laws, Scottish Evidence, J.T. Maxwell.

127 R. Mitchison, 'The creation of the Disablement Rule in the Scottish Poor Law', in T.C. Smout (ed.), *The Search for Wealth and Stability: Essays in Economic and Social History Presented to M.W. Flinn* (London, 1979), 199–217.

128 For a detailed account of Scottish–English differences see A. Patterson, 'The poor law in nineteenth-century Scotland', in D. Fraser (ed.), *The New Poor Law in the Nineteenth Century* (London, 1976), 171–93.

129 I. Levitt and T.C. Smout, *The State of the Scottish Working Class in 1843: a statistical and spatial enquiry based on the data from the Poor Law Commission Report of 1844* (Edinburgh, 1979), ch.9; T.C. Smout, 'The strange intervention of Edward Twistleton: Paisley in depression', in T.C. Smout (ed.), *The Search for Wealth and Stability*, 218–42.

130 S. Blackden, 'The Board of Supervision', 145.

131 G.F.A. Best, 'Another part of the island, 393; PP (HC) 1870 XI, 357, Report of the Select Committee appointed to Enquire into the Operation of the Poor Law in Scotland, q.1102. Blackden, 'The Board of Supervision', n.85 also refers to complaints from local bodies concerning the aggressiveness of the Board.

Local parochial boards tended to be cautious, implementing circulars concerning procedures and standards that were not mandatory, and originated mostly by Henry Littlejohn. Indeed, Littlejohn's personal role was instrumental in extending the Board of Supervision's administrative reach. His visits to Aberdeen, Alloa, Arbroath, Ardrossan, Banff, Bo'ness and Broughty Ferry – and through the remainder of the alphabet to Wick – were part of a systematic inspection of Scottish ports considered to be in the front line of a potential cholera epidemic in 1871 because of their trading links to the Baltic. Littlejohn was sent to all twenty-one ports to inspect their sanitary conditions and emergency preparations for the likely cholera outbreaks. He compiled a written report, as the Board of Supervision annual report noted:

> [Littlejohn] invariably communicated a copy of his Report to the Local authority concerned, accompanied by such special instructions as seemed requisite. Much additional advantage, however was derived from the Commissioner's [Littlejohn's] personal intercourse with the local officials, the information and advice which his experience enabled him to convey, and the impetus and direction which his authority gave to the efforts that were being made. We have every reason to think that upon the whole the intentions of the Privy Council and the Board were effectively carried out. Fortunately, no case of Cholera occurred in Scotland.[132]

To reinforce its Medical Officer's efforts to improve the sanitary condition of Scottish burghs, the central Board of Supervision in Edinburgh used shrewd financial inducements in the form of medical grants to improve standards of care both in poorhouses and by public health measures, including vaccination after 1863.[133]

Overview

Throughout the first half of the nineteenth century Scottish medical and clerical energies were frequently preoccupied with the relationship between disease and destitution. For decades until the 1860s, Edinburgh – the epicentre of the Scottish Enlightenment and the fulcrum of the disease–destitution debate – was paralysed in terms of long-run strategies to deal with public health and poverty. Yet at no time in its recent history was Edinburgh, nor indeed other major Scottish burghs, in greater need of decisive leadership, for here was an ancien régime, still governed by patronage and guided by moral force, but confronted by modernity in the shape of new forms of economic organisation and social structures. The pace of industrialisation and urbanisation increased health risks and lowered life expectancy as density and proximity in the city created hazardous environmental conditions for its residents and incomers alike. Migrants, often

132 PP (HC) 1873 XXIX, 613 Board of Supervision, 27th Annual Report, xxiv–xxv.

133 Outdoor medical relief remained at the discretion of parochial boards, and in this regard the Board of Supervision was inevitably limited in what it achieved. See S. Blackden, 'The development of the Scottish Poor Law medical service, 1845–1914', *Proceedings of the Royal Physicians of Edinburgh*, 20 (1990), 349–54; S. Blackden, 'The parochial medical service in nineteenth century Scotland', *Social Science History Medical Bulletin*, 38 (1986), 21–4.

already debilitated by years of extreme poverty, mingled in conditions suited to endemic disease. Epidemic disease was itself a permanent threat if only an occasional visitor. Buildings, constructed in a different age and for different purposes, were colonised at densities for which they had never been intended; they were overcrowded death-traps, and the agencies that formerly had provided some care and support – principally, the Church, voluntary organisations, and the family – were incapable of doing so as resources were stretched from thin to non-existent.

The dismantling of some elements of Scottish political relations with London and fundamental fractures in the Church of Scotland over the nature and causes of poverty meant that decisive political leadership at the national level was lacking. Consequently, until some of the medical and philosophical issues were clarified, micro-management of towns and cities was the only available option; no strategic vision could be implemented until greater clarity emerged on such fundamental issues as how disease was transmitted, or how resources should be allocated to care for the chronically ill or the temporarily unemployed. In short, public health policy in Edinburgh, as in Scotland generally, was enmeshed with a number of complex and unresolved social policy matters. So, if local micro-management seemed an option, with burghs developing local solutions for local problems, then this too was not without complications, as corrupt corporations brought local administration into disrepute. Parallel systems of local government – the Town Council and the Police Commission – co-existed in Edinburgh, as in most major Scottish burghs. However, this also provided the opportunity for a new breed of professional public servants to emerge as civic authorities began to embrace wider responsibilities. From mid-century, Medical Officers of Health were a nascent force. Chief among these was Henry Duncan Littlejohn, MD.

CHAPTER 3

Littlejohn's inheritance

Edinburgh citizens 'borrowed' the idea of a police commission from Glasgow. Echoing the situation in the west, the reasoning was that the rapid expansion of the city required a new financial and administrative model to cope with the increased levels of infrastructural investment. Householders were wary of the 'despotic municipal rule by self-elected councillors' which had accumulated significant debts in connection with the development of Edinburgh's New Town, so a new agency, the Edinburgh Police Commission, was set up in order to address the problems of urban scale and complexity which the city faced in the new century.[1] Between its establishment in 1805 and 1856 the Police Commissioners provided a powerful parallel administrative regime to the Town Council during a period when the Town Council's indebtedness and financial mis-management cast a long shadow over the city which eventually provoked a political crisis in the 1830s that necessitated a rescheduling of debts and the sale of public assets.

Many, including the powerful Merchant Company of Edinburgh, saw the establishment of a police commission as a distinctively Scottish creation whose wide-ranging civil jurisdiction extended the civil liberties of the majority by promoting regulation and order. In this sense the move to establish a police commission was a product of the Scottish Enlightenment, whereby man could increasingly and more effectively control and improve his environment, and where active citizenship in the form of participation was considered crucial to social progress. As an attempt to regulate public utilities, frame new laws for an increasingly commercial society, and in terms of civic duty, police commissions were direct descendants of Adam Smith's *Lectures on Jurisprudence*, Kames'

1 D.G. Barrie, *Police in the Age of Improvement: Police Development and the Civic Tradition in Scotland, 1775–1865* (Cullompton, 2008), 33–7, 81. Two Acts, 2 and 3 Will. 4, cap. 65, and 3 and Will. 4, cap. 77, one for royal burghs and the other for parliamentary burghs, replaced the self-perpetuating system of appointment to town councils with a voting system based on a £10 p.a. property qualification. For early police administration see J. McGowan, *Policing the Metropolis of Scotland: A History of the Police and Systems of Police in Edinburgh & Edinburghshire, 1770–1833* (Musselburgh, 2011); A. Dinsmor and R. Urquhart, 'The origins of modern policing in Scotland', *Scottish Archives: The Journal of the Scottish Records Association*, 7 (2001), 39–42; A. Dinsmor and A. Goldsmith, 'Scottish policing – a historical perspective,' in D. Donnelly and K. Scott (eds), *Policing Scotland* (Cullompton, 2005), 42; D. Donnelly, *Municipal Policing in Scotland* (Dundee, 2008); G. Morton, 'Identity within the Union state 1800–1900', in T. Devine and J. Wormald (eds), *Oxford Handbook of Modern Scottish History* (Oxford, 2012), 480–82. For further details on national statutes see R.M. Urquhart, *The Burghs of Scotland and the General Police (Scotland) Act, 1833* (Motherwell, 1989), and R.M. Urquhart, *The Burghs of Scotland and the Police of Towns (Scotland) Act, 1850* (Motherwell, 1989).

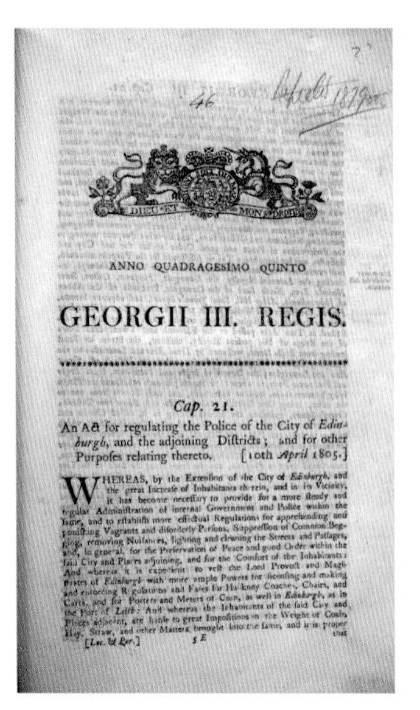
ANNO QUADRAGESIMO QUINTO

GEORGII III. REGIS.

Cap. 21.

An Act for regulating the Police of the City of *Edinburgh*, and the adjoining Diſtricts; and for other Purpoſes relating thereto. [10th *April* 1805.]

WHEREAS, by the Extenſion of the City of *Edinburgh*, and the great Increaſe of Inhabitants therein, and in its Vicinity, it has become neceſſary to provide for a more ſteady and regular Adminiſtration of internal Government and Police within the ſame, and to eſtabliſh more effectual Regulations for apprehending and puniſhing Vagrants and diſorderly Perſons, Suppreſſion of Common Begging, removing Nuiſances, lighting and cleaning the Streets and Paſſages, and, in general, for the Preſervation of Peace and good Order within the ſaid City and Places adjoining, and for the Comfort of the Inhabitants: And whereas it is expedient to veſt the Lord Provoſt and Magiſtrates of *Edinburgh* with more ample Powers for licenſing and making and enforcing Regulations and Fares for Hackney Coaches, Chairs, and Carts, and for Porters and Meters of Corn, as well in *Edinburgh*, as in the Port of *Leith*: And whereas the Inhabitants of the ſaid City and Places adjacent, are liable to great Impoſitions in the Weight of Coals, Hay, Straw, and other Matters brought into the ſame, and it is proper that

[Loc. & Per.] 5 E

3.1 An Act for Regulating the Police of Edinburgh 1805
This was the first of many Local Acts between 1805 and 1856 empowering Police Commissioners to manage the physical and moral environment in Edinburgh. [Source: ECA, Local Acts]

writings on the economic and social context of the law, and Hume's recognition of the role of government as an enforcer of new laws.[2]

Property was at the heart of the issue of police administration in Scotland. Adam Smith noted as much: 'The acquisition of valuable and extensive property … necessarily requires the establishment of civil government.'[3] As urbanisation advanced, the moral economy and the paternalism associated with it were increasingly out of step with the market economy. The eighteenth-century constabulary system[4] for protecting property, watching and warding, was considered not fit for purpose because the funding levels provided insufficient manpower to deal with the perceived increase in theft, anti-social behaviour and the numbers of homeless and poor in the burghs.[5] The initial result was the Glasgow Police Act, 1800. Edinburgh followed suit[6] in 1805 in what was the first step towards the management of public health and the appointment of Henry Duncan Littlejohn as Medical Officer of Health.

Coming as it did just a decade after the French Revolution, the elected nature of the Police Commissions was highly significant. The concept of local public bodies mediating between the individual and the state was important in early nineteenth-century Scotland, embedded as it was in Enlightenment views of a more representative form of government.[7] Based on the votes of householders whose property value was equivalent to a yearly rental of at least £10, each ward elected Resident Commissioners who held fortnightly meetings locally, and referred matters to meetings of General Commissioners for the city on an alternating fortnightly cycle.[8] Public order was a central concern in the

2 A. Smith, *Lectures on Jurisprudence* [1762] (Oxford, 1978), 331; Lord Kames, *Sketches of the History of Man*, Book II (repr. Indianapolis, 2007), 88; D.N. MacCormick, 'Adam Smith on law', in K. Haakonsen (ed.), *Adam Smith* (Aldershot, 1998), 197, 225; D. Lieberman, 'The legal needs of a commercial society: the jurisprudence of Lord Kames', in I. Hont and M. Ignatieff (eds), *Wealth and Virtue: the Shaping of Political Economy in the Scottish Enlightenment* (Cambridge, 1983), 203–34.

3 A. Smith, *Wealth of Nations*, Book V.i.b, 711 (R.H. Campbell and A. Skinner edn, Indianapolis, 1981).

4 Edinburgh South Districts, Leith (both 1771), Canongate (1772), Greenock (1773), Port Glasgow (1775), Dumfries (1787), and Aberdeen (1795) each obtained Local Police Acts but were more concerned with a limited policing conception of watching. See Barrie, *Police*, 23–76 on policing activities before 1800, and for Aberdeen, R. Tyzack, '"No mean city"? The growth of civic consciousness in Aberdeen with particular reference to the work of the Police Commissioners', in T. Brotherstone and D.J. Withrington (eds), *The City and its Worlds: Aspects of Aberdeen's History since 1794* (Glasgow, 1996), 150–3.

5 K. Carson and H. Idzikowska, 'The social production of Scottish policing', in D. Hay and F. Snyder (eds), *Policing and Prosecution in Britain* (Oxford, 1983), argue that police administration was developed as part of the machinery to deal with the wandering poor.

6 45 Geo. 3, cap. 21, An Act for regulating the Police of the City of Edinburgh, and adjoining Districts; and for other Purposes relating thereto. [10 April 1805] 78 sections.

7 However, D.G. Barrie, *Police*, 137, rejects G. Morton's claim that this was 'the beginnings of self-administration of civil society'. Surprisingly, no great importance is attached to police civil administration by authors in T. Griffiths and G. Morton (eds), *A History of Everyday Life in Scotland, 1800–1900* (Edinburgh, 2010), 205, 214–15, 240, 269.

8 45 Geo. 3, cap. 21, sections 4–16. Ward boundaries were described in detail. For an account of a later ward-based system of administration, see C.A. Williams, 'The Sheffield Democrats' critique of criminal justice in the 1850s', in R. Colls and R. Rodger (eds), *Cities of Ideas: Civil Society and Urban Governance in Britain, 1800–2000* (Aldershot, 2004), 96–120.

decision to develop a ward-based system of local administration.[9] Powers were assigned to General Commissioners to deal with vagrants and beggars, and 'for all other Purposes connected with the Preservation of Peace and good Order'. Appointed by the Commissioners, the Superintendent of Police was also to oversee the billeting of troops, and one Officer of Police in every ward was 'to be properly armed and mounted on Horseback'.[10] But the Act also had greater ambitions. These included 'the general Safety and Comfort of the Inhabitants of the said City', the prevention and removal of 'Nuisances and Obstructions', and 'enforcing the rules ... as to lighting and cleaning the streets and passages'.[11]

It was within these general structures of urban management that public health was increasingly defined. Though lighting and cleaning powers for parts of the city had previously been vested in the magistrates, these were applied unevenly and irregularly. From 1805 lighting and cleaning responsibilities were unified in the Police Commission, with systems of inspection, reporting, courts, and penalties. Streets were the locus of much of this early public health activity, and effective urban management was achieved by enshrining clear principles, responsibilities and duties in ways that could be implemented. If regulations governing weights and measures for the sale of hay, coals, and bread seemed like micro-management, and if byelaws restricting the sale of dung – the property of the General Commissioners – or the operation of hackney carriages seemed inconsistent with prevailing principles of political economy, then this was because the Commissioners acknowledged that public and private interest were not always in alignment.[12] Indeed, they recognised in 1805 that the unbridled operations of the market had insidious effects on the public's health; there were significant external diseconomies with consequential costs to the public purse. By insisting that dangerous buildings should be fenced off, and if necessary demolished at the owner's expense, the Commissioners did no more than formalise powers already available through the Dean of Guild Court. The difference was that after 1805 there was a body of inspectors whose duty it was to report such dangerous structures, pavement encroachments and obstructions to the thoroughfares, and who were funded through a revenue stream derived from a systematic enumeration and regular re-valuation of property in the city.[13] When complemented with administrative support and judicial processes with a system of fines and imprisonment, the Edinburgh Police Act, 1805, introduced a new era of public administration. Central to that vision was the public health of the city.

With the introduction of ward-level elections in 1805 and clearly defined lines of responsibility for urban management, it was recognised among the Edinburgh property-owning classes that liberty under the rule of law could

9 Public order had been a concern before police commissioners were appointed. See, for example, ECA Bailie Court Processes, Box 412 11–17, 1783, Procurator-Fiscal *v.* W. Thomson for rioting; and NRS JC7/41, Justiciary Court, 13 March 1781, 9 April 1783 concerning Edinburgh rioters and sedition. We are grateful to A. Lewis for these references.

10 The City Guard comprised a lieutenant, two sergeants, two corporals, two drummers and thirty men who were billeted by the Superintendent.

11 45 Geo. 3, cap. 21, sections 12–13; 17–19.

12 Sections 51–55.

13 Sections 28–29, 32–33, 36–37, 40–43, 56, 61–65, 73–75.

be enhanced by public participation in local government. This view was well established in Edinburgh, where enlightenment notions of 'civil society' were associated with active engagement in the public sphere.[14] Consequently, 'a gradual extension of the police system over our towns trained the people to expect and to exercise elective privilege'.[15] Less philosophically, financial crises had dogged the development of the New Town, and so a distancing between Town Council and Police Commission suited the purpose of the propertied middle classes and, no doubt, the Glasgow precedent was a factor, too. Urban rivalry was nothing new.

The system of police commissioners

The Edinburgh Police Act, 1805, imported an administrative template which set out the geographical extent and jurisdictional reach of a newly established police commission.[16] The Act defined how the physical and financial assets, and the functional organisation of the city, should be managed in relation to public order and urban environmental issues. One of the most innovative features was the election of two Resident Commissioners in each of the thirty wards. Resident Commissioners were empowered to appoint ward inspectors, collectors of assessments (property taxes), police officers and watchmen and could deal summarily with minor infractions of regulations. They also reported on the discharge of their duties to the city-wide General Commissioners – one was elected for each of the thirty wards – which acted as a strategic body, proposing changes in urban management, nominating individuals to sub-committees, liaising with the Town Council, and acting as a civil court. The membership of the Police Commission in 1824–25 is shown in figure 3.2 when, interestingly, Littlejohn's father, baker Thomas Littlejohn, was the Resident Commissioner for the 15th Ward and his paternal grandfather, David Littlejohn, a baker in the Canongate, was elected as the Resident Commissioner for the 19th Ward in 1826–27. An interest in public affairs and urban management in Edinburgh was something that the Littlejohn family shared and Henry Littlejohn would have known almost from birth (1826).

Borrowing powers, authority to enter into contracts with gas and water companies, to own property, and to raise revenue from assessments on property were also among the powers enshrined in the Act of 1805, which required officers to keep minutes and accounts, and a daily log of breaches of regulations. The commissioners' actions, authorised during the lifetime of the Police Commission between 1805 and 1856 by several Local Acts of Parliament, constructed an embryonic framework of public health management for the city of Edinburgh which had significance both for the activities of Henry Littlejohn as Police

14 R.J. Morris, 'Civil society and the nature of urbanism: Britain, 1750–1850', *Urban History*, 25 (1988), 289–301, referring to Adam Ferguson, *Essay on the History of Civil Society* (1767).

15 H. Cockburn, *Memorials of His Time* (Edinburgh, 1856), 170, quoted by D.G. Barrie, '"Epoch-making" beginnings to lingering death: the struggle for control of the Glasgow Police Commission, 1833–46', *Scottish Historical Review*, 86 (2007), 253, brackets added. Barrie, *Police in the Age of Improvement*, 284, notes that eighteen further burghs adopted Police Acts in the twenty years following the Edinburgh decision.

16 45 Geo. 3, cap. 21.

POLICE ELECTIONS.

The following List gives the names of the General and Resident Commissioners of Police for the ensuing year, whose elections, being *unanimous*, were completed in *one* hour. When more than one person, for each office, is voted for within the first hour, the poll-books must continue open for four days. In 22 out of the 30 Wards, however, there has been unanimity. It is also understood, although the returns cannot be made until Thursday evening, that Mr John Alexander, surgeon, will be re-elected for the 1st ward; Mr J. F. M'Farlane, surgeon, for the 5th; Mr William Murray, baker, for the 21st; and Mr John Grubb, for the 25th. In most of these wards, the poll is kept open on account of contests for Resident Commissionerships. Those marked thus * have been newly elected. The rest have all been *re-elected.*

Ward.	General Commissioners.	Resident Commissioners.
2.	John Lees, tobacconist, Lawnmarket.	John Russel, brushmaker, and Archibald Thomson, merchant.
3.	Thomas Sawers, baker, Lawnmarket.	John Lauder, merchant, Luckenbooths, and Samuel Aitken, bookseller.
4.	Andrew Scott, clothier, North Bridge.	Robert Scott, druggist, South Bridge, and John Robertson, bookseller.
6.	*Andrew Hunter, merchant, Bristo Street.	Robert Gray, saddler, and Robert Christie, tobacconist.
7.	Alex. Ross, linen-merchant, South Bridge.	James M'Kay, jeweller, South Bridge, and Robert Grieve, furniture-printer, South Bridge.
8.	Thomas Allan, Banker, Charlotte-square.	James Stewart, W. S. Charlotte Street, and Andrew Rutherford, advocate, do.
9.	J. W. M'Kenzie, W. S. Frederick-street.	David Ramsay, W. S. and Robert Kinnear, bookseller.
10.	David Murray, W. S. Hanover-street.	John Robertson, merchant, Frederick Street, and Alexander Greenhill, advocate, Queen Street.
11.	Wm. Young, W. S. Great King-street.	Robert Hunter, advocate, and Alexander Monypenny, W. S.
12.	*Wm. Douglas, W.S.	George Gardner of the Customs, and Alexander Stevenson, S. S. C.
13.	John Menzies, shoemaker, Hanover-street.	Dr Maclagan, George Street, and M. A. Fletcher, advocate, Queen Street.
14.	*Mathew Walker, spirit-dealer, Register-street.	William Purves, clothier, Prince's Street, and James Leechman, silk-mercer, Prince's Street.
15.	William Bathgate, grocer, James'-square.	Thomas Littlejohn, baker, Leith Street, and Charles Kennedy, surgeon, Catherine Street.
16.	*Joseph Gordon, W.S. London-street.	Thomas Ponton, builder, London Street, and James Brownlee, advocate, Hart Street.
17.	*Andrew Kerr, upholsterer, 21, Greenside-place.	Alexander Muckle, merchant, 1. Calton, and John Neil, brassfounder, Greenside Lane.
19.	James Bartram, brewer, Pleasance.	John Blues, tanner, and David Arthur, jun. toolmaker.

3.2 Election of Edinburgh General and Resident Police Commissioners, 1824–25
Littlejohn's father, Thomas, represented the 15th Ward. [Source: *The Scotsman*, 30 June 1824, 505]

Surgeon and for the form and structure of his *Report.* The scope and aspirations, as well as the shortcomings, of nascent public administration in Edinburgh are essential to understanding the appointment of Littlejohn, first as Police Surgeon and then as Medical Officer of Health.

The Police Act, 1805, embraced only those districts not previously served by the Town Guard who continued to discharge watching and lighting duties in the Canongate and southern districts of the city. But on Hogmanay 1811, riots by gangs of 'ferocious banditti' resulted in muggings and the death of a police officer.[17] Subsequently, 68 persons were arrested; three men were executed and five transported for their offences.[18] The shock waves that reverberated through the City Chambers on New Year's Day 1812 were a catalyst for a prompt response from the Town Council and Magistrates, who concluded that the 'present system of police is totally inadequate' and 'a new bill [should be] brought into parliament, with every possible despatch' to ensure 'a more efficient police force'. The track record of council financial mis-management produced general distrust among the public. The council's ability and probity were questioned in relation in the administration of the sizeable tax revenues and expenditures necessary for a new system of policing. Moreover their legitimacy as an elected body was in several respects questionable. The result was a decision to empower a police commission to undertake the responsibilities of ensuring public order and to 'watch' over the welfare and amenity of Edinburgh citizens.

Building on the administrative structure established in 1805, the Act of 1812 extended the system of representation and executive powers throughout the city. The chain of command from Superintendent of Police to Inspectors then to Officers was robust and largely unchanged throughout the period, with

17 *The Edinburgh Annual Register*, January 1812, 1–3.
18 W.W. Knox, 'The attack of the "Half-Formed Persons": the 1811–12 Tron Riot in Edinburgh revisited', *Scottish Historical Review*, 91:2 (2012), 287–310.

codes of conduct introduced and sanctions applied where officers were found to have committed misdemeanours such as drinking on duty, or being the subject of bribes.[19] Transgressors faced dismissal. Occasionally the upper limit upon police commission borrowing levels was adjusted so that they could build new premises, while the enumeration of inhabitants and numbering and naming of houses and streets provided an improved and enduring baseline for municipal management in decades to come. It is difficult to escape the conclusion that the police commissioners carved out a central role for themselves in Edinburgh in the first half of the nineteenth century and so provided a framework of urban management that reached in to the daily lives of all citizens. Accordingly, the emphasis that has been placed on the role of voluntary organisations in the construction of the public sphere should not be overstated.[20]

If the constitutional structure of the Police Commission over the next half-century closely resembled that of 1805, the scope of the commissioners' regulatory apparatus expanded appreciably. Cleaning, lighting and watching responsibilities formed the guiding principles in 1805, as the commissioners demonstrated their early commitment to public health and public order. The state of the streets was 'watched' and recorded daily. Broken lamps were reported; 'unfortunate females labouring under disease' were 'to have an opportunity of being kept secluded from Intercourse with Society' by being sent to the Bridewell prison and given 'a chance of returning to more virtuous Habits'.[21] Beggars and vagrants were moved on either to prison or 'the boundaries of the county', and powers were granted to shop owners to enclose areas (called piazzas) in front of their premises so as to prevent 'nuisances ... which in the Evening and at Night are Receptacles for idle and disorderly Persons of various Descriptions'.[22] Watch houses were provided in every ward. Weights and measures, and schedules of legitimate charges for carting and carriage, provided a form of surveillance that was consistent with medical policing: watching preceded the formulation of recommendations to pre-empt the adverse impact of the actions of individuals on others, and on the public interest generally. It was an approach equally consistent with the contemporary Benthamite principles of utility and the centuries-old Scottish principle of 'nichtbourheid' enshrined in the activities of the Dean of Guild Court whereby owners of buildings that adversely affected the light, safety or general amenity of others could be required to alter or remove the offending structure.[23]

Between 1805 and 1854 twenty Edinburgh Improvement Acts, with over 1,100 sections, were approved by Parliament.[24] In addition to the 1805 Act, the

19 Six months after the passage of the 1805 Act the police establishment included: 1 superintendent, 6 inspectors, 12 sergeants, 8 constables, 86 watchmen, equivalent to one officer per 615 persons. D. Barrie, *Police*, 150.

20 R.J. Morris, 'Urbanisation in Scotland', in W.H. Fraser and R.J. Morris (eds), *People and Society in Scotland, vol. II, 1830–1914* (Edinburgh, 1990), 73–102; G. Morton, *Unionist Nationalism: Governing Urban Scotland, 1830–1860* (Edinburgh, 1999), 35–7.

21 45 Geo. 3, cap. 21, section 72.

22 45 Geo. 3, cap. 21, sections 22–25, 30.

23 R. Rodger, 'The evolution of Scottish town planning' in G. Gordon and B. Dicks (eds), *Scottish Urban History* (Aberdeen, 1983), 71–91.

24 There were also Local Improvement Acts to improve communications and clear individual sites which had an impact on the quality of the built environment.

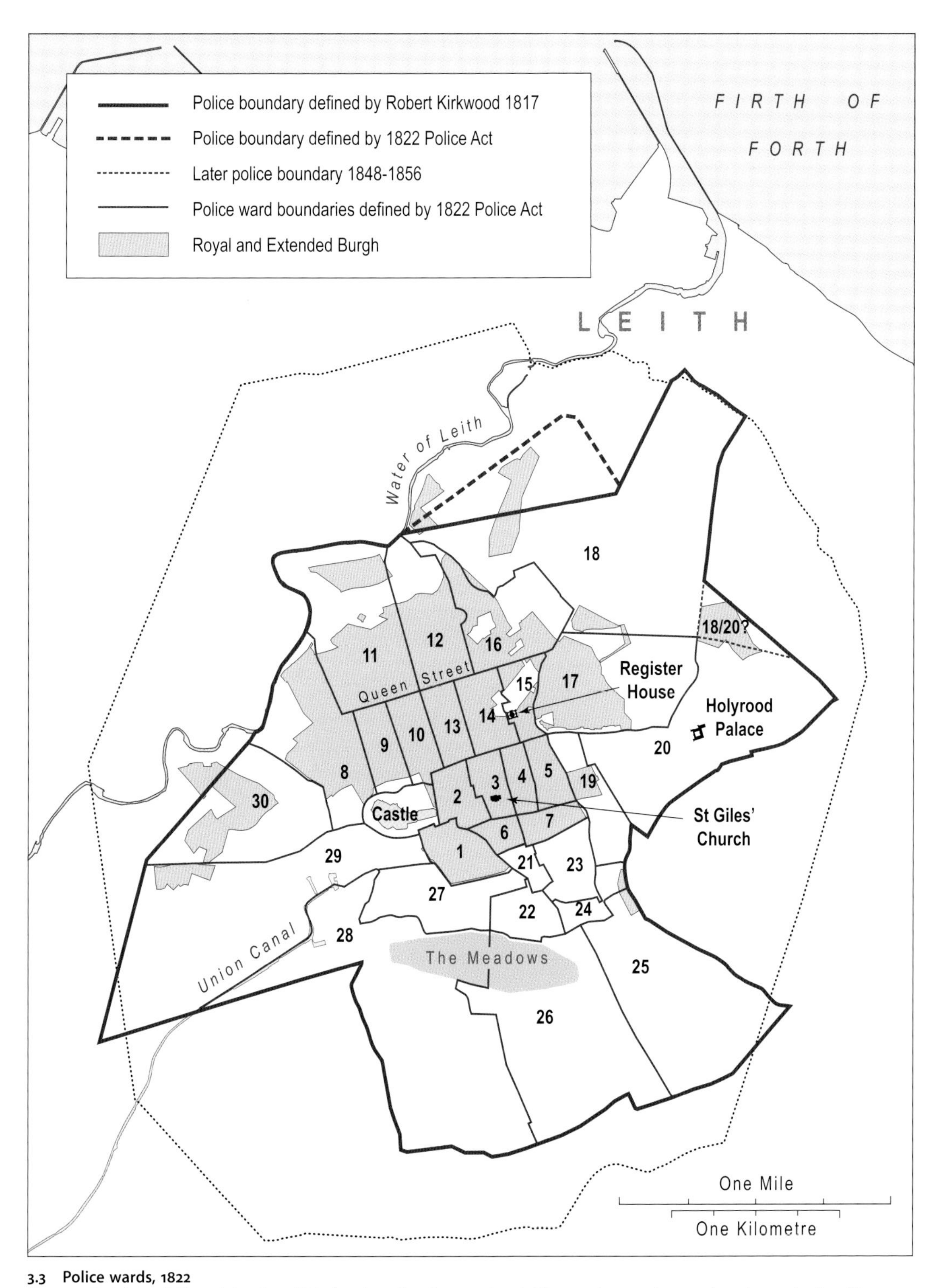

3.3 Police wards, 1822
[Sources: R. Kirkwood, Plan of the City of Edinburgh and its Environs (1817); OS six-inch maps (surveyed 1852); 3 and 4 Geo. IV c. 78, section 3]

most important of these in relation to public health were the 731 clauses of the Local Acts of 1812, 1817, 1822, 1832, 1837, 1848 and 1854.[25] Thus, while the Town Council's activities were largely confined to refinancing the municipal debt, and patronage for university and church positions, based on the 1805 template an ever more elaborate web of environmental control and public health measures was woven into the system of Police Acts.[26] In 1812, for example, long and detailed clauses dealt with buildings in a dangerous state, street obstructions, and the loading of vehicles, while others, in a finely balanced concept of the public interest, proposed penalties where flower pots were positioned precariously on window sills.[27] If, as in 1817, explicit regulations relating to the storage of gunpowder were self-evidently in the public interest, controls relating to weights of coal sold, or the schedule of charges for hackney carriages, were also incorporated into a system of regulation that required the Superintendent of Police to act 'for the public Interest, for the removal of all nuisances within the Limits of Police, and for Remedy of any Act or Neglect whereby the Safety of the Lieges may be endangered'.[28] Safety as an element of the public interest figured prominently in the Act of 1817, as it did in the system of police administration generally, and in an intriguing link between public interest and income redistribution, fines levied for infringements to regulations were available to feed and clothe inmates of the Bridewell prison.[29]

The defence of the public interest was also the principle increasingly invoked to legitimise intervention in areas that were normally considered sacrosanct. The vulnerable in society were also considered to be worthy of protection. In particular, efforts were made to protect customers from unscrupulous traders and brokers. From 1822 dealers in second-hand goods had to be registered, partly to limit the trade in stolen goods, but also to deter them from preying on unsuspecting persons. And by 1848 pawnbrokers and publicans had to be distinct, both in terms of business organisation and location. Furthermore, dealers in second-hand goods were obliged to record in a ledger all items bought and sold, and would be fined if they re-sold goods within seven days or dealt with minors under the age of 14.[30] Protection of the public from deception and gambling was the explicit intent of clauses inserted in 1832 dealing with 'Thimblers,

25 See Local Acts: 52 Geo. 3, cap. 172; 57 Geo. 3, cap. 33; 3 Geo. 4, cap. 78; 2 Will. 4, cap. 87; 7 Will. 4, cap. 32; 11 and 12 Vict., cap. 113; 17 and 18 Vict., cap. 118. In addition 3 and 4 Will. 4, cap. 46, An Act to enable Burghs in Scotland to establish a general System of Police was public statute and was also available to the City of Edinburgh. However, this Act drew heavily on the working and experience of the police commissioners in Glasgow, Edinburgh, Aberdeen, Dundee, and Paisley, and so there was no need for the city of Edinburgh to adopt its sections.

26 J.C. Williams, 'Edinburgh politics, 1832–1852', Edinburgh Ph.D. thesis (1972), 50–2.

27 52 Geo. 3, cap. 172, sections 63–66. The expense of these parliamentary bills was considerable. Barrie, *Police*, 130 notes that between 1822 and 1836 the cost was £9,315, or almost £750,000 in 2012 prices.

28 57 Geo. 3, cap. 33, sections 21, 26–30.

29 52 Geo. 3, cap. 172, section 94 (1812).

30 3 Geo. 4, cap. 78, section 76 (1822); 11–12 Vict., cap. 113, sections 140–54. *The Scottish Jurist*, 30 (1858), 478–80 recorded a notable case involving Janet Williamson in 1858, convicted of the re-sale of hair. Apprehended and convicted within two hours, she subsequently sought £400 compensation for wrongful arrest and 'oppressive' treatment, and brought an action against the Superintendent of Police for wrongful prosecution.

Chain-droppers, loaded Dice Players and all other Persons whatsoever who induce or entice any person or persons to play Games of Hazard', who if found guilty should be 'convicted for Fraud or Imposition'.[31]

Animals in the city posed an increasing public nuisance. Mad dogs and animals were the initial focus of legislation in 1832, though quite how a £1 fine for 'disobedience' would be defined, or collected, must have been problematical. Undoubtedly a nuisance to traffic and pedestrians, animals attracted further attention from the commissioners after the Act of 1832 required those who sold 'unwholesome meat' to be charged and, if found guilty, fined the substantial sum of £5 for each offence.[32] The meat was to be buried or destroyed. So seriously was this offence regarded that a further Act in 1837 even specified very precisely how the officers should publish notices relating to diseased meat: the typeface was to be of 'Roman Characters and at least three inches in Length and of a proportional Breadth, in black Letter upon a White Ground'.[33] Markets, of course, had long been an area of considerable interest for town councils throughout Britain, since rents for booths and taxes on produce were sources of town revenues.[34] But if concern over the quality of meat led logically to control over slaughtering, the Edinburgh Police Commissioners missed an opportunity to do so in 1832 when their powers were extended, and it was only in the following year when the general statute which applied to all royal burghs in Scotland provided for shambles or slaughterhouses 'in the suburbs or other proper and convenient Place of any Burgh'.[35] Despite detailed regulations, the Inspector of Cleansing, Alexander Murray, considered slaughterhouses and the meat trade generally in 1847 to be among 'the more obvious defects in the Police Acts', and the following year a further Police Act stipulated that 'no Butchers [*sic*] Meat, Fish, Poultry or other Article of Food of an unsound or unwholesome Description, or adulterated Butter, Meal, Bread or any other Article of adulterated Food' should be presented for sale.[36] Not for the last time the intervention of a knowledgeable municipal official suggested ways to improve public health practice, even if the regulations were frequently flaunted.

Diseased meat was a specific nuisance and was one that subsequently figured prominently in Littlejohn's *Report* (see chapter 4). The Police Commissioners

31 2 Will. 4, cap. 87, section 37 (1832).

32 2 Will. 4, cap. 87, section 36, 38–9.

33 7 Will. 4, cap. 32, section 23 (1837).

34 For earlier controls on markets see ECA SL80/2/1, Town Council Minutes, 1 April 1767; 28 January 1784. An early report on slaughterhouses, with recommendations, was compiled on 1 August 1770. A. Lewis' references are gratefully acknowledged on these points. See also 22 Geo. 3, 1783, sections 1 and 3.

35 See 3 and 4 Will. 4, cap. 46, sections 111–12 (1833). Control over slaughtering in Edinburgh relied on the relevant clauses of the Acts of 1837 and 1848. To announce the opening of a slaughterhouse 'the beating of a Tuck or Drum or other usual mode of Proclamation' once a day for seven days was to take place; thereafter, it was unlawful for individuals to slaughter beasts for private or institutional consumption.

36 A. Murray, *Nuisances in Edinburgh with Suggestions for the Removal Thereof Addressed to the General Commissioners of Police* (Edinburgh, 1847), 4; See 11 and 12 Vict., cap. 113, section 113 (1848). See *The Scotsman*, 2 November 1842, 3c on Alexander Murray, journalist and elected Liberal councillor for the First Ward, and Inspector of Cleaning 1845 until his death in 1853. For a detailed appreciation of this able public servant, see *Caledonian Mercury*, 1 December 1853, 3d; *The Scotsman*, 30 November 1853, 2f.

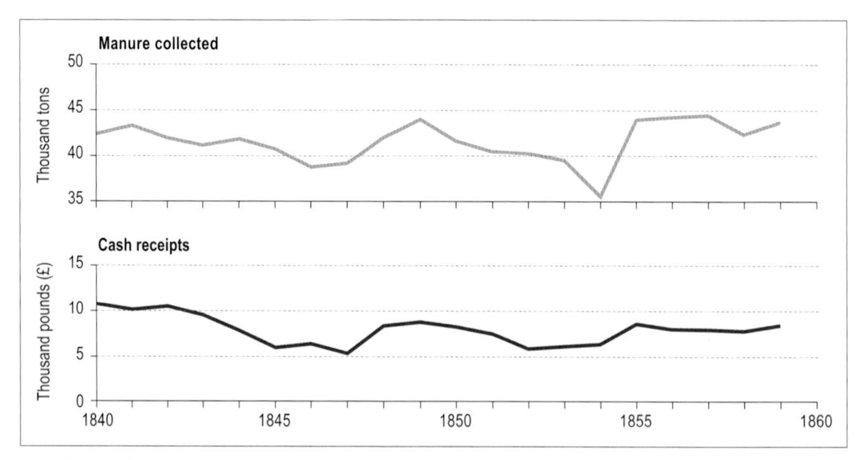

3.4 Street cleaning: manure revenue account for Edinburgh, 1840–59
There was sufficient revenue from the municipal monopoly of street manure sweepings to fund the Cleaning Department in the early Victorian period.
[Source: ECA EDP9 25/3 Report by Committee … of the Police Establishment. Submitted 28 June 1859, 11]

blazed a regulatory trail in many other areas that were to figure in Littlejohn's deliberations. Prominent among these were smoke and water pollution, the latter considered a pernicious hazard since contaminated water was difficult to detect. Though not itself part of the system of police regulation, a decision of the Town Council to promote a Local Act in 1819 led to the formation of the Edinburgh Joint Stock Water Company[37] as a private company supplying running water to the city from the nearby Pentland hills.[38] Almost immediately, and to protect the public against water pollution, clauses were framed to deal particularly with the chemical discharges of gas companies where

> any Washings or other Waste Liquids, Substances of Things … into any River, Brook or Running Stream, Reservoir Aqueduct Feeder, Pond, or Spring Head or into any Drain, Sewer or Ditch … whereby the said Water, or any part thereof, shall or may be soiled, fouled, or corrupted, then and in each and every case the Person or Persons so offending shall forfeit and pay every such Offence the Sum of Two Hundred Pound.[39]

Edinburgh streets were offensive. Polluted water and malodorous waste matter accumulated in the pock-marked and cobbled streets, and tenement dwellers made matters worse by throwing their refuse into the street below:

> The practice of throwing out foul Water and other Filth upon the Streets is a Nuisance which the occupiers of houses divided into separate floors or flats, and having no Communication with the common Sewers, cannot at present easily avoid.[40]

37 See 59 Geo. 3, cap. 116 (1819).
38 J. Colston, *The Edinburgh and District Water Supply: a Historical Sketch* (Edinburgh, 1890).
39 See 3 Geo. 4, cap. 78, sections 41, 90 (1822) and 2 Will. 4, cap. 87, sections 50–52 (1832).
40 3 Geo. 4, cap. 78, sections 97–9.

This type of nuisance was addressed in 1822 by an Act 'for washing, cleansing and lighting the Streets'; it empowered landlords to connect to the street drains and sewers subject to the consent of the ground-floor proprietors. Foul odours also emanated from dunghills, a cash crop of accumulated animal manure and human excrement collected in each ward and harvested by the police commissioners to defray expenses associated with their work. The commissioners also laid claim to the solid dirt, ashes, and offal from slaughterhouses to boost their revenues, and even paid the burgh of Canongate yearly sum of £60 for rights over the dung, or 'fuilzie', of that burgh.[41] These dunghills leeched into the watercourses of the city, creating both a nuisance and a furore over both the 'foul burns' of Edinburgh in the 1830s and 1840s and the carting of dung through the streets of the city.[42] The process was described by Henry Austin:

> The Craigentinny Meadows at Edinburgh were the most successful example of the utilisation of sewage by open irrigation. Two hundred and sixty acres of land were irrigated by the 'Foul Burn' which took the drainage of half of Edinburgh to the meadows where pumps were used to spread the slurry. The irrigation was continued all year round except for Sundays. The fields rotated every three weeks with the land receiving the most manure producing the biggest crop.[43]

The Cleansing Department spent about £12,000 each year on the streets, employed between 100 and 140 scavengers depending on the season, and removed 20–30,000 tons of manure annually, using the Union Canal to transport it to farmers. By 1843, the Inspector of Cleaning was able to claim, proudly, that 'the whole town [was] cleansed every day'.[44]

Chimney smoke was a common feature of Edinburgh; indeed, the city laboured under the sobriquet of 'Auld Reekie' or 'Old Smokey'.[45] From the outset in 1805, police commissioners were charged with ensuring that the fire risk from domestic chimneys be minimised, and the city moved promptly in 1824 to establish the first municipal fire brigade in Britain as a result of the catastrophic Tron fire that year which destroyed 400 homes in the High Street and caused 13 deaths, two of them fire-fighters.[46] The commissioners were also alert to the

41 3 Geo. 4, cap. 78, section 85;

42 PP (HC) 1857 XX, 2262 (2) Report on Means of Deodorizing and Utilizing Sewage of Towns, by H. Austin, 15–16, 44, 51, 77, 94, 96, 101, 103; and PP (HC) 1857–58 XXXII, 2372 Royal Commission to Inquire into Best Mode of Distributing Sewage of Towns. Preliminary Report, 13–17, compared Edinburgh's treatment of sewage favourably to various places in England and to Milan. Edinburgh possessed the most extensive irrigation using open ditches in Britain. See also C. Hamlin, 'Environmental sensibility in Edinburgh, 1839–40: the "fetid irrigation" controversy', *Journal of Urban History*, 20 (1994), 311–39.

43 PP (HC) 1857 XX, 2262, Report by Henry Austin, 44–6.

44 PP (HC) 1844 [572] XVII, Royal Commission for Inquiring into State of Large Towns and Populous Districts. First Report, Evidence of Alexander Ramsay, 'Further Evidence', 729. See also ED9 25/3, Report XVII, 28 June 1859.

45 Chambers, *The Concise Scots Dictionary* (Edinburgh, 1996 edn), 549–50.

46 For an extended account of the fire see R. Chambers, *Notices of the Most Remarkable Fires in Edinburgh: from 1385 to 1824* (Edinburgh, 1824), 54–74; S. Ewen, 'Professional elites and urban governance: chief fire officers in late Victorian British municipalities', in S. Couperas, C. Smit and

dangers of industrial smoke pollution, and were given powers as early as 1822 to encourage industrial firms to re-cycle the fumes from their chimney stacks:

> Owners and Occupiers of all Steam Engines, and of all Iron foundries, Glass works, Gas Manufactories, Distilleries, Breweries, and other Manufactories wherein Furnaces are used, already erected … shall within Six months from the passing of this Act adopt the Method now practised, or some good and efficacious Method, of consuming and burning the Smoke arising therefrom, so far as the same can be done, so as to prevent the same occasioning any Nuisance which can be avoided.[47]

To combat this threat to life and property, regulations were introduced to curtail the frequency of domestic chimney fires which were regarded as a nuisance, and tax assessments were raised in 1832 to enable fire stations to be constructed in the wards of the city and so extend the spatial tentacles of urban administration.[48] Eventually in 1848, and again in 1855, the police commissioners printed and sent a notice to 112 industrial premises encouraging the installation of equipment to combat the polluting effects of their smoke emissions.[49]

Between 1805 and 1854 a raft of detailed clauses in the Police Acts aimed to deter what would now be called anti-social behaviour in a bid to inculcate a sense of common purpose and to construct what was later termed good citizenship.[50] At least this was the evidence of those brought to court and convicted when between 1842 and 1847 almost four out of every five convictions were for theft, disorderly conduct, or assault.[51] Piecemeal, the accretion of police powers produced a patchwork of official controls both in moral and physical environments. By 1848, detailed offences carrying a penalty of up to £2 occupied more than two parliamentary statute pages in relation to section 181 of the Act.[52] Mind and body were both targeted. Profane or coarse books, importuning, and indecent exposure were among the new offences punishable with a fine, and if the prescribed times of day for carpet beating, furniture removals and entertainment were not observed, again fines were imposed. Individual convenience took a lower priority than communal interests. Similarly, in what was one of the first attempts to control parking and loading, the Police Act, 1812, defined a cart loading more than 30 yards from the

D.J. Wolffram (eds), *In Control of the City: Local Elites and the Dynamics of Urban Politics, 1800–1960* (Leuven, 2007), 151.

47 3 Geo. 4, cap. 78, section 94. Non-compliance led to a £50 fine, and the same requirements applied to new and old machinery alike.

48 2 Will. 4, cap. 87, sections 70–74 (1832); 7 Will. 4, cap. 32, section 27 (1837); 11 and 12 Vict., cap. 113, sections 77–79 (1848). Police stations and other buildings could also be acquired or built.

49 ECA ED9/1/13, Police Commissioners, General Minutes of General Commission, 13 August 1855, 100–3. The principal culprits were 17 brewers, 13 engineering firms, 8 corn mills, 8 foundries, 8 printers, 7 tanners, and 5 saw mills.

50 H.E. Meller, *Patrick Geddes: Social Evolutionist and City Planner* (London, 1990); A. Warren, 'Sir Robert Baden-Powell, the Scout movement and citizen training in Great Britain, 1900–1920', *English Historical Review*, 101, no. 399 (1986), 376–98.

51 ECA 9/25/2/13, Half Yearly Report and Return of Crimes since the year 1841 (1848). House-breaking constituted just 2.1% of convictions, assaults and robberies 0.13%; and forgery and counterfeiting 0.27%.

52 9 and 10 Vict., cap. 365, section 181 included, for example, offences presumably aimed at children – throwing stones, 'making a slide on ice or snow', pulling door-bells, kite-flying.

delivery address as an offence.[53] These sections were expanded in 1848 to embrace the rules of the road: both 'not driving on the left' and 'not passing on the right' constituted breaches of regulations warranting a fine, as was 'furiously driving a horse or carriage', another legacy of the 1812 legislation and a progenitor of the modern offence of driving without due care and attention. Behavioural conditioning was part of the agenda of Edinburgh police commissioners.

Mindful of fever and epidemic disease, sections of the Acts were conceived within the context of medical policing, that is, as a series of preventative measures. This was particularly so for regulations pertaining to 'Keepers of Lodging houses for the lower Orders' who, when their customers remained confined to bed for days on end, persistently failed to report cases of illness. From 1822, pressure was put on them through a system of fines to report such cases to the police, but it was only in 1848 that a registration system for lodging-house accommodation was drafted by the Police Surgeon, Dr George Glover, put in place by the commissioners, and overseen by the Inspector of Cleansing.[54] This regime introduced the concept of 'ticketing', a relationship between the size of rooms and the number of occupants permissible within:

> It shall be lawful to the said Inspector [of Cleansing] from time to time to fix and determine the Number of Lodgers who shall be accommodated in each Apartment of such Lodging house, and by a written or printed Certificate signed by him to license such Lodging house ... and to order that a Ticket containing the Number of Lodgers for which each Lodging house or Apartment accordingly ... and to order that a Ticket containing the Number of Lodgers for which each Lodging House or Apartment is licensed and any rules or Instructions made by the Commissioners regarding Health, Cleanliness or Ventilation, shall be hung up or placed in a conspicuous Part of each Apartment into which Lodgers are received.[55]

This pattern of lodging-house regulation heavily plagiarised the earlier legislation of 1846, which was implemented vigorously by Dr William Henry Duncan, the newly appointed Liverpool Medical Officer of Health. It was not the last time that the Liverpool–Edinburgh axis proved influential.[56] A crucial distinction, however, was that in Liverpool there existed from an early stage a health committee to oversee public health policy; in Edinburgh and London the ticketing regime failed to emulate Liverpool in this regard.

53 52 Geo. 3, cap. 172, section 64.

54 ECA Boxes 00/01/20, A/14, Regulations on Lodging Houses drawn up by the Surgeon, and ED 9/25/2/2, Proposed byelaws as to Lodging-houses, prepared by the Surgeon.

55 11 and 12 Vict., cap. 113, section 199 (1848). For details of the later Dublin and Glasgow ticketing system, see C. Eason, 'The tenement homes of Dublin: their condition and regulation', *Journal of the Statistical and Social Inquiry Society of Ireland*, Vol. X Part LXXIX (1898/99), 383–98; J.B. Russell, 'On the "Ticketed Houses" of Glasgow', *Proc. Royal Phil. Soc. of Glasgow* (1888), 19; Glasgow Municipal Commission, *Evidence* (Glasgow, 1904), Fyfe, Q.782–924; Myles, Q.2150–2393; McCallum, Q.2401–45; Kelso, Q.3964–4024.

56 11 and 12 Vict., cap. 113, section 199 is longer yet very similar in its language and provision to that of 1846 for Liverpool: 9 and 10 Vict., cap. 127, section 125, An Act for the Improvement of the Sewerage and Drainage of Liverpool, and for Making Further Provisions for the Sanitary Regulation of the Borough. See P. Laxton, 'Fighting for public health: Dr Duncan and his adversaries, 1847–63', in S. Sheard and H. Power (eds), *Body and City: Histories of Urban Public Health* (Aldershot, 2000), 78–9.

Controlling high-risk locations was a logical approach towards the management of public health. Progressively, even aggressively, the Edinburgh police commissioners extended their reach as they attempted to manage overcrowded flats. Within the tenement block itself, common stairs below the tenant's flat were to be swept daily and washed once a week and, where flats were vacant, the tenants directly above were responsible for sweeping and washing the stairs, passages, and landings.[57] The responsibility was placed squarely on the individual in 1832, and, from 1848, the Police Commission obtained wide-ranging powers to make byelaws 'for cleansing Houses and buildings in which contagious Diseases have appeared', and for 'watering, sweeping, and cleansing of closes, thoroughfares ... and employing any Process of disinfection'.[58]

Isolating fever cases was central to the Scottish conception of medical policing (see chapter 2), and that of William Alison in Edinburgh in particular. Indeed, the Royal Infirmary's 'most vital contribution to public health', it was claimed, was the admission and thus isolation of fever patients which between 1817 and 1830 numbered over 6,500 cases.[59] The contagion of numbers put such immense pressure on the resources of the infirmary that additional premises, the Queensberry House barracks, were required on an emergency basis, with administrative responsibility transferred to a Fever Board in 1830. Described as the 'guardians of the public health', the Fever Board immediately came under extreme pressure with a cholera outbreak in 1832 and typhus epidemics in 1837, 1838 and 1839.[60] Against this background, a series of Police Acts dealing with preventive measures to reduce the risk of fever, and indirectly to relieve pressure on medical resources in the city, made sense. Through a framework of byelaws designed to reduce unpleasant smells, the Police Commission subscribed to widely held beliefs about polluted air as the cause of infection, and so their focus on specific causes of air quality, complemented by a forward-looking approach towards water quality, was designed to cleanse and purify both places and people.

Undoubtedly, the stipulations of the Police Acts were side-stepped; many sections were unenforceable, and the corruption of police commissioners in 1820 reached the status of a public scandal.[61] The poor, it was claimed, found the intrusion of the police 'offensive'.[62] Had it been otherwise then the mid-century need to develop a more systematic urban management, first under a Police Surgeon and then a Medical Officer of Health, would not have been necessary. So regulations were honoured in the breach, rather than in the letter of the law, and yet the content of the Acts reveals the ambition of the Police Commission to improve the public's health.

57 2 Will. 4, cap. 87, section 45 (1832).

58 11 and 12 Vict., cap. 113, section 37 (1848).

59 Quoted in H. Macdonald, 'Public health legislation and problems in Victorian Edinburgh', Edinburgh Ph.D. thesis (1971), 6. See also PP (HC) 1819 II, 449, Select Committee to consider Validity of Doctrine of Contagion in Plague, Minutes of Evidence, J. Mitchell, 88–90.

60 *New Edinburgh Almanac*, 1839, 539; *The Scotsman*, 15 February 1837. For a general treatment of typhus see C. Creighton, *A History of Epidemics in Britain* (London, 1965, 2nd edn).

61 G. Morton, *Unionist Nationalism*, 35, n.58.

62 PP (HC) 1844 [572] XVII, Royal Commission into State of Large Towns, Evidence of Alexander Ramsay, 6 October 1843, 727.

The Police Surgeon as public health administrator

More than twenty committees operated under the new and amended clauses proposed by the series of Police Acts passed between 1805 and 1856.[63] Different committees were concerned with, for example, cleaning, lighting, smoke, and parks; there was no integrated approach to public health, and so medical involvement remained locked in reactive mode, rather than in a pro-active one.[64] From the outset in 1805, therefore, small and occasional payments were made to several doctors and surgeons for medicines and services rendered, initially in connection with the commissioners' responsibilities for the health of police officers, and prisoners in the Bridewell.[65] Commenting on the expert medical advice obtained in 1823 from two giants of Scottish public health, Drs William Gairdner and Douglas Maclagan, the commissioners stated that, 'these Gentlemen have been very assiduous and it cannot be too often repeated that Medical Visitors, above all others ought to be encouraged'.[66] Yet there was no systematic or on-going engagement of medical experts with public health issues; their role remained a pragmatic one. Even though the Cleaning Committee in the 1820s increasingly turned to Dr Alexander Black, the tendency remained for him to be consulted by the individual sub-committees as problems arose, not as someone involved in the systematic development of health policy.[67] Black's position gradually became formalised, first in 1824 when he was described as 'surgeon to Police establishment, 227 High Street', then in 1827 when listed alongside the police commissioners, and finally by 1834 when his salary was paid from the Police Commissioners' General Establishment funds.[68] Despite this, his position remained on a consultative basis albeit on a widening spectrum of public health matters in the 1830s and 1840s.[69] Only in 1848 was the term Police Surgeon used officially, although by then it had assumed common currency.[70]

Five reasons for this lack of coherence in early public health administration in Edinburgh stand out. First, based on the 1805 template, a gradual extension of police commissioners' spheres of operations spawned new committees: the General Committee was established in 1805, and was followed by committees for

63 ECA ED9/1/1 – 23, Edinburgh Police Commissioners Minutes, 1805–56.

64 ECA ED9/25/2/4, Report of the Special Committee appointed by the Police Commissioners to examine and enquire into the management of the affairs of the Establishment in the various departments thereof, 1838, revealed many slack administrative procedures and recommended various reforms especially relating to the revenues of several departments.

65 ECA MYBN 322B, Police Establishment Accounts, 1805–1811; Accounts, 1806–07, 3, Accounts, 1807–08, 7; Accounts, 1808–09; Accounts, 1809–10, 7; Accounts, 1810–11, 4; Police Establishment Accounts, 1819–21, 5.

66 ECA ED9/1/5, General Commission Minutes, 24 November 1823.

67 ECA ED9/22/3, Letter Books, 1822–26; 1 September 1824.

68 *The General Post-Office Annual Directory for 1824–25* (Edinburgh, 1824), 16; *The Edinburgh Almanac or Universal Scots and Imperial Register for 1827* (Edinburgh, 1826); ECA MYBN 322B, Police Establishment Accounts, 1833–34, 4–8.

69 ECA ED9/23/1–2 Indexes to Minutes, 561–62. For 1842–45 for examples, see ECA ED9/23/1 where 4th sequence, 1842–45 for matters relating to Pavements 14–16, 103–104, 128–129, 163–166, 184–185; Manure 41–42, 113, 115; Fever Board 101; Smoke 85–86, 170; Lamps 33–35, 178–180; Scavengers 157; Water and Manure Tanks 79; Urinals 43–44; Sweeping Machines 48; Surgeon 87–88.

70 An earlier reference was made in 1843 by the Inspector of Cleaning, A. Ramsay, see PP (HC) 1844, 572, Royal Commission for Inquiring into State of Large Towns, 727.

Weighing (1806), Cleaning (1819), Billeting (1819), Watching (1820), Lighting (1820), Law (1820), Fire Engine (1824), Paving (1832), Committee on Bills (1833), Finance (1838), and several others. Alexander Murray, Inspector of Cleaning, remarked perceptively in 1847 that 'Among the evils connected with the cleaning of Edinburgh, there is none more remarkable than the multiplicity of Boards'.[71] The incrementalism of this federal structure meant that there was no centralised responsibility for health; organisationally, city management was fractured. As Dr Alexander Wood, one of the General Commissioners, observed, this resulted in a lack of coordination in public health policy that adversely affected the poor of the city, a situation only rectified in 1872 with the formation of a Health Committee.[72] Second, responsibility for epidemic disease was further divided between the various parochial boards in the city (for cleaning inside homes); the Police Commission (cleaning courts and streets); and the Fever Board with its city-wide responsibilities for coordinating action and which swung into operation only when a full-blown epidemic was declared. Third, lacking detailed civil registration data before 1855 on the causes of death, there was no agreed empirical basis for a policy regarding public health in Edinburgh, nor indeed anywhere else in Scotland.[73] True, there had been occasional studies by organisations and institutions such as the Fever Board and Royal Infirmary, and by public figures such as James Stark,[74] whose data found their way during the 1840s into national publications through editorials in the *Journal of Public Health* and into international networks of public health discourse through letters exchanged with William Henry Duncan, the Medical Officer of Health for Liverpool.[75] Civil registration in Scotland was dogged until 1855 by medical disputes concerning the nosology[76] of disease and an insistence by the Royal Colleges that, in contrast to England, only doctors should record the cause of death. Fourth, the on-going national debate concerning poverty (see chapter 2), poor relief, and the nature of epidemic disease perpetuated delays in public health policy. Locally, a series of fifteen lectures in 1844 by the Edinburgh advocate James Simpson raised the profile of public health in a plea for 'proper guardianship'; he called for the 'appointment of a Medical Officer of Health whose sole duty it should be to

71 A. Murray, *Nuisances in Edinburgh*, 20.

72 A. Wood, *Report on the Condition of the Poorer Classes of Edinburgh* (Edinburgh, 1840), ix–xi.

73 A. Cameron, 'The establishment of civil registration in Scotland', *Historical Journal*, 50 (2007), 37–95.

74 J. Stark, *Report on the Mortality of Edinburgh and Leith, for the months of January and February 1846* (Edinburgh, 1846) and 2 others for 1846, and similarly for mortality in volumes for 1847 and 1848. See also J. Stark, *Inquiry into some points of the sanatory state of Edinburgh; the rate of mortality of its inhabitants since 1780 etc.* (Edinburgh, 1847); and J. Stark, 'Contribution to the vital statistics of Scotland', *Journal of the Statistical Society*, 14 (1851), 48–87.

75 *Journal of Public Health and Monthly Record of Sanitary Improvement*, 1 (1848), 194, 268–9, 277; and vol. 2 (1849), 106. See also in the same volume, 215–16, and 283–9; Liverpool Record Office 352 HEA 1/1, letter Duncan to Stark, 9 November 1849. Duncan's pivotal position in the community of public health experts is demonstrated by his exchange of pamphlets and statistics with sanitarians such as Stark in Edinburgh and others in Manchester and Glasgow. Duncan also received and relayed material to Lemuel Shattock in Boston, USA. See LRO, 352 HEA 1/1, Duncan to Shattock, 14 December 1849, to whom he sent 15 pamphlets on Liverpool and materials on Edinburgh and Glasgow.

76 Nosology is the branch of medical science relating to the classification of disease.

visit at all times the whole town, but especially the places where disease is most likely to break out, and to advise the means of relief and prevention'.[77] Finally, there was a strong reluctance among commissioners to spend public money on the management of public health. This erupted in strongly worded letters from the Police Surgeon, Dr William Tait, in 1844 and 1845 in relation to his claim for increased pay.[78] Tait complained that his allowance of 1 shilling per patient amounted to 'just about the sum that is allowed to a common constable; and surely there is a great difference in the value of the services of the two.' The commissioners refused; Tait resigned. Only when the commissioners reviewed the implications of their decision and the lack of medical cover for the health of the police did they reverse their decision; Tait withdrew his resignation.[79] The episode was symptomatic of the penny-pinching attitude which characterised the commissioners' approach to public health throughout the first half of the nineteenth century, and even after the appointment of Littlejohn in 1854.

Nowhere was this fractured administrative structure and parsimonious attitude to expenditure on public health more apparent than when Alexander Ramsay, an expert witness with 19 years experience as Inspector of Lighting and Cleansing in Edinburgh, gave evidence to the Royal Commission on the Health of Towns in 1844.[80] He described the city as 'lamentably defective in its sanatory regulations', adding that it 'must ever be so, until medical police shall have a statutory existence'.[81] He gave two reasons for his opinion: first, that police intervention was not justifiable by statute unless a public health crisis already existed – Ramsay called it an 'excitement regarding epidemic disease'; second, since there were no standing orders designed to anticipate an epidemic, there was inevitably a further delay while gangs of men and sufficient materials were assembled and the fumigation of rooms got under way. What frustrated Ramsay was that, though it was a dangerous process and required supervision, cleaning was quick, effective, and the expense 'a mere trifle'.[82] On a single day,

77 J. Simpson, *Brief Reports of Lectures Delivered to the Working Classes of Edinburgh: on the means in their own power of improving their character & condition* (Edinburgh, 1844), 15. A collection of 15 lectures as reported in the *Edinburgh Weekly Chronicle and Scottish Pilot*, 16 December 1843 to 13 April 1844. Lecture 4, 6 January 1844, pp. 13–16, included 'Sanatory Improvement – Officers of Health', and lecture 15, 13 April 1844, pp. 57–60, 'Condition and Health of Towns – Sanatory Legislation'.

78 ECA MYBN 322B, Police Establishment Accounts, 1832–58, various dates. Dr Alexander Black remained in post until his death in 1852, sharing responsibilities first with William Tait (1842–48) and then with George Glover (1848–55).

79 ECA ED9/1/10?, General Commissioners Minutes, 11 May, 1 June, 13 July, 24 and 31 August 1846, ff. 83–4, 91–2, 98, 127–8, 132. Sergeants of police also claimed (11 May 1846, f. 84) that they deserved a pay increase.

80 Ramsay subsequently was appointed as manager of the Edinburgh Water Company in 1845 and was in post for at least 25 years, during which time eight of the nine Edinburgh reservoirs were built. See *The Scotsman*, 23 April 1869, 3a–e.

81 PP (HC) 1844 572, Royal Commission for Inquiring into State of Large Towns and Populous Districts. First Report, Minutes of Evidence, Alexander Ramsay, 6 October 1843, 726, Q.4. The Royal Commission was chaired by Lyon Playfair, who had detailed knowledge of Edinburgh municipal management.

82 PP (HC) 1844 572, Ramsay, 726, Evidence, Q.4 (*sic*), actually Q.5. Based on his experience, and on specific examples drawn from cleaning operations in an outbreak of fever in 1838, Ramsay demonstrated how cleaning flats eliminated the spread of fever.

3.5 Alexander Ramsay, Inspector of Lighting and Cleansing
Ramsay was a highly knowledgeable municipal official who subsequently managed the Edinburgh Water Company.
[Source: J. Colston, *The Edinburgh and District Water Supply: A Historical Sketch* (1890)]

30 October 1843, 24 men cleansed and lime-washed 41 staircases, 28 rooms, 13 closets, and 57 passages.[83] With labour, materials, and depreciation, the costs of cleaning each of these 139 spaces was between 9*d.* and 1*s.*, and the fumigation 2*d.* per apartment. In eight weeks in the autumn of 1843, 2,343 spaces were cleansed at a total cost of £42, equivalent to 4¼*d.* (1.8p) each.[84] The process of fumigation involved closing all doors and windows and then, with 2 ounces of sulphuric acid poured over 4 ounces of a mixture of 'one part of black oxide to four of muriate of soda', chlorine gas was produced which quickly permeated all crevices in a room. After 8–10 minutes the windows and doors were opened. The speed of the operation put the residents to minimal inconvenience, and they clamoured for such treatment whenever fever was known to be in the vicinity.

Because such cleaning exercises were undertaken as part of a public health emergency, the cost was borne by the police commissioners in line with their cleaning responsibilities. Ramsay, as Inspector of Cleansing, was frustrated at this expensive crisis management, and argued that the money would be better spent on the salary of 'a stipendiary Medical Officer', which, with a few elementary regulations and an annual campaign to lime-wash properties, would mean that 'the periodical attacks of fever, with which all large towns are visited, would be much less frequent in their occurrence and greatly less severe in their character'.[85] This was a finely judged nineteenth-century version of cost–benefit analysis, and a powerful call in 1843 'to establish in Edinburgh a medical police for this purpose'.[86] The expenditure involved, it was claimed in an echo of Edwin Chadwick's *Report on the Sanitary Condition of the Labouring Population of Great Britain* (1842), was justified in terms of enabling hundreds of families who otherwise would become a permanent burden on charity to provide for their own support.

In the 1840s, despite the existence of detailed police regulations and sanctions in many theatres of operations, pragmatism was the hallmark of sanitary policy. It was not surprising, therefore, when in June 1845, and months only since the lime-washing campaign, the Medical Relief Committee of the City Parochial Board again reported to the Town Council on 'the increase of Fever and disease in the City and Suburbs' and instructed their parochial Medical Officers to report properties where fever existed to the Inspector of Cleaning. In a clear move that demonstrated the limited authority of the Police Surgeon, the General Commissioners requested that he 'afford every assistance to the Inspector'.[87] Indeed, office-holders themselves had only a partial understanding of their responsibilities. This was evident when Dr George Glover, Tait's

83 *The Scotsman*, 14 February 1844, noted Ramsay had 185 men on his cleaning staff. PP (HC) 1844 XX, 557, Report of the Royal Commission for Inquiring into the Administration and Practical Operation of the Poor Law in Scotland.

84 PP (HC) 1844 572, Ramsay, post-script, 729, 9 October 1843. Ramsay calculated that the total cost for cleaning and fumigating all the houses in Edinburgh valued at under £4 rent, in addition to all those affected by fever, a total of 7,600 houses, would be £221.

85 PP (HC) 1844 572, Ramsay, 726, Evidence, Q.4 (*sic*). See also 'Further Communication', 727–9. Ramsay's successor as Inspector of Cleaning, Alexander Murray, *Nuisances in Edinburgh*, 21–2, repeated the point that direct intervention by the municipal authority was an essential defensive measure.

86 PP (HC) 1844 572, Ramsay, 'Further communication', 729.

87 ECA ED9/3/5, Cleaning Committee Minutes, 12 June 1845, 5 July 1845, ff. 193–5.

CHOLERA RETURN.
No. 7
FOR THE COMMITTEE OF THE ROYAL COLLEGES OF PHYSICIANS AND SURGEONS.

NAME.	Age and Sex.	Occupation of Patient, or of Parent or Husband, in the case of unemployed children or females.	Circumstances, previous Health and Habits.	Street, No., or Part of Close, and Floor.	State of Cleanliness in and near the House.	Whether, where, and when, in a Cholera locality previously, or in communication with the sick.	Day and Hour of Seizure.	Day, Hour, and Nature of Event.	Whether any Premonitory Stage, and what.	Whether a Gastro-enteric affection only; or Collapse and Spasms; or Consecutive Fever also.	Where treated.	CHIEF TREATMENT.
Mrs Bennet	60	Husband dead	good Intemperate	Two Storied house ground floor [illegible]	Very Clean	house situated two hundred yards distant from the village, both from Cholera locality	Nov. 4th at 11 a.m.	Died Nov. 5th at 2 a.m.	None	Collapse and Spasms	at home	Laudanum and peppermint water Brandy Heat to Surface

Remarks, especially on the apparent Origin, Pathological appearances, and Treatment.

Signature H. D. Littlejohn M.D.

CHOLERA RETURN.
No. 8
FOR THE COMMITTEE OF THE ROYAL COLLEGES OF PHYSICIANS AND SURGEONS.

NAME.	Age and Sex.	Occupation of Patient, or of Parent or Husband, in the case of unemployed children or females.	Circumstances, previous Health, and Habits.	Street, No., or part of Close, and Floor.	State of Cleanliness in and near the House.	Whether, where, and when, in a Cholera locality previously, or in communication with the sick.	Day and Hour of Seizure.	Day, Hour, and Nature of Event.	Whether any Premonitory Stage, and what.	Whether a Gastro-enteric affection only; or Collapse and Spasms; or Consecutive Fever also.	Where treated.	CHIEF TREATMENT.
John Greenlaw	24	Wrought at Paper Mill as Joiner	Good Intemperate	Two Storied house upper flat	Very Clean	lived with No. 7 his Mother in law	Nov. 4 at 1 p.m.	Died Nov. 5th at 6 a.m.	purging for eight hours previous	Collapse and Spasms	at home	Laudanum and peppermint water Calomel and [illegible] Brandy with heat to surface and friction

Remarks, especially on the apparent Origin, Pathological appearances, and Treatment.

Signature H. D. Littlejohn M.D.

CHOLERA RETURN.
No. 9
FOR THE COMMITTEE OF THE ROYAL COLLEGES OF PHYSICIANS AND SURGEONS.

NAME.	Age and Sex.	Occupation of Patient, or of Parent or Husband, in the case of unemployed children or females.	Circumstances, previous Health, and Habits.	Street, No., or part of Close, and Floor.	State of Cleanliness in and near the House.	Whether, where, and when, in a Cholera locality previously, or in communication with the sick.	Day and Hour of Seizure.	Day, Hour, and Nature of Event.	Whether any Premonitory Stage, and what.	Whether a Gastro-enteric affection only; or Collapse and Spasms; or Consecutive Fever also.	Where treated.	CHIEF TREATMENT.
Margaret Locke		lived with step father a Carter	good Temperate	New Town one storied house Clay floor	clean	In a Cholera locality	Nov. 4th at 2 p.m.	Died Nov. 5th 11 a.m.	None	Collapse and Spasms	at home	Laudanum and peppermint water Calomel Tincture of Cannabis Ind.

Remarks, especially on the apparent Origin, Pathological appearances, and Treatment.

Signature H. D. Littlejohn M.D.

3.6 Widow Bennet dies of cholera, 2 a.m., 5 November 1848
One of 23 cholera returns signed by Dr Littlejohn for the joint committee of the RCPEd and RCSEd. [Source: RCPEd]

successor as Police Surgeon, tabled a report in 1848 in which he stated that, contrary to the claims of the Inspector for the Poor, under Clause 118 of the Police Act the Superintendent of Police had no powers to close lodging-houses but only to 'take proper measures' to ensure that these were 'fumigated, washed or cleaned' under the supervision of any medical practitioner'.[88] These were turf wars over jurisdiction and, inevitably, over the financial liability to pay for the implementation of public health measures. For example, Glover's report identified a list of lodging-houses in urgent need of cleaning and fumigating and which the Cleaning Committee considered an expense they could reclaim from the Parochial Board, who in turn possessed a different list of insanitary lodging-houses and made arrangements with private contractors to clean them.

In early October 1848 a cholera outbreak concentrated the collective minds of Edinburgh officials. Belatedly, the Inspector of Cleaning was authorised to engage an additional task force of scavengers and fumigators. These were among the 'Measures for Prevention of Cholera' that occupied hours of Cleaning Committee time, and also included a systematic division of the city into areas. Dr Glover was also authorised to access the records of the Royal Infirmary, dispensaries

88 ECA ED9/3/5, Cleaning Committee Minutes, 11 February 1848, ff. 207–10.

and parochial boards in order to study the epidemiology of fever outbreaks. Crucially, the language of the Cleaning Committee revealed the seriousness of the cholera outbreak: it was referred to increasingly as the 'present emergency' and the 'prevailing epidemic'. There was a real sense of urgency: meetings took place every other day for almost a fortnight as the Cleaning Committee sought to contain the outbreak. The Royal College of Physicians expressed concern to the Town Council, and the president wrote to Edwin Chadwick at the Board of Health to convey their view that little could be achieved without the cooperation of the Parochial Boards.[89] The Inspector of Cleaning was urged by the Cleaning Committee to be more active; obligations of inhabitants were to be 'strictly enforced'; and in what proved to be a highly significant move, the committee empowered their Medical Officer, Dr Glover, to carry out powers under section 201 of the Police Act, 1848, though this was to be regarded as a temporary measure and that 'no undue expence [*sic*] be imposed on the public'.[90]

This decision, authorising yet limiting Glover's powers, proved to be significant. It demonstrated the futility of public health administration where several authorities coexisted in barely disguised hostility; nor was it helpful that there were poisoned relations between the Medical Officer and the administrative authority, first in the form of the Police Commission and later as the Town Council. The Cleaning Committee agreed:

> as a temporary measure that in all special cases when intimation is made that certain localities require to be fumigated, and the houses and persons of the Inhabitants cleansed, that their Medical Officer be authorised to carry out the powers contained in the 201 section of the Act.[91]

However, Section 201 clearly stated that:

> where the inhabitants of such Houses or Apartments shall not have taken due Precaution against such Disease, and where there may be reasonable Apprehension of such Disease spreading or continuing, it shall be lawful for the Commissioners to cause and direct all proper Measures to be taken for the Fumigation or Disinfection and cleansing of such Houses or Apartments … it shall be lawful for any Superintendent, Inspector or other Person appointed by the Commissioners to enter into any such House or Apartment, and to do or assist in doing or causing to be done all Matters and Things for the Purposes aforesaid.[92]

Alexander Ramsay, 'the active head of the lighting and cleansing department' in Edinburgh, had stated in 1843 that he hoped to live to see the day a Medical Officer would be in charge of sanitary policy in the great cities of Britain.[93]

89 Royal College of Physicians Minutes (RCPE) September 1844 to October 1851, Meeting of Council, 6 October 1848. See also RCPE General Minutes, 1843–51, 3732–50, for further details of the cholera outbreak.

90 ECA ED9/3/5, Cleaning Committee Minutes, 31 October 1848, f. 235.

91 ECA ED9/3/5, Cleaning Committee Minutes, 31 October 1848, f. 235.

92 11–12 Vict., cap. 113, An Act for more effectually watching, cleansing, and lighting the Streets of the City of Edinburgh and adjoining Districts, for regulating the Police thereof, and for other Purposes relating thereto [14 August 1848].

93 *The Scotsman*, 30 December 1843, 3b; *Caledonian Mercury*, 25 December 1843, 3f.

Fifteen lectures by James Simpson, subsequently published in the *Edinburgh Weekly Chronicle* and *Scottish Pilot* between December 1843 and April 1844, attracted capacity audiences to the Cowgate Chapel (seating 1,700) and added to the clamour for an officer of health to be appointed. Years of yearning for extended medical powers suddenly seemed a possibility. As Simpson stated, 'with the numberless advantages of such an appointment, the expense would be a mere bagatelle'.[94] The public health emergency in 1848 forced the police commissioners to devolve more power to their Medical Officer; they activated section 201 with limitations only as to period and 'undue expence [*sic*]'. Glover interpreted literally the phrases in section 201 to 'direct all proper measures' and to assist in 'all matters and things for the purposes' of the 'reasonable apprehension of such disease spreading'. He sought to fast track the internal cleaning of insanitary homes where fever was present, and in the absence of sufficient manpower at the disposal of the Inspector of Cleaning, had meetings with the officials of the Parochial Board and led them to believe that the Cleaning Committee would meet the costs of this exercise. Glover also contracted directly and on his own authority for men and materials to undertake the cleaning of 46 closes and passages in the Old Town.[95] Alexander Murray, Ramsay's successor as Inspector of Cleaning, complied with Glover's directions as to which properties were to be cleaned, but understood from Glover that the Parochial Board would pay for the operations. Within hours of activating Clause 201, the Cleaning Committee rescinded their decision. They 'directed Dr Glover to suspend his operations with regard to Cleaning' forthwith and instructed Mr Murray 'to clean the exteriors wherein it appears necessary to him, and the interior of the houses when ordered by the Parochial Authorities'.[96] It was a decision to reinstate the *status quo* – that is to say, fragmented responsibility for the public's health.

If this censure increased the tension between Glover and the Police Commission, the stakes were raised further in a subsequent, wide-ranging review in 1849 of his conduct during the cholera crisis. Statements were submitted, documents attached, and the Cleaning Sub-Committee made an eleven-point report. They noted the absence of a centralised agency, such as a board of health, capable of providing a coherent city-wide strategy for public health. But whereas they commended Glover for his 'most carefully and minutely' compiled statistical data on the cholera outbreak, and recommended he should receive additional pay for his efforts, the committee also concluded that 'it would be better that our Surgeon was kept exclusively to his duties as police Surgeon'.[97] This was a direct consequence of pressure applied by a Committee of Enquiry of the Royal Colleges of Physicians and Surgeons, who were concerned that the cholera returns sent to them by Glover were inconsistent with those he forwarded to London and the Board of Health.[98]

94 J. Simpson, *Brief Reports*, 15.

95 ECA ED9/3/5, Cleaning Committee Minutes, Report of G. Glover, 6 November 1848, ff. 240–1.

96 ECA ED9/3/5, Cleaning Committee Minutes, 6 November 1848, f. 243.

97 ECA ED9/3/5, Sanitary Committee Minutes, 19 January 1849, ff. 253–64.

98 ECA ED9/3/5, letter, Sutherland to Smith, 12 January 1849; Smith to Patterson 15 January 1849; Glover to Lindsay, 18 January 1849, ff. 256–63. See also *The Scotsman*, 21 October, 3b; 8

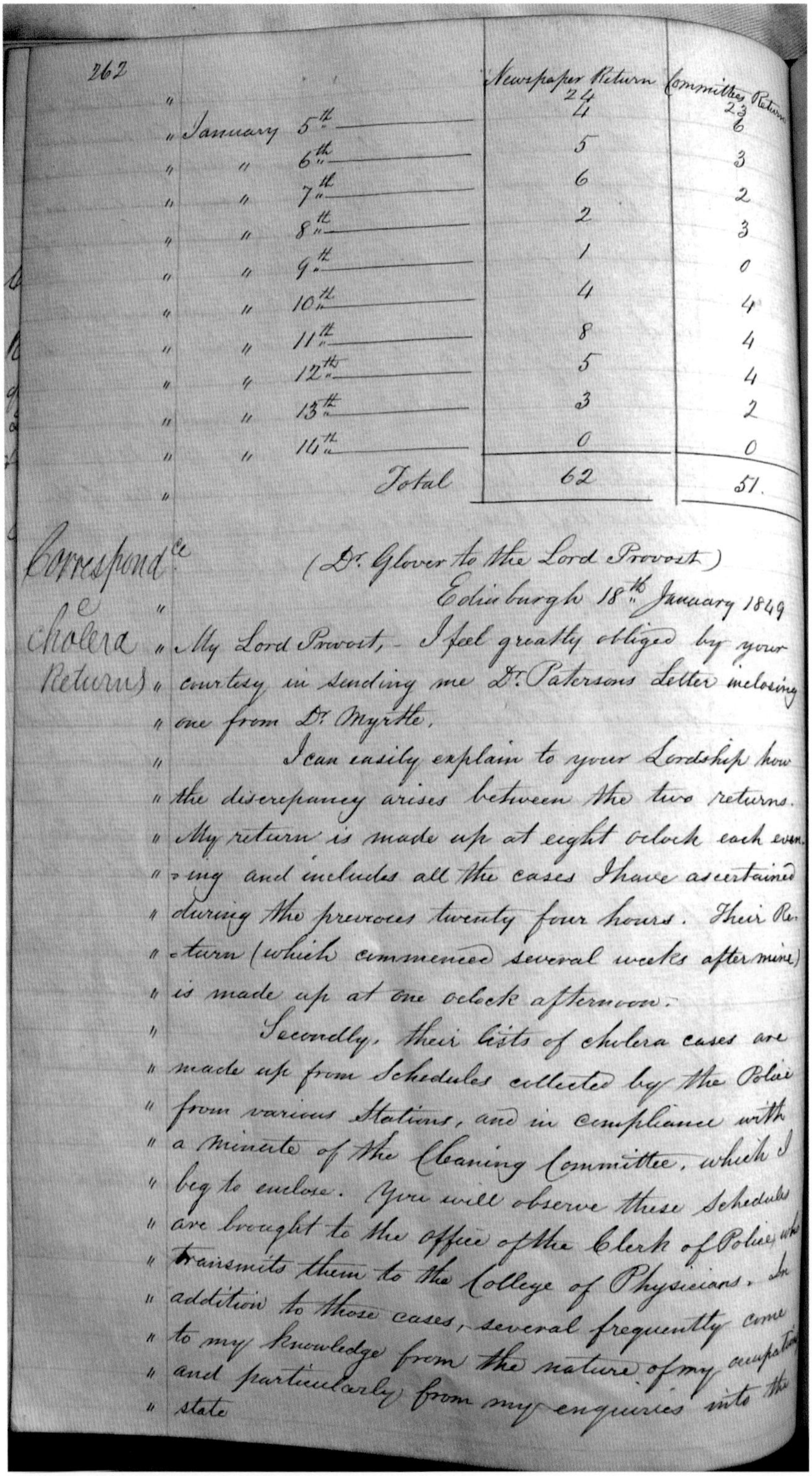

262

	Newspaper Return	Committees Return
	24	23
January 5th	4	6
" 6th	5	3
" 7th	6	2
" 8th	2	3
" 9th	1	0
" 10th	4	4
" 11th	8	4
" 12th	5	4
" 13th	3	2
" 14th	0	0
Total	62	51.

Correspondce
Cholera
Returns

(Dr. Glover to the Lord Provost)

Edinburgh 18th January 1849

My Lord Provost, — I feel greatly obliged by your courtesy in sending me Dr. Patersons Letter inclosing one from Dr. Myrtle.

I can easily explain to your Lordship how the discrepancy arises between the two returns. My return is made up at eight oclock each evening and includes all the cases I have ascertained during the previous twenty four hours. Their Return (which commenced several weeks after mine) is made up at one oclock afternoon.

Secondly, their lists of cholera cases are made up from Schedules collected by the Police from various Stations, and in compliance with a Minute of the Cleaning Committee, which I beg to enclose. You will observe these Schedules are brought to the office of the Clerk of Police, who transmits them to the College of Physicians. In addition to those cases, several frequently come to my knowledge from the nature of my occupation and particularly from my enquiries into the state

3.7 Police Commission Cleaning Committee, 1849
Letter from Dr George Glover explaining why his cholera returns differed from those published in the newspapers. This was one of his many disputes with his employer. [Source: ECA ED9/3/5/262]

Glover, and the office of the Police Surgeon, emerged battered and belittled by the investigations of the Cleaning Committee which instructed him to avoid the wider-ranging, pro-active role of a Medical Officer and to keep to the conventional duties of Police Surgeon. Simultaneously, while Glover's grasp of the epidemiology of fever, of the advisability of isolation and disinfection, and his meticulous statistical schedules were commended and rewarded financially, in recognition of his efforts, the committee publicly censured him for both his interventions and the expenses he had incurred.[99] A later enquiry by the Joint Finance and Sanitary Committee reviewed Glover's actions, and recognised that he had authority for most if not all of his actions.[100] Glover and the office of Police Surgeon were embroiled in a power play between the Cleaning Committee and its chairman, Dr Alexander Wood, and with the Parochial Boards over their respective spheres of cleaning operations and the financial burdens associated with these. The Cleaning Committee were at odds with the Finance and Sanitary committees over the legitimacy of Glover's actions, and the Town Council, who had appointed Glover as Police Surgeon, had no control over him since he operated under powers assigned in Local Acts to the police commissioners. Finally, and significantly, the Royal Colleges of Physicians and Surgeons saw Glover's actions as usurping one of their own responsibilities, liaison with the Board of Health in London. Beneath these organisational turf wars between committees were deep-seated personality conflicts, specifically between Dr Wood and Dr Glover.

With the cholera epidemic in retreat in 1849, confused lines of administrative control prompted Glover to obtain clarification of his duties. He wrote to the chairman of the Cleaning Committee:

> Sir, I beg respectfully to call the attention of the Cleaning Committee to the circumstance that I am frequently called upon to discharge duties connected with the Sanitary State of the City, and for which I have no authority from the commissioners, as they form no part of my duties as laid down by the Board. I will therefore feel obliged by the Cleaning Committee giving such instructions in this matter as they may deem proper. I am &c.[101]

The committee 'were of the opinion that the duties referred to [in respect of the Sanitary State of the City] are not within the prescribed duties of the Surgeon of Police, but that it is necessary and proper that these duties should be performed by the Dr and that he should be allowed suitable remuneration therefore'.[102] Within days the full Sanitary Committee endorsed this view, recognising explicitly that the Police Act, 1848, had increased Glover's duties, but

November 3bc; 6 December, 3b; and 20 December 1848, 3f, for a discussion of the sensitive issue of the publication of mortality statistics, especially during the cholera outbreak.

99 ECA ED9/3/5, General Commissioners Minutes, 9 October 1848; Sanitary Committee Minutes, 12 February 1849; Cleaning Committee Minutes, 14 October, 27 October, 31 October, 4 November, 6 November and 15 December 1848, 19 January 1849, 1 February 1849, 9 July 1849; Report by the Sub-Committee on Dr Glover's Cholera Accounts, ff. 278–9.

100 ECA ED9/3/5, Joint Finance and Sanitary Committee Minutes, 28 February, 5 March and 8 March 1849, ff. 289–90.

101 ECA ED9/25/2, letter, Glover to the Cleaning Committee, 23 August 1849, f. 335.

102 ECA ED9/25/2, letter, Sub-Sanitary Committee to Glover, 25 August 1849, f. 336.

directed him 'to perform all Medical duties and inspection of nuisances required by the Board or any of its committees, or in which the Inspector of Nuisances may require his evidence'.[103] Glover's independence of action and that of the office of the Police Surgeon was circumscribed as a result.

The Water of Leith affair

Just how far public health policy was paralysed both by uncertainty caused by disputes regarding the causes of poverty and the agency responsible for poor relief can best be seen at local level. Police Acts, however well-intentioned, created confusion in terms of local administration. Medical policing, the approach favoured by Alison (see chapter 2) based on monitoring and anticipating epidemic disease, was thwarted by the limited and belated powers of action assigned to the Police Surgeon. This frustrated Drs Tait and Glover throughout the 1840s, and beyond. As experienced physicians, both knew that a more expansive and interventionist role was effective; their respective Inspectors of Cleaning, Ramsay and Murray, were also convinced of the efficacy of the cleaning and fumigating campaigns, and the statistical evidence left little doubt that the cull of cholera could be reduced. However, tensions existed between sanitary officials and councillors. These arose mainly because the under-funding and crisis management of political masters was in direct opposition to the programme of public health measures preferred by the medical officials and sanitary officers. In essence it was an enduring theme of Victorian local government: short-term financial expediency contrasted with long-term forward planning. Dr Tait resigned over pay as a result of the tension, although he was appeased subsequently and retracted his letter; Dr Glover was incensed at the inquisition he endured over expenses incurred in the legitimate discharge of his duties, as he saw them. In both cases, the limited ambition of the Cleaning Committee, and its short-term approach to insanitary housing, unsettled both doctors, and in Glover's case eventually led to his dismissal.[104]

When a further Edinburgh Police Act was under consideration in 1853, it presented Glover with another opportunity to make his views known both on the nature of sanitary policy and the role of a Medical Officer. Following a survey in 1853 by D. and A. Stevenson that left no doubt about the unsatisfactory state of the Water of Leith – it received a high proportion of the untreated sewage of the city and over one hundred drains discharged directly into the river – legislation to address the situation was promoted by the Police Commission with the full support of the Town Council and the Lord Provost, Duncan McLaren, chair of the Sanitary Committee.[105] The problems were the mill dams and races that impeded the water flow, particularly in the summer, trapping sewage in pools, as at Coltbridge. Occasionally, as in April 1848 gangs of up to 50 unemployed men cleaned out the bed of the river in return for a daily meal ticket.[106] Two

103 ECA ED9/25/2, Sanitary Committee Minutes, 12 September 1849, ff. 341–4.

104 Both men were also highly regarded as police surgeons. *The Scotsman*, 27 October 1847, 2g observed: 'Dr Tait … died last night of fever, which, it is thought, he caught a few days ago in the course of his private practice.' As Police Surgeon 'he gave the greatest satisfaction'.

105 D. and A. Stevenson, *Report to the Police Commission of the City of Edinburgh* (Edinburgh, 1853).

106 *The Scotsman*, 8 April 1848, 3cd and 26 April 1848, 3e.

3.8 Water of Leith village: low water volume
The river bed above and below the mill was eventually paved in order to improve water flow. In this view downstream Trinity Church commands this sensitive part of the Edinburgh townscape and was part of a conservation debate in the 1950s. [Source: RCAHMS]

3.9 Water of Leith, 1852
This was the disputed stretch of the river over which Dr Glover and Lord Provost McLaren clashed.
[NLS OS 1852]

proposals were forthcoming from the engineers: the removal of obstructions in the bed of the river, and an intercepting sewer to collect the sewage and deposit it downstream beyond the city boundary.[107] Despite strong objections from Leith Town Council over the inevitable pollution of the harbour that would result, these proposals formed the basis of the Edinburgh Improvement Bill in 1854.[108] Dr Hector Gavin, the Medical Superintending Inspector of the General Board of Health in London, then made a site visit.[109] He was given access to the drainage plan for the Water of Leith, and accompanied by the Lord Provost to the river. Gavin then met Glover for further discussions:

107 P.J. Smith, 'Pollution abatement in the nineteenth century: the purification of the Water of Leith', *Environment and Behavior*, 6 (1974), 8–9.

108 17 and 18 Vict., cap. 118, Edinburgh Police Amendment Act, 1854.

109 Dr Hector Gavin succeeded Dr John Sutherland as Editor of the *Journal of Public Health and Monthly Record of Sanitary* in 1849 and thus further established his credentials as a public health expert. Gavin (1815–55) was born in Edinburgh, apprenticed to the Royal College of Surgeons of Edinburgh aged 16, and became a Fellow (FRCSEd 1838). His working life was entirely based in England, where he was a firm advocate of the Public Health Acts, and made recommendations regarding Newcastle, Dundee and London.

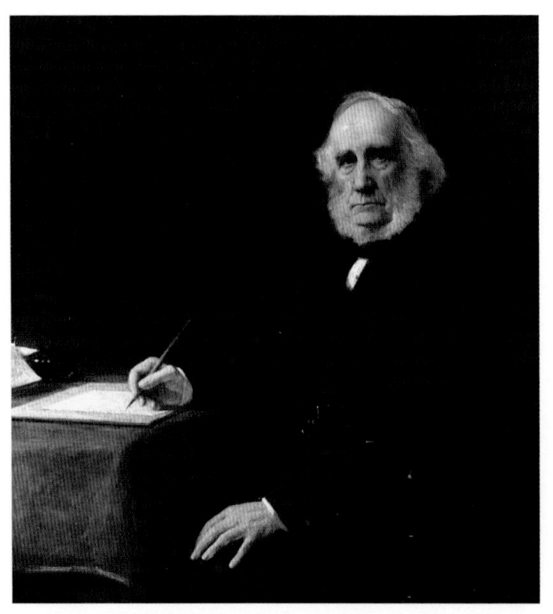

3.10 Duncan McLaren (1800–86)
Draper, and successively councillor, bailie, treasurer, Lord Provost (1851–54) and Liberal MP (1865–81). An energetic Free Church member, he was a powerful advocate of free education, and one of the founders of the Heriot Free Schools in 1836. Artist George Reid, 1881. [Source: CAC]

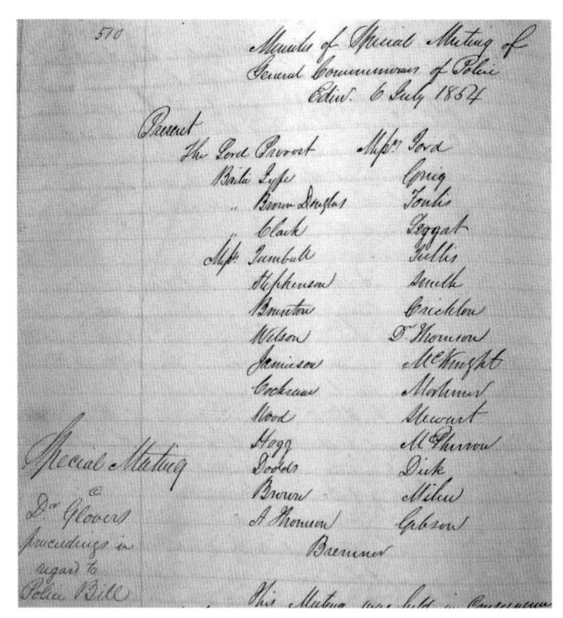
510
Minutes of Special Meeting of General Commissioners of Police
Edin. 6 July 1854

Present
The Lord Provost
Bailie
Brown Douglas
Clark
Mr Turnbull
Stephenson
Brunton
Wilson
Jamieson
Cochrane
Wood
Hogg
Dodds
Brown
A Thomson
Greig
Leggat
Smith
Crichton
Dr Thomson
McKnight
Mortimer
Stewart
McPherson
Dick
Miller
Gibson
Bremner

Special Meeting re Dr Glover's proceedings in regard to Police Bill

3.11 A special meeting of the General Commissioners of Police
This meeting, with only a single absentee, was convened on 6 July 1854 to examine Dr Glover's actions in relation to the Water of Leith bill. It was the prelude to his summary dismissal and to the appointment of Dr Littlejohn. See fig. 3.12.
[Source: ECA ED9/1/12/510]

> I subsequently accompanied Mr George Glover, Surgeon of the Edinburgh Police, over the district of the Village of the Water of Leith, examined the village, its drainage, and the state of the bed of the river …[110]

Glover's expert and local knowledge could not be disregarded by Gavin since from time to time the Board of Health in London had sought his opinion on other sanitary issues.[111] In their private walk along the banks of the Water of Leith Glover conveyed his misgivings about the Bill. The proposals failed to address the nuisance caused by the low volume of water in the river bed, and did not provide relief for the village by the Water of Leith since impurities would continue to flow into the river in its upper reaches.[112] It was not a sufficiently comprehensive measure to achieve its objectives. Gavin then took expert advice from an engineering inspector who considered the proposal both 'unfavourable on engineering grounds' and 'greatly more expensive than necessary', and these

110 ECA ED9/1/12, letter, Gavin to Board of Health, 1 May 1854.

111 ECA ED9/1/12, Police Commissioners General Minutes, Glover to Clerk of the Police Commissioners, 3 July 1854, 'P.S. – I may add, that since 1848, on application from the Board of Health in London, I have frequently furnished them with information on sanitary subjects.' One such instance was in connection with the Slaughter Houses Removal Bill, see ECA ED9/1/12, Police Commissioners General Minutes, 11 March 1850.

112 ECA ED9/1/12, Transcript of Notes by Dr Glover submitted on 21 March 1854 to the law agent for the Bill and copied by Dr Gavin in his report to the Board of Health.

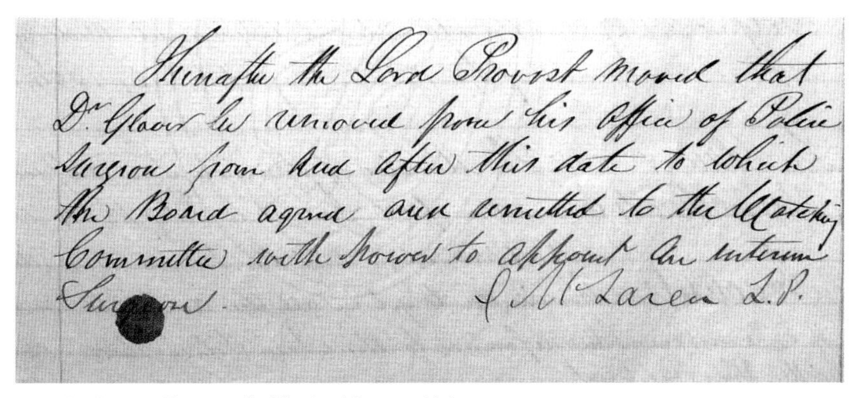
Thereafter the Lord Provost moved that Dr. Glover be removed from his Office of Police Surgeon from and after this date to which the Board agreed and remitted to the Watching Committee with Power to appoint an interim Surgeon.
J McLaren L.P.

3.12 Dr George Glover sacked by Lord Provost McLaren
Glover was not given an opportunity to defend himself against McLaren's allegations.
[Source: ECA ED1/12/513]

reservations necessarily formed part of Gavin's report to the Board of Health regarding the Bill before Parliament. Never slow to find fault with Edinburgh Town Council, *The Scotsman* joined the dispute when it noted that the district that would most benefit from the proposed improvements 'contains a large proportion of wealthy inhabitants and proprietors'.[113]

Closely questioned by the parliamentary committee concerning the reservations in Gavin's report,[114] the Lord Provost identified that in part their concerns originated from Glover, whom he also suspected of lobbying to insert a clause relating to the terms of employment of a Medical Officer of Health.[115] Though the Bill became law without any additional clauses, the Police Commission, led by the Lord Provost, were incensed at Glover's disloyalty, as they saw it, a viewpoint shared by the editorial in the Tory newspaper, the *Caledonian Mercury*.[116] Even though Glover had been absent from all but one of the preparatory meetings for the Bill,[117] the Council held him to account by reviewing all the relevant correspondence, and promptly published a report despite the fact that Glover himself was not given an opportunity to defend his

113 *The Scotsman*, 13 May 1854, quoted in S.C. Oliver, 'The administration of urban society in Scotland, 1800–50, with reference to the growth of civic government in Glasgow and its suburbs', Glasgow Ph.D. thesis (1995), 189.

114 PP (HL) Journals, 11, session 86, 31 January 1854 to 16 December 1854, 236; *Evening Courant*, 20 June 1854, 2f.

115 ECA ED9/3/5, Sanitary and Drainage Committee Minutes, 29 June 1854. *The Witness*, 28 June 1854, 2g, reported that 'Dr Glover, surgeon to the Police Establishment, has, through his law agent, given notice of the following clause to be added to the Edinburgh Police Bill on the third reading, which was fixed for yesterday (Tuesday). The clause, it will be observed, prevents the Police Board from removing Dr Glover from his situation of their own authority.' This assertion was never put to Glover, who subsequently also showed that the revised clause had originally been inserted in the General Police Act for Scotland, 1850, and into several Local Acts in England.

116 *Caledonian Mercury*,10 July 1854, 2a strongly supported the Police Commissioners.

117 ECA ED9/1/12, Special Meeting of the General Commissioners of Police, letter Glover to the Drainage Committee, 6 July 1854, f. 512, notes that he was present at only one meeting, although the minutes of this meeting were not included in the Special Meeting papers to consider his position.

actions.[118] Beginning with his handling of the cholera outbreak in 1848, this was the culmination of a long-running dispute regarding the powers and jurisdiction of the Police Surgeon.[119] It proved a fatal episode. Glover was dismissed, peremptorily, on 8 July 1854.

For Edinburgh, and Glover's successor, the episode produced a very unhealthy legacy of suspicion and antagonism towards the office of Police Surgeon. This was compounded by the poisonous remarks that inevitably followed in the printed *Report of the Drainage Committee*. It began with a very public account from Glover in the press which was highly critical of the Lord Provost.[120] Even before the official announcement of his dismissal, Glover defended his position in a letter to the editor of *The Witness*:

> Sir, Your paper of to-morrow will probably contain a report of the Police Board held yesterday, at which, on the motion of the Lord Provost, after a lengthened statement made by him in reference to my connection with 'the Edinburgh Police Improvement Bill, 1854', I was at once removed from my office of Police Surgeon.
>
> I have not been afforded the opportunity requested in the communication from me, which was read at the meeting, of answering the accusations brought against me by the Lord Provost; indeed many of them have only come to my knowledge to-day through the report of that meeting. I can only therefore, in the meantime, ask that, along with the report of his speech, you will allow me through your columns, to request my friends and the public to suspend their judgement until my statement in reply is before them. – I am, &c. Geo. Glover.[121]

The Scotsman commented that, 'the Board is at all times an extremely arbitrary body, but in this case they have excelled themselves in offering so bold a defiance to common notions of justice and fair dealing'.[122] In a more extended defence a fortnight later, Glover refuted absolutely the accusation by the Lord Provost that he, Glover, had intervened directly with Lord Shaftesbury in an attempt to insert a revised clause in the Police Bill. Glover stated he:

> would leave the Lord Provost to explain as best he can the gross mis-statement on this point which he so pertinaciously urged upon the Police Board and which, along with the charge of having given information to the Board of Health, constituted the grounds for my dismissal.[123]

Glover also defended himself by noting that it was the Lord Provost who had first drawn attention to some of the misgivings about the Water of Leith

118 ECA ED9/3/5, Special Meeting of the General Commissioners of Police, Minutes, 8 July 1854, ff. 510–14; *Report by Drainage Committee of Commissioners of Police on the remit made to them respecting Dr Glover, Police-Surgeon*, 8 May 1854 (Edinburgh, 1854), 1–12, and comments on the Report by Dr Glover, ED 9/3/5 Police Commissioners General Minutes 6 July 1854, f. 511.

119 There were already a number of markers against his name when this major dispute arose. See, for example, the issue of an unanswered letter of 31 January 1850 from the Commissioner of Woods. See ECA ED9/1/12, Police Commissioners General Minutes, 31 January 1850.

120 *The Witness*, 12 July 1854, 3cd.

121 *The Witness*, 8 July 1854, 3b.

122 *The Scotsman*, 8 July 1854, quoted in Cameron, thesis, 190.

123 *The Witness*, 22 July 1854, 3a.

drainage scheme, and that he had deliberately misrepresented events. Glover also named both the patient and the police officer in order to contradict the Lord Provost's claim that he had created a fictitious patient in order to avoid an appearance before the Cleaning Committee.[124] By means of wilfully inaccurate and duplicitous accounts of events, the Lord Provost had embarked, Glover claimed, upon character assassination, and by re-opening previous disputes about the motives of the Police Surgeon had developed what would nowadays be recognised as constructive dismissal. According to the *Edinburgh Evening Post*, Glover was 'Burked' and thrown 'upon the world without a character'. Shortly after his dismissal, Glover left his house in Fettes Row to take up employment in London as an Inspector of Health at a salary of £800, five times his pay as Edinburgh Police Surgeon, and in the following year wrote an influential report on lodging-houses in London.[125]

The drama was played out in the committee meetings of the Police Commission, and in the press. Glover knew he could turn to *The Witness* to get his point of view across since that newspaper took its title from John Knox's words 'I am demanded of conscience to speak the truth', and was outspoken in defence of individuals against institutions.[126] The *Edinburgh Evening Post* was less objective. It campaigned against the Lord Provost, Duncan McLaren, in what was a personal vendetta. 'No public man in this city has ever been so highly paid in *kind*,' the newspaper stated in relation to the Lord Provost, describing him as crafty, cruel and 'unscrupulous.'[127] The *Edinburgh Evening Post* continued:

> the Police-Commissioners dismissed the Surgeon of the Establishment, on the mere *ex parte* representations or personal assurances of the Lord Provost. His Lordship made certain charges, avowedly founded on facts within his own peculiar knowledge, about Dr Glover, and when one or two of the respectable members *hinted* that it would be right to hear what the Dr had to say in reply to his accuser, before proceeding to pass sentence, his Lordship insisted that there should be no delay – that explanation or trial was an idle farce – and, accordingly, the victim was duly offered up a sacrifice to his Lordship's post-haste vengeance.[128]

This 'outrageous abuse of authority', though levelled at Duncan McLaren personally, was also directed at the supine behaviour of other members of the Police Commission. 'It is through them,' the *Post* continued, 'that his Lordship

124 *The Witness*, 22 July 1854, 3c.

125 *Edinburgh Evening Post and Scottish Record* (afterwards *Evening Post*), 12 July 1854, 2h, 16 August 1854, 3bc, and 23 September 1854, 3a; PP (HC) 1854 XLV, Report on Common and Model Lodging Houses in the Metropolis, also quoted in G.S. Jones, *The Eternal Slum: Housing and Social Policy in Victorian London* (London, 1971), 166. The term 'Burked' refers to William Burke (1792–1829), Irish-born murderer hanged in Edinburgh in 1829 on the king's evidence of his accomplice William Hare. After his term of office, Glover went on to enjoy a career as an entrepreneur and inventor of gas meters, winning gold and silver medals at international exhibitions. See *The Times*, 21 April 1880, 10g (gold medal, Sydney Exhibition); 28 October 1884, 10b (George Glover and Co. silver medallists at the Health Exhibition); 13 August 1885 10a: George Glover and Co., gold medallists for gas equipment at the International Inventions Exhibition).

126 B.T. McCrie, *Life of John Knox* (Edinburgh, 1831), 5th edn, vol. 2, 104.

127 *Edinburgh Evening Post*, 12 August 1854, 2h.

128 *Edinburgh Evening Post*, 12 August 1854.

3.13 William Tennant Gairdner (1824–1907)
Gairdner wrote the definitive text book on public health. He was a strong supporter of the appointment of Littlejohn, and endorsed his methodology on sanitary districts when he moved to Glasgow as part-time MOH there (1864–72) and Professor of Medicine (1862–99).
Dr R.O. Adamson, photographer.
[Source: RCPEd]

has dismissed Dr Glover, condemning him unheard,' and it likened the police commissioners 'to the crouching serfs of Russia, living in fear of the vituperative knout wielded by the Lord Provost as their local Czar':

> Surely what would scarcely be tolerated by parasites and slaves on the banks of the Neva, will not be deliberately countenanced by independent Commissioners or free citizens on the shores of the Forth.[129]

The hyperbole seems strange to modern eyes. It was a language of defamation which in the twenty-first century might well result in court cases and compensation claims.[130] Publicly to accuse the Lord Provost as having served up 'a farrago of falsehoods' and 'a gross imposition on the credulity and facility of the Police Board' raised the temperature locally, especially as the *Edinburgh Evening Post* also accused McLaren of having in mind a family member, Littlejohn, as Glover's replacement.

In fact, Henry Littlejohn's impressive testimonials were on the table only days after Glover's sacking.[131] The speed of Littlejohn's appointment was also linked to a more expansive approach to public health, as sought by the Royal College of Physicians of Edinburgh. The tone and substance of the RCPEd's report was characteristic of a profession acutely conscious of its social status and professional interests, yet blithely unaware of the political realities in Edinburgh in the 1840s and 1850s.[132] A letter from the RCPEd's committee considering the appointment of a Police Surgeon claimed that:

> the duties were too numerous and diversified for one man to perform, and that they should be performed by a principal surgeon of high professional skill to perform the Medico-legal and the sanitary duties of the office at a salary suited to his occasional service, and a resident assistant to do the ordinary duties. The College feared the [Police] Commission were not aware of the importance of the duties of the office in offering so low a salary as £155. In Liverpool the salary of £800 was given to the surgeon of police.[133]

The Special Remits committee of the Police Board simply side-stepped the issue by stating that it was 'inappropriate to open up so large a matter', and any more fundamental reforms were promptly shelved.[134]

129 *Edinburgh Evening Post*, 12 August 1854.

130 *The Scotsman*, 13th January 1855, 3a Glover won £250 damages in a libel case against Professor Syme, Professor of Surgery.

131 *Edinburgh Evening Post*, 16 August 1854, 3bc. The *Evening Post* accused the Lord Provost of being absent from the committee when the Royal College's recommendations were received, and for not allowing the memorial from 260 signatories in support of Dr Tod to be considered for the position of Police Surgeon, and thus of endorsing Littlejohn's candidacy.

132 ECA ED9/1/ 12, 525. This meeting of the Police Board set up the consultation with the Royal Colleges. At the same meeting the Police Board approved by a majority of two the Lord Provost's motion to fix the surgeon's salary at £155 rather than McKnight's proposal of £200. It was another instance of the Lord Provost's will prevailing. For an account of the Police Surgeon's duties as suggested by the RCPEd, see *The Witness*, 9 August 1854, 3d.

133 *Evening Courant*, 1 August 1854, 3a, reporting a meeting of the Police Board, 31 July 1854. Brackets added.

134 *Evening Courant*, 1 August 1854, 3a, citing the Minutes of the Joint Meeting of the Finance, Law and Special Remits Committee and the Watching Committee, 11 July 1854.

Littlejohn's testimonials were glowing.[135] He had been nominated as a Fellow of the Royal College of Surgeons just ten days after Glover's dismissal and was proposed and seconded for the post of Police Surgeon by two of the most influential medics of the time, William T. Gairdner and Douglas Maclagan.[136] Gairdner, Littlejohn's highly respected university lecturer, had been promoted from pathologist to the senior position of physician to the Edinburgh Royal Infirmary in 1853, and was a specialist in the emerging field of public health; Maclagan was an expert in forensic medicine and toxicology, had recently published *Contributions to Toxicology, Cases of Poisoning* (1849), and was the leading figure in a field central to the work of a Police Surgeon.[137] Though Littlejohn's detractors considered him too young – 'fresh from school'[138] – in a powerful field of six applicants,[139] Bailie Morrison's statement proposing Littlejohn referred to his impressive credentials:

3.14 Andrew Douglas Maclagan (1812–1900) aged about 50
Maclagan was Professor of Medical Jurisprudence (1862–97), and like his father, President of both Royal Colleges (Surgeons 1859, Physicians 1884). He was knighted in 1886. J. Moffat, photographer, Princes Street. [Source: RCPEd, Aesculapian Club Collection]

> His qualifications were of a very high character, and were … much greater than they had any reason to expect, considering the small amount of salary offered, and the large amount of duties attached to the office. He had no doubt they had all read the testimonials of the various candidates, and, therefore, it would be a waste of time in [*sic*] him [Morrison] to go over those of Dr. Littlejohn. He need only say regarding them that they were all from gentlemen of the highest professional standing, and men who were entitled to the highest consideration at their hands. These testimonials all spoke of Dr Littlejohn in the most flattering terms. Besides having had the highest medical education, he appeared to have paid particular attention to medical jurisprudence, and to have had such opportunities as few young men had of practical study in the Infirmary. Both of these branches of study, they all knew, were peculiarly valuable in an office of this kind, and would tend very much to add to the efficiency of the person occupying this post. He had, therefore, very great pleasure in proposing this gentleman. He was sure that all who had seen him would be satisfied of his active habits and enthusiastic love of his profession, He was persuaded that, if the Board, appointed Dr Littlejohn as Police Surgeon, they would have reason to congratulate themselves on having appointed an eminent man to that office.[140]

135 *Evening Courant*, 15 August 1854, 3b, reporting meeting of the Police Board, 14 July 1854.

136 RCPE, Minutes 1846–65, 25 September 1854, 737.

137 G.A. Gibson, *Life of Sir William Tennant Gairdner: With a selection of papers on general and medical subjects* (Glasgow, 1912); Obituary: 'Sir William Gairdner', *British Medical Journal*, 6 July 1907, 53–9; *Oxford Dictionary of National Biography* (*ODNB*) entries for Sir A.D. Maclagan and W.T. Gairdner. Maclagan was appointed Professor of Forensic Medicine and Public Health at Edinburgh University in 1862. Ian Rankin, *Tooth and Nail* (London, 1998), 87, provides a dialogue between a dental pathologist and Detective Inspector John Rebus in which the policeman is asked whether he knew that the earliest chair of Forensic Medicine had been founded at Edinburgh University. We are grateful to Jane Laxton for this reference.

138 *Evening Courant*, 15 August 1854, 3b. The distinguished veterinary surgeon, Councillor William Dick sought, but failed, to introduce an age barrier of 50 to discriminate against the youthful, 28-year-old Littlejohn.

139 *The Witness*, 16 August 1854, 1g. The other five candidates were James D. Pridie (Stockton); Robert Tod (Edinburgh); John Warnock (Belfast); Louis Foucart (Glasgow); W.J. Thompson (Arbroath).

140 *The Scotsman*, 16 August 1854, 3d.

The Police Board endorsed Littlejohn by a vote of 17 to 9.[141] As Police Surgeon he inherited a mental landscape in which the political economy of medicine was an integral part of both 'stormy' national debates over the Poor Laws and civil registration, and of local political fractures of fundamental significance to a public servant in mid-Victorian Edinburgh.[142] Embedded in these grander frameworks were specific running sores, literally, as with the 'foul burns' (streams) controversy in 1839–40, the cholera epidemic of 1847–48, and environmental controversies over nuisances such as the polluted Water of Leith in the 1850s, and indeed the eventual re-absorption in 1856 of the Police Commission itself into the extended jurisdiction of the Town Council (see chapter 4).[143]

The language of despair concerning the public health of Edinburgh emerged into a state of near-paralysis – 'the evil is too monstrous for cure by ... superficial means'[144] – as newspaper columns reported the intractability of fever in the 1840s and 1850s. These were 'verbal weapons of control', designed to highlight environmental problems and symptomatic of a deeper social and political malaise in mid-century Edinburgh.[145] To subdue the turmoil of public health administration, to diminish suspicion concerning the role of the Police Surgeon, and to establish a track record of dependability based on an empirical platform were Littlejohn's priorities.

From Police Surgeon to Medical Officer of Health

The debacle over Glover exposed for all to see the weakness of the Police Commission as managers of Edinburgh's public health. McLaren had bungled the affair, and a body of rattled commissioners had closed ranks, avoided the health issues that Glover had revealed, and rid themselves of 'an unfaithful servant'. Glover's error was to offend his masters by blowing the whistle after warnings not to exceed his terms of employment. If the commissioners thought that in Littlejohn they would have a more malleable if over-qualified young Police Surgeon they were only partly correct. Certainly, as his subsequent career testifies beyond question, Littlejohn had a strong sense of duty to his employers, though he was also an astute political operator in pursuit of his goals for the health of the city.

The Police Commission was aware that its days were numbered (see chapter 4). In Glasgow, the extension of the municipal area in 1846 led promptly to the demise of the Police Commission there, with the Town Council assuming its

141 ECA ED9/1/12, 14 August 1854, 542–43.

142 For the wider context see R. MacLeod, 'The anatomy of state medicine: concept and application', in F.N.L. Poynter (ed.), *Medicine and State in the 1860s* (London, 1968), 199–227.

143 P.J. Smith, 'The foul burns of Edinburgh: public health attitudes and environmental change', *Scottish Geographical Magazine*, 91 (1975), 25–37; C. Hamlin, 'Environmental sensibility in Edinburgh 1839–40: the "fetid irrigation" controversy', *Journal of Urban History*, 20 (1994), 311–39. For a contemporary view see R. Forsythe, *Foul Burn Agitation* (Edinburgh, 1840), and for the English sanitarian view, see J. Sheail, 'Town wastes, agricultural sustainability and Victorian sewage', *Urban History*, 23 (1996), 189–210.

144 W. Chambers, *Report*. 1.

145 See M. Douglas, 'Environments at risk', in B. Barnes and D. Edge (eds), *Science in Context* (Cambridge, 1982), 265.

responsibilities.[146] In Edinburgh, following Glasgow once again, it was inconsistencies in the way police and council jurisdictions were applied to areas of the city that delayed the introduction of a unitary authority until 1856, though fumbled attempts were made to do so in 1848.[147] The issue was 'whether the community was better served by specialist boards or by a multi-purpose Town Council'.[148] When, in 1856, the Police Commissioners did eventually stand down after 51 years, it meant that for the first time municipal and police boundaries and jurisdictions corresponded exactly, and parallel legal and administrative bodies gave way to a unitary local authority.

3.15 William Henry Duncan, MD (1805–63), MOH for Liverpool
Duncan was the first MOH in Britain (1847–63). His responsibilities and terms of employment informed the appointment of an MOH in Edinburgh (see pages 94–5).
[Source: Liverpool University Library Special Collections]

The timing of Littlejohn's appointment as Police Surgeon was highly significant in another sense. The response to the health crises of the 1840s had utterly altered the municipal climate in England. W.H. Duncan, another student taught by W.P. Alison, had begun to fashion a public health department in Liverpool from 1847 with a regulatory system that was emulated, or at least cited as a model, in Scotland. Duncan was a consummate collector of statistics based in large measure on civil registration data. His first report, on the dramatic years of typhus and cholera, 1847–49, was published in 1850.[149] Other English cities followed. Yet in Scotland an evidence-based approach to public health administration was not possible without reliable death certification – described as 'shameful deficiency'.[150] A succession of attempts to copy English civil registration failed until the Registration (Scotland) Act, 1854, came into force in 1855.[151] Dr James Stark, subsequently the statistician to the Registrar-General for Scotland, had published a series of quarterly bills of mortality for Edinburgh in the late 1840s, though these were collected in keeping with an older tradition of political arithmetic rather than intended for practical use in the promotion of public health.[152] In 1852 W.T. Gairdner and James Warburton Begbie published a significantly timed and perceptive pamphlet on mortality statistics. The Medico-Statistical Association, of which they were joint secretaries, urged the collection of mortality data that would be of clear benefit to medicine, rather than crude bills of mortality based upon dubious nosologies of the cause of death. Twenty-three of their members, including Alison, Struthers and Christison, were:

> invited to inscribe in the schedules, not, indeed, trivial details, but the fullest possible statements as to the more important morbid phenomena, and the

146 9 and 10 Vict., cap. 289, 27 July 1846, An Act to Extend the Municipal Boundaries of Glasgow; D.G. Barrie, *Police in the Age of Improvement*, 224–8. Dundee followed suit in 1851. See L. Miskell, 'From conflict to co-operation: urban improvement and the case of Dundee', *Urban History*, 29 (2002), 369–70.

147 See Chapter 4, Localism and the legislative debacle. The Police Commission itself did not object to a proposal for its own abolition and did not vote against a motion to this effect.

148 The phrase is from R. Tyzack '"No mean city"?', 151, where in 1871 the Aberdeen parallels with Edinburgh are striking.

149 W.H. Duncan, *Report to the Health Committee of the Borough of Liverpool, on the Health of the Town during the years 1847–48–49–50, and on Other Matters within his Department* (Liverpool, 1851).

150 *The Scotsman*, 13 May 1854, 2h.

151 A. Cameron, 'Civil registration in Scotland', 378–9.

152 Stark, author of several works on the weather and of religious tracts, as well as author of unfounded assertions about the healthiness of Edinburgh, was not engaged in public health issues as was William Farr, holder of his equivalent office in London.

> particularity of the causes of death. ... The schedules embracing the details of individual cases are, therefore, in no respect like the very brief and unsatisfactory data on which the bills of mortality, and other registers of causes of death, have hitherto been furnished. They are rather to be as a series of compendious, but authentic and interesting, medical histories, – in themselves, replete with materials for study and reflection, and rendered accessible for this purpose by the copious and complete index to be found in the register.[153]

Gairdner and Begbie's *Report* was, in effect, a blueprint for death certification which provided data on the social circumstances of the deceased and a cause of death which was capable of critical analysis, replacing the single cause approach of the Registrar-General (in England) with a more subtle description of the underlying causes or 'morbid conditions'.[154]

Scotland was nowhere mentioned by Gairdner and Begbie, though they were well aware of the implications of their *Report* for the debate about Scottish civil registration and the form that death certification might take. The Medico-Statistical Association was short-lived and soon was absorbed into the Edinburgh Medical-Chirurgical Society of Edinburgh, but its existence and influential membership demonstrates a concern for statistics that would serve both medicine generally and public health administration in particular. Among that group of members was Henry Littlejohn, a contemporary and fellow student of both Begbie and Gairdner. Though only two years his junior, Littlejohn was a great admirer of Gairdner, whose lectures he attended, and who was later a colleague in the extra-mural Edinburgh Medical School.[155] Gairdner was clearly an outstanding intellect with a sharp eye for detail, and a developing interest in public health; he was Medical Officer of Health for Glasgow from 1863 to 1872, a post he held part-time while also holding the Chair of Medicine at Glasgow University from 1862 to 1899. In the late 1850s he was gathering material, including some extraordinarily modern research that involved linking census enumerators' books and death certificates, for his influential *Public Health in Relation to Air and Water*, published in 1862, a year that was to prove the turning point when Henry Littlejohn was appointed Medical Officer of Health for Edinburgh with the strong endorsement of Gairdner.[156] Like Glover, and indeed Alison before him, Gairdner and his circle demanded an evidence-based approach which required sound and appropriate statistics. Civil registration, in some measure, would meet that need in Scotland from 1855. It was a view that was reflected in the very first sentence of the *Report* that in 1865 was to make Littlejohn's name.

153 W.T. Gairdner and J.W. Begbie, *First Report of the Medico-Statistical Association* (Edinburgh, 1852), 4.

154 Their critique of 'old age' and 'diarrhoea' as 'causes' of death is made with reference to bills of mortality, a phrase which sums up for them the older tradition of mere tabulation, and data from Begbie's father who was medical advisor to the Scottish Widows Fund and Life Assurance Society. The former 'cause', a lazy usage, greatly exaggerated 'pure senile exhaustion and decay', and the latter simply obscured the many conditions of which diarrhoea was really a symptom. W.T. Gairdner and J.W. Begbie, *First Report of the Medico-Statistical Association*, 6, 11.

155 *ODNB*, entry by G.A. Gibson, rev. T. O'Neill, on Sir William Tennant Gairdner; G.A. Gibson, *Life of Sir William Tennant Gairdner.*

156 Littlejohn also used record linkage of census and civil registration data as a technique to establish accurate rates of death at the district level.

Thus two major developments pushed the development of municipal sanitary administration a step further: the introduction of civil registration in 1855 at last gave Scotland the possibility of systematic mortality data, even if it fell far short of what some in the medical profession sought;[157] and the transfer of police powers to the Town Council in 1856 which placed sanitary powers within a unitary authority with enhanced legitimacy and correspondingly greater fiscal leverage due to improvements in the local taxation system under the Valuation Act, 1854.[158]

Another structural change was introduced in 1856 when the Board of Supervision, the administrative arm of the Poor Law in Scotland, acquired sanitary and public health responsibilities.[159] Though based in Edinburgh, its impact on local public health policy should not be overstated, but it did add another political voice to the clamour for change. Increasingly it was appreciated that monitoring the course and location of infectious diseases, as well as regularly inspecting infected houses, were necessary sanitary duties for medical authorities. Gairdner in particular agitated for such a system, an approach not unlike that which Glover had briefly operated as Police Surgeon in the emergency of the typhus and cholera years of 1847–48. In 1854 or 1855 Gairdner proposed, unsuccessfully, that the Parochial Board should set up a system of inspection for epidemic disease.[160] In 1858 he tried again, this time writing to Littlejohn in his capacity as Police Surgeon. Gairdner's letter, intended to be private, was circulated among councillors and passed against his wishes to the newspapers. 'But the only effect,' as he put it in a long letter to the *Scotsman* in January 1861, 'was a little temporary agitation, and a remit to the Lord Provost's Committee, where the affair went to sleep again.'[161]

In the turbulent aftermath of the Glover debacle and during a decade of significant structural changes as a result of the introduction of civil registration, property valuation and the status of the Town Council, Littlejohn, still in his twenties, acquired experience as both Police Surgeon and Crown witness in criminal cases involving forensic medicine.[162] Familiarising himself with public

157 17 and 18 Vict., cap. 80, Registration of Births, Deaths and Marriages (Scotland) Act, 1854.

158 17 and 18 Vict., cap. 91, Lands Valuation (Scotland) Act, passed 10 August 1854.

159 A. Wohl, *Endangered Lives: Public Health in Victorian Britain* (London, 1983), 199–200. The headquarters of the Board of Supervision were in George Street, Edinburgh and Dr H.D. Littlejohn was a commissioner and medical adviser to the Board of Supervision, 1873–1908.

160 He even offered to conduct a report for the Board, but the proposal was rejected as outside their powers.

161 *The Scotsman*, 21 January 1861, 3b. This 2,000-word letter, a favourable response to a leading article (*The Scotsman*, 18 January 1861, 2b) on sanitary developments in Leith and Provost Lindsay's promotion of a Sanitary Bill, describes his inspections of the domestic circumstances of ten fever cases he had encountered in the Infirmary. This had led him to despair of a regime which did little more than clean and regulate the streets and closes: 'But most unquestionably the great work of sanitary inspection and reform, which must go on *inside* the houses, and not *outside*, is not even begun; nay, it cannot be begun till the medical profession, who alone know the evils, are systematically brought into communication with the authorities.' For Gairdner's letter of 1858, whose purpose was to warn that in the absence of any provision by the parochial authorities, the Infirmary could not cope with a major fever epidemic such as that of 1847, see *The Scotsman*, 6 January 1858, 6.

162 Lord Cowan praised Littlejohn on his evidence during the trial of Agnes Cameron for child murder, *Evening Courant*, 13 November 1855, 2fg.

health administration and political agendas, Littlejohn also learned during the 1850s how to operate in public affairs, building up his contacts in medicine and other realms of public life. Councillor Ford, chairman of the Lighting and Cleaning Committee was impressed with a report he requested from Littlejohn.[163] He was indeed 'the coming man'.

Building regulation and the politics of public health

The popular explanation for the decision to appoint a Medical Officer of Health conventionally links it to the collapse of three tenements, numbers 99, 101 and 103 High Street, on 24 November 1861.[164] Thirty-five inhabitants lost their lives, buried in the double level of cellars by the rubble from the floors above (figs 3.16–3.17). Each body was conveyed to the Police Surgeon in Fishmarket Close,[165] where Littlejohn examined each and subsequently reported upon the cause of death:

> HENRY DUNCAN LITTLEJOHN, M.D., surgeon of Edinburgh Police. – I saw all the bodies enumerated in the list, No. 23 of precognition, after they were brought from the ruins to the Police Office, except Nos. 30 and 34, who were removed alive from the ruins to the Infirmary by my directions, where they died, and I saw them there. I examined all the bodies, and the result of that examination is, that it is my opinion the persons died from the following causes, viz., 1, 2, 3, 7, 8, 9, 20, 21, 22, 23, 24, 30, and 34, from direct violence; and 4, 5, 6, 10, 11, 12, 13, 14, 15, 16, 26, 28, 29, from direct violence and suffocation; and 17, 18, 19, 25, 27, 31, 32, 33, and 35, from suffocation alone. Declares that, as directed by the magistrates on the Sabbath afternoon at four, I gave most particular attention to the state of the various bodies which were dug out of the ruins after that day, and I have no doubt whatever that all of them must have died within a few minutes after the fall. – All which is truth.[166]

Littlejohn's evidence was reproduced in a report prepared by the Procurator-Fiscal and from which it emerged that the tenement collapse was an accident waiting to happen. Rather than dwellings built of stone on rock foundations, in reality many tenement inhabitants, including those at Paisley's Close, were living like troglodytes in two levels of windowless cellars with crumbling walls. The overall condition of the housing stock was a matter of fundamental concern. Following the tenement collapse a disaster fund was opened and, it is claimed, a petition presented to the Town Council to appoint a Medical Officer.[167]

163 *The Scotsman*, 21 October 1857, 3ab.

164 See, for example, http://www.ancestry.co.uk/blackfriars.pdf

165 In 1858 Littlejohn's office moved upstairs to the first floor of the Police Buildings opposite the City Chambers.

166 NLS, l.c.2243, Precognition of witnesses examined at the instance of the Procurator-Fiscal for the City of Edinburgh, regarding the falling of the tenement, nos 99–103 High Street, on November 24, 1861, 41. The Procurator-Fiscal is the Crown prosecutor in Scotland and fulfils the same role as that of coroner in England.

167 To mark the centenary of the appointment a plaque was unveiled at 24 Royal Circus, Littlejohn's residence from 1866 to 1914, on 2 October 1962, and a memorial lecture delivered by Professor F.A.E. Crew at, appropriately, Adam House, Chambers Street – one of the new thoroughfares that ultimately resulted from Littlejohn's *Report*. Several newspapers featured the event: *The Glasgow*

	Names of Deceased	*Age*
1	David Skirving, Cabinetmaker	54
2	Margaret Bain or Skirving, wife of No. 1	50
3	Mary Skirving, daughter of No. 1	24
4	William M'Luskie, shoe manufacturer	48
5	Hannah M'Luskie, wife of No. 4	48
6	Bridget M'Kinnon, servant to No. 4	21
7	Agnes Gardner	55
8	John M'Donald, son of Alexander McDonald, compositor, 129 Rose Street	12
9	William M'Donald, Ditto	7
10	Barbara Sutherland or Mackay, widow	65
11	Robert Weir, Mason	48
12	James Irving, shop porter	38
13	Elizabeth M'Kerracher, or Irving, wife of No. 12	43
14	Flora M'Laren or M'Kerracher, mother-in-law of No. 12	88
15	Agnes Irving, daughter of No. 12	2
16	Catherine Irving, Ditto	2 months
17	John Gunn, cooper	50
18	Mary Donaldson or Gunn, wife of No. 17	48
19	Jane Gunn, daughter of No. 17	21
20	John Gunn, junr., jeweller, son of No. 17	18
21	Elizabeth Bannerman or M'Kay	82
22	Alexander Mackay, tailor, son of No. 21	56
23	Joan Sutherland, granddaughter of No. 21	14
24	Isabella M'Lennan or M'Kenzie, wife of James M'Kenzie, Gullan's Close	45
25	John Geddes or Durward, printer and commercial traveller	50
26	Helen Stewart or Geddes, wife of No. 25	38
27	Georgina Wells, staymaker	20
28	Christina Ferguson, staymaker	25
29	Walter Ferguson, brother of No. 28	8
30	John Bruce, shoemaker	54
31	Mary Walker or Bruce, wife of No. 30	48
32	Catherine Bruce, daughter of No. 30	3
33	Jessie Bruce, Ditto	17
34	Elizabeth Drysdale, or Aird, or Beveridge	50
35	Body unidentified, supposed to be Isabella Mackay	25

Table 3.1 List of persons killed by the falling tenement at 99–103 High Street, 24 November 1861
[Source: *Precognition of witnesses examined at the instance of the procurator-fiscal for the city of Edinburgh* (1862) 56]

Understandably, the disaster did cause considerable public anxiety. The presentation of a petition to the Council would certainly have been recorded in the Council minutes and widely reported in the press. Yet no such record exists. Further, that any such public petition would demand a Medical Officer seems implausible.

Herald, 2 October 1962, 8; *Edinburgh Evening News*, 1 October 1962, 4; *The Scotsman*, 2 October 1962. The *Herald* and the *News* hung their stories on the collapsed tenement. Crew's lecture, 'Centenary of appointment of the first Medical Officer of Health for the City of Edinburgh', was published in *Scottish Medical Journal*, 8 (1963), 53–62. Crew, in a well-rounded review of Littlejohn's life and career, makes no mention of fallen tenements.

The real explanation and significance of the tenement collapse is far more complex, and political. The collapsed tenement sensitised the issue of housing quality, and of social inequality, among the general public.[168] Earlier in 1861, building trades workers formed a limited company, the Edinburgh Cooperative Building Company, to provide soundly built accommodation for working men's families.[169] The company became significant providers of housing over the ensuing decades, and the 'Colonies' as they still are affectionately known – Stockbridge, Leith, Abbeyhill, Dalry, Restalrig – were each built on the fringes of the city as a direct response to the failure of the housing market to provide for this skilled segment of the labour force. The Edinburgh Cooperative Building Company initiative raised the profile of housing quality as a political and moral issue, especially in relation to a world inhabited by unskilled and casual workers and their families in the High Street, Cowgate and the Old Town closes. Their insanitary living conditions were condemned as unacceptable in a civilised country by religious leaders, many of whom were drawn from the evangelical wing of the Free Church of Scotland and who, through their urban missions and pamphleteering, championed the interests of the poor. Dissatisfaction was expressed, too, with a system of lax building control that allowed landlords to rack-rent their properties by taking income from tenants without maintaining the physical state of the Edinburgh housing stock. The agency responsible for monitoring building safety was the Dean of Guild Court; it was witheringly criticised by Sir John McNeill, revered surgeon, long-standing chief administrator of the Poor Law in Scotland, diplomat and privy councillor: he described how the court dealt 'most tenderly with the property of its friends'.[170]

What had happened was that the deaths from the tenement collapse fused concern over housing conditions with wider public health anxieties concerning sanitary conditions. Suddenly, debates about the nature of environmental health were conducted in a context readily understandable to the general public. 'Having been palpable to the eyes, it has had greater effect on the public mind,' is how a letter writer to *The Scotsman*, Henry Johnston, described the event.[171] One immediate result of public sympathy for the bereaved was to establish a disaster relief fund by public subscription; another was the initiative of eleven professional men with desirable New Town addresses, including Douglas Maclagan, to spearhead a Building Association with 100 subscribers of £100 to promote a programme of 'Building appropriate Houses in eligible situations' and 'at moderate rents' to 'supply the wants of the Working Classes'.[172] But this was palliative care.

168 The term 'sensitised' is used with reference to the work of S. Cohen, *Folk Devils and Moral Panics: the Creation of Mods and Rockers* (London, 1972), 9. See also H.P. Becker, *Outsiders: Studies in the Sociology of Deviance* (New York, 1963).

169 R. Rodger, *Edinburgh's Colonies: Housing the Workers* (Argyll, 2011). None of the approximately 2,500 properties has yet been demolished.

170 *The Scotsman*, 26 February 1862, 3.

171 *The Scotsman*, 5 February 1862, 3b.

172 *The Scotsman*, 17 December 1861. For an account of the public meeting to establish the disaster fund see *The Scotsman*, 27 November 1861, 3.

3.16 Collapsed tenement, 24 November 1861
City officials were well aware of the perilous state of many tenements in the Old Town before the disaster occurred at Paisley Close, 99–103 High Street.

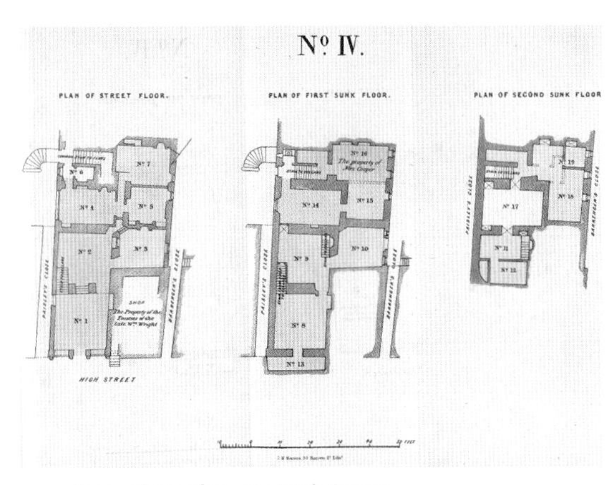

3.17 Floor plans of 99–103 High Street
The published report of the disaster gives a vivid impression of the sub-divided living arrangements and the prevalence of cellar dwellings in the Old Town.
[Source: NLS *Precognition of witnesses … Edinburgh* (1862), Plan IV, l.c.2243]

More significantly, though, the tenement disaster developed its own political momentum in conjunction with the issue of public health. Beginning just hours after the event, witness statements were taken from 88 persons, including testimony from Littlejohn in his role as Police Surgeon investigating sudden deaths and reporting to the Procurator-Fiscal. It emerged that, some months before the disaster, there had been concern regarding the state of the High Street property. The evidence of the civil engineers James Leslie and David Stevenson was heard and, crucially, that of George Cousin, surveyor, who had warned nine months previously that the middle of the three tenements, number 101, 'was in want of some repairs'.[173] Non-expert testimony was also recorded: a workman, Gavin Greenshields, warned of the dangerous condition of the tenement, and was threatened and then dismissed as a result of his revelations.[174] Even before the publication of the 'Precognition' on the disaster by the Procurator-Fiscal, there was a torrent of adverse public comment about the state of housing and health in Edinburgh. A paper on the housing conditions of the working classes by Dr Alexander Wood, vice-president of the Royal College of Physicians, was read to the Architectural Institute of Scotland on 13 January 1862. A number of prominent Edinburgh men then took part in the discussion – William Chambers, Duncan McLaren, the Revd Dr Begg, Dr Sellar, Mr Cousin and Mr Lessels.[175] Indeed, Chambers took up the same subject in his lecture to the Architectural Institute of Scotland two weeks later, and the letters pages of the *Courant* and the regular Town Council meetings were dominated by the state

173 NLS, l.c.2243, Precognition of witnesses, 5. For a report see the *Courant*, 5 February 1862, 2f.
174 *Courant*, 11 February 1862, 2ab.
175 *Courant*, 14 January 1862 2f–3a; *The Scotsman*, 14 January 1862, 2g–3c. David Cousin and John Lessels later combined as the architects for the improvement projects that stemmed from the Edinburgh Improvement Act, 1867, itself a product of William Chambers' election as Lord Provost in November 1865. See chapter 5.

3.18 Sir John McNeill (1795–1883)
McNeill was a diplomat and surgeon, and chairman of the Board of Supervision, 1845–68. Calotype by David Octavius Hill and Robert Adamson, 1845. [Source: SNPG]

of housing for some months.[176] The *Courant* carried leaders on the tenement disaster, focusing first on the activities of the Relief Fund, and then calling for more rigorous monitoring and controls regarding the structural strength of buildings.[177]

Despite this public concern, it was Sir John McNeill's powerful introductory comments from the chair at an open meeting in the Queen Street Hall on 25 February 1862 to consider 'Dwelling-houses for the Working Classes' that re-calibrated the issues of housing and health. He poured scorn on the idea that voluntary efforts would resolve the housing question, and demanded that another agency, the Town Council, be more explicit about its plans to address ruinous and insanitary housing.[178] McNeill was also damning about the Procurator-Fiscal's Precognition because there was no cross-examination of witnesses to discover the actual causes of the collapse, nor to assign responsibility for it, nor to develop a strategy to prevent such events in the future.[179] McNeill's skills as a diplomat were well honed, but it was difficult to escape the logic of his speech: that the Town Council and its committees were paralysed by process rather than preoccupied with policy.

For the reading public it was the words of two ministers, reproduced at length in *The Scotsman* that struck a particular chord early in 1862. The New Greyfriars' minister, the Revd William Robertson, provided poignant accounts of living conditions based on his Old Town mission work extending over twenty years, most graphically in the case of a dying man who endured human excrement dripping through from the floor above on to his face, and in another case, of a flat in Morocco Close, Canongate, 'with neither window nor chimney', below ground level, and with 'the floor damp and slippery'.[180] The Revd Dr Candlish also linked housing and health:

> The state of many of the dwellings of the working classes of Edinburgh is a disgrace to a Christian city, injurious to health and morality, and calculated to originate and diffuse disease, and to counteract the various means adopted for the physical and moral elevation of the population.[181]

The issue had so gripped the public consciousness, and the public's conscience, that the political agenda in 1862 was colonised by the public health issues raised in the aftermath of a housing disaster. For example, Dr Alexander Wood's attack on the Dean of Guild Court stung the Clerk to the Court to write to *The Scotsman* in a damage limitation exercise to show how, insofar as it was

176 For Chambers' lecture see *Courant*, 30 January 1862, 3cd; for Town Council meetings see *Courant*, 22 January 1862, 2d–g; 1 February 1862; for letters see *Courant*, 25 January 1862, 3cd; 7 February 1862, 2d; and 22 February 1862, 2f. See also Report by Mr Patterson of the Metropolitan Building Association on new working-class housing in Edinburgh, *Evening Courant*, 24 February 1862, 2f.

177 *Evening Courant*, 1 February 1862, 2f; 11 February 1862, 2ab.

178 *The Scotsman*, 26 February 1862, 2f.

179 ECA Council Minutes, vol. 283, f. 446, 4 March 1862, notes from a decision of the Queen Street meeting a deputation was formed to promote healthier living condition for the urban poor.

180 *The Scotsman*, 26 February 1862, 3c. Robertson did not think there was a city in Britain with insanitary and environmental problems of such severity as those in Edinburgh and, in a name-dropping moment, reported that Lord Shaftesbury had said so in a conversation with him.

181 *The Scotsman*, 26 February 1862, 3c.

legitimate to do so, this planning agency had been in pro-active mode since the tenement disaster:

> Since the unfortunate occurrence in High Street, fifty cases of ruinous tenements have been visited and inspected by the Dean of Guild Court. Five or six of these have been condemned and taken down, and the others have been repaired or are in the course of being put in order.
>
> The community ... should know that it is not the duty of any Court to ferret out cases to be brought before it. The Dean of Guild Court knows nothing, and ought not to know anything of any case until brought before it by the proper officer. Were it otherwise, the Court would exceed its proper functions by becoming an informer, and would be far more disqualified for the discharge of its duty.[182]

The politics of public health administration had thwarted Glover as Police Surgeon and continued unabated as the Town Council took over from the Police Commission in 1856. 'A systematic and well-prepared effort [was] being made to "pack" the council with men rather unaccustomed if not somewhat unable to think for themselves,' was how the process was explained; the term 'sectarianism' was used to describe the results.[183] The quality and qualifications of councillors nominated in several wards was lamented in a *Scotsman* leader:

> more or less in every very ward meeting ... the spirit of sectarianism has shown itself rampant, and the question uppermost in the minds of most of the electors ... has been not whether the candidates were men of sense and business, likely to promote the good of the city, but whether they worship in this or that church – rather, whether they are submissive to some particular ecclesiastical clique ... all the animosity is between different bodies of Presbyterians.[184]

If there was an expectation that after the 1856 election 'the new Town Council will early direct its attention to the sanitary affairs of the city', there was also a premonition of the events of 1862 that identified two crucial issues: confused lines of administrative responsibility and the highly sensitive issue of the sanctity of private property rights. A newspaper leader explained:

> When a tenement, for whatever cause, happens to be taken down, the Paving Board is entitled to prevent its re-erection beyond certain limits, for the widening and improving of thoroughfares – but this is a very partial and casual means of improvement. The sanitary officers of the city ought to have powers of condemning buildings erected in a manner or position prejudicial to the health of the city, as full and summary powers of the Dean of Guild Court. As long as this is not the case, all our efforts must fall far short of the desirable consummation of placing the town in a satisfactory sanitary condition.[185]

By the time he was sacked in 1854, Glover had already identified the salient fact that reliance on a Police Surgeon who was restricted to the medical care of the police force and prisoners, and to dealing with fever emergencies,

182 *The Scotsman*, 5 March 1862, 7a–f.
183 *The Scotsman*, 29 October 1856, 2f.
184 *The Scotsman*, 18 October 1856, 2f.
185 *The Scotsman*, 18 October 1856, 2g.

could not help to further sanitary administration. Gairdner had not used this term in his letters to the newspapers but – like Littlejohn, Begbie, and other supporters of medically supervised sanitary administration – he almost certainly envisaged a Medical Officer such as was already found in Liverpool, London and other English towns. This was not a view shared by Edinburgh Town Council. For several years following Glover's dismissal theirs was a more conventional understanding of public health based upon stricter controls over drainage, waste disposal and condemned insanitary buildings.[186] Consequently, it was from an 'admirable' Report tendered by a sub-committee on Cleaning and Lighting to the newly elected Town Council in 1857 that draft clauses were formulated in a manner strongly reminiscent of the former Police Commission regulations and fines for infractions.[187] Little progress was made until March 1861 when the Town Council approved the ten clauses of a new Bill drafted by the Lord Provost's Committee and, significantly, sent copies to the Lord Advocate and Provost William Lindsay of Leith. From October 1861, the sanitary condition of the city regularly appeared, sometimes two or three times each month, on the Town Council's weekly agenda.[188]

Further pressure for action accumulated from an important development on 13 November 1861, almost two weeks before the tenement disaster, when a 'memorial signed by nine of the city clergy' on the sanitary condition of the city was submitted to the Council.[189] Chastised in the *Scotsman* for 'retiring to the New Town or suburban retreats', the 'pastors' accurately identified the lack of a water supply as the principal evil.[190] This development resulted in a resolution that the Lord Provost and magistrates should seek a meeting with the Lord Advocate, the principal legal agent in Scotland, 'to induce him to bring in a general police bill for Scotland'.[191] By Christmas Eve 1861 he had agreed do so.[192] In conjunction with the concurrent interest of Edinburgh, Glasgow and Leith to obtain new police powers, the Lord Advocate's positive decision owed much to the 'pick and mix' approach proposed in the new legislation which enabled 'any Town to adopt such clauses as may be considered suitable for its special circumstances, without being obliged, as under the present General Police Act for Scotland (1850), to adopt the whole enactments'.[193]

186 NLS APS 1.77.122, Letter from Henry Johnson to the Lord Provost, 15 May 1856. Based on a survey of 159 closes Johnston advocated more light, air, good paving, better water supply, public privies, better cleaning, and stronger obligations on landlords.

187 ECA SL46/1, Minutes of the Cleaning Committee, 14 July 1857; *The Scotsman*, 15 July 1857, 4c. For details of the ten clauses in *The Scotsman* described as an 'admirable' report see *The Scotsman*, 3 April 1861, 6cd.

188 ECA SL25/1/1, Lord Provost's Committee, Scroll Minutes, 13 November 1861 and 11 December 1861. There are no full council minutes for this period. It would appear that either no record was taken or, more likely, it has not survived. The first entry is the induction of Mr Marwick as Town Clerk. Nevertheless, the items themselves are often of great value and as a general picture of business perfectly adequate. Decisions were recorded.

189 ECA SL1/1/282–283, Minutes of the Town Council, 2 April 1861; *The Scotsman*, 20 November 1861, 7cd; 1 January 1862, 2bc.

190 *The Scotsman*, 1 January 1862, 2b.

191 ECA SL25/1/1, Lord Provost's Committee, 13 November 1861, item 5.

192 ECA Box 00/01/21, Lord Provost's Committee, Report, 12 March 1862.

193 13 and 14 Vict., cap. 33, Police of Towns Act, 1850.

Addressing local priorities

These, then, were the embryonic stages leading to the complicated birth of the General Police (Scotland) Act, 1862.[194] Between January and March 1862 the original ten clauses in the proposed Police Bill were amended and expanded by the Lord Provost's Committee to 12, 14 and, in March 1862, to 16 clauses, mostly dealing with drains, cesspools, and soil-pipes, and a more active role as overseer for the municipal authorities.[195] While these deliberations were taking place early in 1862 *The Scotsman* kept up media pressure on the Town Council in a fine display of investigative journalism. In one account the newspaper disparaged the Town Council for its 'most lame and impotent' approach to sanitary improvement; in another passage it sought 'emphatic action', pleading for justice rather than benevolence in relation to rights of 'poorer brethren'; it mocked the Lord Provost for his 'inconsistency of thought which in one breath earnestly wishes for public support and is thankful for having got it'.[196] Quantification, a by-product of the valuation reform in 1854, was also introduced to the reading public: in 1857, they were informed, 26% of Edinburgh houses had no water connection, and, in 1861, that '30,000 people living in our closes in the Old Town were without the slightest household sanitary conveniences' – equivalent to 18% of the entire population of Edinburgh.[197] Powerful critiques of ideas emerging from the Town Council for improving sanitary conditions, such as the removal of upper tenement storeys and clearing alternate closes, were published in the press. One particular letter displayed a fine understanding of landlordism. Henry Johnston pointed out that compulsorily requiring landlords to introduce water supply to their rented tenements would force 'a test of worthlessness', that is, an assessment of whether the cost of providing water would be so great that non-compliance and compulsory purchase might be the better option, thus enabling the Town Council to acquire sites for improvements.[198] Just as *The Times* had played an important critical role, publishing letters and leaders about the state of the River Thames and the need for a pure water supply for London, so *The Scotsman* assumed an instrumentality in the process of public health agitation in Edinburgh, particularly during the 1860s.

In parallel with their deliberations concerning the new Police Act, the Town Council also considered the appointment of a Medical Officer. In October 1861, before both the decision to proceed with a Police Bill, and the High Street

194 25 and 26 Vict., cap. 101, Burgh Police (Scotland) Act, 1862 (Lindsay Act). The full title showed the complexity of the topic: An Act to make effectual Provision for regulating the Police of Towns and populous Places in Scotland, and for lighting, cleansing, paving, draining, supplying Water to and improving the same, and also for promoting the Public Health thereof. Eventually the Burgh Police Act, 1862, mushroomed to 449 clauses and understandably, therefore, involved complicated negotiation.

195 ECA Box 00/01/21, Lord Provost's Committee, Reports for 29 January 1862; 12 February 1862. An original printed report of the 16 clauses is in the Report for 12 March 1862. A contentious proposal was that all houses rented at £8 annually were to have sewer connections and water supply.

196 *The Scotsman*, 1 January 1862, 2b.

197 *The Scotsman*, 5 February 1862, 3b.

198 *The Scotsman*, 5 February 1862, 3b. Henry Johnston showed a keen sense of economics in his letter to *The Scotsman*, identifying that the capital value of tenements might well decline and that the council could acquire properties at low cost.

disaster, Councillor James Ford, a long-standing member of the Lighting and Cleaning Committee and a persistent advocate of sanitary causes, proposed a motion at Council 'to consider and report upon the advisability of organising through our own Medical Officer, in conjunction with the Medical Officers of the Parochial Board, a scheme of supervision over the public health of the city, with a view to prompt and remedial measures, when emergencies do arise'.[199] Ford's speech was a detailed report on sanitary progress in Edinburgh, quoting statistics on sewerage, water supply, and mortality rates for 1855–60 for several Scottish towns, as supplied by Gairdner, 'whose services as a sanitary reformer I am forward to acknowledge'.[200] By using the phrase 'our own Medical Officer', Ford revealed that he regarded the Police Surgeon's sphere of operations as already those of a fully fledged municipal Medical Officer of Health.

Ford was mistaken in his assessment of the Police Surgeon's role but he had put his finger on the enduring tension between the need for local political and administrative control of public health matters, not least over expenditure, and the medical imperatives of managing epidemic disease. In his letter to *The Scotsman* in 1858 Gairdner referred to the inability of the hospitals to provide emergency accommodation for fever patients, and stressed the need for on-going community and preventive medicine over short-term solutions to medical crises. Gairdner had long despaired of a regime which did little more than clean and regulate the streets and closes: 'unquestionably the great work of sanitary inspection and reform ... cannot be begun till the medical profession, who alone know the evils, are systematically brought into communication with the authorities.'[201] This was precisely what William Alison, Gairdner's and Littlejohn's mentor, meant by medical policing, and Gairdner accordingly viewed the work of William Lindsay, Provost of Leith, in promoting a General Police Bill for Scotland with both hope and admiration. Leith, in Gairdner's view, was developing a sanitary regime that had much to teach Edinburgh:

> She has organised a Sanitary Association to inform and instruct the public mind, to initiate ideas of improvement, and to keep public bodies alive to their sense of duty. She now demands, through Provost Lindsay, the powers necessary to give effect to her aspirations.[202]

The Scotsman shared this view: 'Leith may be proud of a Provost who even vigorously attempts so great a public good. Edinburgh has a Provost who once talked much of his great interest in such matters but who has yet done nothing in them; who cannot, in fact, even help us to keep our streets clean.'[203] The General Police (Scotland) Act, 1862, known as the 'Lindsay Act' to commemorate the Leith Provost's initiative, made available selectively, or in their entirety, police and sanitary powers to all Scottish burghs.[204]

199 *Evening Courant*, 9 October 1861, 2g. The issue was remitted to the Lord Provost's Committee.
200 *The Scotsman*, 9 October 1861, 7d.
201 W.T. Gairdner, 'Sanitary Inspection in Scotland', 2,030-word letter to *The Scotsman*, 21 January 1861, 3b.
202 *The Scotsman*, 21 January 1861, 3b.
203 *The Scotsman*, 18 January 1861, 2b.
204 25 and 26 Vict., cap. 101, General Police (Scotland) 1862 (Lindsay Act).

Crucially, as first published on 21 March 1862, the Bill gave no power to town councils to appoint a Medical Officer.[205] A report on the Bill from the Lord Provost's Committee, dated 14 May, was presented to Edinburgh Council on 20 May.[206] It listed those provisions which would benefit the city without the expense of a Local Bill. The Edinburgh input to the Lindsay Bill can be tracked in detail. Upon a copy of its first printing, sent by the Council to Messrs Maitland and Gifford, their legal advisors, were inscribed their proposed amendments and additions. Against Clause 105, concerning the appointment of an Inspector of Nuisance, Gifford penned the crucial observation: 'Commissioners should have power to appoint one or more Medical Officers of health,' and, beneath it, wrote: 'Note. See as to defining duties of officers of health.'[207] The most detailed examination of the Bill came from the Lord Provost's Committee, which also reported on the appointment of a Medical Officer. The unequivocal recommendation, unanimously approved when the full Council considered the report, was that a Medical Officer should be appointed forthwith:

> It is not expedient that the adoption of additional sanitary measures be delayed until a legislative Act shall be obtained ... and agree to recommend to the Council to appoint a medical practitioner of skill and experience *ad interim* ... to be called the officer of health.[208]

The Town Council was in no doubt that existing powers under the Edinburgh Police Act, 1848, in conjunction with amendments passed in 1854 and the Nuisances Removal (Scotland) Act, 1856, were sufficient: an appointment could be made under existing legislation. There was, in their view, no need to await the outcome of the Lindsay Bill.

Edinburgh's influence on the Bill was also achieved through its new Town Clerk, James Marwick, who was invited, with Provost Lindsay and the Crown Agent, Andrew Murray, to spend time in London with the Lord Advocate. Marwick subsequently recalled:

> I accordingly went with Mr. Murray to London, and devoted much time and labour to recasting and adjusting the bill. Provost Lindsay was with us, of course, and all the representations of burghs and deputations in regard to the bill were referred to us. We were then able to place the result of our work

205 PP (HC) 1862 (57) IV, 199–356. The Bill, with 438 clauses and 5 schedules, was published and first read in the House of Commons on 21 March 1862. Clause 105 allowed for the appointment of an Inspector of Nuisances. The reports in *Hansard* are no more than selected summaries of debates, but the newspapers reported the scrutiny of the Bill and the details of amendments in full, the *Evening Courant* in a 13,000-word supplement. Clauses 99–113, which included the provisions for the appointment of officers passed 'without any observation', *The Scotsman*, 26 June 1862, 5 a–f.

206 *The Scotsman*, 21 May 1862, 6d.

207 ECA Box 00/01/21. See also *Memorial of the Lord Provost, Magistrates, and Town Council of the City of Edinburgh with the Opinion of Counsel* (no date: [1862]) This printed report, with questions by the Lord Provost's Committee on how the Town Council should respond to the Lindsay Bill, is annotated by Messrs Maitland and Gifford (in different coloured inks) indicating their legal advice. A revised version incorporating the lawyers' amendments in print is also extant. It illustrates the way the council promoted its interests in Parliament. Both Maitland and Gifford were appointed as Law Lords. ECA Box 00/01/21.

208 *The Scotsman*, 21 May 1862, 6d, item 14. Another intriguing issue was raised, the construction of a town hall, and was destined to haunt many a council meeting subsequently.

3.19 William Lindsay (1819–84), Provost of Leith, 1860–66
As a burgh with the motto 'Perseverance' Leith Town Council and its provost campaigned actively for affordable housing and improved sanitary conditions. J.A. Horsburgh, artist. [Source: CAC]

> in the Lord Advocate's hands, explaining to him that we felt much hampered by the fact that the bill, as originally submitted to him, had been introduced and printed; but that, while not wholly satisfied with the result, it was the best we could do.[209]

With a willing Town Clerk well versed on the Bill through his daily work and a Lord Advocate warmly disposed to the measure, it was perhaps unsurprising that Marwick's journey south to press for the inclusion of the Edinburgh Council's views on various clauses should be successful. Whether the changes were due to Marwick's input alone is unclear, but the result was that when the Bill came before the House of Commons for debate on the second reading on 24 June 1862, a new clause, number 111 enabling a Medical Officer of Health to be appointed, had been inserted by the Lord Advocate.[210] The Bill received a second reading in the House of Lords in early July, a third reading in the Commons on 22 July, and in the Lords on 24 July and 1 August; no discussion took place on the insertion of the powers to appoint a Medical Officer of Health.[211] The Bill received royal assent on 7 August 1862.[212]

This detailed sequence reveals important aspects about the position of the Edinburgh Town Council in relation to the development of public health policy. After a hesitant start between 1857 and 1861 they were active contributors to the development of the legislation in 1861 and 1862. The Council not only knew that the General Police Bill made unobstructed progress through Parliament, but their officers and legal advisers were actively involved in that process, suggesting clauses and amending others. The Council's agenda was to achieve a simplification of the many Police Acts under which sanitary administration functioned and, as a relatively recently formed single Council authority, to shelter under the wing of a general statute in order to avoid the direct costs of a private Act. There

209 NLS R.178.a, Sir James Marwick, *A Retrospect* (Glasgow, privately published [1905]), 73. Marwick had declined the Town Clerkship of Dundee and later made his name as Town Clerk of Glasgow, 1873–1903. He had been a councillor in Edinburgh in the 1850s. See *ODNB*.

210 See *Hansard*, vol. 166, col. 544; PP (HC) 1862 (133) IV, 357–534; *Hansard*, vol. 167, cols 13–14, 282, 1127; *Hansard*, vol. 168, cols 726, 1,078; PP (HC) 1862 (236) IV, 535–44. The clause read as follows:

> 111 The Commissioners may, if they think fit, appoint a Person of competent Skill and Experience, who shall be styled the 'Officer of Health,' and whose Duty it shall be to ascertain the Existence of Diseases within the Limits appointed to him, especially of epidemic, endemic and contagious Diseases, and to point out any local Causes likely to occasion or continue such Diseases or otherwise injure the Health of the Inhabitants, and to point out the best Means of checking or preventing the Spread of such Diseases, and from Time to Time, as required by the Commissioners, to report to them upon the Matters aforesaid, and to perform any other Duties of a like Nature which may be required of him; and the Commissioners shall fix the Salary to be paid to such Officer, and shall pay such Salary out of the Police Assessment hereby authorized to be levied; and the Commissioners may with the Approval of One of Her Majesty's Principal Secretaries of State, remove any such Officer of Health, or, with the like Approval, discontinue any such Officer.

211 The relevant four sections in the Bill, 104–107, became five, 109–113, in the Act where a Medical Officer could be appointed under section 111.

212 *Hansard*, 3rd series, 168, col. 282, 14 July 1862. Lord Redesdale, who steered most *local* sanitary Bills through Parliament, recorded his opinion that Lindsay's Bill tried to do too much and would fail.

was, too, a direct involvement by the Council, as evidenced by the insertion of Clause 111 concerning the appointment of a Medical Officer of Health which, though introduced belatedly, cannot have been a surprise to them since their own committee's report had recommended this in May, fully two months before the passage of the Act. In much the same vein, the Edinburgh sub-committee's report regarding the job description of the officer of health, itself bearing a strong resemblance to that of the Liverpool Sanitary Act, 1846, and presumably relayed through a Duncan–Gairdner liaison, found its way into the 1862 Act in a language bearing the hallmarks of plagiarism.[213] This episode and others also revealed the consultative process between local and central government, and the constructive role of the Lord Advocate's office.

Despite this careful attention to its legislative interests, the popular opinion of the Town Council was of a dilatory body on sanitary affairs. This may have been a legacy of the McLaren years, at least as far as the constant carping of the newspapers is concerned, but even the kindest observer would have regarded Edinburgh's steps towards a medically supervised, modern public health department as reluctant. Gairdner's barely concealed complaint that the Council had a habit of anaesthetising issues by remitting them to committees was reminiscent of earlier criticisms of their predecessors, the police commissioners, and it was repeated many times in the full rhetorical tones of newspaper leader writers. Nowhere was indecision more apparent than in the minutes of the Lord Provost's Committee to which sensitive issues were often referred.[214] On only two of the twenty-two occasions between March 1861 and December 1862 when sanitary matters came before the committee were decisions reached.[215] This administrative paralysis within the council was combined with a grudging attitude to expenditure on public health, even though 'much expense [was] incurred ... for Local Acts which would have been quite unnecessary had there been a good general Act in operation throughout'. As *The Scotsman* thundered, Edinburgh exhibited 'ignorance, inertia, prejudice, economy, vested interests, routine, and like obstructives stood as a formidable succession of walls and ditches against the assault of invading reform'.[216]

A Medical Officer appointed

Given the divisions between reformers and conservatives within the Council, and between the Council and influential medical opinion, it comes as no surprise that the appointment of Henry Littlejohn as the first municipal Medical Officer of Health in Scotland was a messy, contested affair, with foot-dragging masquerading as principled objection and, yet again, amid arguments over the salary.

213 9 and 10 Vict., cap. 127, section 125, An Act for the Improvement of the Sewerage and Drainage of Liverpool, and for Making Further Provisions for the Sanitary Regulation of the Borough.

214 In an intriguing exchange in the council chamber, reported in *The Scotsman*, 25 June 1862, 6c, Bailie Mossman considered a complaint over the two-month delay in a response from the Lord Provost's Committee regarding Littlejohn's salary as unwarranted.

215 ECA SL25/1/1, Scroll Minutes of Lord Provost's Committee, 19 December 1860 to 28 September 1863.

216 *The Scotsman*, 18 January 1861, 2b.

The formal process of making an appointment began at a council meeting on 1st April 1862 and was not concluded until eleven meetings later, on 28 October 1862, one week before a new council was elected. Uncertain whether the Lindsay Bill would be passed in the current Parliament, the Lord Provost, Francis Brown Douglas, proposed that a Local Bill should be prepared to consolidate all extant police and sanitary powers. It should contain a clause to appoint a Medical Officer of Health, as existed in many English towns, and as proposed in the new Glasgow Police Bill.[217] For the first time the council was presented with the crucial issue: were the powers to appoint a Medical Officer to be drawn from the local Police Act of 1848?; or from a new and as yet undrafted Edinburgh Police Bill?; or from the Lindsay Bill, which was still to receive its second reading in Parliament? The Local Act could be invoked immediately and gave the Council control over the appointment; a new Local Act would incur considerable expense; and the Lindsay Bill was deemed less than satisfactory because its provisions currently contained no power to appoint a Medical Officer, and its passage in any case was uncertain. These three options presented the Lord Provost's Committee, the inner cabinet of the council, with a dilemma complicated further by the fact that Paliament would not be in session during the summer and that impending local elections would return a new council in November 1862. The council's room for manoeuvre was, therefore, very limited.

The proposal from the Lord Provost to draft a Local Bill was consistent with deliberations in the council during the previous twelve months. It, and the matter of the appointment of a Medical Officer, was referred in April 1862 to the Lord Provost's Committee, and six weeks later, in mid-May 1862, the full council had before them the committee's recommendation to appoint such a person, together with a list of his proposed duties. These duties were loosely modelled on those of Liverpool: namely, to present a record of the causes of death, gained monthly from the registrars and arranged in districts; to report on his findings from time to time; to encourage co-operation with parochial authorities and their surgeons, the dispensaries and others in the medical profession, in order to monitor and prevent epidemic disease; and to work with the Inspector of Nuisances, and all others, to clean, ventilate and improve poorer and crowded areas.[218]

If, finally, in May 1862 matters seemed to be coming to a climax, the Lord Provost applied the brake: he 'did not wish to urge this matter to a decision' at that meeting, adding that the appointment 'would, of course, involve a salary; at the same time he believed the public would cheerfully meet the expense, as the whole community would receive the benefit of the reports of such an officer.'[219] He took this step for a simple reason: the council meeting on 20 May 1862 took place just two days before the revised Lindsay Bill was printed prior to a full debate in the House of Commons.[220] Had the Bill been mauled, or thrown out, then realistically one of the three options before the council would have

217 ECA Council Minutes, vol. 284, 106–7; *The Scotsman*, 2 April 1862, 7d.

218 ECA Council Minutes, vol. 284, 224.

219 *The Scotsman*, 21 May 1862, 4c.

220 PP (HC) 133, IV, 357,0 22 May 1862. Police and Improvement (Scotland) Bill [as amended in committee] to make more effectual provision for regulating the police of towns and populous places in Scotland.

been closed. There was still a strong possibility that the Bill would proceed to the statute book before Parliament recessed for the summer. The long-drawn-out process towards the codification of police powers in Edinburgh, begun in February 1861, would thus be completed in a matter of a few weeks.

No councillor, indeed no informed Edinburgh citizen, could have been ignorant of the consolidation of police powers proposed under the Lindsay Bill. The *Courant*'s 13,000-word account of the clauses ensured that detailed information was in the public domain.[221] So the absence of any reference to powers to appoint a Medical Officer can be explained in three ways: some councillors thought, rightly, that they already possessed such powers; some confused, or deliberately conflated, the post of Police Surgeon with that of Medical Officer; and some had simply not thought about the need to legitimate the Medical Officer's post under the authority of specific legislation. Almost certainly there were councillors in all three categories.

The progress towards the appointment of Littlejohn as Medical Officer of Health was complicated by these possibilities and the shifting alliances that resulted from questions surrounding the status and salary of the post. In a lengthy statement at a Council meeting on 29 July, nine days before the Lindsay Act received the royal assent, Dr James Alexander, member for St Cuthbert's ward, raised the question of the Police Surgeon's salary, which he proposed in a formal motion should be raised from £150 to £250.[222] He drew on a long statement from Dr Littlejohn about his remuneration and his onerous duties, which included: the medical charge of an increased number of prisoners; work in relation to the Reformatory Schools Act; and registering all cases of sudden death. None of these duties had been required at the time of his appointment in 1854.[223] Following an acrimonious debate, Alexander's motion was defeated by 15 votes to 8, essentially because some councillors were aware that the Lord Provost's Committee was already considering wider issues than the surgeon's salary – the Lindsay Act was all but passed except for the House of Lords' consideration of minor Commons' amendments. 'They were all agreed,' said Bailie Johnston, 'as to Dr Littlejohn's merits, and had the highest opinion of them. At the same time he regretted this motion had been made, seeing the Lord Provost's Committee at present had under consideration other questions connection with the medical service of the town, and it was desirable that no one point in the case should be prematurely decided.'[224] James Ford made matters even clearer: 'The Council had something better in store for Dr Littlejohn. … [I] entreat Dr Alexander, as a friend of Dr Littlejohn, to withdraw the motion.' Only two days after this debate the Lindsay Bill received its final reading in Parliament, with Clause 111 giving power to appoint a Medical Officer inserted. By proceeding as they did, the

221 *Evening Courant*, 26 June 1862, 5 a–f.

222 ECA MYBN 322B, Police Establishment Accounts, 1832–58. The Police Surgeon's salary had been £155 since May 1851.

223 *The Scotsman*, 30 July 1862, 4b.

224 *The Scotsman*, 30 July 1862, 4b. The Lord Provost further commented that the terms and conditions of employment of a council employee were a matter of confidentiality and most appropriately dealt with in the Lord Provost's Committee. In so doing he simultaneously ensured control of the issue of an appointment.

Lord Provost and senior councillors had avoided the cost and trouble of drafting a Local Bill and gained such powers as they needed through a General Act at the expense of Westminster rather than of Edinburgh ratepayers. The issue of improvements, police powers and an officer of health appeared to be resolved.

Late in August 1862 a formal proposal from the Lord Provost's Committee, based on the recommendation they had made on 1 April, was tabled: a Medical Officer should be appointed with a salary of £500, and a clerk who was to receive £50.[225] No decision was sought, and the only discussion surrounded an objection raised to a joint appointment of Police Surgeon and Medical Officer by Councillor Dr John Cochrane, and no doubt prompted by professional medical interests intent on demarcating a strategic role for the Medical Officer and a more administrative one for the Police Surgeon.[226] Although the Lord Provost's Committee had finalised its proposal, at a further meeting on 9 September 1862 the council deferred all discussion of the matter.[227]

With the appointment still unresolved, attention turned to a single key issue: should the functions of a Police Surgeon be conjoined with the duties of a Medical Officer? Significantly, as with earlier public health matters, battle lines were drawn not on a party basis but on factional manoeuvrings between shifting alliances of councillors, with some determined to avoid further expenditure on public health and others opposed in principle to conflating the two posts on the grounds that no one man could do both jobs. As the *Scotsman* commented:

> Edinburgh is not famous for agreement among its citizens either on general or local topics of interest. Party feeling usually runs high, and the ecclesiastical element which is made perforce to interfere in matters utterly beyond its province, usually imports sectarianism and bitterness into every public question.[228]

Anticipating the decisive council meeting and sensitive to the likely turn of the debate, W.T. Gairdner had sought the advice of Dr Duncan in Liverpool. He passed Duncan's reply to the *Scotsman*, which obliged by quoting it in a leading article published the day before the crucial council meeting. Whatever Gairdner's own views on the detailed issues, the *Scotsman* came down firmly against the Lord Provost's proposal to combine the two posts:

> Dr Duncan, Officer of Health of Liverpool, is, however, peculiarly qualified to advise on this point … He says 'It is undesirable that private practice should be combined with the duties of Officer of Health.' Why? Because in a place, like Liverpool, where 'the greater part of the dwellings of the working classes are in the hands of parties who have a more lively sense of the privileges than of the duties attaching to property … the combination of private practice would be quite incompatible with the efficient and impartial discharge of duties of Officer of Health.' There is no escaping from the result of this argument, so that Dr Duncan's letter is the most telling testimony we have seen against the proposal of the Lord Provost's Committee.[229]

225 ECA Council Minutes, vol. 284, 21 August 1862, 429.

226 *The Scotsman*, 22 August 1862, 2de.

227 ECA Council Minutes, vol. 284, 14–15. Dr Alexander gave notice of a motion that the offices of Police Surgeon and Medical Officer 'be not conjoined'.

228 *The Scotsman*, 22 September 1862, 2cd.

229 *The Scotsman*, 29 September 1862, 2b–d.

Duncan's expert view, as presented by *The Scotsman*, focused on a conflict of interest. Edinburgh councillors were concerned, however, about the conflation of two public offices, not about the combination of public service and private medical practice. Correspondence between Duncan and Gairdner makes it absolutely clear that any conflict of interest applied only in small towns, where the salary of the Medical Officer of Health was unlikely to afford a decent living to the incumbent, and so private practice would be an essential addition to his income.[230] In larger cities, such as Liverpool and Edinburgh, the combination of the two posts of Police Surgeon and Medical Officer was both desirable and affordable. In presenting the Duncan correspondence as it did, *The Scotsman* skewed the local debate over the issue and stoked up opposition to the Lord Provost's proposal to conjoin the two positions. In relation to the substantive issue of the Medical Officer's powers, Duncan actually wrote: 'I see no objection to the duties [being] associated with those of the Surgeon of Police.'[231] For a medical man educated in Edinburgh and in close correspondence with many of the most influential public health figures Britain, as well as being consulted by others abroad such as Lemuel Shattuck in Boston, Duncan's expert knowledge of public health administration may not have been informed by the latest manoeuvrings in the Edinburgh Council Chamber or every aspect of the Police Surgeon's post, but he knew what constituted a conflict of interest.[232]

Thus the *Scotsman*, whether maliciously or mischievously, by conveying Duncan's view as opposed to the joint public health posts, certainly influenced the tone and conduct of the debate. In so doing, the newspaper used verbal weapons of control to construct a climate of suspicion and distrust that enabled factionalism to flourish among council members. Even the normally implacable Littlejohn was exasperated and, a few months later in his first appearance before the newly elected council, reminded them of the 'discouragements' he had endured.[233] Indeed, during seven months between April and October 1862 and in the course of eleven council meetings, all reproduced verbatim in the newspapers and including details of his salary and professional credentials, Littlejohn said nothing as his accountability and probity came under scrutiny. Only when in post and in front of a new slate of elected councillors did he allow himself one word of comment, 'discouragements', and that as part of his endeavour to elicit the unequivocal support of the new council.

230 Liverpool Record Office 352 HEA 3: Medical Officer of Health Letter Books, vol. 3, folios 216–17, 280 and 331–2. Duncan first wrote to Gairdner on 29 June 1861 sending copies of his published reports and giving details of sanitary operations in Liverpool. In February 1862 he thanked Gairdner for a copy of his new book, *Public Health in Relation to Air and Water*. The letter quoted here was sent on 15 August 1862, though it was a delayed reply to Gairdner's questions because Duncan had been 'in the Country'.

231 Liverpool Record Office 352 HEA 3: Medical Officer of Health Letter Books, vol. 3, folio 332.

232 Liverpool Record Office 352 HEA 1/1, folio 289–92, Medical Officer of Health, Letter Books, vol.1, Duncan to Shattuck, 14 December 1849. Duncan sent parcels of documents to Shattuck containing statements chiefly concerned with Liverpool sanitary conditions and regulations, and also forwarded packets of documents received from Dr J. Stark in Edinburgh, and from Glasgow and Manchester officials and medical experts. Shattuck's subsequent *Report of a General Plan for the Promotion of Public and Personal Health* for Boston, published in 1850, referred to Stark's Reports on Mortality in Edinburgh and Leith for 1847 and 1848 (footnotes on 147–8) and reproduced the table of mortality from Stark's *Edinburgh Medical and Surgical Journal*, 70 (1848).

233 *The Scotsman*, 19 November 1862, 5f.

A joint appointment of Police Surgeon and Medical Officer presented a further dilemma, and another excuse for prevarication. The Police Surgeon was appointed under a Local Act. To whom was a new Medical Officer to be accountable? Under the Lindsay Act it would be the Home Secretary and not someone in the locality, and certainly not the Lord Provost, as had been the case in the Glover affair. The prospect of power over a city official transmitted to an authority outwith Edinburgh was unpalatable to many and raised anew the spectre of interference from the Board of Health in London. As the Lindsay Act went through its legislative passage, the council continued to regard the powers of the Medical Officer to be competently discharged under the 1848 Act but ideally sought to appoint the Medical Officer under the Lindsay Act – why else were they intent in promoting Clause 111? Paradoxically, in the list of clauses in the Lindsay Act marked for adoption by Edinburgh, Clause 111 was missing.[234] This muddle was grist to the mill for those seeking to delay further the appointment of a Medical Officer, and to *The Scotsman* which mounted a powerful advocacy of the benefits of having the Home Secretary as the ultimate arbiter:

> The report of the Lord Provost's Committee, about to be considered by the Council … recommends the Council to keep the Officer of Health in a dependent and subordinate position; and to secure this the more effectually, recommends the appointment of an officer under an act passed in 1848, to discharge duties prescribed under an act of 1862 …[235]

Terrier-like, *The Scotsman* in the same article identified another clutch of issues: public probity, and accountability. These had a resonance beyond the boundaries of Edinburgh since they were part of an emerging culture of audit as municipal expenditure in Britain spiralled upwards in the 1860s, partly as a result of responsibilities originating from Westminster itself.[236] A Medical Officer, the *Scotsman* proclaimed, needed absolute protection from the 'caprice or revenge' of local parties whose interests might be adversely affected by his actions in the legitimate pursuit of his duties. As the newspaper explained:

> A Bailie may establish a manufactory injurious to health, and it will scarcely quicken the operations of the Medical Officer against him to know that the Bailie has a powerful backing in the Council, and can expose him to great annoyance and possible loss of situation … where the bread of the officer and his family is, not once in a lifetime, but daily and hourly, perilled by the act? It cannot be hoped, then, that the duties of an officer of health will be fearlessly and independently discharged except by a man who can afford to be independent.[237]

234 A printed list of all clauses in the Lindsay Act, indicating in print those intended for adoption by Edinburgh, is dated 17 October 1862. Clause 111 is not marked for adoption, even though some clauses are marked in manuscript.

235 *The Scotsman*, 29 September 1862, 2bc.

236 See, for example, W.H. Fraser, 'Municipal socialism and social policy', in R.J. Morris and R. Rodger (eds), *The Victorian City, 1820–1914: A Reader in Urban History* (Harlow, 1993), 258–80; R. Millward, 'The political economy of urban utilities', in M.J. Daunton (ed.), *Cambridge Urban History of Britain*, vol.3, *1840–1950* (Cambridge, 2000), 315–50.

237 *The Scotsman*, 29 September 1862, 2b.

On 30 September 1862 matters came to a head. Lord Provost Brown Douglas was armed with several documents: the reports of the Lord Provost's Committee; three separate statements from Littlejohn about his duties and emoluments; copies of the Lindsay Act, 1862; information obtained by the Town Clerk from Liverpool, and copies of the Liverpool Sanitary Act, 1846 'as amended in 1854, defining the duties of the Medical Officer of Health in that town'. With all these items tabled, the Lord Provost formally proposed the appointment of a Medical Officer of Health.[238] Dr Littlejohn would be appointed under Clause 111 of the Lindsay Act, would be full-time except for his teaching in the medical school, and would be paid £500 annually. Glowing references were read from the presidents of both the Royal Colleges of Surgeons and Physicians. Interestingly, there is no record of any discussion about other candidates; the favoured insider was appointed.

The Lord Provost's statement, like most speeches in council, is absent from the official minutes, but was quoted in full in the newspapers. Two reporters, from *The Scotsman* and the *Courant*, evidently had excellent shorthand, or compared notes, because they published identical accounts of the Lord Provost's speech, which was designed to mollify opposition to the post, and to stress the council's continued cautious approach to expenditure. But Lord Provost Brown Douglas' statement was thoroughly muddled about the legislative Act under which Littlejohn was to be appointed; Brown Douglas twice contradicted himself in his statement. He concluded his speech, weakly, by saying that 'he thought the committee had sufficient grounds for the report they had made'.[239]

This explains why, in the voluminous archival record on the adoption of clauses in the Lindsay Act and careful comparison with provisions already available in Local Acts, there is no sign in 1862 of any council intention to adopt Clause 111 under which a Medical Officer of Health could be appointed. Indeed, there is every sign as late as mid-October 1862 that the Lord Provost's Committee intended *not* to adopt it.[240] Not only did they think the appointment could be made under Local Acts; they also thought that would avoid any influence from London over their Medical Officer.

But none of the Provost's reassurances discouraged opposition. Two motions – one to defer the whole business, another to increase the Police Surgeon's salary but not to conjoin the two jobs – were defeated, the latter quite narrowly by 14 votes to 11. A motion by Professor William Dick, Littlejohn's nemesis in 1854, opposed the proposal 'on economical grounds' and was lost 17:16, only by the casting vote of the Lord Provost. Most accepted the decision, although Councillor John Hope gave notice of a formal protest.[241]

238 ECA Council Minutes, vol. 285, 30 September 1862, ff. 49–55. *The Scotsman*, 30 September 1862.

239 *The Scotsman*, 1 October 1862, 2e.

240 ECA Box 00/01/21. There survive at least three printed lists of the 159 clauses (out of 449) proposed for adoption by Edinburgh. One list, a printed proof dated 15 September 1862, is signed by James Marwick; he underlined the number of each clause to be adopted, deleted eight others and added five. Clause 111 is not listed. Another, dated 17 October 1862, lists all clauses in the Act and has those for adoption asterisked or marked in manuscript. Clause 111 was not asterisked.

241 ECA Council Minutes, vol. 285, 55. Hope 'protested against the foregoing appointment and took instruments in the Clerk's hands', meaning he would table an official 'Reasons of the Protest'.

Littlejohn was installed as Medical Officer of Health, but the dust did not settle immediately. At the next council meeting Hope, seconded by Alexander, moved that the minutes be not approved. His 'Reasons of the Protest' were tabled: that one man could not do both jobs; that duties defined by the Lindsay Act should be kept separate; that in any case the council had not yet decided to adopt the relevant part of that Act; and that a council 'at the close of its career' should not make appointments for its successors. Hope was technically correct about Clause 111 of the Lindsay Act, though one Councillor offered to propose its adoption on the spot. His first objection also had substance. In most circumstances, and especially given Littlejohn's own complaints about his onerous duties – though, in truth, the complaints were really about the remuneration rather than the effort demanded – the case for appointing a second man was a reasonable one.

Councillor Hope's attempt to scupper the appointment was only defeated by 21 votes to 16.[242] In the last week of the council's life Hope made a last-ditch stand. His real purpose was presumably to have the objections formally recorded in the minutes. His Reasons for Dissent, co-signed by councillors Peter Miller and David Curror, amounted to two main points: that the Police Surgeon already did all the duties that were proposed for a Medical Officer of Health; and, that the cost was unreasonable:

> Because, acting under the powers contained in Clause 36 of the Police Act of 1848, there has already been appointed a Police Surgeon whose business it is to discharge all the necessary duties prescribed by the different clauses of that Act having reference to the removal of nuisances, the preservation of the Public Health, and the prevention of Contagious, Infectious, or Epedemic [*sic*] diseases; and that the list of duties which the present Police Surgeon undertook to discharge when he was appointed, along with the other duties which have since been imposed upon him under subsequent Acts of Parliament, embrace all the duties which this Council is authorised, or have any legal authority to require the said Surgeon of Police to perform ... [and that] the creation of a new office without any additional duties to be performed beyond what the Police Surgeon is at present bound to perform, and giving him an additional salary of £395 [*sic*] a-year for discharging these duties under another appointment is a gross misapplication of Police funds.[243]

This time the vote was 18 to 8 against the dissenters.

The model for this new approach to public health administration was Liverpool, and parallels with the disputed appointment of Dr W.H. Duncan as the first English Medical Officer of Health are striking. Like Duncan, Littlejohn's credentials were rarely questioned; indeed both men were highly regarded. The disputes centred on three issues: whether it was appropriate that they should have other paid work, in Duncan's case private practice, which would render them, in effect, part-time; the amount of their salary; and who should sanction their removal from office – the local council or the Home Secretary?[244] Thus, the ubiquitous conflict between public medical service and private commercial

242 ECA Council Minutes, vol. 283, 93–5. Twenty-one was the highest number of votes in several divisions on Littlejohn's appointment; 57% of the vote and 50% of the whole council.

243 *The Scotsman*, 1 October 1862, 2e.

244 P. Laxton, 'Fighting for public health: Dr Duncan and his adversaries', 59–88.

medicine was negotiated in public through arguments about the salary of a Medical Officer of Health. The episode also exposed conflicts within Edinburgh's political and medical classes who had no better idea as to the terms and conditions of a public Medical Officer than did English cities in the 1840s.

The carping over Littlejohn's appointment as the Medical Officer for Edinburgh spilled into the local elections in 1862 as candidates roused a rabble of ratepayers to protest against new expenditure. A rowdy meeting in the Nicolson Street Temperance Hall, for example, was assured that the candidate had opposed expenditure on 'a new officer altogether – an officer of health' on the grounds that 'it was quite uncalled for, that it was distasteful to the ratepayers, and that the expense would not be repaid by the advantage to the community'.[245] The election offered the prospect of change for the better – 'it could scarcely be for the worse,' claimed *The Scotsman*.[246] Lord Provost Douglas was persuaded not to stand again, either in that role or as a councillor, as a result of the efforts by our 'best citizens' to redeem the character of the city and its corporation. Douglas' prevarication, and his unvarying tactic to remit policy documents and initiatives to his inner cabinet, produced a sense of frustration with his vacuous term of office. As the newspaper concluded:

> Last year's elections did much, this year's will do as much more as is necessary to destroy the impression produced on the country and the Parliament that the community of Edinburgh has been fairly reflected in the sectarianism, contentiousness, and double-dealing of recent Town Councils.[247]

If factionalism and sectarianism were features of local political jostling over sanitary policy in Edinburgh in 1861 and 1862 there was a silver lining, an 'engrossing topic of interest last year on which wonderful unanimity was expressed'. Public attention was arrested by the tenement disaster and, fearful of the implications of the 'calamity', 'Whig and Tory, Liberal and Conservative, Established and Free Churchmen, forgot for a time the wide gulfs which separated them, and by public meetings and deputations showed our Town Council that they were in earnest about the matter, and that remedies must be found and applied for the clamant evils which existed.'[248] The review of the year railed at the inconsistencies in public affairs: of assurances about adequate legislation yet demands for new powers; council concern for economical expenditure yet 'the usual amusements of deputations to London … to which councillors are never averse'; and parliament intent upon the independence of the Medical Officer, accountable to the Home Secretary, but not similarly intent upon the public accountability of local councillors.[249]

As it happened, Edinburgh got a man who discharged *four* jobs: Police Surgeon, university lecturer, City Medical Officer, and Medical Officer to the

245 *The Scotsman*, 29 October 1862, 6bc. Meeting for St Leonard's ward, 28 October 1862. Interim Councillor Macnish had indeed voted against the appointment by exercising the ward politician's natural instinct for economy rather than on instructions from his constituents.

246 *The Scotsman*, 24 September 1862, 2b.

247 *The Scotsman*, 22 September 1862, 2b.

248 *The Scotsman*, 22 September 1862, 2c.

249 *The Scotsman*, 22 September 1862, 2cd.

Board of Supervision. His professional credentials were impeccable; his track record as Police Surgeon was excellent. Littlejohn assumed the post of Medical Officer of Health in Edinburgh with a significant stock of public goodwill. *The Scotsman* hailed the appointment – loudly demanded by the great public meeting in the Queen Street Hall and also by a deputation from that meeting to the Town Council.[250] Expectations were also high after a protracted period of 'muddling in bumbledom' by the Town Council, though Edinburgh was not alone in this regard.[251] Upon Littlejohn's zeal, *The Scotsman* claimed, will depend 'whether we are to continue in our present degraded condition, or … attain a position more in accordance with modern civilisation.'

Littlejohn appeared before the new Town Council and presented his first report. Delivered verbally, it was a long and detailed assessment of the prevalence of smallpox in the city and of the steps he had taken to deal with it. His report left no doubt that in just two weeks Edinburgh could see a modern Medical Officer of Health in action.[252] Astonishingly, Hope and Miller rose to move that 'the appointment of Dr Littlejohn as officer of health … be recalled'. They lost that vote by 23 votes to 2, with 8 abstentions, some of which were expressions of contempt for the move. The two medical men, Alexander and Cochrane, expressed admiration for their newly appointed colleague. The 'coming man' had arrived.

250 *The Scotsman*, 22 September 1862, 2c.

251 C. Hamlin, 'Muddling in Bumbledom: on the enormity of large sanitary improvements in four British towns, 1855–1885, *Victorian Studies*, 32 (1988), 55–84.

252 *The Scotsman*, 19 November 1862, 5f. Littlejohn's 1,300-word Report includes a statistical digest of the weekly progress of the disease, ranges over such issues as lodging-houses, hospital accommodation, liaison with the Parochial Boards, observations on the effect of behaviour of different classes on the disease, and a list of places for vaccination of the poor with the days of the week when they were open.

CHAPTER 4

'The property of the public': the *Report* acclaimed

> To register the progress of sanitary reform is about as tedious an affair as recording the movement of a glacier. From year to year the reports of the Medical Officer of the Privy Council upon Public Health tell the same melancholy tale to a coldly-apathetic community. The bane is demonstrated, and, in general, its antidote prescribed, with masterly clearness and with official punctuality. But the public listens to the lecture, and returns to its avocations even less deeply roused to a sense of its own remissness, than if the lecturer had been a Little Bethel missionary and his subject Kamstchatka.
>
> *Edinburgh Evening Courant*, 22 September 1864

Littlejohn's *Report* was formally presented to the Town Council on 15 August 1865, and was simultaneously published for the general public. It had been long expected. In the summer of 1864 Littlejohn had completed an investigation of the cow byres in the city, the results of which were published in *The Scotsman* in November 1864.[1] Three weeks later the printed version was tabled at a council meeting fully nine months before it appeared word for word in his *Report*.[2] This, Littlejohn explained, he did for two reasons: 'first, that I was anxious to show the manner in which I was prosecuting my enquiries, so as to render my report as complete as possible; and, secondly, because the management of our dairies was at present exciting a great deal of public attention.'[3] In other words, he had used the public concern over the cattle disease that was endemic in the Edinburgh byres to trail his *Report* and assure those remaining doubters about his office that he was at work looking after their sanitary interests.

Councillors were impressed. Bailie Alexander moved a vote of thanks to Littlejohn: 'He had never seen a report on which a greater amount of labour had been expended …' It was approved unanimously. Councillor Ford noted characteristically that he had reported on the state of the byres seven years previously but that nothing had been done. Was this report to go to a committee? Alexander urged the Council to wait: 'it was the desire of Dr Littlejohn that it should lie on the table till another report of his on the improvement of the closes of the Old Town should be laid before the Council.'[4] That was indeed the next item of business. It was a 3,200-word summary of Littlejohn's manifesto for the most

4.1 The *Report* presented to the Town Council, 15 August 1865
[Source: ECA, Council Minutes, vol. 291, 15 August 1865]

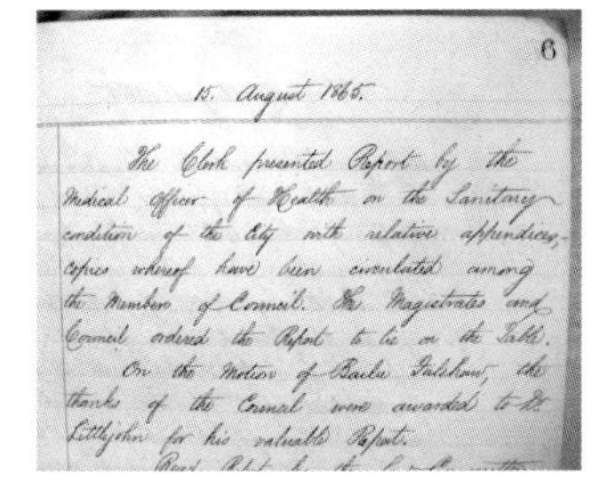

6

15. August 1865.

The Clerk presented Report by the Medical Officer of Health on the Sanitary condition of the City with relative appendices, copies whereof have been circulated among the Members of Council. The Magistrates and Council ordered the Report to lie on the Table.

On the Motion of Bailie [illegible], the thanks of the Council were awarded to Dr Littlejohn for his valuable Report.

1 The article in *The Scotsman*, 30 November 1864, 7ab, is, word for word, pages 50–56 of the *Report*. *The Scotsman* provided a long summary.

2 *Evening Courant*, 21 December 1864, 6a. The only surviving copy of this 18-page report is at ECA SL12/287 (2).

3 *Evening Courant*, 30 November 1864, 2c; *The Scotsman*, 21 December 1864, 7a.

4 *The Scotsman*, 21 December 1864, 7a.

pressing of all Edinburgh's sanitary problems, the foul condition of the closes in the Old Town. It illuminated for the first time Littlejohn's thinking and his method. Rather than appealing to commercial self-interest by using the language of health economics, he sought the humanity and charity of his fellow citizens. In this short extract from what was to be his final *Report*, we can see Littlejohn's clear understanding of the habits of the poor in the insanitary closes and decaying tenements, and his repeated emphasis on their poverty. These are modest but precisely targeted measures for improvement, not idealistic schemes. Fourteen passages, about two-thirds of the text, found their way into the *Report* of 1865, in most cases with only a few words changed.

These early glimpses of the *Report* helped to fuel the public debate on the sanitary condition of Edinburgh. In his recommendations to the council in December 1864 Littlejohn stated that clause 210 of the Lindsay Act, giving powers to enforce the introduction of a piped water supply and WCs into houses, had only been adopted by the Town Council on 28 October 1864, two years after it had been listed for adoption by the Lord Provost's Committee. But he regretted that it was being used in the Old Town: 'Since then I find that only two or three closes have been ordered to be proceeded with, and I must express my gratification that more has not be attempted; for I cannot imagine a more disastrous condition of matters for the poorer districts of our city than the general introduction of water-closets, so long as the present system of house accommodation obtains.'[5] Months later, in August 1865, Dr James Stark drew attention to the fact that the council was reviving clause 210 and issuing notices to proprietors of working-class housing to install water-closets despite warnings not to press ahead with it: 'in so far as it is applicable to … Edinburgh, most sanitary reformers are agreed that it should be allowed to fall into abeyance. The Magistrates cannot plead that they have not been warned … for Dr Littlejohn, their own medical inspector, in that able report which he laid before them in December last, specially pointed out the evils which had already resulted from the introduction of water-closets into a house newly erected for that very class.'[6] The central arguments in the 1865 *Report* fell on receptive ears, not just because the issues had been long debated but because Littlejohn had trailed them very effectively.

At what stage in 1865 these separate reports, and Littlejohn's statistical analysis of the city, assumed the form of the final *Report* is not known. It may be that he did not have a fixed plan for the work in late 1864. His comment that what he presented to the council on 20 December 1864 was 'a *resumé* of a portion of my General Report on the Health and Sanitary State of Edinburgh, which is at present being printed for circulation among the members' is tantalising. Did he mean that the short report on the sanitary condition of the closes was being printed following a spoken presentation at the meeting – an oral presentation being necessary if members did not have printed copies – or was he referring to the larger work, which could hardly be described as 'being printed'? Whatever

5 *The Scotsman*, 21 December 1864, 7b. For Littlejohn's argument against the introduction of WCs into the poorest accommodation see his *Report*, 109.

6 *Evening Courant*, 5 August 1865, 3d.

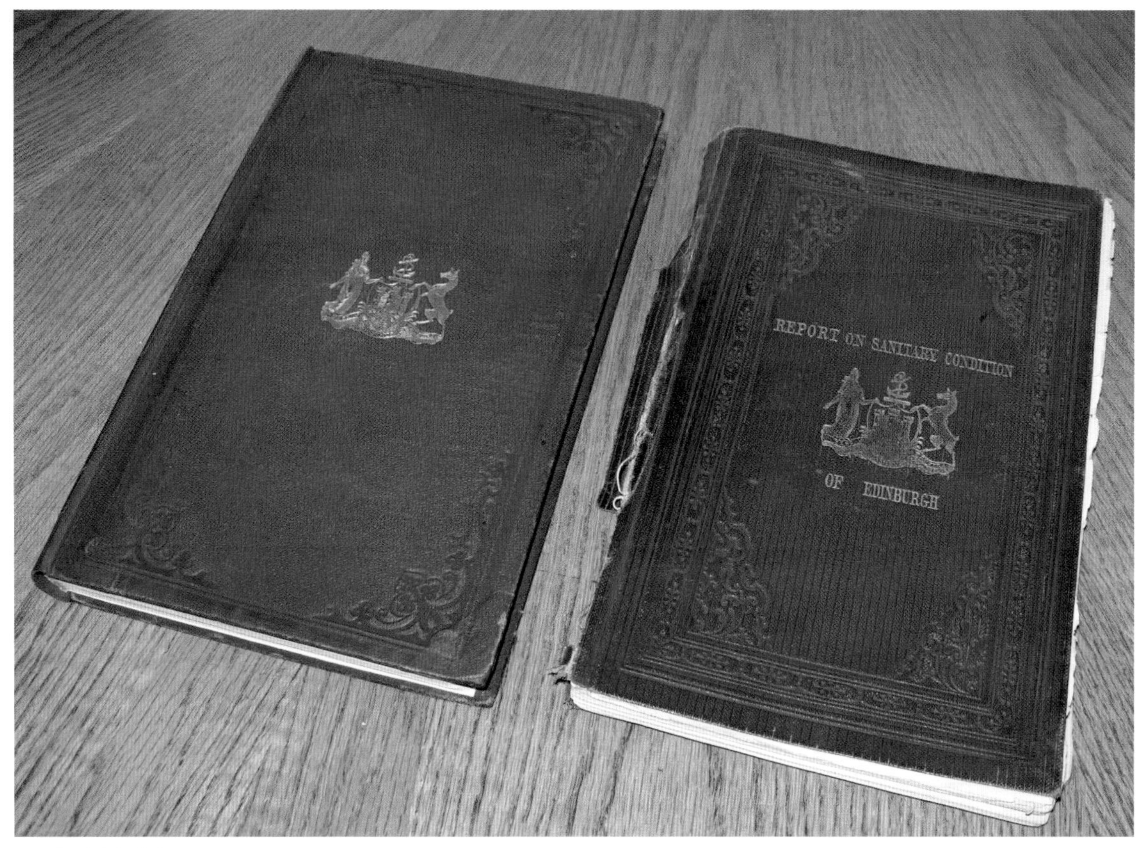

4.2 Littlejohn's *Report*
The two editions are identifiable by their distinctive bindings, with the first printing on the left and a slightly revised second printing on the right, a facsimile of which is reproduced at the end of this book. [Source: ECA]

the case, several months before its publication, the work was widely known and keenly anticipated.

The day after the Council received the *Report* on 15 August 1865, the *Evening Courant*, by this time as powerful a voice for sanitary reform as *The Scotsman*, marked the publication with an editorial:

> There is probably no other city in the kingdom now so well informed of what is needed to be done; and we trust our Town Council ... will now devote itself thoroughly to the needed reforms. A suspension of sectarian quarrels for the next five years would enable the Town Council to make Edinburgh the healthiest as well as the most beautiful city in Europe. ... Dr Littlejohn's report is intended not so much to prescribe the cure for existing evils as to present an accurate and minute diagnosis of the disease. But as a good diagnosis is the true foundation of all safe treatment, we must rejoice to possess this report as the first real step towards a remedy.[7]

7 *Evening Courant*, 16 August 1865, 4f.

The same day the *Caledonian Mercury* began an eleven-part serialisation of the *Report* and two days later the *Courant* began its ten-part serialisation.[8] The official return of newspaper stamps listed the circulation of the *Mercury* and *Courant* as 24,500 and 242,000 respectively.[9]

The precise story of the printing and publication of the *Report* is hard to reconstruct from the small number of surviving copies and the accounts of the Edinburgh Police Department. It was first issued bound in hard covers, green cloth, and with the city arms embossed in gold. It seems likely that the first print run – there could have been several – was complete well before the *Report* was formally presented to the council in August 1865. The accounts for 1865–66 record payments to Johnston's, the map printers, for maps supplied between January 1864 and June 1865, and to John Pairman for engraving the diagrams between February and June 1865. Alexander Colston, the printer, was paid £157 on 12 August 1865, which suggests a large print run: even at 2*s*. 6*d*. (12.5p) each, that would cover 1,000 copies.

Soon afterwards, perhaps within days, more copies were printed with a soft cover and some redesigning of the title and decoration, and more significantly several revisions to the text. We can imagine Littlejohn calling at Colston's printing works in Rose Street on his way from his house in York Place to his High Street office, armed with last-minute revisions. In some surviving copies he corrected a printing error introduced at the second printing as a result of his changes. Twelve of the 22 copies found in a worldwide search of public and institutional libraries are of the first printing, the remainder the soft-cover version.[10] The differences are fully described in this edition. The bibliographical evidence is not necessarily conclusive; in one copy maps supplied for the first printing were used in the second – why waste them? – and one survivor from the first printing was bound in the soft-cover style. In other respects, however, we have two consistent variants of the *Report*. Why? A simple explanation would be that demand was under-estimated. But one of the second printing, presented by Councillor J.H. Stott on 18 August 1865, suggests that copies from the second printing were available three days after the *Report* was formally released to the council and the press.[11] The Town Clerk, James Marwick, certainly did his best to increase demand. In a letter accompanying three copies for the City Parochial Board in mid-December 1865 he offered to supply 250 copies for £15, 'or at a rate of 14d. per copy'. The Board, which consisted of about 30 members, 'seemed

8 *Caledonian Mercury*, 1865: 16 August, 4a–c; 18 August, 3a–d; 21 August, 4a–c; 22 August, 4a–c; 23 August, 3bc; 24 August, 3ab; 25 August, 4a–c; 26 August, 5c–f; 28 August, 4a–e; 29 August, 4a–c; 30 August, 4ab. The Appendix and diagrams are omitted. Some tables are reproduced as conventional text; others are omitted. The main text of 47,600 words is reproduced in full. *Evening Courant*, 1865: 18 August, 3a–e; 21 August, 5cd; 22 August, 3a–d; 23 August, 3a–d; 24 August, 2c–f; 25 August, 6a–d; 28 August, 2d–f; 31 August, 6f–7b; 1 September, 6f–7b; 2 September, 7b–d. The *Courant* also made the same omissions but, curiously, the 600-word conclusion was not printed.

9 *Evening Courant*, 21 December 1865, 4a.

10 All of these have been examined. A further copy in the College of Physicians of Philadelphia was only available on the payment of a substantial fee, which was declined.

11 This is one of two copies in the Edinburgh City Archives. Although it was once the property of the Edinburgh Council Library, it carries the inscription 'Scottish Property Investment 102 South Bridge 18 August 1865 From J H Stott'.

to be [of] the prevailing opinion that 250 copies were too many, some members suggesting that fifty copies were sufficient, others considering that the copies sent were quite sufficient'.[12] The chairman, David Curror, was persuasive and in the event they ordered 50 copies.[13]

Even more difficult to pin down is the Council's scheme to spread Littlejohn's *Report* among the less affluent in the city. In October 1865 Councillor John Hope – 'a very provocative "party man" upon occasions' as *The Scotsman* once called him while observing that in sanitary matters his sympathies were sound[14] – tabled one of his many long motions, that

> the Council having received with much satisfaction the Report on the sanitary condition of the City of Edinburgh by Dr. Littlejohn ... and sensible that nothing will so much facilitate the carrying out of its suggestions as enlisting the public sympathy in its favour, and understanding that copies of the Report without the Map, but including pages 56–60, and p.69 of the Appendix, can be supplied by the Printer in a suitable cover at a shilling per copy, direct a People's Edition of a thousand copies to be cast off at that rate so as to make said Report accessible to the public at an easy rate, and request the booksellers of the City to give all facility for the circulation of this edition.[15]

The matter was approved and, of course, remitted to the Lord Provost's Committee, who after setting a maximum cost of £50 sat on the matter for about six months.[16] The cryptic decision recorded in the index to their (no longer extant) minutes for 23 March and 4 July 1866 – 'Printed for Council to be sent up to City Chambers' and 'Pay out. Sell to Booksrs at 9d. and advertise' – tells us little more than that some copies were printed. No advertisements have been found in the Edinburgh newspapers, and only five copies of the abbreviated 1866 edition have been located, two of them unbound proofs. Either the 'people' devoured their copies so eagerly that most were destroyed, or few of them read it because few were printed. The 1866–67 accounts record 'Paid Alex. Colston & Son on 3d Aug. 1866 for additional Copies of Report on the Sanitary Condition of the City by the Medical Officer of Health; 10th November 1865 – £52 1[*s*.]' and 'Paid W. & A. K. Johnston on 12th April 1867 for additional Copies, plan of City, to accompany Dr Littlejohn's Report on the Sanitary State of the City; 8th Augt to 19th Oct. 1865—[£]18'. So it may be that the cryptic entry in the Lord Provost's Committee minutes refers not to the popular edition but to the printer's long overdue bill. The Council also failed to pay Johnston's, the map makers, in reasonable time.

12 *The Scotsman*, 20 December 1865, 8c.

13 ECA SL8/1, Minutes of the Parochial Board, Volume E, 439.

14 *The Scotsman*, 13 November 1860, 2b.

15 ECA SL1/1/291, 333, Council Minutes, 31 October 1865. Hope had already tabled a long (and, to other councillors, irksome) motion on the smoke nuisance, but the press failed to report this one; *The Scotsman* reporting that seven motions by Hope 'were all postponed' as councillors left the room and the meeting adjourned inquorate. *The Scotsman*, 1 November 1865, 8a, and *Caledonian Mercury*, 1 November 1865, 4b. *The Courant*, 1 November 1865, 8a, merely noted that the Lord Provost's Committee were 'to consider what steps should be taking for printing a cheap edition of Dr Littlejohn's report'.

16 EDA SL25/1/1, Scroll Minutes Lord Provost's Committee, 3, 15 and 29 November 1865; 3 January, 23 March and 4 July 1866.

3rd November 1865	
1. Remit as to printing cheap Edition of Medical Officer's Report	remit to Bailie Hill; Treasurer & City Clerk to carry out limiting, the Maximum Cost to £50.
15 November 1865	
6. Letter Colston & Son as to their contract for Printing 9. Peoples edition of Dr Littlejohn's Report	[blank]
Wednesday 29th November 1865	
6. Medical Officers Report	[blank]
3 January 1866 ctd	
16. Cheap edition of Medical Officer's Report	[blank]
23rd March 1866 ctd	
19. Printing Report of Medical Officer	Printed for Council to be sent Officer up to City Chambers
4th July 1866	
2. Remit to print cheap edition of Medical Officer's Report (31st Oct. 1865)	Pay out. Sell to Booksrs at 9d. and advertise

Table 4.1 Scroll minute (agenda books) entries of the Lord Provost's Committee relating to a popular edition of Littlejohn's *Report*
Note: The agenda items are on the left; any decisions were recorded on the right, though it was common to leave the space blank. [Source: ECA SL25/1/2]

At a Council meeting on 9 July 1866 the clerk read a report by the Lord Provost's Committee that 'an edition of 1000 copies of the Report by the Medical Officer of Health have been printed, and that the Committee have directed that copies be furnished to the Booksellers at 9d. to be sold to the Public at 1/– each. Only 500 have been bound and the expense of printing this Edition and binding 500 copies has cost per Estimate £52. 1/.'[17] This transaction appears in the accounts with the dates 3 August 1866, when Colston was paid, and 10 November 1865, and would normally indicate the date on which the goods were supplied. Whatever the case, the council were selling the report well below what it cost to print it.[18] As a publishing venture Littlejohn's *Report* seems to have received the same muddled, vacillating and incompetent treatment from the Lord Provost's Committee, as with many other issues connected with the sanitary reform of Edinburgh.

The *Report* did not go unnoticed by national sanitary authorities. It was immediately reviewed by John Simon, Medical Officer to the Privy Council, in his annual report published in March 1866.[19] Curiously, while Simon's

17 ECA SL1/1/293, 217, Council Minutes, 9 July 1866. The *Courant* baldly stated that 500 additional copies of the Medical Officer's report had been printed, giving the impression that these were simply to satisfy further demand for the 1865 edition. *Evening Courant*, 10 July 1866, 3b.

18 If binding was half the cost of a volume then the manufacturing cost was 1*s*. 5*d*.; if binding was a third of the manufacturing cost then a bound volume cost 1*s*. 3*d*.

19 PP (HC) 1866 XXXIII, 421 [3645], Eighth Report of the Medical Officer of the Privy Council. With Appendix.

commentary contains details of individual cases of destitution and on police inspections of defective housing – taken from unacknowledged sources but not from Littlejohn – it bears signs of a lofty Metropolitan assessment lacking appropriate local knowledge: 'Dr Littlejohn is not called Medical Officer. He is chief Medical Officer of police and professor of forensic medicine. His report for 1865 contains a multitude of curious facts about Edinburgh.' On one issue, however, Simon had been primed: 'The new Scotch Police Act [1862] can be adopted either in whole or in part, and is only with reference to privies adopted in Edinburgh. There seems to be fear lest its adoption should endanger some civic privileges, and a new local bill now in preparation will probably be preferred. The important clause against overcrowding (sect. 443.) is not adopted, and what local law there was did not seem to give Dr Littlejohn, the medical inspector, much power.'[20]

Others were more impressed than Simon. Edward Mapother was appointed the first Medical Officer of Health for Dublin in 1864, the year when civil registration began in Ireland. In 1867, revising his *Lectures on Public Health*, he wished to demonstrate the difficulties of correlating cholera and fever, with pauperism and untrapped cesspools. Littlejohn's *Report* provided what he needed: 'The difficulty of explaining the ravages of cholera in a city, by reference to the relative number of filth depots, or of the proportion of pauperism in various districts, is shown in the following table, arranged from one by Dr. Littlejohn of Edinburgh, whose recent publication is, perhaps, the most comprehensive sanitary report ever issued in these kingdoms.'[21] This endorsement from a pioneering sanitarian in Edinburgh's rival capital is particularly interesting given the tardy introduction of civil registration in Ireland as well as the late appointment of a Medical Officer; Dublin is in many ways a more appropriate comparator than provincial cities in Britain.

Public opinion and the Edinburgh newspapers

The public conversation over the sanitary condition of Edinburgh had filled the columns of the city's newspapers for decades. Regular and full reports of proceedings in the Police Commission, the Town Council and the Parochial Boards were supplemented by trenchant editorial comment, a constant supply of correspondence, and vivid accounts of public meetings, lectures and sermons. For even to the casual reader of the press the physical and social state of the city was inescapable. It was an open debate and a disputatious middle class of avid newspaper readers with acute legal, theological and political minds constantly watched those responsible for sanitary conditions and the care of the poor. Thus the newspapers have a triple role in this story. Firstly they informed. Secondly they pushed the debate, shaming local politicians into responding, though with modest results, exposing their sectarian behaviour and the petty squabbling debates, and assessing the quality of political discourse with some

4.3 Alexander Russel (1814–76): Editor, *The Scotsman*, 1846–76
Russel was a vigorous liberal who used his editorial position to write powerfully on sanitary reform. [Source: *Cassell's Old and New Edinburgh*, vol. I, (London 1880), 285]

20 *Eighth Report of the Medical Officer of the Privy Council*, 64, both quotations.

21 E.D. Mapother, *Lectures on Public Health, delivered at the Royal College of Surgeons* (Dublin, 1867), 474. On Edward Dillon Mapother see L.M. Geary's article in the *ODNB*.

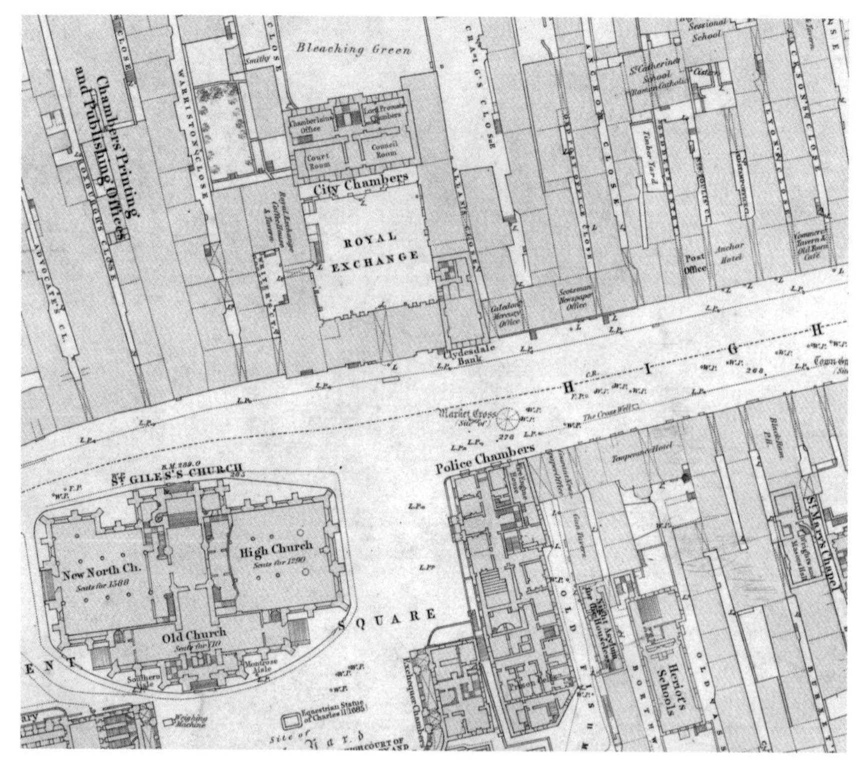

4.4 The nexus of power: town council, police and newspapers' offices
The Police Chambers and the City Chambers were opposite each other in the High Street; the *Caledonian Mercury*, *Evening Courant* and *Scotsman* offices were adjacent. William Chambers' printing and publishing business can be seen close by. [Source: NLS OS 1852]

rigour.[22] And thirdly they assembled the historical record so that the story can be told. For historians they provide what official records have in large measure failed to record: a full account of the debate and an understanding of attitudes adopted and postures taken. Three instances from may be taken as typical. The minutes of the Police Commission recording the dismissal of Dr George Glover in 1854 (see chapter 3) consist of 39 words, excluding a printed report on the case; *The Scotsman* reported the debate verbatim in 2,800 words. The minutes of the Town Council on the appointment of Littlejohn in 1862 employ 900 words, mostly to record formal motions and votes; again *The Scotsman* reported the acrimonious debate in over 5,900 words. The debate in the House of Commons in June 1862 on the Lindsay Bill was accorded 1,164 words in Hansard; 11,900 words in *The Scotsman* and a full-page supplement of about 13,000 words in the *Evening Courant*.[23] This full reporting was also a reflection of local demand for this information.

22 Sectarianism was the basis of party in the published results of Edinburgh elections. Candidates were identified as 'Non-intrusionist', 'Moderate Churchman', 'Dissenter', 'Roman Catholic'. See, for example, *The Scotsman*, 2 November 1842, 3c.

23 ECA ED9/1/12, 510–13; *The Scotsman*, 8 July 1854, 3gh; ECA Council Minutes, vol. 285, 49–55; *Evening Courant*, 26 June 1862, 5a–f; *The Scotsman*, 26 June 1862, 6–7; 29 September 1862, 2b–d.

At this crucial time in the sanitary debate the two leading papers, *The Scotsman* and the *Edinburgh Evening Courant*, had campaigning editors capable of penning or commissioning sharp, well-targeted editorial comment. It is worth noting the proximity of the leading newspaper offices to the Town Council's City Chambers and the Police Office. In the 1850s and 1860s, *The Scotsman*, *Edinburgh Evening Courant*, *Caledonian Mercury* and *Edinburgh Evening Post* were all produced within a few yards of the Chambers. Alexander Russel, as editor of the *Scotsman* from 1846 to 1876, was a liberal, popular in Edinburgh and in London, but not one enslaved to a party line. His constant attacks on Lord Provost Duncan McLaren were part of a festering quarrel with him starting with the 1847 Parliamentary election and came to a head in 1856 when McLaren sued Russel and *The Scotsman* for libel. The £400 and costs awarded against Russel were promptly paid by public subscription.[24] The *Courant* was equally keen to promote the sanitary cause. From December 1864 to 1868 it was edited by Francis Espinasse (1823–1912), an Edinburgh-born protégé of Carlyle, who had edited the *Manchester Examiner* in the 1840s and was able to see the Edinburgh political scene with the detachment of a journalist experienced in the radical politics of an industrial city.[25]

4.5 The new *Scotsman* office
The newspaper moved on 14 May 1862 to number 32 in the recently formed Cockburn Street. See also fig. 5.6.
[Source: Cassell's *Old and New Edinburgh*, vol. I, (London 1880), 284]

The *Report* in summary

A synopsis of the *Report* affords the best way to judge Littlejohn's priorities, strategy and methodology. What follows is a condensed commentary in which his statistical methods, selection and deployment of data, mode of argument, and choice of words are appraised. Littlejohn's incisive prose is crystal clear, even to the modern reader not always familiar with Victorian usage, but his choice and form of language require explanation and guidance. His forensic turn of mind and his canny political skills require explanation and guidance. One of the reasons the *Report* made such a strong impact on his readers in Edinburgh and beyond was Littlejohn's ability to go to the heart of the matter. He was strategic, politically pragmatic and never careless or flabby in presenting his case; objections were anticipated, statistics were accompanied by appropriate cautions, and the loose ends of obfuscatory prose were eliminated. A man used to tangling with lawyers in the courts – indeed with a reputation for terrifying inexperienced barristers – did not write the keystone document for the reform of mid-Victorian Edinburgh without making his case watertight.

Littlejohn's table of contents, with its long titles and elaborated sub-headings, may be taken as his summary of the *Report* and a guide to its structure. Excluding the extensive appendices, eighteen distinct sections or chapters are listed. In the text most of these sections run on without starting on a new page, and their titles,

24 C. Matthews, 'Russel, Alexander', in *ODNB* (Oxford, 2004).

25 W.J. Couper *The Edinburgh Periodical Press* (Stirling, 1908), vol. 2, 31–5. Couper describes Espinasses's tenure as 'notable' and says that among the enterprises he conducted to rescue the *Courant's* finances was 'the investigation he conducted into the state of the poor in the city' (p. 34). Asa Briggs describes him as 'a well-known Victorian journalist'; 'The Longman Family' in *ODNB*. Espinasse had been secretary to the Lancashire Public Schools Association, whose members included Thomas Carlyle and William Chambers. *The Scotsman*, 15 December 1849, 4d.

which are not always exactly as worded in the list of contents, are presented in capitals to distinguish them from sub-sections. However, the structure of the *Report* is not immediately clear. The last five sections seem intended to be a single chapter – Sanitary Requirements of the City – with four sub-sections including the Conclusion which, curiously, has a heading in smaller type than other sections. This lack of clarity must have occurred to Littlejohn himself, for in the second printing the sections in the table of contents are arranged in two parts under new headings: 'The Sanitary State of Edinburgh' and 'Sanitary Requirements of Edinburgh'. Thus Littlejohn intended the second part to be recommendations following his analysis in the first part, though the word 'recommendations' is used with important caveats (see below).

A quantitative analysis of Littlejohn's text is instructive. The eighteen sections vary considerably in length (Table 4.2), and in large measure this must reflect the author's view of their significance for his purpose; not necessarily their intrinsic importance as public health issues, but their priority in Littlejohn's strategy for convincing his readers, particularly those in a position to influence the evolution of policy and practice in these matters. His emphasis was on matters amenable to short-term action by civic authorities for long-term benefit to the health and welfare of the community as a whole. To that extent, although writing strictly as a public servant, Littlejohn presented his 'suggestions'[26] not as the sort of recommendations that might be found in an official enquiry today – in which failure to carry through the recommendations would be seen as a political decision subject to censure if the consequences turned out to be damaging – but as the offerings of an official whose authority derives from the utter clarity and cogency of his analysis and the evidence selected for that purpose. Thus there is comparatively little discussion of the details of disease, mortality and epidemics; the figures are largely left to speak for themselves. On the other hand about 17% of the *Report* is devoted to drainage and water supply, matters easily understood and capable of rapid and effective improvement through investment in public works. Strikingly long – nearly 14% of the wordage – are the sections on cow byres and diseased meat. The issue of unfit meat was topical, and Littlejohn had been involved as a witness in several cases in the courts. The *Report* was an irresistible opportunity to put his case against those professional brethren who refused to see it as a threat to public health. Again these were matters amenable to solution by relatively inexpensive regulation. In addition to several elaborate diagrams and tables, almost 10% of the text comes under the section on 'Density of the Population'. Littlejohn placed great emphasis on his ecological and topographical approach to his subject. Public health, in its widest context,

26 'It is upon these broad grounds that I respectfully venture to urge upon the Magistrates of this City the necessity of maintaining a thorough inspection at our Slaughter-houses and Markets, and of enforcing the suggestions which my visitation of the Byres of the City has led me to make.' (p.61); 'I found that the masters had anticipated the requirements of the Act, and were willing to adopt any suggestions that would tend to the comfort of their men, and to greater cleanliness in the manufacture.' (63); 'Such are the suggestions which I beg to offer for the sanitary improvement of Edinburgh.' (116); 'I believe the suggestions offered will materially tend to this result. In the present day, there are two hopeful signs that its accomplishment may be looked upon as certain.' (117). In the list of contents the word is used three times: 'Suggestions for their Improvement', 'Suggestions for proper Supervision', 'Suggestions as to Extramural Interment'.

	pages	*words*	*% words*
Report on the Sanitary Condition of Edinburgh [Introduction]	6.5	3,179	6.7
Description of Sanitary Districts	12.5	2,776	5.9
District Mortality from Disease [Mortality of the Sanitary Districts]	5.5	1,048	2.2
Epidemics [History of the Sanitary Districts]	2.0	581	1.2
Density of the Population	17.5	4,561	9.7
Trades and Occupations, and their Influence upon Health	4.5	1,777	3.8
Sanitary Condition of the Byres	6.5	3,365	7.1
Sale of Diseased Meat	5.5	3,046	6.5
Sanitary Condition of the Bakehouses	5.0	2,280	4.8
Amount of Population Engaged in Trades and Occupations, and the Mortality in 1863	4.5	775	1.6
Public Institutions	4.0	1,733	3.7
Drainage and Water Supply	17.0	7,869	16.7
Intramural Interment	7.0	3,252	6.9
Sanitary Requirements of the City	1.5	383	0.8
The New Town	6.5	3,616	7.7
The Old Town	8.0	3,902	8.3
Southern Suburbs	1.0	477	1.0
Conclusion	5.0	2,539	5.4
Total	120	47,159	100.0

Table 4.2 The organisation of Littlejohn's *Report*
The titles in brackets are from the table of contents where they differ significantly from the main text. The length of each 'chapter' given in pages (to the nearest half page) includes diagrams and tables. The length in words excludes tables and headings. This analysis is based on the second printing.

is presented holistically and through a close geographical and environmental analysis of local distributions. In short, what may appear to the modern reader an unconventional choice and balance of topics was carefully designed to have the maximum practical effect. Henry Littlejohn did not indulge in empty rhetoric. He used forensic language for a practical purpose and a wider strategy.

This approach differed from that of Chadwick, Simon, Duncan, and other leading English sanitarians. Littlejohn's priorities were strategic and pragmatic. He was also alert, in an Alisonian way, to a holistic view of poverty and aware that strict regulation and technical solutions were inadequate. Above all he knew he must not be George Glover; he should stick to his terms of reference and avoid preaching, a hard thing to do in Edinburgh. He identified over and again with his fellow citizens – a telling phrase – in what is possible rather than ideal.[27] This was a man with very well-tuned political and social antennae. The early 1860s might be seen as being at the cusp of the emergence of the expert.

27 The word 'citizens' appears nine times in the *Report*, three times with a possessive pronoun: 'our citizens', 'our philanthropic citizens' and 'my fellow-citizens'.

Littlejohn could still engage over issues that would later be regarded as outside his area of authority. He had first-hand knowledge of a wide range of specialist areas; there was more than a little justification for his appearance as omniscient.

Littlejohn's spatial framework

The mortality data available from 1855 through civil registration of deaths were useful but limited in their published form. To monitor the pattern and progress of disease a Medical Officer required constant access to the civil register itself so that the information could be presented in a manner of his choosing. So Littlejohn's first task was to gain access to civil registers; it was one of the original stipulations in the job description that the Medical Officer of Health should receive monthly returns from the registrars.[28] The district registrars returned copies of the registers to Dr James Stark, statistical superintendent at the General Register Office, but were *employed* by the Town Council. To extract the information Littlejohn needed it had to be forwarded weekly to the Police Office, for which service the registrars demanded additional payment.[29] It was an administrative barrier to progress towards the acquisition of accurate mortality data, but it was not as Duncan had found in Liverpool in 1847. In practice the medical officer could either to pay a clerk to visit the registrars weekly and make copies of entries in the registers, or have the Town Council instruct the registrars to supply copies, with or without payment. The obstacle in Liverpool had been the demand for payment, excessive in some cases, for supplying copies to the Medical Officer of Health, Dr Duncan.[30] Littlejohn proceeded patiently and correctly through the Lord Provost; his problem was to get the council to act on his repeated requests for access to the returns. His letter was read to the

28 The Lord Provost's Committee recommended to council in May 1862 [Council Minutes, vol. 284 p. 224, 20 May 1862] that the first duty of the Medical Officer 'shall be to arrange with the proper authorities for the classification into convenient localities within reach of the Registrars' Districts and the diseases causing mortality therein, and for monthly returns thereof by the Registrar; to receive and digest and report the same or the results from time to time.' See *Caledonian Mercury*, 22 August 1862, 2f. The confused and obscure language suggests that the Lord Provost's Committee had no clue what this might mean in practice.

29 The post of Registrar was often taken as a lucrative additional source of employment for professional men. There were frequent complaints in the newspapers that they (and indeed the staff of the Registrar-General's department as a whole) held sinecures, that they were not always available for working people to register births and deaths, and medical men who filled out and returned death certificates were not paid at all. These eventually pushed the Town Council to investigate the matter formally: Report of sub-committee of the Lord Provost's Committee on application of registrars for increase of salary, 29 August 1864, ECA SL1/1/288/118.

30 W.H. Duncan took up his post as Britain's first Medical Officer of Health on 1 January 1847 and was soon faced with the task of monitoring what would be the worst urban mortality crisis since the seventeenth century, yet he had a ten-month battle with the ten registrars who covered the borough of Liverpool. The registrars demanded £25 a year for providing weekly returns. The issue was finally settled with the help of the Registrar-General and several legal opinions in late October 1847. The registrars accepted £13. The following year their notorious ring leader, Charles Chubb, who had originally demanded a shilling per entry from the Health Committee (about £100 *per annum* in 1847), was convicted and jailed for making false entries. Liverpool Record Office, Health Committee Minutes, vol. 1, 239, 294, 307–8, 316, 349, 374, 412–13 and 423. *Liverpool Mercury*, 11 June 1847, 8cd and 19 December 1848, 5b–d.

council on 13 January 1863 and remitted to the Lord Provost's Committee 'with power to advise and direct Dr. Littlejohn as to the various matters connected with his department that may from time to time require consideration'.[31] The committee then sat on the matter. It was on their agenda for four meetings between 14 January and 11 February 1863, but the record of their decision is blank in three cases; in the other the clerk wrote 'Delay'. Littlejohn's letter (or did he write more than once?) was again considered on 19 May at a 15-minute meeting before a full council. At last there was a decision: 'Remit to Clerk to arrange with Registrars for Returns on payment of £5 each.'[32] The matter was not raised at the council meeting.

Another barrier was that the five registration districts were ill-designed for Littlejohn's purpose: they were too large and they cut across well-established social districts. Nineteen new sanitary districts were drawn up, designed to reflect the social geography of the city that was recognisable by the inhabitants (see fig. 4.6). As far as possible, each was socially and geographically distinctive. Most are still used to describe Edinburgh today. It is not surprising that they remained unchanged until 1882, when the municipal boundary was extended.[33] They were specifically designed to convey the broad pattern of the sanitary geography to councillors and opinion makers, not for day-to-day administrative purposes.

Comparison with Glasgow raises important questions about the administrative significance of districting as a component of public health management. Less than three months after the publication of the *Report*, W.T. Gairdner, as Professor of Medicine at the University of Glasgow and Medical Officer for that city, described the system of 54 sanitary districts in Glasgow in the following terms:

> The principle of the sub-division is not very dissimilar from that which has been applied by Dr. Littlejohn in the City of Edinburgh, and which is so ably expounded and turned to account in his late admirable Sanitary Report. There is, however, one difference between Dr. Littlejohn's plan and mine, viz., – that he has evidently not made it an object to preserve any approach to a relation between the districts as regards population; whereas I have aimed, among other objects, at having the whole of the districts requiring special Sanitary superintendence so divided, that in seasons of emergency they may be placed under the charge of individual Medical Officers, district inspectors, &c., with some degree of convenience and consistency, as parts of a system.[34]

The Glasgow districts were first planned by Gairdner in January 1864 and were made up of blocks of enumeration districts in the 1861 census. They did

31 ECA Council Minutes, vol. 285, 370, 13 January 1863.

32 ECA SL25/1/1, Scroll Minutes of Lord Provost's Committee: 14 and 21 January; 4 and 11 February, and 19 May 1863.

33 In August 1869 a commission appointed under the Municipal Elections Amendment (Scotland) Act, 1868, published a plan and written description of proposed alterations to the boundaries of the 13 municipal wards of Edinburgh. The number of wards was to remain the same, as were their names, although the boundaries of St Andrew's and St George's wards were altered. See *The Scotsman*, 31 July 1869, 7a and 11 September 1869, 1bc.

34 *Memorandum from the Chairman of the Sanitary Committee, to Accompany a Map of the Sanitary Districts of Glasgow. By the Medical Officer of Health. November, 1865* (Glasgow, 1865), 3.

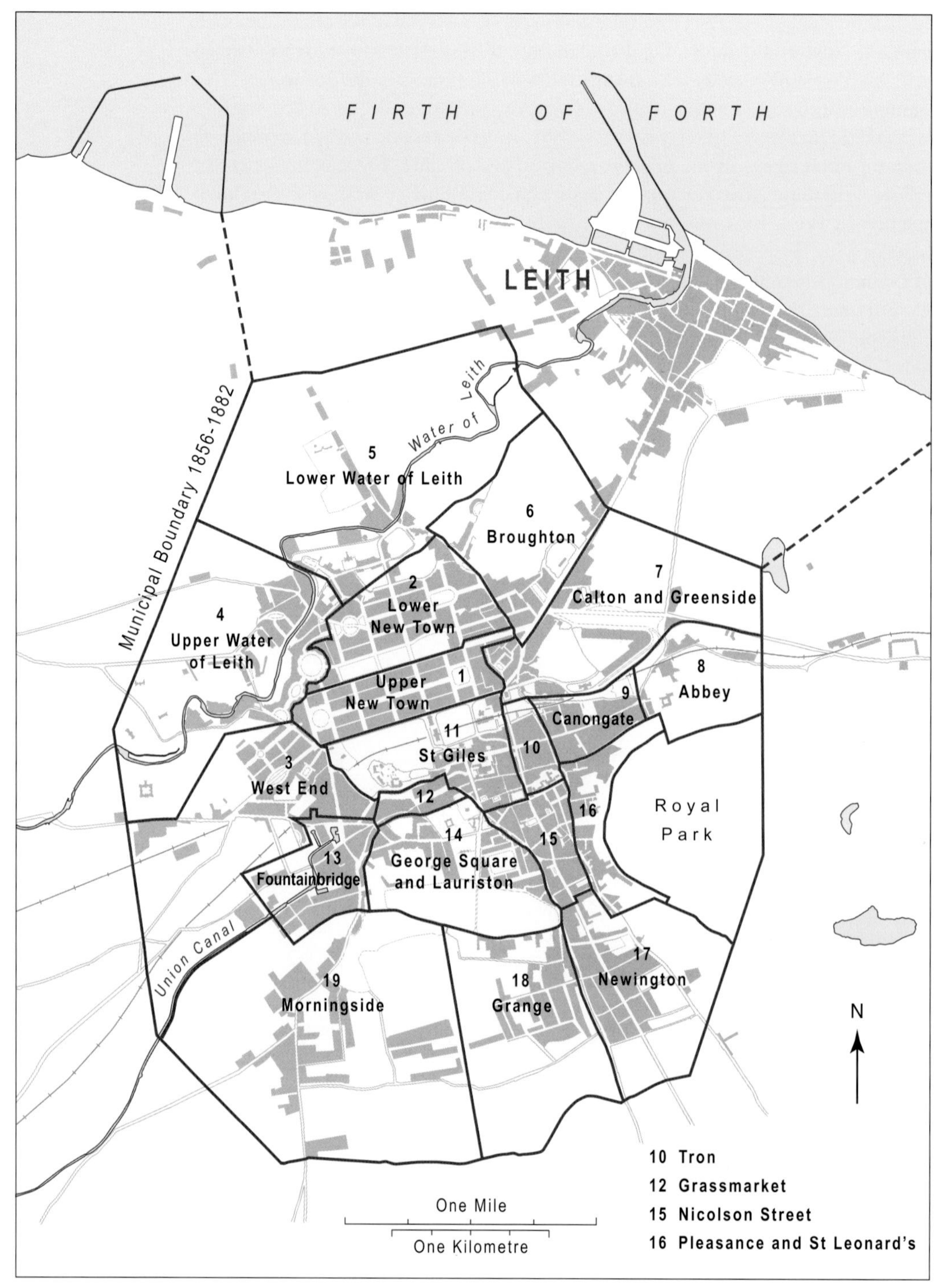

4.6 The New Sanitary Map of Edinburgh, *c.*1865

In 1863 or 1864 Dr Littlejohn created 19 sanitary districts. They provided an improved basis for understanding the mortality and morbidity of the city, and accorded closely with contemporary understanding of the social topography of Edinburgh.
[Source: from the *Report*]

not survive long; Gairdner revised them in 1871, creating 24 districts on much the same lines as Littlejohn's in Edinburgh.[35] It was a way of deploying district medical inspectors to best advantage and also for monitoring the progress of epidemics in detail. Gairdner was not only Littlejohn's supporter for his post in Edinburgh and, briefly, his teacher, but in his *Public Health in Relation to Air and Water* demonstrated the same insistence on, and appropriate statistical and geographical basis for, monitoring public health. The dual problems were to design a way of districting the city which matched as closely as possible its social geography rather than obscuring it, and at the same time to deploy data from the decennial census in order to estimate the population at risk and to calculate mortality rates. There appears to have been no attempt by the Registrar-General for Scotland to construct registration districts with such local needs in mind. As Gairdner put it in 1871, in terms Littlejohn might well have used, 'I had long ago remarked, that the ten Registration Districts formed a subdivision geographically compact enough, but for sanitary inquiries utterly useless, and even misleading, inasmuch as almost every one of these Registration Districts comprises a population not less varied in character than that of the city itself.'[36] It was also necessary to collect and organise vital data, especially about mortality, and, where appropriate and feasible, morbidity. That way, 'hot spots' of disease could be identified and presented consistently over several years in a way that the public could understand. Reasonably large sanitary districts removed the danger of statistical noise. Glasgow was two and a half times the size of Edinburgh, so in 1871 its sanitary districts housed, on average, 20,435 persons compared with 10,333 in Edinburgh.[37] On statistical grounds and for practical sanitary and epidemiological purposes it was important to establish sufficiently large sanitary districts.

At the start of the *Report* Littlejohn described – in his case one should say systematically dissected – the geography of the city. This emphasised his insistence on ecology and topography as the first approach to understanding the social condition of the city and things that he could do very little about – the given structure, as it were. It was not only the rationale for his re-districting of the city but also the lecturer's way of ensuring that his readers would see the rest of the *Report* in relation to familiar streets and neighbourhoods. This was also Littlejohn as a structuralist – a classifier in a relatively new classificatory climate. The basic demographic data, with much emphasis on density, are presented first, district-by-district, and with less discussion of disease than one might expect.

The most extraordinary view of Littlejohn's social area analysis of Edinburgh is provided in Table IV of the appendix to the *Report*. Here he presented, in effect, a spreadsheet with 35 columns of data and 1,062 rows, in which the rows represent streets, parts of streets, closes, wynds, courts and institutions. Of the

35 Glasgow City Archives LP1/13: Sanitary Department, Glasgow, *Annual Report on the Health of the City, for the year 1871. By W.T. Gairdner, M.D., Medical Officer; and on the Operations of the Sanitary Department, for the Year ending 30th April, 1872*. By Kenneth M. MacLeod, *Sanitary Inspector* (Glasgow, 1872), 15–30.

36 Sanitary Department, Glasgow, *Annual Report, 1871*, 16.

37 The 24 Glasgow sanitary districts remained unchanged from 1871 to 1903. See O. Checkland and M. Lamb (eds), *Health Care as Social History: the Glasgow Case* (Aberdeen, 1982) 8.

36,108 cells, only 10,433 (28.1%) contain data and of these 3,185 contain a single '1'. But they are so arranged geographically within the sanitary districts as to allow concentrations of disease to be seen at a glance, at any scale, simply by amalgamating selected rows. The best clue as to when Littlejohn completed this huge tabulation – March 1864 – comes from the record of payment to the clerk who wrote it out for the printer.[38]

Placing the city under the microscope in this way left Littlejohn exposed to the imperfections of his data. At all levels he was dependent on census enumerations whose undoubted inaccuracies would have been greater in some districts than others, as well as being out of date for the purposes of his birth and death rates. While questions about the completeness of registration data and the accuracy of death certification still remain, few would have been more aware of these issues than Littlejohn.

Byres, butchers and bakehouses

Littlejohn's pages on food production occupy 18.4% of the entire *Report*, and 26.3% of the analytical and descriptive sections. This requires some explanation. Bakehouses had recently been concerning the government as a significant public health problem requiring regulation. Littlejohn's father and grandfather had been bakers and confectioners in Canongate and Leith Street and indeed the business continued into the late 1960s. So he also wrote from personal experience. As for the cow byres, they had long been a source of complaints about the nuisance they caused, but were accepted as a necessary inconvenience for the supply of fresh milk they provided. Ordinarily a short section on regulating their cleanliness might have sufficed but in the early 1860s the topic of cattle and meat had become a major cause of public concern in Edinburgh, in particular about the contested connection between the presentation of diseased animals for slaughter and the sale of their meat in local shops and markets.[39] In 1857, in the same year that he founded the New Veterinary College in Drummond Street, John Gamgee, the controversial but highly talented veterinary surgeon, began to expose the extent of disease in the byres. He was fiercely opposed by the founder of the Edinburgh Veterinary College (1823), the reactionary Professor William Dick, who was also a member of the Town Council and accustomed to his position as the accepted authority on veterinary matters. The dispute divided opinion in the city and caused factious squabbling in the Town Council since it employed the market inspectors as well as owning the slaughter-houses at Fountainbridge, the only abattoir permitted in the city under the Edinburgh Slaughter-houses Act, 1850. The dispute also found the veterinary and medical profession taking opposite sides in the debate as well as in several prominent prosecutions of butchers for the sale of bad meat – meat 'of an unsound or unwholesome Description, or in a

38 'Paid Alexander Harris for writing Return by Medical Officer of Health of Population and Mortality of the City, 80 pages, large size; March 1864.' Harris was paid £4 on 23 June 1865. ECA Edinburgh Police Accounts, Whitsunday 1864 to Whitsunday 1865, 130.

39 This is explored in P. Laxton, 'This nefarious traffic: livestock and public health in mid-Victorian Edinburgh', in P.J. Atkins (ed.), *Animal Cities: Beastly Urban Histories* (Farnham, 2012), 107–71.

4.7 The Edinburgh slaughterhouses, 1910
The municipal abattoir, opened in 1853 to replace all private slaughterhouses, was replaced in 1910 by a new facility at Slateford. Beyond the fortress-like gates the gable of Chalmers Buildings (1855) is just visible. Tollcross Primary School now occupies the yard. Photographer James Henderson. [Source: ECL]

State unfit or unsuitable for Human Food', as the Police Act, 1848, section 115, put it. All this lies behind Littlejohn's comment in December 1864, when he first presented his findings about the byres to the Town Council, 'that the management of our dairies [is] at present exciting a great deal of public attention'.[40] So he, too, was bound to give it full attention.

The report on the byres, including its elaborate appendices, was printed and presented to the council in November 1864 and was incorporated in the final *Report* unchanged except for a few minor editorial amendments. Thus the second paragraph of the original text began 'During the past summer I have inspected 171 byres'. The reference to the summer when Littlejohn did his fieldwork had to be removed before publication of the *Report* in the autumn of 1865.

Fieldwork and painstaking personal investigation were the foundation of almost everything Littlejohn wrote. The size of the task he set himself in inspecting the byres can be judged thus: in 1900 Liverpool had two inspectors of cowsheds and milkshops covering the 437 cowsheds in the city which housed about 5,900 beasts. In that year they made 4,415 inspections of cowsheds, or about 10 visits a year for each cowshed. Thus, a full-time inspector made about 550 visits over three months.[41] Henry Littlejohn, as just part of one of his several jobs, inspected 171 byres in about the same time, but his visits are unlikely to

40 *Caledonian Mercury*, 22 December 1864, 2g.

41 E.W. Hope, *Report on the Health of the City of Liverpool during 1900* (Liverpool, 1901), 51 and 113. Cows per byre in Edinburgh 1864, 12.2 per shed; in Liverpool 1900, 13.5 per shed.

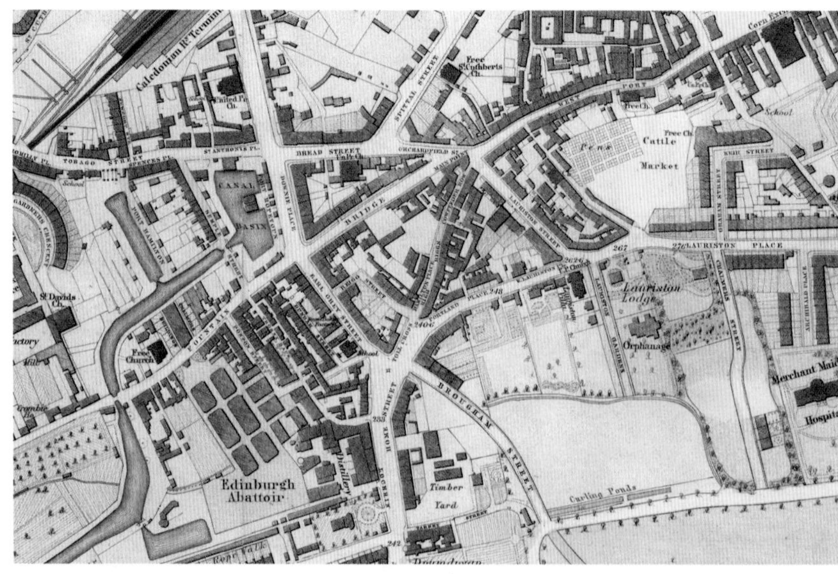

4.8 Meatland
The cattle and meat trades of mid-Victorian Edinburgh were concentrated in a district between the Grassmarket and the Union Canal, with the cattle market in the congested area of the West Port and the municipal slaughterhouse in Fountainbridge. [Source: NLS Lancefield 1861]

have been as perfunctory as those of the Liverpool men. These were structured interviews with standard questions – a very modern form of investigation – but there would doubtless have been conversations.

The section on the sale of diseased meat was written later than that on byres and in a distinctly harder tone. It was a reflection on Littlejohn's experience as the leading prosecution witness in several trials of butchers in the Police Court, where he and Gamgee had clashed with the witnesses for the defence, notably Dr Alexander Wood and William Dick. That experience explains not only his tough judgment on 'a well-known class of Butchers' who had committed 'the most open fraud', but also the words 'What could my client do?' – a sarcastic reference to the defence counsel's attempt to excuse the sale of meat from a diseased cow.[42] Littlejohn was writing with passion after frustrating days in court listening to what he knew to be self-serving and often duplicitous testimony. He had taken on the powerful interests in the meat and cattle trade and did not afford them the sympathy he clearly showed to many of the dairymen. When, in November 1864, Littlejohn published his *Report on the Condition of the Byres* it was approved unanimously by the Town Council.[43] As a concise outline of the problem with clear recommendations it was a masterpiece. Littlejohn left the council in no

42 *Report*, 57.

43 A sole surviving copy has recently come to light in Edinburgh City Archives, SL12/287 (2), and we are grateful to the City Archivist, Richard Hunter, for bringing this to our attention. It was reproduced (without the Appendices) in *The Scotsman*, 30 November 1864, 7ab, summarised in the *Evening Courant*, 30 November 1864 2c, and just under half of it was reproduced in the *Caledonian Mercury*, 1 December 1864 4d. In the final 1865 *Report* Appendix VI is a simple table with the number of cows in the city in 1857 and 1864; in the original 1864 Report it contained an extract from a

4.9 William Dick (1793–1866)
Founder of the Edinburgh Veterinary School in 1823 (later the Royal Dick Veterinary School). Dick was a longstanding police commissioner and town councillor and a voluble conservative voice. John Dunn, artist.
[Source: The University of Edinburgh Fine Art Collection]

4.10 John Gamgee (1831–94)
Founder of the New Veterinary College in Drummond Street (1857). An exponent of systematic scientific approaches to veterinary medicine, Gamgee inevitably clashed with the reactionary William Dick. [Source: courtesy of the Ramsay Head Press]

doubt that public agitation was amply justified.[44] It was indeed. On Christmas Eve 1864 a pantomime in the Princess' Theatre amused the audience with topical local references: 'The diseased meat question is particularly referred to,' observed a critic, 'and the best is made of the same subject in the harlequinade.'[45] Diseased meat had become a *cause célèbre*.

One of Littlejohn's strengths was his understanding of the tradesman's view and of the economic consequences of sanitary improvement.[46] As the appendix to the *Report* shows, only 5% of the city's milk supply arrived by railway. So

speech by Councillor Ford, taken from *The Scotsman*, 6 May 1857, 3d, describing and enumerating the dairies in the city.

44 *Evening Courant*, 30 November 1864, 2c; *The Scotsman*, 21 December 1864, 7a. With some justification Councillor Ford noted characteristically that he had reported on the state of the byres seven years previously but that nothing had been done.

45 *Caledonian Mercury*, 26 December 1864, 2e. The detailed review in *The Scotsman*, 26 December 1864, 3a merely refers to 'some happily conceived local allusions' to the meat question.

46 Littlejohn's section in his *Report* which dealt with the mutual benefits of public abattoirs to the public and butchers was subsequently quoted directly in the *Brisbane Courier*, 1 October 1895, 3g.

his report thus begins by balancing the contribution of the dairymen to the local economy against the welfare of the community:

> While care should be taken not to hamper with teasing restrictions a branch of industry which contributes so much to the general comfort, it should never be forgotten that the importance of the traffic, as shown by the amount of capital invested in it, is due to the patronage of the inhabitants, who have a right to demand that the milk they pay for should be clean and of good quality, and at the same time that the cows should not be so kept as to prove a source of public nuisance.[47]

As the appendix to the *Report* shows, dairy cattle were to be found in most parts of the city (Figure 4.11), with concentrations around Fountainbridge near the slaughter-houses and on the northern fringe of the New Town. Mostly they were not purpose-built milking parlours; many were ill-adapted stables rented from neglectful landlords. 'In such places, properly enough constructed to accommodate a few horses, half of whose life is spent in the open air, we usually find double the number of cows doomed to spend their entire existence. I have often remarked how much better the horse is tended than the cow, which is the more delicate and sensitive animal.'[48] This state of affairs, said Littlejohn, would continue 'so long as the trade in question is in the hands of persons possessing little means, and who cannot afford to pay a rent for proper premises'. The trade needed capital invested in purpose-built premises. Nevertheless, he described in unflinching terms the foul nuisance that the byres were to the public and, more significantly, the danger they were to the cattle and thus the interests of the cowkeepers themselves. Many dairymen were unwilling to accept that disease among their stock had anything to do with their husbandry or the state of their premises. Littlejohn was also concerned about the poor quality of milk due to the poor feeding and housing of cows.

While Littlejohn tempered his strictures towards the dairymen with some sympathy he had no time for the dishonest men who brought animals to the dead meat market. Needing hard data on mortality in the dairies he turned to the Slaughter-house books, which he found defective because they did not say from where beasts had come. Dairymen kept quiet about the matter, so a 'system of secrecy is thus established, and the only clue to be obtained as to the healthiness or otherwise of our Dairies, is to be found in the number of diseased animals brought to the Slaughterhouses by certain butchers. But dead meat can be brought into the city from all quarters, and at all hours.'[49] In other words, Littlejohn had already learned from his extensive contacts in the trade the truth of the widespread claims that a significant amount of meat from diseased animals was on sale in the city and that it reached the markets by subterfuge. The precise way this happened is described in the section of the *Report* on diseased meat.

47 *Report*, 50.

48 *Report*, 51.

49 As John Gamgee put it, 'If an outbreak of human cholera or smallpox occurs, we set to work and drain, ventilate, and vaccinate; but as cattle proprietors wish to preserve secrecy ... nothing is done.' 'The Scope and Objects of the Veterinary Profession ... Introductory Lecture delivered in the New Veterinary College', *Edinburgh Veterinary Review and Annals of Comparative Pathology* 6 (1864), 709.

Littlejohn set out seven clear recommendations about the byres for the council to consider: byres should be registered with an assigned capacity as, he might have added, lodging-houses had been a decade earlier; they should be inspected and keepers obliged to observe remedies ordered; they should be supplied with adequate water; manure should be removed weekly 'as in Paris'; disease among stock should be notified; the history of every dead cow brought to slaughter should be recorded, and the dressing of the carcase viewed by an inspector; and that no meat should be sold in the city unless inspected at the slaughter-houses.[50]

Most of all, Littlejohn expressed his views that cow-keeping should be banned from the whole of the central parts of the city, and that those on the periphery required regulating.[51] Again he drew on experience and admiration for long-established methods of environmental management in Paris: 'No doubt an outcry would be raised by the Dairymen that an attempt is being made to ruin them, were regulations introduced here similar to those which have been in force for nearly 20 years in Paris.' As the son and grandson of Edinburgh bakers he could write with feeling that the 'Bakers ... have been lately placed under stringent regulations as to the cleanliness and ventilation of their work-shops, and it cannot be expected that the Dairy trade ... can much longer be exempted from the operation of the law of progress.'[52]

The diseased meat question continued to exercise Edinburgh through 1865–66, when the nationwide epidemic of rinderpest or cattle plague devastated the city's byres. Butchers continued to be prosecuted, and debates over the nature and size of the risk of diseased meat to the public were reignited several times during the ensuing forty years, most notably during the late 1880s and the mid-1890s, when the links between tuberculosis in the human population and TB in cattle were investigated. Littlejohn was a witness for the Departmental Committee on Pleuro-Pneumonia and Tuberculosis, 1888, an expert witness in the 1889 Glasgow prosecution, and a witness for the Royal Commission into the Effect of Food Derived from Tuberculous Animals on Human Health, 1896.[53] While his extensive evidence to these inquests reveals a man embracing the advancing bacteriological science in a flexible and pragmatic way, it also shows a realistic public officer fully aware that, without constant vigilance, cattle dealers, cowfeeders and fleshers would tend always to put private profit before the public good. The politicians, parliamentary enquiries and the interest of the newspapers in the cattle trade and the diseased meat question waxed and waned, but for the medical officers and their inspectors there was a constant struggle to regulate

50 *Report*, 55–6. Littlejohn was to be a notable advocate of compulsory notification by the medical profession.

51 At a meeting convened by the Lord Provost to discuss his improvement scheme, the influential Free Church minister Dr James Begg stated that 2,000 cows were kept within the burgh, occupying land which should have been available for people and polluting the atmosphere. He advocated powers 'to prevent cows being kept within the town at all'. *The Scotsman*, 10 March 1866, 7b.

52 *Report*, 55.

53 PP (HC) 1888 XXXII [C. 5461–I] 536–42, Q.7599–7751; *Public Health* 2, 1889–90, 78 and *The Glasgow Herald* 29 May 1889, 9i–10a; PP (HC) XLVI, [7992] 88–98. In Glasgow in May 1889, and as so frequently over more than 30 years, Littlejohn was cross-examined for the defence by John Comrie Thomson.

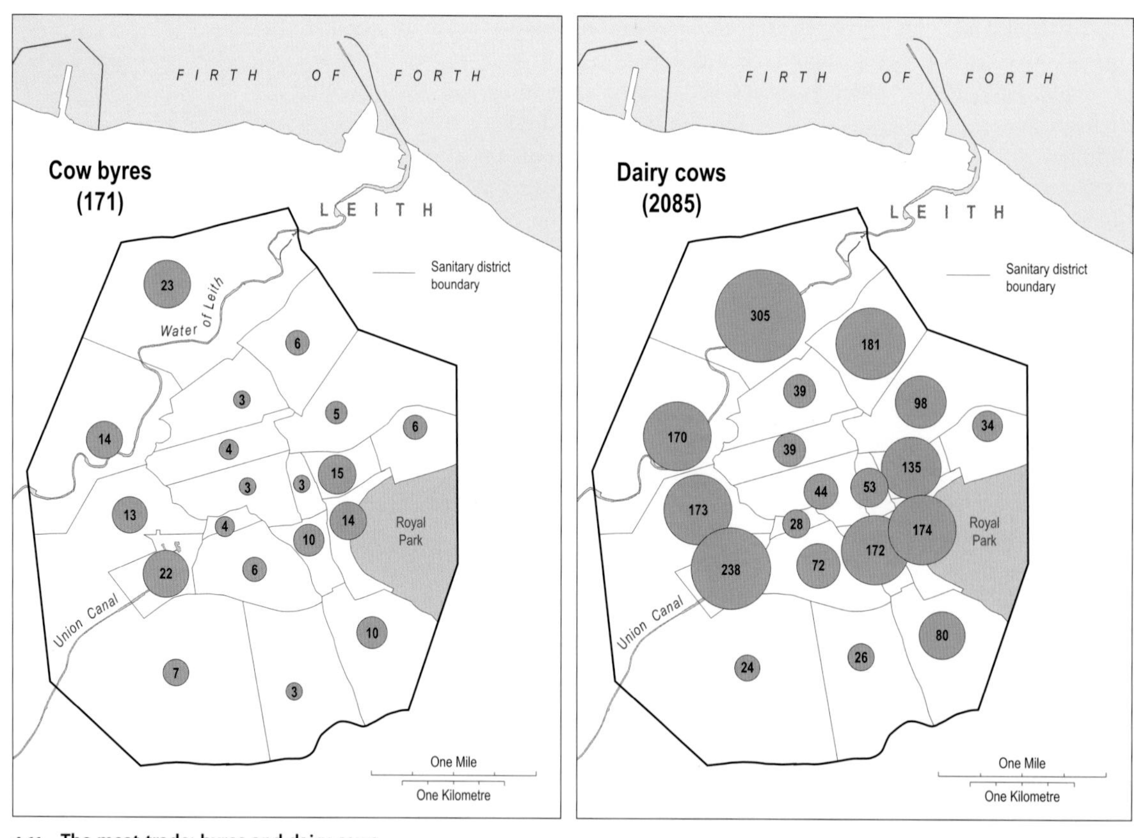

4.11 The meat trade: byres and dairy cows
In the summer of 1864 Littlejohn visited all the dairies in the city and reported their condition to the Town Council in November 1864. [Source: *The Report*, Appendix]

the trade. The fundamental questions about food supply and public health are nearly all to be found distilled in Henry Littlejohn's *Report*.

The discussion in the *Report* of bakehouses begins with the law, the only basis for the Medical Officer of Health to interfere in the trade. The Bakehouse Regulation Act, 1863, had only nine clauses and defined a bakehouse as any place making bread, biscuits or confectionery for profit (section 2). It stipulated that: no person under 18 shall be employed in a bakehouse between 9 p.m. and 5 a.m. (section 3); that all interior walls and ceilings should be painted, varnished or limewashed at least every seven years, and washed in hot water with soap at least every six months; that there should be adequate ventilation and freedom from effluvia (section 4); that there should be no sleeping in bakehouses (section 5); that local authorities were to enforce the Act in places of 5,000 inhabitants or more, instructing Medical Officers or inspectors of nuisances to police its sanitary provisions (section 6).[54] So the first part of Littlejohn's discussion reproduced sections 4 and 5 of the Act which he had had printed for circulation among the

54 26 and 27 Vict., cap. 40, 13 July 1863. Sections 1 and 7–9 dealt with the title and enforcement matters.

trade.[55] He added a warning of his own: that 'your premises will be officially inspected, from time to time'.

As a baker's son Littlejohn saw the importance of this matter and applied his usual energy to its regulation. But again the council showed little interest in taking an initiative. In May 1863, as the Bakehouses Regulations Bill was before a committee in Parliament, the clerk to the Lord Provost's Committee minuted its view in these terms: 'The provisions of this Bill dont [*sic*] apply to circumstances of Edinburgh – not necessary therefore to take any action.' The following January they were obliged to 'instruct the Medical Officer to issue such circular as he thinks necessary calling the attention of the Bakers to the provisions of the Act relative to cleanliness & ventilation'.[56] The instruction was at the prompting of the Medical Officer himself, who used his observation of a bakery causing a nuisance as an opportunity to suggest that the council enforce the Bakehouses Act and allow him to circulate its provisions.[57]

The Bakehouse Regulation Act was the government's response to reports in 1862 and 1863 from Seymour Tremenheere on working conditions and health hazards in bakehouses. These addressed a growing concern that bakehouses were a threat to health and welfare. In a report to the Home Secretary, examining the operation of the Act, Tremenheere published local inspection reports returned by Scottish towns in 1865. That for Edinburgh was submitted by Dr Littlejohn in December.

> In the small bakehouses much dust, much want of ventilation, and sulpherous emanations from the oven injurious to men. 'Important that dough should not be exposed to emanations either from persons sleeping in workshop, or from defective drainage.' ... Masters had, in most cases, anticipated the requirements of the Act, and willing to adopt any suggestions that tend to the comfort of their men or to greater cleanliness in the manufacture.[58]

Twenty Scottish towns received Tremenheere's questionnaire but only eleven replied. Of these, Edinburgh, Glasgow and Kilmarnock were the only ones to offer comments in their returns. Littlejohn gave the number of bakehouses as 200, of which 14.5% were found to be dirty, 18.0% with imperfect ventilation and 39.5% with privies in the workshop. Many had defective drains. Under 'Result of Inspection', Littlejohn stated, 'The utmost cleanliness insisted upon'. Compared with Littlejohn's expert and informative answers, returns for other towns were either opaque or plainly misleading. The town clerk of Leith, while admitting that the last inspection had been eleven years before, stated 'Bakehouses examined by inspector, and no cause found for making formal report'. The town clerk of

55 The circular was printed on 4 February 1864: ECA Police Accounts, Whitsunday 1864 to Whitsunday 1865, p. 38.

56 ECA SL25/1/1, Scroll Minutes of Lord Provost's Committee, 11 May 1863; ECA SL25/1/2, Scroll minutes of Lord Provost's Committee, 6 January 1864.

57 *Caledonian Mercury*, 12 January 1864, 3b. He may have approached the council earlier on this matter: on 15 December 1863 the Town Council letters from the Operative Bakers' Society drawing attention to the Bakehouses Act and from the Medical Officer (by implication on the same subject) were referred to the Lord Provost's Committee; *Evening Courant*, 16 December 1863, 5d–f.

58 PP (HC) 1866 LXVI (394) 373. The relevant appendix is on page 20. The Return is a paraphrase of Littlejohn's answer, but a passage in quotation marks is verbatim.

Falkirk, claiming that the last inspection was 23 April 1866, simply wrote 'No contraventions of the Act'.

How successful Littlejohn was in monitoring the state of the bakehouses is an open question. Once the Health Committee was established in 1873, with considerable independence, an inspector could be appointed: 'On the recommendation of the Public Health Committee, the Council appointed four inspectors under Dr Littlejohn, and the inspectors of markets, to be inspector of nuisances under the Public Health Act, under the Doctor's direction, for the execution of the Public Health Act, the Bakehouses Acts, and the Adulteration of Food and Drink Act.'[59] There is little sign that in the years following 1863 bakers were pursued in the courts like the butchers, though Littlejohn himself referred a case through the Lord Provost to the Procurator-Fiscal in April 1864; it may have been a test case, a warning to others.[60] Indeed five years later the editor of the *Scotsman* published a strong attack on the Town Council for its failure to regulate the bakehouses. Noting that the 1863 Act was 'framed in the spirit of the Factory Acts' and that its powers were 'intrusted to the local authorities', he posed pointed questions:

> And in what manner have they fulfilled their task? Have they freely but fairly mulcted every slovenly and avaricious baker whose premises are unwashed, and whose men toil in a pestilential atmosphere? Have the £1, £2, £5, £10, £20 fines been so frequent and effectual that these evils have been put down, and are historical? How stands it in other cities we do not know, but there is reason to doubt whether here, in Edinburgh, the 'Bakehouse Regulations Act,' with all its philanthropic and penal machinery, has accomplished much good, and whether the Act is more than a dead letter, so many benevolent words – neither a terror to the wicked, nor a comfort to the suffering.[61]

The silence from the Edinburgh Council following this embarrassing assault seems to endorse the *Scotsman*'s view and was doubtless uncomfortable reading for Dr Littlejohn who had in his *Report* demonstrated a comprehensive understanding of the trade and again used his knowledge of Paris to demonstrate the environmental aspects of bakehouses. On the whole he had found bakehouses clean and their workers healthy. Three-quarters of them were under dwellings whose tenants were, he noted, kept warm and dry.

59 *The Scotsman*, 15 August 1873, 3e.

60 SL25/1/2, Scroll Minutes of Lord Provost's Committee, 1 April 1864 (item 14) and 27 April 1864 (item 11). We have found no record of the case coming to trial.

61 *The Scotsman*, 29 January 1869, 2bc. The leading article was a response to a survey of bakery workers in 1868. There were well over a thousand bakers in Edinburgh and Leith; the writer doubted that the journeymen answering the survey were a random sample. They may even have been exaggerating. 'Out of one hundred and thirty-three working or "operative" bakers … of Edinburgh and Leith who were asked whether they considered the Act beneficial, one hundred and three answered that it was not so; and many of them stated that there was required a Government inspector to see to the faithful observance of its provisions. … Being asked when the bakehouses in which they worked were last inspected, these men answered with surprising unanimity, "Never to my knowledge," "Never," or "Not in my time." So many, too, replied "Three years ago," that it is a probable inference that the local authorities, full of zeal of novelty, then made a spasmodic effort to do their duty.'

The meat and milk trades, water supply, sewerage and burial of the dead, all posed risks to the health and welfare of the population at large. Doubtless to some degree this applied to the manufacture of bread and biscuits, but the chief concern here is for the health of the workers – the sanitary condition of the workplace, the heavy loads they sometimes had to carry, and the air they breathed. He was right to describe the Bakehouses Act as 'framed in the spirit of the Factory Acts'.

Occupational health in context

The detailed attention to byres and bakehouses is incorporated in a wider discussion of the relationship between the Edinburgh economy and public health. This section of the Report starts with the 'Trades and occupations, and their influence upon health' (p. 45) and finishes with an analysis entitled 'Amount of population engaged in trades and occupations, and the mortality in 1863' containing an elaborate table of occupational groups by age and cause of death (pp. 69–71). This is an intriguing approach by Littlejohn. A modern analysis would concentrate on social, and particularly ethnic issues, such as Irish and Highland immigrants who were disproportionately represented among the poorest casual labourers but about which he says almost nothing. Many early Victorian health reports did indeed chart squalor and epidemic disease in relation to immigrants, notably poor Irish. But not Littlejohn, despite the presence of some 8,000–10,000 Irish in the city heavily concentrated in the poorer parts of the Old Town.[62]

What Littlejohn does do is to distinguish Edinburgh from other cities such as Leith and Glasgow, and by implication, places beyond Scotland – Manchester, Birmingham, Belfast, for example – where heavy industry had a malign influence on the urban environment and health. 'Edinburgh, as is well known,' he continued, 'has no pretensions to be a manufacturing city. Its peculiar situation, and its distance from the sea, may help to account for this while, at an early period, the establishment of a University and of the highest Courts of judicature, appear to have diverted the attention of the inhabitants from mercantile pursuits.'[63] In fact, Edinburgh had a considerable amount of industrial production but for the most part in small workshops rather than large factories.[64] It lacked the mass of low-paid workers employed in the mills, docks and shipyards which characterised other cities of its size. Moreover, as a capital city it had a greater concentration of gentry and aristocracy whose 'pretensions' for their city did not favour large-scale manufacturing.[65] Littlejohn's view of an insanitary city extended beyond inadequate drainage, sewers and water supply to include poor amenity and intolerably unpleasant environment. A city such as

62 The word 'Irish' appears only three times in the *Report* (pp. 27, 80) and never pejoratively. 'Highlands', 'Highlander' and 'immigrants' are not found in the text. Littlejohn avoided any line of argument about the poor which used their origins as a cause of their degradation.

63 *Report*, 45.

64 R. Madgin and R. Rodger, 'Inspiring capital? Deconstructing myths and reconstructing urban environments, Edinburgh 1860–2010', *Urban History* 40:3 (2013), explore the extensive and durable nature of industrial interests in Edinburgh.

65 R.Q. Gray, *The Labour Aristocracy in Victorian Edinburgh* (Oxford, 1976).

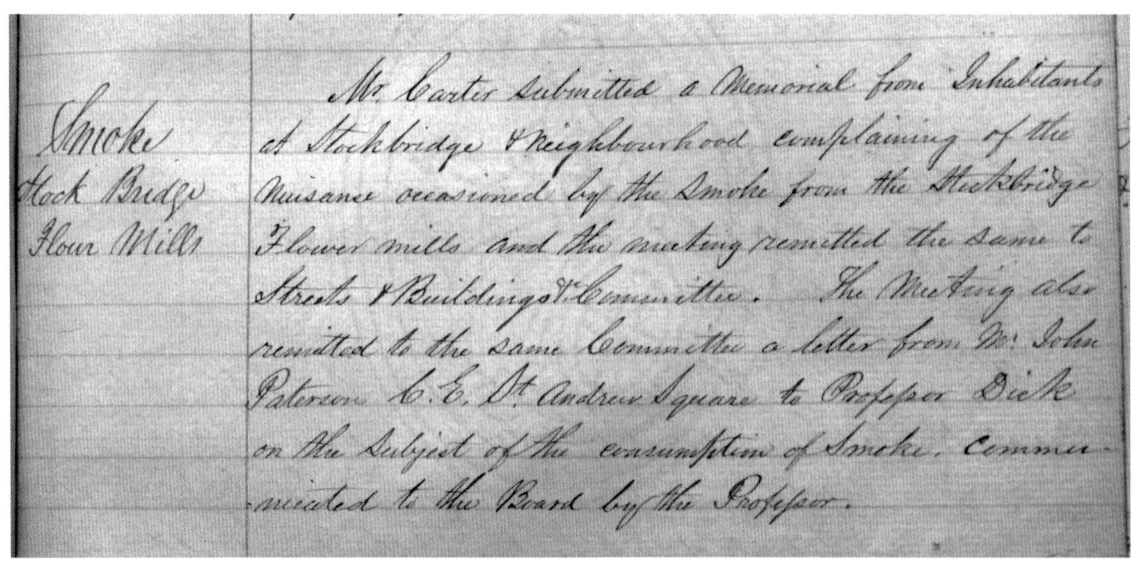

Smoke
Stock Bridge
Flour Mills

Mr Carter submitted a Memorial from Inhabitants of Stockbridge & Neighbourhood complaining of the Nuisance occasioned by the Smoke from the Stockbridge Flower mills and the meeting remitted the same to Streets & Buildings &c Committee. The Meeting also remitted to the same Committee a letter from Mr John Paterson C.E. St Andrew Square to Professor Dick on the Subject of the consumption of Smoke, communicated to the Board by the Professor.

4.12 Smoke pollution, Stockbridge Flower (*sic*) Mills, 1855
Residents objected to this source of pollution and sought council intervention to mitigate its effects.
[Source: ECA, Police Commissioners Minutes, 1855; *The Scotsman*, 3 November 1855, 3]

Edinburgh was at greater risk of being 'disfigured by large manufacturing works'. He took this opportunity to draw attention to the new gas works chimney in the Canongate – at 342 feet high it was from 1846 to 1898 the tallest structure in the city[66] – and another new tall chimney at the Caledonian Distillery in Dalry. Anticipating modern planning considerations, Littlejohn was arguing that such developments were not just eye-sores (his word), but by intruding into residential areas they injured health and depreciated neighbourhoods. 'Unfortunately, in this country, no supervision is exercised over the plans of buildings intended for the purposes of trade,' was a surprisingly forward-thinking opinion in the report of a public officer.[67] Health at work, he declared, was just as needful of 'the supervision of a sanitary officer' as the streets and homes of the city.[68] To make his point sting he used his knowledge of France to expound the virtues of a system of planning and environmental policing. Moreover, such a system should use the expert knowledge abundantly available in Edinburgh, and he named two distinguished medical colleagues, Robert Christison and Douglas Maclagan, as consultants who were beyond reproach in the city.

66 *Caledonian Mercury*, 9 November 1846, 2d. For an exhaustive description see *The Civil Engineer and Architect's Journal*, 14 (1850), 35. It was demolished in 1898: *The Scotsman*, 28 June 1911, 7b. Its 250-foot replacement stood from 1896 to 1911. *The Scotsman*, 28 June 1911, 8g. See also *Nelson's historical and descriptive hand-book to Edinburgh* (1858), handbook section, 29, although this erroneously gives the date of construction as 1847 – it was in fact November 1846.

67 *Report*, 46. The Dean of Guild Court adjudicated on matters of 'nichtbourheid', or amenity, regarding existing buildings, but it was not until 1880 that its jurisdiction included new buildings and areas outside the ancient and extended royalties of the city.

68 *Report*, 67.

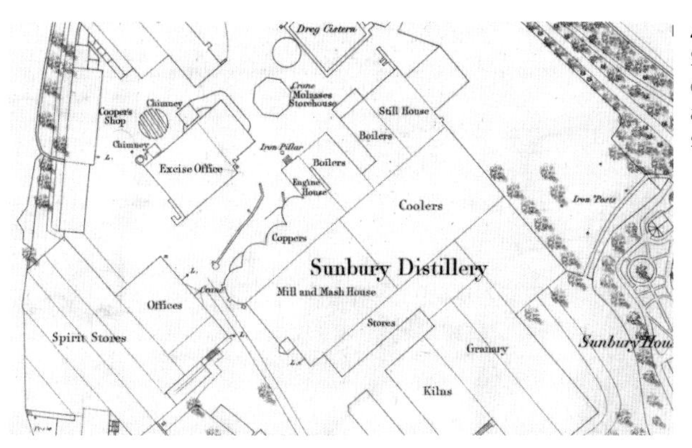

4.13 Sunbury Distillery, Dean Village
Sunbury Distillery closed as a result of a prosecution for smoke pollution and relocated at Dalry, near Haymarket station. [Source: NLS OS 1852]

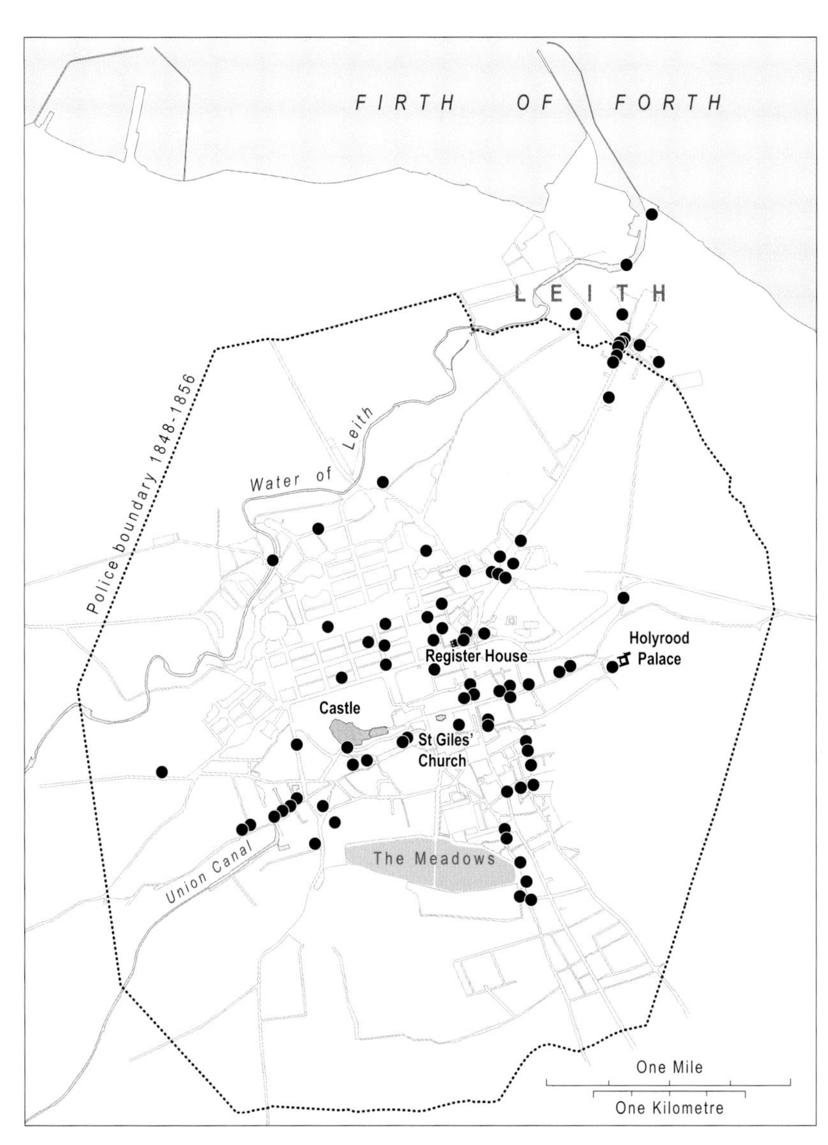

4.14 Smoky businesses: spatial distribution of polluters, 1855
The map locates those industrial premises and organisations that were sent nuisance notices by the Police Commissioners under section 230 of the Edinburgh Police Act 1848. They were requested to make every furnace 'consume or burn its own smoke'. [Source: ECA ED 9/1/13/100–103]

This emphasis on amenity – a word used twelve times in the *Report* – extended to smoke pollution:

> For this there is a sufficient remedy in the Smoke Nuisance Abatement Act, which, however, appears to be a dead letter with us, because, at all hours of the day, we have our city breweries, located in poor overcrowded localities, and a large number of the printing establishments in the New Town, polluting the air with their smoke. From this state of matters, a double evil results, not only in the air being contaminated, and the appearance of the town disfigured, but an obstacle is placed in the way of the free ventilation of the houses in the neighbourhood. Householders will rather have their apartments ill-ventilated, than expose themselves and their furniture to contact with smoke.[69]

Industrial smoke not only disfigured; it had a knock-on effect on domestic ventilation. The smoke legislation that Littlejohn called a dead letter was the Smoke Nuisance (Scotland) Act, 1857, and many of his readers were aware of years of desultory attempts by the Police Commission to prevent industries from emitting excessive smoke.[70] First the commissioners had printed a warning notice encouraging firms to install equipment to consume their smoke. Then, quoting section 230 of the 1848 Act, the commissioners increased the pressure on 112 smoke polluters by issuing warnings to desist, and finally in 1855 they sought to assess the effectiveness of the law by taking a test case to the Sheriff Court.[71] Their victim was the Sunbury Distillery in Dean Village, and the case may have contributed to the decision to close the works.[72] The Town Council continued the commissioners' pursuit of smoke polluters: statutory notices were issued against 12 parties in December 1857 and a further 61 in January 1858.[73] Meanwhile, as in every other large town, almost every newspaper contained an advertisement from firms offering devices to consume smoke.[74]

69 *Report*, 48.

70 20 and 21 Vict., cap. 73, 25 August 1857. It was amended in 1861 and 1865. The full title, An Act for the Abatement of the Nuisance arising from the Smoke of Furnaces in Scotland, alerts us to the fact that nineteenth-century smoke regulation was restricted to industry. Under section 94 of the Edinburgh Police Act, 1822, 'Owners and Occupiers of all Steam Engines, and of all Iron foundries, Glass works, Gas Manufactories, Distilleries, Breweries, and other Manufactories wherein Furnaces are used, already erected … shall within Six months from the passing of this Act adopt the Method now practised, or some good and efficacious Method, of consuming and burning the Smoke arising therefrom, so far as the same can be done, so as to prevent the same occasioning any Nuisance which can be avoided.' See chapter 3. The penalty for guilty parties was £50. A proposed stronger clause (146) in the Edinburgh Police Bill, 1848, was deemed impractical by the government assessor of the Bill but survived as clause 230.

71 ECA ED9/1/13, General Police Minutes, 9 July 1855. Of the 107 businesses identified the offending smoke polluters were, by trade, brewers 18%; engineers 16%; foundries 11%; printers/publishers 9%; flour mills, tanners both 8%; saw mills 5%; glass manufacturers 4%; plumbers, railways and blacksmiths each 3%; chemicals and 14 other industries 1% each.

72 *Caledonian Mercury*, 30 October 1855; *The Scotsman*, 23 April 1856, 2h and 28 May 1856, 3b. The firm relocated to Dalry where the chimney survives and passengers at Haymarket station can still identify a plaque dated 1855 high up on the gable of the Caledonian Distillery building.

73 *Caledonian Mercury*, 7 April 1858, 3b.

74 For an overview of smoke pollution and control see S. Mosley, *The Chimney of the World: A History of Smoke Pollution in Victorian and Edwardian Manchester* (Cambridge, 2001).

Littlejohn recognised that smoke pollution was not entirely the fault of industry – he described the Infirmary as 'a great offender' – but he says nothing about domestic smoke which must have contributed substantially to air pollution. His strong remarks on the widespread disregard of the Smoke Nuisance Abatement Act were aimed at a popular target. At a council meeting on 31 October 1865 John Hope began a long motion by citing three specific pages of the *Report*: 'Whereas the Officer of Health refers in his report to the annoyance and injury which the city and its inhabitants sustain by reason of smoke, pp. 48, 74, and 106, and points out that the Smoke Nuisance Abatement Act, though a sufficient remedy, is a dead letter in the city.'[75] The motion was remitted to the Streets and Buildings Committee 'to obtain from the Superintendent of Streets and Buildings and the Medical Officer of Health a report as to the cases of smoke nuisance which they think require attention'. This was the usual method for shunting an inconvenient issue out of sight. Littlejohn, however, reported as requested with a list of neighbourhoods most affected by industrial smoke but informed the council that no evidence had been reported by complainants sufficient to satisfy a court. His report elicited no discussion but a statement from the Lord Provost, William Chambers, that 'he was convinced from the experience of his own firm, that smoke could be consumed on the premises' and so he would work to put a stop to industrial smoke pollution.[76] Others did not regard smoke as a high priority, however. Councillor Hope, in appearing to be obsessed with the matter, did not help. He failed on four occasions to get his long rambling motions on smoke discussed in the council.[77] In a powerful editorial listing the topics in Littlejohn's *Report* it regarded as urgent, the *Scotsman* poured contempt on self-regarding councillors: 'There would still remain ample opportunities for the individual members of Council who wished to distinguish themselves by attacking minor abuses – such, for example, as the imperfect enforcement of the Smoke Nuisance Prevention Act.'[78] For many, however, it was far from a minor abuse. A regular correspondent to the *Scotsman*, hoping for action under the recently passed Provisional Order, expressed his indignation:

> There is no greater nuisance in Edinburgh than the chimneys of printing offices and manufactories vomiting forth black smoke, hiding the light of the sun at noon, substituting for atmospheric air an irrespirable gas, and finding its way through every open window into our rooms, destroying the furniture and rendering valueless the skill of the housemaid … The West End is rendered intolerable by five great chimneys belching forth smoke … the chimney of the

75 *Caledonian Mercury*, 1 November 1865, 4b.

76 *Caledonian Mercury*, 6 December 1865, 2g. It was the last item in a three and a half hour meeting on 5 December 1865.

77 At council meetings on 29 September, and 9, 16 and 31 October 1865: *The Scotsman*, 30 September 1865, 3ab; 10 October 1865, 2h; 17 October 1865, 8e; and 1 November 1865, 8a. Five years earlier an editorial had paid Hope a backhanded compliment: 'We need not quarrel outright … with Mr John Hope (a very provocative "party man" upon occasions) because, with preternatural refinement of olfaction, he scents the Caledonian Distillery in every breeze that blows in upon him through his open bed-room window. Rather let us be thankful to him for teaching us, though in a crotchety way, the double lesson, that bed-room windows ought to be opened, and that the air entering them ought to be kept as pure as may be.' *The Scotsman*, 13 November 1860, 2ab.

78 *The Scotsman*, 1 November 1865, 2cd.

> mill opposite Donaldson's Hospital formally consumed its own smoke, and might still be made to do so. The natural extension of the town to the West is thus interrupted, and even the fine buildings now erecting on the Coates property will long be found objectionable ... a series of steam engines have been erected, chiefly in connection with printing offices, behind Queen Street; and in certain not unusual directions of the wind the smoke pours down upon them ... chemical works, sugar refineries, and maltings are rapidly covering with their brick walls and smoky chimneys the ground long vacant; so that, in whatever direction the wind blows, Edinburgh is sure of smoke.[79]

Firms were warned or prosecuted in the 1860s and beyond for adding to Edinburgh's notoriously polluted atmosphere, though both smoke consumption and observation of offence remained difficult technical and legal problems.

At just over a page, the last section of the *Report*, on the economy and employment, might appear perfunctory. It is really little more than an explanatory comment on the three-page table which follows (pp. 69–71). The table itself represents an extraordinary piece of research. Wishing to know both the occupational composition of the city by sex and to compare it with the causes of death among persons in the same categories of employment, Littlejohn set about analysing the complete manuscript returns of the 1861 census: 'the laborious process of going over the returns seriatim' involved over 168,000 entries on more than 6,700 pages. He placed 61,373 individuals into categories of his own devising, into which he could then tabulate 959 persons who had died in 1863 'whose occupations could be determined satisfactorily'. The deceased were also tabulated in four age categories. The data for his huge 'spreadsheet' appendix must have been extracted from the census at the same time, including for every close and court the number of persons under and over five years of age. Littlejohn was under no illusions about the limitations of these hard-won data, which seemed to be a taster for his readers – 'interesting, as affording a specimen', as he put it. Several phrases suggest that he would like to have carried his analysis further but was restrained by the time and cost required to do that.

Littlejohn realised that spreading the deaths in a single year over a matrix of 47 occupations by eight causes of death was unlikely to produce any clear patterns, just statistical noise. There is little reason to believe that being a cooper or a brewer, despite the coincidence of the two trades, carried such exceptional risks of mortality, or that bricklayers were immortal because nobody described as such happened to die that year. He was also well aware that expressing deaths in 1863 as a percentage of population in 1861 where the number of deaths was tiny and the number in each occupation was likely to have a significant margin of error whether from the census (the denominator) or the death register (the numerator). With his systematic mind he simply turned over every stone. Perhaps the chief value lies in the enumeration of occupations presented separately for the New and Old Towns, a shorthand for north and south of a line extended east and west along Princes Street. This simple division of the city, he explained, was to avoid the labour and pitfalls of presenting results for each of the 19 sanitary districts – as if this stupendous labour, even with the help of a clerk, was a short cut!

79 *The Scotsman*, 5 November 1867, 7b.

Of approximately 50,000 males in gainful employment in 1861, Littlejohn selected about 77% – the working classes as he saw them. In rejecting the classification used for the census as 'too minute for such a purpose as the present' he was being polite; for almost any serious analysis of Victorian society the classification adopted by the British census takers was flawed. Instead Littlejohn used easily understood descriptions of working-class occupations. Interestingly, while most of his data are in sufficient agreement with those of the Registrar-General, even allowing for clerking errors and unavoidable ambiguities in interpreting occupational descriptors, others are seriously at odds. Littlejohn found more than two and a half times as many bookbinders and cabinet-makers, and nearly twice as many blacksmiths.[80] To a statistician this exercise may have its limitations. Nevertheless, in its comprehensive approach it represents a fundamental shift from carefully applied sanitary statistics towards a strikingly modern form of social science. Characteristically cautious, Littlejohn was underselling his achievement with the phrase 'interesting, as affording a specimen'.

Public institutions

A recurring theme in the *Report* is the need to move medical institutions, especially the new infirmary, from cramped and insalubrious sites to open areas beyond the central area of Edinburgh. While Littlejohn's tabulation of mortality in institutions is useful, his chief concern in this short section was to assess whether the public institutions were serving their designated purpose with proper regard to health. He was well qualified to do so having not only trained, worked and taught in hospitals but also being a Police Surgeon. There was nothing inherently unhealthy about where hospitals were to be found, he said, but he regretted the dilapidated state of many of the charitable institutions for the elderly and sick poor. He again urged the combination of the three Poor Law authorities, at least for the purposes of maintaining a workhouse. Being personally involved in the plans for a new poorhouse at Craiglockhart, and working intimately with the Parochial Boards and their medical officers, his view carried considerable weight. Above all, Littlejohn insisted on the sanitary contribution of the hospitals, not just for regular medicine and surgery but also for convalescence from acute and chronic diseases, and maternity services for the poor whose homes were so dangerous for confinement and childbirth.

Victorian Medical Officers of Health were accustomed to treating the population in public institutions separately. Workhouses, often filled with the elderly sick and infirm, and hospitals could inflate the mortality of a district and mask that of the resident population. Dr W.H. Duncan demonstrated this in the first published report as Medical Officer of Health for Liverpool. While six major public institutions contained less than 2% of the population, they contributed over 10% of the mortality between 1848 and 1850. The crude death rate for Abercromby ward was about 24 but would be 72 if the Workhouse within its

80 Categories such as clerks, shopkeepers, porters and labourers are impossible to extract from the published returns and must be hidden under other categories. HC (PP) [3275] 1864, LI, 434–42, Census of Scotland, 1861, Population Tables and Report, vol. 2 (1864), 310–18.

boundary were included.[81] If the military personnel in the castle are discounted the proportion of the population of Edinburgh in 1861 in public institutions was still higher than in Liverpool in 1851, possibly because the list of long-established charitable hospitals was not strictly comparable to Duncan's limited list.

Since the removal of cases of epidemic disease to separate hospitals was strongly recommended by Alison in the 1820s, there might seem little that was particularly new in Littlejohn's approach. However, informed by Duncan's analysis of institutional deaths in Liverpool and armed with statistical data derived from the recently introduced civil registration in Scotland, he forcefully argued that by locating hospitals on the urban fringe this made a dual contribution to public health: it both provided more accurate mortality statistics for the central districts themselves and, by removing fever cases directly diminished the likelihood of infection among the general public.

Drainage and water supply

By far the longest section of the *Report* is Littlejohn's consideration of water and drainage (Table 4.2). It is certainly a faithful reflection of the amount of newsprint and public debate on this matter over the preceding two decades, though some, if not most, of that public concern was about the filthy state of the Water of Leith. Littlejohn's priorities, however, were rather different. He sought simple and effective measures, carefully designed, to reduce disease and mortality, and took his cue from his highly regarded lecturer, W.T. Gairdner, who explained the 'evils' of defective water supply in his published lectures on public health:

> Sometimes the source may be a well perhaps three doors off – the evil is then not very great, that is to say, if the houses are not high; but the evil even then becomes very great if, as in the Old Town of Edinburgh, you build your houses eight or ten, nay, even twelve or fourteen storeys high, and at the same time make no provision for carrying up to them this necessary of life. … The rich do not greatly feel the evil. Their wants are supplied after a fashion, and they allow a large poor population to grow up in a state of neglect and helplessness as regards one of the first necessities of a healthy life.[82]

Gairdner admonished the city for its failure to supply clean water to the poor:

> In Edinburgh we are deeply to blame in respect to the water-supply of the poor, and are largely responsible for the filthy and neglected state in which they live. … If we want an illustration and a type of the evils of scanty water – not of impure water, for we have always had, fortunately, access to water which is tolerably pure – we can hardly find a better one than this good and fair city of ours, which was one of the first in this country to bring water from a distance, but is likely to be one of the last, unless we bestir ourselves much more than hitherto, to make a full and free use of the cleansing and health-giving element.[83]

81 Calculated from data in W.H. Duncan, *Report to the Health Committee of the Borough of Liverpool on the Health of the Town, and on other matters within his department* (Liverpool, 1851), 90.

82 W.T. Gairdner, *Public Health in Relation to Air and Water* (Edinburgh, 1862), 158–9.

83 W.T. Gairdner, *Public Health*, 159–60.

In any assessment of the sanitary condition of a city the supply of clean water and the disposal of effluent are prime concerns. Littlejohn's starting point was the distinctive topography of Edinburgh and its environs, using three dramatic cross-sections to demonstrate the obstacles to drainage. Nowhere was this better illustrated than in the case of the main sewer which ran along the ridge from the castle to the lower end of Canongate but which carried little more than storm water and surface effluent from street drains. A short paragraph stated the paradox and central problem for the city: while the completion of drainage works in the city dealt effectively with rainfall conveyed in splendid new sewers that ran through the poorest districts, as far as waste disposal was concerned it might as well never have existed since the closes the poor inhabited were not connected to sewers. Accordingly, cleaning in these districts continued to rely on carting waste to nearby parishes.[84]

If drainage was a prerequisite to sanitary improvement it was not itself the solution. In fact, Edinburgh's distinctive domestic architecture required a local solution, as Littlejohn proceeded to demonstrate in detail. Supplying water and sewerage to terraced houses was technically straightforward and relatively cheap; English towns had made great progress against epidemic disease by connecting individual houses to sewers in the 1840s and 1850s. According to Littlejohn: 'to enforce the introduction of conveniences, would be attended with the worst results. In England, where the poorest houses are self-contained, and necessarily small, with a court behind, in which the convenience is placed, the system works admirably.'[85] By contrast, to introduce waste pipes and a water supply to decaying and increasingly overcrowded multi-storey tenements was both complicated and costly. Though there was an adequate supply of mains water – 'One of the most satisfactory circumstances connected with the sanitary condition of Edinburgh' – as Littlejohn explained, this applied only so far as providing a water main at the entrance to each tenement.[86]

The principal technical problem which dogged the sanitary improvement of the city, especially in the hilly Old Town, was how to install pipes, water-closets, and drains in domestic property. Leaving this to market forces and in the hands of developers and landlords was hazardous, even for decent dwellings. Powers to compel landlords to provide these basic sanitary facilities were sought, and then omitted, from legislation in 1848, and only became available in Lindsay's General Police Act, 1862, section 210. Though the council adopted some of the provisions of this Act it was dilatory over this crucial clause 210.

To appreciate the resistance to such a compulsory power and why it became both significant and controversial, it is necessary to return to the 1840s, when far-sighted attempts to regulate sanitary and environmental problems were frustrated by vested interests and administrative incompetence.

84 *Report*, 76. For the persistence of this practice into the twentieth century in certain European cities see G. Massard-Guilbaud and R. Rodger (eds), *Environmental and Social Justice in the City: Historical Perspectives* (Cambridge, 2011), 155–88.

85 *Report*, 79.

86 *Report*, 90.

Localism and the legislative debacle of the 1840s

Just as in 1805, when Edinburgh Town Council had mirrored Glasgow in the formation of a Police Commission to regulate public order and environmental health, so in October 1847 the council began the process completed by the Glasgow Municipal Boundaries Act, 1846, to decommission its police authority.[87] Lord Provost Adam Black proposed that Edinburgh take powers to regularise its administrative geography and to extend its regulatory powers, particularly its sanitary powers.[88] Whereas Glasgow had a single Act for these purposes, Black promoted two Bills in November 1847. The Edinburgh Municipality Extension and Transference of Police and Paving Bill was to provide geographical coherence to the administrative area and thus 'confer on all the inhabitants equal rights and privileges with equal burdens'.[89] The absurdity of different jurisdictions existing within the city meant that a shopkeeper on South Bridge and his brother a few hundred yards farther along on Nicolson Street were subject to different inspectorates and sentenced for any trading infringements by different magistrates.[90] Figure 4.16 shows the legacy of ancient jurisdictions and inconsistent boundaries which had long ceased to have any relevance to the topography of the city, leaving properties under different authorities from their immediate neighbours and in some cases forming islands within a different jurisdiction.[91]

A House of Commons Select Committee conveyed their incredulity at the complex administrative geography when they examined an Edinburgh witness[92] in connection with the proposed boundary extensions:

> Mr Logan – Police purposes into how many wards are the Police Boundaries divided?
>
> A There are 32 Wards of Police.
>
> Q For Parliamentary purposes and Electoral purposes into how many wards is the Parliamentary Borough divided?
>
> A Into Eleven wards.
>
> Q And for the Municipal Elections, Elections of Members of the Town Council into how many wards is the Ancient and Extended Royalty divided?

87 9 and 10 Vict. 1846, cap. 289, Municipal Boundaries of the City of Glasgow Act, 1846, section 2. See also D.G. Barrie, *Police in the Age of Improvement: Police Development and the Civic Tradition in Scotland, 1775–1865* (Cullompton, 2008), 226–34. For details of the 1805 Glasgow Act see chapter 2.

88 The legislative complexity of what was proposed persuaded councillors to urge the Lord Provost, Adam Black, to continue in office beyond his term. See *The Scotsman*, 9 October 1847, 2b; 20 October 1847, 2f and 3c.

89 ECA EDP25/1/XXII, *Report of the Lord Provost's Committee regarding Proposed Bills for extending the Municipal Boundaries and for Improving the Sanitary Condition of the City* (Edinburgh, 1847), 3. Inconsistencies remained in the proposals in relation to the way the Annuity Tax, Parochial Board and the Dean of Guild Court functions were to operate.

90 J. Sinclair, *Case for the Extension of the Municipal Boundary of Edinburgh and the Transference of Powers of the Police and Paving Boards to the Town Council* (Edinburgh, 1855), 45–6. More generally, Sinclair provides an extensive account of public administration in Edinburgh.

91 Like Edinburgh, Leeds also experienced police administration that was not consistent with the boundaries of the city. See R. Baker, 'On the industrial and sanitary economy of the borough of Leeds in 1858', *Journal of the Statistical Society of London*, 21 (1858), 427–43.

92 HC/CL/PB/2/15/5, Municipality Extension bill, Opposed Private Bill Committee Evidence, 1847–48, vol. 5, group 7.

A Into five.

Q Then for the purpose of returning the Commissioners for the Southern Districts into how many wards are those districts divided?

A Into eight wards, eight Southern Districts.

Committee – For what purpose?

A For the purpose of electing Commissioners for the Southern Districts.

Committee – The 32 Wards of Police that you first mentioned comprise the Southern district?

A Yes they do.

Mr Logan – So that the Parliamentary City of Edinburgh is for its various Electoral purposes divided into 56 different varying wards?

4.15 Adam Black (1784–1874), Lord Provost, 1843–48, MP, 1856–65
During Black's leadership the administration of the city was consolidated under the Town Council. John Watson Gordon Artist, 1847. [Source: CAC]

Lord Provost Black's Edinburgh Municipality Extension Bill proposed the absorption of Portsburgh, Calton, Canongate, the most populous parts of the St Cuthbert's parish, and the southern districts of the city within their jurisdiction so as to streamline administration within what, in modern terminology, might be considered a unitary authority.[93]

The second Bill proposed by Black, the Edinburgh Police Consolidation and Sanitary Improvement Bill (267 sections) was intended to give the council powers previously invested in the Police Commission in relation to water, drainage and environmental responsibilities. Black specifically mentioned powers to compel proprietors to make connections to sewers, and to provide the 'Dwellings of the Poorer Classes with Water and Water-Closets'.[94] The two council Bills were indissolubly linked: without the Municipal Extension Bill the council had no powers over most of the police territory, and without the Improvement Bill they had no administrative machinery to carry out the functions of the police.

Prompted by Black's initiative, the police commissioners responded a fortnight later with their own Bill (280 sections) – the Edinburgh Police (Amendment and Consolidation of Acts, and Police and Sanitary Improvement) Bill. Though claims were made that the Police Bill was 'drawn up without any reference'[95] to that of the Town Council, and that there was no 'collision' (presumably the *Mercury* meant 'collusion'), the fact that the Lord Provost chaired both the Police Commission and the Town Council and that some councillors were also police commissioners shows the extent of confusion in the city – 'muddling in bumbledom' – over sanitary matters.[96] A correspondent to the *Caledonian Mercury* commented on this 'flood of legislation':

93 A disadvantage of a separate police jurisdiction was the need, and cost, to renew powers from time to time through a parliamentary bill. This became an issue across Britain, as recognised by the appointment of a Select Committee to Consider the Expediency of Adopting a More Uniform System of Police in England and Wales and Scotland. See PP (HC) 1852–53 (715) XXXVI, 115, Second Report, with Minutes and Evidence.

94 *The Scotsman*, 27 November 1847, 1g.

95 *The Scotsman*, 28 October 1847, 4c.

96 The phrase comes from C. Hamlin, 'Muddling in Bumbledom: on the enormity of large sanitary improvements in four British towns, 1855–1885, *Victorian Studies*, 32 (1988), 55–84. In May 1848 the parliamentary agents, Messrs Spottiswoode and Robertson, requested the burgh chamberlain to pay £350 for preliminary expenses for the new Municipal Bill and simultaneously £350 for the new Police Bill before parliament. See *Caledonian Mercury*, 18 May 1848, 4b.

> Here, then, we have the unseemly sight of two public boards quarrelling with each other, at the public expense, and in this pugnacious attitude going up to Parliament, each with bill in hand, and neither the one nor the other deigning to ask the opinions of their constituents about measures which so vitally concern them.[97]

Although there were similarities of language and intent in the two Improvement Bills, they were significantly different in detail.[98] For example, in the case of the crucial power to introduce water into every dwelling the relevant section of the commissioners' Bill was considerably longer and more technical than the corresponding section of the council's Bill (169).[99] The council had much less day-to-day experience of sanitary matters.

Both the commissioners' and the council's Bills were announced in the local press[100] during November and December 1847, with summaries of intended powers, and their publication prompted the involvement of an official legislative scrutineer, Edinburgh advocate Robert Macfarlane, to give a formal notice to examine the three Local Bills on 17 February 1848. This interval of two months enabled Black to mount a public relations initiative by publishing a 15-page pamphlet in January 1848 entitled *A Vindication of the Municipality Extension and Police and Sanitary Bills Proposed by the Town Council* to coincide with the two-day meeting specifically devoted to the council Bills.[101] As well as reporting the hearing in full *The Scotsman* gave strong endorsement: 'The whole pamphlet should be in the hands of all who wish to understand a question which has been much misunderstood and misrepresented.'[102]

Black's sense that current arrangements were not only irrational but unjust was also evident in his *Vindication* since, as he indicated, three-fifths of the inhabitants of the city were deprived of the opportunity to serve as councillors; conversely, the remaining two-fifths shouldered the burden of office.[103] Though Lord Provost Black made it clear that if the Municipal Extension Bill failed the council's other Bill, the Edinburgh Police (Amendment and Consolidation of Acts, etc) Bill was a dead letter. Nevertheless, in a 'Memorandum' attached to the published Bill, Black explicitly encouraged 'Public Bodies and others' to suggest amendments to the proposed clauses.[104] Exactly a month later an anonymous, and tendentious, pamphlet was published contesting the desirability of the

97 *Caledonian Mercury*, 25 January 1848, 3b.

98 This did not prevent residents' confusion over the bills: see *Caledonian Mercury*, 24 January 1848, 3b letter from 'A Hereditor and Tenant'.

99 For a comparison of the proposals in the two Bills see *House of Commons Journal*, 103, 1847–48, pp.142–43; 166–67; 206, 214, 219, 226, 231, 240, 250, 271, 276, 508, 527, 544–45, 659, 712, 743, 893, 898, and 920. To complicate matters further there was also a separate Improvement Bill for Leith – The Leith Municipality and Police Trusts, Markets, Paving, and Sanatory Improvement Bill – and part of the cleaning activities of Leith were concerned with limited areas of Edinburgh.

100 *Caledonian Mercury*, 11 November, 1d; 18 November, 4b; and 9 December 1847, 3c–e.

101 *Caledonian Mercury*, 20 January 1848, 3de.

102 *The Scotsman*, 22 January 1848, 3cd.

103 A. Black, *A Vindication of the Municipality Extension and Police and Sanitary Bills Proposed by the Town Council* (Edinburgh, 1848), 4–5. See also *Caledonian Mercury*, 17 January 1848, 1c, and *The Scotsman*, 22 January 1848, 3cd.

104 'Memorandum' attached to the Council's bill – see previous note.

council's Bill. *Remarks on the Lord Provost's Vindication* claimed that 'Important public bodies', said to represent to 80,000 'respectable and intelligent members of the community', viewed Black's Bill as high-handed since public consultation had not taken place, as unfair because it retrospectively imposed debts incurred by Edinburgh on citizens outwith its boundaries, and as discriminatory as it denied residents in the adjacent districts the opportunity to participate fully as office-holders in the county area.[105] These were misgivings shared by lawyers, administrators, Leith residents, and even some of Black's fellow councillors.

In an exercise which further demonstrates the significance of local consultation in framing legislation before it reached Westminster, a process too often overlooked by historians, all three of these Bills went before a government surveyor, Robert Macfarlane.[106] The hearings were held not in a public building but in a private hotel rented for the purpose.[107] From 17 to 19 February 1848 lawyers and agents for interested parties appeared before Macfarlane in a loosely structured hearing. Black's brisk presentation of the arguments for the council's Bills was followed by evidence obtained from powerful opponents of the legislation – several loan companies, the Union Canal, the Earl of Moray, agents for the neighbouring districts directly affected, and County Road Trustees.[108] On the same day as he gave evidence to Macfarlane's enquiry at the Royal Hotel, Saturday 19 February, Professor William Alison convened a distinguished committee of the Royal College of Physicians which reviewed the public health provisions then under consideration in England and their relevance to the council's and commissioners' Bills.[109] The physicians generally approved of the sanitary proposals in the two Edinburgh Bills, though aware of their limitations, but regretted that there was no mention of the appointment of a Medical Officer of Health. Somewhat disingenuously given the coverage in the newspapers, pamphlet wars and debates in the public sphere, Macfarlane claimed that 'virtually no separate proceedings or discussion have taken place on the subject of this Bill'.[110] Not only was this not the case, the Town Council had agreed to

105 ECA Box 398, Bundle 20, *Remarks on the Lord Provost's Vindication of the Municipality Extension and Police and Sanitary Bills* (Edinburgh, 1848), 1–22.

106 Robert Macfarlane was appointed under 9 and 10 Vict., cap. 106, Local Acts, Preliminary Inquiries Act, 1846, which directed that local and private Bills should be examined by a surveyor appointed by the Commissioner of Woods, Forests, Land Revenues, Works and Buildings before proceeding to Parliament. Macfarlane (1802–80) was later Lord Ormidale, High Court judge. For Macfarlane's Report see HL/PO/JO/10/8/1663 and 1664b.

107 HL/PO/JO/10/8/1690; Evidence (1,109 questions to 12 'Promoters' of the bill which included Alexander Murray, David Cousins (sic), James Stark and William Allison (sic); and 11 'Objectors'.

108 ECA Box 398, Bundle 19, Edinburgh Municipality Extension and Transference of Police and Paving, Minutes of Evidence taken by the Surveying Officer; *The Scotsman*, 19 February 1848, 3bc. See also J. Sinclair, *Case for the Extension of the Municipal Boundary of Edinburgh*, 45–6.

109 *Report by the Committee of the Royal College of Physicians appointed to consider any Bills that may be brought into Parliament for the Improvement of the Health of Towns and the applicability of Such Measures to Scotland* (Edinburgh, 1848), 6–7, 10. The committee included Professors Christison and Gregory, Dr Spittal, and Dr James Stark, later first Superintendent of Statistics at the General Register Office for Scotland. See also *The Scotsman*, 23 February 1848, 3e.

110 PP (HC) 1847–48 (135) 423, Report, 23 March 1848.

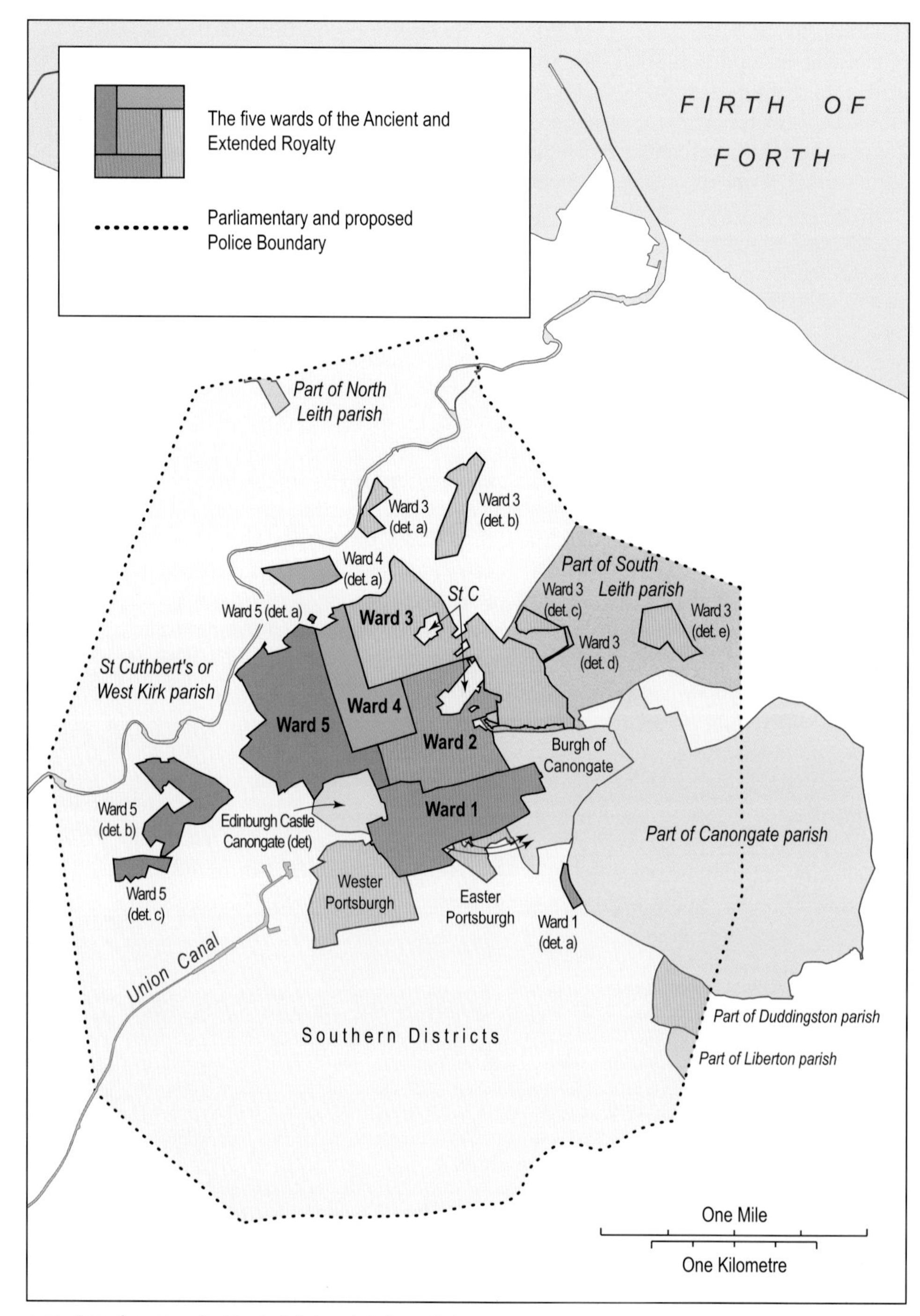

4.16 Boundary complexities in Edinburgh before 1856

After the Police Commissioners and the Town Council were merged in 1856 the municipal boundary was extended to coincide with the parliamentary boundary and 13 wards were created. Before the new arrangement, elections and administration were based on a confusion of ancient burgh boundaries and police wards (see fig. 4.17). The Ancient Royalty was the term for the Old Town; it was 'extended' in 1767 and 1809.

[Source: Ordnance Survey 1:1056 sheets surveyed 1851–52]

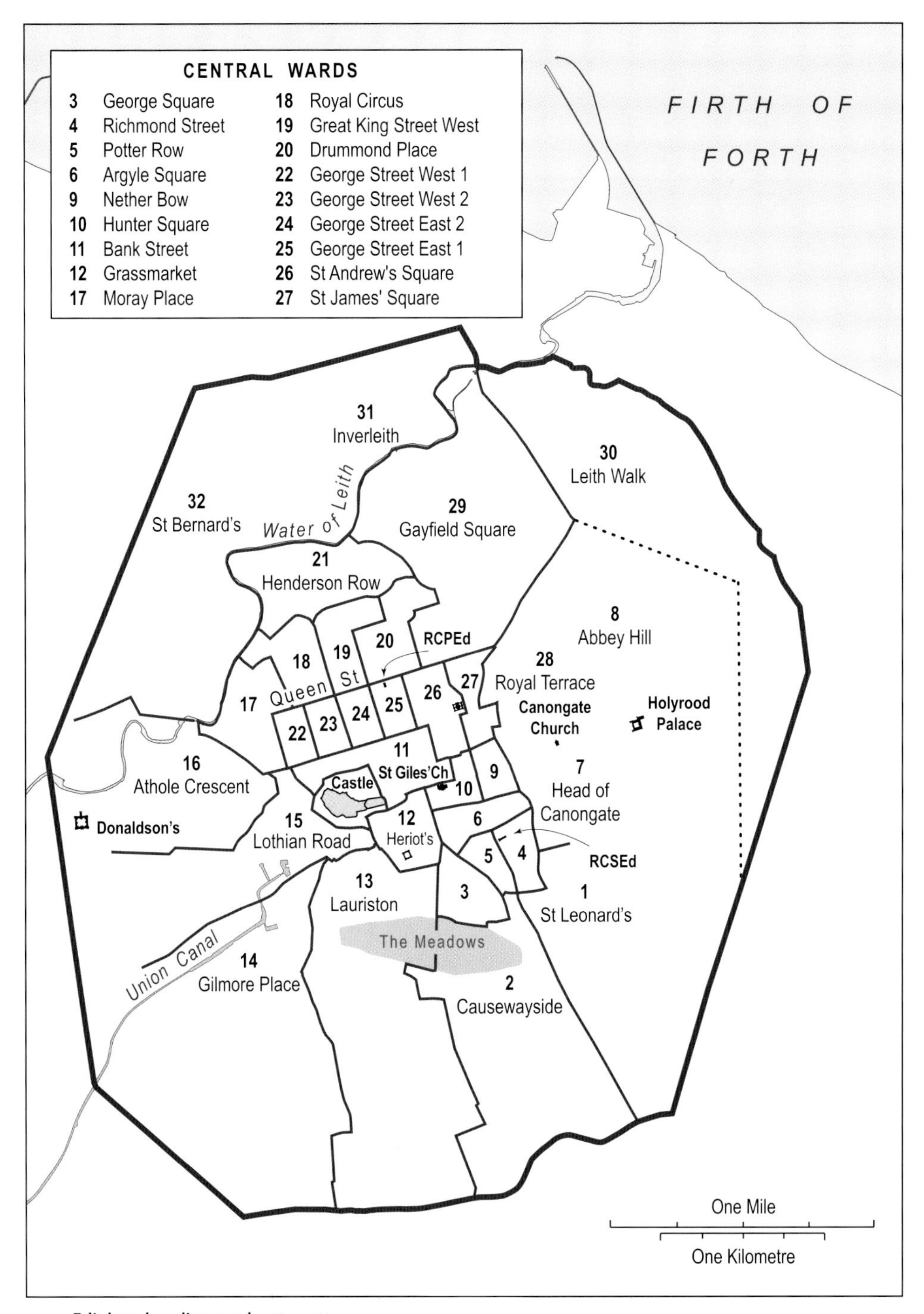

4.17 Edinburgh police wards, 1837–56

The Police Commission was first established by the 1805 Police Act with six electoral wards. The number and arrangement of wards was revised by subsequent Acts in 1812 (26 wards), 1822 (30 wards; see fig. 3.3), 1832 (2 wards added) and 1837 (32 new wards). No map of the ward boundaries is known so they are here based on descriptions in the Local Acts. It has not been possible to locate the precise boundaries of some wards in unbuilt areas.
[Source: Edinburgh Police Acts 1837, section 2, and 1848, section 6]

Process	*Town Council's Municipality Bill*	*Town Council's Sanitary Bill*	*Police Commissioners' Sanitary Bill*
Petition for a bill	3 Feb. 1848	3 Feb. 1848	3 Feb. 1848
Bill presented, i.e. 1st reading	4 Feb. 1848	4 Feb. 1848	4 Feb. 1848
Referred to Committee of Selection, i.e. 2nd reading	11 Feb. 1848	14 Feb. 1848	15 Feb. 1848
Petitions against Bill	14, 17, 18, 21 Feb.; 12 May 1848	18, 21, 22, 28, 29 May 1848	18, 21, 22, 28 Feb. 1848
Local consideration of Bills (Macfarlane Report)	17–19 Feb. 1848	17–19 Feb. 1848	17–19 Feb. 1848
Reported	22 May 1848	22 May 1848	28 June 1848
Report considered, amendments agreed			12 July 1848
Passed, i.e. 3rd reading			19 July 1848
Passed by Lords with 35 amendments			8 Aug. 1848
Considered and agreed			10 Aug. 1848
Royal assent			14 Aug. 1848

Table 4.3 Edinburgh parliamentary Bills, 1848

make concessions to various objectors.[111] Without an unequivocal endorsement locally, and without the blessing of the government's legal scrutineer, the prospects for the passage of the council's Bills were not good. Nor were they improved when powerful individuals and organisations lined up during the committee stage of the Bill in the House of Commons to petition against the municipal extension. Prominent among them were the Liberal politician and major Edinburgh landowner, Sir Thomas Dick Lauder, and the Dean of the Faculty of Advocates, but it was the combined assault by four railways companies, two roads authorities, and the representatives of both the Southern Districts and Canongate which torpedoed the proposals.[112] The committee of the House of Commons concluded that the case for the extension was not convincing, or as they put it, 'the preamble of the bill was not proved', and accordingly rejected the proposals by a majority of 7 to 2.[113] The congruence of the physical boundaries of the parliamentary and municipal burgh was logical, but the extension of the civil and criminal jurisdictions of Edinburgh to the adjacent districts was deemed not justified. The Municipality Extension Bill failed to get a second reading on 17 May 1848. The Town Council's Police Bill was withdrawn immediately.

The *Scotsman*'s pessimistic expectations for the bills were confirmed:

111 *Caledonian Mercury*, 20 April 1848, 3b. Inhabitants of the Canongate burgh negotiated six concessions.

112 HC Papers 1847–48 (103), 214, 226, 240, 508; 1847–48 (135) 423; Report, 23 March 1848.

113 *The Scotsman*, 20 May 1848, 3a.

4.18 Alexander Wood MD (1817–84)
Wood was a police commissioner (1846–53), and leading promoter of sanitary reform in Edinburgh. As a Free Church member with a strong conscience he led campaigns to improve the housing of the poor. [Source: RCPEd]

> In every attempt hitherto made in Edinburgh to obtain improvements in drainage and similar matters, private interest – or, more properly speaking, a landlord interest – has been more powerful than the interests of the community; and the consequence has been the adoption of abortive half measures.[114]

This was a reference to the vested interests of railway companies and landlords in defeating attempts to obtain compulsory powers to require sewer connections. Macfarlane's Report, based on the public enquiry he chaired, also sided with the proprietors: 'all houses below a certain rental ought to be expressly exempted from the burthen of the expense of the introduction into them of water and pipes.'[115]

The failure of one council Bill and the withdrawal of the other cleared the way for the Police Commission to proceed with its Bill, which became law on 15 August 1848.[116] After detailed scrutiny in parliament, sections dealing with compulsory powers over landlords regarding water supply and drainage were removed from what became the Edinburgh Police Act, 1848. For almost two decades builders and proprietors were absolved from sanitary obligations that were widely acknowledged as essential in the late 1840s. Until 1867, the provisional order under which Edinburgh eventually adopted such powers, police regulation was almost exclusively based on the provisions of the 1848 Police Act.

The political consequences of the legislative confusion of 1848 were highly significant. In part it was conditioned by forces beyond the city's control as, for example, when a select committee in 1852 considered urban administration by police authorities at a national level and so slowed the reforming stimulus.[117] More directly, local control was consistently sought over the actions of employed officials, as with the Lord Provost's action in 1854 to dismiss the Police Surgeon Dr George Glover for overstepping his powers. Central–local tensions also surfaced when a Police Commission committee, convened by the tenacious councillor, Dr Alexander Wood, reported on a draft Public Health (Scotland) Bill in 1849 and objected vehemently to the proposed centralising powers of a General Board of Health in London.[118] In a mood that was firmly anti-Chadwickian, the committee thought it 'highly objectionable' to locate such powers in London where the servants under the English board were not 'conversant with the laws of Scotland and the habits and character of the Scottish

114 *The Scotsman*, 8 December 1847, 3a. The editorial referred to the First Report of the Metropolitan Sanitary Commissioners [PP (HC) 1847–48 [888] xxxii] trusting 'that its findings will be applied across all towns in the kingdom'.

115 PP (HC) 1847–48 (135–26) 29.

116 11 and 12 Vict., cap. 113, Edinburgh Police Act, 1848 (formerly Edinburgh Police (Amendment and Consolidation of Acts, and Police and Sanitary Improvement) bill). Comparison of clauses at the Committee stage shows significant alterations to the language of the bill.

117 PP (HC) 1852–53 (715) XXXVI, 115, Select Committee to Consider the Expediency of Adopting a More Uniform System of Police in England and Wales and Scotland. The Municipal and Police powers were amalgamated by 19 and 20 Vict., cap. 32, 'An Act to extend the municipal boundaries of the City of Edinburgh, to transfer the powers of the commissioners of Police to the Magistrates and Council, and for other purposes relating to the municipality of the said city'.

118 Report by the Sanitary Committee of the Commissioners of Police on the Public Health (Scotland) Bill, 1 May 1849.

population'.[119] Anti-centralisation sentiments surfaced during an attempt to carry out the provisions of the Nuisances Removal and Diseases Prevention Act[120] in Edinburgh. Wood's powerful critique in 1849 of the legislation for England and Wales meant there was no appetite in the city to extend sanitary powers beyond the codification which emerged from the Edinburgh Police Act, 1848. Localism, however, could be a double-edged weapon, as when conservative elements in the council chamber opposed change, and a generation elapsed, therefore, before a general Public Health Bill was contemplated, first for Scottish burghs in 1862, and for Scotland as a whole in 1867. The 1840s are critical, therefore, to an understanding of the administration of public health both before and after Littlejohn's appointment.[121]

Clean water

As Edinburgh expanded it needed, and obtained, additional reservoirs and waterworks, but that was not the priority for sanitary reform: the problem was to get clean water into homes. In 1857 the redoubtable chairman of the Cleaning Committee, Councillor Ford, had put it starkly:

> The total number of dwelling-houses in Edinburgh is 31,980. Of these there are 23,822 supplied with water, leaving 8158 unprovided. We have thus 41,000 of our population to whom an accessible and abundant supply of water is utterly unknown. What a desideratum in human existence is here for this Council to grapple with and supply; and how is this great work to be accomplished?[122]

Landlords were not prepared retrospectively to install water pipes in old tenements since most were either of solid stone or crumbling. All this Littlejohn saw clearly:

> The houses ... in the great majority of cases, were never intended for this sanitary improvement. They are of great age, many of them as strong as fortresses, and others so old as already to be falling to pieces, with walls hardly able to maintain themselves erect, much less to stand the operations of the sanitary engineer.[123]

Piped water also raised the spectre of social and environmental justice. The issue was who would pay for the introduction of water-closets bearing in

119 Report by the Sanitary Committee, 1849, 7. See also G.F.A. Best, 'The Scottish Victorian city', *Victorian Studies*, 11 (1968), 329–58; PP (HC) 1884–85 [C. 4409], Royal Commission on the Housing of the Working Classes, Evidence, D. Crawford, Q.18,488–91 and W.S. Walker, Q.18,262,

120 11 and 12 Vict., cap. 123, Nuisances Removal and Diseases Prevention Act, 1848.

121 The Public Health (Scotland) Act, 1867 first empowered town councillors and police commissioners to form urban sanitary districts.

122 *The Scotsman*, 6 May 1857, 3cd.

123 *Report*, 80–1. The phrases 'strong as fortresses', 'so old as already to be falling to pieces, with walls hardly able to maintain themselves', and 'much less to stand the operations of the Sanitary Engineer' were penned for a report to the council on 20 December 1864, ECA SL2/187(1), *The Scotsman*, 21 December 1864, 7b. For a discussion of the way Littlejohn was bounced in to reporting on the sanitary condition of the closes before his full *Report* was completed, see above page 102.

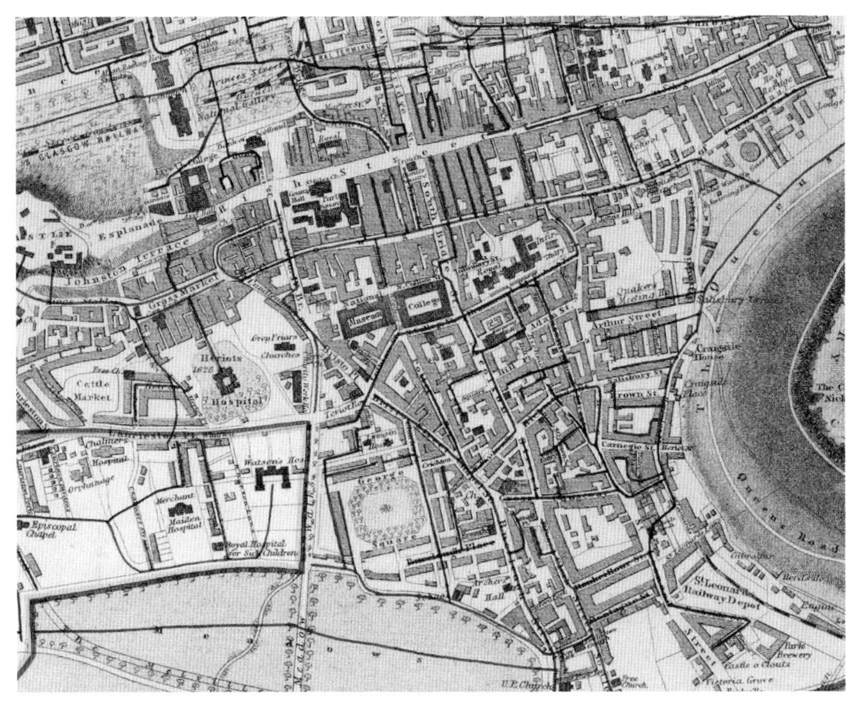

4.19 Street drains in central Edinburgh, 1869
An *ad hoc* and partial arrangement that creates a false impression of a system or network but which is in reality only storm drainage. Most tenement properties were not connected to the drains.
[Source: NLS Drainage Plan of Edinburgh and Leith, 1869]

mind that two-thirds of Edinburgh houses were worth less than £10 *per annum* rental. To Councillor Bryson's comment that, 'The people would pay for them', Bailie Johnston replied, 'Thus it is you increase the charge on the poor', and especially discriminate against poor women who constituted over a quarter of all household heads in properties rented at below £10 per annum.[124] To the physical and social character of tenements a cultural argument also fuelled opposition to the compulsory introduction of water supplies. Littlejohn observed, 'The poor require preliminary education in keeping their houses and stairs clean, before they can be trusted in the manner proposed.'[125] Where tenements were connected to the water supply it was abused, as in one case where an examination revealed pipework choked with '14 knives, 1 putty do., 9 forks, 6 tablespoons, 1 dozen teaspoons, old blankets, cloths (sundry), 2 shoe-brushes, filth.'[126] It was confirmation, if any were necessary, of an investigation in 1858 that tenants were unaccustomed to sanitary appliances and that this resulted in a 'greater degree of damage'.[127]

124 *Caledonian Mercury*, 4 March 1863, 4ab.
125 *Report*, 80.
126 See note 104: Henry Littlejohn Report to Council on 20 December 1864, reported in *The Scotsman*, 21 December 1864, 7b.
127 *Report of the Committee of the Working Classes of Edinburgh on the Present Overcrowded and Uncomfortable State of their Dwelling Houses*, with an introduction and notes by Alexander

An economic context was also a barrier to supplying water to every dwelling. The method of waste disposal which operated in Edinburgh substituted labour for capital investment in domestic water technology, with residents carrying clean water up stairways and taking their sewage and other waste down the same stairs to the street, from where some 100–150 scavengers were employed daily to remove the waste. Approximately 150,000 tons of solid waste was disposed of each year in this way. Because the commissioners had a monopoly of this 'police manure', as the solid waste and street sweepings were called, they sold it to farms as fertiliser, and the receipts, estimated as £7,000 annually, funded the cleaning operations of the city (see chapter 3).[128] Although Littlejohn himself extolled the sanitary virtues of this daily cleaning regime, the revenue from the police manure system so appealed to the council that they endorsed the existing arrangements and retreated from any confrontation with property owners.[129] For these reasons Littlejohn's opposition to the use of clause 210 of the Lindsay Act, 1862, to compel the installation of water-closets in tenement homes might initially seem a retrograde step but was both logical and practical.[130] While there was an adequate water supply, there was not yet an adequate system of waste water and sewage disposal in 1865.[131]

Faced with these obstacles and the futile and dangerous schemes for installing water-closets without water, Littlejohn recommended practical and inexpensive solutions, measures which would certainly benefit public health even if they lacked the political appeal of grander schemes. As he noted in 1866, 'the ventilation of sewers has not been lost sight of by our authorities, but with 800 untrapped street cesspools in our midst, to form ventilation shafts would be a work of supererogation'.[132] So more modest yet productive suggestions were forthcoming from Littlejohn: the provision of street urinals, of publicly maintained lavatory blocks, of domestic sanitary engineering to trap drains and isolate cesspools from dwellings, and of lighting on common stairs so that they could be kept clean, were all practical improvements, easily realised, and which offered considerable sanitary benefits.[133] No single approach to the water and drainage issues was appropriate, as government medical inspectors Dr George Buchanan and John Netten Radcliffe confirmed when justifying the continued use of dry earth closets in Burnet's Close in 1874: 'for some time to come the

Macpherson, Secretary to the Committee (Edinburgh, 1860), 14.

128 C. Hamlin, 'Environmental sensibility in Edinburgh 1839–40: the "fetid irrigation' controversy', *Journal of Urban History*, 20:3 (1994), 311–39; P.J. Smith, 'The foul burns of Edinburgh: public health attitudes and environmental change', *Scottish Geographical Journal*, 91:1 (1975), 27, fig. 2. There were irrigated meadows at Lochend, Craigentinny, Dalry, Roseburn, Craigmillar and Blackford.

129 In a paper read to the National Association for the Promotion of Social Science on 12 October 1863, published in their *Transactions* (London, 1864), 513–18, and again with fuller quotations from reports on Liverpool and Manchester in Henry D. Littlejohn, *On the Cleansing Operations of Edinburgh, as Compared with Other Towns* (Edinburgh, 1865).

130 *Report*, 109.

131 See *Evening Courant*, 11 October 1864, 4a–d; 12 October 1864, 4e; and 13 October 1864, 2d; *The Scotsman*, 24 October 1866, 8b; *Caledonian Mercury*, 23 October 1866, 3bc. Although in some periods, including the autumns of 1864 and 1866, there were complaints of shortages especially in the southern suburbs.

132 *The Scotsman*, 28 February 1866, 6d, Henry Littlejohn, Letter to the Editor.

133 See page 143.

old tenements of the city will have to be dealt with each upon its own merits as respects such disposal, and no uniform system will be practicable.'[134] Despite reservations about compulsory powers, clause 210 of the 1862 Act was invoked on almost a hundred occasions between 1864 and 1869 to enforce water-closet connections to the sewers, over 25% of which were located in the New Town.[135] It was evidence of a willingness to use different legal means to achieve appropriate local solutions to the water and drainage problems, and an astute reading of the political climate within which Littlejohn had to operate. He concluded, pragmatically, 'there is abundant scope for the compulsory introduction of conveniences' and though there were particular streets where 'it would be most injudicious to enforce the regulation', other streets and entire districts – Broughton, Calton, and Water of Leith – 'afford ample scope for improvement' in the introduction of water-closets.[136]

Rather than some grand design or overarching theory, Littlejohn's pragmatism was the result of a fragmented administrative structure in which there was no separate Health Committee which could unify public health policy. This fragmentation was both a strength and weakness: strength in that once Littlejohn's credentials were established it was difficult for parties to gainsay his empiricism and the actions derived from that; and weakness, insofar as more decisive interventions were not directly authorised by a powerful council committee for almost twenty years of his professional life as Police Surgeon and Medical Officer. On balance, the strengths of his personal standing probably outweighed the advantages of a Health Committee, and when that was finally approved it was very much on Littlejohn's own terms.[137]

No report on the city's drainage and water supply would have been possible without some reference to the Water of Leith – 'a great open sewer' running through Edinburgh which 'emits offensive odours' in close proximity to many of the most exclusive residences in the city.[138] Industrial effluent polluted the river, but more seriously, industrial demands for water along its course seriously reduced the volume of flow in what was more of an ambitious stream than a river. Littlejohn defused the clamorous expectations of New Town residents to address the condition of the Water of Leith in three ways: by noting that death rates were not high given the social composition of those clustered along the banks of this 'water'; that winter and summer death rates showed no discernible change as might have been expected in warmer months; and that the causes of death associated with 'sewage exhalations' – diarrhoea, dysentery, and fever – were not observably higher in these areas. Methodical in his analysis, Littlejohn selected a triangular area – India Place, Saunders Street and Kerr Street (see fig. 4.20)

134 PP (HC) 1874 [C. 1066], 'Report by Mr J. Netten Radcliffe on Certain Means of Preventing Excrement Nuisances in Towns and Villages', Reports of the Medical Officer of the Privy Council and Local Government Board, new series 2, supplementary reports (1874) 158 and plates I–IV. On public privy blocks see also PP (HC) 1870 [C. 208], 'Report by Dr Buchanan and Mr J. Netten Radcliffe on the Systems in Use in Various Northern Towns for Dealing with Excrement', Twelfth Report of the Medical Officer of the Privy Council (1870) 131–33, and plate XV.

135 ECA Council Scroll Index to volumes, 289–300, 26 July 1864 to 7 December 1869, 206–11.

136 *Report*, 81.

137 See chapter 5.

138 *Report*, 86.

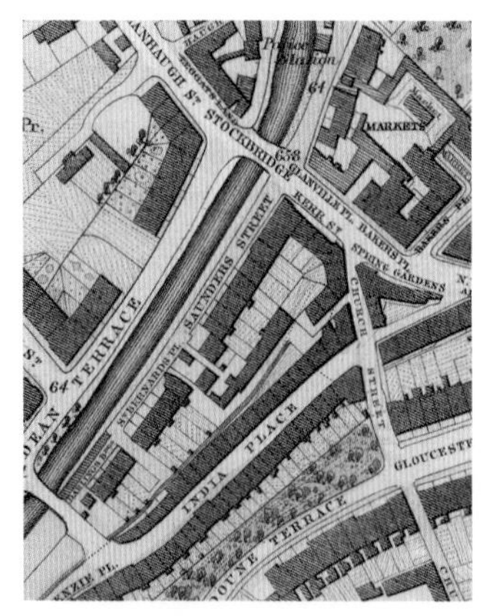

4.20 Littlejohn's mortality test
Littlejohn demonstrated that mortality in Kerr Street, Saunders Street and India Place was not raised by their proximity to the Water of Leith. [Source: NLS Lancefield 1861]

– notorious for the impurities in the stream and showed that, though higher than the waterside areas generally, the death rates and infant mortality rates were not attributable to disease associated with malodorous conditions.

The exercise, repeated on the north side of the Water of Leith, showed a closer association with overcrowding than any other causal factor. This was the statistical prelude to a set of astute conclusions: the purification of the Water of Leith was 'an important sanitary measure'; the removal of industrial production along the banks should be undertaken in due course; and 'my object' Littlejohn concluded, 'has been to warn the public against supposing, that the sanitary measures in question will have any material influence in diminishing the rate of mortality … Lower than at present, we can hardly expect it to be.'[139] In terms of epidemiology, since 'no marked connection could be proved between it [mortality] and sewage emanations',[140] Littlejohn showed agnosticism in relation to miasmatic theories of disease transmission, and greater emphasis on the social conditions in which the poor were housed. However unpleasant, smell did not cause disease, whether from irrigated meadows, proximity to cow byres, or according to access to air, as in Dickson's Court.[141] In three pages on the Water of Leith, Littlejohn deflected insistent demands over several decades from wealthy residents to invest in purification, while simultaneously putting down a marker that industrial users should literally clean up their mess, and showing concern for the overcrowded inhabitants of the area who, unlike many poorer people, were ideally placed to have water-closets introduced to their homes. It was a convincing instance of political economy combined with medical jurisprudence.

Cemeteries: 'a sanitary measure of no small importance'

Overcrowded burial grounds were a major concern to the Victorian sanitary reformers. Old parish graveyards were closed in many English towns in the 1840s following official reports on interment in urban areas by a select committee chaired by William Mackinnon (1842) and Edwin Chadwick (1843), and the activities of George Walker's National Society for the Abolition of Burials in Towns.[142] Scotland, however, lagged behind England in closing town burial places, and Littlejohn made this a major topic of his *Report*. The closure of Greyfriars churchyard, the burial ground for the Old Town, was, he claimed, 'a sanitary measure of no small importance'.[143] His central idea, that there should be a new cemetery beyond the built area of the city, indeed beyond its municipal boundary,

139 *Report*, 88.

140 *Report*, 81.

141 *Report*, Appendix, District of Tron, Dickson's Court.

142 PP 1842 (HL) (327) X and PP (HL) 1843 [509] XII, Select Committee on the Improvement of the Health of Towns, 'Report on Effect of Interment of Bodies in Towns', 349–563; Edwin Chadwick, *A Supplementary Report on the Results of a Special Inquiry into the Practice of Interment in Towns* (London, 1843). The standard literature on sanitary reform in early Victorian Britain has surprisingly little to say about burial grounds, and almost nothing about Scotland, which is habitually missing from several books and theses whose titles proclaim an interest in public health 'Great Britain'. Far more is to be found in the cultural history of burial practices, notably in the context of grave robbing and the Anatomy Acts: see especially R. Richardson, *Death, Dissection and the Destitute* (London, 1988).

143 *Report*, 94.

was not new. Indeed, there had been several such proposals in Edinburgh over the preceding decades. What distinguished his approach was his insistence that a cemetery should be in public hands, so that the poor could afford to bury their dead and that the local authority could fulfil their legal responsibilities under the Burial Act.[144] In conveying this message Littlejohn demonstrated his characteristic understanding of public opinion and forensic deployment of evidence. The problem of disposing of the dead in cities was a lifelong concern, and Littlejohn was an early proponent of cremation.[145]

Disposing of corpses in already crowded churchyards, especially in their public sections, involved disturbing existing graves, frequently with revolting practices which were not only a health hazard but which gave offence to those attending the burials of friends and family members. In December 1831 the Lord Provost had suggested that part of the Meadows, then still inadequately drained, might provide a cemetery.[146] The following year, a proposal to establish an elaborate cemetery at Hunter's Bog on the slopes of Arthur's Seat addressed the growing demand for funerals to take place in well-ordered burial places, away from the fetid air of the town, surrounded by nature, and ornamented with fine architecture; it would be, as the promoter put it, 'the *Père la Chaise* of Edinburgh'.[147] This idea, too, came to nothing.[148]

Early proposals were chiefly concerned with the practical issue of overcrowding and the consequent indecencies in old burial grounds. Littlejohn, who like Chadwick understood the economics of disposal of the dead, was equally concerned with those matters but was troubled by the effect on the poor of closing graveyards. Following the closure of Greyfriars churchyard they were at the mercy of the private cemetery companies. The funerary market was competitive, and Littlejohn's comment that soon after Warriston Cemetery was

144 18 and 19 Vict., cap. 68, Burial Grounds (Scotland) Act, 1855. Under section 10, following the closure of a burial ground by Order in Council, the Parochial Board was obliged to provide alternative ground.

145 The Edinburgh Cremation Society was inaugurated in the City Chambers on 3 February 1910 with Sir Henry Littlejohn as its first president, his son Professor Harvey Littlejohn as one of the vice-presidents and his niece Isabella Spring Brown as a member of the Executive Council. See *The Scotsman*, 4 February 1910, 10c. In the discussion the sanitary arguments, including the dangers of cholera and fever from close proximity to graveyards, were set against continuing public suspicion and opposition. Edinburgh's first crematorium at Warriston opened in 1929, so Littlejohn was cremated in Glasgow where a crematorium had been opened in 1895. In 1911 the total number of cremations in Scotland was 30: *The Scotsman*, 18 May 1911, 11a. By the day Littlejohn died in 1914 only 530 persons had been cremated in Scotland.

146 *The Scotsman*, 14 December 1831, 3a.

147 *Caledonian Mercury*, 28 April 1832, 3a. Although described as a public cemetery, it is unlikely that the writer meant a cemetery in public ownership and management. These ideas for spacious cemeteries beyond the town limits may appear at the onset of the first cholera epidemic in Britain but they more likely reflect changing tastes and sensibilities. Mount Auburn, the first American woodland cemetery, opened in 1831. Its relationship to Père la Chaise and to public health (its chief promoter was Professor of Medicine at Harvard) are discussed in D. Schuyler, *The New Urban Landscape: the Redefinition of City Form in Nineteenth-century America* (Baltimore, 1986), 37–56. Père la Chaise was established in 1804 as a government response to crowded and insanitary burial grounds in Paris: Schuyler, *The Redefinition of City Form*, 49.

148 *The Scotsman*, 14 December 1831, 3a; 14 January 1832, 4b; 25 February 1832, 3f; *Caledonian Mercury*, 28 April 1832, 3a.

opened in 1843 'the state of the money-market' encouraged the flotation of four more cemeteries in 1845 was entirely correct. These 'cemetery utilities', as Julie Rugg has termed them, like the gas and water companies and transport undertakings, were quoted daily on the Edinburgh Stock Exchange. They were pure investment opportunities, responding to a market for a certain quality of funeral; they were not public health initiatives.[149] In addition to the Edinburgh Cemetery Company's facility at Warriston, the five cemeteries (see fig. 4.22) opened in 1846 added an area more than twice that of all the old burial grounds put together: the Newington Necropolis at Echo Bank and Dalry Cemetery (both by the Metropolitan Cemetery Association), Dean Cemetery (Edinburgh Western Cemetery Company), Rosebank (Edinburgh and Leith Cemetery Company), and Grange (Southern Cemetery Company).[150]

In a characteristically pithy and judiciously worded passage Littlejohn set out his manifesto for dealing with burial of the dead:

> It is high time that this subject should be carefully considered … Should we be threatened with any pestilence, I feel convinced that Government would not hesitate for a moment in peremptorily preventing all intramural interment … I would propose that our City Parishes should combine to provide … a public Cemetery of large extent at some distance in the country, and of easy access, where the land would be cheap, and in which the rate of interment could be made as reasonable as possible, so as to meet the necessities of the poorest inhabitants. This is, in my opinion, a more crying want than a public park for any district of the city, and it is to be hoped that the scheme will meet with ready approval in these enlightened days of sanitary improvement, when even our Poorhouses are removed outside the city boundary.[151]

There is insistent, almost admonishing language here for the Town Council: it is 'high time' for action; central government would not hesitate to take the steps he recommends; this problem is more urgent that the luxury of a public park; these are 'enlightened days' so by implication to delay on this matter was to be unenlightened. This was but one of several matters – his appointment, diseased meat, water supply, and now burials – in which the vacillation and squabbling of the council were a scandalous obstacle to social and environmental improvement. This is a major lesson: that Victorian social progress was in large measure

149 As a result of the attractive dividend paid by the Edinburgh Cemetery Company, the other four companies, 'tastelessly eager to carve up the city', floated within days in a frenzied scramble for business. J. Rugg, 'The rise of cemetery companies in Britain, 1820–53', Stirling University Ph.D. thesis (1992), 215 and 219–21.

150 With the exception of Dean Cemetery, these cemeteries were finally purchased by Edinburgh Corporation between 1987 and 1994.

151 *Report*, 99. On the same page, in a passage added 'since these remarks were penned', Littlejohn noted the purchase of 230 acres from the Craiglockhart estate for £29,000 by the City Parochial Board (*The Scotsman*, 18 April 1865, 3a) for a new poorhouse and suggested that the remaining land would make a good site for a public cemetery. The chairman of the Parochial Board, David Curror, solicitor and town councillor 1859–64, remarked that 'Some of the more important of his suggestions to the Parochial Boards have happily been anticipated by the City Parish in the purchase of Craiglockhart, and some other may yet be accomplished realities there', *The Scotsman*, 26 September 1865, 4cd. The 'Proposed Site of West End Park' appears on the maps in the *Post-Office Edinburgh and Leith Directory* for 1864–65 and 1865–66.

the responsibility of local authorities, but that these bodies often failed their citizens. When the City Parochial Board met to consider Littlejohn's proposal for a cemetery at Craiglockhart the chairman, David Curror pointed out that Littlejohn,

> has overlooked one clause of the Burial Grounds Act, which provides that in cities like this the Town Council is constituted the Parochial Board to carry into execution the provisions of the Act. Hence you see that that Act does what he regrets has not been done – it combines all our parishes for its purposes. It is the Town Council who is to shut up existing churchyards in Edinburgh and to provide suitable cemeteries for all the parishes; and the provision is a wise one. The Council is trustee for all citizens alike, without regard to parochial boundaries.[152]

Naturally Littlejohn was perfectly aware of where the responsibility lay.

Although Littlejohn presented the closure of old churchyards as a health issue, it is not entirely clear whether he was endorsing the conclusions of the reports of 1842–43 that miasmas from buried corpses were a cause of disease, fever in particular, or whether he was mostly concerned with the lack of accommodation during epidemics. No new space was created between 1820 and 1843, during which time *at least* 100,000 corpses had to be accommodated in the 19 (mostly full) acres of the seven old churchyards and burial grounds.[153] The section of the *Report* on interments draws attention to the 'lessons taught us by the Cholera',[154] and Littlejohn clearly regarded cemeteries as a general sanitary threat when they were close to dwellings. Even if scientifically dubious, this approach was understandable in the light of the management of burial places, whether old churchyards or new cemeteries.[155] Time and again he raised the dangers of cholera, doubtless having in mind the spectacle and smell of the open pits in which bodies had lain exposed, often for several days – a practice commonly condemned in other cities.[156]

Littlejohn again pressed for a public cemetery a year after the publication of the *Report*. In a statement to the council on 4 September 1866 he reminded them of what he had said, that the law required them to facilitate speedy burial of the dead, that the closure of the old city churchyards would raise the burial fees in the cemeteries, and that the poor would be unable to pay to bury their

152 *The Scotsman*, 26 September 1865, 4c.

153 St Cuthbert's, Greyfriars, Canongate, St John's and Holy Trinity churchyards, and New Calton and East Preston Street burial grounds. The Quaker and Jewish cemeteries were tiny.

154 *Report*, 93.

155 See below for his findings on the matter in 1883. A modern visitor to some of these cemeteries, now rarely used for burials, and in which the dangers are from insecure monuments and drug users rather than the odours of rotting flesh, might not appreciate their busy state in the Victorian era. Mistaken miasmatic theories of disease were not required to regard them as offensive to worried citizens inclined to be offended.

156 Dr George Glover described this practice in Canongate churchyard in December 1848, and it was one of the more serious objections to intramural burial raised by a report for the Liverpool Health of Towns Association which was generally sceptical of the medical dangers but intolerant of the nuisance and offence caused by insufficient space for burials in the built areas of the town, *The Scotsman*, 27 December 1848, 3g; *The Liverpool Health of Towns Advocate*, 1 March 1847, 167–68.

4.21 Greyfriars churchyard: closed by Littlejohn
The churchyard today contains the tombs of the affluent; the communal graves of the poor remain invisible. In the 1860s Greyfriars was already considered full, and Littlejohn decided to prohibit further burials after 1863. He acknowledged the decision forced the poor into the hands of the commercial cemetery companies.

dead. Only the corporation, he said, could act in this matter, and in epidemics it was an urgent public health matter.[157]

In October 1866, less than a month after chiding the council for not taking up his recommendation to establish a public cemetery, Littlejohn warned of the lack of burial space for cholera victims. The Lord Provost's Committee reported to the council 'on a letter from the Medical Officer of Health as to public interments, the results of various conferences ... between representatives of the committee and directors of the various cemetery companies.'[158] It was agreed that the six private cemeteries would inter, 'on application of the Public Officer of Health' and 'in rotation', those who had died of cholera. The Town Council would meet the cost.[159] Littlejohn, who was given full powers to act in the matter, was clearly driving this arrangement, and although the reports say that members of the Lord Provost's Committee had negotiated with the companies, there are clear

157 *The Scotsman*, 5 September 1866, 8a.

158 *The Scotsman*, 3 October 1866, 6d.

159 *The Scotsman*, 3 October 1866, 6d; *Evening Courant*, 3 October 1866, 4f. The reports make it clear that the long-standing arrangement with the Parochial Boards would not be affected. In this case the 'local authority' was the Town Council.

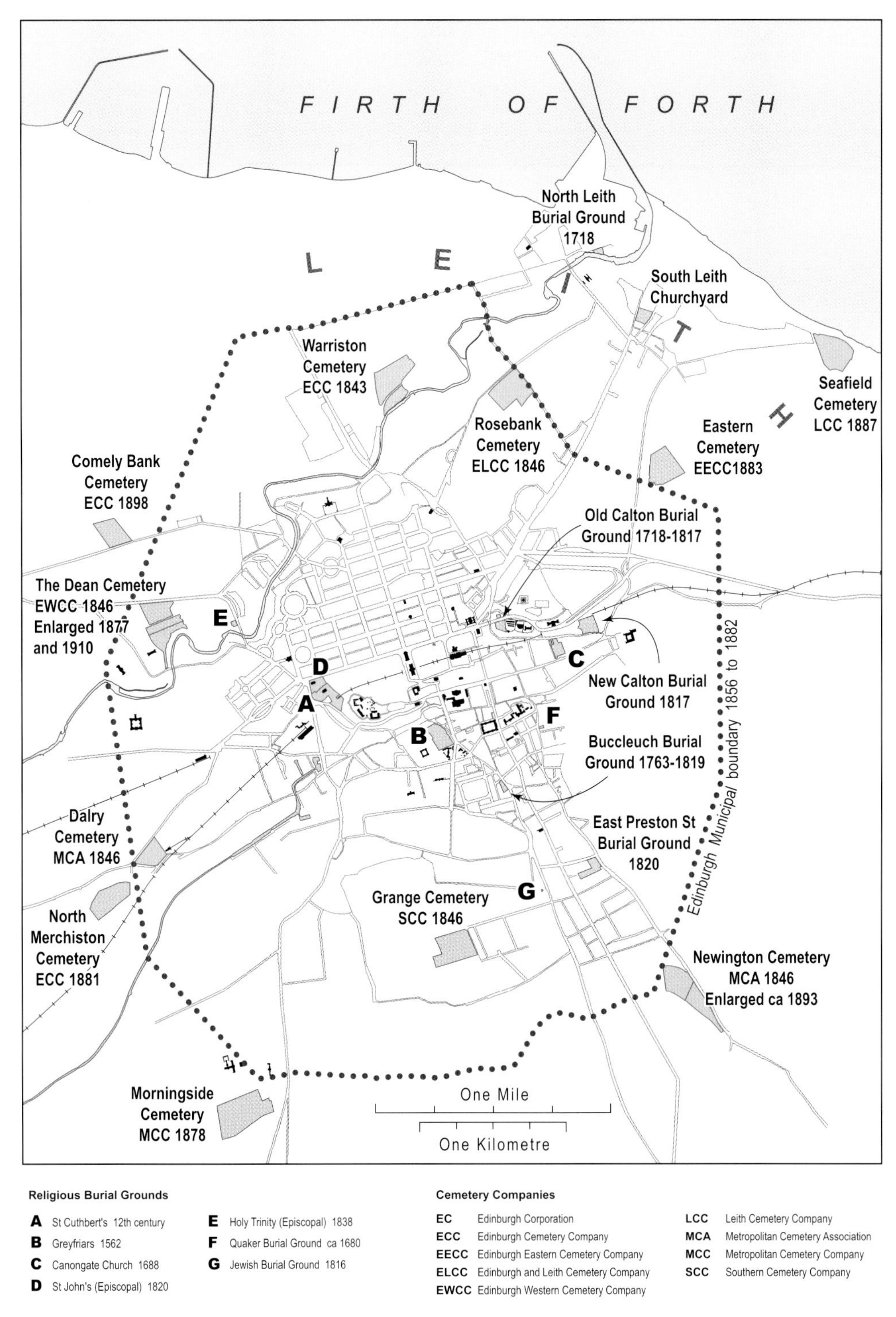

4.22 Edinburgh cemeteries

The joint-stock cemetery companies established a ring of burial grounds around the city in 1843–46. More commercial cemeteries were added, and some enlarged, from 1877, but no municipal cemetery was established until 1959.

indications that this was all Littlejohn's doing.[160] The rates for burials were agreed as the minimum for a standard interment at each cemetery, ranging from 11 shillings at Warriston, Newington, Dalry and Rosebank to 20 shillings at Dean. In the year ending 29 June 1867 the council paid for approximately 400 burials.[161]

In his *Report* Littlejohn indulged his keen interest in the history of the city's burial grounds beyond what was strictly necessary for his purpose. Members of his extensive family were interred in several of them, but his historical research may have been a means to capture the attention of the many readers who extolled their city through its past. As a brilliant anatomist and dissector, Littlejohn also had good reason to understand an aspect of graveyards with particular significance in Edinburgh, the consequences of grave robbing.[162] Even before the Anatomy Act, 1832, not all stolen cadavers for sale to medical schools were taken from graveyards, but fear of disinterment led to elaborate attempts to secure graves. His claim that the Act had stopped disinterment entirely is certainly the judgment of one who should know.[163]

Littlejohn's recall of the attempt to force the closure of Canongate churchyard in 1848 was probably drawn from personal knowledge. At that time he was a newly qualified doctor helping out at the New Town Dispensary to treat cholera cases. It would certainly have coloured his views on the question.[164] J.G. Blaikie, the General Police Commissioner for the ward and a local resident, had been so alarmed at the state of the churchyard that he called in George Glover, the Police Surgeon, and the Police Superintendent to investigate. Glover described finding open pits with bodies lying uncovered for days until the pits were sufficiently full to be covered. Even when covered, some with only five inches of soil, they stank abominably. Glover had concluded that because many fatal cases had occurred in the Canongate, and he considered the state of the churchyard to be 'a nuisance and dangerous to the neighbourhood'.[165] Blaikie wrote to the Town Council describing the revolting condition of the yard, enclosing Glover's sworn testimony and that of another doctor, and asking for advice. In another instance of impotence caused by administrative areas, the Lord Provost replied that Canongate was outside his jurisdiction and that he should try the Sheriff instead.[166] An angry public meeting demanded the closure of all but private

160 *Caledonian Mercury*, 2 October 1866, 3a.

161 The location and number of the burials could doubtless be ascertained from the cemetery records, but the total amount paid in that year was £227 2*s.* 6*d.* (4,452.5 shillings). *Abstracts of the Accounts of The Edinburgh Police Establishment, for the Year ended at Whitsunday 1867; including payments made up to 29th June 1867, of expenses incurred within the Year* (Edinburgh, 1867), 19. It seems unlikely that the exclusive Dean Cemetery accepted cholera victims from the lower classes.

162 *Report*, 94.

163 There was a continuing shortage of corpses in Victorian Edinburgh and some were shipped in from Ireland. We are grateful to Dr S. Sturdy for information on this point. See also E.T. Hurley, 'Whose body is it anyway? Trading the dead poor, Coroner's disputes, and the business of anatomy at Oxford University, 1885–1929, *Bulletin of the History of Medicine*, 82:4 (2008), 775–818, who shows in a later period how the shortage of bodies affected the transport of corpses for miles around Oxford. See also R. Richardson, *Death, Dissection and the Destitute*.

164 *Report*, 92. Two cases in the New Town in November 1848 signed by Littlejohn are among the cholera returns preserved in the Royal College of Physicians, Edinburgh.

165 *The Scotsman*, 27 December 1848, 3g; *Caledonian Mercury*, 4 January 1849, 3e.

166 *The Scotsman*, 27 December 1848, 3g.

burials and squarely blamed the Canongate and Kirk authorities, calling for the dismissal of the Kirk Recorder and, in the case of one protester, quoting passages from 'the work of Dr Walker, published in London ten years ago' to denote best practice. In the event the churchyard remained open with new personnel, reformed practice, and the deposit of several hundred tons of soil over the worse northern parts of the ground.[167] In the very same week, and not unnoticed by the Edinburgh press, the magistrates in Glasgow (three Bailies and the Lord Provost) ordered the closure of three private cemeteries in Calton and Bridgeton using powers under the new Nuisances Removal Act, 1849.[168]

Littlejohn seems to have found it hard to establish accurate numbers of interments in the city. His table (p. 95) and the accompanying commentary (pp. 97–8) were significantly revised for the second printing, but by 1866 when the abridged edition was published they had been revised again in the text, though there were no further changes to the table. The revisions and additions are indicated in the notes to this edition of the *Report*.

Reviewing Littlejohn's *Report* as a whole, the editor of the *Caledonian Mercury* drew particular attention to Littlejohn's comment that a public cemetery was, in his opinion, 'a more crying want than a public park for any district of the city'.[169] 'There are few reflective persons,' wrote the editor, 'who will call in question either the clamant nature of the want or the accuracy of the opinion formed with regard to it ... as there are very few reflective persons, however, in our present Town Council, it is just possible that, not withstanding their officer's facts and opinions, they will keep on talking about Meadow improvements, the West End Park, bells for St Giles', or Mr Chambers' antique hobby, the erection of "The Old Cross".'[170]

The failure of the local authority to tackle the cemetery issue continued to frustrate Littlejohn. The firm suggestion in his *Report* for a public cemetery beyond the municipal limits prompted no response. In 1866 he presented a formal reminder to the council of their responsibilities: 'Among the duties which fall to be discharged by the local authority in such an emergency as the present is, in the words of the Act of Parliament, to provide for the speedy interment of the dead.'[171] The recommendation was as crystal clear as the argument

167 *The Scotsman*, 6 January 1849, 3g and 4d; *Caledonian Mercury*, 4 January 1849, 3e. On 31 January 1850 the Office of Woods and Forests wrote to Dr Glover to ascertain whether the works had been completed to his satisfaction. He failed to answer and in June was instructed by the Police Commissioners to do so. ECA ED9/1/12/74, 3 June 1850.

168 *Glasgow Herald*, 8 January 1849, 2c–e. The *Herald* reported the three-hour sitting in full detail, rightly recognising its significance. The report illustrates vividly the issues involved in closing private cemeteries. No compensation was awarded on the grounds that factories and the like were frequently closed when they were deemed a nuisance. For the Edinburgh summary, see *Caledonian Mercury*, 11 January 1849, 3b. The Nuisances Removal Act, 11 and 12 Vict. cap. 123, was passed on 4 September 1848 and gave powers to stop nuisances; and under an amending Act, 12 and 13 Vict. cap 111, 1 August 1849, gave powers under section 9 to the General Board of Health to regulate or close burial grounds, but did not extend to Scotland. See W.C. Glen, *The Nuisances Removal and Diseases Prevention Acts, 1848 & 1849* (London, 1849), 3rd edn, and for the Act see http://www.archive.org/stream/nuisancesremova02glengoog#page/n5/mode/1up

169 *Report*, 99. See also *The Scotsman*, 18 April 1865, 3a; 19 April 1865, 2cd.

170 *Caledonian Mercury*, 30 August 1865, 2bc.

171 *The Scotsman*, 5 September 1866, 8a.

supporting it. The response was to convey the impression that they were hearing it for the first time: 'After some conversation it was agreed to remit the letter for consideration to the Lord Provost's Committee to confer with other public bodies if necessary, and to report.'[172] When at last the council established a Public Health Committee in December 1872, Littlejohn had a stronger power base and thus a more effective way of carrying out investigations and presenting recommendations to the full council. In 1874 the city, supported by eminent medical witnesses, went to court to force St Cuthbert's Parochial Board to close the public sections of its burial grounds in Lothian Road, Buccleuch Street and East Preston Street. They were successful; but this, yet again, simply made the lack of public provision worse. The council seemed happy to take action against others but incapable of providing the solution.

In 1883 Littlejohn once again urged the question of a public cemetery by presenting a formal report to the Public Health Committee. In characteristic style, after rehearsing the central arguments in the 1865 *Report*, he set out the results of a scientific survey of the private cemeteries authorised by the committee. Between 30 March and 12 April 1882, with the expert assistance of the superintendent of Greyfriars churchyard, he visited six of the private cemeteries and made 324 borings to ascertain the depth of burials. It was a damning judgment on the private cemeteries. Eleven of the 30 burials bored in Dalry Cemetery were less than two feet from the surface, one just eight inches deep. In England, Littlejohn observed sharply, a minimum of four feet had been mandatory 'for a great number of years'; and he agreed with 'the most recent authorities' that it should be six feet. By demonstrating these lax practices he was attempting to convince the council that the private cemeteries were not to be trusted with the interment of the mass of ordinary citizens who did not possess private plots or mausoleums.[173] Regretting that these cemeteries had not been placed outside the city boundary for they were now 'more or less surrounded by residences', he recommended annual inspection. But even this full frontal assault achieved almost nothing with the Town Council who, faced with pleas from the Trades Council, medical opinion and their own Public Health Committee to establish a public cemetery outside the municipal boundary, batted the report back and forth to the committee, unprepared to make a decision in principle until every last detail was before them.[174] Suggestions at a meeting of the Trades Council that the matter was being delayed because members of the Town Council, and especially the Health Committee, had interests in the private cemetery companies were strongly refuted. 'All members of the Committee were agreed,' said Bailie Clark convener of the Public Health Committee, 'as to the necessity of such a cemetery at a suitable time and in a suitable place.'[175] This

172 *The Scotsman*, 5 September 1866, 8a.

173 *The Scotsman*, 3 January 1883, 9bc. The sixth private cemetery was Dean, owned by the Edinburgh Western Cemetery Company whose cooperation was less than full. Littlejohn was unable to work there until late June and his public strictures on them in his report led the company to publish their letters to him; *The Scotsman*, 4 January 1883, 2e. Littlejohn's ashes were buried in the Dean Cemetery in 1914 and a memorial seat to him was set up near the family plot in 2004.

174 *The Scotsman*, 21 February 1883, 5g and 7 March 1883, 5f.

175 *The Scotsman*, 7 February 1883, 9a.

very public failure to heed the considered advice of the Medical Officer of Health occurred some 18 months before the Lord Provost boasted (to loud applause) at a public dinner that Edinburgh 'was perhaps the healthiest large city in the world' and that its 'citizens and Corporation did all they could for the preservation of health and life, and that under the direction of the Medical Officer of Health, their esteemed friend Dr Littlejohn – (Hear, hear, and applause.)'[176] The private companies opened further cemeteries in the nineteenth century, and Littlejohn continued to admonish them into the twentieth. The first municipal cemetery in Edinburgh was opened in 1960.[177]

Littlejohn as a social scientist

When the National Association for the Promotion of Social Science held its annual congress in Edinburgh in 1863, Professor Robert Christison as president of the public health section benefited from the services of his outstanding former student, Henry Littlejohn, as local secretary.[178] Established in July 1857 by an influential group of liberal figures, notably by Lord Brougham, founder of the *Edinburgh Review*, the NAPSS defined its aim as 'to unite together as far as possible the various efforts now being made for the moral and social improvement of the people'.[179] The Association was led by 'an extraordinarily distinguished group of public figures interested in social reform'.[180] Among them were leading sanitarians, including William Farr, Sir James Kay-Shuttleworth, Thomas Southwood Smith, Edwin Chadwick, John Simon, Richard Cobden, John Bright, John Stuart Mill, and the Earl of Shaftesbury, as well as influential businessmen, churchmen, and prominent campaigners for women's rights.[181] The organisational structure adopted by the NAPSS, though modelled on the British Association for the Advancement of Science, sought to be more inclusive in order that disparate organisations acted with greater cohesion in relation to social improvement. This was a reaction to the earlier Health of Towns Association which, though it had 'a key role in equating public health with

4.23 Sir Robert Christison (1797–1882)
Christison held the chair of medical jurisprudence and medical police and was one of Littlejohn's university teachers. His distinguished career was reflected in his election as President of both the RCPEd and RCSEd, and in 1875 as President of the British Medical Association.
[Source: Wellcome Library, London]

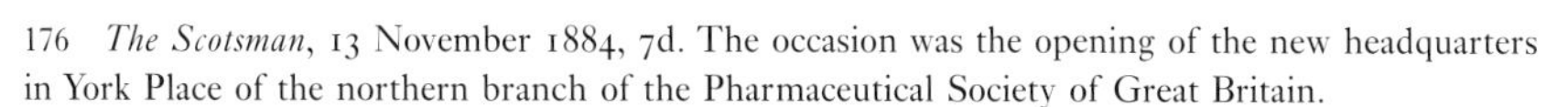

176 *The Scotsman*, 13 November 1884, 7d. The occasion was the opening of the new headquarters in York Place of the northern branch of the Pharmaceutical Society of Great Britain.

177 A Dundee newspaper ran a 'News in Brief' story which simply read: 'Sir Henry Littlejohn has been passing severe strictures upon the Edinburgh cemeteries', *Courier and Argus*, 10 February 1900, 6a. Mortonhall Cemetery, opened in 1960, was the first municipally owned cemetery; the Corporation also two took over two previously privately owned cemeteries (Corstorphine Hill and Saughton) between 1987 and 1994 (see http://www.lands-tribunal-scotland.org.uk/decisions/LTS.COMP.1997.04t007.html) under compulsory purchase orders during the liquidation proceedings of Edinburgh and Essex Property Management Limited.

178 In addition to Public Health the other four sections of the NAPSS were jurisprudence and the amendment of the law; education; social economy; and punishment and reformation. Christison was professor of medical jurisprudence and public health, and co-authored the standard text on public health, *The Medico-Legal Examination of Dead Bodies* (1839) before concentrating on toxicology.

179 L. Goldman, *Science, Reform, and Politics in Victorian Britain: the Social Science Association, 1857–1886* (Cambridge, 2007), 27–34.

180 M.W. Flinn, 'Introduction' in A.P. Stewart and E. Jenkins, *Medical and Legal Aspects of Sanitary Reform* (Leicester repr., 1969), 21. Stewart spoke at the Birmingham meeting of the NAPSS.

181 *The Times*, 14 October 1857, 7e–8f provides an account of the inaugural meeting in Birmingham Town Hall.

sanitary improvement', was no more capable than the General Board of Health of providing a focus for public health reform beyond the narrow technocratic approach to drains, sewerage and smoke abatement.[182] The NAPSS provided a bridge, therefore, between the sanitary mission of the 1840s and a wider social and civic vision of public health in the 1860s. No doubt the Edinburgh contingent which attended the Birmingham meeting in 1857 – the Revd Dr James Begg, the Revd Dr Thomas Guthrie, Dr E.C. Seaton, Robert Chambers, Dr John Sutherland, and Professor James Pillans – were instrumental in relaying the proceedings to the Edinburgh citizenry. So when Littlejohn acted as local organiser for the public health section of the NAPSS meeting in 1863 he was aligned on a national stage with social scientists who, as Christison explained in his presidential address, regarded public health as a branch of social science.[183]

This national context provides a clue to Littlejohn's approach to public health based not on a narrow technical branch of sanitary provision but on a holistic or interdisciplinary dimension to urban society and its ills. Littlejohn was concerned in his *Report* with the systematic study of society and social relationships in Edinburgh. His first priority was to develop a better understanding of the social areas of the city. Even *The Scotsman* understood the utility of more accurate statistics: 'They [mortality tables] throw a strong light on the condition of the population. They show how abundance or scarcity of employment, cheap or dear bread, cold or hot seasons, affect the general health.'[184] The energetic physician James Stark, later to become Registrar-General for Scotland, began from 1846 to revive the eighteenth-century practice of publishing monthly bills of mortality for Edinburgh and used the same classification of diseases as in the London Bills of Mortality.[185] He issued blank certificates to all physicians who completed them stating the cause of death; these were then collected by burial officials and returned to Stark to be collated as monthly city-wide mortality figures. Littlejohn, however, needed to track mortality at a local or district level to produce a meaningful analysis of the social geography of disease in the city. So it was essential first to record deaths and causes of death at the level of individual streets. Only then could he reassemble the data for areas which more faithfully reflected the social character of the various districts of the city.

In describing the geography of disease, Littlejohn's second priority was to provide a historical context. This long run perspective was frequently to be found in the *Report*. In doing so, Littlejohn's purpose was both to remind readers, and councillors, of the recent history of epidemic disease and of its potentially disastrous consequences for an insanitary city, as was the case within recent memory in 1847–49. It was also to provide a robust and incontrovertible empirical basis with which to withstand the inevitable sniping his *Report* could expect from those disinclined to increase council spending. Littlejohn's 'data-rich' research

182 R. Paterson, 'The Health of Towns Association, 1844–1849', *Bulletin of the History of Medicine*, 22 (1948), 373 (Cambridge, 1998), 249–57.

183 *The Times*, 15 October 1863, 5a.

184 *The Scotsman*, 18 March 1846, 3c.

185 *The Scotsman*, 18 March 1846, 3c. The article also provides information relating to the collection of mortality data between 1739 and 1794, and notes that the Edinburgh approach was similar to that in London.

produced a hard-copy Victorian version of a modern spreadsheet. He re-worked civil registration data, analysed unpublished enumeration books for 1861, and exploited personal data in hospital admission records and burial registers. He even personally checked the records of the slaughterhouses. With no qualified assistance other than a part-time clerk, and using only a slide rule or logarithmic tables, he produced comparative statistical data for each of his nineteen newly defined sanitary districts. The results, mostly in percentages to two decimal points, have been cross-checked and shown to have very few errors, some of which were those of the printer. It is fair to state that no city in nineteenth-century Britain was subjected to a more detailed public health analysis than Littlejohn's work on Edinburgh.

The breath-taking scale of Littlejohn's empirical undertaking itself is sufficient to mark it out as fundamentally different from that of earlier investigations of public health.[186] In many ways his approach paralleled that of his teacher, William T. Gairdner, who explored the use of census returns and applied similar methods of districting and record linkage in his textbook on public health before moving in 1863 to Glasgow as professor of medicine and Medical Officer of Health.[187] However, these two men, who stand together in the similarity of their geographical and statistical approaches towards public health investigation, had rather different personae: Littlejohn, the public man, was more comfortable in the messy world of municipal politics; Gairdner was more at home in the world of academia.

Littlejohn's empiricism was complemented by his fieldwork skills as a geographer, coupled with his oral interview skills and acute understanding of the social contours and boundaries of the city.[188] The result was first-class social investigation by a man with a penetrating analytical mind and values driven more by an adherence to the Hippocratic oath to relieve suffering than by a preoccupation with death and its causes. Like his mentor, William Alison, morbidity rather than mortality was a key concern for Littlejohn, as the various sections of his *Report* make clear.[189] The methodological and statistical rigour of Littlejohn was driven by an imperative to improve public health *administration*, and, unlike Edwin Chadwick or even Henry Duncan in Liverpool, data collection had a very clearly defined purpose for him, and was one reason why Littlejohn remained influential in public life long after his *Report* had been published.

Public engagement was a significant aspect of Littlejohn's duties, and the impact of the *Report* further enhanced the stature of the man. He was acknowledged as an expert on social statistics, and his peers – men such as

186 An exception is Professor W.T. Gairdner who focused in Glasgow on rates of change rather than crude numbers of population, and who journeyed to London to exploit the manuscript enumerators' books for that purpose.

187 W.T. Gairdner, *Public Health in Relation to Air and Water* (Edinburgh, 1862), 344–51; W.T. Gairdner, *Memorandum for the Chairman of the Sanitary Committee to Accompany a Map of the Sanitary Districts of Glasgow by the Medical Officer of Health* (Glasgow, 1865).

188 *The Broadford Courier and Reedy Creek Times*, 3 December 1897, 5h, provides an account of how a young Australian medical student was encouraged by Littlejohn to undertake 'a lot of practical work' which included 'inspection of butchers' shops, bakehouses, dairies etc., sewage works, etc.'.

189 See C. Hamlin, 'Could you starve to death in England in 1839? The Chadwick–Farr controversy and the loss of the "social" in public health', *American Journal of Public Health*, 85:6 (1995), 856–66.

Gairdner, Mapother, and his obituarists – recognised this. International awareness of the Littlejohn *Report* was forthcoming in an India Office publication – a Sanitary report from Bengal, Madras and Bombay[190] – and his views were sought by the Registrar-General on questions relating to the Census (1871), by royal commissioners and departmental officials investigating the relationship between diseased food and human health (1866, 1888, 1896), on rivers pollution (1873), and as an expert witness to royal commissions on the Housing of the Working Classes (1885), and on the Notification of Infectious Diseases (1876). Littlejohn's *Report* was acknowledged through his weekly health reports published in the Edinburgh press, and as a result of his numerous contributions on public health presented to the Board of Supervision in Scotland. There were over 600 citations to Henry Littlejohn in the *British Medical Journal* alone – equivalent to more than one per month during the fifty years following the publication of the *Report* – and he fulfilled an important role for some years as the President of the State Medicine section of the British Medical Association.[191] Presidential roles were also fulfilled for the United Kingdom Police Surgeons' Association, British Institute of Public Health, and the Society of Medical Officers of Health for Scotland, as well as for local and Scottish organisations.

Littlejohn sought to ensure that his readers understood that community health was inseparable from public policy, and that public administration was designed to relieve suffering, and to address and mitigate forces which could damage the health of local inhabitants.

190 Report on Measures Adopted for Sanitary Improvements in India, together with Abstracts of Reports for 1868 Forwarded from Bengal, Madras and India [T.G. Hewlett] (India Office Paper 6017: London, 1870), 251–53.

191 Abstracted from the *British Medical Journal* index.

CHAPTER 5

Urban management in the age of Littlejohn

'The object of this Report,' Littlejohn stated in his conclusion, is 'to deal with those obstacles to the well-being of society.'[1] He was in no doubt that the principal 'obstacle' to sanitary and environmental improvements was 'that no one can interfere *in limine*', by which he meant that as things stood municipal intervention was only possible once a nuisance had developed. In Littlejohn's words: 'it is not until the house becomes uninhabitable that the authorities can interfere.'[2] Policy was reactive, not pro-active. In the wealthy Grange suburb no consultation took place with the City Engineer over the design and direction of drains, and only when 'some defect is ascertained' were his services as the responsible municipal officer required. Similarly, landlords had routed drains under sleeping quarters rather than incur the greater expense of constructing them on the exterior of new tenement property. Crucially, city authorities could not interfere *in limine* – from the outset – but only after such properties were tenanted and the consequences of defective design had become apparent.

Littlejohn stated that 'private rights should succumb to the efficient control of a central authority'.[3] His view of municipal intervention was entirely consistent with contemporary ideas of liberalism, since for the state to function prior knowledge of those it sought to govern was essential.[4] This was precisely how the initial sentence of Littlejohn's *Report* began, by recognising that with civil registration in 1855 'it first became possible to ascertain with precision' the condition of the population. Quantification and categorisation, hallmarks of Littlejohn's methodology throughout his *Report*, increasingly became the *credo* of municipalities, Edinburgh included, as each grappled with expanding responsibilities in the second half of the nineteenth century. A developing audit culture also demanded accountability for significant increases in Victorian public expenditure. The plea for supervision from the beginning of a project was, therefore, an implicit appeal to local taxpayers and elected officials for greater efficiency in public administration by anticipating problems and so limiting public and private expense in the longer term. It struck at the heart of local

1 *Report*, 119.

2 *Report*, 118.

3 *Report*, 118. More specifically this was a comment on broadening the terms of reference of the Dean of Guild Court from an arbiter of nuisances in part of the city to the monitor of building control throughout the extended city.

4 See P. Joyce, *The Rule of Freedom: Liberalism and the Modern City* (London, 2003), 20–97 for an extended discussion on this point. See also, M.J. Daunton, *Trusting Leviathan: The Politics of Taxation in Britain, 1799–1914* (Cambridge, 2001), 58–76.

government, then and now. Prudence dictated intervention from the outset of any development as an insurance against later catastrophic expenditure; this precautionary principle was Littlejohn's compass. Rarely, however, was there a consensus for major infrastructural projects; councillors and ratepayers alike argued that such schemes added unnecessarily to local taxation. Nonetheless, Littlejohn concluded:

> No district should be built upon, and no house should be erected, until a drainage plan has been prepared and submitted for approval to the Magistrates, in whom all sewers should be vested.[5]

Ordering society through 'common-sense regulation' from the outset benefited inhabitants because it released them from the tyranny of the landlord, diminished their exposure to ill-health, and enabled them to function more actively as members of society. Regulation meant that the streets were clean, noxious industrial fumes were controlled, and exposure to occupational hazards limited; it meant that an industrious population was less susceptible to ill-health and to the consequential downward spiral of interrupted employment.[6] The wealth of nations was dependent on the health of nations.

Littlejohn's approach represented medical jurisprudence in action: anticipating public health concerns and recommending administrative initiatives to address them. Reciprocity was also involved, since the citizen's right to receive assistance 'naturally involves the *counter right* of inspection, by duly qualified and *responsible* agents'.[7] While Littlejohn recognised the expert knowledge of engineers, inspectors, cleaning and other municipal officials and the staff under their supervision, he was also frustrated by the administrative structure within which he had to operate. He argued for the consolidation of executive authority, pointed to the inconsistencies between the way parochial boards dealt with paupers, and the inequalities that resulted. He urged that the city, St Cuthbert's and Canongate parochial boards be amalgamated and also noted jealousy between parish officials in the existing arrangements. From 'a glance at the map' the 'three great divisions' of the city were recognisable, but from a sanitary point of view the city had to be treated as an integrated whole, with different arguments presented to appeal to each area.[8] The desirability of a unitary authority was a theme which had been seized upon by *The Scotsman* a few months earlier in 1865: 'Unity is simplicity; and Edinburgh is not so large a place that a united and simplified administration of parochial relief would be cumbrous and unwieldy.'[9] In relation to poor relief, Littlejohn concluded that 'A better example of the benefit to be derived from centralization and union can hardly be given', and then moved the focus to turf wars and struggles among the City, the County Road Trusts, and proprietors 'all with separate interests, in the struggle for which, the general good is not subserved'.[10] This critique of the structure of public administration,

5 *Report*, 118.
6 *Report*, 118.
7 W.P. Alison, *Observations on the Epidemic Fever* (1844), 31, quoted by L.S. Jacyna in *ODNB*.
8 *Report*, 100.
9 *The Scotsman*, 19 April 1865, 2cd.
10 *Report*, 118.

allied to the comments about the toothless power of municipal departments at the outset of construction projects, was equally relevant to the field of public health.

Littlejohn was careful, however, not to trample on the sensibilities of various interest groups. The data, he claimed, would allow philanthropists to target 'their enquiries into the social condition of our poor'. He strongly approved of the efforts of women missionaries, noted the contributions of 'several important sanitary agencies', and observed that:

> we find ourselves surrounded by religious agencies busying themselves in attending to the higher interests of the masses in the most devoted manner, and at great outlay. Bitter complaints have been made as to the poverty of the results obtained by such multifarious and strenuous endeavours.[11]

This was a well informed and highly intelligent official commenting politely, if critically, on the ineffectual nature of voluntary agencies to address fundamental social problems. Littlejohn was not surprised at their lack of success: it was 'no wonder, when we reflect on the overwhelming disadvantages against which the missionary and philanthropist have to contend', but it was also a statement that only by engaging with the public's health could such deep-seated problems be addressed. Littlejohn's recommendations amounted to a blueprint for municipal reform: they were fundamental, structural, and considered the long term in contra-distinction to the short-termism of voluntary and religious bodies. As *The Scotsman*'s editorial noted:

> The Report is a chart for the sanitary reformer to steer by; it is full of most valuable practical suggestions – suggestions based on painstaking personal investigation combined with competent professional knowledge. Our civic authorities are certainly bound either to follow the advice of their officer of health or to prove to the satisfaction of the inhabitants, who pay for that advice, that they are justified in not acting upon it.[12]

The concluding 'suggestions' were modern in their conception of what would now be called efficiency gains, designed as they were to streamline administrative structures and utilise specialist knowledge. They also demonstrated an awareness that as the municipal tentacles became increasingly extended to every aspect of daily life, then, without efficient and expert executives, vested interests would paralyse the city as individuals sought to promote their own agendas rather than communal ones.

The poorer classes and the city

Throughout his *Report* Littlejohn showed empathy for the poor. His was not a class-based analysis but one which focused on the disadvantaged and disempowered; it was founded on a utilitarianism that justified intervention because of the comfort and well-being it sought for all the inhabitants of Edinburgh. The emphasis in the *Report* was on reducing death rates in the

11 *Report*, 120.

12 *The Scotsman*, 6 September 1865, 2c.

Old Town where the poorest congregated and 'whose cause we are pleading'.[13] The language of the *Report* departed fundamentally from the judgmental tone of Chadwick's *Sanitary Report* where character defects and a culture of blame often targeted the poor and the Irish.[14] Littlejohn acknowledged that the poor were crowded and badly housed, and offered insight and local knowledge to explain that they were not always complicit in their condition. For example, the construction of homes by philanthropic and voluntary agencies was admirable for the 'industrious workman' they housed, but the unintended consequence was a filtering down in the city centre and ever greater concentrations of the very poor. By removing a particular class of industrious tenants from the Old Town to the edge of the built-up area – as at Rosebank, Rosemount, Chalmers' Buildings, or Stockbridge colonies – the labouring class who remained in the Old Town were less likely to learn and benefit from the precepts and practices of the labour aristocracy (see fig. 5.1).[15] Builders were allowed 'to run up skeleton houses of the most rickety description and faulty sanitary construction',[16] and Littlejohn produced stinging indictments of the design and materials to make this point.[17] He took few prisoners in his section on drainage where, with considerable originality, he argued powerfully that water disposal, not water supply, was the major engineering problem.[18] Another target for critical comment was parochial authority. In addition to their squabbling territoriality, noted already, they were mean in giving poor relief. Littlejohn observed:

> The pittances that are given to paupers through the proverbial economy of [parochial] boards, representing the rate-payers of our city, are only intended to allow of life being maintained at a legal flicker, and by no means at a steady flame.[19]

'Injustice' was the term used by Littlejohn to describe the stance of authority towards the poor. He also recognised that the living conditions of the poor and 'its attendant evils – mental depression, imperfect nourishment, scanty clothing, and ... intemperance' had an adverse effect, and that it was hardly surprising that the poor resorted to the public house.[20] As an expert witness to the Select Committee on the Poor Law (Scotland), Dr Alexander Wood, later put it, 'I think the condition of the poorer classes is not only bad, but is becoming every day worse in Edinburgh.'[21] Decency in daily life was problematical in over-crowded

13 *Report*, 117.

14 The word 'Irish' appears only three times in the *Report*.

15 *Report*, 41, 108, 111.

16 *Report*, 33.

17 Three years after Littlejohn's *Report* improved housing design was also uppermost in Alexander (Greek) Thomson's proposals for the Glasgow Improvement Trust competition in 1868. See B. Edwards, 'Thomson – pioneer of sustainable architecture?' *The Architectural Review*, 205 (1999), 81.

18 S.N. Serneri, 'Water pollution in Italy: the failure of the hygienic approach, 1890s–1960s', in C. Bernhardt and G. Massard-Guilbaud (eds), *The Modern Demon: Pollution in Urban and Industrial European Societies* (Clermont Ferrand, 2002), 157–78, shows how the management and purification of water once it had been used was a major problem in Italian cities.

19 *Report*, 42.

20 *Report*, 41.

21 PP (HC) 1868–69 XI, Report from the Select Committee on the Poor Law (Scotland), evidence of Dr A. Wood, Q.5017.

5.1 Model dwelling, 1850s
Rosebank Cottages, with Rosemount in the background, were attempts to address unhealthy working-class housing conditions and provide an acceptable rate of return to builders. [Reproduced by permission of John Reiach]

homes; temptation and vice were never far away. It was a thankless task and 'a mere waste of words' to exhort the poor to consider temperance and God's judgment.[22] Not surprisingly, then, sanitary regulations were disregarded, and it was useless to enforce them by means of the strong arm of the law. Persuasion and incontrovertible evidence were the way forward, and these were the distinctive characteristics of Littlejohn's methodology as revealed in his *Report*.[23]

Environmental and social injustices formed an important theme in the *Report*, though not accorded a separate section in it. Littlejohn displayed an eye for the aesthetic by noting how smoke 'disfigured' the city. This was the case with a still-visible chimney stack in Dalry, an attempt by Scotland's largest distillery to disperse emissions, and in the Canongate where in order to limit smoke

22 *Report*, 42.
23 NLS APS 1.77.122, Letter from Henry Johnston to the Lord Provost, 15 May 1856. In a manner that anticipated some of Littlejohn's field work, Johnston undertook a survey in the winter of 1855–56 of all 159 closes running from the Lawnmarket, High Street and Cowgate and sent his findings to the Town Council in a 37-page report.

5.2 Caledonian Distillery, Haymarket, 1855
Founded by Graham Menzies and Co., owners of Sunbury Distillery, the Caledonian Distillery was the largest in Scotland and became part of Distillers Co. in 1884. The still-house chimney, photographed from a train on the Edinburgh and Glasgow railway line, is still standing. [Source: RCAHMS]

pollution 'a chimney-stalk had to be erected, of such gigantic proportions as to form a landmark and eye-sore from what quarter soever the city is approached'.[24]

What concerned Littlejohn was the absence of regulation at the initial building phase over developments which had an adverse and long-term effect on health. By also astutely referring to the consequences of the Dalry pollution for elite residences in the West End he understood that political alliances might be necessary to counteract the actions of businessmen. Interfering in the legitimate profit-making activities of middle-class manufacturers while attempting to improve environmental health was a delicate balancing act. This was the case in France, too, and Littlejohn made several envious references to it in the course of his *Report* because, as early as 1810, no factory in France could be built without plans approved by a scientific committee who assessed the proposed activity in relation to its impact on nearby dwellings.[25] In addition, there was also a system of classification in place in France that determined which manufacturing activities could be conducted legitimately in central districts, and which should be exiled to the margins of the city. Littlejohn showed an awareness of the medical literature and practice in relation to public hygiene in which the French were

24 *Report*, 46, 89–90. The chimney 'stalk' itself was the result of litigation brought by the Town Council and the owner of the richly manured Craigentinny meadows where rentals were adversely affected by waste dumped from the gas works. Rather than compel the gas works to relocate to a rural site at a modest rent, the company was obliged to construct a chimney, with the effect that 'one of our poorest localities' was subjected to smoke pollution for decades.

25 See *Report*, 46, 48–9, 54, 63.

5.3 New Street gasworks from the Calton Hill, 1868
The 'hideous chimney-stalk', as Littlejohn described it, was built as a result of a law suit to remove noxious fumes affecting mainly east Edinburgh. [Source: RCAHMS]

world leaders in the early decades of the nineteenth century.[26] Doubtless he had absorbed such ideas during his short sojourn in Paris following graduation, but there were enough parallels with Duncan's public health regime in Liverpool, the city at the forefront of British policy initiatives in this area, to indicate that he was also well versed in public health management methods south of the border.[27]

Invariably, Littlejohn's language was that of the obedient public servant. Time and again he adopted deferential tones towards his employers, the Town Council – 'my civic superiors'.[28] Hence his statements, 'I respectfully venture to urge upon the Magistrates of this City the necessity of maintaining a thorough inspection at our Slaughter-houses and Markets', and 'Such are the suggestions which I beg to offer for the sanitary improvement of Edinburgh' are typical of a conciliatory language intended to gain the confidence and support of politicians. Cleverly, and no doubt deliberately, Littlejohn admitted his own fallibility. He stated in relation to meat quality: 'I am conscious of the imperfect character of professional knowledge,' and, with humility, recognised that his decision to close Greyfriars churchyard for burials had knock-on effects on funeral costs which imposed hardship on the poor.[29] When considering the issue of food quality and

26 By coincidence the first Department of Hygiene was set up in Munich by Max von Pettenkofer in 1865, although there is no direct evidence to link it to Edinburgh.

27 Experience from other cities was also incorporated with more observations about London than Glasgow, and information on Liverpool and Paris frequently deployed to provide another frame of reference.

28 *Evening Courant*, 3 July 1863, 2e, letter from Henry Littlejohn concerning the Vaccination Bill.

29 ECA SL44/1, Scroll Minutes of the Plans and Works Committee, 1861–68, 12 and 19 February 1863.

diseased meat, he was generous in regard to the butcher, the baker and every other maker, commenting that 'the tradesman judges by what may be called '*tactus eruditus*', that is, by feel, and that 'Medical knowledge cannot compete with the tact gained by the lengthened experience of tradesmen'.[30] Littlejohn was courteous to those whom he regarded as well meaning, if misdirected.

A tale of two cities: the *Report* concluded

In the language of a public servant, Littlejohn offered in the Conclusion his 'suggestions … for the sanitary improvement of Edinburgh'. These were of two types: those where improvements 'can only be properly dealt with by the municipality' without delay, and those where the inhabitants should undertake the improvements. This second group of suggestions referred to the 'modern part of the city', the New Town, where private citizens were themselves expected to remove cesspools and fit modern water-closets with suitable sewer connections. Such measures were expected to have little impact on mortality but would improve comfort. The first group of suggestions related principally, but not exclusively, to the four central districts of the Old Town, and involved improved paving, cleaning, various measures to reduce overcrowding, and the creation of new streets cutting across the closes to improve cleaning and communications. Keen to give credit where it was due, Littlejohn recognised the contribution of several agencies to recent improvements in the sanitary condition of the Old Town, specifically in relation to improved water quality, limitations of refuse accumulations in and around houses, periodical lime-washing of courts, the slaughtering of animals in a new public abattoir, and improved medical attendance and public dispensaries.

Unusually, and in a move more familiar to the audit culture of the late twentieth century, Littlejohn suggested target death rates which he considered achievable. He proposed that the four central Old Town districts should reduce their death dates to 25 per 1,000, thus saving 312 lives annually, and that the city overall should achieve a level of 23.82 per 1,000, a reduction of 6.2%. Littlejohn's confidence stemmed from two major capital projects: the expenditure of £40,000 on a purification scheme for the Water of Leith; and construction by the City Parochial Board of a poorhouse in the country. Statistically, the removal of paupers, with their predisposition to infirmity and especially to epidemic disease and thus to higher death rates, would itself exert downward pressure on the mortality rates in the Old Town.

The New Town–Old Town distinction was familiar to contemporaries.[31] Indeed, Littlejohn himself argued that such a division had much to commend it both in the minds of the public because it would be easily understood and, administratively, because it would simplify jurisdictions. However, the persistent reference throughout the *Report* to conditions in the New Town served another,

30 *Report*, 58–9.

31 See, for example, *The Scotsman*, 14 November 1864, 8a letter from Dr James Cowan pleading for less money to be spent on the adornment of the New Town and more on the conditions prevailing in the Old Town.

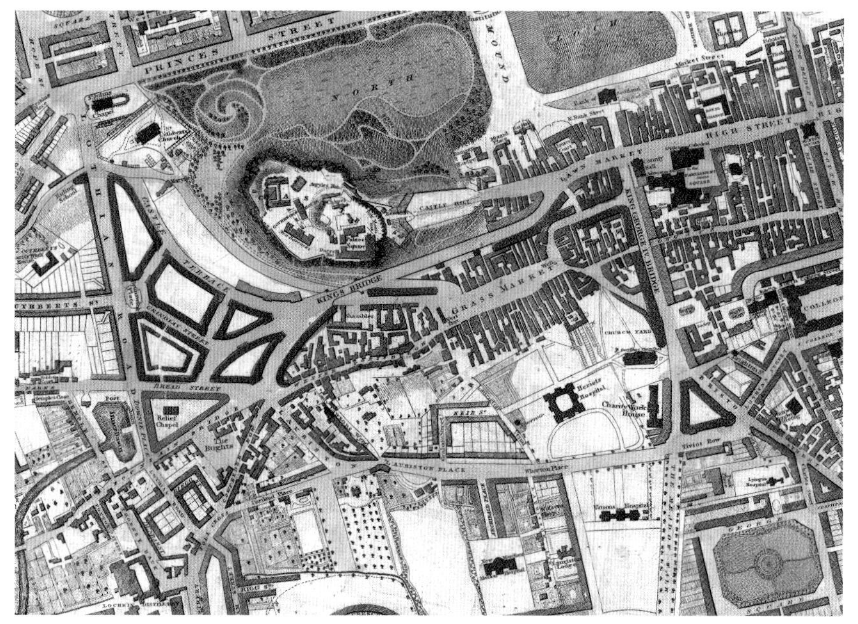

5.4 Victoria Street 1827 and proposed improvements, 1829–31
The street improvements of the 1820s foreshadowed the schemes of the 1860s. They also added to the city's indebtedness and fuelled the anxiety over capital projects such as those in 1867.
[Source: NLS Wood 1831]

overtly political, purpose. It demonstrated that all was not well in the New Town, and that residents there also had much to gain in terms of their comfort and amenity through improvements funded from local taxes. The sale of diseased meat and the carting of excrement and carcasses were nuisances for New Town dwellers, as was the encroachment of workshops in the back lanes of fashionable streets, rather like those identified by Booth in central London. All gave cause for environmental concern.[32] Hence the Water of Leith scheme, a long-running source of complaint for the New Town inhabitants, offered environmental improvements and in doing so built a consensus around the need for public action on both sides of Princes Street. There was an implicit contract in Littlejohn's conclusion: environmental and public health benefits would accrue to all members of Edinburgh society, irrespective of status.

Like many of his class Littlejohn was deeply conscious of the historical development of Edinburgh. '[M]en of taste,' it was claimed, agreed 'that a noble opportunity for embellishing the Old Town had arrived' with the city improvements of the 1820s and 1830s.[33] The collective memory and communal identity of the city were closely identified with its buildings. 'Our closes are objects of historical interest,' he proclaimed; they 'excited the astonishment of strangers' and were 'the subject of comment by travellers.'[34] Houses in Edinburgh were 'the

32 See *Report*, 8–9, compared to the main streets of the New Town, the death rates in the side streets of the upper and lower New Town were respectively 17% and 42% higher.

33 *Caledonian Mercury*, 3 April 1841, 3c.

34 *Report*, 111.

highest in the world' and resembled a 'rabbit warren', so to reduce their height to four storeys, as in the New Town, would 'interfere somewhat with the noble outline of the High Street'. It was a phrase reminiscent of many in Lord Cockburn's *Letter to the Lord Provost on the Ways of Spoiling the Beauty of Edinburgh* (1849), and showed Littlejohn ahead of his time concerning the importance of civic societies and conservation principles.[35] Indeed, his approach anticipated by a quarter of a century that of Patrick Geddes' 'conservative surgery', or selective demolition and renewal, and its corollary of maintaining a degree of housing density in order to sustain neighbourhoods and communities, and thus local businesses.[36]

The aesthetic aspect of 'our chief street' was recognised by Littlejohn as attractive to 'holiday tourists' who, voyeuristically, roamed through the nearby closes and subjected the poorer districts to greater scrutiny than elsewhere. He noted that 'there are few cities in the empire which are subjected to a more searching examination by tourists, and there are fewer still in which the objects of chief interest lie in the dirtiest and most squalid streets'.[37] With a strong sense of the historical legacy associated with the Scottish built environment, Littlejohn recognised that tenement living in 'upright streets' was a product both of feudal tenure and the solidity of stone construction, and that unlike English terraced housing, this 'fixed and immobile capital'[38] was an impediment to upgrading Scottish housing. Concerning the modernisation of the Edinburgh housing stock, Littlejohn concluded that many tenements were 'so old as already to be falling to pieces, with walls hardly able to maintain themselves erect, much less to stand the operations of the sanitary engineer'.[39]

This sense of historical continuity permeated Littlejohn's *Report*. The cholera epidemics from the 1830s, foundation of private cemeteries in Edinburgh in the 1840s, evolution of public utilities and philanthropic housing, knowledge of individual clauses of local improvement acts, and specific statutes such as the Smoke Nuisance Abatement Act and the Bakehouse Regulation Act, 1863,[40] each

35 Littlejohn's awareness of the quality of the built environment pre-dated the foundation of the Cockburn Society (1875), the romantic refurbishment of the Castle (1886) and St Giles' (1871) sponsored, respectively, by William Chambers and William Nelson, and the concept of 'conservative' or selective surgery as an approach to conservation, as preached later by Patrick Geddes. See J. Johnson and L. Rosenburg, *Renewing Old Edinburgh: the Enduring Legacy of Patrick Geddes* (Argyll, 2010); J. Gifford *et al.*, *The Buildings of Scotland: Edinburgh* (Harmondsworth, 1988 edn), 106; R.J. Morris, 'The capitalist, the professor and the soldier: the re-making of Edinburgh Castle, 1850–1900', *Planning Perspectives*, 22 (2007), 55–78. The Society for the Protection of Ancient Buildings was formed by William Morris with John Ruskin's collaboration in the 1870s; Glasgow had a Ruskin Society (1880) and a Kyrle Society (1882).

36 B. Edwards, 'Thomson – pioneer of sustainable architecture', 80–4, explains the principle of preserving sufficient density to sustain small shops and businesses, while renewing houses was enshrined in at least one of the Glasgow improvement proposals.

37 *Report*, 111–12. The poor of Paris, London, Dublin, Liverpool and Glasgow are noted as not being on the tourist trail: had they been, it was thought that public health improvements would have been more likely as they would have been subjected to greater scrutiny.

38 The phrase comes from D. Harvey, 'The geography of capitalist accumulation: a reconstruction of the Marxian theory', in R. Peet (ed.), *Radical Geography* (Chicago, 1977), 263–92.

39 *Report*, 81–2.

40 28 and 29 Vict., cap. 102, Smoke Nuisance (Scotland) Act, 1865; 26 and 27 Vict., cap. 106, Bakehouse Regulation Act, 1863.

provided a convincing context for what followed in the *Report*. In a brisk reference to the building mania[41] of 1825 and the ensuing crisis 'which not only stopped the building that was going on, but arrested for the long period of thirty years the extensions of the city', Littlejohn observed, acutely, that 'imperfect notions prevailed as to the internal and external drainage of houses'.[42] In a thinly veiled attack on the building industry and its legacy of shoddy practices during boom periods, Littlejohn commented: 'When unhealthy competition prevails in the building trade and houses are erected with undue haste, many points of essential importance to their sanitary condition are very apt to be overlooked, while others ... such as external decoration, receive an undue amount of attention.' The durability of the housing stock meant that scamped building had a long-term legacy, the effects of which were intensified because there was 'no definite drainage' plan for the city. By noting that 'the faulty planning of the better class of houses' was a risk to health and the quality of life, Littlejohn demonstrated that sanitary improvements benefited all classes.[43] Time and again his statements were supported with a historical context so that his 'suggestions' were both practical and convincing, and also avoided the sensationalism of a single event such as a collapsed tenement in the High Street in 1861 (see Chapter 4).[44]

Earlier achievements by both the Improvement Commission to clear older properties and form the new Victoria Street in the 1830s (fig. 5.4), and by the Railway Access Company to form (Lord) Cockburn Street in the 1850s, were beneficial. But for Littlejohn they also 'provided valuable hints as to the best method of improving our closes and wynds', namely by 'piercing the closes with an airy street'. In a diagram of his proposal, Littlejohn demonstrated how keeping to a contour line parallel to the High Street would transect the long, narrow closes of the Old Town and expose them to light and air and, crucially as far as Littlejohn was concerned, to the activities of the cleaning department.[45] Specifically, Littlejohn's clearance proposals were in a rectangle formed by Niddry Street to the west and St Mary's Wynd to the east, and bounded on the southern and northern edges by the Cowgate and High Street. With a density of 646 persons per acre, arguably the most overcrowded in Europe, fourteen closes would be bisected, and some of those inhabitants displaced by clearances would find new accommodation lining the newly formed street.[46] Other advantages would ensue: cellars would provide wash-houses for the poor of the district; the latest sanitary designs would be incorporated in the new homes; cleared areas would become playgrounds for children; and traffic would be more efficiently managed since games and gossip would be removed from the main thoroughfares.

41 See also R. Rodger, *The Transformation of Edinburgh: Land, Property and Trust in the Nineteenth Century* (Cambridge, 2001), 82.

42 *Report*, 101–2.

43 *Report*, 105.

44 R.S. Neale, *Bath: A Social History, or, a Valley of Pleasure yet a Sink of Iniquity* (London, 1981), on the elite in Bath, and Charles Booth's survey of London both make a similar point about how socially mixed and inter-dependent the apparently wealthy areas were. See R. O'Day and D.E. Englander (eds), *Mr Charles Booth's Inquiry: Life and Labour of the People in London Reconsidered* (London, 1993).

45 *Report*, 112–13.

46 *The Scotsman*, 25 September 1858, 2.

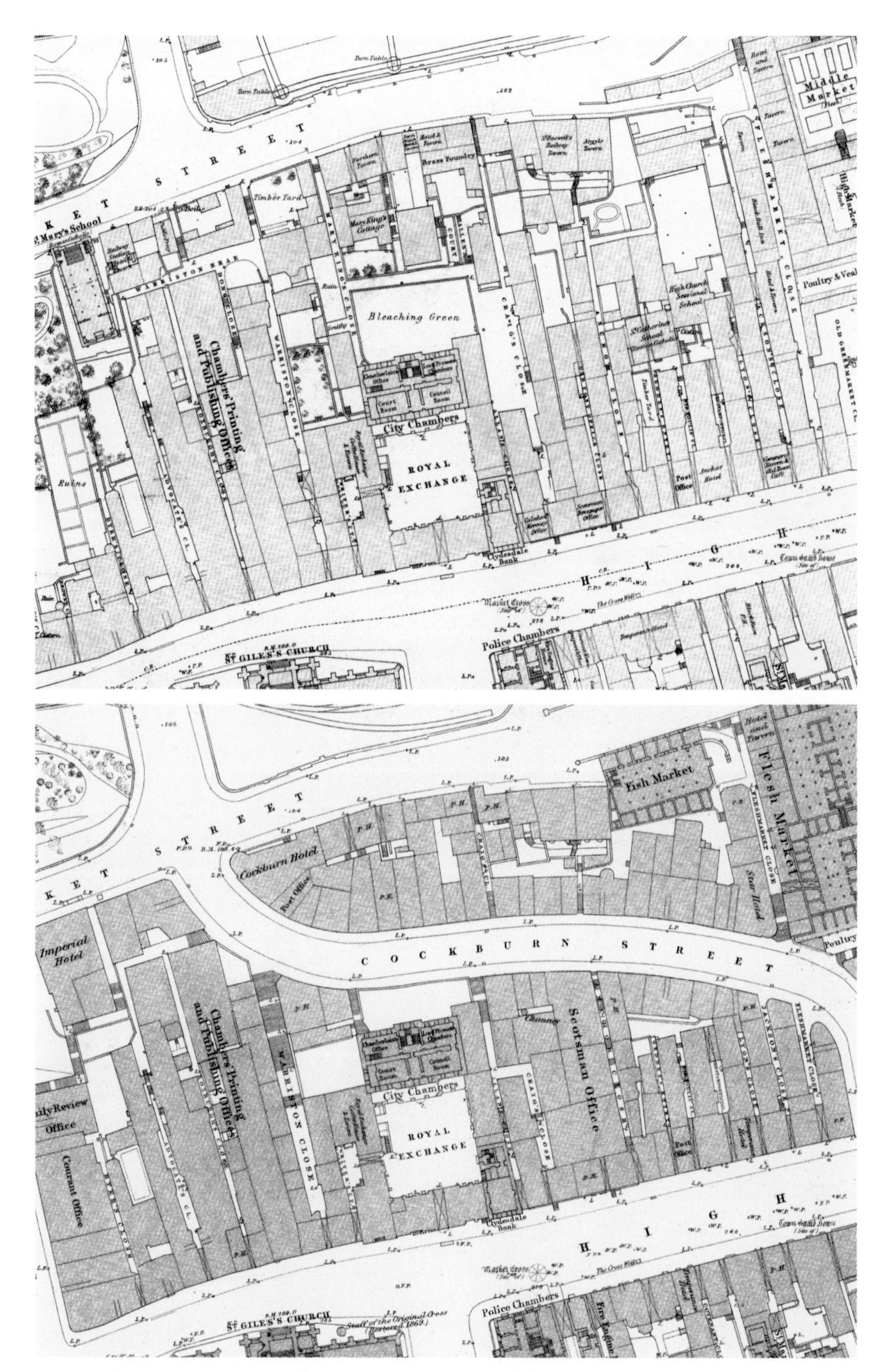

5.5 Cockburn Street before and after Improvements of 1859–64
The prime motive of early improvement schemes was to improve traffic circulation and, in this case, access to the new Waverley station. The gradient of this new 'S' shaped street, echoing the success of the earlier Victoria Street, was adapted in the 1860s scheme. 1852 (top) and 1877 (bottom).

5.6 Cockburn Street: Improvements, 1856
Cockburn Street presented an opportunity to re-use ancient and decaying 'lands', and introduce the 'modern' Scots baronial architectural style. It was mostly completed between 1859 and 1864.

The clearance programme proposed by Littlejohn was likened to the conduct of war: logistical planning was essential in any campaign to address the sanitary problems of an area.

Since the development of the New Town in the late eighteenth century Edinburgh citizens had been obsessed with levels of municipal expenditure, and, in another demonstration of his historical awareness, Littlejohn countered two potential objections to his improvement proposals on the grounds of expense. Firstly, although an improvement tax would be required, there was no need for expensive buildings and adornment, since the object of the proposals would be to remove 'a stain and a reproach … on account of the misery and wretchedness of the dwellings of our poor'.[47] Secondly, the civil engineering involved was simpler and thus cheaper in comparison to a diagonally constructed street running across the contour.

In under five pages, Littlejohn's conclusion exhibited its Enlightenment credentials. It was a reasoned summation of material systematically collected and analysed, with conclusions drawn and recommendations offered. It was didactic in its political and moral tones, though not overbearingly so, and holistic in reviewing the inter-relationships between technology, engineering, medicine, political economy, human behaviour, history, religion, topography, hydrology, and the environment. A year later, Councillor Ford's testimonial to Littlejohn's qualities was printed in glowing terms in the *Evening Courant*: 'an able and

47 *Report*, 113–14.

arduous public servant ... night and day he was at work, and he had shown an amount of practical commercial knowledge that really astonished him.'[48] The contemporary description of Littlejohn as 'one of the greatest public health authorities of our time',[49] and the *Report* as 'monumental'[50] seems entirely justified.

How, then, did the 'suggestions' and empirical findings in his *Report* inform civic policy in the years immediately following publication? In what follows, demolition, street improvements, water supply and drainage are each considered in some detail in the five or so years immediately after the publication of Littlejohn's *Report*. The *Report* was not a prescriptive or staged programme for urban management; it set out a series of logical and inter-related practical actions intended to improve the quality as well as the length of life. Morbidity was just as important as mortality in Littlejohn's thinking. Community health and well-being were guiding principles; grand gestures and flagship projects were of less significance than value for money and the resolution of environmental problems. The methods adopted to achieve these objectives shed light on municipal politics and personalities, inform understanding about the role of the expert in a period after 1870 when local government responsibilities mushroomed, and provide insights into how the concept of the civic evolved.

City Improvements

A leader in the *Edinburgh Evening Courant* in September 1864 announced, with heavy irony, that 'To register the progress of sanitary reform is about as tedious an affair as recording the movement of a glacier.'[51] Yet two years later the same newspaper printed a series of ten articles by William Anderson on the 'The Poor of Edinburgh and their Homes',[52] which so touched the public that donors sent money to the newspaper to relieve the local poor, and the articles were reprinted as a book.[53] The *Courant* was tapping into a mood, prevalent in Edinburgh in 1866, which recognised a serious social issue.

The housing issue gripped the Edinburgh public in the aftermath of the publication of the Littlejohn *Report,* which had been acclaimed in the press and by the Town Council. Implementation of some of the conclusions might have seemed reasonably straightforward, therefore, especially when William Chambers, the respected publisher and long-time campaigner for housing improvement, was persuaded to stand for election on the understanding that he would be nominated as Lord Provost and that various public health measures would follow. On entering the council chamber in November 1865 after his

48 *Evening Courant*, 24 November 1866, 8d.

49 *The Glasgow Herald*, 2 October 1914.

50 *The Lancet*, 10 October 1914, 913–14.

51 *Evening Courant*, 22 September 1864, 2ab.

52 *Evening Courant*, 26 October 1866, 2ef; 10 November 1866, 5ab; 21 November 1866, 5ab; 28 November 1866, 5a–c; 10 December 1866, 3ab; 19 December 1866, 5a–c; 26 December 1866, 5a–c; 2 January 1867, 2fg; 12 January 1867, 5b–d; 19 January 1867, 5ab.

53 W. Anderson, *The Poor of Edinburgh and their Homes* (Edinburgh, 1867).

election success 'to much applause and cheering', Chambers declared there was no case for 'embellishing the town'; instead he commented:

> there has been a most valuable sanitary report made by Dr Littlejohn, an indefatigable public officer whom Edinburgh is very fortunate in possessing, and some of whose views, as respects opening up the Old Town by cross and diagonal streets through the more dense and confined masses, cannot be too soon carried out.[54]

Chambers continued in a vein intended to enlist support and disarm potential critics: 'To spend a hundred thousand pounds, or even two hundred thousand, carefully and wisely ... would be for Edinburgh not only true economy, but an excellent investment. We live and can flourish only through our reputation for amenity and salubrity.'[55]

Four days after his election on 11 November 1865 Chambers, accompanied by David Cousin, the City Architect and Superintendent of Works,[56] began an arduous three-month winter programme of visits to closes in the Old Town with the intention of producing a clearance plan.[57] Chambers explained his methods:

> I have perambulated the closes of the Old Town. I have scrutinised every one of them on the north side of the High Street, from the North Bridge to New Street; and on the south side, from the Old Fishmarket Close to St John Street. Besides going up and down these closes, looking into every accessible hole and corner, and sometimes ascending stairs to see the condition of dwellings, I have gone to the tops of the taller buildings, in order to get a good bird's-eye view of the whole concern.[58]

Away from the taller buildings, at street level, the dilapidated state of the central area of the Old Town was captured by photographers such as James Balmain on behalf of the Improvement Trust, Thomas Begbie, and A.A. Inglis.

Chambers' method emulated Littlejohn's, and the motives were not dissimilar. Few, if any, could challenge evidence acquired systematically, and subsequent recommendations to the Town Council, and any defence to a House of Commons committee in association with a Bill to authorise an Improvement Trust, would be the more robust for his fieldwork. Just three weeks after his inaugural speech, Chambers presented a preliminary 'Statement to the Town Council Respecting Sanitary Improvements' in which he gave, in considerable detail, locations for new streets. One of these was for a diagonal street to run from the top of Leith Wynd,

54 *Evening Courant*, 11 November 1865, 5a–d.

55 *The Scotsman*, editorial, 11 November 1865, 2d.

56 For David Cousin's appointment as Superintendent of Works see identical reports of the Town Council meeting of 18 May 1847 in *The Scotsman*, 19 May 1847, 3c and *Caledonian Mercury*, 20 May 1847, 4b. There were 10 or 11 applicants of which four were proposed for election. Cousin only won on a third vote, 16 to 14. For obituaries see *The Scotsman*, 4 September 1878, 4; *Evening Courant*, 4 September 1878.

57 *The Scotsman*, 15 November 1865, 2e. Chambers' efforts were described as 'immense personal labour.' See ECA SL/158/1, Report by the Sub-Committee of the Lord Provost's Committee as to the Sanitary Improvement of the City, 23 March 1866.

58 ECA SL158/1, The Lord Provost's Statement to the Town Council Respecting Sanitary Improvements, 5 December 1865, 2. A copy is also available in the National Library of Scotland, 3.1919 (6).

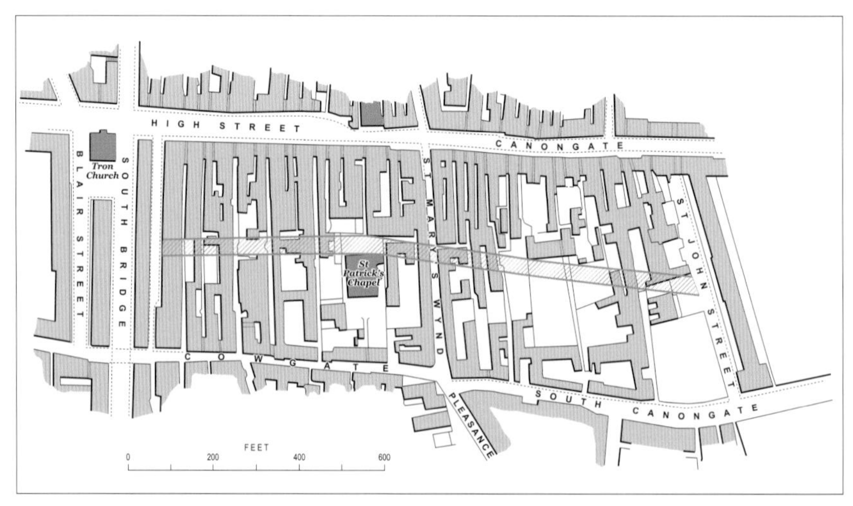

5.7 Littlejohn's concept for opening up the closes
By including this, the only coloured lithograph in the *Report*, Littlejohn sought to convince his readers of a basic principle: 'by simply piercing the closes with an airy street, you let in light, ventilation, and also the scavenger.' [Source: *The Report*, 112]

now Jeffrey Street, northerly towards the foot of Halkerston's Wynd, a close which ran parallel to North Bridge. The new street was to pass between the model housing at Ashley Buildings and John Knox's church, and cut across a series of closes: Little Grant's, Baron Grant's, Hope's, Trunk's, Monteith's, Sandiland's, Chalmers', Barringer's, Paisley's, Bailie Fyfe's, Morrison's, North Gray's, Bishop's, Carrubber's, and Halkerston's Wynd.[59] Fourteen closes were exposed, and, as Littlejohn had explained previously, 'By simply piercing the closes with an airy street, you let in light, ventilation, and also the scavenger.'[60] Chambers put his own stamp on the Littlejohn proposals (*Report*, p. 112). He explained,

> Dr Littlejohn has sketched a plan for perforating the denser clumps by new streets running at right angles to the closes. My proposal has a higher and more economic aim. By going, for example, right across the closes from the middle of Niddry Street to the middle of St John Street, you would serve no great end as regards convenient thoroughfare; and you would also run through the centre of breweries, which are not detrimental to health, and the purchase of which would involve heavy expenditure. In all my projected alterations, I have endeavoured to avoid costly properties, and also kept the thoroughfares for traffic steadily in view.[61]

Chambers' 'outline sketch', as he called it, forcibly expressed his commitment to 'sanitary improvement', 'the primary idea from which I cannot be diverted'.[62]

59 ECA SL158/1, Lord Provost's Statement, 5 December 1865, 3.

60 Littlejohn, *Report*, 112. In the second printing of the *Report* the metal type was misplaced, introducing an error. The word 'best' was moved so that the phrase then read 'piercing the closes best with an airy street'. Littlejohn corrected this error by hand when sending complimentary copies.

61 ECA SL158/1, Minutes of the Sanitary Improvement Committee, 21 November 1865, 3–4.

62 ECA SL158/1, Lord Provost's Statement, 5–6.

Rightly, he also anticipated that the expense of an improvement scheme would present a considerable political challenge, and so stated, 'I would like to be perfectly candid … the inhabitants will need to submit to a small tax for a few years.' He then sought to reassure local taxpayers on the issues of cost and corruption:

> On one point I can give an assurance. If the thing is done in my time, I promise that the works shall be carried on without fear or favour, or, in other words, free from that species of jobbery of which the citizens, from experience, entertain a salutary horror.[63]

In his Explanatory Statement to the full Town Council Chambers attempted to head off political opposition with an explicit 'back me or sack me' challenge:

> no one will expect that I should go on if the great features of the project are disapproved of, or frittered away to insignificance or … be rendered abortive by protracted formalities and discussion.[64]

The motion on 13 February 1866 to authorise the Lord Provost's Committee to take such steps as necessary to bring the improvement scheme into being was approved unanimously. The matter was then referred to a sub-committee to 'mature' the scheme. Within a week of the first meeting of the five-man committee, the city architect, David Cousin, had produced a modified scheme involving just five of the eleven areas originally proposed by Chambers, costed on the basis of the purchase of 18–20 years of rentals at £119,615 compared to Chambers' original proposals costed on the same basis at £230,000.[65]

Littlejohn's *Report* in August 1865 and Chambers' post-election declaration in December 1865 initiated months of intense public discussion.[66] These included comments from a meeting of West Port residents; alternative proposals from Roderick Coyne based on costings for the earlier Cockburn Street scheme;[67] lectures from Dr Alexander Wood to the Working Men's Club and Institute, and to the Royal Society of Arts by Alexander Ramsay, Manager of the Edinburgh

5.8 William Chambers (1800–83)
As Lord Provost (1865–69) Chambers piloted the 1867 Improvement Scheme in the face of considerable opposition, not least in the council itself.
J. Horsburgh, artist.
[Source: Scottish Borders Council Museum and Gallery Service]

63 ECA SL158/1, Lord Provost's Statement, 9.

64 ECA SL158/1, Lord Provost's Explanatory Statement, 13 February 1866.

65 ECA SL158/1, Minutes of the Lord Provost's Committee relative to the Sanitary Improvement of the City, 31 January 1866; Lord Provost's Explanatory Statement, 13 February 1866. Estimates took account of road and parliamentary costs, and of revenue generated from land sales. While the compensation at 18–20 years' purchase was recognised as unduly generous in various cases, no reduction was attempted for what might have been a lower number of years as a purchase price given the dilapidated nature of many of the properties, or of additional rateable value attributable to the improved properties that would result, or for the reduced incidence of crime and poverty that were presumed to result from the clearance programme.

66 For a brief survey see P.J. Smith, 'The rehousing/relocation issue in an early slum clearance scheme: Edinburgh, 1865–1885', *Urban Studies*, 26 (1989), 100–14.

67 See NLS K.77.a.11(5), R.A.F.A. Coyne, Estimate and Prospectus of the Annexed Plan of Sanitary and City Improvements, 25 January 1866. Overall costs of 13 elements of the scheme were £426,792. Coyne's calculations suggest that the addition to local taxation would be 3*d*. per £ for 50 years. The proposals include a tunnel from King's Stables Road to the Mound, and a diagonal new street from the Cowgate to Canongate at the north end of St John's Street. Coyne was a civil engineer and subsequently Superintendent of Works for the council between 1872 and 1890.

Water Company.[68] Members of the City Parochial Board applauded chairman David Curror as he expressed 'hearty wishes for the success of [Chambers'] contemplated sanitary improvements'.[69] By contrast, Peter Miller, an Edinburgh magistrate, proposed that the 'principle that should guide us in reconstructing the Old Town' was 'to obliterate the closes and wynds altogether', rather than to perpetuate them by 'mere piercing of the closes by cross streets'.[70] Public interest was stimulated also by *The Scotsman*'s editorial comments on the sanitary state of the Old Town and the *Courant's* report of a meeting of the Architectural Institute of Scotland in the City Chambers on 26 February 1866 which was held to discuss the sanitary improvements.[71] The public realm was fully engaged with the issue of the improvement scheme.

Of course, Chambers himself fuelled debate for his proposals in February 1866 by seeking legitimacy in an 'Explanatory Statement' through a process recognisable in modern times as a public consultation exercise. The issues were then taken up with vigour by a succession of public and private interests in March 1866.[72] The Incorporated Trades of Edinburgh scrutinised Chambers' proposals, commenting block by block and adding a few suggestions; the Royal College of Physicians expressed 'pleasure in co-operating' and also offered constructive ideas; the University Senate 'earnestly hope[d] that the complete plan of the Lord Provost will be carried into effect'; the Chamber of Commerce gave 'cordial support'; and the Building Trades Employers 'heartily approved' of the general features of the plan; the Edinburgh Road Trust stated that they considered the improvement 'very necessary'; and, predictably given their primary interest in the welfare of the poor, both the Destitute Sick Society and the City Parochial Board were strongly supportive of Chambers' proposals, the latter stating that 'sanitary improvements should not be delayed for one hour'.[73] The official resolutions from these powerful public agencies enabled Chambers to comment in March 1866 that he was 'encouraged by almost universal support'[74] and, in face-to-face meetings in the council chamber later that month, the individuals delegated by their organisations again strongly supported his proposals.[75]

68 *The Scotsman*, 27 November 1865, 2cd; 1 December 1865, 4c; 7 December 1865, 2c; 11 December 1865, 5ef; 13 December 1865 8a–d. Ramsay demonstrated his competency by being promoted from journeyman gardener to district overseer of scavengers, and then to Inspector of Cleaning before becoming manager of the Edinburgh Water Company. See *The Scotsman*, 7 May 1869, 5c.

69 *Evening Courant*, 1 January 1866.

70 NLS, Bc7.44, P. Miller, *Suggestions for the Sanitary Improvement of the Old Town of Edinburgh* (Edinburgh, 1866), 4.

71 *Evening Courant*, 27 February 1866, 8a–c. Speakers included David Cousin (chair: councillor and architect), H.W. Cornillon (Secretary), Lessels, J. Dick Peddie, Milne, Muir, McGibbon, Mathieson, James Richardson, James Gowans, Revd Dr Nisbet, R.A.F.A. Coyne, and D. Curror.

72 ECA SL158/1, Report by the Sub-Committee of the Lord Provost's Committee as to the Sanitary Improvement of the City, 23 March 1866, Appendix.

73 ECA SL158/1, Report by the Sub-Committee, 23 March 1866, Appendix VII.

74 *Evening Courant*, 14 March 1866, 6ab, account of Town Council proceedings.

75 *The Scotsman*, 27 March 1866, 8cd. The institutions represented included the Merchant Company, University, Chambers of Commerce, Royal College of Physicians, Architectural Institute of Scotland, Destitute Sick Society, City Parochial Board. Others who spoke included Dr Andrew

While this public consultation process was taking place, parallel meetings with local residents were specially convened at the ward level in March and April 1866.[76] This early version of a local planning enquiry differed radically from those of modern times: Chambers himself attended, and promoted, his plans, facing the hostile audience in lively and, at times, rowdy meetings.[77] Topics covered included the details of street plans, construction and parliamentary costs and, in the words of John Miller junior (St Bernard's ward), the 'remodelling the Old Town Streets in so imperial a manner, he [Provost Chambers] had gone far beyond the necessities of sanitary improvement'.[78] Indeed, with only St Andrew's and Canongate showing any confidence in the Town Council, all other wards condemned Chambers' proposals for their extravagance, arguing that they did not deal with the most congested districts, that existing powers were sufficient, and that the proposals were too hastily conceived.[79]

Simultaneously, private opposition to the improvements was also mounting in 1866.[80] A powerful critique from one letter-writer, 'Watchman', published before the ward meetings were fully under way, provided considerable ammunition for the opponents of Chambers' scheme: 'The evils of overcrowding … existing in our closes will simply be removed to other districts of the town.'[81] 'Watchman' argued that speculators would be encouraged by generous compensation and re-development opportunities, and the Lord Provost's increasingly dictatorial manner, together with the cost of the parliamentary Bill, all added to misgivings about the scheme. Squeals of anguish came from property owners; it was unreasonable, they claimed, to have their assets compulsorily purchased without any consultation.[82] It was much simpler, argued 'Watchman' in agreement with a Mr Miller of Leithen, just to knock down one side of every close. *The Scotsman*, too, claimed that Littlejohn, in suggesting a new street parallel to the High Street, had confused '*openness*' with '*thoroughfare*' and that circulation and mobility in the city would be enhanced significantly with an 'S' shaped second Cockburn Street to link districts between the Tron and the Queen's Park.[83]

The critique from 'J.M.L.', another correspondent, was that the enforcement of simple sanitary regulation and the installation of decent water-closets, dust shafts, lime-washing, and cleaning were more important than street works. With more than a hint of sarcasm towards Chambers' planning aspirations, J.M.L. commented: 'there is no doubt that it is a fine thing in print to knock down

Wood, Dr Gairdner, A Working Man, Professor Bennett, Dr Dunsmure, Bailie Falshaw, Thomas Lansdale, Professor Christison, Professor Spence, Dr Masson, Dr Begg, ex-bailie Johnston.

76 *Evening Courant*, 27 March 1866, 8a–d, reports from ward meetings throughout the city.

77 *Evening Courant*, 27 March 1866, 8a–d. Reports of meetings in Canongate, St Stephen's, Calton, Broughton, Newington, St Cuthbert's, and St Bernard's wards.

78 *Evening Courant*, 27 March 1866, 8d.

79 ECA SL158/1, Report by the Sub-Committee of the Lord Provost's Committee, 23 March 1866, Appendix IX. St Cuthbert's Ward made no return.

80 *Evening Courant*, 8 March 1866, 2f. See the exchange between R.A.F.A. Coyne and J.D. Marwick, Town Clerk.

81 *Evening Courant*, 20 March 1866. The 'existing powers' was a reference to clause 210 of the General Police (Scotland) Act, 1862 (Lindsay Act). See chapter 3.

82 *The Scotsman*, 13 March 1866, 5e, letter from 'An enquirer.'

83 *The Scotsman*, 27 November 1865, 6cd.

old houses wholesale, and build new streets by the dozen, quite "à la Napoleon III",' but to expect people to change their habits 'you might as well try to wash the negro white.'[84] 'Edinensis' agreed with another correspondent who claimed, wrongly, that local taxes in Edinburgh were already 'quite as high, if not higher, than in Glasgow or London'.[85] He reminded readers that in March 1866 Chambers' scheme was not the only one on the table, and cited rivals by Coyne, Bailie Miller, and the Architectural Institute. As another *Courant* correspondent noted, 'The plans of the Lord Provost and Bailie Miller are Utopian; that of Mr Coyne admirable, with perhaps a few alterations in detail; while that of the Architectural Institute is a barefaced piece of plagiarism of all the important features of Mr Coyne's plan.'[86]

Another line of attack on the improvement scheme was personal, conducted with dripping sarcasm by the *Courant* a few days after the Lord Provost had made an important statement to the Town Council in March 1866. Chambers, the *Courant* commented, 'takes credit to himself', thus usurping the true authorship, that of Littlejohn. The newspaper applauded his ability to spend money on housing improvement, and quipped that it was others' money, and with regard to Chambers' urgency, jibed:

> Unless we push on at once, Mr William Chambers will retire without his fame. No 'Chambers' Street' affixed to the corners of some stately and salubrious diagonal will carry down his name to the grateful wayfarers of future generations. No new edition of Walford's 'County Families' will be able to insert 'Sir William Chambers, Knight,' at the point where the name of our present Lord Provost appears in the genealogic roll of his ancient line.[87]

Littlejohn's *Report*, endorsed from all quarters in the autumn of 1865, was in danger of being side-lined as voters associated clearances with Chambers, and opposed the tax implications as well as the technical and practical implications of his proposals. The focus had switched; public health had become synonymous with street improvements and, in the eyes of many, was tarnished by association with Chambers. The meticulous empiricism of the Littlejohn *Report* was overlooked as personal attacks against the Lord Provost came from residents across the city and through the columns of the newspapers. Alternative schemes emerged, and this focus on the improvement project threatened to marginalise Littlejohn's comprehensive approach towards sanitary improvements. Attacks were aimed at Chambers on the grounds that thousands would be displaced; that the estimates of costs were too low; that proper enforcement of sanitary legislation would suffice; and that poverty lay at the root of the problem.[88] Even

84 *Evening Courant*, 29 March 1866, 6c.

85 *Evening Courant*, 27 March 1866, 6e, commenting on the letter from 'An Old Citizen', 24 March 1866, 5c.

86 *Evening Courant*, 6 April 1866, 6b, letter from W.L.R. (W.L. Rollo of the *Burghs Reform Newspaper*).

87 *Evening Courant*, 27 March 1866, 2cd. It was the case that Chambers expressed concern about timing. He stressed that if action were not taken in early 1866 then a Bill could not come before Parliament until 1868. See *Evening Courant*, 23 March 1866, 4b.

88 ECA SL158/1, Report by the Sub-Committee of the Lord Provost's Committee, 23 March 1866. See *Evening Courant*, 27 March 1866, 8ef for a summary.

in his nine-page report to the Town Council on 23 March 1866 in which he stated 'a remarkable unanimity as to the necessity for immediate and vigorous action' and recommended that the best professional advice be obtained to take the proposals forward, Chambers devoted almost 60% of his report to refuting objections to his proposals. His irritation of a few days previously showed. On that occasion, during the St Andrew's ward meeting in the Royal Hotel, one misconception of the improvement scheme after another was voiced from the floor.[89] Chambers' report was his opportunity to get his retaliation in before all wards had held their meetings.

Despite the misgivings of the public, Chambers maintained the political momentum in the spring of 1866. The Lord Provost's Sub-committee approved a five-point plan: to proceed with an improvement scheme; to defray the cost with a tax not exceeding *2d.* in the £ – equivalent to a 0.83% addition to the local tax rate; to take professional advice on the details of the scheme; to obtain parliamentary authority for the plan; and to proceed only block by block.[90] These proposals were then put on the same day, 6 April 1866, to the full Lord Provost's Committee, where two amendments were tabled.[91] Chambers city improvement proposals were narrowly approved, by a 5–4 majority. Next, the full Town Council considered the five-point plan, dispatched two amendments, and they, too, approved the Chambers proposals, 21–16.[92] This was hardly the ringing endorsement that he might have expected on his election day and after such a positive reception of Littlejohn's *Report*. Chambers had been conciliatory during the meeting when confronted by seven further hostile reports from ward meetings tabled just as the Town Council convened and, faced by a plea from one of the senior councillors, Bailie Falshaw, to heed the wards and step back, he responded:

> I am willing to modify or throw aside my own notions, and leave the matter to the professional advisers who may be employed, including the Officer of Public Health. I would fix on the worst block first, say that between Niddry Street and St Mary's Wynd, or that between the North Bridge and Leith Wynd, and get one completed before we meddle with another. Could anything be more moderate than that?[93]

The Town Council vote approved the levy of *2d.* rate for twenty years 'payable in equal proportions by Landlord and Tenant' to finance the improvements, and to proceed toward the preparation of plans and estimates with professional assistance in relation to the technical and legal details.

With the crucial council vote in favour of the improvement scheme on 9 April 1866, there then followed a period of relative calm. This was, firstly,

89 *Evening Courant*, 23 March 1866, 3d–f.

90 SL158/1, Minutes of the Lord Provost's Sub-Committee as to the Sanitary Improvements of the City, 23 March and 6 April 1866.

91 SL158/1, Minutes of the Lord Provost's Committee, 6 April 1866.

92 SL158/1, Minutes of the Town Council, 9 April 1866. Predictably this was not the end of discontent, with further sniping in the letter columns of the press, and in council, where a tetchy row broke out over the issue of whether the procedures leading up to the vote were constitutional. See *Evening Courant*, 25 April 1866, 6a–d.

93 *Evening Courant*, 10 April 1866, 6a–f.

Edinburgh, 6 April 1866.
At a Meeting of the Lord Provost's Committee. Present: the Lord Provost, Bailie Falshaw, Bailie Miller, Bailie Handyside, Bailie Russell, Dean of Guild Shennan, Treasurer Callender, Councillor Kay, Councillor Ford, Councillor Mossman.
The Sub-Committee's Report of 23d ulto., with the relative Minutes thereon, were read.
The Minute of the Sub-Committee of this date having been also read and considered, the Lord Provost, seconded by the Dean of Guild, moved the adoption of the Resolutions engrossed in the Sub-Committee's Minute of this date.
Bailie Falshaw, seconded by Bailie Russell, moved as an amendment: "That while the committee are all the opinion that the time has now come when important sanitary and other improvements should be effected in the City, yet, having regard to the opposition which has been offered to the proposed improvements at the several Ward meetings, the Committee do not feel themselves warranted in proceeding with any general scheme of improvement."
Bailie Handyside, seconded by Bailie Miller, moved as an amendment: "That while the Committee are of opinion that the time has now come when important sanitary and other improvements should be effected in the City, yet, seeing that the public have not had a specific plan before them showing the precise improvements proposed to be executed, and the order in which it is proposed to execute them with accompanying estimates, resolved:

5.9 The Town Council decision to proceed with the City Improvement Scheme, 1866
[Source: ECA SL158/1, Council Minutes, 6 April 1866]

because the reappearance of cholera in May focused attention on public health measures for several months, with Littlejohn offering practical steps to combat the outbreak which by October had claimed 28 lives.[94] Chambers opportunistically observed that he 'regretted that they were not better prepared in the way of sanitary improvement'.[95] Secondly, city technical staff were preoccupied with the details of gradients and alignments associated with the improvement proposals and these attracted little interest from newspapers. The lull in public debate was short-lived, however, and interest was soon rekindled in the press by the publication of the revised improvement proposals (see figs 5.10, 5.11 and 5.13). The appointment in May 1866 of John Lessels[96] was specifically requested by the city architect, David Cousin, and jointly they developed a preliminary draft for St Mary's Street which was presented by Lessels himself to a meeting of the full Town Council on 31 July 1866.[97] Small wonder, then, that there was considerable

94 For a lengthy reports on the measures and the outbreak generally, see *Evening Courant*, 10 April 1866, 6a–f; 9 August 1866, 3a. For the tally of cases, see *Courant*, 24 October 1866, 5b.

95 *Evening Courant*, 9 May 1866, 8a.

96 *Dictionary of Scottish Architects*, entry for John Lessels. A contradictory entry under David Cousin gives the date of appointment as 17 March 1868. See http://www.scottisharchitects.org.uk/architect_list.php?asnme=lessels&asstr=&astwn=&ascnt=&asctr=

97 ECA SL158/1, Minutes of the Lord Provost's Committee, 30 July 1866. The Cousin and Lessels' plan was considered, with revised costings, and a map printed by W. and A.K. Johnston, at a scale of 3.31 inches to the mile. See also *Evening Courant*, 1 August 1866, 4d. Cousin is credited

Block	Locality	Number of families	Value under compulsory purchase (£)
1	From Halkerstone's Wynd to Leith Wynd	429	33,000
2	From Leith Wynd to Big Jack's Close	516	44,745
3	East Side of St Mary's Wynd to Miln's [*sic*] Close	381	28,480
4	Niddry Street to St Mary's Wynd	450	41,250
5	Stevenlaw's Close to Old Fishmarket Close	255	19,200
6	Adam Square to Brown Square	327	54,000
7	Cowgate, High School Wynd, and High School Yards	70	4,740
8	Grassmarket (both sides)	182	17,500
9	Detached portions of West Port and King's Stables	89	8,120
10	Lady Lawson's Wynd, West Port, &c	75	8,800
11	Canongate (both sides)	213	14,400
12	Nicolson Square to Bristo	143	23,280
13	Pleasance to Nicolson Street	127	9,480
	Total	3,257	306,995

Table 5.1 Compulsory purchase: the numbers and probable costs of displacing families as a result of the improvement scheme
[Source: *Edinburgh Evening Courant*, 21 Aug 1866, 6e]

public interest when the *Courant* set out details, block by block, with costs and the numbers of inhabitants to be displaced, the improvement scheme as presented and approved on 17 August 1866 by the Lord Provost's Committee as the body to whom the responsibility had been devolved.[98]

Cousin's and Lessels' Report was printed for public consultation, and it and the plans were available for public inspection in the council chamber during August 1866.[99] This consultative process was much admired by *The Glasgow Herald*, although it considered the scale of the Edinburgh proposals a 'mere bagatelle' compared to their own improvement scheme.[100] This assessment might

with planning St Mary's Street, Blackfriars Street, Jeffrey Street and Chambers Street. Cousin was previously appointed as Superintendent of Works – see reports of the Town Council meeting in *Caledonian Mercury*, 20 May 1847, 4b. He won the nomination for Superintendent of Works on a third vote, 16 to 14.

98 *Evening Courant*, 21 August 1866, 6a–e.

99 University of Edinburgh Special Collections, Q.d7/18, D. Cousin and J. Lessels, *Plan of Sanitary Improvements of the City of Edinburgh* (Edinburgh, 1866). Cousin and Lessels acknowledged the input to the revised report from the Architectural Institute of Scotland, and the Lord Provost's 'almost daily' contribution.

100 *The Glasgow Herald*, 12 November 1866, 2c–e. The Glasgow Improvement Act, 1866, ultimately resulted in 39 new streets. Chamberlain's Birmingham clearances were begun ten years later and on an area half that of Glasgow. See C.M. Allan, 'The genesis of British urban development with special reference to Glasgow', *Economic History Review*, 18 (1965), 598–613; J. Lindsay (ed.), *Municipal Glasgow: Its Evolution and Enterprises* (Glasgow, 1914), 48, 50–7; S. Chisholm, 'The history and results of the Glasgow City Improvement Trust,' *Proceedings of the Royal Philosophical Society of Glasgow*, 27 (1895–96), 39–56.

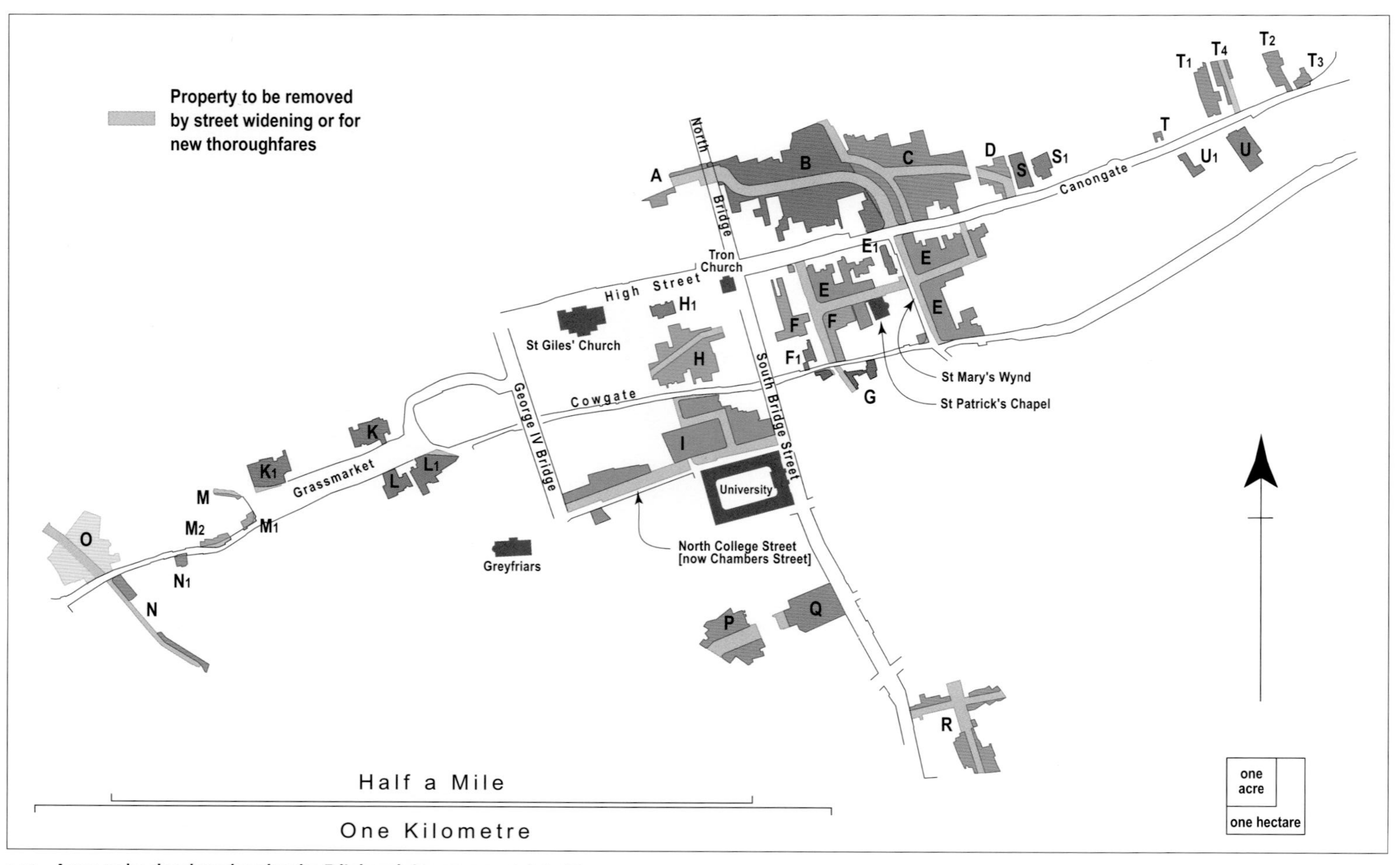

5.10 Areas to be developed under the Edinburgh Improvement Act 1867
This map summarises the areas of property and streets to be acquired under the Improvement Act.
[Source: redrawn from Cousin's and Lessels' six detailed maps three of which are shown in figures 5.10, 5.11 and 5.13]

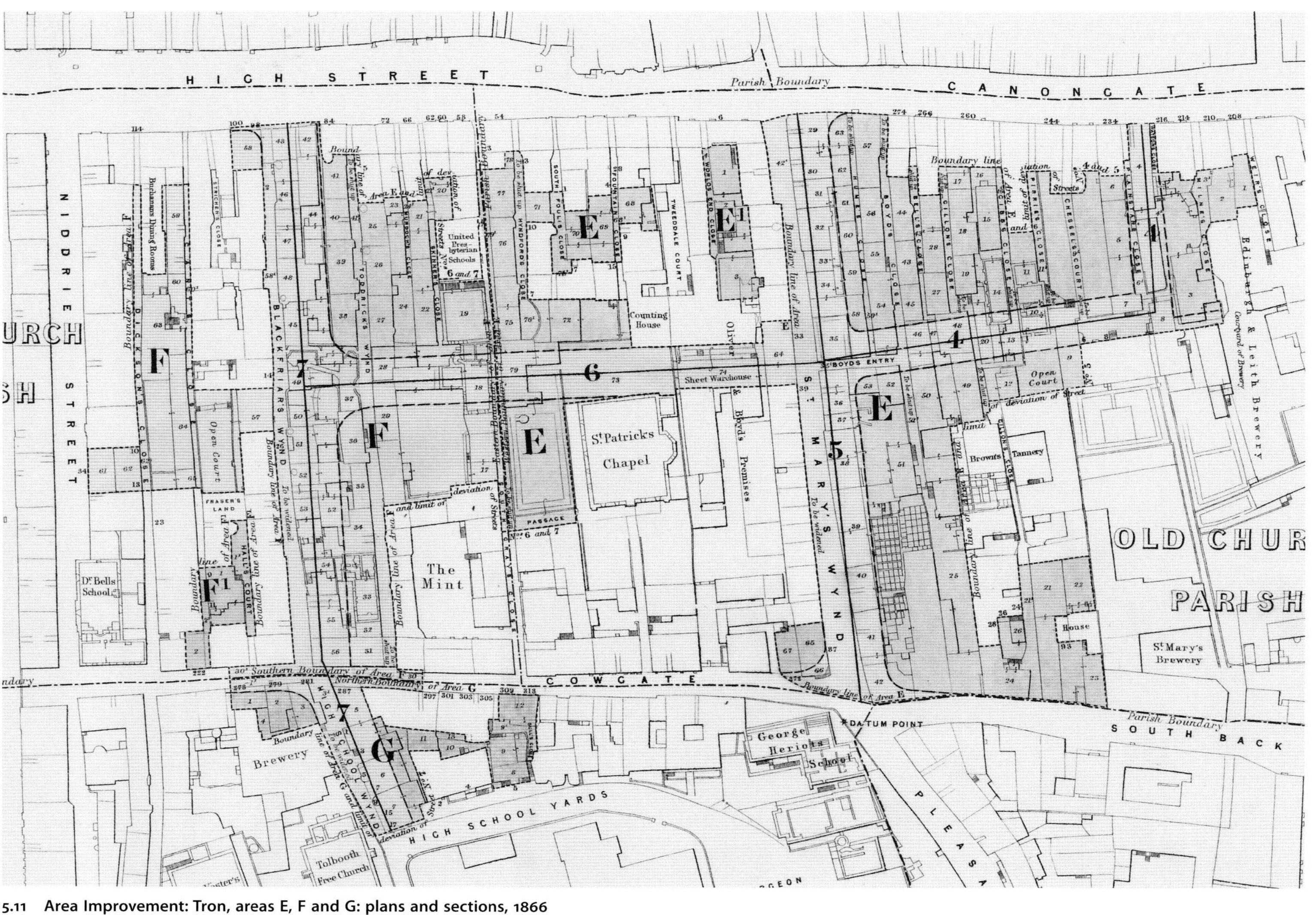

5.11 Area Improvement: Tron, areas E, F and G: plans and sections, 1866

Cousin's and Lessels' scheme for improving one of the densest concentrations of the poor in the Old Town. The letters refer to the areas in Figure 5.12, and the many numbers in small type refer to the hundreds of properties that the City authorities had to acquire to implement the improvements. See also figures 2.1 (Irish population), 5.7 (Littlejohn's proposal).

well have been tinged with envy since the levy on local residents to pay for the Glasgow scheme, approved earlier in the year, produced a backlash at the polling booths in September 1866 when Lord Provost Blackie was unceremoniously ejected by the electors, an outcome that could scarcely have escaped the notice of Chambers and his fellow Edinburgh councillors.[101] The cost of the Edinburgh scheme, £306,995, was to be offset by selling building stances to 'enterprising builders', leaving a deficit of about £200,000; the architects claimed that 'the total number of families likely to be displaced is 3257, of which three-fourths would get accommodation in the new houses to be erected'.[102] If subjecting the proposals to further public scrutiny in the intimidating surroundings of the council chamber was a device to avoid referring the matter yet again to the critical words of the wards, it was only a partial success.[103] The municipal elections were just weeks away, and the letters columns of the *Courant* and *Scotsman* were increasingly colonised by concerns about the clearances. One critic identified a misrepresentation in the Cousin and Lessels plans:

> It is surely a mistake to call them sanitary improvements. It is more properly a plan for certain architectural alterations, or it may be embellishments, of the old part of the town. I am decidedly opposed to such alterations, or to the imposition of tax on the inhabitants for that purpose.[104]

The departure from Littlejohn's vision of sanitary improvement was considerable. The architects proposed, and the Town Council eventually approved, a major capital project, whereas Littlejohn had been at pains to point out an array of minor and relatively inexpensive improvements – lavatory blocks and improved drain design being just two – which could make a considerable difference. Also, Cousin and Lessels did not focus on the most congested districts, which both Littlejohn and Chambers had identified as the priority. There was, then, a disjuncture between the expert *Report* produced by Littlejohn and embedded in Chambers' initial proposals, and the design stage, since the architects Cousin and Lessels adopted different principles when developing their plans. These did not stress 'opening out' sites, as did Littlejohn, but emphasised displaced inhabitants occupying new housing built on cleared sites. Another inconsistency concerned timing. By law, the Glasgow Improvement Act, 1866, limited to 500 the number of inhabitants displaced in any six-month period.[105] This guarantee was cited by Chambers as part of damage limitation in reply to his critics.[106] Such a constraint meant that Cousin's and Lessels' intention to remove 3,257 families, or about 15,000 people, and construct 2,955 homes would take many years to complete.

101 Allan, 'The genesis of British urban development', 604. Councillors subsequently admitted that the Glasgow Improvement Trust was so unpopular that they could not visit the clearance areas unaccompanied.

102 *Evening Courant*, 29 August 1866, 6a. The figure of 75% for re-housing those displaced was particularly high compared to displacements elsewhere.

103 *Evening Courant*, 29 August 1866, 6d. The leader writer recommended that more account should be given to local views 'than was manifested on a late occasion'.

104 *Evening Courant*, 2 October 1866, 4d.

105 In Scottish burghs the term Improvement Act is reserved for schemes such as street works; Police Acts have a wider remit, often restraining behaviour, and rarely concerned with capital projects.

106 ECA SL158/1, Report of the Sanitary Sub-Committee, 23 March 1866.

There was little prospect of the scheme being self-financing, which was why, in April 1866, the Town Council had approved a *2d.* in the £ levy on property to fund the improvements. The likelihood was that unless building anticipated demolition those few houses which were built each year would be rented at levels affordable only by the better off working class and the problems of the density of the poor would be shifted to another area of the city. It was simply a matter of demand far outstripping the supply of homes for the poor. Eventually this shortfall in funding had to be met from an increased levy on property, and, though the estimated cost of the improvements continued to escalate, Councillor Ford provided a telling rebuke to the economism of some councillors. He remarked that, although the total cost of the improvement proposals had escalated from £230,000 to £305,000 and finally to £542,000 in October 1866, the overall municipal assessment had fallen by a third in a decade, from *2s.* 3½*d.* to *1s.* *6d.* in the £ of rental value.[107] Councillors, like their constituents, were paying less in local taxation than for many years.

The revised improvement plan of Cousin and Lessels was considered by the Town Council in a series of meetings, the most important of which were on 8 October 1866, when they voted in favour of the revised plans, and on 27 November 1866, when they agreed to finance it with a levy of an extra *4d.* in the £ on landlords and tenants.[108] Hostility to the proposals continued, during which two opposing motions, though defeated, secured substantial support. With more than a hint of impatience, the Lord Provost on 27 November noted,

> We have approved the plans as they stand; Parliamentary notices have been given embracing the whole; books of reference showing the names of proprietors and occupants are made up; engraved plans depicting every morsel of property to be touched, are ready for being deposited on Friday 30th, the last day that such can be done; the bill to correspond with these details is in type, and just needs the final deliverance of the Council regarding assessment for its completion. … My own resolution is, to go to the House of Commons with the plans in all their integrity, and so far stand or fall by them.[109]

Chambers also promised that if no enterprising builders came forward he would himself 'claim the honour of being permitted to erect the first tenement'.[110] The *Evening Courant* delighted in this offer, reproaching the doubters Councillors Stott, Lewis, Fyfe, and Colston by name, and urging them to 'Go ye and do likewise'.[111] Chambers lambasted others for sitting in council for years and bringing forward no proposals themselves, despite claiming to support sanitary reform, and scorned yet more elected representatives for believing that there was suitable existing legislation to secure sanitary improvements while having

107 These figures relate to reports to the Lord Provost's Committee on 13 February, 17 August, and 28 November 1866.

108 *Evening Courant*, leader, 28 November 1866, 2b.

109 *Evening Courant*, 28 November 1866, 7c. The Lord Provost wrote to the two Edinburgh MPs, Duncan McLaren and James Moncrieff, on 14 November explaining the basis of his proposals.

110 ECA SL158/1, Report by the Sub-Committee of the Lord Provost's Committee as to the Sanitary Improvement of the City, 23 March 1866.

111 *Evening Courant*, 28 November 1866, 2b; *4d.* in the £ was equivalent to an extra tax of 1.67%, and was below the Glasgow levy of *6d.* in the £.

5.12 East end of the Grassmarket showing the foot of the West Bow, 1856
This early photograph captures an area of the city densely packed with poor and migrant populations, and the missions that ministered to their needs. See also Figure 2.4. Thomas Keith, photographer.
[Source: ECL]

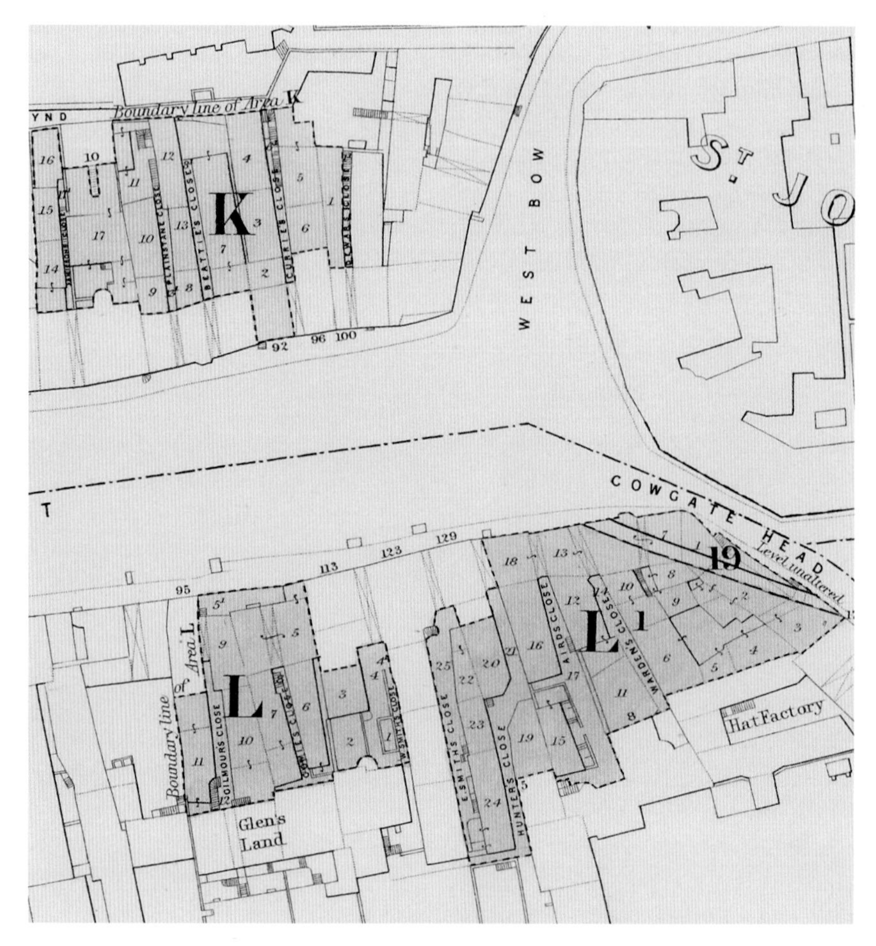

5.13 Area improvement: Cowgatehead, areas K and L
The scheme for the eastern part of the Grassmarket shows the substantial parts of property to be improved were located behind the façades. This is the area of the Keith photograph in Figure 5.12.

made no effort to identify such powers. His taunting of Councillor Lewis caused derisory laughter when he revealed how, despite his well-known opposition to clearances, Lewis had recommended, and Chambers adopted, the proposals to open up Simon Square, yet Lewis continued to oppose clearance schemes. And finally, just before the vote was taken on 27 November, Chambers admonished his opponents for having approved the outline plans on 8 October and then taking seven weeks to debate the finance issue, just hours before the deadline for these details were required for the parliamentary Bill. It was a deliberate filibustering attempt by the doubters to wreck the legislation. In summing up, Chambers confronted his opponents, stating that if his proposals were not approved it was 'an end for ever to any improvements to the Old Town of Edinburgh'. He concluded by saying that 'I leave the responsibility of the decision with the Council, and wash my hands of it'.[112]

5.14 The Improvement Scheme in stone, 1867
The commemorative plaque in St Mary's Street identifies the first building constructed under the Edinburgh Improvement Act 1867, and the initials high above it, DC/JL, also in St Mary's Street, refer to the architects David Cousin and John Lessels.

Applause for Chambers' speech was followed by a vote: 23–15 in favour of the improvement scheme. The announcement was greeted with 'unusually enthusiastic' cheering, and once it had subsided, Councillor Ford called for 'one more cheer' to be given with equal enthusiasm.[113]

The majority was clear but the opposition remained resolute. For the next three months William Anderson's ten articles on 'The Poor of Edinburgh and their Homes' hit the headlines.[114] There was continued sniping at the Chambers' clearance proposals. Property owners convened a meeting at 5 St Andrew Square, a list of opponents of the Bill was published repeatedly, frequent anonymous letters critical of the proposals appeared in the press, and adverts were placed showing where in the city residents could sign a petition opposing the Bill.[115] After a month of activity by opponents, the *Courant* commented:

> It will be observed that the remonstrance against the City Improvements Bill, which has been signed by upwards of 4000 residents, lies at several places mentioned in the advertisement, in another column to-day and to-morrow, to give those an opportunity of signing to who may yet wish to do so.[116]

The House of Lords committee considering the provisions of the Bill noted that compulsory purchase powers were granted for ten years over '430 houses occupied by about 14,170 persons of the labouring classes' and that the inconvenience caused would be addressed by limiting evictions to 500 persons in any six-month period, or by building temporary homes for those displaced if alternatives did not exist. Optimistically, the Lords committee concluded: 'With these provisions no Inconvenience is anticipated.'[117] Despite considerable opposition, by 19 March 1867 the Bill had progressed through its various stages,

112 *Evening Courant*, 28 November 1866, 7c, The Lord Provost's speech.
113 *Evening Courant*, 28 November 1866, 7c.
114 The articles were reprinted as W. Anderson, *The Poor of Edinburgh and their Homes* (Edinburgh, 1867).
115 *Evening Courant*, 29 December 1866, 3d; Adverts: 7 and 19 February 1867, 1a.
116 *Evening Courant*, 19 February 1867, 2e.
117 House of Lords Library, HL/PO/JO/10/9/627, Report from the Committee on the Edinburgh Improvement Bill, 13 May 1867.

was approved, and received the royal assent on 31 May 1867. The *Courant* leader commented:

> The City of Edinburgh Improvement Bill was before a committee of the House of Commons yesterday as an unopposed bill. There are, of course, many who object strongly to the measure, but the opponents have not gone the length of asking to be heard against it in its progress through Parliament. The proceedings before the committee yesterday were therefore to a great extent formal, and after a verbal alteration on one of the clauses, the bill was ordered to be reported to the House of Commons.[118]

After a period of preliminary planning, the clearances began on the north-east corner of St Mary's Wynd, exactly one year later, on 31 May 1868.[119]

Remarkably, only nineteen months had elapsed between the publication of Littlejohn's *Report* and the passage of the Edinburgh Improvement Act, 1867.[120] Littlejohn's *Report* was instrumental in providing a consensus upon which Chambers' political commitment capitalised to secure the successful passage first through the council committees, and then in parliament.

Re-structuring urban administration

The Edinburgh Improvement Act, 1867, heralded another change: the rise of the expert.[121] To advance the improvement scheme, Chambers relied on respected professionals. He involved the experienced City Architect, David Cousin, and the up-and-coming architect, John Lessels, at each stage of the process – from draft plans to detailed specifications, from property acquisitions to the displacement and re-housing of inhabitants. In addition to architects, physicians, chemists, and engineers were drawn into the decision-making process concerning urban sanitation. This shift to involve expert knowledge was an unintended consequence of the improvement process. Respect for Littlejohn's *Report* had secured a platform for subsequent expert knowledge, and for professionals such as Cousin and Lessels; they and Chambers were the inheritors of political goodwill established by Littlejohn. The statistical revolution initiated by civil registration facilitated a level of public debate that was more sophisticated in its use of data to support an argument. After Littlejohn, mere opinion was no substitute for informed judgment.[122] It was the Town Clerk and the City Architect who accompanied the Lord Provost to meet parliamentary committees when Local Bills in 1867 and 1869 were under consideration in London, in contrast

118 *Evening Courant*, 15 March 1867, 2b. Chambers, Marwick and Lessels attended the session, as did the Lord Advocate and Edinburgh MP (1859–68) James Moncrieff.

119 *Evening Courant*, 14 April 1868, 2e.

120 30 and 31 Vict., cap. 44, Edinburgh City Improvement Act, 1867.

121 See G. Massard-Guilbaud, 'French local authorities and the challenge of industrial pollution c.1810–1917', in R.J. Morris and R.H. Trainor (eds), *Urban Governance: Britain and Beyond since 1750* (Aldershot, 2000), 153, for wider European perspectives.

122 This is not to suggest that Littlejohn was without opinions of his own, as his evidence to royal commissions and other investigations indicated. When asked direct questions about his own views he was characteristically direct. To command support and thus a chance of implementation his *Report* required evidence and not opinion.

to proceedings over the Water of Leith drainage in 1854, when Glover, the Police Surgeon, was marginalised.[123]

The balance of power in council was informally under revision as the role of experts encroached on the autonomy of council committees and the power of their conveners. Technical issues increasingly moved discussion beyond the capabilities of laymen, who were gradually confined to areas of principle and precedent rather than practice. Littlejohn himself put the matter succinctly some years later. Rather than appoint individuals with knowledge of the building trades as sanitary inspectors, as was originally the case, he preferred individuals with special training and a diploma, as in England, or north of the border, from the Sanitary Institute in Scotland.[124] The increasing scale and complexity of civil engineering schemes for water and drainage in Edinburgh, as in many British cities, required a command of technical details. For example, as part of the argument about improvements, Cousin and Lessels produced a table of gradients for the streets affected, showing just how their plans would aid the flow of traffic.[125] Thereafter, it was difficult for critics to suggest different routes for street improvement without similar calculations; only Coyne, an engineer himself, was able to do so.

Knowledge conveyed greater power from the 1860s and Littlejohn and Chambers both used this skilfully to inform the public in their attempts to secure support in advance of political developments. Through the newspaper columns, even before his *Report* was published, Littlejohn's weekly mortality statistics cleverly kept the issue of public health in the mind's eye of the public. Chambers' impassioned address on housing improvement following his successful election in 1865 was another example of media management. Newspapers were instrumental in this process, therefore, and presented complex arguments to the reading public through both editorial comment and the letters columns, as with the moral and ethical ideas presented by a regular correspondent, 'Civis', in the *Caledonian Mercury* in November 1866 about the unacceptable actions of landlords in relation to overcrowding:

> A house owner has no more right to crowd a vast number of human beings together for gain with the certainty of generating misery, pestilence, and death, and thus ruinously affecting his neighbours' and public rights and interests, than he has to convert his house into a menagerie or a fever hospital. A coach proprietor is restricted by law to carrying only a limited number within a vehicle of certain proportions, although the occupancy is only for a transient period. In the transmission of emigrants to our colonies and foreign parts, stringent regulations under official superintendence are made to prevent overcrowding.[126]

If Chambers and Littlejohn were adept in their management of the press, it could also be a double-edged weapon, as when in the letters columns of

123 See p XX
124 PP (HC) 1884–85 [C. 4409], Royal Commission on the Housing of the Working Classes, Scotland. Vol.5, Minutes of Evidence, Q.19,046.
125 D. Cousin and J. Lessels, *Plan of Sanitary Improvements of the City of Edinburgh* (Edinburgh, 1866), 20–1.
126 *Caledonian Mercury*, 29 November 1866, 2a.

the *Courant* the views of numerous well-informed correspondents produced a political momentum sufficient to marshal over 4,000 signatures in opposition to the Chambers' proposals, and in 1866 nearly derailed the improvements.[127] Thus within a few years of the removal of the 'tax on knowledge' in 1855, as the duty on newspapers was called, citizens, councillors and city officials participated in an informed exchange of views which ensured a degree of vigilance in the public sphere.

Perhaps most significant, though, was the comprehensive manner of newspaper reporting. Verbatim accounts of council meetings were commonplace, and cross-checking between the Edinburgh newspapers confirms the excellent shorthand skills of reporters whose comprehensive accounts of council business were superior in both quantity and quality to those available in the formal council minutes. Thus, for example, on the day Littlejohn's *Report* was published the *Caledonian Mercury* reported the 43 items of business on the agenda of the Town Council, and though the *Scotsman* covered only half of these, both provided over 13,000 words.[128] The level of knowledge about local developments, therefore, far exceeded that of the twenty-first century.[129] Important, lengthy documents such as the 13,000-word account of the clauses of the General Police Act, 1862, were reproduced in their entirety, and Littlejohn's *Report* and William Anderson's 'The Poor of Edinburgh and their Homes' were reproduced in serial form, cumulatively adding to public discussion and political momentum.[130] The crucial council debate on 27 November 1866 at which the 23:15 vote was cast in favour of the Improvements was the subject of a 1,000-word leader and 14,000-word verbatim account of councillors' speeches. Householders with a vote certainly knew their elected representatives well through their utterings in the council chamber and exchanges in print.

The rise of the municipal expert was in part a consequence of the emergence of an audit culture.[131] The ward basis of elections for 'Resident Police Commissioners' in the first half of the nineteenth century was an earlier attempt to restrain the more ambitious financial projects of Edinburgh Town Council. Accountability became a central issue for town councils generally as they increasingly assumed wider powers in the provision of services and amenities, and Edinburgh was no exception. The memory of substantial long-term debts incurred for improvement schemes in the not too distant past – the New Town, North Bridge, George IV Bridge, and in the 1850s Cockburn Street – encouraged an attitude of parsimony towards any form of public expenditure.

Not surprisingly, perhaps, the result in Edinburgh was a paralysis in matters of public health compounded by parking issues in sub-committees. The Town Council was drowning in its own administrative structures; lengthy agendas and

127 *Evening Courant*, 19 February 1867, 2e. *The Scotsman*, 19 February 1867, 1f carried a list of 12 locations where the 'remonstrance against the bill' could be signed.

128 *Caledonian Mercury*, 16 August 1865, 2e–g; 3a–f; *The Scotsman*, 16 August 1865, 6a–d.

129 An analysis of word lengths relating to 14 local matters of Town Council business on 20 December 1864 was reported in over 8,500 words by both *The Scotsman* and the *Caledonian Mercury*, both 22 December 1864, respectively, cols 2f–3c and 7a–d.

130 The pattern continued with reports of approximately 70,000 words on the House of Commons and House of Lords Select Committees on water.

131 See M.J. Daunton, 'Introduction' in M.J. Daunton (ed.), *The Cambridge Urban History of Britain*, vol. 3, *1820–1950* (Cambridge, 2000), 14–29.

limited demarcation over executive responsibility for policy were a recipe for inaction. This did little for the standing of local councillors, as was certainly the case under Francis Brown Douglas, Lord Provost during the discussions over the local and general police bills in 1862.[132] By consistently remitting business to the Lord Provost's Committee, and then deferring action there, he so seriously damaged the reputation of the council that he was persuaded not to stand for election in 1862. Brown Douglas was not alone, however. An inspection of the agenda items for the Lord Provost's Committee shows 'delay' or 'no action' as the most common entries in the early and mid-1860s.[133] This, and the absence of formal minutes for the Lord Provost's Committee, reveals much about the workings of an inner cabinet compared to the full council with its regular committee meetings. The Lord Provost's Committee almost certainly met informally, sometimes privately, and without all members aware of such meetings.[134] In a newspaper jibe at the paralysis in the political structures shortly after Littlejohn's *Report* was published, a columnist remarked: 'if half the time and enthusiasm which that body [the Town Council] wastes in petty and personal squabbling about matters of no practical interest were devoted to consideration of the sanitary condition of the city, we should be at once a more peaceable and healthier community.'[135]

In short, the conduct of Town Council business did little to inspire confidence and was another reason why the opponents of the Chambers' improvement scheme were both suspicious and vociferous. As the letters columns of the three main Edinburgh newspapers reveal, the public was distrustful of the conspiratorial atmosphere, and while generally approving of public health improvements in principle, were conservative in relation to major capital projects because they were often distrustful of councillors' motives and averse to the secrecy they associated with the council decisions.

Divided expert medical opinion also complicated public health policy. This was partly because medicine was itself split into specialist sub-divisions and societies, and not without its own feuding factions.[136] Running through the various public health issues from 1840 to 1870 was the influential figure of Dr Alexander Wood, elected as Police Commissioner and town councillor, and chairman of the Cleaning Committee which was often at odds with both police surgeons, Glover and Littlejohn. He accused Glover of transgressing the bounds of his authority during the cholera outbreak in 1848 and, in another demonstration of self-importance, persistently sought to promote the activities of the Cleaning Committee (see chapter 3). The distinguished physician Wood envied the forensic surgeon Littlejohn's success and reputation, and accused the younger man of high-handedness in assuming a role as sanitary 'legislator for Scotland'.[137] Indeed,

132 See chapter 3.

133 ECA SL25/1/1–2, Agenda Books of the Lord Provost's Committee, 1862–66. Chambers used the Lord Provost's Committee and sub-committees to greater effect.

134 The meetings also tended to be fixed 15 or 30 minutes before full meetings of the Council so as to help the Lord Provost to manage the business.

135 *The Scotsman*, 6 September 1865, 6cd.

136 See J. Jenkinson, *Scottish Medical Societies, 1731–1939: Their History and Records* (Edinburgh, 1993), Appendix 1; I. McIntyre and I. MacLaren (eds), *Surgeons' Lives* (Edinburgh, 2005), 136–7.

137 *The Scotsman*, 29 June 1863; entry for Alexander Wood in the *ODNB*. See chapter 3 on the Wood–Glover tensions.

little divided the medical fraternity more than disputes over whether and how the Police Surgeon's role was different to that of Medical Officer of Health, complicated as that was not just over duties, but over which legislation governed the appointment, and whether a continuation of private practice was ethical. Wood's long-term tenure as chairman of the Cleaning Committee made structural changes to public health policy in Edinburgh highly unlikely, committed as he was to its limited activities and opposed to the expansive responsibilities of a Medical Officer of Health. Littlejohn's pre-emptive approach to public health was at odds with the reactive and pragmatic Wood, concerned as he was with cleaning courts and sweeping streets to relieve the distress of the poor.

In Edinburgh, as Littlejohn explicitly recognised in the conclusion to his *Report*, the responsibility for public health was fragmented among a number of committees and semi-autonomous parochial board chairmen controlling their respective fiefdoms. The stasis in public health policy in the pre-Littlejohn era is the more understandable in such a context, as was the sniping which subsequently imperilled the clearance schemes proposed by Chambers.

Politics and the quest for organisational efficiency

Littlejohn's central theme in the conclusion to his *Report* was the need for monitoring construction projects at the approval or initial stage – *in limine*. In his *Report* he despaired of the disorganisation caused by fragmented responsibilities. While he acknowledged the contribution of voluntary organisations to the social capital of the city, Littlejohn remained sceptical of their overall impact. For example, to leave infectious children in the community was unwise; to retain them in an institution unnecessarily was undesirable. Yet to admit them to a hospital or home meant that their infected clothes were destroyed so they could not leave unless there was a sufficient stock of garments available from the donations made by voluntary organisations and visitors. Ultimately, the responsibility fell to the public authorities, and it was an example of how the uncertainty of private funds required a more systematic public response.[138]

Whether Chambers was influenced by the indirect effects of public decisions is unclear. What was apparent was that even before the Improvement Act had become legislation he promoted the idea of rationalisation in the management and relief of the poor in Edinburgh. He convened a meeting in the City Chambers in April 1867 to discuss the 'practicability and expediency of adopting measures to simplify, economise, and concentrate the action of public charities of Edinburgh, as well as to improve the condition of the really deserving poor'.[139] Subsequently Chambers reminded the interested parties that 'What we want is sound administrative action', and that sectarianism, one barrier to the rationalisation of charity,

138 *Evening Courant*, 24 November 1866, 8d. The first Edinburgh Hospital for Sick Children opened in Lauriston Lane with 20 beds and a dispensary in 1860, and was granted a royal charter by Queen Victoria in 1863. See D. Guthrie, *The Royal Edinburgh Hospital for Sick Children, 1860–1960* (Edinburgh, 1960).

139 *Report on the Condition of the Poorer Classes of Edinburgh and of their Dwellings, Neighbourhoods and Families* (Edinburgh, 1868), xi. Compiled by Dr Alexander Wood, it was a powerful assembly of 92 men – medical, legal and clerical representatives and other inhabitants of the city.

had to be addressed. This was a view advanced by the distinguished anaesthetist Sir James Young Simpson to a packed Queen Street Hall meeting in March 1868 when he 'rejoiced that all sects and denominations were represented at that day's meeting'.[140] It was a diplomatic nod to the entrenched and shifting religious divisions which permeated Edinburgh's political alliances. Even though there was a very significant Roman Catholic population (see Figure 2.1) in mid-nineteenth-century Edinburgh[141] this was less a Catholic–Protestant rift, as in Glasgow, Belfast and Liverpool, and more because 'all the animosity [was] between different bodies of Presbyterians'.[142] A *Scotsman* editorial noted how councillors were elected not on whether they were 'men of sense and business likely to promote the good of the city and its institutions, but whether they worship in this or that church – rather, whether they are submissive to some particular ecclesiastical clique.'[143]

Littlejohn's methodology certainly influenced the deliberations of the committee set up by Chambers to consider the condition of the poorer classes of Edinburgh. The connection between poverty and health, empirically revealed by Littlejohn, was explicitly acknowledged by the 92-man committee in the first two pages of their report. Littlejohn's sanitary districts also formed the basis of their analysis. Proposed remedial measures included house-to-house visitations of the poor, another feature of Littlejohn's empirical approach, and a reliance on statistical data.[144] Sir James Simpson deployed quantitative indicators of poverty when speaking to the Queen Street Hall meeting, estimating that £100,000 per year was spent on the destitute and that this could be reduced by a third by pooling effort and reducing administrative overheads.[145] Simpson then posed a moral dilemma to the packed audience:

> ... they had 6000 dogs in Edinburgh to whom lodging and meat were bestowed to a great extent. Let them do the same to the human animal, who deserved it much better than dogs, and they would accomplish all they required. (Applause.)[146]

The 'remedies calculated to restore the lapsed classes', as proposed in the printed report that resulted from Chambers' initiative, were many. Some

140 Letter from Chambers to Sir H.W. Moncrieff, 28 March 1868, reported in the *Evening Courant*, 1 April 1868, 6a–e; Sir James Y. Simpson, 'Destitution in Edinburgh', speech to a meeting in Queen Street Hall, 28 March 1868, reported in the *Evening Courant*, 1 April 1868, 6c.

141 In 1861 the Irish-born were 5.2% of the population of the parliamentary burgh. Despite the large chapel in Cowgate (fig. 5.11) not all were Roman Catholics.

142 *The Scotsman*, 18 October 1856, 2f. See A. I. Dunlop, *The Kirks of Edinburgh: the Congregations, Churches, and Ministers of the Presbytery of Edinburgh, 1560–1984* (Edinburgh, 1988), 8.

143 See *The Scotsman*, 24 November 1866, 8b. A correspondent commented, 'The Roman Church has always been remarkable for diving down into the very depths of defilement', sending its clergy to live among the 'flock of the High Street and the Cowgate', and while 'We send missionaries to live among savages ... that is paradise in comparison'. Protestant 'pastors' were said to live in more comfortable districts.

144 *Report on the Condition of the Poorer Classes*, 2–4. See also, *The Scotsman*, 20 February 1868, 7.

145 The official figures was £112,500, equivalent to a tax of '13 shillings per head for every man, woman and child in the city.' See *Report on the Condition of the Poorer Classes*, 45, compiled by Dr Alexander Wood.

146 Sir James Y. Simpson, 'Destitution in Edinburgh'.

conveyed the tone of self-help, such as greater sobriety, savings banks, cooperatives, and 'rational recreation'. Echoing Littlejohn's Conclusion to his *Report*, other remedies could 'only be enforced by law and authority'. Thirteen proposals were advanced under this heading, most unexceptionable and few original. First identified was 'to run streets through the densest blocks', described as Provost Chambers' plan, but others such as the closure of unfit housing, refurbishment, reduced density, improved drainage, and the erection of public washing houses, owed much to Littlejohn's research, and added little. Other proposals were simply vague or part of a wish list: to improve education, suppress begging, reform the poor law, and regulate the liquor trade.

Beyond setting up the meeting to consider the condition of the poorer classes of Edinburgh, and speaking to its initial meeting, Chambers' involvement in the initiative was slim. Though no doubt concerned to achieve a degree of rationalisation in charitable effort, it is not unlikely that in the aftermath of the acrimonious public debate over his improvement proposals, this was an astute move to give stakeholders a louder voice in topics of public interest, and thus to heal wounds. It was also an indication of how sensitive the political climate of the 1860s was, both in terms of the shifting alliances within the council chamber, and in the mobilisation of political action through the press. Even with the strongest of political endorsements, as Chambers enjoyed on his election, and with the unanimous support for an expert analysis of public health, as provided by Littlejohn, the implementation phase of policy was stymied by fears of excessive public expenditure and a multiplicity of practical objections. Indeed, the political calendar almost invariably showed filibustering tendencies prior to council elections in November when, exhausted by months of in-fighting, indecision, and ill-grace, the retiring council approved in its last gasp such contentious issues as the appointment of a Medical Officer, the negotiations over the Police Bill and Lindsay Act in 1862, and final approval of the Improvement Scheme in 1866.

The foundation of the Health Committee

However, the final remedial suggestion struck an important note of agreement with Littlejohn's *Report*, and again it was concerned with organisational efficiency. This was a recommendation for the 'appointment of a sanitary committee of the Town Council' to be 'composed of those who understand such matters, and who are not likely to be influenced by the selfish clamours of house proprietors'.[147] It was almost certainly a recommendation drafted by the compiler of the report, Dr Alexander Wood, given his involvement in demarcation disputes between the Cleaning Committee, the Sanitary Committee, the Police Surgeon and the Parochial Boards. Wood was not simply self-seeking in foregrounding this suggestion, though he almost certainly considered himself the front-runner for the chairmanship of the enlarged Sanitary Committee which the report recommended. It was another four years before that administrative consolidation took place, by which time Wood, already jilted, had turned his attentions to the Tramway Company as its chairman.

147 *Report on the Condition of the Poorer Classes*, 66.

If Littlejohn was frustrated by the fractured nature of the committee structure and decision-making process in the council, his opportunity to have a direct and positive influence on its future character arose in 1872. A motion by Littlejohn's longstanding ally, Bailie Lewis resolved, 'That it be remitted to a Special Committee to report on a better organisation for accomplishing the Sanitary business of the City under the Public Health Act.'[148] The Special Committee comprised four councillors, the Burgh Surveyor and Littlejohn. Rather conservatively, they considered that areas of committee responsibility for cleaning and lighting, and streets and building should not be altered, but recommended a new committee, to be called the Sanitary Committee, which should coordinate public health matters in the city.[149] Indeed, to signal this intent it was at its next meeting renamed the Public Health Committee, and confirmed its areas of responsibility as:

1. The supervision of burying grounds
2. The supervision of lodging houses and overcrowding
3. The prevention of smoke nuisance
4. The consideration of all proposals to establish new manufactories and the supervision of manufactories already established
5. The inspection of workshops, bakehouses, cowhouses, stables and pigsties
6. The adulteration of food and diseased meat
7. The prevention or mitigation of epidemic disease, including the establishment and administration of hospitals &c.

Littlejohn's fingerprints were all over the process of establishing a Public Health Committee. Diplomatically cautious in not usurping the terms of reference of existing committee chairmen, yet tactically astute by securing discrete areas of responsibility for a new committee, the sphere of operations for the new Public Health Committee were almost a carbon copy of the sub-headings of his own *Report*. Its first meeting 'resolved to ask Dr Littlejohn to report to the next meeting of the Committee what are his duties and what arrangements he would suggest by means of increase to or re-organization of his Staff to carry his duties into effect.'[150] It was a significant step. Just two weeks later Littlejohn's prompt written response on 7 January 1873 formed the first entry in the Minute Book of the new Public Health Committee. On a purely practical level Littlejohn subsequently reported through a single committee which had the power to act quickly when matters were considered urgent and, if it did not involve great expense, Littlejohn could act independently and without referring to the Town Council.[151] This was an emphatic vote of confidence in Littlejohn and in the position of Medical Officer of Health, and was a radical change

148 ECA SL26/1/1, Minutes of the Public Health Committee, Report, 6 September 1872.

149 ECA SL26/1/1, Minutes of the Public Health Committee, 17 October 1872, item 1, reported in *The Scotsman*, 22 October 1872.

150 ECA SL26/1/1, Minutes, 17 December 1872 and ECA Box 00/01/20/E74. A seven-page printed statement dated 7 January 1873 provides the first entry in the Minutes of the new Public Health Committee.

151 For example, where water dripped from a cesspool or water-closet, the defect could be repaired on Littlejohn's authority and charged to the rates. See PP (HC) 1884–85 [C. 4409], Royal Commission on the Housing of the Working Classes, Scotland. vol. 5, Minutes of Evidence, Q.19,006.

from the situation when Glover, Littlejohn's predecessor as Police Surgeon, was unambiguously instructed to intervene in public health matters only during an epidemic emergency. So it was to the Public Health Committee that Littlejohn made regular reports concerning mortality in the city, and proposed measures to anticipate a cholera outbreak, or when he sought to develop policy, as, for example, concerning the notification of infectious diseases. Equally, the Public Health Committee turned directly and increasingly to Littlejohn over matters which drew on his expertise, and he subsequently described the relationship as one of 'full support'.[152] By these means the paralysis in public health policy which had plagued his predecessors as police surgeons was minimised. New monitoring systems were put in place through regular reports from the Medical Officer of Health, and the inspectorate, whom he was empowered to appoint, was also required to make daily reports on its activities.[153] The administrative pendulum had swung: the political influence in health policy was in decline, and that of the expert was in the ascendant. Public health had become a major administrative arm of a modernising municipality.

The politics of water

No issue in Edinburgh caused more political turbulence than the condition of the Water of Leith, though the central issue was the sluggish rather than the turbulent nature of its flow. Littlejohn's *Report* was framed against a highly sensitised yet divided arena populated by politically active New Town residents. Just as the inter-departmental character of the improvement scheme brought out the need for restructuring civic administration, so the condition of the Water of Leith revealed conflicting interests between councils that made for administrative inefficiencies in water and drainage management.

In the aftermath of the cholera epidemic of 1848–49 the conviction that polluted water was a carrier of contagion prompted efforts to improve the quality of the Water of Leith.[154] In the 1850s this involved discussions between the town councils of Edinburgh and Leith, and the Leith Harbour and Dock Commission, but disagreements over costs meant that a proposed intercepting sewer was not built; minor changes in the weirs to improve the flow of the river resulted only in making the Water of Leith 'a more efficient open sewer'.[155] The issue of water quality resurfaced in 1861 when the councils agreed a drainage plan but then squabbled again, both over the expense and over the significance of the results of chemical analysis which showed unpleasant but relatively harmless industrial pollutants and more alarming discharges of human excrement into the

152 PP (HC) 1884–85 [C. 4409], Royal Commission, Minutes of Evidence, Q.18,953, 19,024.

153 *The Scotsman*, 8 January 1873, 5d; 6 February 1873, 5b.

154 For a discussion of Alison's views on the origins of infection in the context of John Snow's demonstration that cholera was a water-borne disease, see M.W. Flinn, Report on the Sanitary Condition of the Labouring Population of Great Britain by Edwin Chadwick, 1842 (Edinburgh, 1865) 63. It was arguments over remedies for the state of the Water of Leith in 1853–54 that placed Dr George Glover's conduct as Police Surgeon under intense scrutiny.

155 P.J. Smith, 'Pollution abatement in the nineteenth century: the purification of the Water of Leith', *Environment and Behavior*, 6 (1974), 9.

Water of Leith and its tributary streams. Eventually, with a vocal wealthy class of New Town residents complaining of their malodorous neighbourhood, the matter was referred in 1864 to the Lord-Justice General who adjudged that all property owners in the catchment area of the river should pay equally towards costs, thus endorsing the argument of Leith Town Council.[156] Soon after, and despite heated public opposition and constant council in-fighting that culminated in the resignation of the City Treasurer,[157] the Edinburgh and Leith Sewerage Act, 1864, was passed, and a new supra-organisational body, the Sewerage Commission, was to prevent 'injurious' matter being discharged into the Water of Leith, 'ordinary sewage excepted'.[158] The commissioners set about the task of constructing the interceptor sewer but, since the new body was a toothless force, upstream industrial polluters continued to use the river as an open drain, and the downstream municipalities, Edinburgh and Leith, were not compelled to control 'ordinary sewage'. The neutering of the Sewerage Commissioners was almost inevitable because only a few years earlier, in 1856, the absorption of police powers as part of the extended jurisdiction of Edinburgh Town Council meant the concession of powers to another unelected body was highly unlikely. As Bailie Johnston explained: 'to invite the authority and red-tapeism of official men to override the liberties of the free-born citizens of this kingdom' was unrealistic.[159] Whatever the reality about the emergence of expert knowledge, in some quarters faceless and unaccountable men had no place in decisions affecting the revenue and expenditure of Edinburgh citizens. The basic principle was '*local provision, for local wants, locally identified*'.[160] 'No taxation without representation' was as appropriate at the local level as it was in state formation.

This, then, was the contentious local political and jurisdictional battleground in which Littlejohn's *Report* was published in 1865.[161] His findings, that death rates were not noticeably higher in the two sanitary districts adjoining the Water

156 P.J. Smith, 'Pollution abatement', 9–17. Edinburgh Town Council opposed this because, as the larger authority, more of the cost would fall on their ratepayers.

157 Letter from David Curror, City Treasurer and councillor, to the Lord Provost, 1 April 1864, resigning on the constitutional and procedural grounds that he was unable to discharge his responsibilities because council business was considered in secret by a sub-committee, and that he was excluded and refused sight of the documents relevant to the Water of Leith drainage scheme, despite being named as a promoter of a Bill to which he was opposed. See *Evening Courant*, 2 April 1864, 2f.

158 27 and 28 Vict., cap. 53, An Act for the Purification of the Water of Leith by Interception and Conveyance into the Sea of the Sewage falling into the same, and otherwise; and for other purposes [30 June 1864]. The Edinburgh and Leith Sewerage Act, 1864, was described by a correspondent to the *Evening Courant*, 7 November 1864, 8c as 'the greatest improvement that was ever made upon Edinburgh'.

159 *Evening Courant*, 19 February 1862, 6ab.

160 The phrase comes from E.P. Hennock, 'Central/local government relations in England 1835–1900', *Urban History Yearbook*, 9 (1982), 38–49, especially 39, Hennock's emphasis. See also M. Ogborn, 'Local power and state regulation in nineteenth-century Britain', *Transactions of the Institute of British Geographers*, 17, 2 (1992), 215–26.

161 *Caledonian Mercury*, 7 July 1865, 2a–c, provided a list of expenses associated with the attendance of various Edinburgh officials in London in connection with the Sewerage Bill. This led to appeals against the 'reckless expenditure' relating to the 'Water of Leith job' heard in the Sheriff Court in August 1865, just weeks before the publication of Littlejohn's *Report*. See *The Scotsman*, 11 August 1865, 2fg, and 23 August 1875, 2e–g. Similar complaints were made in relation to the Edinburgh and District Water Bill in 1869, *The Scotsman*, 23 October 1969, 3bc.

of Leith, and that in those streets adjoining the river diseases such as diarrhoea, dysentery and fever were not particularly prevalent, ran counter to popular opinion. Poverty, it was clear, was a more convincing explanation of the patterns of mortality and morbidity alongside the Water of Leith, as the analysis of data on the socio-economic character of the inhabitants convincingly indicated.[162] Littlejohn's conclusion should not have been surprising. His monthly tables of mortality, summarised in 1864 by a solicitor for the benefit of a committee of the House of Lords considering the Edinburgh and Leith Sewerage Bill, showed that only four out of nineteen Edinburgh districts had lower overall mortality rates than the two Water of Leith districts, and among infants, only seven had lower rates than those of the Water of Leith districts. Littlejohn's data and judgment went unchallenged: the Water of Leith constituted a health hazard, but was not a killer.[163] It was an instance of how the early release of detailed information, over a year before the publication of the full *Report*, contributed materially to policy debates. Given the political sensitivity of the Water of Leith drainage issue, Littlejohn's hallmark, meticulous research, steered a careful course between three earlier investigations[164] and took account of a royal commission investigation which subjected the sewage disposal of Edinburgh to a more detailed scrutiny than in any other town or city in Britain.[165] Delicately worded, Littlejohn's take on mortality in the Water of Leith districts, when it did eventually appear over a year later in his Conclusion, defused potential opposition to his *Report* from New Town residents concerned about pollution and local taxation levels because it had already become part of the official record, as presented to Parliament. Small wonder, then, that the *R eport* concluded: 'In the modern part of the City, there is less call for interference on the part of the authorities.'[166]

As a lifetime resident of the New Town, Littlejohn was acutely aware of the inhabitants' quest for value for money in local services, and of their capacity to scrutinise the council's expenditure. His *Report* was compiled during the period of office of Lord Provost Charles Lawson (1862–65),[167] who was noted for his lavish entertainment and the trappings of office, and published during a vitriolic and sustained attack on politicians' expenses and experts' fees. During 1865 two

162 *Report*, 86, Littlejohn notes that the unpleasant smells on the northern fringe of the city are to some extent the result of spreading sewage on the fields, not due only to the condition of the Water of Leith.

163 *Evening Courant*, 16 June 1864, 4c.

164 See reports by D. Stevenson and C. MacPherson, *Report ... Relative to the Drainage of the Water of Leith* (Edinburgh, 1861); C. MacPherson, *Report to the Sub-Committee of the Lord Provost's Committee on the Water of Leith Improvement* (Edinburgh, 1863); M. Thomson, *Report as to the Cause or Causes of the Offensive Smells in the West Side of the City, and from the Water of Leith* (Edinburgh, 1863).

165 See PP (HC) 1865 XXVII, 3472, Royal Commission on Sewage of Towns, 3rd Report, Appendix 5, Report by Stevenson Macadam on the Contamination of the water supply of Leith by the sewage of Edinburgh and Leith, 1–62. Macadam brought the Water of Leith issue into the public glare with a paper entitled 'The pollution of the Water of Leith by the sewage of Edinburgh and Leith' to the Social Science Association at York, 1864, a version of which was also published as 'On the contamination of the water of Leith by the sewage of Edinburgh and Leith (London, 1865). See *Evening Courant*, 28 September 1864, 2d–g.

166 *Report*, 116.

167 Anon., *The Lord Provosts of Edinburgh 1296 to 1932* (Edinburgh, 1932).

scandals involving Edinburgh officials brought the issue of public probity to the fore. Both involved Henry Callender, initially in his role as City Treasurer, when councillors Stott and Lewis accused him of 'cooked accounts',[168] because, without appropriate receipts, he sought and obtained the approval of the Treasurer's Committee to write off city debts.[169] In the second episode, in the summer of 1865 and just weeks before Littlejohn's *Report* was published, Callender in his new role as Treasurer to the Water and Sewerage Commissioners authorised payments to the value of almost £10,000 to council employees and expert witnesses for expenses incurred in 1864 while appearing in London before a parliamentary committee in connection with the Water and Sewerage Bill. The individuals were named and shamed.[170] The law agent's and civil engineers' fees accounted for almost half of the expenses, but it was the payment of fees rather than expenses to salaried Edinburgh officials, Marwick, Macpherson and Paterson, that was considered excessive and which excited opposition.[171] A present of an inkstand costing £63, the equivalent of a labourer's yearly wage, also charged to the public purse, was a source of further annoyance. Thus, according to *The Scotsman*'s correspondent, one-sixth of the anticipated £60,000 intended to complete the water and sewage works was spent on fees and out-of-pocket expenses. The *Caledonian Mercury* leader observed:

> We have not space today to sum up the magnificent accounts paid out of the pockets of the New Town ratepayers, with so much prodigality, to Bailies and Councillors who profess themselves working for the public good, nor to the appalling sums paid to lawyers, Parliamentary agents, civil engineers, and others, whose evidence was no doubt deemed essential to the completion of the job; we solicit attention, however, to such payments as the following, and in the name of common sense and common justice we ask our New Town friends, who are the sufferers, what on earth these men did, or could have done, to merit such sums?[172]

This angry leader in the *Mercury* led to appeals against the 'reckless expenditure' relating to the 'Water of Leith job', and a case was brought in the Sheriff Court. Although that appeal was eventually rejected, it demonstrated the highly charged political atmosphere in which Littlejohn's *Report* was published, and the care needed on his part to avoid hostility towards it from a powerful group of electors and councillors.[173]

Littlejohn himself was the target of cost savings even before he was in post in 1862. The need for a Medical Officer was itself questioned on the grounds that the city already had such an officer, the Police Surgeon. Littlejohn's salary was on several occasions also a source of friction, even though his pay was significantly

168 *Caledonian Mercury*, 7 July 1865, 2a–c.

169 The accuracy of and receipts for the Police Accounts were the central issue over Treasurer Henry Callender's activities. See *The Scotsman*, 25 January 1865, 7b–f; 28 January 1865, 7ab; 15 February 1865, 6a–c; 29 March 1865, 6c; 30 March 1865, 8ab.

170 *The Scotsman*, 10 July 1865, 7.

171 These three officials were Town Clerk (Marwick), Superintendent of Streets and Buildings (Macpherson), City Assessor (Paterson).

172 *Caledonian Mercury*, 7 July 1865, 2b.

173 *Caledonian Mercury*, 31 October 1865, 4a–d.

lower than that of equivalent officers in Liverpool and Glasgow.[174] Because Littlejohn's approach was focused on morbidity rather than on mortality, that is to say, on the impact of disease rather than crude death rates, he concentrated on a wide range of public health strategies, many of which cost little and were organisational in nature. For example, the appointment in 1864 of four meat inspectors was at a modest cost of £500.[175] The enforcement of regulations on coffee and other foodstuffs was based on Littlejohn's experience that, far from preventing suppliers ply their trades, it was in dealers' own interests 'to furnish a purer article'.[176] Throughout his *Report* Littlejohn was emphatic that tighter controls across a spectrum of public health areas would enhance the living and working conditions of city dwellers and thus strengthen their resistance to infection. Incrementally the quality of life, and life expectancy itself, would be improved. It was both logical and cost effective, for example, to improve the standards of cow byres since the quantity and quality of milk would be increased, with benefits to both consumers and producers.[177] Littlejohn was withering in his condemnation of law officers and any official who connived at abuses to regulations. His condemnation extended equally to racketeers in the meat and dairy trade: 'When an offender of humble status was caught, he was left by the trade to his fate; but when an influential member of the craft was detected, a powerful defence was organized.'[178] Without mechanisms for regulatory enforcement the public health mission was weakened and citizens exposed to greater morbidity, and thus a subsequent charge on the poor rates. Moreover, had William Dick in 1863 been conscientious in his veterinary duty to inspect animals imported at Leith, a major source of local livestock infection would have been closed, or at least reduced.[179] The issue of diseased cattle also revealed a changing of the guard in terms of municipal administration: Gamgee the scientist superseded Dick the pragmatist.[180] The appliance of science was Gamgee's strength, and this resonated with the preventative or precautionary principle that ran through the Littlejohn *Report* as a prudent, cost-effective, systematic public health strategy. It constituted what, in current terms, might be called joined-up government.[181]

174 Though Littlejohn's salary more than tripled on his appointment as Medical Officer of Health, rising from £155 to £500 annually in 1862, despite the positive reception of his *Report* it remained at that level until 1875 when it rose to £750.

175 ECA SL45/1, Slaughter-houses Investigation Committee, 25 March 1864.

176 *Report*, 60.

177 A. Cunningham and B.A. Thorpe, 'The milk supply of the city of Edinburgh', *Journal of Hygiene*, 19 (1920), 107–14, concluded that when compared major to European and American cities between 1885 and 1917 bacterial content was high, but not abnormally so, but that it was of an undesirable nature. The results point to 'the necessity of educating the producer and distributor in the principles underlying the production of clean milk and emphasise the importance of proper control of the industry'.

178 *Report*, 58.

179 P. Laxton, 'The nefarious trade', in P. Atkins (ed.), *Animated Cities: Urban Historical Insights into Human–Animal Interaction* (Cambridge, 2012), 107–72. See also *The Scotsman*, 1 August 1863 7b; 5 August 1863 7d; 5 August 1863 7d; 8 August 1863 3b; 10 August 1863 3b; 25 August 1863 3c; 26 August 1863 4ab; 27 August 1863 3a.

180 'John Gamgee' entry by S.A. Hall in *ODNB*.

181 A visiting Australian student, Dunkley 'took out a course of Public Health under Dr Littlejohn' in 1893 and obtained direct knowledge by visiting nuisance sites in Edinburgh. Dunkley joined Public

Elsewhere the *Report* identified various areas for effective yet inexpensive improvements to property, some of which could be charged to landlords so that public expense could be avoided altogether. This was the case with paving and draining closes so as facilitate cleaning. Littlejohn drafted a sentence, not subsequently included in the *Report*, that paving tenement courts and providing a water supply to them would facilitate a daily flushing practised in Parisian streets.[182] Absentee landlords and their factors were later acknowledged by Littlejohn to be a particular problem for the sanitary authorities in that they frequently kept their properties in a poor state of repair and required constant vigilance as a result.[183] The fragmented nature of ownership, often among several landlords within a single tenement, was a distinctively Scottish feature and made, and still makes, collective decision making on maintenance problematical.[184]

Detailed observation and technical advice obtained from the relevant experts were embedded in the *Report* at various points, as with the suggestion to construct water-tight cesspools at an additional building cost of just £2 each so as to prevent leakages into the water courses. Here, too, the *Report* showed awareness of value for money and sought where possible to transfer the costs to private builders and landlords.[185] Similarly, untrapped drains, sewers, rhones, and overflow pipes were a conduit for contamination as sewage gases forced noxious smells and waste back into the home. The *Report* identified these as targets for private action rather than public expense.[186] This was hardly a frontal assault on property owners, but it was a signal that the council was not going to burden the public expense with necessary improvements to private property. In two other practical suggestions to improve amenity Littlejohn argued, first, that cellars could be usefully re-used as washing-houses where 'the poor could have their clothes satisfactorily and frequently cleansed',[187] and, second, that the introduction of gas lighting would significantly aid cleaning in common stairs. As for drinking fountains in the city, only 10% were located in the four central districts, Canongate, Tron, St Giles' and Grassmarket; a more generous provision would improve health and amenity in these poorer districts.[188] There were plainly social and environmental inequalities and injustices in the city.

Enquiries by Littlejohn revealed that tenement dwellers in the city centre were often unable to obtain water except at public wells and only then for a limited period each day, especially in summer. They were seriously inconvenienced as a

Health department inspectors on Littlejohn's recommendation 'to go round the city and investigate all sorts of complaints.' *Warragul Guardian*, 3 December 1897, 6h; *Broadford Courier and Reedy Creek Times*, 3 December 1897, 5h.

182 *The Scotsman*, 21 December 1864, 7b. Fourteen passages (1,558 words) from the report Littlejohn presented to council on 20 December 1864 (3,206 words) appeared unchanged at various points in the *Report* of 1865.

183 PP (HC) 1884–85 [C. 4409], Royal Commission on the Housing of the Working Classes, Q.19029–30.

184 R. Rodger, *The Transformation of Edinburgh*, 69–76.

185 *Report*, 84. Littlejohn argued that with the main streets sewers completed cesspools should no longer be constructed at all.

186 *Report*, 107. See also comments on cleaning cisterns.

187 *Report*, 113.

188 *Report*, Table XII, 61.

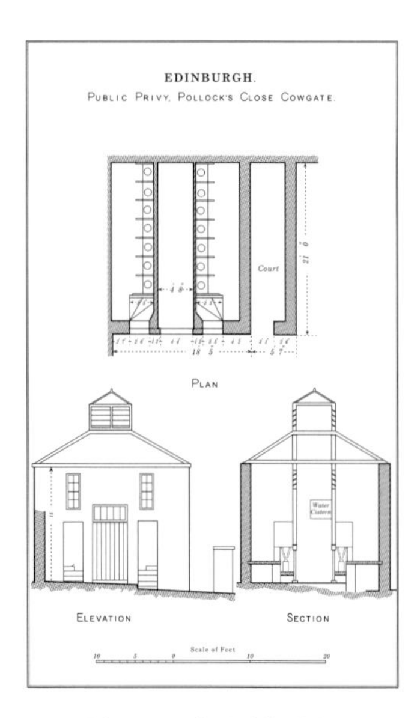

5.15 Diagram of a Public Privy, Pollock's Close, Cowgate, 1869
To introduce water-closets was technically difficult in multi-storey tenements. Littlejohn's *Report* identified inexpensive means to improve housing amenity, and the introduction of toilet blocks was one such proposal to improve sanitation with minimum disruption to residents.
[Source: Re-drawn from a Report to the Medical Officer to the Privy Council, 1869]

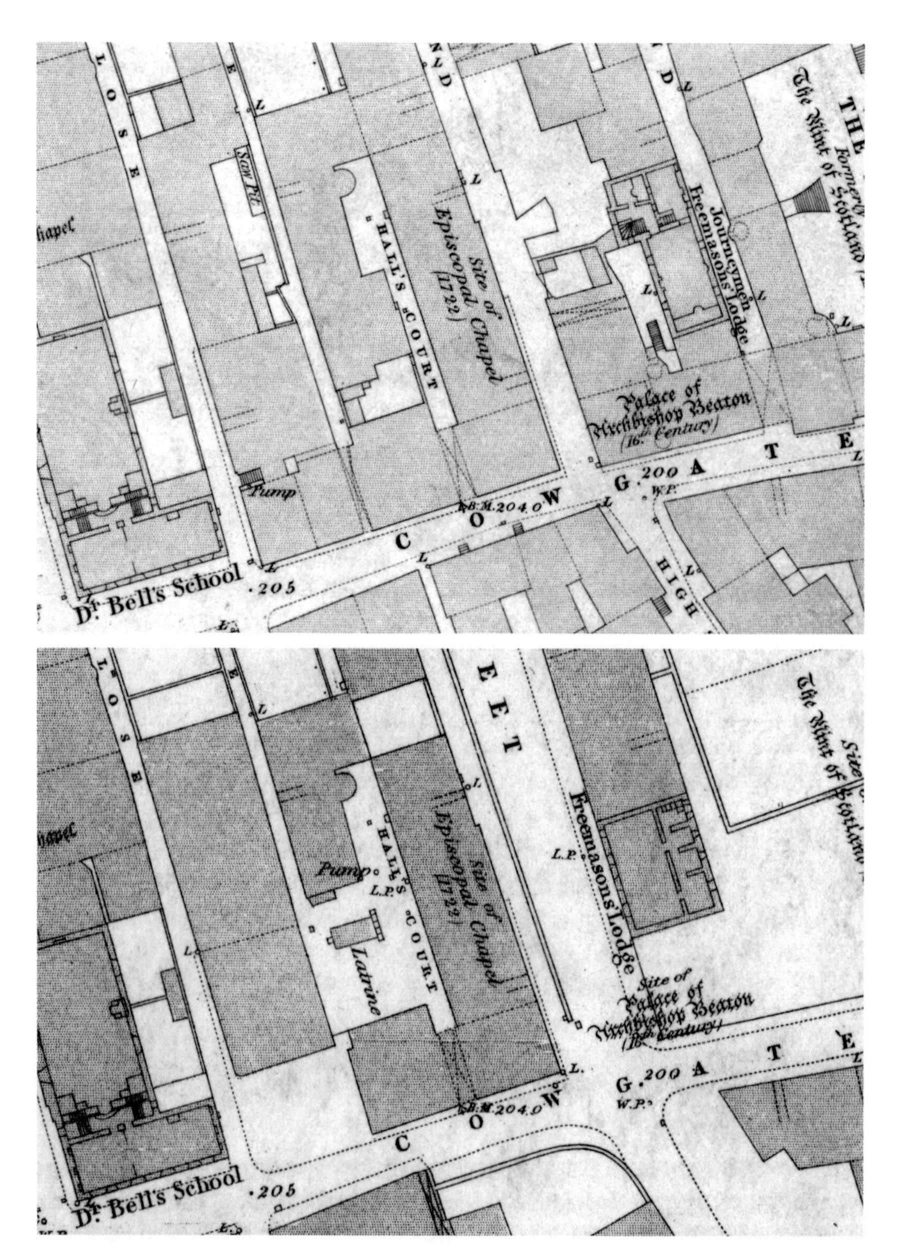

5.16 Hall's Court, 230 Cowgate in 1852 (top) and 1877 (bottom)
By opening up a court and building a latrine block significant sanitary improvements were achieved in Hall's Court, as elsewhere in the city. [NLS, OS maps, 1852 and 1877]

result; long queues formed in the streets for the public wells. As to sanitation in Edinburgh, a Privy Council enquiry in 1869 observed: 'In what way the removal of refuse from these tenements [of the poorer population] can best be effected has at all times been a problem difficult of solution.'[189] The Privy Council Report continued:

> it is evident that there is more risk in having them [water-closets], as in Edinburgh, upon a common stair or in a passage within the tenement, than there is in placing them, where in poorer parts of English towns they are almost always found, wholly outside the house.[190]

Littlejohn's position was very clear: water-closets without sufficient water were a public health nuisance.[191] His survey of the Edinburgh drainage in 1866 predictably echoed the findings published in 1865, and were reiterated in 1869 when, before a select committee in London, he confirmed that he had been 'compelled to refuse' applications for water-closets because of the shortage of water supplies.[192] His recommendations in 1865, therefore, made all the more sense: where modern facilities could be provided, so much the better, but 'in the meantime, enforce greater cleanliness in the closes, and supply them with a greater number of public conveniences'.[193] Progressively, blocks of water-closets were introduced for inhabitants, in Hall's Court, Canongate, Pollock's and Baird's Closes, and in many other tenement courtyards in the ten years following the *Report*, and public urinals became more widely available throughout the city.[194]

Despite Littlejohn's view on water disposal, water supply was a major political issue in Edinburgh. It was not just a matter of concern to the central districts inhabited by the poor of the Old Town: a number of middle-class residents in the southern suburbs of Grange wrote frequent letters of complaint to the council and the newspapers.[195] Littlejohn acknowledged that, by the 1860s, crude quantities of water supplied compared favourably with other cities. Alexander Ramsay, the manager of the Edinburgh Water Company, stated that daily per capita consumption in 1868 was 37 gallons in Edinburgh compared to between 14 and 17 gallons in Nottingham, Norwich, Derby and Sunderland, 20 gallons in Manchester, 42 in Glasgow, 70 in Dublin, and 110 gallons per person per day in Oxford.[196] But rate of flow and volume of delivery were two different matters. This was because, firstly, the environmental inequalities noted by Littlejohn

189 *Twelfth Report of the Medical Officer to the Privy Council* (1869), Report on the Systems in Use in Various Northern Towns for Dealing with Excrement, 133 noted that the sale of manure by the city cleaning department, whose monopoly this trade was, realised some £7,000 p.a., thus financing almost half (47%) of the department's £15,000 annual expenditure on cleaning.

190 *Twelfth Report of the Medical Officer*, 132.

191 *Report*, *The Scotsman*, 23 October 1869, 3b.

192 *The Scotsman*, 20 December 1865, 6d, and letter from G.H. Girle, 17 March 1866, 7c. Tenants in Dickson's close petitioned to have their closets restored to them following closure on Littlejohn's orders affecting 120 inhabitants.

193 *Report*, 81–2, 109.

194 See T. Fraser (Burgh Engineer) and H.D. Littlejohn, Table 16 February 1874.

195 J. Colston, *The Edinburgh and District Water Supply: a Historical Sketch* (Edinburgh, 1890), 100.

196 J. Colston, *The Edinburgh and District Water Supply*, 101–3, quoting a letter, 1 June 1868, from Alexander Ramsay. See also *The Scotsman*, 12 March 1869, 6a–c; 23 April 1869, 3a–e.

meant that only certain parts of Edinburgh received water during the summer months; and secondly, because there were serious losses in terms of leakages from defective stopcocks in tenement flats, estimated by Ramsay to be about 33%; and, thirdly, because the Edinburgh Water Company themselves acknowledged that ¾-inch pipes were too narrow and pressure insufficient to supply water to all floors in a tenement.[197] Turning on the tap in a ground-floor flat deprived residents above of a water supply.[198] So although there had been considerable investment by the Edinburgh Water Company in the 1840s and 1850s[199] there was an enduring problem of retrospectively fitting toilet accommodation within the 'highest houses to be seen in the world', as Littlejohn once described Edinburgh tenements.[200] The introduction of water was complicated by a pattern of multiple ownerships within tenements and made no easier by landlord absenteeism and a house-factoring system which stressed revenues rather than amenities.

In 1869 a 'water war' broke out in Edinburgh.[201] The issues were ones central to, and in some respects a direct consequence of, the Littlejohn *Report* as it related to fresh water supply, drainage and sewerage. The contentious issue was how far, in the form of dividends, should shareholders in the Edinburgh Water Company benefit from the supply of water to the city's residents? Put in modern terms the question was: should water supply be privatised? A proposal was developed to convert the monopoly of the Edinburgh Water Company to that of a public utility in the form of the Edinburgh and District Water Trust.[202] The Bill presented to parliament caused considerable ratepayer hostility, firstly over the likelihood of increased charges, possibly by as much as 50%; secondly because their was no assurance of improved water supply; and, thirdly, since charging took no account of the size of home it was seen as a tax on the poor. The Edinburgh and District Water Bill came before select committees of the House of Commons and the House of Lords, with evidence provided by Lord Provost Chambers, Littlejohn, Ramsay, and other Edinburgh experts.[203] *The Scotsman* carried numerous strongly worded and critical letters, rowdy council meetings debated the issues, there were advertisements opposing the Bill, and local petitions articulated ratepayer opposition.[204] A compromise, including a generous 6% preferential annuity to replace dividends on the capital stock of the Water Company, was struck on the terms of the public

197 A. Ramsay, evidence to the Select Committee of the House of Commons, Q.2030–46, quoted in J. Colston, *Edinburgh and District Water Supply*, 117–18, 144.

198 *The Scotsman*, 21 April 1869, 3d; Littlejohn, *Report*, 92.

199 The reservoirs were Glencorse (1822), Threipmuir (1847), Harlaw (1848), Bavelaw (1848), Clubbiedean (1850), Torduff (1851), Loganlea (1851), Bonaly (1857), Harperrig (1859).

200 Littlejohn used the phrase in a report to council, see *The Scotsman*, 20 December 1864, 7a–c, and later in the *Report*, 112.

201 Letter from W. Law, *The Scotsman*, 21 April 1869, 3d.

202 The councils of the neighbouring burghs of Leith and Portobello were also involved.

203 For a list of witnesses for the corporation, see Colston, *Edinburgh and District Water Supply*, 114.

204 *The Scotsman*, letters 24 April 1869, 6f; 28 April 1869, 7a; 4 May 1869, 2c; 6 May 1869, 7ab. See reports of Council 12 May 1869, 7b–d, and 19 May 1869, 7a.

takeover between the company and the council, and the Edinburgh and District Water Act received the royal assent on 24 July 1869.[205] It was the starting gun for a second front in the war over water. Within two weeks Chambers had announced his resignation over the manner in which Water Trust appointments were skewed towards councillors and their cronies,[206] and, in an echo of the City Improvement Act, 1867, expenses of £10,860 incurred by city officials to secure the Water Act were reported at the first meeting the new Water Trust and became a recurrent theme in the local elections in the autumn of 1869.[207]

Local election meetings in 1870 made no mention of the St Mary's Loch project to build additional water storage capacity forty miles away in the Scottish borders for Edinburgh and its neighbours, Leith and Portobello. The local landowner, Lord Napier, Governor of Madras, initially replied to an enquiry in 1868 by Lord Provost Chambers in a cooperative tone, but later instructed his lawyers to protect his water rights in relation to the loch.[208] Although the St Mary's Loch proposal had been shelved during discussions on the transfer of water operations to the Edinburgh and District Water Trust, the issue attracted immediate and vigorous opposition once the parliamentary bill was published early in 1871. Littlejohn was one of a number of notable Edinburgh figures in support of the project, designed as it was to anticipate rising demand for water in the city. Other supporters included ex-Lord Provost Chambers, his successor William Law, and the provosts of Leith and Portobello. The medical profession as represented by Professor Sir Douglas Maclagan and Dr Alexander Wood, and a distinguished list of water and civil engineers which included J.F. Bateman, J.M. Gale, Sir John Hawkshaw, Dr Frankland, and Stevenson Macadam also favoured the St Mary's scheme.[209] Critics convened a public meeting in Queen Street Hall in February 1871, and considered due process to have been breached since the citizenry had not been consulted about the proposed new source of water for the city, challenging the entire scheme on the grounds that it was excessively expensive, unnecessary, and inferior in water quality to supplies in the nearby Pentland Hills. Portobello and Leith councils unanimously supported the proposal to obtain water from St Mary's Loch; Edinburgh councillors after three, five-hour days of debate narrowly supported it by a vote of 22:19. After thirteen days of consideration, the Bill was approved by a committee of the House of Commons in May 1871, although this only stimulated further opposition. As a contemporary and long-serving member of the Water Trust commented:

> Since the celebrated Disruption of the Church of Scotland in 1843, party feeling in Edinburgh had never run so high, nor was it so embittered, as in

205 32 and 33 Vict., cap. 144, Edinburgh and District Water Act, 1869. The transfer was effective from 15 May 1870.

206 William Chambers' term of office expired in November 1869.

207 *The Scotsman*, 27 October 1869, 5c–f. Report of Edinburgh and District Water Trustees meeting. See also the *The Scotsman*'s 23 October 1869, 3bc account of the election meeting in St Stephens' ward on 22 October 1869 at which all the councillors' and officials' expenses were read out.

208 Letter, Lord Napier to Chambers, 31 October 1868, quoted in Colston *Edinburgh and District Water Supply*, 108–9. See also *ODNB*, entry on Francis Napier, which notes his interest in public health matters and correspondence with Florence Nightingale.

209 Colston, *Edinburgh and District Water Supply*, 132.

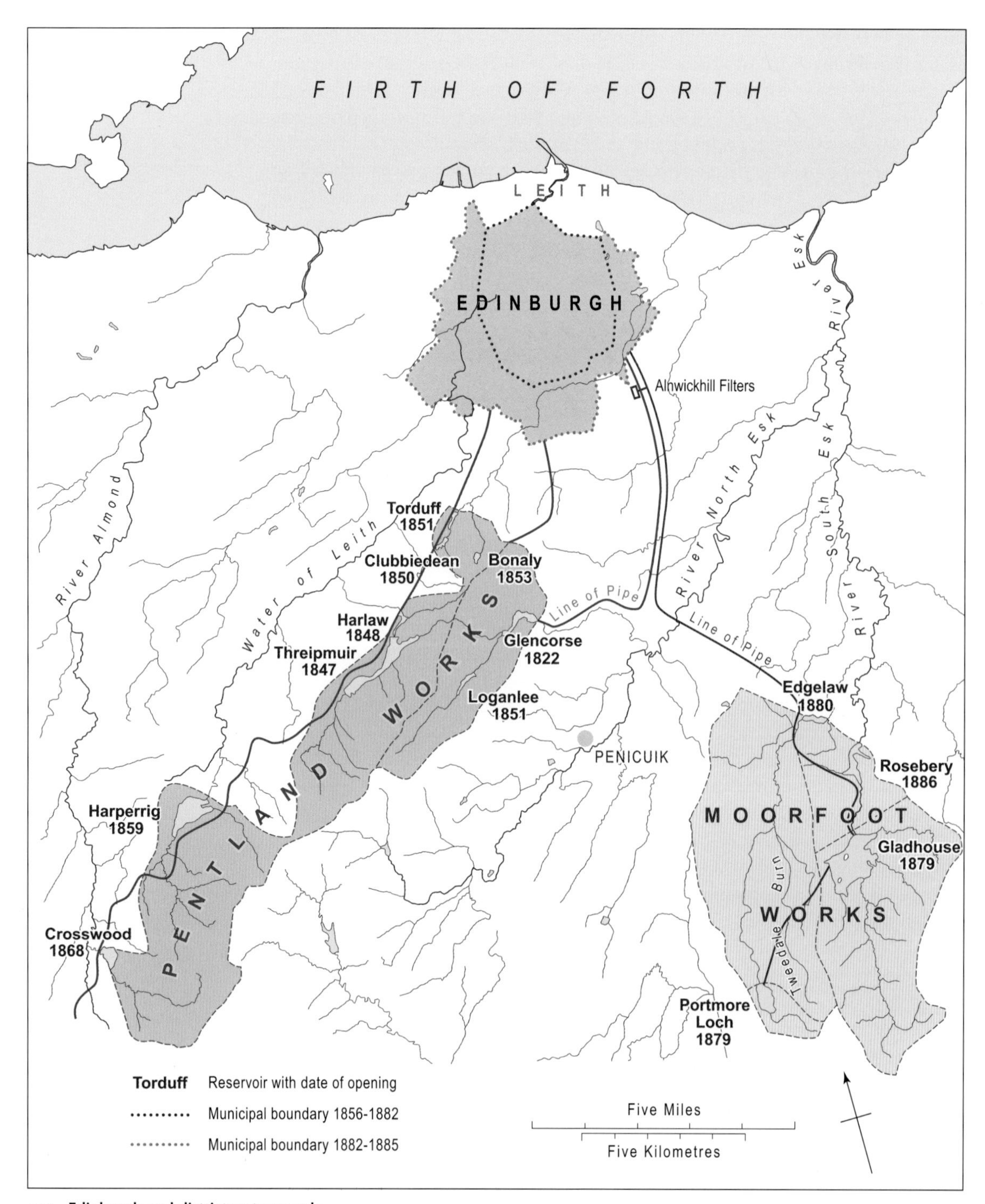

5.17 Edinburgh and district water supply
Edinburgh and Leith drew their water from less than 20 miles away in the Pentland and Moorfoot Hills.
[Source: adapted from J. Colston, *The Edinburgh and District Water Supply: A Historical Sketch* (Edinburgh 1890).

> this great water struggle. Indeed, some personal friendships were in danger of giving way to private animosities. The opponents of the measure had … secured the public ear. The newspapers, as a rule, were on their side; and no step that could be taken to produce a popular clamour was left unadopted.[210]

No longer was there a phoney water war. Five weeks later, in June 1871, the House of Lords refused to allow the Bill to proceed further. Fewer leakages and better use of existing water supplies in the Pentlands were the flimsy explanations for the decision offered by the Lords, but, more likely, it was 'the most determined opposition' that Lord Napier instructed his lawyers to mount which torpedoed the project.[211] Clever public relations and inventive correspondents had caused a reversal of the Commons' decision, and the ensuing ward elections confirmed the popularity of the Lords' refusal to proceed with the St Mary's Loch project.

The result was an 'infusion of the opposition element into the elective body' with implications for both the Water Trust and the Council where a 'continual strife' characterised business for some time. Indeed, the legal position of the Edinburgh and District Water Trust was described as a 'great obstacle to future progress' because Lord Gifford, considering an appeal on the liability for costs for the failed Bill, adjudged that since the promoters were trustees and not councillors or directors, then parliamentary costs incurred in the unsuccessful effort to obtain new sources of water supply for the city rendered the trustees personally liable for £19,000. The Court of Session upheld this interpretation by a 3 : 1 majority; they concluded that the trustees had no powers under their Act to apply or borrow funds for the purpose of proposing a water Bill.[212] Though not directly a result of Littlejohn's *Report*, the search for a more efficient urban management had produced an impasse and it was ten years before any new reservoirs were constructed. One thing had been achieved, however: control over water supplies was no longer in the hands of a private company, and Littlejohn's vision of equity and justice in the provision of environmental health was one step further advanced.

Between 1805 and 1856 the Edinburgh Police Commission took overall control of matters relating to environmental health. Their terms of reference were wide-ranging, and they discharged summary justice through a system of fines and custodial sentences as determined by the actions of a single magistrate, normally a town councillor (see chapter 3). However, though full of good intentions, the commissioners lacked an effective system of enforcement for their expanding jurisdiction during decades of unprecedented population growth, and their roles were assumed by the Town Council from 1856. Public concern over issues such as epidemics, water quality, diseased meat and the insanitary condition of streets and closes required a more systematic enforcement to be effective. Only gradually was this realised as environmental health gained greater acceptance. The appointment of Littlejohn as Medical Officer of Health in 1862

210 Colston, *Edinburgh and District Water Supply*, 135. This was an instance where an icon, the flea *Daphnis pulex*, served as a logo or emblem of protest. The water flea, said to carry impurities, was reproduced on walls, in newspaper columns and indeed presented as an anonymous correspondent.

211 Colston, *Edinburgh and District Water Supply*, 110.

212 Decisions of the Lord Ordinary, 5 December 1871, and the First Division of the Court of Session, 8 March 1872.

and the publication of his *Report* in 1865 were crucial steps in that process, demonstrating as they did the inter-connectedness of many facets of the public's health. Littlejohn's thorough research and dispassionate analysis ultimately persuaded politicians and the public to endorse projects to form new streets, to clear congested sites for housing, to improve systems of inspection for meat and other foodstuffs, and to monitor water quality, though none of these steps was achieved without rearguard action to block or subvert such initiatives. Despite such opposition, the relationship between the private and public spheres was revised. An increasing awareness of inequality and injustice underpinned public intervention as the legitimacy of private actions came under greater scrutiny, especially in relation to the sanitary condition of housing. Administratively, the enlargement of an inspectorate reporting to Littlejohn tightened the reporting process and facilitated the issue of notices and the commencement of legal processes in the 1860s. What had been a complicated administrative jigsaw in the 1860s became a more streamlined and hierarchical management structure after 1872 when the Public Health Committee was formed. Thereafter the Medical Officer need only confer with a single committee and was empowered to take a number of decisions on his own initiative. Complemented by the expertise of the city architect (Cousin), water manager (Ramsay), physicians (Gairdner) and scientists (Gamgee), Littlejohn's professional standing and his expert knowledge convinced the council committee to trust their advisors and to shape policy on the basis of evidence rather than mere opinion.

CHAPTER 6

Littlejohn and public health in Edinburgh after 1865

On Saturday 4 April 1885, Dr. H.D. Littlejohn, MD walked fifty yards from his office in the High Street to appear in the Edinburgh City Council Chamber as a witness before the Royal Commission on the Housing of the Working Classes.[1] Within minutes he had confirmed to the chairman, Sir Charles Wentworth Dilke, MP, that there had been a marked reduction of 32.1% in the average death rates in the city between 1865 and 1883 (see Fig 6.1).[2] Littlejohn might also have informed the chairman that not only had the average fallen significantly but the divergence between death rates in the sanitary districts had been reduced by almost 38%.[3] Though crude death rates are just that – a crude way of measuring mortality since no account is taken of age structure – Littlejohn was positive in his evidence that, across the city, Edinburgh inhabitants had benefited from improvements to their living conditions.[4] His target death rate of 25/1,000 for the five central districts of Abbey, Tron, St Giles', Canongate and Grassmarket had been achieved in Abbey and St Giles', with the three other central districts registering a death rate in 1883 ranging from 27 to 29/1,000. Sir Charles Dilke observed that the death rates declined in the central districts because of falling population levels, thus reducing density per acre, and this was exactly the rationale for de-crowding enshrined in the Edinburgh Improvement Act, 1867, and the outcome predicted by Littlejohn in the conclusion to his *Report*.[5]

Within seven years of the first site for improvement being cleared, 80% of the total expenditure for the project had been committed.[6] Indeed the compression of Improvement Trust activity (see fig 6.2) coincided with one of the most active periods of private sector housebuilding for some years, and the symbiotic nature of public and private building was not lost on the Improvement Trust:

1 PP (HC) 1884–85 [C. 4409], Royal Commission on the Housing of the Working Classes. Vol. 5 Scotland, Minutes of Evidence, Littlejohn, Q.18,939–19,058, and Appendices A–C.

2 The Edinburgh mean death rates fell from 25.3 to 19.0 per 1,000 between 1863 and 1883; the Glasgow figures fell from a mean death rate of 30.5 in 1861–70 years to 26.5 per 1,000 for the years 1881–84. See PP (HC) 1884–85 [C. 4409], Royal Commission, Evidence, Collins, Morrison, Q.19,326.

3 The respective figures for the mean and standard deviation in 1863 were 25.3 and 7.4, and, for 1883, mean 19.0 and standard deviation 4.6. The change in density, that is in persons per acre, showed a overall increase in the city from 94.5 to 101.0.

4 For a wider discussion of this point see N. Williams, 'Death in its season: class, environment and the mortality of infants in nineteenth-century Sheffield', *Social History of Medicine*, 5:1 (1992), 71–94.

5 *Report*, 117. Abbey sanitary district was the exception with a rising population and density 1861–81.

6 ECA SL64/3/6, Accounts of the Improvements Trustees. From 1875 improvement expenditure was scaled back each year.

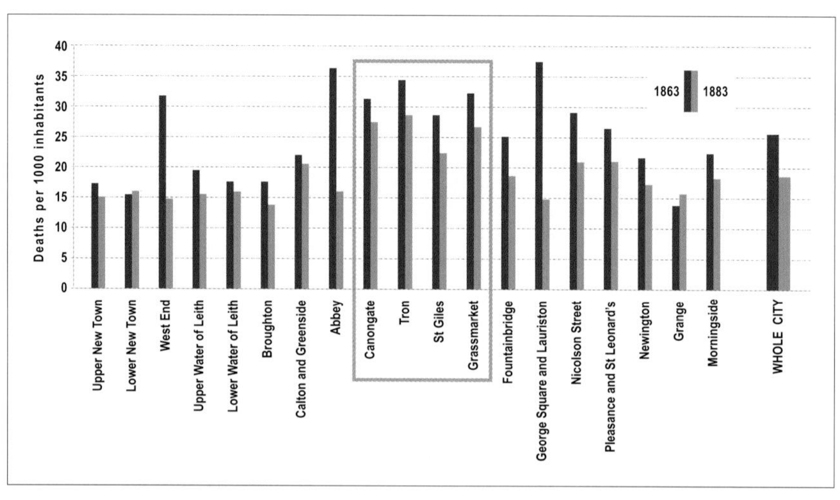

6.1 Death rates in Edinburgh sanitary districts, 1863 and 1883
Deaths in 1863 and 1883 per 1,000 inhabitants in relation to the population at the preceding census (1861 and 1881) for each sanitary district, and with the four central districts distinguished in a box. The high mortality in West End and in George Square and Lauriston in 1863 was due to the presence of poorhouses. [Source: PP (HC) 1884–85 C.4409, evidence of H D Littlejohn, appendix B]

> The work of removing so many tenements in so short a time has been made easy by the extensive building for the working classes for some years past in the suburbs; these new buildings give accommodation for a large number of the more provident of the working classes.[7]

The Royal Commission on the Housing of the Working Classes of 1884–85 struggled to understand Scotland. The definition of a house perplexed the commissioners; the extent of urban regulation firmly embedded in Local Acts surprised them; and the discharge of legal duties and responsibilities by differently named officers, and the irrelevance of slum clearance Acts widely used in England – the Cross and Torrens Acts – meant they were unable to come to terms in just two days with what was later described as 'another part of the island'.[8] It was perhaps understandable, therefore, that they would concentrate on improvements and death rates. For example, to consider the Improvement Trust activities a limited success because death rates did not fall dramatically or exclusively in the central areas where most of the clearances took place is to misunderstand the Littlejohn agenda to address morbidity as an element inseparable from medical jurisprudence.[9] Clearances formed only one of his many suggestions for the

7 ECA SL64/1/1, Trustees' Minute Books, 6 December 1870. Glasgow Municipal Commission on the Housing of the Poor, *Report* (Glasgow, 1904), 13 noted that when, as in the economic depression of the 1880s, demand from landlords for new rental accommodation was not forthcoming, it was very difficult to sell off sites cleared by the Improvement Trust. It took the Glasgow Improvement Trust thirty years to complete its work.

8 G.F.A. Best, 'Another part of the island', in H.J. Dyos and M.J. Wolff (eds), *The Victorian City: Images and Realities*, vol. 2 (London, 1973 edn), 389–412; G.F.A. Best, 'The Scottish Victorian city', *Victorian Studies*, 11 (1968), 329–58.

9 P.J. Smith, 'Slum clearance as an instrument of sanitary reform: the flawed vision of Edinburgh's first slum clearance scheme', *Planning Perspectives*, 9 (1994), 1–27.

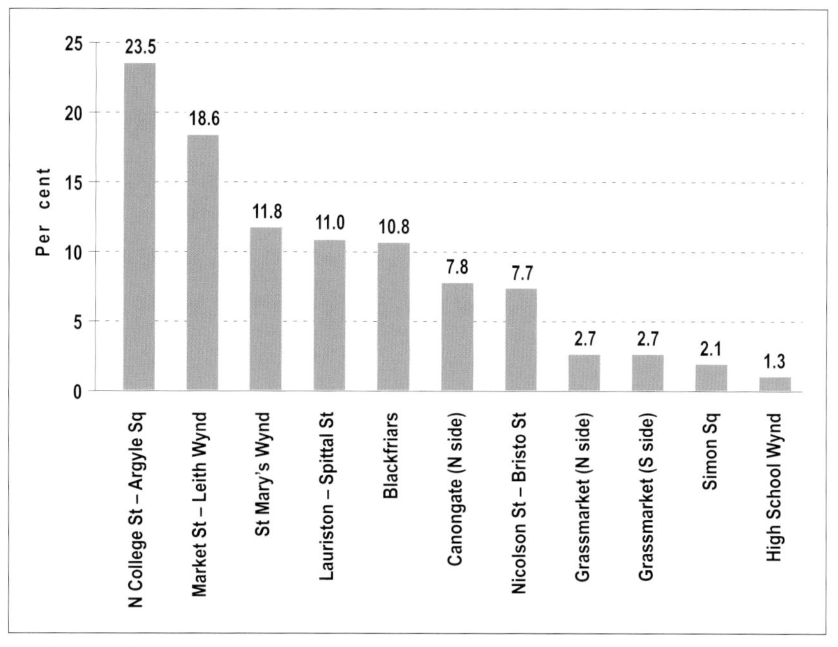

6.2 Edinburgh Improvement Trust: expenditure by area, 1867–89
Most of the Improvement expenditure was concentrated in the period 1869–79, though some elements of the proposal were never begun. Some small-scale projects are omitted from the chart for reasons of clarity. [Source: ECA SL64/3/6]

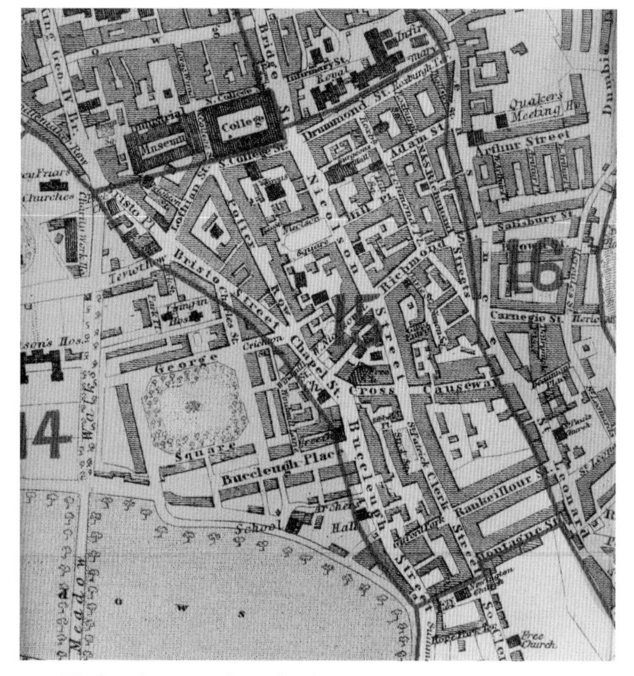

6.3 Nicolson Street: sanitary district 15
Detail from Littlejohn's map of new sanitary districts.
[Source: *The Report*, map]

improved public health in Edinburgh. Indeed, the feasibility of improvements was dependent upon the prospect of a safe and pleasant environment for politically powerful elements in the city in the 1860s and 1870s, and ratepayer opposition and value for money permeated not just Chambers' Improvement proposals but the Water of Leith and St Mary's Loch water supply schemes too.

With an increase in population of 36% between 1861 and 1881, and no increase in the boundaries of the municipality, the density of the inhabitants was certain to rise. Central clearances combined with suburban expansion to reduce the disparity between the least and most overcrowded districts between 1861 and 1881. The Tron church (district 10), previously a symbol of urban regeneration in 1824 after a fire,[10] and again in 1860 at the head of the newly formed Cockburn Street, was once more a beacon of modernity in the 1870s at the heart of a district cleared of insanitary tenements, and the subject of the greatest population reduction (43.2%) in the city.

With the population decline in the central districts were the poor simply caught in some form of urban centrifuge that expelled them to the margins of the city? Though such an experience is mainly associated with the development of twentieth-century council housing estates, the process began in the 1870s with migrations to the districts neighbouring those most affected by the Chambers' Improvements Scheme. The Nicolson Street sanitary district, already the second most densely populated before the clearances started, was 5.3% more so by 1881, on a par with the Tron before the demolitions; and the Pleasance and Leonard's district experienced a 69% rise in density between 1861 and 1881 to equal overcrowding in all but one of the inner-city sanitary districts prior to the demolitions (see fig. 6.1).[11] Also on the fringes of the clearance programme both Abbey, and Calton and Greenside districts experienced appreciable additions to their populations, though from fairly modest density levels in 1861. The knock-on effects of increasing population density was also experienced on the perimeter of the city with some spectacular changes in the southern suburbs of Morningside, Grange, and Newington, and in the West End district most of which had been sparsely settled before 1861.

Put differently, the changing patterns of density in the central sanitary districts reflected the displacement caused both by the actions of the Improvement Trust and by the operation of the housing market. As the wealthier sections of society continued their flight to outer suburban and the latest western New Town developments, their properties were sub-divided and occupied by skilled workers and a petit bourgeoisie comprising clerks and shopworkers; simultaneously, builders for the first time began to construct purpose-built tenement blocks with up to sixteen flats which were affordable by skilled and semi-skilled manual workers in regular work. It was the homes of these workers that were colonised in a process now known as 'filtering-up' by those displaced by clearances under the Improvement Act.[12] This was exactly what Littlejohn claimed: that there was enough slack in the housing market for the displaced to find homes. He made

10 S. Ewen, *Fighting Fires: Creating the British Fire Service, 1800–1978* (Basingstoke 2010), 30–50. The Edinburgh Municipal Fire Brigade was formed as a result of the Tron church fire.

11 PP (HC) 1884–85 C.4409, Royal Commission, Littlejohn, Q.18,939–19,058, and Appendices A–C.

12 For further characteristics of the skilled workforce, see R.Q. Gray, *The Labour Aristocracy in Victorian Edinburgh* (Oxford, 1976).

the point that the sheriff only ever removed inhabitants once he, Littlejohn, had certified there was 'house accommodation of a similar class in other districts of the city'.[13] Since Littlejohn and the Burgh Engineer, Thomas Fraser, published a table in 1874 detailing each of the nineteen sanitary districts in 132 columns and cataloguing in minute detail the types and locations of water-closets and ventilation systems for eight rental categories, it is reasonable to assume that they and their four sanitary inspectors knew with some precision the state of the rental market.[14] Filtering-up for the poor in the central districts of Edinburgh certainly did not involve moving directly into new tenements, but it did result in taking over those properties vacated by a labour aristocracy which migrated, for example, to the five 'colony' developments (Stockbridge, Hawthornbank, Restalrig, Abbeyhill, and Dalry) of 914 dwellings completed by the Edinburgh Cooperative Building Company between 1862 and 1872, and into the new tenement 'estates' along Dundee Street and Fountainbridge in the developing industrial zones to the west of the city.[15] In the early 1870s, James Steel's new Caledonian and Orwell tenements in Dalry accommodated almost 3,500 residents on census day, 1881, equivalent to a quarter of those dislocated by the Improvement Trust, and across the railway tracks on streets running off the spine of Dundee Street another 900 souls were housed in speculative working-class housing.[16] As a result, the internal migration of skilled and regularly employed workers vacated rooms for the casually employed in the central districts.

In 1878 the City of Glasgow Bank failed and forced two-thirds of Glasgow businesses in the building trades into bankruptcy. The financial crash caused the Improvement Trustees to be left with unsaleable land.[17] With an excess of empty tenement housing – vacancies were over 10% – why clear more land?[18] So, 'Raised up to purify and purge the City, to sweep away slums and dens of pestilence, they [the Improvement Commission] were forced to remain the owners of some of the meanest property within the[ir] jurisdiction.'[19] By contrast, in Edinburgh relocation for the dislocated was not so problematical because the more diversified local economy insulated the trustees against the worst of the Glasgow experience.[20] This is not to claim that there was not hardship in the

13 PP (HC) 1884–85 [C. 4409], Royal Commission on the Housing of the Working Classes, Evidence of Dr Littlejohn, Q.18,996, Appendix B.

14 *Return by the Burgh Engineer showing the number of Dwelling-Houses within each of the 19 Sanitary Districts into which the City is divided provided with Water-Closet accommodation, the means adopted for Ventilating the same, and Water Supply, &c., with Supplementary Return by the Medical Officer of Health of the rate and amount of Mortality and causes of Death in each District* (Edinburgh, 1874).

15 R. Rodger, *Edinburgh's Colonies: Housing the Workers* (Argyll, 2011), 85.

16 PP (HC) 1883 LXXXI, Census of Scotland, 1881, City of Edinburgh.

17 Glasgow Municipal Commission on the Housing of the Poor, *Report* (1904), Evidence of T. Binnie, Q.7,011. The Improvement Trust difficulties were exacerbated rather than caused by the bank failure, since Glasgow building bankruptcies in 1877 were already four times the average of 1870–76. See *Edinburgh Gazette*, bankruptcy notices 1877, and NRS CS318, concluded sequestrations, 1870–77.

18 A.K. Cairncross, *Home and Foreign Investment 1870–1913: Studies in Capital Accumulation* (Cambridge, 1953), 29–31.

19 J. Bell and J. Paton, *Glasgow. Its Municipal Organization and Administration* (Glasgow, 1896), 225.

20 R. Rodger, 'Wages, employment and poverty in the Scottish cities, 1841–1914', in G. Gordon (ed.), *Perspectives of the Scottish City* (Aberdeen, 1985), 25–63; R. Rodger, 'The Victorian building

1880s; for many there was an imperfect fit in Edinburgh between the demand for and supply of homes at affordable prices. Housing in the new industrial suburbs came at a price that was usually beyond the reach of those ejected from Old Town properties. More seriously, and in a preview of later social problems in inter-war council housing estates, the relocated poor became detached from the social and community support mechanisms crucial to their survival – charity organisations, church missions, the pawnbroker, and kin and friendship networks. Little direct evidence of this domestic stress remains in relation to the work of the Improvement Trust, though twentieth-century studies suggest such disruption was considerable.[21]

Since the decline in death rates was not confined to the districts most affected by clearances, and to differing degrees was evident in all other areas of the city, it is reasonable to conclude that the various initiatives proposed by Littlejohn had some impact. Cumulatively his threats and nudges were sufficient. He did not have to bring the full weight of the Public Health Committee and the letter of the law to bear when cesspools or cisterns dripped: a letter sufficed. With the new regime of inspection, prosecutions for food contamination declined progressively.[22] Littlejohn offered support, though not usually advocacy, for the public works projects which would improve water supply and drainage, and appeared before official bodies and enquiries to promote good practice across a spectrum of public health initiatives. The empirical mission was ratcheted up even further as a 132-column table for each of the nineteen sanitary districts indicated areas for intervention. Case by case, Littlejohn's public health principles could be implemented through his familiarity with public health legislation. When asked in 1885 by the commissioners enquiring into working-class housing whether he required more powers Littlejohn, in typically direct terms, replied: 'Undoubtedly not.'[23] Littlejohn monitored property and mentored individuals; he trained his staff to apply rigour and consistency. For each district, and for each home in each district, and for seven different rental categories, the number of water-closets, types of ventilation, and location of water supplies in the tenement were recorded, and in reply to a question about the strength of his four-man sanitary inspectorate, his only regret was that it was not sufficient for him to develop the kind of on-going detailed tabulations he had provided for the Commissioners.[24]

industry and the housing of the Scottish working class', in M. Doughty (ed.), *Building the Industrial City* (Leicester, 1986), 151–206.

21 See, for example, M. Young and P. Willmott, *Family and Kinship in East London* (London, 1957); S. Damer, *From Moorepark to 'Wine alley': the Rise and Fall of a Glasgow Housing Scheme* (Edinburgh, 1989); M. Miller, *The Representation of Place Urban Planning and Protest in France and Great Britain, 1950–1980* (Aldershot, 2003), 242–98.

22 ECA ED006/1/1a contains the published annual reports and returns from the Superintendent of Police, 1865 to 1881. The returns give figures for the preceding six years and thus cover the whole period from 1859 to 1881. The data for 1855–60 are in ECA ED006/1/19. *Report and Returns as to Crimes, Offences, and Contraventions and to Cases of Drunkenness, within the Police Bounds of the City of Edinburgh, during the Six Years ended with 1860. Prepared for the Magistrates and Council, by Thomas Linton, Superintendent of Police, 1861*, 17. For 1852 (the first year in which Thomas Linton compiled crime statistics for publication) to 1854 see *The Scotsman*, 29 April 1857, 4c.

23 PP (HC) 1884–85 [C. 4409], Royal Commission, Q.19,019.

24 PP (HC) 1884–85 [C. 4409], Royal Commission, Q.19,018–23.

The persistent nature of environmental inequalities can be seen from Table 6.1. One-third of Edinburgh homes with water-closets in 1874 lacked a water supply to flush the toilet; in the worst cases – Canongate, Grassmarket, and St Giles' – it was twice as common, with the Tron district not far behind.[25] Another indicator showed the social composition of the Edinburgh population according to housing valuations or assessments.[26] Some districts, notably Newington and Pleasance/St Leonard's, had virtually inverse social pyramids: only 19% of Newington inhabitants occupied a house valued below £15, and only 17% of those in Pleasance/St Leonard's did not live in such accommodation. Elsewhere (George Square, Broughton) there was a strong presence of rentals in the £15–50 range, but more striking is the absence of upper-class properties in six districts, each with less than 5% of the housing stock in the £50 p.a. or more category (Table 6.2).

From subscriber lists, voting rolls, and letters to the newspapers it is evident that the most vocal and active citizens in mid-Victorian cities were from the educated and professional elements, and their absence in particular wards did little to redress the environmental inequalities disproportionately found in these wards.[27] What is surprising, and only evident from a detailed scrutiny of the Burgh Engineer's and Littlejohn's data, is that the districts most resembling the social composition of Edinburgh as a whole were suburban Morningside and the West End, where the graceful tenements of the third New Town were offset by the meaner tenement apartments built among the spaghetti of railway lines in the Dalry and Gorgie areas.

What emerges from the data published by Littlejohn in 1874 is that it was too soon to see changes in the social structure and environmental health of Edinburgh. By 1885, when the Royal Commission on the Housing of the Working Classes took evidence, Littlejohn was able to report a decline in death rates across the city. Parallel to the cost-effective public health initiatives which Littlejohn commended with a view to reduce morbidity, were important independent contributions to health and welfare. These were promoted by charities and mutual societies. As the *Quarterly Review* observed:

> No array of statistics, no sanitary reports, no highly-coloured descriptions in novels ... can convey an adequate conception of the horrors of the gregarious life of the poorest of our town population to those who have never visited the haunts themselves.[28]

Henry Littlejohn's achievements owed much to his predecessors, and to other agencies. Sanitary reform was cumulative and not attributable to one man. Many medical men (Alison, Glover, Wood, Gairdner) and city officials (Ramsay, Marwick, Patterson) had recognised the importance to the public's health of

25 *Return by the Burgh Engineer showing ... Water-Closet Accommodation*, 16 February 1874.

26 This was based on annual rental values, used for local taxation purposes.

27 For a contemporary view of local inequalities see Environment Agency, R&D Technical Report E2-067/1/TR, Environmental Quality and Social Deprivation (Bristol, 2003).

28 *Quarterly Review*, 107, April 1860, 269, quoted in an editorial in *The Scotsman*, 31 May 1860, 2a on a collection of publications about housing for the working class. The editorial caught the eye of Dr W.T. Gairdner who made use of it in his lectures on *Public Health in Relation to Water and Air* (1862), 171.

No. of sanitary district	Name of sanitary district	Houses without water-closets	All dwellings	Percentage of dwellings without water-closets
I	Upper New Town	191	1,667	11.5
II	Lower New Town	418	2,621	15.9
III	West End	217	3,072	7.1
IV	Upper Water of Leith	1,125	2,763	40.7
V	Lower Water of Leith	284	1,293	22.0
VI	Broughton	253	1,359	18.6
VII	Calton and Greenside	986	2,635	37.4
VIII	Abbey	279	840	33.2
IX	Canongate	1,858	2,353	79.0
X	Tron	1,205	1,956	61.6
XI	St Giles'	1,835	2,677	68.5
XII	Grassmarket	789	1,069	73.8
XIII	Fountainbridge	1,348	2,809	48.0
XIV	George Square and Lauriston	366	1,960	18.7
XV	Nicolson Street	1,701	4,582	37.1
XVI	Pleasance and St Leonard's	997	3,991	25.0
XVII	Newington	293	1,815	16.1
XVIII	Grange	57	1,155	4.9
XIX	Morningside	117	996	11.7
Totals		14,319	41,613	34.4

Table 6.1 Water-closets lacking water supplies by sanitary district, 1874 (%)
[Source: *Return by the Burgh Engineer. Water and Water Closets in the City ... Edinburgh, February 1874*]

cleaning and infection control, and Littlejohn extended that by systematically analysing occupational and environmental health and suggesting administrative improvements. The introduction of civil registration, revised arrangements for local taxation, and substitution of police commissioners by town councillors provided a basis for legitimate intervention by civic authorities. Voluntary efforts, too, made a significant impact on the health of the poor, notably through the work of the Night Asylum for the Houseless. In the quarter century before 1867 it provided over 313,000 bed nights for the 'houseless poor', of whom 23.5% were Edinburgh-born.[29] Together the Night Asylum and the House of Refuge (Queensberry House) provided 750 soup rations daily, though even this impressive amount was considered sufficient only for the poor of the High Street and, following prompts from Littlejohn in 1866 to the Lord Provost

29 *Report on the Condition of the Poorer Classes of Edinburgh and of their Dwellings, Neighbourhoods and Families* (Edinburgh, 1868), 35, compiled by Dr Alexander Wood. After the Edinburgh born, the most numerous of the houseless poor were from Lanarkshire (14.4%), Ireland (14.0%), England (9.0%), and Midlothian County (6.1%).

Sanitary district	Annual valuation (%) less than £15 p.a.	£15–50 p.a.	over £50 p.a.
Pleasance and St Leonard's (16)	82.6	17.1	0.1
Canongate (9)	66.1	29.9	3.4
Tron (10)	61.3	34.0	2.6
Fountainbridge (13)	59.8	34.4	3.6
Abbey (8)	56.0	39.4	3.7
Grassmarket (12)	45.9	42.6	6.6
Calton and Greenside (7)	44.1	41.2	12.5
Nicolson Street (15)	44.1	54.6	0.8
West End (3)	42.8	32.9	21.8
Lower Water of Leith (5)	38.7	40.7	15.3
St Giles' (11)	35.5	52.7	10.8
Upper Water of Leith (4)	31.5	28.2	34.5
Broughton (6)	23.4	56.9	15.3
George Square and Lauriston (14)	21.6	62.9	9.8
Upper New Town (1)	19.6	29.9	39.9
Newington (17)	19.2	52.8	20.0
Lower New Town (2)	14.9	45.2	33.0
Grange (18)	11.4	48.8	28.1
Morningside (19)	8.9	34.9	49.8
Edinburgh	34.8	41.4	19.1

Table 6.2 Distribution of Edinburgh housing stock, 1874
[Source: *Return by the Burgh Engineer. Water and Water Closets in the City … Edinburgh, February 1874*]

and to the Lighting and Cleaning Committee to provide more soup kitchens, public subscriptions were obtained to provide for western areas around the Grassmarket.[30] Three new soup kitchens were established 'during the recent [1866] cold and inclement winter', and it was these which, the Cleaning Committee believed, were 'the means, to a great extent, of averting cholera and other diseases, and thereby preserving the city in a comparatively healthy condition'.[31] Further efforts from the Edinburgh Association for Improving the Conditions of the Poor were made to check morbidity. Its annual meeting in April 1869 heard how throughout the city 1,227 men and women had volunteered as visitors to 1,143 families during the first three months of 1869, and that in addition to assistance for beggars, finding work for the unemployed, and assisting the destitute, 44,232 meals costing £300 had been provided by Canongate Soup

30 *The Scotsman*, 24 October 1866, 8a–d. See *Evening Courant*, 28 January 1867, 1cd for the list of subscribers to the Soup Kitchen Fund for the Relief of the Industrious Poor.
31 *Caledonian Mercury*, 21 March 1867, 3b.

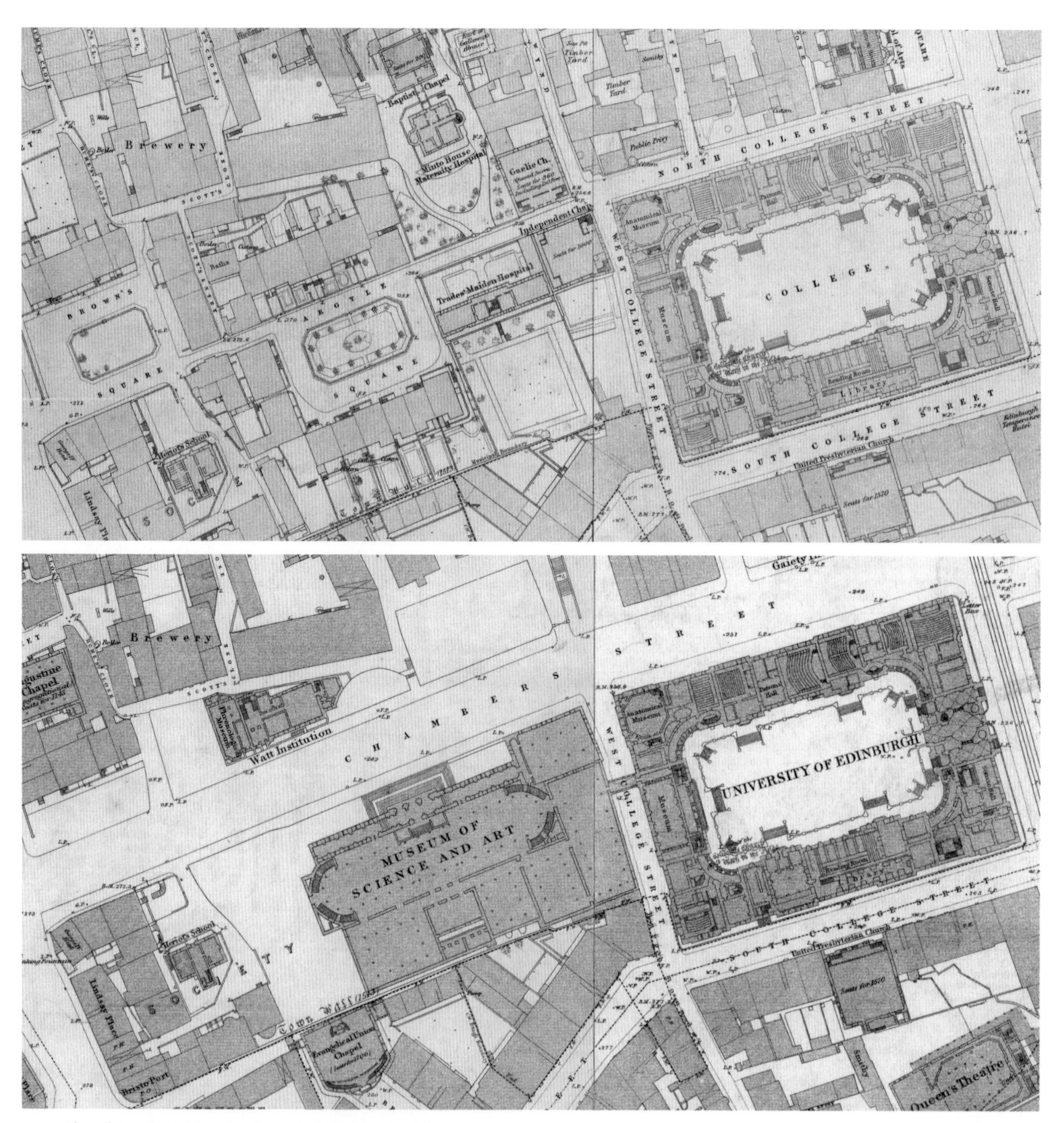

6.4 Chambers Street in 1852 (top) and 1877 (bottom)

The primary motivation for the creation of Chambers Street was to provide a more spacious approach to the Museum, opened by Prince Albert on 23 October 1861. The major displacements were the Trades Maidens Hospital and housing in Brown and Argyle Squares. [Sources: NLS OS 1852 and 1877]

6.5 A prospect of Chambers Street, 1861
Prince Albert laid the foundation stone for the Museum of Science and Art (now the National Museum of Scotland) on 23 October 1861. It was originally intended to place a statue of him on the street, as this perspective watercolour by David Cousin, with figures by Sam Bough, shows, but it was the statue of William Chambers that was eventually erected there in 1891. See fig. 6.6. [Source: NMS]

Kitchen.[32] Numerous voluntary societies and church organisations, therefore, provided support to bolster the poor and infirm in their survival strategies, not least against the climatic rigours of Edinburgh winters. So, too, did the three Parochial Boards of the city, financed through a tax on residents and collected with the rates. Their efforts cushioned the adverse impact of poverty and social deprivation on the health of paupers in the city, the majority on whom (61%) were born outwith Edinburgh.[33]

Despite his forensic analyses and practical suggestions, Littlejohn's advice was not always heeded. He was on the losing side over the furious debate concerning the St Mary's Loch water supply which the Edinburgh and District Water Trust sought in 1871. Overtaken by the clearance programme of Chambers, some less spectacular but nonetheless significant proposals in the *Report*, for example those concerning the design of drains and re-routing waste pipes, were gradually implemented though usually through the actions of builders and contractors. In relation to cemeteries, Littlejohn advanced the same arguments for a quarter of a century following his appointment in 1854. With reference to

32 *The Scotsman*, 6 April 1869, 5a–d, equivalent to 490 meals per day. Littlejohn had written to the Lord Provost previously on the need to provide soup kitchens for the poor during the winter months to prevent disease. See *The Scotsman*, 24 October 1866, 8a.

33 Abstract of Return to Parliament as to Birth Places of Paupers chargeable to the Parish of Edinburgh, quoted in *Report on the Condition of the Poorer Classes of Edinburgh*, 34. The Parochial Board also helped 352 illegitimate children.

the passages in his *Report*, that under the Burial Grounds Act, 1855 the Town Council was obliged 'to provide for the speedy interment of the dead', the issue became more pressing as cholera reached the city in 1866. Victims became more numerous, and so Littlejohn reiterated:

> Last year [1865] I endeavoured to impress on the Council the necessity of their procuring ground suitable for a public cemetery so as to afford to the poor of this city adequate provision for the disposal of their dead. From inquiries I had made I had come to the conclusion that the churchyards were so over-crowded as to demand, in the interests of public health, that they should be closed. I also pointed out that with the shutting of the churchyards, the rates of the cemeteries would be raised to a prohibitive standard so far as the poor were concerned.[34]

The closure of all nineteen churchyards, confirmed in 1874 following an appeal to the Sheriff Principal by St Cuthbert's Parochial Board, delivered a monopoly to the private cemetery companies, but it was only an emergency in 1882 that forced the council to be more receptive. This was a tip off to Littlejohn that bodies were being buried in shallow graves in Dalry Cemetery and then exhumed and re-interred in vaults. After clandestine night-time borings by Littlejohn and his staff of 324 holes in six private cemeteries in the city, 33% were found to be at a depth of less than 3 feet.[35] The burials issue brought into alignment Littlejohn's concern for the public's health, respect for the poor, and prudent public expenditure. For over fifty years he sought to control what in 1911 a distinguished member of the newly formed Edinburgh Cremation Society called the 'insanitary graveyard process'.[36] Littlejohn encountered perennial obstruction and delay by councillors over the issue of public cemeteries and, if it was probably not the reason for his commitment to and advocacy of cremation as president of the Scottish Burial Reform and Cremation Society, the procrastination of council officials would probably have inclined him to that view anyway.[37]

Wider perspectives

It was, and has remained, easy to link the Littlejohn *Report* directly with Chambers Street and the city improvement project. After all, they were separated only by months. But this is a simplistic connection, perpetuated in local folklore

34 *The Scotsman*, 3 January 1883, 6a, Littlejohn urges that there should be a public cemetery providing a 'means of interment for the poorest of the inhabitants at the lowest possible rates'. The matter occupied the Health Committee for several months in 1883.

35 *The Scotsman*, 3 January 1883, 9bc. In Dalry cemetery the shallowest grave was 8 inches from the surface, and in the Grange cemetery, the shallowest was 20 inches.

36 *The Scotsman*, 18 May 1911, 11a. Statement by Sir James R. Simpson, professor of midwifery and nephew to Sir James Y. Simpson. J.R. Simpson was killed in a motor accident, *British Medical Journal*, 1, no. 2885, 15 April 1916, 572–4.

37 With no cremation facilities in Edinburgh at the time of Littlejohn's death on 30 September 1914 he had to be cremated at the Glasgow Crematorium, and was the 530th person to be cremated since it opened. Edinburgh cremations accounted for 35% of the business of the Glasgow Crematorium. See *The Scotsman*, 21 May 1911, 7c; 5 June 1912, 10; 22 November 1912, 6d; 9 December 1913, 6g; 11 December 1914, 3e; 20 November 1915, 8.

and published work, and a conflation with another quite separate event in Chambers Street, the opening of the Museum of Science and Industry to visitors in 1866.[38] In fact the museum, now the National Museum of Scotland, was a cultural project with its own history, authorised and funded a decade earlier in 1854 with a £7,000 subvention from the British Treasury.[39] Prince Albert laid the foundation stone of the Museum and the new General Post Office on the same day in October 1861 (see Figure 6.5).[40]

City improvement was nothing new in Edinburgh, and in April 1863 fifty merchants and farmers tabled proposals before the Town Council for a tunnel from Market Street (Waverley Station) to the Cowgate to avoid the steep gradients involved in carting goods to the Grassmarket.[41] More typically, street widening was involved, and in the 1860s a sinuous new thoroughfare, Cockburn Street, was still under construction, as its date-stamped buildings show (see fig. 5.6). The significance of this new building programme and the displacement of 4,000 people was heightened after the attention of the Edinburgh reading public had been drawn to the modernisation programme in Paris, commissioned by Napoléon III and led by the Seine prefect, Baron Georges-Eugène Haussmann, between 1852 and 1870.[42] *The Scotsman* made explicit links between street improvements and sanitary conditions: 'as towns increase, stronger obligations are continually laid upon local guardians of the public health to maintain the requisite sanitary conditions.'[43] This, indeed, was the legitimation of civic intervention. Like spokes of a wheel, the new boulevards radiated outwards from centre to suburb, and offered imperial Paris 'immunity from epidemics … and from the rage of Red Republicanism'. Opening up lines of communication and control 'resembles the operations of actual warfare', Littlejohn explained when presenting his plan of attack on insanitary areas.[44] This Parisian parallel coincided with proposals for street improvements in Edinburgh in 1864.[45] David Cousin, the city architect, submitted a 'sketch plan' on 10 August 1864 at the request of the Lord Provost and senior councillors to widen the street

38 D. Keir (ed.), *The Third Statistical Account of Scotland: The City of Edinburgh* (Glasgow, 1966), 930. The new building was a fusion of the Industrial Museum of Scotland with objects from the Great Exhibition in London in 1851, and the Natural History Museum of the University of Edinburgh. See G.N. Swinney and D. Heppell, 'Public and privileged access: a historical survey of admission charges and visitor figures for part of the Scottish National Collections', *Book of the Old Edinburgh Club*, 4 (1997), 69–70; G.N. Swinney, 'Reconstructed visions: the philosophies that shaped part of the Scottish national collection', *Museum Management and Curatorship*, 21 (2006), 128–42.

39 PP (HC) 1854 XL, 172, 417–456 [1–40]. Treasury Minute, 7 April 1854, 434, Civil Service Estimates, etc., for the year ending March 1855. The assistance of Geoff Swinney in explaining the origins of the National Museum of Scotland is much appreciated.

40 *The Scotsman*, 24 October 1861, 2e–g.

41 *The Scotsman*, 16 February 1863, 5c; 29 April 1863, 7a; 8 May 1863, 2d; 11 May 1863, 6f; and 29 July 1863, 7c. The city architect also commented on the cost and feasibility of these but concluded a private company was more appropriate. Only that portion of land below the High Street itself was in the possession of the Town Council.

42 A. Sutcliffe, *The Autumn of Central Paris: the Defeat of Town Planning, 1850–1970* (London, 1970).

43 *The Scotsman*, 29 February 1864, 3a.

44 *Report*, 114.

45 *Caledonian Mercury*, 17 August 1864, 3a.

6.6 Statue of William Chambers, Chambers Street
John Rhind 1891, artist.

(subsequently Chambers Street) from George IV Bridge to South Bridge to give improved access to the Industrial Museum (see figs. 6.4–6.5).[46] Another project proposed a street from George IV Bridge in front of the stalled building site for the Industrial Museum through Brown Square and Adam Square, crossing South Bridge and extending eastwards by demolishing the north side of Infirmary Street to link up with St Mary's Wynd as a major road interchange. With the Industrial Museum underway, an ensemble of public buildings was envisaged for a new Town Hall, Merchant's Hall, and College Hall considered in a concept recognisable nowadays as a civic quarter. Other public improvements were proposed: a widening of Candlemaker Row to ease access to the Grassmarket; a similar treatment of Lady Lawson's Wynd to improve access from Lauriston Place north-westwards to the Main Point and beyond; an entirely new street penetrating Potterrow to link it with Nicolson Street and Bristo Street; and another new street from John Knox's House in the High Street curving westwards to Leith Wynd so as to improve access to the New Town.[47]

Here, then, in 1864 was an embryonic improvement project long before the Chambers improvement scheme was even contemplated. It was conceived so as to have minimum impact on historic sites, to respect property rights, to involve no major civil engineering works and thus minimise costs to local taxpayers, and to provide for improved retail possibilities. It bore more than a passing resemblance to the suggestions contained in Littlejohn's *Report* and, significantly, was contextualised in terms of the regular health reports that were presented by him through the press to the citizens of Edinburgh. Continuities rather than changes were more in evidence in Edinburgh's public health history. By providing the press with previews of his *Report,* Littlejohn was able to inform and influence public debate and, crucially, to prepare the ground for a favourable reception to the published version.

As a coherent set of principles and suggestions to improve the health and well-being of the city, Littlejohn's *Report on the Sanitary Condition of Edinburgh* owed debts to his mentor, William Pulteney Alison, and his predecessors as Police Surgeon, particularly George Glover. There can be no doubt, either, that the systems developed by Henry Duncan, the Liverpool Medical Officer of Health (1847–63), were also highly influential, as was the thinking and friendship of Littlejohn's lecturer and Glasgow's Medical Officer of Health (1863–72), William Gairdner. Each in their different ways contributed to the emergence of a systematic approach to public health to which Littlejohn added his own rigour. Although it was some years before pioneering research conclusively identified the bacteriological mechanisms by which diseases were transmitted, Littlejohn was by

46 *Evening Courant*, 17 August 1864, 4a–c; *Caledonian Mercury*, 17 August 1864, 3a. It is worth noting that when the Industrial Museum was opened, far from being an 'improvement scheme', it was criticised as a site of moral depravity. A 'Scot Abroad' noted that 'on going into this magnificent building full of amorous school boys and girls whose sole object in coming seemed to be to look at one another', while another visitor commented that the museum was 'a place of assignation for juveniles'. See G.N. Swinney, '"I am utterly disgusted …" – the Edinburgh Museum of Science and Art effecting (sic) moral decline?', *Review of Scottish Culture*, 16 (2004), 78–9.

47 *The Scotsman*, 16 February 1863, 5e; 29 April 1863, 7a; 8 May 1863, 2d; 11 May 1863, 6f; 29 July 1863, 7c.

6.7 Professor Sir Henry Littlejohn, MD, LLD, FRCSEd
Sir George Reid painted this portrait to be presented to Littlejohn by his pupils on his retiral in 1907. The painting captures the authority and determination of the man. [Source: SNPG]

no means an adherent to the prevailing miasmatic theories of infection, preferring to focus on observation and fieldwork to identify and address identifiable unhygienic practices through changes in urban administration.[48] Hippocratic principles and pragmatism were the hallmarks of his approach, underpinned by empirical evidence and sensitivity to local conditions.

What emerged from Littlejohn's work was the close interconnection of community health and public administration. This was the very essence of medical jurisprudence, a field in which Alison excelled, and in which both Littlejohn, and Glover before him, encountered institutions and regulations which impeded and occasionally blocked their professionally based recommendations. Foremost among these rigidities were the many committees and sub-committees of the Town Council, packed as they were with individuals who were genuine in their intentions and even sympathetic to Littlejohn's arguments, but who were constrained by political considerations or religious affiliations. Littlejohn's *Report* with its emphasis on evidence and deductive reasoning heralded the emergence of the technical expert – the engineer, public analyst, surveyor, inspectorate, fire and police chiefs, and the medical officer – even if the town clerk's dynasty remained intact for some time to come.[49] As the compilation in 1874 of an elaborate table of housing data with its 132 columns and twenty rows shows,[50] Littlejohn worked effectively with Thomas Fraser, the burgh engineer; he also developed good working relations with the manager of the Edinburgh Water Company, Alexander Ramsay, and with the numerous inspectors employed by different council departments. As a commercial baker's son, Littlejohn knew well the pressures businessmen experienced as they sought to make a living. There was, then, in Littlejohn both a street-wise Edinburgh resident with a deeply ingrained sense of the city's history and administration, and a networked operator, hard-wired in to medical circles and establishment connections.[51] His office was within a stone's throw of all three main Edinburgh newspapers and, as noted earlier, just 50 yards from the council chambers.

48 On the contribution of the 1860s to pre-Koch germ theories see J.K. Crellin 'The dawn of the germ theory: particles, infection and biology', in F.N.L. Poynter (ed.), *Medicine and Science in the 1860s* (London, 1968), 57–76. On the contribution of, and application to, animal medicine, see M. Worboys, 'Germ theories of disease and British veterinary medicine, 1860–1890', *Medical History*, 35 (1991), 308–27.

49 M. Niemi, *Public Health and Municipal Policy Making: Britain and Sweden, 1900–40* (Aldershot, 2007), 1–24; S. Ewen, 'Chief officers and professional identities: the case of fire services in English municipal government, *c.*1870–1938', *Historical Research*, 81, no. 211 (2008), 123–49; J. Moore and R. Rodger, 'Who really ran the cities? Municipal knowledge and policy networks in British local government, 1832–1914', in R. Roth and R. Beachy (eds), *Who Ran the Cities? City Elites and Urban Power in Europe and North America* (Aldershot, 2007), 37–69.

50 The 132 columns were different measures of the quality of water and water-closet provision in each of the 19 sanitary districts and a total row for the city overall.

51 *Evening Courant*, 28 April 1863, 1a–c. Advertisement from the Lord Provost (as Convenor of the General Committee) for the annual meeting of the National Association for the Promotion of Social Science, 7 October 1863. Littlejohn was one of those responsible for organising the Public Health section of the meeting. The General Committee listed occupies 1½ columns with many clergy, medical men, lawyers, and councillors, and is a census of the academic and general establishment. See also the networks associated with the *Report on the Condition of the Poorer Classes of Edinburgh and of their Dwellings, Neighbourhoods and Families* (Edinburgh, 1868), xi.

Above all else, what emerged from Littlejohn's *Report* was a public dialogue about what constituted the meaning of 'civic'. It was one thing to promote amenity and salubrity; few would oppose that, and it was regarded as important to rank Edinburgh highly in a wider European context. Promoting place promoted business.[52] 'The prosperity of Edinburgh,' observed one writer, 'is entirely dependent upon its character for healthfulness and amenity.'[53] Littlejohn was acutely aware that visitors to the city would carry away an impression which might be unfavourable if public health was compromised and the streets encountered by tourists were unpleasant or dangerous.[54] As a columnist in *The Scotsman* explained shortly after the publication of the *Report*: 'Any passing tourist even who [*sic*] penetrates into the historical recesses of the Old Town needs no evidence beyond that of his eye and nose to convince him of the existence of influences seriously adverse to health. He sees and smells that this fair Edina … has within her bosom plague spots of deadliest virulence.'[55]

Tourism and the international reputation of the city were one thing; it was quite another, however, to consider public health as a civic project, something desirable in itself because it brought an enriched quality of life to all citizens. In this respect, Littlejohn was a public health missionary, an unswerving believer in the good that resulted from more efficient public health administration precisely because it benefited all the inhabitants of Edinburgh and sidelined sectional interests. If anything, there was positive discrimination in that the poor stood to gain most from the differential social impact of his various sanitary proposals. That 'fever is never entirely absent'[56] and that there were 'nurseries of fever breeding places of pestilence' was well known but never described 'so distinctly or carefully as by Dr Littlejohn. The great merit and value, indeed, of his admirable report … is that it enables us to lay our finger on every black spot in the city, and to say that, until this and this is cleansed, the sin of blood-guiltiness lies upon us.'[57]

The *Report* was an excuse for the press to develop a culture of blame for the unhealthiness of the city, the responsibility for which they placed firmly on the inhabitants and their civic heads, though Littlejohn himself was careful to avoid such accusations. By 'clearly and mercilessly exposing neglects and defects', there was a challenge to civic authorities, implicit in Littlejohn's prose and explicit in that of the newspapers, to follow the advice of their medical officer. *The Scotsman* wryly noted: 'We do not engage a physician merely to tell us that we are ill, but to act on his instruction so as to get well.' Should little come of his 'valuable practical suggestions' then few would be surprised, but it was clear where blame would lie: with the civic authorities. There were too many officials,

52 ECA ACC 378, Edinburgh Exhibition Trust, Minutes 10 July 1888, f. 2, composition of committee. From the 1860s the city of Edinburgh began actively to court international conferences and exhibitions See R. Rodger, 'The 'Common Good' and civic promotion: Edinburgh 1860–1914', in R. Colls and R. Rodger (eds), *Cities of Ideas: Civil Society and Urban Governance in Britain, 1800–2000* (Aldershot, 2004), 144–77.

53 *The Scotsman*, 6 September 1865, 2c.

54 *Report*, 11–12, 111.

55 *The Scotsman*, 6 September 1865, 2c.

56 *Report*, 27.

57 *The Scotsman*, 6 September 1865, 2c.

responsibility was fractured, zeal for change was counteracted by apathy, and positive action was constrained by 'the bonds of red tape, and the paralyzing influences of conflicting jurisdiction'. In a withering indictment of localism and the small-mindedness of officials, *The Scotsman* columnist used the phrase 'the obstructiveness of our Fords' to denote the 'perpetual palliatives and annual whitewashings' which passed for a public health policy in 1865 – a reference to Councillor Ford's and others' preference for disinfecting closes and dealing with the symptoms rather than the causes of ill-health. Ultimately, though, blame was a collective matter: because of its topography, Edinburgh 'ought to be one of the healthiest cities in the world and … it is our own fault that it is otherwise.'[58] If the City Council had the power but lacked authority, the reverse was true of Littlejohn; he possessed ample authority but did not seek power.

Public health, as Littlejohn's *Report* showed convincingly, cut across almost every sphere of public activity – drainage, water supply, waste disposal, ventilation, overcrowding, diseased meat, ports and the importation of food, sale of goods, markets, inspections, street cleaning, occupational disease, epidemics, isolation hospitals, notification of certain diseases, burials, site visits, civil engineering, transport planning, staffing, record keeping, and annual reporting. Public health was not just a part-time activity but one that required constant vigilance and frequent liaison with municipal departments. As a consequence, from the 1860s public health formed part of the DNA of local government in Edinburgh. It is abundantly clear that in Edinburgh, as in many cities, modern local government emerged through public health departments.

When his *Report on the Sanitary Condition of Edinburgh* was published in 1865, Littlejohn was just 39, three years into the job as Medical Officer of Health, and an employee of Edinburgh Town Council as Police Surgeon for just over a decade. There were 43 further years of public service ahead, and these were guided by what was described soon after the publication of the *Report* as a chart by which the sanitary reformer should steer.[59] What could not have been anticipated was that it would be that same sanitary reformer who would do just that while concurrently discharging his duties as Medical Adviser to the Crown in Scotland, lecturing in medical jurisprudence at the Royal College of Surgeons and Edinburgh University, and acting as a commissioner and medical adviser to the Board of Supervision and from 1897, the Scottish Local Government Board. The objective of Littlejohn's *Report,* as defined by him, was 'to test for the first time by reference to the mortality, the sanitary condition of the portions of the city inhabited by the richer and poorer classes'.[60] Informed medical opinion in *The Lancet* subsequently described Littlejohn's research as 'monumental'.[61] This was no exaggeration. He was also described as 'one of the greatest public health authorities of our time' and as 'one of Edinburgh's and of Scotland's great men'.[62]

58 *The Scotsman*, 6 September 1865, 2d.

59 *The Scotsman*, 6 September 1865, 2c.

60 *Report*, 5.

61 *The Lancet*, 10 October 1914, 913–14.

62 *British Medical Journal*, 10 October 1914, 648–50; *The Glasgow Herald*, 2 October 1914.

REPORT ON SANITARY CONDITION

OF EDINBURGH

Identifying the different editions of Littlejohn's *Report*

Although not all of them are in their original state, the printing and revisions of Littlejohn's *Report* can be described from the small number of surviving copies. There were three printings:

1. **The first printing** of 1865 in hard boards and green sand-grain book cloth with only the arms of the City of Edinburgh embossed in gold on the front. The title is on the spine: 'REPORT ON SANITARY CONDITION OF EDINBURGH'. There was no index. In the fold-out coloured map of the sanitary districts the title is 'Plan of | EDINBURGH, | Leith & Suburbs;'.

2. **The second printing**, also issued in 1865 in a softer binding with more elaborate decorative tooling on green dot-and-line grain book cloth with the title as well as the arms in gold on the front. There is no title on the spine. In the fold-out coloured map of the sanitary districts the title is 'Plan of | EDINBURGH, | Leith & Suburbs; | BY | W. & A. K. JOHNSTON | GEOGRAPHERS & ENGRAVERS | *TO* | THE QUEEN'. Below the scale bar is added '1865'.

3. **The 1866 edition**. A popular abridged edition in purple cloth on soft boards with a label carrying an abbreviated title on the front: 'REPORT | ON | THE SANITARY CONDITION OF EDINBURGH | BY | THE MEDICAL OFFICER OF HEALTH.' The title page has the date 1866. It lacks the fold-out map of the sanitary districts and most of the appendix. It was referred to in the Town Council as 'a People's Edition'. Only five copies are known in libraries and archives.

This facsimile reproduces the second printing which incorporates most of the passages of additional text. Marginal notes describe differences in the two other printings (see pages 434–8); the editors hope that these notes are comprehensive and that this constitutes a variorum edition. Taken together the revisions demonstrate the care taken by Littlejohn to check both text and statistics. Some of the corrections involve a second decimal place. A significant change in the 1866 edition was the replacement of the running head 'REPORT' with sectional running heads, sometimes repeated over three or four pages, in nine cases running across two facing pages, but mostly for a single page only. They indicated Littlejohn's summary of the contents.

REPORT

ON THE

SANITARY CONDITION OF THE CITY OF EDINBURGH.

REPORT

ON THE

Sanitary Condition of the City of Edinburgh,

WITH

RELATIVE APPENDICES, &c.

BY

HENRY D. LITTLEJOHN, M.D.,

F.R.C.S.E.,

MEDICAL OFFICER OF HEALTH FOR THE CITY.

EDINBURGH:

PRINTED BY COLSTON & SON.

MDCCCLXV.

CONTENTS.

REPORT.

Sanitary State of Edinburgh.

Sanitary Requirements of Edinburgh.

APPENDIX.

Vital Statistics.

Appendix No. II.

Statistics of Cows and Byres.

DIAGRAMS, &c.

REPORT

ON THE

SANITARY CONDITION OF EDINBURGH.

When the Act for the Registration of Births, Deaths, and Marriages was extended to Scotland in 1855, it first became possible to ascertain with precision the mortality of our cities and towns, and to compare it with that of the surrounding country districts, in which, from the scantiness of the population, and the purity of the air, the mortality was believed to be at the most favourable standard. Edinburgh (the exact limits of which had been determined in 1832) was divided by Commissioners into seven districts, to each of which a Registrar was appointed. The principle of the division appears to have been determined by the ordinary Municipal Wards. The number of registration districts, however, having been found to be inconveniently large, were, in 1859, reduced to five. These embraced the whole Parliamentary area (which is identical with the Municipal) and also the landward part of the Parish of St Cuthbert's, which for registration purposes was included in the first district, or that of St George's. This district comprised also, on the north, the suburb of Stockbridge, the village of Water of Leith, the West End of the Town, the Lothian Road, and portions of Fountainbridge and of the Grassmarket. The New Town to the north, Canonmills, Broughton, Leith Walk, and the Calton Hill, with adjoining Terraces, were included in district No. 2, or that of St Andrew's. In the third, or Canongate district, were the Canongate, the Abbey, a portion of the Pleasance, and of the High Street, below the Tron Church. The fourth, or St Giles's district, contained the High Street, and the adjacent Closes and Wynds above the Tron Church, a portion of the Grassmarket, and all the south parts of the city, as far as the Meadows, bounded on the one side by Fountainbridge and on the other by Nicolson Street. The last district was named Newington, and, in addition to the suburb bearing that name, included a portion of the Pleasance, and the streets lying between it and Nicolson Street, the suburbs of Grange and

Morningside, and a portion of Fountainbridge. The following table shows the various portions of the City, and also the Municipal Wards, which are included in the registration districts, the population of which, as at 1861, is also given :—

Names of Registration Districts.	Population in 1861.	Portions of City included.	Municipal Wards.
1. St George's...........	42,068	Stockbridge, Water of Leith, West End, Lothian Road, Portions of Fountainbridge and Grassmarket, and the Landward part of the Parish of St Cuthbert.	3. St Bernard's. 4. St George's. 10. St Cuthbert's.
2. St Andrew's.........	38,731	New Town, Canonmills, Broughton, Leith Walk, Calton Hill.	1. Calton. 2. Broughton. 5. St Stephen's. 6. St Luke's. 7. St Andrew's.
3. Canongate............	30,169	Canongate, Abbey, Portions of Pleasance and High Street, and Cowgate, Landward part of Parish of Canongate.	8. Canongate.
4. St Giles'..............	29,679	High Street and Cowgate above Tron Church, Portion of Grassmarket, and District to the north of Meadows.	9. St Giles'. 11. George Square.
5. Newington............	29,797	Portion of Pleasance, Newington, Grange, Morningside, Portion of Fountainbridge.	12. St Leonard's. 13. Newington.
Total Population, ...	170,444		

But a reference to the accompanying map will show how faulty this division is. Two points of importance appear to have been entirely overlooked :—1st, The convenience of the public, who were called upon, under pains and penalties, to obey the enactments of a troublesome law, the benefits of which to the people at large, were not very manifest ; and, 2d, The obvious importance of making the registration divisions subservient to the purpose of testing the mortality of special districts, so that the authorities might have their attention directed to the parts of the city which stood most in need of sanitary improvement. No fewer than 43 streets are divided by the present registration districts, and the inhabitants are thus necessarily put to much inconvenience. Again, from the peculiar division adopted, it is a matter of difficulty to determine the exact registration district of a locality, and tabular guides have been provided for this purpose for the use of the medical profession and the Registrars themselves. The difficulties experienced by the public can easily be imagined. We have, for example, Princes Street in three registration districts, as also the Cowgate. A portion of Canonmills is in St George's, and the Registrar's office is in the Lothian Road; while another is in St Andrew's, the office of which is in North St Andrew Street, and comparatively near. Similar inconsistencies prevail in other parts of the city, and especially in the wide-spread district of Newington. Indeed, the almost daily instances of annoyance which have come under my notice, experienced especially by the poorer and more ignorant classes of the community from the present arrangements, have convinced me of the necessity of diminishing the number of the districts. Were they limited to two—one for the Old Town, south of the great line of Princes Street, and the other for the New—the division would be easily remembered, and as clearly understood. But, again, the statistical data furnished by two such districts would be more valuable than those gathered from the five districts of the present arrangement, which range in no definite direction, but divide in two important sub-divisions of the city, and include others which differ widely in character, site, and population. Indeed, I found that the statistics which I had prepared on the basis of the present division were valueless, as affording a test of the mortality of the various portions of the city. Even with regard to the weekly statements of the mortality which I submitted to the Town-Council, numerous enquiries were addressed to me as to the signification of the names of the districts, and what they represented. And I could not but consider the complaint a well-founded one, that, in the case of Newington, for example, only a small proportion of the mortality registered weekly in that district was drawn from the suburb of that name, while by far the greater part came from the village of Morningside, in which there are two large asylums, and also from the poor, badly-drained district of Fountainbridge, which is separated from Newington by at least a mile and a-half. It soon became apparent that a fresh arrangement must be made, and the question came to be, what plan should be adopted in a new division of the city into what might be called sanitary districts, which might be of use, not merely for such a temporary purpose as the publication of an Annual Report, but might serve as the basis of a scheme of sanitary improvements, by enabling the authorities to ascertain with precision the district mortality? The Municipal Wards, though sufficiently restricted in size for useful comparison, were faulty as regarded their eccentricity of outline and the distribution of the population. Similar disadvantages, along with great disproportion in relative extent, were found to weigh against the parochial division. The one finally adopted will be found figured in the accompanying map of the city, which represents the parliamentary area divided into 19 districts. In framing it, my first object was, by uniting portions of the registration districts of St George's and St Giles', to constitute a special district of Grassmarket and West Port—localities memorable in the medical history of Edinburgh. And again, by joining portions of the districts of St George's and Newington, to form a district of Fountainbridge, a well-marked locality, with special sanitary requirements. By following the stream of the Water of Leith from its entrance within the Parliamentary boundary at Coltbridge until it leaves it at Bonnington, the district of the Water of Leith was marked out,—of importance, not only as bearing upon the recent discussions as to the purification of the stream, but also as indicating the plain which runs northward from the hilly range on which the New Town is built. This is well seen in the elevation section of the city at p. 44. The district is large, and a considerable population is grouped along the banks of the Water of Leith. It became advisable, therefore, to sub-divide it into an upper district, comprising the villages of Dean and Water of Leith, and the important suburb of Stockbridge, and a lower, which included Henderson Row, Canonmills, and Bonnington. The remaining districts were comparatively easily mapped out. The configuration of the New Town naturally resolved it into two sub-divisions, an Upper and a Lower New Town, the one consisting of the plateau on which Princes Street, George Street, and Queen Street stand; the other, the various streets sloping to the north. These were numbered first and second. The gap left between the district of Fountainbridge and the Upper Water of Leith formed the third district, and was named West End. The districts of the Water of Leith constituted Nos. 4 and 5; while that of Broughton, No. 6, ranged from the Beaverhall and Bonnington Roads to Leith Walk, in the one direction, and from Pilrig Street to Broughton Street on the other. The rest of the New Town to the east was thrown into a district, the seventh, called the Calton, comprehending the Calton Hill, Greenside Street, St James' Square, and also that portion of the city between Leith Walk and Lochend. The well-marked ridge of the Old Town (see plan, p. 77), was divided into four divisions of regular gradation in elevation, forming the eighth, ninth, tenth, and eleventh districts. The level surrounding the Abbey of Holyrood, and stretching eastwards as far as the Parliamentary boundary, was named the Abbey. From the Horse Wynd to St Mary's and Leith Wynds, and including on either side, north and south, the North and South Back of Canongate, we have the well-defined district of Canongate, properly so called. The Tron comprehended that block of closes and wynds between the Bridges, on the one hand, and the western boundary of Canongate, on the other, and stretching north and south from the Physic Gardens to Drummond Street. The highest elevation of the ridge was included in the district of St Giles, which was bounded on the north by the New Town, and on the south by the University and the Grassmarket, which constituted district No. 12. Fountainbridge was No. 13. Lauriston, including George Square and the park of the Meadows, formed district No. 14. The densely-peopled localities to the south of the University, and bordering on Nicolson Street, were named after that street, and composed district No. 15, while the range of streets sloping to the east from the Pleasance to Arthur's Seat, and stretching southwards from the Canongate, formed the well-defined district of the Pleasance and St Leonard, No. 16. The southern suburbs were divided into the three districts of Newington, Grange, and Morningside, respectively Nos. 17, 18, and 19. It only remained to indicate, as district No. 20, the landward or county portion of the parish of St Cuthbert, reaching from the sea shore far to the south of the city, the boundaries of which could not be shown in the map.

	Registration Districts.	Sanitary Districts.
NEW TOWN, North of Princes Street.	I. St George's, part of. II. St Andrew's.	1. Upper New Town. 2. Lower New Town. 3. West End. 4. Upper Water of Leith. 5. Lower Water of Leith. 6. Broughton. 7. Calton and Greenside.
OLD TOWN, South of Princes Street.	I. St George's, part of. III. Canongate. IV. St Giles'. V. Newington, part of.	8. Abbey. 9. Canongate. 10. Tron. 11. St Giles'. 12. Grassmarket. 13. Fountainbridge. 14. George Square and Lauriston. 15. Nicolson Street. 16. Pleasance and St Leonard's.
SOUTHERN SUBURBS.	V. Newington, part of.	17. Newington. 18. Grange. 19. Morningside.

The preceding table shows the distribution of the new districts in the Old and New Town, and also their relation to the present registration division.

Such an arrangement enables us to test, for the first time, by reference to the mortality, the sanitary condition of the portions of the city inhabited by the richer and poorer classes. As a preliminary step, a correct list of the streets, lanes, and closes, &c., had to be drawn up, a task of no little difficulty, as there was none in existence, the accuracy of which could be depended upon. This list had again to be sub-divided, so as to form miniature directories for each of the various sanitary districts. The exact amount of the population in each district had next to be ascertained. On turning to the Registrar-General's Report on the population of Scotland, the sole information available for my purpose was the gross population of the five registration districts, as given in Table (p. 2), and to my surprise, I ascertained that at the last census, 1861, the city had not provided itself with a copy of the returns for each street, court, and close,—a document not only essential for the furtherance of sanitary inquiries, but also of great municipal interest. The remedy was to make a copy from the census, which, as the property of Government, had been deposited in the New Register House; and I received the authority of the Magistrates and Council to solicit the permission of the Registrar-General for Scotland, to have a copy made. This was at once granted, and the population column in Table III. of the Appendix (Sanitary Districts and their Vital Statistics) gives the results of the inquiry, which was attended with no little difficulty, as the returns lay just as they had been originally sent in, and from the manner in which they had been made up, the population of main streets had been confused, in some instances, with that of their offshoots, such as closes, courts, and lanes. The mortality of the districts was now ascertained by allocating the deaths, as furnished by the weekly returns of the five local Registrars of Births, Deaths, and Marriages, which had been placed at my disposal. In attempting this, however,—and in order to give a true statement of the mortality of Edinburgh, or of any of the sanitary sub-divisions, so as to admit of satisfactory comparison,—it was necessary, in the first place, to strike off the deaths of persons not belonging to Edinburgh, and who were merely resident in it for a short period, not sufficient to give them, so to speak, a right of domicile. As the seat of a medical school, and of a great hospital, presided over by men of the first eminence in their profession, this city has been the favourite resort of the sick and maimed—a class the mortality of which is well known. A record of such deaths could throw no light on the sanitary condition of Edinburgh, and it could not be maintained that the mortality in question was that of citizens. Secondly, the residences of all persons belonging to Edinburgh, dying in our hospitals, had to be ascertained, so as to permit of the deaths being carefully distributed over their proper districts. Thus it would be impossible to ascertain the mortality of any of our closes were we to restrict our attention to the deaths registered as occurring in the locality. The class of deaths which it is of most importance for a sanitary officer to be acquainted with would escape his notice, as, from their infectious nature, parties suffering from them (and this is especially true of the poor) are drafted at once to our Infirmary, and in the event of death would just increase the special mortality of the institution, and afford no information as to the locality whence they came. Both these points have been attended to, in drawing up the statistics in the Appendix to this Report; and to give some idea of their importance, it may be mentioned that, out of a total mortality during 1863 of 4592, the number of strangers who died within the Royal Infirmary, having come there soliciting medical and surgical advice, was 172, or 3.74 per cent, while the number of deaths of those who had been admitted to this institution from all parts of Edinburgh was 348, or 7.57 per cent.

The smaller the numbers that the statistician has to deal with, the greater the care necessary to insure accuracy; and in striking the mortality ratio of such places as our closes, with a limited population and a comparatively small mortality, we would continually be led into error were we to decide on their sanitary condition from such data. It is not merely necessary to know the exact number of deaths in such places, but also the *character* of the deaths, that is, the nature of the fatal diseases ought to be ascertained before any comparison is instituted. Accordingly, under each street, &c., will be found, not only the gross mortality, but also the deaths from various diseases, all of more or less interest in determining the place of any locality in the scale of salubrity. Special care was taken with regard to the important class of fevers, the deaths from which were carefully analyzed and classified under four leading types; also with regard to diphtheria, which, as a new scourge, has attracted of late so much attention. Another column was devoted to the number of paupers, and persons dependant on paupers, found scattered over the city. No one can visit our poorer districts without being impressed with the poverty of their inhabitants, and it appeared to me that it would be interesting, as well as important, to be able to compare the mortality of any place with the number of inhabitants in the receipt of parochial relief. The residences of the paupers were obtained from the respective parishes, and to the numbers thus allocated were added,—1st, The dependants on each pauper; 2d, The parochial apprentices; and 3d, Those paupers domiciled in Edinburgh but in receipt of relief from other parishes. By this means the character of the population in our closes and wynds was in some measure ascertained, and aid was afforded in judging of the value of their gross mortality.

In such an inquiry as this, touching the sanitary condition of an ancient metropolis, it was felt that the area of investigation was continually extending in the desire to give as accurate an estimate as possible. Previous writers had not enjoyed the advantages conferred on me by my official position, and these in turn prompted to fresh inquiries. Thus, having availed myself of the population of the last census, and of the special mortality for 1863, I was impressed with the necessity of appealing to other data than those afforded by a single year of average sickness, and I thought it possible, by investigating the history of former epidemics, and ascertaining the localities where their ravages were greatest, to be able to give, as it were, the sanitary history of the new districts, during a long series of years, and at junctures when such localities were clearly put to the test. Our great epidemics of Cholera naturally presented themselves to my mind. But on making inquiry after the records of the first in 1832, I found, to my regret, that none were available, and that, with an efficient staff of medical men, all strenuously and gratuitously working for the public good, no local history of the epidemic had been written, and that the very records of the Cholera Hospitals had disappeared. With regard to the second epidemic in 1849, I was more fortunate, as, in the library of the Royal College of Physicians, I found two large volumes of cholera returns from the city and county. These, to the number of nearly 700, were found to be available; the exact residences of the patients, both in hospital and in private practice, with few exceptions, being specially mentioned.

Edinburgh is notorious for its epidemics of fever, and in the books of the Royal Infirmary careful records are kept of the number of cases in each year, and also of the residences of those admitted to the charity. This latter point has received special attention from the present excellent superintendent, Mr M'Dougal, who was appointed in 1847. The last great epidemic occurred in the years 1847 and 1848, when the patients belonging to the city treated in our Hospital amounted to 6181. These cases of fever will be found, in the tables, to be carefully allocated over the city. For the purpose of comparison, the total admissions of fever cases into the same institution during 1857-58, just ten years after, have been added in a separate column.

DESCRIPTION OF SANITARY DISTRICTS.

1. UPPER NEW TOWN.

Population—10,930.	Death-Rate—17·38. / Birth-Rate—20·58.	Excess of Birth-Rate—3·2.

THIS district comprises that portion of the New Town which was built first, and is now nearly 100 years old. The streets are wide, and the houses, which are of excellent dimensions, were a great improvement on the small confined dwellings of the Old Town. The main streets, viz., Princes Street, George Street, and Queen Street, are now gradually being filled with shops, and the population is thus diminishing. At the same time, the mortality of the district is increased from the number of lodging-houses, peopled by valetudinarians, attracted to the city for medical advice. The intermediate streets, Rose Street and Thistle Street, are inhabited by the better class of workmen; and the mortality of these streets rises to 20.49 per 1000. Were these removed from the district, the total mortality would be lowered by 2 per 1000, and would stand at 15.68. But what is remarkable, there would be no diminution in what may be termed the infantile mortality. It would rise from 68 per 1000 to 69.5. It was to be expected that the infantile mortality in these densely-peopled streets would be higher than that of the entire district. The following table shows that this is not the case:—

	Population 1861.			Mortality 1863.			Death-Rate per 1000.		
	Above 5 years.	Under 5 years.	Total.	Above 5 years.	Under 5 years.	Total.	Above 5 years.	Under 5 years.	Total.
Upper New Town	10,166	764	10,930	138	52	190	13·57	68·	17·38
Side Streets	3,464	390	3,854	53	26	79	15·30	66·66	20·49
Remainder	6,702	374	7,076	85	26	111	12·68	69·5	15·68

The density of the population is 90.3 persons to the acre, and if the vacant spaces of St Andrew Square and Charlotte Square be subtracted, we have 94.8 as the ratio to the inhabited acre. The whole district is thoroughly drained, but in the side streets there is still a great lack of conveniences. The construction of the houses is such as to admit of their easy introduction, and a peremptory order should be issued for this sanitary improvement. At the same time, the adjacent stable lanes should be properly levelled, and the surface drainage improved.

2. LOWER NEW TOWN.

Population—14,024.	Death-Rate—15·47. / Birth-Rate—23·24.	Excess of Birth-Rate—7·77.

The whole of this district lies on the slope of the ridge of the New Town. Although the exposure is northern, and the population is denser than that of the previous district, the mortality, both adult and infantile, is less. This is to be accounted for by the smaller number of invalids from a distance, who undoubtedly swell the mortality of the Upper New Town. Included in this district, to the eastward, is the ancient village of Broughton, now entirely surrounded by houses of the better classes. According to the original plan of this part of the City, a street, with houses for persons of humbler rank, was placed between the more fashionable streets; and in this district there are two which, along with the remains of Broughton village, demand special notice, viz., Jamaica Street and Cumberland Street. The following table shows their population and mortality, and the influence they have in increasing the death-rate of the district:—

	Population 1861.			Mortality 1863.			Death-Rate per 1000.		
	Above 5 years.	Under 5 years.	Total.	Above 5 years.	Under 5 years.	Total.	Above 5 years.	Under 5 years.	Total.
Lower New Town	12,936	1,088	14,024	155	62	217	11·98	56·98	15·47
Side Streets	3,307	420	3,727	54	28	82	16·32	66·66	22·
Remainder	9,629	668	10,297	101	34	135	10·49	50·9	13·11

3. WEST END.

Population—7,748.	Death-Rate—31·88. / Birth-Rate—25·68.	Excess of Death-Rate—6·2.

This district, stretching as it does to the Parliamentary boundary, comprises a large amount of unoccupied land. Of late years, a considerable amount of building has been going on, and the population must have increased in a marked ratio since 1861. Taking the last census returns, however, the density of the population was 22 to the acre, but in the inhabited portions of the district it rises to 44. The large mortality is accounted for by the presence of the St Cuthbert's Poorhouse or Union. If this be subtracted, the death-rate is at once diminished, as is shown in the following statement:—

	Population 1861.			Mortality 1863.			Death-Rate per 1000.		
	Above 5 years.	Under 5 years.	Total.	Above 5 years.	Under 5 years.	Total.	Above 5 years.	Under 5 years.	Total.
West End	7,036	712	7,748	173	74	247	24·58	103·93	31·88
Poorhouse	469	34	503	81	28	109	172·7	823·53	216·7
Remainder	6,567	678	7,245	92	46	138	14·01	67·84	19·04

We have only one intermediate street, strictly so called, viz., William Street, between Melville Street and Coates Crescent. It also requires the same sanitary measure as the corresponding streets in the preceding districts. As to the drainage, the eastern portion is thoroughly drained, and the main lines of sewers being now completed, no difficulty will be experienced in supplying the wants of an extended inhabited area.

4. UPPER WATER OF LEITH.

Population—12,332.	Death-Rate—19·46. / Birth-Rate—33·81.	Excess of Birth-Rate—14·35.

The stream of the Water of Leith runs through the city for a distance of three miles, and a considerable population lines the banks for the greater portion of its course. Above, we have the educational establishments of Donaldson's Hospital, Watson's Hospital, and the Orphan Hospital, and the old village of the Water of Leith; and below, we have the modern suburb of Stockbridge, with a mixed population of the poorer and the richer classes. In marking out the district, I anticipated some diversity of opinion as to its limits. In the present arrangement there are included several streets of the New Town, which are situated on the southern bank of the stream. So much notoriety has been acquired by this district of late years, that I judged it right, in estimating the effects of the Water of Leith on the public health, to include within it the houses on both banks, and I took care that only those streets were taken from the Lower New Town in which the effluvia from the stream had been felt and complained of. Portions of these streets are as close to the stream as streets lower down, such as India Place, which could not be excluded from any arrangement the basis of which was the Water of Leith; and higher up the stream, it was found impossible to divide the village of the Water of Leith into two parts. The district as a whole is thinly peopled, and the inhabited portion of the district forms but a third of the area: the density of the population varies, therefore, from 29 in the acre to 88. The village of the Water of Leith, occupying both banks, with an area of 10 acres, has a density of population of 151·8 to the acre, and a death-rate of 23·72 per 1000. The inhabitants are poor, and the houses are for the most part of imperfect construction, in bad repair, and deficient in sanitary appliances. It is exposed to the full influence of the emanations from the stream, and as the inhabitants are generally poor and imperfectly fed, they offer a good test of the insalubrity of the district. Lower down at Stockbridge we have a very dense population; indeed about India Street it rises to 516·7 in each acre, and a little farther off the average is 336·9 persons to the acre. The drainage goes directly to the Water of Leith—the natural outlet. In the neighbourhood of Dean Street the drainage is imperfect, but this will no doubt be remedied as the operations connected with the drainage scheme of the Water of Leith are advanced.

5. LOWER WATER OF LEITH.

Population—3,866.	Death-Rate—17·58. Birth-Rate—25·86.	Excess of Birth-Rate—8·28.

This is mainly a rural district, with a limited population, chiefly confined to the southern bank of the stream. It contains the remains of the ancient village of Canonmills, in which many of the houses still preserve the wretched character of the poorer class of country dwellings of the last century.

The drainage is satisfactory, having a ready fall towards the Water of Leith. Huntly Street has been excavated, at some points, to such a low level, in the desire manifested by the proprietors to increase the house accommodation, that the under flats are periodically flooded with sewage forced back by the stream. Such underground dwellings should be used simply as cellars. The influence of Canonmills on the mortality of the district is seen in the following Table :—

	Population 1861.			Mortality 1863.			Death-Rate per 1000.		
	Above 5 years.	Under 5 years.	Total.	Above 5 years.	Under 5 years.	Total.	Above 5 years.	Under 5 years.	Total.
Lower Water of Leith	3,504	362	3,866	42	26	68	11·98	71·82	17·58
Canonmills	764	120	884	9	13	22	11·78	108·34	24·88
Remainder	2,740	242	2,982	33	13	46	12·05	53·72	15·42

6. BROUGHTON.

Population—5,672.	Death-Rate—17·63.	Excess of Birth-Rate—7·22.
	Birth-Rate—24·85.	

This district partakes of a similar character to the last. The population is not dense; it is chiefly accumulated towards the municipal boundary in Leith Walk, and also at the opposite side, where the district abuts upon those of the Lower New Town and Calton. But even about Moray Street and Shrub Place, where the houses are inhabited by the poorer classes, the death-rate is only 19 per 1000, and that for children under five years, 26. The district is thoroughly drained.

7. CALTON AND GREENSIDE.

Population—10,984.	Death-Rate—22·12.	Excess of Birth-Rate—8·56.
	Birth-Rate—30·68.	

This district, which takes its name from the Calton Hill, and the ancient village of Greenside, has a large population. It is not, however, densely peopled, except at two points, viz., the sub-districts of Greenside and St James Square. In the one, the ratio is 361 to the acre, in the other it rises to 524.

The following table shows their respective mortality :—

	Population 1861.			Mortality 1863.			Death-Rate per 1000.		
	Above 5 years.	Under 5 years.	Total.	Above 5 years.	Under 5 years.	Total.	Above 5 years.	Under 5 years.	Total.
Whole District	9,739	1,245	10,984	156	87	243	16·	69·87	22·12
St James Square, &c.	2,163	292	2,455	36	23	59	16·64	78·77	24·03
Greenside	2,872	508	3,380	54	36	90	18·83	70·8	26·6

Some objection may be made to the apparently arbitrary separation of St James Square, and neighbouring streets, from the Upper New Town. What weighed with me, however, was the configuration of the ground, and the similarity of the population to that of Greenside. The drainage of both is connected, and is equally unsatisfactory. Until this be remedied, an important sanitary measure, viz., the introduction of conveniences, cannot be enforced. The localities are well suited for it, although some difficulty may be experienced in certain parts of the St James Square sub-district, on account of the excessive sub-division of the houses.

8. ABBEY.

Population—2,237.	Death-Rate—36·65.	Excess of Birth-Rate—17·44.
	Birth-Rate—54·09.	

We now come to four districts, each rising in elevation, by regular gradation. This is well seen in the section at p. 77. The large sewer, the Foul Burn, runs through it for a considerable distance, quite uncovered. Some explanation may thus be afforded of the large mortality, which is remarkable, when we take into account the limited population, its scattered character, and low density. Another fact, however, must not be forgotten, viz., that it is the first district with a poor population with which the miasmata from the celebrated irrigated meadows first come into contact. It is satisfactorily drained.

9. CANONGATE.

Population—12,200.	Death-Rate—31·23.	Excess of Birth-Rate—12·78.
	Birth-Rate—44·01.	

This is a well-defined district, comprising the Canongate, properly so called. It is densely inhabited by a poor population, who crowd the numerous closes. It contains numerous public works (chiefly built on the garden ground of the older houses), including the City Gas Works. There is also an old churchyard, and the district workhouse. The drainage is complete.

10. TRON.

Population—11,636.	Death-Rate—34·55.	Excess of Birth-Rate—7·56.
	Birth-Rate—42·11.	

Here the population is most densely clustered, and the houses are most closely packed. As many of the closes are common to the High Street and Cowgate, portions of both these thoroughfares had to be included. To the north, the district has added to it the large vacant space of the railway station, although the buildings in the district stop abruptly at the Physic Gardens. This space might have been joined either to the Canongate or Calton districts, but as dwelling-houses will never be built upon it, it was considered preferable to secure an uniformity of outline. In estimating the inhabited area of the district, this space has, so to speak, been subtracted, and the density of the population rises to its maximum in Edinburgh, viz., 352.6 to the acre. The drainage is complete. The following is the mortality of its sub-divisions :—

	Population 1861.			Mortality 1863.			Death-Rate per 1000.		
	Above 5 years.	Under 5 years.	Total.	Above 5 years.	Under 5 years.	Total.	Above 5 years.	Under 5 years.	Total.
Cowgate, from South Bridge eastwards	1,236	211	1,447	21	32	53	17·	151·6	36·6
High Street do. do.	5,579	857	6,436	102	138	240	18·3	161·	37·3
Netherbow	668	121	789	4	14	18	6·	115·7	22·8
Leith Wynd and St Mary's Wynd	1,271	216	1,487	17	32	49	13·4	148·1	32·9

11. ST GILES.

Population—15,967.	Death-Rate—28·8.	Excess of Birth-Rate—8.77.
	Birth-Rate—37·57.	

As the Castle had to be included in this district, its outline is somewhat irregular. It was formed, however, on the same plan as the Tron, viz., starting from the ridge of the New Town, and running south as far as College Street. Its population is large, but from its containing numerous vacant spaces, such as the Castle rock and the railway valley in the Princes Street Gardens, the density of its population is much less than that of the two previous districts. But, if we allow for these vacant spaces, the density increases to 234.8 to the acre. The whole district is thoroughly drained. Its worst portion is undoubtedly the upper end of the Cowgate, while the closes in the higher district of the High Street, Lawnmarket, and Castle Hill, improve in character as they rise in elevation. Two sections of this district are given at pp. 44 and 77, the ridge of the High Street determining its centre. The following is the mortality of its sub-divisions :—

	Population 1861.			Mortality 1863.			Death-Rate per 1000.		
	Above 5 years.	Under 5 years.	Total.	Above 5 years.	Under 5 years.	Total.	Above 5 years.	Under 5 years.	Total.
Castlehill	566	71	637	7	10	17	12·4	140·9	26·6
Lawnmarket	1,877	283	2,160	30	31	61	16·	109·5	28·2
High Street to Tron Church	3,467	585	4,052	57	62	119	16·4	106·	29·3
Cowgate to South Bridge	4,415	761	5,176	83	88	171	18·8	115·6	33·

12. GRASSMARKET.

Population—5,227.	Death-Rate—32·52.	Excess of Birth-Rate—14·73.
	Birth-Rate—47·25.	

In this are comprised the West Port and the King's Stables, both outlets from the well-known Grassmarket or Market Place, which gives its name to the district. It is notorious in all our epidemics from the density and character of the population. The main street is wide, and the district is bounded north and south by vacant spaces. The West Port, although narrow, rises rapidly, and the tenements which line it have for the most part a free exposure. The drainage is complete.

The relative mortality is shown below :—

	Population 1861.			Mortality 1863.			Death-Rate per 1000.		
	Above 5 years.	Under 5 years.	Total.	Above 5 years.	Under 5 years.	Total.	Above 5 years.	Under 5 years.	Total.
Grassmarket (proper)	2,276	377	2,653	41	52	93	18·	137·9	35·
West Port	1,933	350	2,283	30	39	69	15·	111·4	30·

13. FOUNTAINBRIDGE.

Population—9,880.	Death-Rate—25·2.	Excess of Birth-Rate—20·34.
	Birth-Rate—45·54.	

This is a level district surrounding the canal, with an outline rather arbitrary. The population and the character of the large proportion of the houses, however, sufficiently mark it out. It is being rapidly built on by houses for the working-classes, and the population must have greatly increased since the last census. The situation, though good, has a most defective drainage; this is chiefly owing to the imperfect levels, and also to the fact that the district is intersected by the Union Canal, below which the chief sewer has to pass. The following is the mortality of its principal thoroughfares:—

	Population 1861.			Mortality 1863.			Death-Rate per 1000.		
	Above 5 years.	Under 5 years.	Total.	Above 5 years.	Under 5 years.	Total.	Above 5 years.	Under 5 years.	Total.
Fountainbridge Street	2,060	337	2,397	41	31	72	19·9	92·	30·
Cowfeeder Row & High Riggs	717	134	851	16	13	29	22·3	97·	34·

14. GEORGE SQUARE AND LAURISTON.

Population—6,593.	Death-Rate—37·46.	Excess of Death-Rate—11·68.
	Birth-Rate—25·78.	

The outline of this district was determined by the formation of the surrounding districts. It contains the ancient village of Portsburgh, and was a suburb of the old town. It is still thinly peopled. It includes the well-known educational establishments of George Heriot and George Watson, and also the City Poorhouse, Greyfriars Churchyard, and the large vacant space of the Meadows. It is thoroughly drained. The district mortality is of course largely increased by the pauper population. The following table shows the effect of deducting the population and mortality of the Poorhouse:—

	Population 1861.			Mortality 1863.			Death-Rate per 1000.		
	Above 5 years.	Under 5 years.	Total.	Above 5 years.	Under 5 years.	Total.	Above 5 years.	Under 5 years.	Total.
George Square and Lauriston	5,959	634	6,593	180	68	248	30·2	107·25	37·61
City Poorhouse	569	52	621	111	19	130	195·08	365·4	209·34
Remainder	5,390	582	5,972	69	49	118	12·8	84·19	19·76

15. NICOLSON STREET.

Population—18,307.	Death-Rate—29·	Excess of Birth-Rate—26·55.
	Birth-Rate—55·55.	

This a well-defined, closely-built-on, and densely-peopled district. In this latter respect it stands second only to the Tron. The character of the population, however, is widely different, and the houses are more moderate in size. The large birth-ratc is accounted for by the presence of the Maternity Hospital. Deducting the births in that institution, the district birth-rate would fall to 38.35, being only 9.35 in excess of the death-rate. The drainage is complete.

16. PLEASANCE AND ST LEONARD.

Population—11,104.	Death-Rate—26·65.	Excess of Birth-Rate—19·99.
	Birth-Rate—46·64.	

This district abuts upon the Queen's Park, and is very open. It has become of late years a favourite site for workmen's houses, and the population has undergone a proportionate increase. Many wretched tenements and courts line the main street, which is no longer the great thoroughfare to the south, and has, at many points, fallen into decay. The comparatively large mortality is thus accounted for.

17. NEWINGTON.

Population—4,955.	Death-Rate—21·79. / Birth-Rate—29·06.	Excess of Birth-Rate—7·27.

This is the oldest and the most densely-peopled of the suburban districts. The rate of mortality is high, from the presence of an old thoroughfare, Causewayside, now fallen into disuse, and which, like the Pleasance, has dragged its population along with it in its downward course. This is shown by the following table:—

	Population 1861.			Mortality 1863.			Death-Rate per 1000.		
	Above 5 years.	Under 5 years.	Total.	Above 5 years.	Under 5 years.	Total.	Above 5 years.	Under 5 years.	Total.
Whole District	4,428	527	4,955	80	28	108	18·	53·13	21·79
Causewayside	1,652	247	1,899	35	16	51	21·19	64·78	26·85
Remainder	2,776	280	3,056	45	12	57	16·21	42 86	18·65

The slope of the district to the south, and its drainage facilities, render it admirably suited for building purposes.

18. GRANGE.

Population—1,886.	Death-Rate—13·78. / Birth-Rate—28·63.	Excess of Birth-Rate—14·85.

This district has been almost entirely formed during the last few years, and its population must have undergone a large increase since the last census in 1861. It presents similar features to the last named, and has now become a township of villas. It is still, however, thinly peopled, and shows a very favourable death-rate, although it contains in its north-eastern corner some houses of old date, and deficient in sanitary appliances. The drainage is satisfactory.

19. MORNINGSIDE.

Population—2,573.	Death-Rate—22·54. / Birth-Rate—15·15.	Excess of Death-Rate—7·39.

This suburb has an unusually high mortality, when we take into account its sparse population and favourable position. At first sight it might be supposed that a sufficient explanation was afforded by its containing a portion of the Royal Asylum for the insane, and also Gillespie's Hospital for the aged; but allowing for this special population and mortality, the death-rate still remains higher than that of the New Town, as is shown below :—

	Population 1861.			Mortality 1863.			Death-Rate per 1000.		
	Above 5 years.	Under 5 years.	Total.	Above 5 years.	Under 5 years.	Total.	Above 5 years.	Under 5 years.	Total.
Whole District	2,378	195	2,573	51	7	58	21·44	35·89	22·54
Asylums	134	...	134	9	...	9	67·16	...	67·16
Remainder	2,244	195	2,439	42	7	49	18·72	35·89	20·09

Nor is the fact accounted for by the presence in the district of such localities as the villages of Morningside, Wrightshouses, and Boroughmuirhead, in the latter of which the population is of the poorer class. By deducting the deaths in these places, the district death-rate is actually increased. The true solution of the difficulty is to be found in the number of invalids who resort to this quarter to escape the biting winds which are so keenly felt in the northern part of the city.

LANDWARD.

Population—2,323.	Death-Rate—41·32. / Birth-Rate—19·8.	Excess of Death-Rate—21·52.

This district contains that portion of the extensive Parish of St Cuthbert, which does not lie within the muncipal boundary. It is of large extent, having an area of 3·127 acres. The Water of Leith flows through it, containing at this portion of its course little sewage, but a large amount of refuse from various manu-

19
20

factories. The mortality of the district is greatly increased by the presence of two lunatic asylums, viz., the large pauper one forming the west division of the Institution at Morningside, and that at Saughtonhall and Balgreen. Deducting this large amount of exceptional mortality, the death-rates fall to 16· per 1000.

	Population 1861.			Mortality 1863.			Death-Rate per 1000.		
	Above 5 years.	Under 5 years.	Total.	Above 5 years.	Under 5 years.	Total.	Above 5 years.	Under 5 years.	Total.
Whole District	2,130	193	2,323	85	11	96	39·9	57·	41·32
Asylums	812	5	817	71	...	71	87·44	...	86·9
Remainder	1,318	188	1,506	14	11	25	10·62	58·5	16·6

It is to be remembered that the population of this district, amounting to 2323, and the attendant mortality, are, in the Reports of the Registrar-General, included under that of Edinburgh, although for what purpose it is difficult to conceive.

DISTRICT MORTALITY FROM DISEASE.

In the year 1863, which we have selected for illustration, there was no unusual mortality, except what was occasioned by Small-pox, which, during the previous year, had visited the city in an epidemic form. The force of the disease was now, however, spent, and it merely left its impress on mortality. This epidemic will be long remembered for the stimulus it gave to legislation on the subject of compulsory vaccination. It is gratifying to reflect that it was owing to the vigorous action taken by the Town Council of Edinburgh, that the attention of the Legislature was called to the subject, and that the Act at present in force was passed through Parliament.

The total number of deaths registered in Edinburgh was 4592. Of these, no fewer than 179 were strangers, who had come to obtain medical and surgical advice, and died in our hospitals, and one death was the result of an accident at our railway station. The remaining 4412 deaths have been classified in the Appendix according to the system of the Registrar-General, and will be found in the succeeding tables to be arranged according to age and sex. They are also distributed under certain leading divisions among the various Sanitary Districts. Some of the diseases demand special notice, while others are of less importance, and it is interesting to observe how the mortality (the percentage of which to the population in 1861 is given) varies in the different districts.

DISEASES OF THE BRAIN.

District		District		District	
George Square and Lauriston	·44	Nicolson Street	·25	Upper Water of Leith	·21
West End	·38	Calton and Greenside	.25	Grange	·21
Morningside	·35	Grassmarket	·24	Newington	·2
Lower Water of Leith	·31	Fountainbridge	·24	Abbey	·18
Landward	·3	St Giles	·22	Pleasance and St Leonard	·18
Tron	·29	Upper New Town	·22	Lower New Town	·15
Canongate	·28			Broughton	·15

In these are not included the deaths from Hydrocephalus or water in the head. The large proportion of paupers who die of diseases of the brain, at once explains why the districts containing our two large Poorhouses should stand highest; and in the Morningside and Landward Districts we have lunatic asylums. The high place of the Lower Water of Leith is quite exceptional.

DISEASES OF THE HEART.

District		District		District	
George Square and Lauriston	·27	Calton and Greenside	·16	West End	·12
Morningside	·23	Fountainbridge	·16	Upper Water of Leith	·12
Upper New Town	·2	Nicolson Street	·16	Broughton	·1
Abbey	·18	Tron	·14	Lower New Town	·06
Canongate	·18	Newington	·14	Lower Water of Leith	·03
Pleasance and St Leonard	·18	St Giles	·13	Grange	...
Grassmarket	·17			Landward	...

It will be interesting, when we have larger data to go upon, to observe the influence exercised by the elevations which our citizens have to ascend before they reach their places of business in the Old and New Town, and such resorts as the University and Courts of Law. The heights are more considerable than is generally supposed, as a reference to the diagram at page 44 will show. The total mortality of the city from these diseases was ·14 per cent. Comparing this with that of other towns with fewer inequalities of position, we find that diseases of the heart caused a mortality in Glasgow of ·11, in Greenock ·11, in Perth ·1, in Leith ·09, and in Paisley ·08 per cent.

DISEASES OF THE CHEST.

Tron	·79	Calton and Greenside	·39	Upper New Town	·18
Abbey	·62	Fountainbridge	·38	Upper Water of Leith	·18
Grassmarket	·61	Nicolson Street	·38	Landward	·17
West End	·54	Pleasance and St Leonard	·36	Lower New Town	·15
George Square and Lauriston	·54	Newington	·28	Lower Water of Leith	·15
St Giles	·52	Broughton	·24	Morningside	·11
Canongate	·43			Grange	·05

Wherever there is poverty, there is generally manifested great inattention to the risk from exposure to cold. At almost all hours of the days or night, we see infants out of doors in our closes during the most inclement weather. This helps to account for the mortality from this class of diseases in the poorer districts, and also in the Poorhouses. St Giles, the highest district in point of elevation, comes next. The exposed situation of the Upper and Lower New Town Districts tells less upon their special mortality than might have been expected. The explanation is to be found in the character of the population. While the mortality of Edinburgh from diseases of the chest was ·38 per cent., it rose as high as ·57 in Glasgow, and ·39 in Greenock, while in the other towns the percentage was as follows:—Leith ·36, Paisley ·33, and Perth ·24 per cent.

PHTHISIS.

Morningside	·42	Canongate	·28	Grassmarket	·21
George Square and Lauriston	·37	Pleasance and St Leonard	·27	Upper New Town	·21
Abbey	·36	Calton and Greenside	·25	Lower Water of Leith	·2
St Giles	·3	Tron	·24	Lower New Town	·19
Nicolson Street	·3	Fountainbridge	·24	Upper Water of Leith	·14
West End	·29	Newington	·22	Landward	·08
Broughton	·28			Grange	...

The mortality from this disease has been separated from that of the class of tubercular diseases, in which it is included by the Registrar-General. The position of Morningside in the table is quite exceptional, depending on the number of invalids, who flock to that suburb during winter and spring. It will be observed that one-half of the districts show a smaller percentage of deaths than that of the whole city, which is ·25. The other towns range themselves in the following order, viz., Greenock ·47, Glasgow ·39, Paisley ·37, Perth ·23, and Leith ·19 per cent.

CROUP.

Grassmarket	·15	Lower Water of Leith	·08	Lower New Town	·02
Canongate	·13	Nicolson Street	·07	Broughton	·02
Tron	·13	West End	·05	Calton and Greenside	·02
George Square and Lauriston	·12	Pleasance and St Leonard	·04	Fountainbridge	·01
St Giles	·11	Morningside	·04	Newington	...
Abbey	·09	Upper New Town	·03	Grange	...
Upper Water of Leith	·08			Landward	...

DIPHTHERIA.

Upper Water of Leith	·21	Nicolson Street	·09	Fountainbridge	·05
Grange	·16	Lower New Town	·07	Upper New Town	·04
Calton and Greenside	·11	Canongate	·07	Grassmarket	·04
West End	·1	Newington	·06	Morningside	·04
Pleasance and St Leonard	·1	Tron	·05	Lower Water of Leith	·03
Abbey	·09	St Giles	·05	Broughton	...
George Square and Lauriston	·09			Landward	...

These two tables are placed together for the purpose of comparison, as it has been supposed that wherever Croup is prevalent, there the mortality from Diphtheria will be found to be the largest. It will be observed, however, that the distribution of the fatal cases of Diphtheria is not affected either by poverty or density of population. With regard to the district of the Grange, it must be remembered that there has been a large increase in the population since 1861.

SCARLATINA.

Fountainbridge	·11	Nicolson Street	·09	Lower New Town	·05
West End	·1	Landward	·08	Tron	·05
George Square and Lauriston	·1	Upper Water of Leith	·06	Morningside	·04
Pleasance and St Leonard	·1	Calton and Greenside	·06	Upper New Town	·03
Grange	·1	St Giles	·06	Lower Water of Leith	·03
Broughton	·09	Grassmarket	·06	Newington	·02
Canongate	·09			Abbey	...

MEASLES.

Tron	·41	St Giles	·13	West End	·04
Grassmarket	·4	Fountainbridge	·09	Newington	·04
Abbey	·31	Upper Water of Leith	·07	Upper New Town	·03
Canongate	·2	Calton and Greenside	·06	Broughton	·02
Pleasance and St Leonard	·2	George Square and Lauriston	·05	Grange	...
Nicolson Street	·15	Lower New Town	·04	Morningside	...
Lower Water of Leith	·13			Landward	...

The uncertain manner in which these diseases affect various localities, is well seen in these tables. It will be noticed that the three first districts in the table of Measles occupy a similar position in that of the Diseases of the Chest.

FEVERS.

Abbey	·22	Calton and Greenside	·11	Grassmarket	·08
Canongate	·16	Nicolson Street	·11	Upper Water of Leith	·06
Grange	·16	Morningside	·11	Pleasance and St Leonard	·06
Tron	·14	St Giles	·09	Upper New Town	·05
Landward	·13	Fountainbridge	·09	Lower Water of Leith	·05
West End	·12	Lower New Town	·08	Newington	·04
Broughton	·12			George Square and Lauriston	·03

The percentage in this table is calculated upon the total mortality from Fevers of all kinds. The poor districts of Abbey, Canongate, and Tron stand first in the list; and it is interesting to observe the gradation in the mortality of the districts in the line of the ridge of the High Street,—the mortality diminishing as the ground rises,—and the districts arrange themselves in the following order—Abbey, Canongate, Tron, St Giles. In the Appendix, Tables Nos. VI. and VIII., the deaths from Fevers have been classified under the four heads of Typhus, Typhoid, Gastric, and Infantile. The mortality from each of these forms of Fever in 1863 are, however, too small in the various sanitary districts, to admit of satisfactory comparison. The following table gives the mortality per cent from Fevers and Diarrhœa and Dysentery, in six Scottish towns:—

FEVER,				DIARRHŒA AND DYSENTERY.			
Leith,	·24	Perth,	·15	Perth,	·1	Paisley,	·07
Greenock,	·22	Paisley,	·11	Greenock,	·08	Edinburgh,	·07
Glasgow,	·17	Edinburgh,	·09	Glasgow,	·07	Leith,	·06

DIARRHŒA AND DYSENTERY.

District	Rate	District	Rate	District	Rate
Tron	·11	Landward	·08	Upper New Town	·05
Grassmarket	·11	St Giles	·07	Lower New Town	·05
George Square and Lauriston	·1	Nicolson Street	·07	Upper Water of Leith	·05
Grange	·1	Calton and Greenside	·06	Lower Water of Leith	·05
West End	·09	Canongate	·06	Pleasance and St Leonard	·05
Abbey	·09	Newington	·06	Broughton	·04
Fountainbridge	·09			Morningside	·04

Abstracting, for the reasons already mentioned, the Districts of George Square and Lauriston, Grange, and West End, the mortality from these diseases is largest in the districts destitute of conveniences, the first nine in order being the worst in this respect in the whole city.

SCROFULOUS DISEASES.

District	Rate	District	Rate	District	Rate
Abbey	·36	St Giles	·19	West End	·11
Nicolson Street	·32	Fountainbridge	·16	Upper Water of Leith	·1
Pleasance and St Leonard	·24	Newington	·16	Upper New Town	·09
George Square and Lauriston	·23	Morningside	·16	Lower New Town	·09
Canongate	·22	Grassmarket	·15	Landward	·08
Calton and Greenside	·19	Lower Water of Leith	·13	Broughton	·05
Tron	·19			Grange	·05

These include Hydrocephalus or water in the head, but not Phthisis, which, on account of its importance, has received separate notice.

PREMATURE DEBILITY.

District	Rate	District	Rate	District	Rate
Grassmarket	·24	George Square and Lauriston	·18	Broughton	·09
Abbey	·22	Lower Water of Leith	·18	Calton and Greenside	·08
Grange	·21	Fountainbridge	·16	Upper New Town	·06
Nicolson Street	·2	Pleasance and St Leonard	·14	Newington	·06
Canongate	·19	West End	·1	Morningside	·04
Tron	·19	Upper Water of Leith	·1	Landward	·04
St Giles	·18			Lower New Town	·03

To the deaths from Premature Debility have been added all deaths under two years which were certified as due to Atrophy. This addition was made on account of the vague manner in which the terms were employed in the death certificates.

EPIDEMICS.

The statistics of a single year, in a city like Edinburgh, are open to the obvious objection that the mortality is too limited to afford accurate data for instituting comparison between such districts as those we have been commenting upon. But Epidemics, whose mission it seems to be to remind us of our sanitary short-comings, attack the population in such numbers, that the lessons they teach admit of being tabulated. The more extended the field of inquiry, the less are the risks of error; and when we deal, not with the deaths alone, but also with the number of persons affected with the special disease, we can look with some degree of confidence to the results. The two following tables illustrate the ravages of the Cholera epidemic of 1848, and the Fever epidemic of 1847-48, calculated on the census returns of 1861:—

CHOLERA EPIDEMIC, 1848.

Grassmarket	1·95	Upper New Town	·18	Lower New Town	·04
St Giles	1·29	Calton and Greenside	·16	West End	·04
Tron	1·16	Nicolson Street	·16	Fountainbridge	·02
Canongate	·72	George Square and Lauriston	·14	Newington	·02
Abbey	·18	Lower Water of Leith	·13	Grange	...
Pleasance and St Leonard	·18	Broughton	·09	Morningside	...
		Upper Water of Leith	·09		

FEVER EPIDEMIC, 1847-48.

Grassmarket	23·91	Fountainbridge	1·2	Lower Water of Leith	·62
Tron	11·34	George Square and Lauriston	1·	Upper Water of Leith	·5
St Giles	11·12	Upper New Town	·8	Broughton	·37
Canongate	5·67	Landward	·78	Grange	·37
Pleasance and St Leonard	1·82	Abbey	·72	Morningside	·31
Calton and Greenside	1·46	West End	·7	Lower New Town	·3
Nicolson Street	1·32			Newington	·21

In both it will be observed that the Grassmarket stands first in order. This is not to be wondered at, when the condition of this district, even in the present day, is looked at; and what it was twenty years ago, when the population was denser, and when the lodging-houses with which this district abounds were imperfectly superintended, can easily be imagined. It has always been the favourite resort of the Irish, and nowhere in the city is their faculty of crowding into small space more characteristically manifested. This explains the high percentage of Fever cases in the great epidemic—that disease being more contagious than Cholera, and spreading like wildfire among a dense population. A good illustration of this is afforded by the district of the Abbey, which is thinly peopled, but the sanitary condition of which is very imperfect. As might have been expected, it exhibits a much higher percentage of cases of Cholera than of Fever. The districts which follow next in order are those in which we have the greatest poverty and the densest population. Fever is never entirely absent from Edinburgh, and its presence would yearly be manifested in the epidemic form, did not the poor enjoy unusual facilities for the early treatment of the sick, and the removal of infected persons to our large Hospital. It is a well known fact—the experiment having again and again been tried in the Infirmary—that if the air become impregnated with fever poison beyond a certain limit, persons coming within its influence fall ready victims to the disease. The history of all our epidemics of Fever has been, that, on the outbreak of the disease, the Irish suffer in the first instance, and the first admissions into the Hospital consist almost entirely of that class. Congregated as they are in lodging-houses, the infection is communicated in all directions, and the disease becomes epidemic. The ordinary inhabitants of the town then begin to suffer, and the Fever having exhausted its victims among the class first attacked, the later admissions consist almost entirely of the Scotch.

Ten years after the Epidemic we have been speaking of, the admissions of persons affected with Fever into the Hospital amounted only to 139, and, for the purpose of comparison, the distribution of the cases throughout the city is here given, and the percentage calculated on the census of 1861. Abstracting the district of George Square and Lauriston, containing the City Poorhouse, which, in a slight epidemic like this, would send many sick applicants to the Hospital, the three districts of St Giles, Tron, and Grassmarket exhibit the highest percentage.

FEVER, 1857–58.

St Giles	·24	Nicolson Street	·04	Upper Water of Leith	·02
Tron	·21	Newington	.04	Canongate	·01
George Square and Lauriston	·14	Lower New Town	·03	West End	·01
Grassmarket	·13	Lower Water of Leith	·03	Abbey	...
Upper New Town	·13	Broughton	·02	Grange	...
Fountainbridge	·06	Calton and Greenside	·02	Morningside	...
Pleasance and St Leonard	·06			Landward	...

DENSITY OF THE POPULATION.

THE density of the population had never been ascertained until, with the assistance of my colleague Mr Macpherson, the area within the Parliamentary Boundary was carefully measured. This was found to contain 4191 acres, and taking the population as at 1861, to give a ratio of 40 persons to the acre. A reference to the map will show, that within the area in question, which was intended to allow for the expansion of the city in all directions, for many years to come, there are large unoccupied spaces, and that the Calton Hill and a large portion of Arthur's Seat are also included. This must be borne in mind, when comparing Edinburgh with other towns whose limits are more compact, and which do not admit of much increase in the number of the inhabitants. If the 243 acres of Arthur's Seat be deducted, the density of the population rises to 42.5. Few data exist for comparing this with other capitals; but the Registrar-General gives the following as the ratio of some of the principal cities of the empire, corrected to 1865:—

Liverpool (borough) ...	93·3	Birmingham (borough) ...	41·9
Glasgow (city)	83·7	London	38·7
Manchester (city)	79·1	Bristol (city)	34·5
Dublin (city)	66·9	Salford (borough)	21·4
Edinburgh	42.5	Leeds (borough)	10·4

Such a table at once shows us the caution necessary in instituting a comparison between towns as to their relative density of population. Believing, as we do, that the crowding together of human beings has a greater effect upon the rate of mortality than is generally supposed,—it is of importance to see that the data submitted for comparison have some points of similarity. Liverpool and Glasgow, for example, have of late years undergone rapid extension, and their area is now almost entirely covered with houses. Their density of population cannot be satisfactorily compared with that of Edinburgh, where the inhabitants are distributed, so to speak, over a widely-extended area, a large portion of which consists of hilly grounds and country fields. By abstracting these, the ratio of Edinburgh would rise as high as 60 persons to the acre. It is only by determining the area and population of special districts that a correct scale of density of population can be formed. The new sanitary districts of Edinburgh were accordingly carefully measured, and their population ascertained by allocating to each street, &c., its population as determined at the census of 1861. The results are given in the following table:—

Tron	314·5	Fountainbridge	95·	West End	22·1
Nicolson Street	286·	Upper New Town	90·3	Newington	21·2
Grassmarket	237·6	Calton and Greenside	39·	Abbey	20·3
Canongate	206·7	George Square and Lauriston	36·2	Grange	7·5
Pleasance and St Leonard	132·2	Upper Water of Leith	29·6	Lower Water of Leith	7·2
St Giles	121·8	Broughton	28·8	Morningside	4·1
Lower New Town	95·4			Landward	·7

Many of these districts include large unoccupied spaces. This is specially the case with those lying on the outskirts. And it was believed that a truer estimate of the relative density of population would be gained by omitting these in the measurement of the area, which, thus restricted, might be termed the inhabited area. In fact, the same measure was applied to these districts for the purpose of comparison among themselves, as was found to be necessary for ascertaining the true place of Edinburgh in a scale which included other large towns. The results will be found in a special column in Table VII., p. 56 of the Appendix.

In the 25th annual report of the Registrar-General, we have the area and population given of the registration sub-districts throughout England, with the exception of those of Liverpool, which is to be regretted, as Liverpool is the most densely-peopled city in the empire, and it would have been interesting to have known the ratio in its poorest localities. On looking over the list, the sub-districts which attract attention, by their density of population, are those of the Metropolis; and a few have been selected along with those which compose the area of the city of London proper. The rate of mortality and the birth-rate per 1000 of the population are calculated for 1862, and the districts are arranged in the order of their density of population.

District.	Area in Statute Acres.	Population 1861.	Proportion of Population to each Acre.	Death-Rate.	Birth-Rate.	Birth-Rate in excess of Death-Rate.	Death-Rate in excess of Birth-Rate.
Whitecross Street (St Luke's)	33	14,778	447·8	26·59	31·8	5·21	...
Berwick Street (St James', Westminster)	25	10,607	424·3	20·55	36·47	15·92	...
St Andrew, Holborn W. (Holborn)	33	12,947	392·3	35·07	34·6	...	·47
St Ann, Soho (Strand)	53	17,426	328·8	18·94	31·68	12·74	...
St Giles, South-West (St Giles)	63	19,483	309·2	38·34	39·21	·87	...
St Clement Danes (Strand)	52	15,207	292·4	31·17	32·55	1·38	...
London City, North-East	92	11,544	125·5	18·62	23·13	4·51	...
Do. do. North-West	72	9,020	125·3	12·75	15·74	2·99	...
Do. do. South-West	67	7,762	115·8	17·78	25·89	8·11	...
Do. do. South	100	8,570	85·7	18·2	25·8	7·6	...
Do. do. South-East	103	8,659	84·	15·	20·56	5·56	...
Total for London City	434	45,555	104·9	16·55	22·15	5·6	

The first four in the list are much more densely peopled than any of the sanitary districts of Edinburgh; and, when the peculiar house accommodation in London is taken into account, it is evident that the small self-contained houses there must be very closely packed. It will be observed that the rate of mortality in these districts does not rise and fall with the density of population. Much of course depends on the poverty of the inhabitants, and where there is destitution along with overcrowding, as in St Giles', the death-rate is high. In other districts, as St Luke's and Westminster, there are public institutions, viz., lunatic asylums and prisons, which largely increase the population, but do not affect the mortality in a corresponding degree. In some of the sub-districts of Edinburgh, the density of population has been determined, and similar results are obtained on comparing their respective rates of mortality.

	Proportion of Population to each Acre.	Mortality.		
		Above 5 years.	Under 5 years.	Total.
Tron, between North Bridge and St Mary's Wynd ...	646	16·95	184·59	39·26
India Place, &c.	553	13·7	106·25	26·33
Greenside	524	18·83	70·8	26·6
St James' Square, &c.	361	16·64	78·77	24·03
Dean Street, &c.	336	17·78	69·07	25·02
Canongate, between St Mary's Wynd and St John St.	331	14·76	122·34	29·47
Village of Water of Leith	151	16·43	62·5	23·72

The districts in which there is the greatest amount of poverty, and where the houses are of a very imperfect description, are undoubtedly the first and the two last in the list. In the Tron sub-district, the density of the population and the rate of mortality are at their maximum. The district next in order, so far as the mortality is concerned, is that of the Canongate; but here the population is much less dense. The inhabitants most comfortably housed are to be found in India Place and Dean Street, but notwithstanding these advantages, the closeness with which the people are packed leads to unhealthiness, and raises the mortality. It has been plausibly urged that this high rate of mortality is produced by their proximity to the Water of Leith; but this explanation is seen to be erroneous when the sanitary condition of the Village of the Water of Leith is inquired into. There the population is of a poor class,—for the most part in miserable cottages, and constantly subjected to the effluvia from the stream, and from mill-lades which pass within a few feet of the dwellings; yet, the rate of mortality is lower than in either of the two districts last named, although there is no comparison in their sanitary condition. The true explanation will be found in the relative density of the population. And this also accounts for the singular fact that the infantile mortality is comparatively low in the village of the Water of Leith, where the children under five years constitute one-sixth of the total population, while in the sub-district of India Place, where the infantile mortality is very high, the population of children under five years is one-seventh.

The only satisfactory method, however, of showing the remarkable manner in which the poorer inhabitants live crowded together in their lofty tenements is by taking a few examples from some of the sanitary districts. From St Giles' I have selected some well-known specimens. The first in the list, Gowanloch's Land, has just been demolished on account of its insecure condition. It occupied an airy situation in the High Street, and its rooms were spacious and well ventilated. The three next occur in one of the worst parts of the city, viz., the Cowgate. In all epidemics they were well known as furnishing to our Hospital a very large number of sick. No. 8 Cowgatehead is inhabited by a better class than that which swarms in the Mealmarket Stairs, which for filth, poverty, and overcrowding are not surpassed in the City.

GOWANLOCH'S LAND, High Street.

	Rooms.	Families.	Children under 5.	Adults.	Total.	Sinks.	Water Closets.
First Flat	9	7	7	21	28	1	...
Second Flat.........	7	5	3	15	18	...	...
Third Flat	7	4	3	12	15	...	1
Fourth Flat.........	8	5	...	12	12	1	...
Fifth Flat	9	6	4	15	19	...	1
Sixth Flat	9	7	6	19	25	1	...
Seventh Flat	9	4	2	12	14	...	1
Eighth Flat.........	2	1	...	3	3	...	...
Total...........	60	39	25	109	134	3	3

COWGATEHEAD, 8 Cowgate.

	Rooms.	Families.	Children under 5.	Adults.	Total.	Sinks.	Water Closets.
First Flat	12	2	...	31	31	2	1
Second Flat.........	13	8	4	31	35	...	...
Third Flat	12	8	4	32	36	...	...
Fourth Flat.........	16	14	11	39	50	...	...
Fifth Flat	7	6	5	22	27	...	...
Total...........	60	38	24	155	179	2	1

Middle Mealmarket Stair.

	Rooms.	Families.	Children under 5.	Adults.	Total.	Sinks.	Water Closets.
First Flat	12	12	10	39	49	...	...
Second Flat.........	11	11	14	40	54	...	...
Third Flat	12	12	10	45	55	...	...
Fourth Flat.........	12	12	11	45	56	...	...
Fifth Flat	12	9	6	28	34	...	...
Total.........	59	56	51	197	248	...	...

Old Mealmarket Stair.

	Rooms.	Families.	Children under 5.	Adults.	Total.	Sinks.	Water Closets.
First Flat	7	3	4	25	29	...	...
Second Flat.........	6	5	1	18	19	...	...
Third Flat	7	7	6	23	29	...	...
Fourth Flat.........	11	7	3	30	33	...	...
Total.........	31	22	14	96	110	...	...

The following houses are situated in the district of Tron, which contains the densest population in the city. Two are to be found in closes, and the third in the main street of the Cowgate. The tenements in Blackfriars Wynd and in the Cowgate are comparatively modern structures.

58 Blackfriars Wynd, High Street.

	Rooms.	Families.	Children under 5.	Adults.	Total.	Sinks.	Water Closets.
First Flat	12	7	5	28	33	1	...
Second Flat.........	13	7	10	20	30	1	...
Third Flat	12	7	4	27	31	1	...
Fourth Flat.........	12	7	8	28	36	...	...
Total.........	49	28	27	103	130	3	...

ELPHINSTON'S LAND, Carrubber's Close.

	Rooms.	Families.	Children under 5.	Adults.	Total.	Sinks.	Water Closets.
Ground Flat	4	4	5	15	20	2	...
First Flat	6	2	4	9	13	...	...
Second Flat.........	...	...	...	...	...	...	...
Third Flat	8	7	4	20	24	1	1
Fourth Flat.........	10	8	7	21	28	2	2
Fifth Flat	10	8	4	23	27	2	2
Sixth Flat	7	6	4	19	23	2	2
Total............	45	35	28	107	135	9	7

SCOT'S LAND, 341 Cowgate.

	Rooms.	Families.	Children under 5.	Adults.	Total.	Sinks.	Water Closets.
First Flat	9	8	8	25	33	...	...
Second Flat.........	11	8	4	22	26	...	...
Third Flat	11	8	10	24	34	...	...
Fourth Flat.........	10	7	8	26	34	...	...
Fifth Flat	7	6	6	16	22	...	...
Back Land	5	5	6	15	21	...	...
Total............	53	42	42	128	170	...	...

The Canongate supplies us with four examples. Purves' Land was found, some years ago, to be in an insecure state, and the top storey was removed, and the walls were repaired. The population of Burns' Land is given, as the house is modern, and of small size, and its inhabitants belong to the working-classes. It has a free ventilation. In Birtley Buildings, and in the solitary instance taken from the district of Grassmarket—viz., Crombie's Land in West Port—we have marked specimens of what will become of our courts and closes, should proprietors be allowed to run up skeleton houses of the most rickety description and faulty sanitary construction. A minute description of these tenements would be tedious, from the sameness of the details. Both are inhabited by the very poor; but Birtley Buildings is a refuge for some of the worst characters in the town. Each room is small and overcrowded; the passages are dark and ill-ventilated. On all sides you have vice in its most repulsive forms. With an Inspector of Buildings, armed with sufficient powers, such monstrosities in dwellings for the poor would never have been permitted. Tried by any standard, they are faulty in the extreme. A similar plea cannot be urged in their behalf as may be put forth for older houses in the city, that at first they were inhabited by a better class, and were not overcrowded, but have sunk gradually into their present condition. Birtley Buildings and Crombie's Land, on the other hand, are modern structures, built specially for the poor, and with an eye to a large rental; hence the small ill-ventilated rooms, and their great deficiency in sanitary comforts.

Hope's Land, 268 Canongate.

	Rooms.	Families.	Children under 5.	Adults.	Total.	Sinks.	Water Closets.
First Flat	5	5	6	12	18	...	...
Second Flat...	10	5	3	12	15	...	...
Third Flat	9	9	4	22	26	...	...
Fourth Flat.........	4	4	5	15	20	...	...
Fifth Flat	4	4	3	13	16	...	...
Sixth Flat	4	2	2	6	8	...	...
Total...........	36	29	23	80	103	...	...

Purves' Land, 327 Canongate.

	Rooms.	Families.	Children under 5.	Adults.	Total.	Sinks.	Water Closets.
First Flat	9	9	7	31	38	1	...
Second Flat.........	10	9	9	28	37	1	...
Third Flat	7	5	4	15	19	...	...
Fourth Flat.........	6	6	7	18	25	...	...
Total...........	32	29	27	92	119	2	...

Burns' Land, North Back of Canongate.

	Rooms.	Families.	Children under 5.	Adults.	Total.	Sinks.	Water Closets.
First Flat	7	3	3	15	18	...	...
Second Flat.........	9	5	8	18	26	...	...
Third Flat	9	5	3	21	24	...	...
Total...........	25	13	14	54	68	...	...

Birtley Buildings, Mid-common Close, Canongate.

	Rooms.	Families.	Children under 5.	Adults.	Total.	Sinks.	Water Closets.
First Flat	8	8	2	17	19	...	...
Second Flat.........	8	8	11	33	44	...	...
Third Flat	10	8	5	27	32	...	...
Fourth Flat.........	9	9	6	24	30	...	...
Total...........	35	33	24	101	125	...	...

DISTRICT OF GRASSMARKET.

Crombie's Land, 50 West Port.

	Rooms.	Families.	Children under 5.	Adults.	Total.	Sinks.	Water Closets.
Street Flat	6	3	4	8	12	...	...
Second Flat.........	11	8	4	26	30	...	...
Third Flat	10	9	8	20	28	...	...
Total	27	20	16	54	70	...	...

The districts already named furnish the best examples of overcrowded tenements; but in all parts of the city, owing to the peculiar construction of the houses, we find, wherever we have a poor population, a great tendency to overcrowding. This is well exemplified in the two following examples :—

The first is taken from the district of Nicolson Street, to the south, and the second from that of Calton and Greenside, and is situated in the New Town. The latter is a modern erection, built on the slope of a hill, with rooms of good ventilating proportions; but the separate houses have undergone repeated subdivisions, until the present state of overcrowding has been attained.

No. 3 East Richmond Street.

	Rooms.	Families.	Children under 5.	Adults.	Total.	Sinks.	Water Closets.
First Flat	10	7	5	30	35	...	...
Second Flat.........	12	10	10	31	41	...	...
Third Flat	13	8	6	29	35	...	...
Fourth Flat.........	12	11	7	35	42	...	...
Fifth Flat	9	7	1	23	24	...	...
Total...........	56	43	29	148	177	...	...

No. 23 St James Street.

	Rooms.	Families.	Children under 5.	Adults.	Total.	Sinks.	Water Closets.
First Flat	13	10	11	38	49	2	1
Second Flat.........	12	9	18	36	54	2	...
Third Flat	12	10	2	24	26	2	...
Fourth Flat.........	13	11	9	27	36	2	...
Fifth Flat	13	10	8	27	35	2	...
Sixth Flat	7	6	4	16	20	1	...
Total...........	70	56	52	168	220	11	1

When any disease is epidemic, these houses speedily become infected; and it is not until the special ailment slowly exhausts itself by attacking all the persons liable to suffer from it, that such tenements may be said to be free from sickness. This is a slow and uncertain process, and should it be going on at Whitsunday, when so many occupants change their houses, it may be indefinitely prolonged.

With reference to these statistics, it must be remembered that, with the exception of Burns' Land and Birtley Buildings, the lowest storey is occupied by shops, and is not included in the enumeration of the flats, which commences with the one above the ground-floor. We have already seen that in Edinburgh the rule is amply borne out that the greater the amount of overcrowding in population, the larger is the mortality; and the same truth is taught by this analysis of special tenements. It becomes, therefore, an interesting question to determine the mortality of their inhabitants in such a year as 1863, characterised by no epidemic or the presence of unusual sickness. The following table supplies the requisite information, not merely as regards the gross mortality, but also as to the character of the various causes of death.

It is certainly remarkable that, of the 163 cases of death from Fever, not one occurred in these the poorest and most crowded houses in Edinburgh, and that only one death took place from diarrhœa, and this is specially noted as having been connected with dentition. Of course the overcrowded state of their population renders them hot-beds of disease in epidemic years, and when Cholera and Fever were raging, these houses attained an unenviable notoriety. Were not unusual facilities presented in Edinburgh—the seat of a medical school—for the speedy treatment of the sick, and the removal of cases of infectious disease to our noble charity, the Royal Infirmary, a single case of fever allowed to run its course unwatched in such tenements would spread contagion on all sides, and the district mortality would be greatly increased.

OVERCROWDED TENEMENTS, AND THEIR VITAL STATISTICS.

NAME.	Height in feet above the sea.	Area in Square Yards.	Population in 1864.			Mortality in 1863.			Brain.	Heart.	Chest.	Abdomen.	Phthisis.	Croup.	Diphtheria.	Measles.	Hooping-Cough.	Scrofulous Diseases.	Diarrhœa and Dysentery.	Old Age, above 60.	Premature Debility.	Other Causes.
			Above 5 years.	Under 5 years.	Total.	Above 5 years.	Under 5 years.	Total.														
Gowanloch's Land	287	292	109	25	134	2	2	4	...	...	1	...	1	...	...	...	...	1	...	...	...	1
8 Cowgatehead	211	365	155	24	179	4	2	6	1	1	1	2	1	...	...	...	...	...	...	...	...	...
Middle Meal Market Stair	216	400	197	51	248	3	5	8	...	...	1	...	...	1	...	2	...	2	...	...	...	2
Old Mealmarket Stair	216	300	96	14	110	4	3	7	...	...	2	...	3	...	...	...	2	...	...	...	...	...
56 Blackfriars' Wynd	200	250	103	27	130	1	1	2	...	...	1	...	...	...	...	...	...	...	...	...	...	1
23 Carrubber's Close	230	353	107	28	135	3	2	5	...	...	3	...	...	...	...	1	...	...	...	1	...	...
Scot's Land, Cowgate	189	250	128	42	170	6	3	9	...	...	2	2	1	...	...	2	...	...	...	...	1	1
Hope's Land, Canongate	210	230	80	23	103	2	1	3	...	...	...	...	1	...	...	...	...	1	...	...	...	1
Purves' Land, do.	212	352	92	27	119	...	4	4	...	...	1	1	...	...	...	...	...	1	...	...	1	...
Burns' Land, do.	133	176	54	14	68	...	1	1	...	...	...	...	...	1	...	...	...	...	...	...	...	...
Birtley Buildings, do.	184	254	101	24	125	1	6	7	1	...	1	...	...	...	...	2	...	1	1	...	...	1
Crombie's Land, West Port	227	167	54	16	70	1	2	3	...	1	...	...	...	...	...	...	...	...	...	...	...	2
3 East Richmond Street	253	285	148	29	177	1	2	3	...	...	1	1	...	...	...	...	...	1	...	...	...	...
23 St James Street	205	438	168	52	220	3	3	6	1	...	...	1	1	...	...	1	...	1	1	...	...	...

LODGING-HOUSES.

Another circumstance must be noticed as aiding in preventing such disasters, viz., the existence of licensed Lodging-Houses, and their careful superintendence by the Police. In Table XII. of the Appendix, p. 61, I have given a statement of the number of these in the various sanitary districts. It will be observed that they exist in largest numbers in the very localities which call for their presence,—the poorest and most densely-crowded districts. The attention of the authorities was early directed to the important subject of regulating the number of the inmates of such houses, and of putting them under the surveillance of the Police. The Lodging-houses were registered and inspected. Their ventilation and cleanliness were attended to by special rules, as to when the windows were to be opened, and as to the sweeping and washing of the floors, and the whitewashing of the walls of the apartments. It was also specially provided, "that in case of fever, cholera, or any other contagious, infectious, or epidemic disease occurring in such Lodging-house, whether to any lodger or to any other person residing or being in such house, the keeper of such house who shall neglect or omit forthwith to give notice thereof to the Superintendent of Police, in order that the nature of the complaint of such person may be ascertained, shall, for every such neglect and omission, be liable in a penalty of not exceeding forty shillings." Since 1848 these houses have been regularly visited by the Police, especially at night, to see that the number of lodgers allowed was not exceeded. At present, and for some years back, they have been under the special superintendence of the Senior Lieutenant of Police, and I cannot but ascribe much of the immunity from epidemic disease enjoyed by the poorer districts of the town to the admirable manner in which the regulations have been enforced.

HOUSES FOR THE WORKING-CLASSES.

The condition of the poor and their miserable dwellings also engaged the attention of the charitable in Edinburgh, and the movement which originated in London, that centre of all noble schemes, for erecting suitable houses for the working-classes, extended to this city. In 1851, the first block of houses was built, and named Ashley Buildings, after the nobleman who had taken such a prominent part in the operations of the Metropolitan Association. No better site could have been obtained for the structure in question. It was placed in the Tron district, in which over-crowding prevails to a great extent, and on all sides it was surrounded by decaying houses, tenanted by the poor. It not only afforded to the industrious workman a greatly improved habitation, but, from its situation, formed an example to surrounding proprietors and tenants of the manner in which such houses should be built and kept in a permanent state of cleanliness. To secure a site, old property had to be removed, and thus, while benefiting the working-classes, the Association directly ameliorated the condition of the Old Town by the erection of houses in its midst, built according to the most approved sanitary plans.

TABULAR STATEMENT of HOUSES for the WORKING-CLASSES, ACCOMMODATION, &c., &c.

No.	NAMES OF HOUSES.	Where situated.	Date of Erection.	Total Cost.	Number of Families.	Lowest Rent.	Accommodation afforded for Lowest Rent.						
							Rooms.	Closets.	Kitchen.	Water-Closets.	Water.	Gas.	Green or Court.
1	Ashley Buildings	Tron	1851	£5,100	70	£3 12 0	1	...	...	$\frac{1}{3}$	1	1	1
2	Pilrig do.	Broughton	1851	6,800	62	5 12 0	1	1	1	$\frac{1}{3}$	1	1	1
3	Chalmers' do.	Fountainbridge	1855	3,600	29	7 0 0	1	1	1	1	1	1	1
4	Dr Begg's do.	Abbey	1860	6,000	66	6 10 0	1	1	1	$\frac{1}{2}$	1	1	1
5	Milne's do.	Tron	1860	2,356	20	8 10 0	1	2	1	1	1	1	1
6	Rosemount do.	West End	1860	11,780	96	7 0 0	1	1	1	1	1	1	1
7	Croall's do.	Abbey	1860	3,600	30	5 5 0	1	...	1	1	1	1	1
8	Patriot hall do.	Upper Water of Leith	1861	4,800	42	9 15 0	2	...	1	1	1	1	1
9	View Craig do.	Pleasance and St Leonard	1861–2	15,000	110	7 5 0	1	1	1	1	1	1	...
10	Prince Albert do.	Do.	1863	19,200	132	9 10 0	1	1	1	1	1	1	1
11	Blackwood's do.	Abbey	1863	3,000	26	7 7 0	1	1	1	$\frac{1}{2}$	1	1	1
12	Prospect street do.	Pleasance and St Leonard	1863	3,600	74	3 0 0	1	...	...	$\frac{1}{5}$	1	1	1
13	Gillis' do.	Nicolson Street	1863	1,800	12	10 0 0	1	1	1	1	1	1	...
14	Clermiston do.	Canongate	1863	1,750	20	7 0 0	2	...	1	$\frac{1}{2}$	1	1	1
15	Rae's do.	Pleasance and St Leonard	1864	2,500	26	6 6 0	1	...	1	1	1	1	1
16	Gladstone do.	Canongate	1864	2,000	32	3 0 0	1	...	1	...	1	1	1

A reference to the preceding table will show that, since 1851, much has been done in all quarters of the city to improve the dwellings of the working-classes, and to relieve the overcrowded Old Town districts. The lowest rents of these houses are there given, and the accommodation afforded. It must be remembered that but few families in each of the buildings are accommodated at the lowest rent; and it may be stated generally that the average rent in the whole of these buildings is from £6, 10s. to £7. Such a sum is a good index of the class which has been benefited by such associations. It was that of the well-to-do industrious workman, who, how much soever he may have suffered from the imperfect houses in the Old Town, could not fail to be an acquisition to the neighbourhood in which he lived, from his notions of cleanliness and propriety. When attracted elsewhere for a dwelling, a vacuum was left, so to speak, in the Old Town, which was quickly filled up by the freemasonry of poverty; and without exaggeration it may be affirmed that the locality was left worse than it was before. Rents necessarily fell, and a poorer population crowded in to supply the places of the former inhabitants. That the working-classes, as a body, have been greatly benefited, there can be no doubt. A visit to almost any of the buildings in the list will convince the most sceptical on this point. But the question is forced upon us—Is a class, which can afford to pay such rents, not capable of being provided with suitable accommodation, on the ordinary principle of supply and demand. Their wants are soon known, and the enterprising builder will supply them fully as well as any association, the members of which, for the most part, look for an adequate return for the money they have expended. The poorer workmen cannot afford to pay the rents just named, and on all sides I have heard complaints that the houses are of a better class than they could afford to occupy. Again, there is the very poor, consisting of the day labourer and the outworker on farms, &c. Such cannot help themselves, and are helpless in a city like Edinburgh. Had societies been formed to assist the poor, by improving their existing houses, erecting more suitable ones at such a rent as they could afford to pay, and, by various agencies, teaching them the plainest lessons of external cleanliness in their houses and stairs, and how to prepare their food in such a way as to secure economy, with the greatest amount of nourishment, they would have benefited at once the lowest classes of the community, and also the poorest districts of the city. A noble example was shown by Dr Foulis, years ago, of what was required, and the best method of helping the poor and the poorer localities. He took a close in the Grassmarket, gutted it, cleaned it thoroughly, and repaired it, in no expensive manner, but in such a way, as to afford comfortable housing for the poor. This close, the Warden's Close, No. 139, has thus been reclaimed. It is placed under such supervision, that the inhabitants are taught cleanliness, and should a new comer not be susceptible of the lesson, after patient trial, he quickly leaves. To this hour, the close in question stands out an oasis amidst the wretchedness and filth that is to be met with in the other closes of that well-known locality. Had this example been followed by our philanthropic citizens who have subscribed so handsomely to the various building schemes, some of the worst localities in the Old Town might have been renovated, crime and pauperism rooted out from them, and the workmen comfortably housed in situations possessing a good exposure and a healthy site. A more admirable situation for such buildings than the district of the Canongate, can hardly be seen anywhere, whether altitude, exposure, or drainage facilities be taken into consideration. Again, by erecting suitable houses, intended for workmen, in good localities, within easy distance of the centre of the town, less time is spent in marketing, and fewer temptations are placed in the path of the workman who may have, on his way homeward, to run the gauntlet of a dozen gin-palaces, and be tempted to delay his return. Were he near his household, the attractions of his home might prove stronger than the call of pleasure. On a wet night, surrounded by companions, he may be unpleasantly reminded that before he reaches his fireside, he has to leave the lighted cheerful town behind. I have known of instances where such temptations proved too strong.

PAUPERISM.

One important element in our overcrowded population must not be overlooked, and that is the amount of pauperism which it contains. In addition to the large number of paupers dependent on the three city parishes, viz., the City Parish proper, St Cuthbert's, and Canongate, we have those belonging to other parishes, but resident in Edinburgh. At p. 60 of Appendix, Table XI., these have been distributed through the various sanitary districts, and the percentage of paupers to the population as at 1861, given in a separate column. It must be remembered, however, with reference to these tables, that three of the districts contain workhouses, viz., West End, St Cuthbert's Workhouse; Canongate, the Canongate Workhouse; and George Square and Lauriston, the City Workhouse; and of course the population of these houses swells the amount of pauperism in each of these districts. The St Cuthbert's Workhouse contains not only persons belonging to Edinburgh, a large portion of which is within the parish, but also persons from an extensive rural area. Neither in the case of St Cuthbert's nor in that of the City Poorhouse has it been possible to allocate the city paupers to their former residences before they became inmates of these institutions. As regards the Canongate, this was of inferior importance, as the sanitary district of that name pretty closely corresponds in extent and configuration to the parochial boundary. It will be observed how readily pauperism gravitates to the poorest districts, and where, as in Canongate, Tron, St Giles, and Grassmarket, we have the greatest overcrowding and the most deficient house accommodation, we have also superadded pauperism and its attendant evils, mental depression, imperfect nourishment, scanty clothing, and in too many instances, intemperance. The large mortality of these districts is amply accounted for, and it is not to be wondered at if in epidemics of cholera and fever, as shown by the same table, the percentages of cases should be universally high. Were the poorest and most degraded of the class removed to better quarters, I am convinced that a great improvement would be effected in our Old Town. So long as there is a population with such a percentage of pauperism scattered through it, the best sanitary regulations are disregarded, and it is useless to enforce them by the strong arm of the law. The pittances that are given to paupers through the proverbial economy of boards, representing the ratepayers of our city, are only intended to allow of life being maintained at a legal flicker, and by no means at a steady flame. Pauperism must be made distasteful, and in the attempt to force applicants to work for their own support, injustice must be done to many. This is inevitable from the present working of the system in Edinburgh, and the limited accommodation afforded in our workhouses. But to speak to the pauper poor of the necessity of cleanliness and the dangers attendant on overcrowding, when they have hardly enough of support to keep soul and body together, is a mere waste of words. The parties truly responsible are the Parochial Boards, who are charged with the support of their poor, and who should take care, if they cannot afford space to accommodate them within their own premises, that the apartments occupied by these dependants be kept decent, clean, and wholesome. Were a large proportion of the poor drafted into a properly-constructed Poorhouse, outside the parliamentary boundary, a double benefit would be conferred at once on the densely-peopled districts of our city, and also on the paupers themselves. It is well known that in too many instances persons claiming parochial relief will submit to the greatest privations rather than allow themselves to be immured within those barrack-like buildings, where they find themselves in the midst of town life, yet debarred from enjoying it. The sounds they hear constantly remind them of their bondage, and the confined dismal spaces allowed to the sexes as airing-grounds help to deepen the feeling. To live huddled together in squalid apartments, and subsist on the poorest fare, is to them paradise in comparison. But had they free scope in fresh country air, and could they be engaged in healthy out-of-door exercise, surrounded with all the enlivening influences of a country life in the neighbourhood of a large town, I am convinced that residence in a workhouse would not be dreaded as it is at present, while the legitimate application of the labour-test would thin the ranks of pseudo-paupers, and secure for parochial relief its legitimate objects. The pauper population would also gain in health. As it is, whenever a pauper in ordinary health enters a workhouse, his chances of life are increased. This is accounted for by the regularity of hours, the dieting, and the careful discipline. But these important hygienic advantages would all be increased in value in a country situation. To effect this highly important change in our parochial administration, as speedily and thoroughly as possible, it would be highly desirable that our three local boards, laying aside all rivalry and jealousy, should combine, and thus not only effect a saving on the general rate, but, at the same time, inaugurate the sanitary improvement of Edinburgh, and increase the comfort and health of the paupers.

INFLUENCE OF ELEVATION ON HEALTH.

An interesting question connected with the distribution of the population is the heights above the sea-level at which the inhabitants are found grouped in the largest numbers, and the effect of elevation on disease, whether sporadic or epidemic. A reference to the section of the city on page 44 will show the remarkable inequalities of the ground on which Edinburgh is built; and, in the following table, the whole of the population within the Parliamentary Boundary, numbering 168,121 persons, has been arrayed in successive elevations from 50 up to 450, according to their residence. In parallel columns the mortality for the year has been distributed in a similar manner, as also that caused by Fever and Diphtheria during 1863, and two epidemics of Fever and Cholera, along with the calculated results per 1000.

32

Height in feet above the sea.	Population 1861.	Total Mortality 1863.	Special Mortality 1863.		Epidemics.		Death-Rate per 1000.			Rate of Cases per 1000.	
			Fever.	Diphtheria.	Fever 1847-8.	Cholera 1848.	Total Mortality 1863.	Fever 1863.	Diphtheria 1863.	Fever Epidemic 1847-8.	Cholera Epidemic 1848.
400—450	854	15	1	...	...	...	17·54	1·17	...	...	...
300—350	3,168	63	2	1	31	12	19·88	·63	·31	9·78	3·78
250—300	30,740	915	24	19	942	111	29·73	·78	·61	30·64	3·61
200—250	70,898	1,853	70	46	3,538	417	26·12	·98	·64	49·9	5·88
150—200	19,432	573	25	25	1,343	86	29·48	1·28	1·28	69·11	4·42
100—150	26,304	560	24	20	218	49	21·28	·91	·76	8·28	1·86
50—100	15,178	297	17	23	83	17	19·56	1·12	1·51	5·46	1·12
1—50	1,547	40	...	...	6	2	25·85	...	...	3·87	1·29
Total,	168,121	4,316	163	134	6,161	694	25·66	·96	·74	37·24	4·12

33

This general table was constructed at a considerable expense of time and trouble. Each district was taken separately, and a similar plan was followed in the enumeration and calculation. From the 19 separate tables thus prepared, the one given above was arranged. From the large accessions of a poor population prone to disease at an elevation of from 200 to 300 feet, comprising among others that occupying the Grassmarket, Cowgate, &c., the influence of height and exposure on the production of disease is not manifest. This is specially seen to be the case with Cholera, which, in the Metropolis and elsewhere, clearly showed the marked influence which elevation had on the number of cases, and the rate of mortality. On taking a single district, however, with marked graduation in its elevation, and a considerable population, more trustworthy results are obtained.

SECTION through the CITY of EDINBURGH from South to North, and extended to the Sea.

The figures denote the height above the sea; and the Vertical is nearly thirteen times greater than the Horizontal Scale.

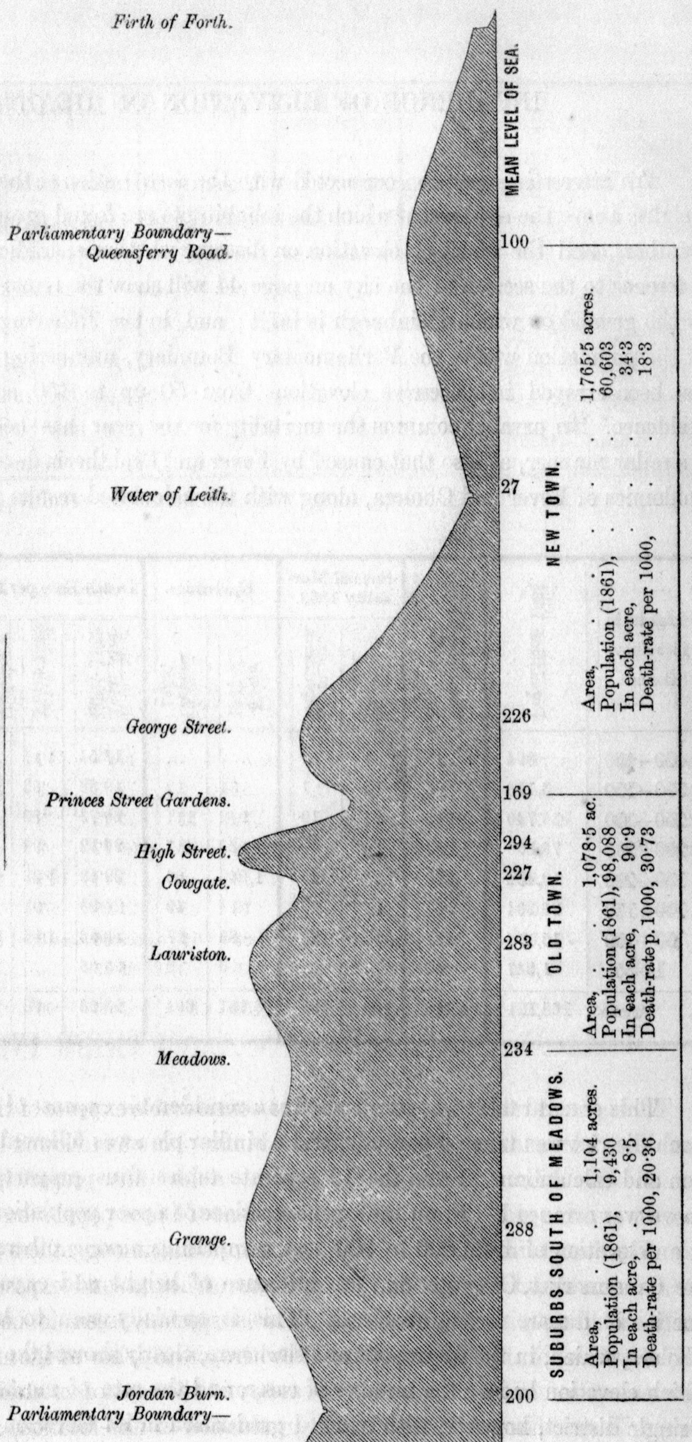

Firth of Forth. — MEAN LEVEL OF SEA.

Parliamentary Boundary—Queensferry Road. — 100

Water of Leith. — 27

George Street. — 226

Princes Street Gardens. — 169

High Street. — 294

Cowgate. — 227

Lauriston. — 283

Meadows. — 234

Grange. — 288

Jordan Burn. — 200

Parliamentary Boundary— — 250

NEW TOWN.

Area, ... 1,765·5 acres.
Population (1861), . . . 60,603
In each acre, . . . 34·3
Death-rate per 1000, . . 18·3

OLD TOWN.

Area, 1,078·5 ac.
Population (1861), 98,088
In each acre, 90·9
Death-rate p. 1000, 30·73

SUBURBS SOUTH OF MEADOWS.

Area, . . 1,104 acres.
Population (1861), 9,430
In each acre, . 8·5
Death-rate per 1000, 20·36

District of St Giles.

Height in feet above the sea.	Population 1861.	Total Mortality 1863.	Special Mortality 1863.		Epidemics.		Death-Rate per 1000.			Rate of Cases per 1000.	
			Fever.	Diphtheria.	Fever 1847-8.	Cholera 1848.	Total Mortality 1863.	Fever 1863.	Diphtheria 1863.	Fever Epidemic 1847-8.	Cholera Epidemic 1848.
400—450	854	15	1	...	...	...	17·54	1·17	...	...	
300—350	1,783	38	1	...	31	12	21·31	·56	...	17·38	6·73
250—300	7,142	188	4	4	641	74	26·32	·56	·56	89·75	10·36
200—250	5,971	209	9	4	1,102	119	35·	1·50	·67	184·55	19·92
150—200	217	10	...	...	1	1	46·08	...	...	4·6	4·6
Total,	15,967	460	15	8	1,775	206	28·8	·93	·50	111·16	12·9

It will be observed that as we proceed from a lower to a higher elevation, there is a regular diminution in the general death-rate during 1863, and also in the rate of cases per 1000 of the population affected in the great epidemics of Fever and Cholera, if the small proportion of the population living at from 150 to 200 feet above the sea level be abstracted. The character and respectability of the population vary, however, with the height at which they live, and there is a marked difference in this respect between that portion of the Cowgate included in the district of St Giles, lying at a comparatively low level, and the higher localities of the High Street, Castle-hill, and the Castle, where undoubtedly the inhabitants live in greater comfort, and enjoy life under better hygienic conditions.

TRADES AND OCCUPATIONS, AND THEIR INFLUENCE UPON HEALTH.

Edinburgh, as is well known, has no pretensions to be a manufacturing city. Its peculiar situation, and its distance from the sea, may help to account for this; while, at an early period, the establishment of a University and of the highest Courts of judicature, appears to have diverted the attention of the inhabitants from mercantile pursuits. When Scotland could boast of a Sovereign, it was also the residence of the Court, and the chief Nobility of the kingdom took up their abode within its walls, attracting at the same time large numbers of the Gentry.

Even the stimulus given to trade throughout the country by the remarkable extension of the railways has but slightly affected Edinburgh, and the enterprise of manufactures has been turned to Leith on the one hand, and Glasgow on the other. So far as appearance and amenity are concerned, few cities could be more disfigured by large manufacturing works. Two which might be named have given rise to much annoyance. Our City Gas Works have unfortunately been placed at such a low level in the district of Canongate, that the fumes of the manufacture rendered almost uninhabitable the houses which skirt the Calton Hill. To remedy this nuisance a new chimney-stalk had to be erected, of such gigantic proportions as to form a landmark and eye-sore from what quarter soever the city is approached. Again, the amenity of the West End as a place of residence has been greatly interfered with by the erection of large premises as a Distillery, said to be the largest in the kingdom. Unfortunately, in this country, no supervision is exercised over the plans of buildings intended for the purposes of trade. Any manufacture, even though it be detrimental to health, can be commenced and got into full operation before it can be stopped by a tedious process of litigation. In France, on the other hand, where much more attention is paid to the hygiène of towns, no manufacture can be begun until the plans and nature of the operations have been referred to a scientific commission, who determine whether the site selected is suitable for the special manufacture, care being taken that none injurious to health are permitted near human dwellings. So early as 1810 all manufactories were there divided into three classes—1st, those that must be kept at a distance from habitations, but which are not prohibited from the outskirts of a town; 2nd, those which may be carried on near human dwellings, assurance in all cases being obtained that the operations of the proposed manufacture could not prove a source of nuisance to the neighbourhood; 3d, those which may remain near dwellings, but are still subject to the surveillance of the Police. Were such a system in operation in this country, Edinburgh would have been saved the infliction of the two evils just referred to. Our large Gas Works would have been removed to the outskirts, or even into the country itself, a tube of sufficient dimension supplying Edinburgh with gas, and the district of Canongate would have escaped the nuisance, and the city the great disfigurement. The site occupied by the Caledonian Distillery would also have been refused, and the interests of the West End would not only have been secured, but enquiry would have been made as to the manner in which it was proposed to carry away the refuse of so large a manufacture. As it is, the refuse finds its way westward for a distance of 300 yards, polluting the atmosphere of the western districts of the city, until it reaches the Water of Leith, flowing eastwards through the city for a distance of three miles, and thus the inhabitants are again subjected to the annoyance. I can see no hardship in the Magistrates having the power, on consultation with such authorities as Professors Christison, Playfair, and Maclagan, to prevent manufactories being established on sites that must lead to the annoyance of the inhabitants, and the impairment of the amenity of the city.

TABULAR STATEMENT of the Number and Distribution of MANUFACTORIES and TRADES.

No.	NAMES OF THE DISTRICTS.	Population 1861.	Printing Establishments.	Breweries.	Distilleries.	Tanneries.	Cabinetmakers.	Coach Works.	Foundries.	Workers in Metals.	Workers in Glass.	Tobacco Manufactories.	Hat Manufactories.	Pipe Manufactories.	Marble Cutters.	Flour Mills.	Oil Manufactories.	Dye Works.	Chemical Works.	Cat-gut Manufactories.	Gas Works.	Builders.	Saw-mills.	Gutta-Percha Works.
1	Upper New Town	10,930	17	...	...	...	...	...	...	9	...	...	...	...	...	...	...	...	...	...	...	...	...	...
2	Lower New Town	14,024	...	...	...	...	2	2	...	4	...	...	...	...	...	...	...	...	1	...	...	1	...	...
3	West End	7,748	1	...	1	...	4	2	...	6	...	...	...	...	...	1	...	...	...	...	...	2	...	...
4	Upper Water of Leith	12,332	...	...	...	1	...	...	...	...	...	...	...	...	...	4	...	1	...	...	...	...	...	...
5	Lower Water of Leith	3,866	...	1	...	3	...	...	...	...	...	...	...	...	...	1	...	1	1	1	...	2	...	...
6	Broughton	5,672	...	...	...	...	...	1	...	...	...	...	...	...	1	...	...	...	...	...	...	...	...	...
7	Calton and Greenside	10,984	7	...	...	...	2	...	...	12	11	...	...	1	2	...	...	...	...	...	...	1	2	...
8	Abbey	2,237	...	3	...	...	...	...	1	1	...	...	...	...	...	...	...	...	1	...	...	...	...	...
9	Canongate	12,200	...	8	...	3	...	...	2	7	2	...	1	1	...	...	...	...	...	...	1	...	...	...
10	Tron	11,636	4	1	...	2	...	...	...	1	...	1	...	...	...	...	...	...	...	...	...	...	...	...
11	St Giles	15,967	9	2	...	...	...	...	...	3	...	...	1	...	...	...	...	1	...	...	...	...	...	...
12	Grassmarket	5,227	...	1	...	3	...	...	...	...	...	2	...	...	...	...	...	...	...	1	...	...	...	...
13	Fountainbridge	9,880	...	2	...	...	...	1	1	6	...	...	...	...	...	1	2	...	...	...	..	2	...	2
14	George Square and Lauriston	6,593	...	...	...	...	...	...	...	...	...	...	...	...	...	...	...	...	...	...	...	...	...	...
15	Nicolson Street	18,307	...	1	...	...	...	...	1	7	...	1	1	...	...	...	1	...	...	..	...	...	...	...
16	Pleasance and St Leonard	11,104	...	3	...	...	...	2	1	1	...	...	...	1	...	...	...	...	...	...	...	1	...	...
17	Newington	4,955	1	2	...	1	...	...	...	...	...	...	...	...	...	...	...	...	...	...	...	1	...	...
18	Grange	1,886	...	...	1	...	...	...	...	3	...	...	...	...	...	...	...	...	...	...	...	1	...	...
19	Morningside	2,573	...	...	...	...	...	...	...	...	...	...	...	...	...	...	...	...	...	...	...	...	...	...
	Total,	168,121	39	24	2	13	8	8	6	60	13	4	3	3	3	7	3	3	3	2	1	11	2	2

The preceding table will give some notion of the principal manufactures carried on in Edinburgh. Our chief trades are undoubtedly printing, brewing, and the manufacture of furniture. The printers are chiefly located in the New Town, while the great brewing establishments are found in the Cowgate and Canongate, around certain wells of great value for their peculiar properties. It is somewhat remarkable, that these are the only sunk wells in use throughout the city. One of the most efficient causes of the health of the poorer districts undoubtedly arises from the water supplied for domestic purposes coming from a distance, and being remarkably pure and uncontaminated. Of late years, a considerable trade has been done in the manufacture of furniture, the chief works of which have been removed to the outskirts. Applying the French classification to the trades mentioned in the table, we find that the great majority can be carried on in close proximity to human dwellings, without risk to health. The chief nuisance connected with them, is the amount of smoke they discharge into the atmosphere. For this there is a sufficient remedy in the Smoke Nuisance Abatement Act, which, however, appears to be a dead letter with us, because, at all hours of the day, we have our city breweries, located in poor overcrowded localities, and a large number of the printing establishments in the New Town, polluting the air with their smoke. From this state of matters, a double evil results, not only in the air being contaminated, and the appearance of the town disfigured, but an obstacle is placed in the way of the free ventilation of the houses in the neighbourhood. Householders will rather have their apartments ill-ventilated, than expose themselves and their furniture to contact with smoke. It is to be regretted that so many establishments are to be found in the Old Town, where the population is most dense. Many of them have been there for centuries, and occupy the same place they did when the city was crowded within the limits of the old fortifications; but now, with opportunities for removal to more suitable localities, it is highly objectionable to have such a trade as that of tanning carried on in close proximity to the High Street and St Mary's Wynd. The same might be said of our large breweries, but in their case, the character of the manufacture is not so offensive, and the wells are the great source of attraction. A more decided opinion can be expressed as to such trades as prepare cat-gut from the intestines of animals. Luckily, there are only two within the Parliamentary boundary, one in the West Port, in a most objectionable situation, and the other in a much less densely-peopled locality at Beaverhall. Both have been made the subject of repeated complaints, but without avail; seeing that a large amount of testimony, ordinary and scientific, was forthcoming, to speak as to the innocuous character of the manufacture. Now, with regard to this trade, the French legislation is very explicit. It is placed in the first class of insalubrious occupations, and is not permitted to be carried on near human habitations, and the reason given for the prohibition was the disagreeable and unwholesome character of the odours.

The keeping of bones and rags for sale has given rise to repeated complaints in the Old Town, where the trade is carried on in confined localities. It can be easily understood that the storing of these articles in an ill-ventilated atmosphere must give rise to unpleasant odours. The nuisance has long been known as a source of annoyance, and a special bye-law was passed in 1848, providing that "all persons dealing in bones and rags shall, at all times, keep their shops and cellars, and other premises, in a cleanly state, to the satisfaction of the Inspector of Cleaning." The next section determines the quantity of bones and rags that may be kept at one time. Unfortunately the rags are defined in it as "woollen;" and as in all such establishments there are rags of other materials besides wool, the bye-law has hitherto proved totally inoperative. The simple remedy is the omission of the word "woollen," or else the addition of the names of the other kinds of rags.

In the New Town the sale of meat, fish, game, &c., is, in many instances, carried on in an offensive manner. The premises are generally located in prominent positions at the corners of streets, and have not been specially constructed for the purposes of the trade. The ventilation and drainage are, in consequence, very defective, and a strong effluvium taints the air of the immediate neighbourhood, and the inhabitants who live above, and the passers by, are subjected to constant annoyance. The carcases of the animals are openly exposed to the heat and dust—a spectacle that may be witnessed in some of our fashionable streets. The Magistrates, in the interests of public decency, have ordered that all meat carried through the city in carts should be covered with a suitable cloth. The same order should apply to the exposure of carcases on the walls of shops, and the premises themselves should be visited from time to time.

Two trades have specially engaged my attention, *First*, That of the Dairyman, which is included in the third-class of the French code, and is of importance in a hygienic point of view, not so much as affecting the health of the workmen employed, as influencing the amenity of the neighbourhood by the odours coming from the refuse of the animals, and from the almost universal want of sanitary precautions, leading to a sickly condition of the cows, and the production of inferior milk. *Second*, Inquiry has been made into the state of the Bakehouses throughout the city. This trade does not figure among the establishments in the three classes,—the unhealthiness of the trade affecting those only who are employed in the production of the bread. Special regulations, however, are in force in France, regulating the use of leaden cisterns and of copper scales, so as to obviate the dangers that result from the action of water on the lead, and from the rusting of the copper. From the first of these dangers we are preserved by the excellence of the Edinburgh water; and from the second by the general use of tinned scales for weighing the flour and dough. The trade, however, has, in this country, been made the subject of a special Act, "The Bakehouses' Act 1863," which provides for the sanitary state of the workshops, and the comfort of the workmen.

SANITARY CONDITION OF THE BYRES.

WHEN inquiring into the Nuisances caused in the City by accumulations of manure, my attention was directed to the Byres,—to their position as influencing the amenity of certain localities, and to their condition as affecting the health of the cows.

I have inspected 171 Byres within the Parliamentary Boundary, and from the tabular statement in the Appendix, p. 69, it will be observed that Byres are situated in all parts of the city.

The number of cows within the municipal area may be estimated at 2085, and allowing £15 as the average price of each animal, we have a total of £31,275. If to this be added the sums expended in the purchase of food, straw, wages of servants, and rent of premises, we can form some idea of the importance of the trade. While care should be taken not to hamper with teasing restrictions a branch of industry which contributes so much to the general comfort, it should never be forgotten that the importance of the traffic, as shown by the amount of capital invested in it, is due to the patronage of the inhabitants, who have a right to demand that the milk they pay for should be clean and of good quality, and at the same time that the cows should not be so kept as to prove a source of public nuisance.

The points to which I paid special attention in examining the Byres, were—

1*st*, Their proximity to human dwellings.

2*d*, Their condition as to cleanliness.

3*d*, Their overcrowding and want of ventilation; and

4*th*, The state of the court where the manure is accumulated.

In the country, no doubt, the odour of a Byre may not be unpleasant, tempered as it is by the accessories of country life; but to be compelled, in a crowded district of a city, to inhale the effluvia of Byres from morning to night, is highly disagreeable,—to some constitutions positively hurtful: and I have no hesitation in saying that Byres under such circumstance are veritable nuisances. In some few instances the Byres were found to be placed actually *under* human dwellings, and proved a source of discomfort to the inhabitants above. But wherever situated, much depends upon the manner in which the Byre is cleaned, whether thoroughly or otherwise. A large proportion of the Dairymen in Edinburgh are persons whose experience has been gained at small farms in the country, where, from the paucity of servants and other causes, strict cleanliness is not maintained. Their careless habits they bring with them to the large towns, where they take no pride in keeping their Byres in good order. It must, however, be confessed, that little is done by landlords in Edinburgh to assist their tenants in improving the condition of their Byres. In a very small proportion of cases are Byres built specially for the purpose. Generally an old stable or an outhouse is selected, without any preparation in the shape of flagging and the formation of proper drains. Whatever paving there may be soon falls into disrepair, and it would tax the energy of any one to keep such a place tidy or dry. Again, even in better localities, the stables no longer being required for horses, and no tradesman offering to occupy them as workshops, they are let as Byres, possibly at a diminished rent. Repairs are not executed, and the cows are kept in a constant state of damp and filth. The neighbourhood, too, is annoyed by the smell of the animals, the manure, and the effluvia arising from the preparation of the food.

In such places, properly enough constructed to accommodate a few horses, half of whose life is spent in the open air, we usually find double the number of cows doomed to spend their entire existence. But in addition to the overcrowding, we have in many cases the light excluded, and along with it most of the ventilation—on the principle, as it was stated to me again and again by respectable cowfeeders, that the darker and the warmer (that is, worse ventilated) the cows are kept, the more milk you are likely to obtain from them. Now, it is well known, that if an animal live in an ill-aired apartment, the more liable is it to be affected with cold on the slightest exposure or fall of temperature. I have often remarked how much better the horse is tended than the cow, which is the more delicate and sensitive animal. But the Dairyman, instead of invigorating his stock by dryness, cleanliness, and judicious ventilation, and thus warding off disease, flies to the opposite extreme, and actually creates the danger he is seeking to avoid.

The chief public complaints that arise as to Byres refer principally to the manure heaps, which are to be found, in the case of stable lanes, immediately in front, or, where the Byre is detached, in a vacant space or court. As regards cows, there is a large quantity of liquid refuse, and this, along with the washings of the Byres, speedily accumulates, and where the paving is imperfect and the drains not properly constructed, the whole area of the court becomes saturated, and cannot be kept in a cleanly state. In dry weather, the smell is offensive; but, at all times, we have the manure fermenting in receptacles, generally of a faulty construction, either too small for the requirements of the place, or with such defective fall that the drainage is inoperative. It is said that the quality of the manure is thereby improved, and I have been informed on good authority that Dairymen have actually obstructed the drains, so as to prevent the escape of the liquid refuse. This may be quite allowable in the country, where the population is thinly scattered, but in densely-peopled localities it should not be tolerated. Here again, however, the landlord is not without blame; premises should not be let for the purposes of a dairy, unless suitable provision be made for cleanliness in an abundant supply of water within easy reach—for where it has to be carried any distance as little will be brought as possible—and also in the formation of a suitable causeway. The drains should be carefully constructed, so as to carry off with facility the surface water. The connection of these drains with the main sewer should be so adjusted as to permit the free discharge of their contents; and the opening of the drains in the court should also be trapped. The most unsatisfactory and unwholesome feature connected with Byres is undoubtedly the condition of their courts or vicinage.

In the course of my inspection, I was much surprised to find that the variations in the number of the cows in the different Dairies was unusually great, indicating a very large mortality. In some cases, I found that Byres had been emptied in consequence of the prevalence of disease, and that the proprietor had either promptly supplied the losses, or, disheartened by a continuance of what is called "ill luck," had relinquished the trade. I saw enough, however, to convince me that a considerable proportion of the mortality must have resulted from the causes to which I have alluded. The Dairymen are most unwilling to allow this, and attribute all their misfortunes to the existence of infectious diseases; and it must be admitted that the best regulated Dairies have been decimated by epidemics. But I believe that the analogy holds good with such diseases as are observed in man in the case of epidemics of cholera, fever, and small-pox, that the more crowded and ill ventilated a locality or a house is, the larger the number of infected individuals, and consequently the larger the mortality. To the Dairymen, many of whom, to do them justice, have made the most of the places they rent as Byres, I specially urged the importance of dryness, improved ventilation, and diminution in the number of the cows, but to little purpose. The invariable answer was, "This disease (pleuro-pneumonia) is very mysterious; when it enters a Byre little or nothing can be done to stop its ravages." But common sense should long ere this have told these tradesmen that nothing is so efficacious in preventing the spread of an epidemic than the early and decided separation of the suspected, not to say the already infected, individual, and that to allow an infected animal to stand in a crowded Byre, crushed up against a wall, damp with its breath and that of its adjoining companions, was to be fulfilling every condition known to be necessary to favour the rapid communication of an infectious disorder. Yet in no Byre did I see a place specially set apart as a sick stall or infirmary, so to speak, where the suspected animal could be safely treated and watched, and by which, in the event of the disease ultimately manifesting itself, the other inmates of the Byre might thus be preserved from infection. No doubt, so long as the trade in question is in the hands of persons possessing little means, and who cannot afford to pay a rent for proper premises, we cannot expect to find such accommodation; and this is one reason among many for desiring to see persons with sufficient capital engaging in the trade, and who can afford to provide every requisite for the satisfactory and successful management of their business.

Indeed, it soon became apparent that graver questions than those of mere Nuisance were involved in this inquiry. There were questions connected with the deterioration of the milk, arising from the faulty construction of the Byres, and also from the prevalence of disease. I willingly acknowledge that, during the last ten years, few complaints have reached me of anything like symptoms of disease having been caused, or been supposed to have been caused, by milk; but when we remember what an important article of diet it is, especially for children, it can easily be understood that milk, when deteriorated in quality, may aggravate, if not actually produce, many infantile disorders, and lay the foundation of weakness and a susceptibility to disease, at a time of life when rapid healthy growth is necessary for proper development. In Edinburgh, and it is now believed to be the case even in London, there is little adulteration, with the exception of the addition of water,—foreign ingredients of a deleterious character never being introduced. A poverty of taste, suggestive of the addition of water, is often observed; but I am convinced that what is complained of as "poor milk," is in reality the produce of cows placed in most unfavourable circumstances for living, and much less for the daily supply of a highly nutritious fluid.

In addition to all this, there is to be found in our markets the flesh of cows who have either died of disease, or have been killed to prevent them from so doing. When I became aware of the great mortality among the cows in Edinburgh, I was anxious to ascertain the rate of mortality of the respective Dairies. This I could hardly expect to obtain from the Dairymen themselves, and I turned to the books of the Slaughterhouses for the information. But I found the records there so far defective, inasmuch as while they mention the name of the butcher at whose instance the animal was killed, or the carcase prepared, they give no information as to the locality whence the animal was brought. The Dairymen are generally unwilling to allow that their Byres have been unhealthy, and this for the very obvious reason, that were it to become known that any unusual mortality existed in a particular Dairy, the public would naturally be chary in supplying themselves from it. A system of secrecy is thus established, and the only clue to be obtained as to the healthiness or otherwise of our Dairies, is to be found in the number of diseased animals brought to the Slaughterhouses by certain butchers. But dead meat can be brought into the city from all quarters, and at all hours. An affected animal has only to be killed, carted out of the Parliamentary Bounds, and the carcase dressed in some part of the county, and brought back in the evening and exposed in any shop, where, unless it chance to excite the suspicion of the Inspector, it is sold to the public at the price of sound marketable meat, and without a word of warning as to its history. Notwithstanding the many excellent changes inaugurated by the Market Committee, I can see no remedy for the present unsatisfactory state of matters, except by enforcing the wholesome rule, that no meat be sold in the city unless it have first been submitted to inspection at the Slaughterhouses, and that the carcases of all cows be dressed in the presence of one or other of the Inspectors. The daily number of such animals slaughtered cannot surely be so large as to prevent this being accomplished; and the duty, I submit, is as important as any official can well be called upon to discharge.

That the Byres or Cow-houses in Edinburgh require strict supervision by our local authorities, was abundantly proved to me during my inspection.

Of the 171 Byres examined, in 11 cases they were placed under human dwellings. As to cleanliness, I noted it as "passable" in 101; while in 70 the want of it was so apparent, as at once to call for remark. The ventilation was pretty good in 61 cases, and "imperfect" (generally the result of overcrowding) in 110, and the condition of the court or of the vicinage was very bad in 100 cases, and only in 71 Byres was it such as to merit the term "clean" being applied to it.

The only clauses in our local Police Act applicable to Cow-houses refer to the length of time manure can be kept in their neighbourhood, viz., for 14 days; but it is carefully specified that this applies solely to "Mews or Stable Lanes." Now, a large proportion of our Cow-houses are situated in courts, passages, and stray unoccupied stances, which can in no sense be termed "Mews or Stable Lanes." And while the efforts of the Inspector of Nuisances (Mr Paterson) and myself have mainly been directed to prevent any extension of the time during which accumulations of manure are allowed to remain, I am clearly of opinion that were this clause [the 194th of the Edinburgh Police Act 1848] enforced, it would enable us to remove many Cow-houses which are veritable nuisances, seriously affecting the health and destroying the amenity of the neighbourhood in which they are placed.

All Cow-houses in close proximity to human dwellings, for reasons I have already stated, should be suppressed, and only those should be permitted by the authorities which are situated in thinly-peopled localities. In France, since 1810, such establishments have been placed under the inspection of the Police, and they are inserted in the third class of insalubrious occupations on account of the bad smells which are occasioned by them. From time to time, in Paris, ordinances have been issued regulating the situation and sanitary condition of the Cow-houses —the last, which consolidated all former enactments, was put in force so long ago as the 27th February 1838. In this country, I regret to say, we have been much more dilatory, and a clause in the Metropolis Amendment Act 25-26 Vict. c. 102, only came into operation on the 1st of November 1862, providing for the due licensing of Cow-houses in London, and is at present enforced by the Medical Officers of Health. The General Police Act for Scotland (Lindsay's Act) passed in the same year, contains no special provision with reference to the registration, situation, size, or ventilation of Cow-houses, but in one clause [141] enforces cleanliness in "stables, byres, and areas connected therewith."

So far as Edinburgh is concerned, no one can compare the summary of the classified list of Byres within the Parliamentary Boundary appended to this report (p.69), with the accompanying map, representing the city divided into 19 Sanitary Districts

—the area and population of which have been carefully determined, without being impressed with the necessity of diminishing the number of our Cow-houses. During the last ten years, they have increased in number, or at least they have become so overcrowded, that instead of accommodating 1797 cows, as they did in 1857, (see Appendix, No. 6), the number of cows in our town Dairies is now 2085, an increase of 288, and this, be it remembered, notwithstanding the facilities afforded by the Railway Companies for the conveyance of milk. It will be seen, however, (see Appendix, No. 7), to what a small extent the Dairymen of Edinburgh have availed themselves of railway communication, and by removing to the pure air of the country, have secured for their cows an improved hygienic condition. No Byres should, in my opinion, be permitted in any part of the New Town, upper or lower—nor in the Canongate, in the Districts of the Tron, St Giles, or Grassmarket, densely peopled as these localities are by the poorest of the inhabitants. I would urge a similar prohibition on those situated in the district of George Square and Lauriston, and of Nicolson Street, and on several Byres in each of the other districts.

Finally, those Cow-houses which are placed in suitable localities should, in my view, be placed under careful supervision, and their sanitary condition regulated by special enactment. No doubt an outcry would be raised by the Dairymen that an attempt is being made to ruin them, were regulations introduced here similar to those which have been in force for nearly 20 years in Paris, a copy of which is given in the Appendix to this Report (page 71). But year by year we find that trades and occupations which in any way influence the public health, whether by the character of the food they supply, or by the emanations with which they pollute the atmosphere, are brought within the reach of legislative enactments. The Bakers, for example, have been lately placed under stringent regulations as to the cleanliness and ventilation of their work-shops, and it cannot be expected that the Dairy trade, so intimately connected as it is with the production of food for the inhabitants in the shape of milk and butcher meat, can much longer be exempted from the operation of the law of progress. I feel sure that the time is not far distant when the Dairymen themselves will be the first to acknowledge the wisdom of any enactments which shall force them to seek purer air and healthier dwellings for their cows, and that the trade will reap the advantage in a greatly diminished mortality in their stock.

I BEG TO SUGGEST—

1*stly*, That all Byres within the Parliamentary Boundary should be registered, their dimensions ascertained, and the number of cows to be kept in them determined, not at the caprice of the Dairyman, but by the size of the building, as measured by the Inspector.

2*dly*, That all Byres should be inspected by the Superintendent of Streets and Buildings; and where the paving or drainage is defective, the proprietor should be compelled to remedy the same, and specially to provide suitable receptacles for the manure.

3dly, That proprietors should be called upon to afford an adequate supply of water for cleansing purposes.

4thly, That the manure from Byres should, as in Paris, be removed weekly, instead of fortnightly.

5thly, That all cases of death among Dairy cows should be notified to the Inspector, whose duty it should be to inquire into the circumstances of the death, and as to the disposal of the carcase.

6thly, That the history of the carcase of every dead cow, brought to the Slaughterhouses, should be entered in a book to be kept for that purpose, and that the carcase itself should be dressed in the presence of the Inspector.

7thly, That no butcher meat should be exposed for sale within the Parliamentary Boundary until it has been examined at the Slaughterhouses by the Inspector.

SALE OF DISEASED MEAT.

It has already been shown in our last inquiry, that an intimate connection exists between the traffic in diseased meat and the healthy or unhealthy condition of town Dairies. When an animal becomes sick, the first question which naturally presents itself to the owner is, "What can I do to cure it?" and the cow is at once put under treatment. By a wise provision of nature, should the illness be severe, the secretion of milk is at once arrested, and all chance of infection by that channel is prevented. If remedies appear to be unable to arrest disease, and should the animal be sinking, it then becomes the interest of the owner to have it killed as soon as possible, before it can be alleged that the animal had died of disease. The cow, such as it is, is then driven, or should it be too weak to walk, it is carted, to the Slaughterhouses, and there despatched. In many cases, however, it is killed in the Byre in which it became ill, and the carcase is taken to the Slaughterhouses to be dressed. So much for a case of ordinary disease. When the illness of the animal at once testifies to the presence of that most virulent infectious disease, which, on account of its attacking very generally the organs of the chest, has been termed "Pleuro-pneumonia," or vulgarly, "Pleura," the owner, knowing from the deadly character of the illness, that remedial measures are of little avail, has the animal at once taken to the Slaughterhouses, or has it killed before removal. The eagerness displayed in bringing such animals to the public shambles is easily explained. It is to enable the carcase to be sold to the public as sound and wholesome meat, and thus secure to the owner an equivalent for the value of his animal. The only other course open to him, is to dispose of the remains to the knacker, the manufacturer of glue, &c., &c., and to suffer a heavy pecuniary loss—the sum received being but a small part of the original value of the animal. In these transactions two parties have been engaged—the Dairyman, on the one hand, and the Butcher, on the other. Generally speaking, the bargain is left open until the result of the official inspection becomes known, everything depending on the vigilance of the public officers. The trade, indeed, closely resembles in its exciting character the running of a blockade, with this exception, that in the case of the traffic in diseased meat, the general public is no gainer from a successful run. On all sides we have deception. The cow, unless its state betray its condition, is palmed off as a healthy animal, and as such it is brought to the public Slaughterhouses. The very fact of doing so, however, has an aspect of honesty. Should the disease be detected, it is at once said, "What could my client do? He had an animal which he suspected of being ill, and he brought it to the test of inspection by skilled officials." The question, however, is, did he declare its condition when it was driven into the shambles? By a well-known class of Butchers, all such precautions are disregarded, and the most open fraud is committed. A cow too far gone to be safely submitted to official inspection is killed, carted secretly out of the city, dressed in some part of the county, and reconveyed into the city, either as an entire carcase, or piecemeal, and exposed for sale. The public often purchase, at the ordinary market price of good butcher meat, what is not fit even for the pig-stye, but only to be boiled down and destroyed.

For many years past, the Magistrates of this city have shown an earnest desire to secure the citizens against such mal-practices, and have, in various Police Acts, introduced stringent clauses, regulating the trade in butcher-meat, and attaching heavy penalties to the sale of diseased carcases. These efforts were attended with little success, until the sweeping measure was passed prohibiting the existence of private shambles; and the trade was compelled to use the public abattoirs at Fountainbridge, which were opened in 1853, and are believed to be the finest in the country. The city was thus at once relieved from the nuisances caused by the numerous private killing-houses, which, from their very number, could not be adequately watched by the authorities; and the meat traffic was subjected to official inspection. Where, however, there is such a strong inducement to commit fraud, constant attempts are made to evade the police enactments. The traffic in the meat of diseased animals was regularly organized, and the traffickers became well known to the authorities and to the trade generally. Detections were made from time to time; convictions were obtained; and the heavy penalties of the Act were enforced.

But the traffic continued. It is, as we have remarked, like blockade-running—highly remunerative; and one successful run will cover the losses incurred in many unsuccessful ventures. When an offender of humble status was caught, he was left by the trade to his fate; but when an influential member of the craft was detected, a powerful defence was organized, and the case was conducted with the greatest possible ingenuity and determination, generally, I am happy to say, without success: the conduct of the officials who seized and condemned the suspected meat having generally been approved of by the Magistrates.

Within the last twelve months, public attention has been specially directed to the subject, in consequence of certain convictions having been obtained through the agency of a new set of officials, appointed to carry out the improved regulations for the management of the Slaughterhouses, and the inspection of our markets. The traffic in the flesh of diseased animals, and the proceedings in our Police Courts, have thus been eagerly discussed in the public prints. These recent cases have differed in no respect from those in which, for the last ten years, I have been in the habit of giving evidence, and in which I felt it to be my duty to corroborate the testimony of the market officials. As specimens of the flesh of diseased animals, nothing more characteristic could be adduced than those appealed to on the occasions in question. The presence of the infectious disease "pleura" was admitted in nearly all the cases, and the localized effects of the disorder were plainly visible on the carcases; and yet evidence at great length was adduced for the defence by respectable physicians and butchers.

It has always, however, appeared to me that the testimony of medical men in such cases is of little weight, unless it can be shown that they have had special opportunities of acquiring a technical knowledge of the appearances presented by various specimens of butcher-meat from an experience more extensive than that gained by the inspection of cooked meat served up at their own tables. Medical knowledge cannot compete with the tact gained by the lengthened experience of the tradesman. As little can the microscope afford reliable aid in giving an opinion in such cases. The examination of muscular tissue by this instrument is never appealed to in similar diseases in the human subject, and no reliance would be placed on its evidence as to their presence. What microscopist could tell by the examination of the flesh of a person's leg whether he was killed by a musket shot, died rapidly of typhus, sank under an attack of cholera, or died worn out by a cancerous affection of some given organ of the body? And yet few would be found who would be hardy enough to advocate the sale of the flesh of animals affected with such diseases. The tradesman judges by what may be called his "*tactus eruditus*." The appearance of the cut section of the meat—the mere touching of it—will in many cases at once inform him of its true character, and if he have in addition an opportunity of seeing the state of the internal organs, he without hesitation expresses an opinion, which to the untrained observer may appear very unreasonable. Other tradesmen are guided by similar indications. The clothier by merely passing his hand across a piece of cloth can tell you its quality and its market price. The shoemaker judges in a similar manner of the hides which he inspects; and the baker, by simply breaking a loaf across, looking at it, and smelling it, comes rapidly to a conclusion which it might take a chemist with his laborious analysis weeks to arrive at. For myself, after a varied experience of more than ten years, I am conscious of the imperfect character of professional knowledge when unaided by examination of the diseased organs, and it is only in flagrant cases, and where I can speak with decision, that I venture to give evidence.

The tradesmen who appeared for the defence in the cases alluded to, were careful to qualify their testimony by adding, that "while, in their opinion, the carcases in question were sound and wholesome, they would not dispose of them to their own customers, as a better class of meat was required by them. It would do for the poor; it was not suitable for the rich." Now, I am quite convinced, from my experience of the traffic, that all classes of the community are liable to eat the flesh of diseased animals. The best tradesman cannot always provide, from his own stock, pieces of butcher meat desired by his customers—certain parts of the animal being generally preferred, and he has to supply them in some way or other. And this can only be done by obtaining what are termed "cow roasts" from tradesmen whose business consists in the obnoxious traffic. Such meat, after being duly trimmed, and having undergone the process of cooking, may present only an unsatisfactory appearance, not such as to attract the serious attention of the eater, while the effects produced by it are obscure—temporary depression—the consequence of the imperfect nutrition afforded by the meat. It is generally urged by the advocates for the traffic, that the flesh in question is not unwholesome, and that to deprive the poor of this as an article of diet would seriously diminish their means of subsistence. The question, however, of the wholesomeness and unwholesomeness of the meat of diseased animals can only be settled in two ways;—first, by the common sense of the public, and second, by a large induction carried on for a series of years, during which a general careful market inspection is maintained over the country.

It stands to reason that the flesh of an animal, the victim of an infectious disorder, and whose blood has become disorganised, and has deposited diseased masses in important organs, cannot be so wholesome as that of a healthy animal. The muscular langour induced by slight illness in our own frames must convince us of the serious impairment of the tissues during severe illness. In the case of the animal, it at last becomes unable to stand, and even when the disease is not so far advanced, its weakness is very marked, and at once attracts attention. To think of the flesh of such a carcase being sold without the slightest information to the public as to its previous history is disgusting.

No doubt we cannot appeal to cases of sudden disease caused by the eating of such flesh—cases of so-called poisoning. But we must remember that the stomach, when in a healthy state, can resist the action of animal poisons, and that it is the continued use, day after day, of meat from diseased animals, that we should expect to be attended with marked results. By the very poor, butcher-meat is seldom partaken of; and among the better class of tradesmen, and the richer classes generally, I believe that, owing to the inspection maintained at the Slaughterhouses and in our Markets, the supply of such faulty meat is intermittent, and under the influence of rest, fresh air, and the invigorating effects of other aliments, the constitution quickly recovers. But I hold myself warranted in attributing to its use many of those instances of indigestion which come on so unexpectedly—characterized by dullness, lassitude, and inability for mental exertion, and which resist the usual remedial treatment.

It would be exceedingly difficult to settle any sanitary question, were we to suspend our action until it could be proved that the nuisance complained of was a cause of death—I mean such proof as would be satisfactory in a court of law. It is only by comparing the ratio of mortality in England now, with what it was before the recent sanitary movement was commenced, that we can judge of the efficacy of modern hygienic measures. No drain could be remedied—no cesspool cleaned—no midden removed, had we to delay our sanitary operations until we could *prove* that the existence of the special nuisances was detrimental to health. And so with regard to the traffic in diseased meat. Let it be so watched as greatly to diminish, if not entirely to stop it, and I am convinced that, like all other means tending to improve the health of the people, the good results will be apparent in a diminished mortality.

But will such strict supervision of the traffic result in a serious interference with the food-supply of the poorer classes? I have no hesitation in answering in the negative. This care for the poor has been a favourite cry when attempts have been made to secure them against fraud. When the legislature determined that the poor man, in purchasing coffee, should really purchase coffee, and not a spurious article compounded of coffee and chicory, similar arguments were employed—that the poor would, under the circumstances, take less coffee; and again, that the mixture was better for them. The evil complained of is the deception which is practised in all such cases. The meat is not ticketed as of inferior quality, and sold at a lower price. The mixture of coffee and chicory was labelled coffee, and sold as such at a largely remunerative profit.

In the case of coffee and other adulterations, a remedy was quickly found in stringent enactments. But, with regard to butcher-meat, it has been argued that diseased animals cannot be replaced by healthier, and that by enforcing the regulations of our local Acts, we stop the supply of an important article of food, and that this cannot be increased. The reverse has been proved by the history of all Acts against adulteration; the faulty producer has seen it to be his interest to furnish a purer article; a healthy competition has been induced, and adulteration has been banished from the trade. This has been the case with bread. Everywhere we find it, with the rarest exceptions, of excellent weight and sound quality. In the poorest districts of our city, the bread, without any supervision being now exercised, is fully up to the standard. A similar result will follow in the case of butcher-meat. Notwithstanding the constant importation of stock from the Continent, we find it daily urged that large districts of our country should be more and more devoted to the rearing of cattle, and less to the production of poor crops,—and it may be expected that our supply of animal food will thus be greatly increased. It is a libel on the skill of our farmers to suppose that no more healthy cattle can be reared. What would be thought of the recruiting sergeant who, in times of peace and plenty, brought for enrolment squads of diseased recruits, and pled as his excuse that the species was degenerating? Again, how careful is the same individual to guard his recruits from infection, knowing well that the fewer he presents for inspection, the less will be his gain. He watches them carefully, and permits no communication with individuals under contagious disease.

Now, let the parties chiefly interested in the question of animal production be convinced that our chief towns are in earnest in insisting upon a sounder quality of beef, and the best results will follow. The rearer of stock will be more careful in selection and in upbringing as regards pasturing and exposure. The cattle dealer will protect his drove with increased caution against the admission of infected animals, and will exercise the sharpest scrutiny in approaching a crowded market, feeling assured that the contact of a single diseased animal may imperil his gains for many a season. He will be the first to call upon the authorities of the market to enforce a thorough inspection of all the cattle presented for sale. The continental agents, aware of the impossibility of attempting to evade the inspection at our ports by introducing unhealthy animals, will make a more careful selection, and will insist on a better class of cattle being forwarded to them for exportation. Lastly, our Dairymen will be still more careful in their choice of cows, while, as we have seen, there will be, year by year, fewer chances of mistake in their purchases. They will feel the necessity of improving the condition of their Dairies as to cleanliness, and ventilation, as well as providing suitable accommodation for any infected animal, thus securing the remainder of the stock from disease. By the public thus standing on their rights, they will not only be the gainers in an improved and increased supply of butcher-meat, but the landowner, the cattle-dealer, and the dairyman will have less disease among their stock, and will thus be equally benefited. The country at large, too, will be profited; for in this matter the smaller burghs are defenceless, as they cannot afford to pay for efficient inspection. They look for protection to the large towns, which have only to act with decision, and the evil will be remedied. It is upon these broad grounds that I respectfully venture to urge upon the Magistrates of this City the necessity of maintaining a thorough inspection at our Slaughter-houses and Markets, and of enforcing the suggestions which my visitation of the Byres of the City has led me to make.

SANITARY CONDITION OF THE BAKEHOUSES.

IN 1863, an Act was passed, placing Bakehouses under the supervision of the authorities. Its provisions had reference—1st, to the age at which persons could be employed in the trade; and, 2d, to the sanitary condition of the workshops. With the first of these, as sanitary officer, I had nothing to do; but on calling the attention of the Magistrates to the Act, I received instructions to see that the sanitary regulations were strictly enforced. For this purpose, I issued a circular to the trade throughout the city, of which the following is a copy:—

"I beg to call your attention to the following Sections of 'The Bakehouse Regulation Act, 1863,' which will now be strictly enforced:—

"IV. The inside walls and ceiling or top of every Bakehouse situated in any city, town, or place, containing, according to the last census, a population of more than five thousand persons, and the passages and staircases leading thereto, shall either be painted with oil or be lime-washed, or partly painted and partly lime-washed: where painted with oil, there shall be three coats of paint, and the painting shall be renewed once at least in every seven years, and shall be washed with hot water and soap once at least in every six months: where lime-washed, the lime-washing shall be renewed once at least in every six months. Every Bakehouse, wherever situated, shall be kept in a cleanly state, and shall be provided with proper means for effectual ventilation, and be free from effluvia arising from any drain, privy, or other nuisance. If the occupier of any Bakehouse fails to keep the same in conformity with this Section, he shall be deemed to be guilty of an offence against this Act, and to be subject, in respect of such offence, to a penalty not exceeding Five Pounds.

"V. No place on the same level with a Bakehouse situated in any city, town, or place containing, according to the last census, a population of more than five thousand persons, and forming part of the same building, shall be used as a sleeping place, unless it is constructed as follows; That is to say, unless it is effectually separated from the Bakehouse by a partition extending from the floor to the ceiling: unless there be an external glazed window of at least nine superficial feet in area, of which at the least four and a half superficial feet are made to open for ventilation: And any person who lets, occupies, or continues to let, or knowingly suffers to be occupied, any place contrary to this Act, shall be liable for the first offence to a penalty not exceeding Twenty Shillings, and for every subsequent offence to a penalty not exceeding Five Pounds."

"I have also to state that your premises will be officially inspected, from time to time."

I was well aware, before commencing my inspection, that nothing had occurred in Edinburgh with regard to the manufacture of bread that called for legislation. Indeed, it was notorious that it was the condition of the Bakehouses in London which directed the attention of the legislature to the subject, and led to the adoption of the stringent measures of the Act. In Paris, the manufacture is carried on under still greater disadvantages, and it is somewhat remarkable that in both capitals the bread should be celebrated for its excellence. For, in Paris and London, where the ground is level, and where the building area is so costly, Bakehouses are generally mere excavations, and are, of course, sadly deficient in light and ventilation. The drainage, too, is inoperative; and the manufacture is carried on under the most disadvantageous circumstances: the health of the workmen suffers, and the bread is prepared in an unwholesome atmosphere. It is consistent with common sense, that all articles of food should be kept in as an untainted air as possible, and that bread—which forms such an important item in the dietary of all classes of society—should be prepared under the best possible conditions. These are, 1st, that the materials (including the water) should be pure and fresh; and 2d, that the dough should not be exposed either to the emanations from persons sleeping in the workshop, or from defective drainage. Owing to the competition which prevails among bakers, and to the improvements effected in the manufacture of flour, the bread now sold in all our large towns is of good quality, which must exercise an important influence on the health of the labouring classes. The present Act has special reference to the other points, not only as bearing upon the cleanliness of the manufacture, but also upon the health of the workmen. These are exposed for many hours continuously to a heated atmosphere, and should the ventilation be imperfect, they suffer at once from the exhaustion produced by the heat, and from the bad effects of vitiated air. The defining clause of the Act is as follows:—"'Bakehouse' shall mean any place in which are baked bread, biscuits, or confectionery, from the baking or selling of which a profit is derived." It is sufficiently comprehensive, and no fewer than 200 workshops were inspected as coming within its scope. These, as shown by the following table, were scattered throughout the Sanitary Districts in very unequal proportions, and it will be observed that their position, cleanliness, ventilation, and general sanitary condition engaged my attention. The results of my inspection are given in a tabular form. I may state that every facility was given to me, both by the masters and men. They felt that the new regulations affecting their trade were designed for their common good; and, with very few exceptions, I found that the masters had anticipated the requirements of the Act, and were willing to adopt any suggestions that would tend to the comfort of their men, and to greater cleanliness in the manufacture.

TABULAR STATEMENT of the NUMBER and CONDITION of the BAKEHOUSES.

No.	NAMES OF THE DISTRICTS.	Population in 1861.	Number of Bakehouses.	Under Dwellings.		Cleanliness.		Ventilation.		Water-Closets.		
				Under.	Apart.	Clean.	Dirty.	Good.	Imperfect.	In house.	Apart.	Absent.
1	Upper New Town	10,930	25	21	4	18	7	24	1	12	6	7
2	Lower New Town	14,024	22	20	2	22	...	18	4	10	11	1
3	West End	7,748	7	4	3	6	1	6	1	5	2	...
4	Upper Water of Leith	12,332	9	6	3	9	...	6	3	5	2	2
5	Lower Water of Leith	3,866	3	2	1	3	...	3	...	1	2	...
6	Broughton	5,672	9	9	...	8	1	7	2	5	2	2
7	Calton and Greenside	10,984	13	8	5	12	1	12	1	6	4	3
8	Abbey	2,237	1	1	...	...	1	...	1	...	...	1
9	Canongate	12,200	9	2	7	9	...	5	4	1	3	5
10	Tron	11,636	6	6	...	5	1	6	...	...	1	5
11	St Giles	15,967	13	10	3	10	3	9	4	6	1	6
12	Grassmarket	5,227	4	3	1	4	...	3	1	...	1	3
13	Fountainbridge	9,880	16	12	4	12	4	12	4	3	5	8
14	George Square and Lauriston	6,593	4	4	...	2	2	4	...	4	...	...
15	Nicolson Street	18,307	40	29	11	36	4	34	6	11	11	18
16	Pleasance and St Leonard	11,104	13	10	3	11	2	10	3	3	4	6
17	Newington	4,955	5	4	1	3	2	4	1	5	...	...
18	Grange	1,886	1	1	...	1	...	1	...	1	...	...
19	Morningside	2,573	1	...	1	1	...	1	...	1	...	...
	Totals,	168,121	201	152	49	172	29	165	36	79	55	67

In Edinburgh, owing to the hilly character of its situation, we have no Bakehouses underground, in the proper sense of the term: that is to say, they are not wholly excavated. To the front they may be under the level of the soil, but to the back they are fully above the level, as the land shelves rapidly; so that, while the front apartments may be imperfectly lighted from gratings in the street, they are fully lighted and airy to the back. Of the 200 inspected, 151 were under-dwellings on the ground-floor, and only 49 were apart. There can be no doubt, however, that wherever it is possible, a Bakehouse should be built apart from other dwellings, so as to admit of free light and ventilation. As in this trade cleanliness is of essential importance, the lighter the workshops the more satisfactory will the manufacture be. But where the Bakehouses were lighted dimly from the street, I always found, in my inspection, that the ventilation was imperfect. Large quantities of dust accumulate at the gratings, and whenever the small windows are opened, this dust falls in large quantities, and damages the flour. Again, with such small apertures, powerful draughts are occasioned, which the workmen cannot stand, overheated as they are; and, in many instances, I was told by the men that they had voluntarily closed the windows, so as to avoid risk from cold. Indeed, the subject of the ventilation of these workshops is a matter of some nicety; because, for the due production of good bread, a certain elevation of temperature is required; and were the workshop too airy, it would be unsuitable for the purpose of the trade. Now, where, as in Edinburgh, the Bakehouses are situated in the ground-floors, it is exceedingly difficult so to regulate the ventilation as to avoid extremes. But there are other disadvantages. In very few instances have I found that the Bakehouses have been built for the purpose. They are merely the kitchen or cellar flats of shops or houses, without any special arrangements for the trade. The oven is placed in a cellar under the street pavement, and the furnace communicates disadvantageously with the nearest chimney, which has not been constructed to carry a large body of flame and smoke. Again, where the draught is defective, the sulphur from the coals is driven back into the Bakehouse, and the men suffer from the emanations. With regard to this, many complaints have been received.

There is certainly an advantage connected with the situation of Bakehouses in the ground-floor, and that is, the tenement above is kept warm and free from damp. One danger, however, which naturally suggests itself, viz., that of fire, is scarcely known in Edinburgh. Mr Mitchell, the Fire-master, informs me that in his experience, which extends over a period of 38 years, he remembers of only two or three occasions of fires taking place in Bakehouses, and these were in consequence of wood igniting which had been left out to dry.

It can be easily understood that, as the drainage of the house above has to pass through the ground-floor, one of the most important points to be attended to in an inspection of Bakehouses is the state of the drain. In many instances this was found to be defective, and proprietors had to be called upon to remedy it. This was usually most effectually done by substituting the earthenware tubular one for the old built drain, which had been laid down when the tenement had been erected.

On the score of cleanliness there was little to complain of. I had seldom to note any lack of it, and I generally found that masters were in the habit of white-washing their premises regularly, and that the Bakehouses of the city were clean and tidy. Out of the total number inspected, 172 merited the title of "very clean;" the title "dirty," as applied to the remaining 29, has reference to the state of the walls of the workshop, and not to the utensils or materials employed. Some of the larger establishments in the New Town are included in this latter class. It was urged by the proprietors that their workshops were kept in such constant employment that the walls quickly became discoloured, and that no time could be set apart for more frequent white-washing. As to this, however, the Act is explicit: "the lime-washing shall be renewed once at least in every six months." The larger the trade, the greater the necessity for cleanliness, and the better able are proprietors to incur extra expense; and there is nothing to prevent the cleansing of the walls being effected during the night.

One circumstance connected with the comfort of the men and the salubrity of the trade came not unfrequently under my notice, viz., the presence and position of conveniences, or their absence. In 67 cases none were provided, in 79 they were situated in the workshop, and in the smaller number of cases—viz., 55—they were placed outside, and with a free ventilation. Now, where a convenience is not properly constructed, or kept clean, it is better for the men and the trade that it should be removed, and that the men should betake themselves to those erected at the public cost. The air becomes tainted, and, from the close proximity to the drain, there is a constant escape of effluvia. When placed outside the premises, these evils are avoided; and there can be no doubt that this is the preferable position. With regard to those situated in the house, I have always insisted on the utmost cleanliness, and in future inspections this will be strictly attended to. Where no conveniences were provided, and where they could be suitably placed, proprietors have at once been called upon to put them in.

In my visits to the various workshops, no evidence was found of unhealthiness in the men, although the trade is one necessarily attended with danger to the organs of respiration. It will be observed, by referring to the table given at p. 67, that the mortality per cent for 1863 was 1.06, (the number of Bakers in Edinburgh at the last census being 1131), and that diseases of the chest constituted a fourth of the total mortality of the class. This is easily accounted for, when we remember how often the men have to leave a heated atmosphere to deliver the bread, not to speak of the constant risk of inhaling particles of flour to which they are exposed. It is to be regretted that Bakers indulge so much in smoking while engaged in the operations of the trade, and this remark applies both to masters and men. It is utterly impossible that perfect cleanliness can, under such circumstances, be maintained; and it is not to be wondered at that Bakers are apt to suffer from delicacy of the chest when, to the special dangers incident to the trade, there is superadded the habitual use of tobacco by even the youngest apprentices. Of course, much depends on the masters, who should insist on the wholesome regulation, that there be no smoking in the workshop. Some excuse might be pled for the men when they were compelled to work for hours at a harassing trade in a debilitating atmosphere. But now, things have changed greatly for the better,—the apprentices and the men no longer sleep on the premises, huddled together in corners; and greater attention is paid to the sanitary condition of the workmen. Within the last few years some new workshops have been built in Edinburgh, and many others have been remodelled on plans of the best description, combining space, ample ventilation, and every convenience which the comfort of the men might require.

AMOUNT OF POPULATION ENGAGED IN TRADES AND OCCUPATIONS, AND THE MORTALITY IN 1863.

In taking the census, special attention has been paid to the occupations of the inhabitants. It is of importance, in estimating the sanitary condition of any city, narrowly to watch the mortality of the large and important class engaged in the various trades and occupations, generally found living in those districts which most urgently demand the supervision of a sanitary officer. During 1863, nearly 1000 persons died whose occupations could be determined satisfactorily. Before, however, the ratio of this mortality to the population could be determined, it was necessary to obtain from the census returns the numbers of those engaged in trades and occupations in Edinburgh at the time of the last census in 1861. These could only be arrived at by the laborious process of going over the returns seriatim. The results were tabulated, not according to the divisions adopted by the Registrar-General, which are too minute for such a purpose as the present, but on a plan which included the principal occupations in which both males and females were engaged throughout the city. A glance at the following tables will explain the arrangement finally adopted. The population and total mortality of each subdivision having been ascertained, the ages at death and the principal special diseases which proved fatal are also noted. Under the head of "Other Causes" were included such causes as accidents, &c., which could not be classed under the other headings. The last column in the tables gives the ratio per cent of the mortality to the numbers employed in the given trade or occupation. An endeavour was made, in constructing these tables, to localise the mortality in the various registration districts, but the inequality of these, as regards outline and character of population, was such as to render the tables of little value. Some more definite plan had to be selected, and the natural division of the city into an Old and New Town was finally adopted as one which promised the most reliable comparison. The boundary line being Princes Street, prolonged eastwards by the terraces on the Calton Hill, and westwards by Shandwick Place and Haymarket, all north of that line was considered the New Town, and the Old Town included all to the south. It would have been interesting to have ascertained the mortality and population of the trades, &c., in the 19 Sanitary Districts; but the smallness of the numbers in each district, and the expense attendant upon the investigation, deterred me from making it. The present arrangement groups larger numbers together, and the value of the results is thus increased, while, at the same time, the effect of the different exposure of the New and Old Town upon the classes in question can be more easily studied. It will be observed that the mortality from diseases of the chest is given in both divisions of the city, but this does not include the deaths from phthisis, which, on account of the importance of the disease, have been classed separately. The total mortality of the working-classes (both sexes) from chest diseases and phthisis was 96 per cent., while in the New Town this rose to 117, and in the Old Town it was only 89. The deaths from fever, again, are separated from those caused by the other diseases of the zymotic class, and are stated in a special column. The mortality from fever in the working-classes (both sexes) throughout the city was 19 per cent. In the New Town the same percentage occurs, viz., 19. This is higher than might have been expected, as in the Old Town, with all its special sanitary disadvantages, the mortality only rises to 21 per cent. As a general rule, in Edinburgh, the working-classes live in an overcrowded state, and this evil prevails largely in the New Town. To it must be attributed the high rate of mortality from fever in the northern part of the city. With reference to these Tables, however, it must be remembered that where there is, as in Edinburgh, a comparatively limited labouring population, the numbers afforded by the mortality tables of a single year are so small as to demand great caution in drawing conclusions, and that it will be only at the expiration of say five years that the mortality will be such as to afford reliable results. At the same time, the Tables are interesting, as affording a specimen of the causes of death in an important class of the community in a year of ordinary sickness. The first includes the whole city, while the others have reference to the city as divided into an Old and a New Town.

General Table for the whole City.

Trades, &c.	Total Population.	Total Mortality.	Age. Under 20.	Under 40.	Under 60.	Above 60.	Diseases. Brain.	Heart.	Chest.	Abdomen.	Phthisis.	Zymotic Diseases.	Fever.	Other Causes.	Mortality, per cent.
Baker	1,131	12	...	2	5	5	4	2	2	2	1	...	...	1	1·06
Blacksmith	2,071	36	3	14	7	12	4	2	4	9	7	3	2	5	1·73
Bookbinder	1,290	14	3	4	3	4	4	1	2	...	5	...	...	2	1·09
Boot and Shoe maker	2,182	40	2	9	18	11	8	7	5	3	8	...	2	7	1·83
Brassfounder	733	15	1	7	3	4	1	2	1	2	7	1	...	1	2·04
Brewer	194	16	2	5	3	6	1	1	5	2	1	1	2	3	8·25
Bricklayer	46	...	...	...	...	...	...	...	...	...	...	...	...	...	...
Brushmaker	115	2	...	...	1	1	...	1	...	...	...	...	...	1	1·74
Butcher	536	12	1	6	4	1	2	2	...	3	2	...	1	2	2·24
Cabinetmaker	3,328	72	2	20	24	26	12	13	14	6	17	1	3	6	2·16
Carter	698	22	4	4	11	3	2	5	2	3	2	1	2	5	3·15
Cattle dealer	87	2	...	2	...	...	...	...	...	...	1	...	...	1	2·3
Chimney sweep	57	3	1	1	1	..	...	...	1	...	1	...	...	1	5·26
Clerk (all kinds)	2,819	42	4	20	8	10	11	7	3	5	10	...	3	3	1·49
Coachmaker	238	4	1	2	...	1	...	2	...	1	...	...	1	...	1·68
Coachman	740	18	...	7	8	3	3	2	3	1	3	...	2	4	2·43
Cooper	167	12	...	1	2	9	...	1	5	2	1	...	...	3	7·18
Coppersmith	29	1	...	...	...	1	...	...	1	...	...	...	...	...	3·54
Dairyman	413	3	...	...	2	1	...	1	...	...	...	2	...	...	·72
Domestic servant (male)	724	15	1	3	5	6	2	...	2	3	1	...	1	6	2·07
Engraver	273	8	3	1	4	...	1	1	...	...	4	...	...	2	2·93
Fishmonger	83	2	...	...	...	2	...	...	1	...	...	...	...	1	2·41
Gardener	563	17	...	3	5	9	5	3	1	2	2	...	2	2	3·02
Glass-cutter and blower	218	7	2	3	...	2	1	...	2	...	3	...	...	1	3·2
Grocer	987	19	1	6	5	7	1	5	2	2	2	2	1	4	1·92
Groom	234	4	...	1	2	1	2	...	1	...	1	...	...	...	1·71
Hatter	127	3	...	...	2	1	...	1	1	...	1	...	...	...	2·36
Hawker (all kinds)	611	9	...	1	6	2	4	1	1	1	2	...	...	...	1·47
Jeweller	382	11	3	1	4	3	2	1	...	1	6	1	...	...	2·88
Labourer (all kinds)	3,657	89	3	19	34	33	13	14	18	12	7	...	4	21	2·43
Mason	1,238	38	2	9	13	14	3	4	7	5	11	...	2	6	3·07
Miller	107	3	...	...	2	1	2	...	...	...	...	...	...	1	2·8
Painter, House	904	15	...	8	2	5	3	1	1	1	5	...	...	4	1·66
Plasterer	357	8	...	1	1	6	1	...	2	2	1	...	...	2	2·24
Plumber	698	5	1	3	1	...	...	...	...	2	2	1	...	...	·72
Printer	1,809	35	6	10	7	12	4	7	1	7	14	...	1	1	1·93
Porter (all kinds)	1,159	46	1	18	6	21	5	4	7	8	2	1	2	17	3·97
Sawyer	157	8	...	1	2	5	...	2	2	...	1	...	1	2	5·1
Shopkeeper (all kinds)	3,111	34	3	17	10	4	6	2	4	3	10	...	3	6	1·09
Slater	195	3	1	1	...	1	...	...	...	1	...	...	...	2	1·54
Tailor	1,692	38	3	12	14	9	5	3	4	7	8	1	2	8	2·24
Tanner	400	9	...	1	4	4	1	...	2	2	2	...	...	2	2·25
Teacher (male)	488	10	1	4	3	2	3	...	1	1	4	...	...	1	2·05
Tobacco & Snuff manufacturer	225	2	1	1	...	...	...	...	...	...	1	...	1	...	·89
Typefounder	374	5	...	1	2	2	1	...	1	...	1	1	1	...	1·34
Watchmaker	209	8	2	2	2	2	...	2	1	...	3	...	...	2	3·82
Wine and Spirit merchant	552	24	1	12	7	4	9	1	2	5	3	...	1	3	4·35
Total,	38,408	801	59	243	243	256	126	101	112	104	163	16	40	139	2·08
Percentage to Population	....	.....	·15	·63	·63	·66	·33	·26	·29	·27	·42	·04	·1	·36	...
Females.															
Domestic servant	13,948	86	21	26	20	19	7	4	10	17	14	3	13	18	·62
Milliner, Dressmaker, & Seamstress	5,388	41	3	24	9	5	7	2	3	4	15	...	3	7	·76
Shop Girl (all kinds)	1,202	9	3	6	...	...	...	...	2	...	4	1	2	..	·75
Teacher	816	4	2	2	...	...	...	...	...	...	4	...	...	...	·49
Washerwoman	1,611	18	1	5	7	5	1	2	4	1	2	...	4	4	1·12
Total,	22,965	158	30	63	36	29	15	8	19	22	39	4	22	29	·68
Percentage to Population	....	.....	·13	·27	·15	·13	·06	·03	·08	·09	·17	·02	·09	·13	...

New Town.

Trades, &c.	Total Population.	Total Mortality.	Age.				Diseases.							Other Causes.	Mortality, per cent.
			Under 20.	Under 40.	Under 60.	Above 60.	Brain.	Heart.	Chest.	Abdomen.	Phthisis.	Zymotic Diseases.	Fever.		
Baker	372	4	...	...	3	1	2	1	...	...	...	...	...	1	1·07
Blacksmith	590	16	1	7	3	5	1	2	2	2	4	2	...	3	2·71
Bookbinder	111	2	...	1	1	...	1	1	...	...	...	...	...	...	1·8
Boot and Shoe maker	539	11	...	3	5	3	1	2	2	1	3	...	1	1	2·04
Brassfounder	142	4	...	2	1	1	...	1	1	1	...	1	...	...	2·82
Brewer	20	3	...	1	1	1	...	...	1	...	1	...	1	...	15·
Bricklayer	15	...	...	...	...	...	...	...	...	...	...	...	...	...	...
Brushmaker	17	...	...	...	...	...	...	...	...	...	...	...	...	...	...
Butcher	108	2	...	...	1	1	1	...	...	...	...	...	...	1	1·85
Cabinetmaker	1,151	31	2	9	9	11	4	3	6	3	9	...	3	3	2·69
Carter	143	7	...	1	4	2	...	3	1	1	...	1	...	1	4·89
Cattle dealer	16	2	...	2	...	...	...	...	...	...	1	...	...	1	12·5
Chimney sweep	22	3	1	1	1	...	...	...	1	...	1	...	...	1	13·64
Clerk (all kinds)	1,493	24	4	9	6	5	6	6	1	3	4	...	1	3	1·61
Coachmaker	122	3	...	2	...	1	...	1	...	1	...	...	1	...	2·46
Coachman	473	11	...	4	4	3	3	1	1	1	1	...	1	3	2·32
Cooper	40	5	...	...	2	3	...	...	2	1	1	...	...	1	12·5
Coppersmith	13	...	...	...	...	..	...	...	...	...	...	...	...	...	...
Dairyman	169	1	...	...	1	...	...	...	...	...	...	1	...	...	·6
Domestic servant (male)	528	12	1	3	5	3	2	...	2	2	1	...	1	4	2·27
Engraver	109	5	3	...	2	...	1	...	...	...	4	...	...	...	4·6
Fishmonger	21	...	...	...	...	...	...	...	...	...	...	...	...	...	...
Gardener	292	7	...	...	1	6	3	3	...	...	...	...	...	1	2·4
Glass-cutter and blower	67	3	...	2	...	1	1	...	...	...	1	...	...	1	4·47
Grocer	382	6	1	1	2	2	...	1	...	1	1	2	...	1	1·57
Groom	117	2	...	1	1	...	1	...	...	...	1	...	...	...	1·71
Hatter	15	...	...	...	...	...	...	...	...	...	...	...	...	...	...
Hawker (all kinds)	2	3	...	...	2	1	3	...	...	...	..	...	...	...	...
Jeweller	139	6	1	1	3	1	2	...	...	...	4	...	...	...	4·31
Labourer (all kinds)	376	19	1	8	8	2	3	2	4	2	5	...	...	3	5·05
Mason	350	18	1	7	5	5	...	...	2	3	7	...	1	5	5·14
Miller	84	3	...	...	2	1	2	...	...	...	...	...	...	1	3·57
Painter, House	305	9	...	6	...	3	2	1	1	...	3	...	...	2	2·95
Plasterer	80	3	...	...	...	3	1	...	1	1	...	...	...	...	3·75
Plumber	220	2	...	1	1	...	...	...	...	...	1	1	...	...	·91
Printer	368	11	1	3	4	3	3	1	...	4	3	...	...	...	2·99
Porter (all kinds)	301	17	1	5	3	8	1	4	3	3	1	1	1	3	5·64
Sawyer	48	2	...	1	...	1	...	...	1	...	1	...	...	...	4·16
Shopkeeper (all kinds)	908	16	...	10	3	3	3	1	4	1	4	...	1	2	1·76
Slater	34	1	1	...	...	...	...	...	...	...	...	...	...	1	2·94
Tailor	382	14	...	4	7	3	2	1	1	4	2	...	1	3	3·66
Tanner	154	5	...	...	4	1	...	...	1	1	1	...	...	2	3·25
Teacher (male)	245	8	...	3	3	2	3	...	1	...	3	...	...	1	3·26
Tobacco & Snuff manufacturer	25	...	...	...	...	...	...	...	...	...	...	...	...	...	...
Typefounder	13	...	...	...	...	...	...	...	...	...	...	...	...	...	...
Watchmaker	67	5	2	2	...	1	...	1	...	...	2	...	...	2	7·46
Wine and Spirit merchant	193	8	...	4	3	1	5	...	...	1	...	...	1	1	4·14
Total,	11,381	314	21	104	101	88	57	36	39	37	70	9	14	52	2·76
Percentage to Population	......	......	·18	·91	·88	·77	·5	·31	·34	·32	·61	·08	·12	·45	...
Females.															
Domestic servant	8,647	49	13	15	11	10	4	2	2	10	9	2	7	13	·56
Milliner, Dressmaker, & Seamstress	1,798	18	...	10	6	2	5	2	1	2	6	...	...	2	1·
Shop Girl (all kinds)	305	1	...	1	...	...	...	...	...	...	1	...	...	...	·33
Teacher	462	3	1	2	...	...	...	...	...	...	3	...	...	...	·65
Washerwoman	429	9	1	2	4	2	...	1	2	1	2	...	1	2	2·1
Total,	11 641	80	15	30	21	14	9	5	5	13	21	2	8	17	·69
Percentage to Population	......	......	·12	·25	·18	·12	·08	·04	.04	·11	·18	·02	·07	·14	...

Old Town.

Trades, &c.	Total Population.	Total Mortality.	Age.				Diseases.							Other Causes.	Mortality, per cent.
			Under 20.	Under 40.	Under 60.	Above 60.	Brain.	Heart.	Chest.	Abdomen.	Phthisis.	Zymotic Diseases.	Fever.		
Baker	759	8	...	2	2	4	2	1	2	2	1	...	...	...	1·05
Blacksmith	1,481	20	2	7	4	7	3	...	2	7	3	1	2	2	1·35
Bookbinder	1,179	12	3	3	2	4	3	...	2	...	5	...	...	2	1·02
Boot and Shoe maker	1,643	29	2	6	13	8	7	5	3	2	5	...	1	6	1·77
Brassfounder	591	11	1	5	2	3	1	1	...	1	7	...	...	1	1·86
Brewer	174	13	2	4	2	5	1	1	4	2	...	1	1	3	7·47
Bricklayer	31	...	...	...	...	...	...	...	...	...	...	...	...	...	...
Brushmaker	98	2	...	...	1	1	...	1	...	...	...	...	...	1	2·04
Butcher	428	10	1	6	3	...	1	2	...	3	2	...	1	1	2·34
Cabinetmaker	2,177	41	...	11	15	15	8	10	8	3	8	1	...	3	1·88
Carter	555	15	4	3	7	1	2	2	1	2	2	...	2	4	2·7
Cattle dealer	71	...	...	...	...	...	...	...	...	...	...	...	...	...	...
Chimney sweep	35	..	...	...	...	...	...	...	...	...	...	...	...	...	...
Clerk (all kinds)	1,326	18	...	11	2	5	5	1	2	2	6	...	2	...	1·36
Coachmaker	116	1	1	...	...	...	...	1	...	...	...	...	...	...	·86
Coachman	267	7	...	3	4	...	...	1	2	...	2	...	1	1	2·62
Cooper	127	7	...	1	...	6	...	1	3	1	...	...	...	2	5·51
Coppersmith	16	1	...	...	...	1	...	...	1	...	...	...	...	...	6·25
Dairyman	244	2	...	...	1	1	...	1	...	...	...	1	...	...	·82
Domestic servant (male)	196	3	...	...	...	3	...	...	...	1	...	...	...	2	1·53
Engraver	164	3	...	1	2	...	...	1	...	...	...	...	...	2	1·83
Fishmonger	62	2	...	...	...	2	...	...	1	...	...	...	...	1	3·22
Gardener	271	10	...	3	4	3	2	...	1	2	2	...	2	1	3·69
Glass-cutter and blower	151	4	2	1	...	1	...	...	2	...	2	...	...	...	2·65
Grocer	605	13	...	5	3	5	1	4	2	1	1	...	1	3	2·15
Groom	117	2	...	...	1	1	1	...	1	...	...	...	...	...	1·71
Hatter	112	3	...	...	2	1	...	1	1	...	1	...	...	...	2·68
Hawker (all kinds)	609	6	...	1	4	1	1	1	1	1	2	...	...	...	·98
Jeweller	243	5	2	...	1	2	...	1	...	1	2	1	...	...	2·06
Labourer (all kinds)	3,281	70	2	11	26	31	10	12	14	10	2	...	4	18	2·13
Mason	888	20	1	2	8	9	3	4	5	2	4	...	1	1	2·25
Miller	23	...	...	...	...	...	...	...	...	...	...	...	...	...	...
Painter, House	599	6	...	2	2	2	1	...	...	1	2	...	...	2	1·
Plasterer	277	5	...	1	1	3	...	...	1	1	1	...	...	2	1·8
Plumber	478	3	1	2	...	...	...	...	...	2	1	...	...	...	·63
Printer	1,441	24	5	7	3	9	1	6	1	3	11	...	1	1	1·66
Porter (all kinds)	858	29	...	13	3	13	4	...	4	5	1	...	1	14	3·38
Sawyer	109	6	...	...	2	4	...	2	1	...	...	...	1	2	5·5
Shopkeeper (all kinds)	2,203	18	3	7	7	1	3	1	...	2	6	...	2	4	·81
Slater	161	2	...	1	...	1	...	...	...	1	...	...	...	1	1·24
Tailor	1,310	24	3	8	7	6	3	2	3	3	6	1	1	5	1·33
Tanner	246	4	...	1	...	3	1	...	1	1	1	...	...	...	1·62
Teacher (male)	243	2	1	1	...	...	...	...	...	1	1	...	...	...	·82
Tobacco & Snuff manufacturer	200	2	1	1	...	...	...	...	...	...	1	...	1	...	1·
Typefounder	361	5	...	1	2	2	1	...	1	...	1	1	1	...	1·38
Watchmaker	142	3	...	...	2	1	...	1	1	...	1	...	...	...	2·11
Wine and Spirit merchant	359	16	1	8	4	3	4	1	2	4	3	...	...	2	4·46
Total,	27,027	487	38	139	142	168	69	65	73	67	93	7	26	87	1·8
Percentage to Population	...	...	·14	·51	·52	·62	·25	·24	·27	·25	·34	·026	·09	·32	...
Females.															
Domestic servant	5,301	37	8	11	9	9	3	2	8	7	5	1	6	5	·69
Milliner, Dressmaker, and Seamstress	3,590	23	3	14	3	3	2	...	2	2	9	...	3	5	·64
Shop Girl (all kinds)	897	8	3	5	...	...	...	...	2	...	3	1	2	...	·89
Teacher	354	1	1	...	...	...	...	...	...	...	1	...	...	...	·28
Washerwoman	1,182	9	...	3	3	3	1	1	2	...	...	...	3	2	·76
Total,	11,324	78	15	33	15	15	6	3	14	9	18	2	14	12	·69
Percentage to Population	...	...	·13	·29	·13	·13	·05	·026	·12	·08	·16	·02	·12	·1	...

PUBLIC INSTITUTIONS.

NAME.	Height in feet above the sea.	SANITARY DISTRICT.	Population 1861.			Mortality 1863.		
			Above 5.	Under 5.	Total.	Above 5.	Under 5.	Total.
Castle	437	St Giles,	816	38	854	11	4	15
Prison	239	Calton and Greenside,	343	5	348	4	3	7
Police Office	278	St Giles,	63	7	70	...	...	...
Royal Infirmary.........	226—239	Tron,	470	8	478	4	1	5
Maternity Hospital ...	264	Nicolson Street,	24	6	30	...	...	...
Sick Children's Hosp.	246	George Square & Lauriston,	22	5	27	1	...	1
Lunatic Asylum.........	260	Morningside,	87	...	87	7	...	7
Deaf & Dumb Institn.	73	...	59	...	59	...	...	...
City Poorhouse	281	George Square & Lauriston,	569	52	621	111	19	130
St Cuthbert's Poorhouse	196	West End,	469	34	503	81	28	109
Canongate Poorhouse...	138	Canongate,	67	4	71	13	1	14
Gillespie's Hospital ...	274	Morningside,	47	...	47	2	...	2
House of Refuge.........	138	Canongate,	405	10	415	14	1	15
Magdalen Asylum	174	Do.	66	...	66	...	...	...
Deanbank Institution	71	Upper Water of Leith,	22	...	22	...	...	...
Original Ragged School	320	St Giles,	85	...	85	...	...	...
Donaldson's Hospital...	200	Upper Water of Leith,	206	1	207	...	...	...
Heriot's do....	290	George Square & Lauriston,	203	1	204	...	...	...
Merchant Maiden do. ..	250	Do.	101	...	101	...	...	...
Orphan do....	185	Upper Water of Leith,	139	...	139	...	...	...
Stewart's do....	162	Do.	83	...	83	1	...	1
Trades' Maiden do....	260	Grange,	53	...	53	...	...	...
Watson's (George) do.	260	George Square & Lauriston,	110	4	114	...	...	...
Watson's (John) do.	264	Upper Water of Leith,	115	1	116	...	...	...

In the above list are included the principal public Institutions of Edinburgh, which have a considerable population of both sexes. An attempt at classification has been made, commencing with the Garrison and our Prisons, and ending with the various charitable educational establishments, which form such an architectural display in and around the city. The Medical Institutions stand second in the list, followed by three Unions or Workhouses. To Gillespie's Hospital, a separate place had to be assigned: for, although it is a charitable institution, it is strictly limited to the aliment and maintenance of old men and women above the age of 55 years. Next in the list are various Reformatories. The House of Refuge accommodates cases of incurable disease, and nightly affords shelter to numbers of the wandering poor. The last sub-divisions comprise the charitable educational institutions. These are maintained in the highest state of efficiency, so far as medical and hygienic superintendence is concerned; and the small amount of their mortality is the best proof of the admirable manner in which so many young people are accommodated and cared for. During the last few years, questions have been raised as to the desirability of the sites of the Castle and Royal Infirmary, for the purposes of a garrison and a general hospital. The exposed situation of the Castle has been considered detrimental to the health of the soldiers; but it is forgotten that our soldiers are picked men, in the prime of life, who ought, in times of peace, to be inured to hardness in a bracing atmosphere. It may safely be affirmed that if a strong man, with all the comforts of a garrison, cannot stand the exposure of the Castle rock, he cannot be expected to camp out at a moment's notice, in the most trying weather, as he may at any time be called upon to do. Such a site affords unusual facilities for drainage, and were greater care manifested in housing the soldiers, and in selecting regiments which had not come directly from the tropics, to occupy this elevated position, the mortality from chest disease, which has occasionally been noted as high, would be greatly diminished. As to the Royal Infirmary, the greater portion is of considerable age, and was erected at a time when sanitary notions were sadly defective. Hence the old or medical part of the house cannot be said to offer a good example of hospital accommodation. The managers of the Charity had plans prepared years ago, on an extensive scale, for a new hospital, a considerable portion of which, intended for the Surgical Department, has already been erected; and the completion of the original design languishes for want of funds. It remains with the public to aid the managers in placing this justly celebrated Charity on a level, so far as accommodation is concerned, with the most recently-planned hospitals of the country. An important question has been raised as to its present site. It has been urged that it is very defective in a sanitary point of view, and that a bold effort should be made to remove the hospital to a freer and less-crowded situation. The present site, however, is less faulty than is generally supposed. It is high, and has a very free exposure, although it is in the close neighbourhood of the densely-peopled districts of the Old Town. When its proximity to the Medical School is considered, and the large amount of new buildings that have already been erected are taken into consideration, the difficulties of removal become insurmountable. No new site can be proposed which offers the advantages of the present one, with the addition of what, in a new situation, would be looked on as indispensable, viz., large airing-grounds for the patients. A strenuous effort should be made to secure the erection of a new medical hospital on the present site, according to the plans of the managers, who are all gentlemen of experience, and have the best interest of the Charity and of the Medical School at heart. In the meantime, its sanitary condition should be put on a more satisfactory footing, by the abolition of cesspools and the careful trapping of every gully,—the site presenting unusual facilities for efficient drainage. The atmosphere of the neighbourhood would be greatly improved by the enforcement of the Smoke Prevention Act. On all sides we have the air tainted by the smoke from breweries. But it must not be forgotten that in this respect the hospital itself is a great offender. The large chimney, most disadvantageously placed between the surgical and medical departments, gives out a large volume of smoke, which is a nuisance to the neighbourhood, and which ought to be consumed, were it only for the amenity of the institution, to say nothing of the importance of not adding to the already vitiated condition of the atmosphere.

Again, the present vacant grounds of the Infirmary are never to be encroached upon by buildings, either of a temporary or permanent character. During epidemics of fever, in which the house accommodation proved too limited for the enormous number of cases, temporary provision was made in the emergency by erecting wooden sheds. There was necessarily great overcrowding, and demands were made upon the resources of the institution for nursing and superintendence, which taxed them severely. It is now understood, however, that the managers have determined never to allow the grounds of the hospital to be occupied by such temporary erections, or to admit more cases of infectious disease than the hospital can reasonably accommodate. This has been intimated to the parties on whom the *onus* lies of providing for the sick poor during the prevalence of epidemic disease, viz., the various Parochial Boards. Accordingly, during the late epidemic of small-pox, the City and St Cuthbert's parishes provided two small hospitals. The danger, however, passed away, and these hospitals have been applied to other uses. It is of importance that a suitable building should be set apart in some central locality as an hospital, which might be useful in any epidemic. The best time for securing such, is when we have good warning of our danger. It is too late when disease breaks out; for, in our crowded closes, any infectious disorder spreads with great rapidity, and the epidemic would have done its worst before a suitable hospital could be improvised. The three Parochial Boards should combine for the purpose indicated, and were no better locality and building to be suggested, the present Canongate Workhouse, standing apart from other houses, and within easy distance of the worst districts of the city, might be looked to, as, sooner or later, an amalgamation of the City and Canongate parishes must take place, and the building would not be required for its present purpose. Were such an hospital provided, our Infirmary would, at all times, be fully able to meet the wants of the city and neighbourhood, and the severity of epidemics would be greatly lessened.

No one can visit the sick poor of Edinburgh without becoming aware of certain deficiencies in our charitable institutions. While great difficulties present themselves in the way of removing the Royal Infirmary to a more salubrious situation, this invaluable institution would be greatly aided by the establishment on an efficient scale of a Convalescent House, which might be placed in the outskirts, and would relieve the Infirmary of the class of cases which suffer most from its present confined situation, viz., those recovering from acute and chronic disease. With such a building might be combined a few wards for the reception and maintenance of incurables, a class of cases whose sufferings might be greatly alleviated by medical treatment and judicious nursing. The miserable houses of the poorer description of the labouring population render the Maternity Hospital an urgent necessity for the preservation of maternal and infantile life, not to speak of the common decencies of life. At present this hospital neither represents faithfully the necessities of a large medical school nor the clamant wants of our poor population. In no institutions has the value of hygienic and sanitary measures been more incontestably shown than in Maternity Hospitals. The building at present devoted to this purpose is, from its age, situation, and internal arrangement, unsuitable, and a new building on an improved plan should be provided. The medical charities of Edinburgh cannot be regarded as on a satisfactory footing, until our Infirmary is completed and there are provided the important adjuncts of a Convalescent Hospital with wards for Incurables, and an enlarged Maternity Hospital.

The sites occupied by our three Workhouses are of an excellent description. Nothing could be more advantageous, in a sanitary point of view, than the position of the City Workhouse, and that of St Cuthbert,—the one occupying an airy and commanding situation immediately to the south of the oldest parts of the city, while the other, in the district of the West End, is only now being surrounded by buildings. No one can visit these institutions, without seeing that they are antiquated structures, their original design having been encroached upon by subsequent additions, and by the introduction of sanitary improvements. The expense attendant upon repeated alterations is proverbial; and there can be but little doubt that, in the case of St Cuthbert, the removal of the Workhouse, and its reconstruction on some other site within its widely-extended parish, would, even on the score of economy, have been a boon to the rate-payers, while it would have secured for the present inmates a freer and healthier exposure in a rural district. It is to be hoped that the Managers of this Charity will follow the example set them by the City Parish, and escape from a position which, though salubrious, is not fitted for the requirements of a Workhouse in the present day.

The Magdalen Asylum, the position of which was in many respects objectionable, has been removed to an admirable site beyond the city. The other institutions call for no remark.*

---

* It may be proper to mention that, in the Table prefixed to the above Chapter, only those Institutions are included whose population was found to exceed 20. The Night Asylum, on account of the migratory character of its inmates, has not been specially referred to, but will be found noticed in the Appendix, St Giles' District, pp. 36, 37.

DRAINAGE AND WATER SUPPLY.

Few cities are more favourably situated for efficient drainage than Edinburgh. A reference to the section of the Parliamentary area from north to south, at p. 44, will show that there is a succession of valleys running parallel to each other, which naturally drain the adjoining heights. The Water of Leith receives the drainage of the New Town, while the Jordan Burn to the south performs the same office for the Southern Suburbs. The intermediate valleys fall rapidly eastwards, and converging towards the Queen's Park, empty their sewage into the Foul Burn, which, on its way to the sea, supplies the well-known irrigated Meadows. The two following sections from east to west, on pp. 77 and 78, show the inclination of the western portion of the City. In the former of these, the ridge of the Old Town, draining naturally to the east, ends abruptly with the Castle Rock; and to the westward the land inclines to the Water of Leith. In the latter, from the summit of the ridge of Lauriston, at Heriot's Hospital, the same inclination is seen, and the drainage passes beyond the Parliamentary Boundary to empty itself into the Water of Leith, as it approaches Edinburgh at Coltbridge. Immediately to the westward of the Castle rock there is a deep and narrow cleft, which communicates directly with the valley of Princes Street Gardens. Through this chasm the drainage of the West Port and Grassmarket passes round the Castle to its natural outlet between the Old and New Towns, and joins the Foul Burn.

For many years past great drainage works have been carried on in the city, and it may now be regarded as satisfactorily drained. In the poorest districts we have large sewers of the best construction. These, of course, fulfil the important sanitary purposes of carrying off the rain-fall, and the drainage of more elevated districts; but so far as the closes are concerned, these drains, for any sewage they convey from such poor localities, might never have existed. This depends at once upon the manner in which the poor live together, and on the system of cleansing which experience has determined as the best adapted for Edinburgh.

Centuries ago, when drains were unknown, and when the inhabitants, to keep themselves within the protection of the city walls, were compelled to add to the height of their houses so as to provide for the increasing population, the only way in which filth could be disposed of, was either by allowing it to accumulate within the houses, or by summarily getting rid of it by bringing it to the street or close. The dangers attending the first of these plans, soon became apparent in the presence of disease, and the recurrence of epidemics; while the second rendered Edinburgh notorious for its odours, especially at night. The great sanitary movement in

SECTION of the CITY along the ridge of the High Street, westwards to the Water of Leith.

The figures denote the height above the sea ; and the Vertical is nearly thirteen times greater than the Horizontal Scale.

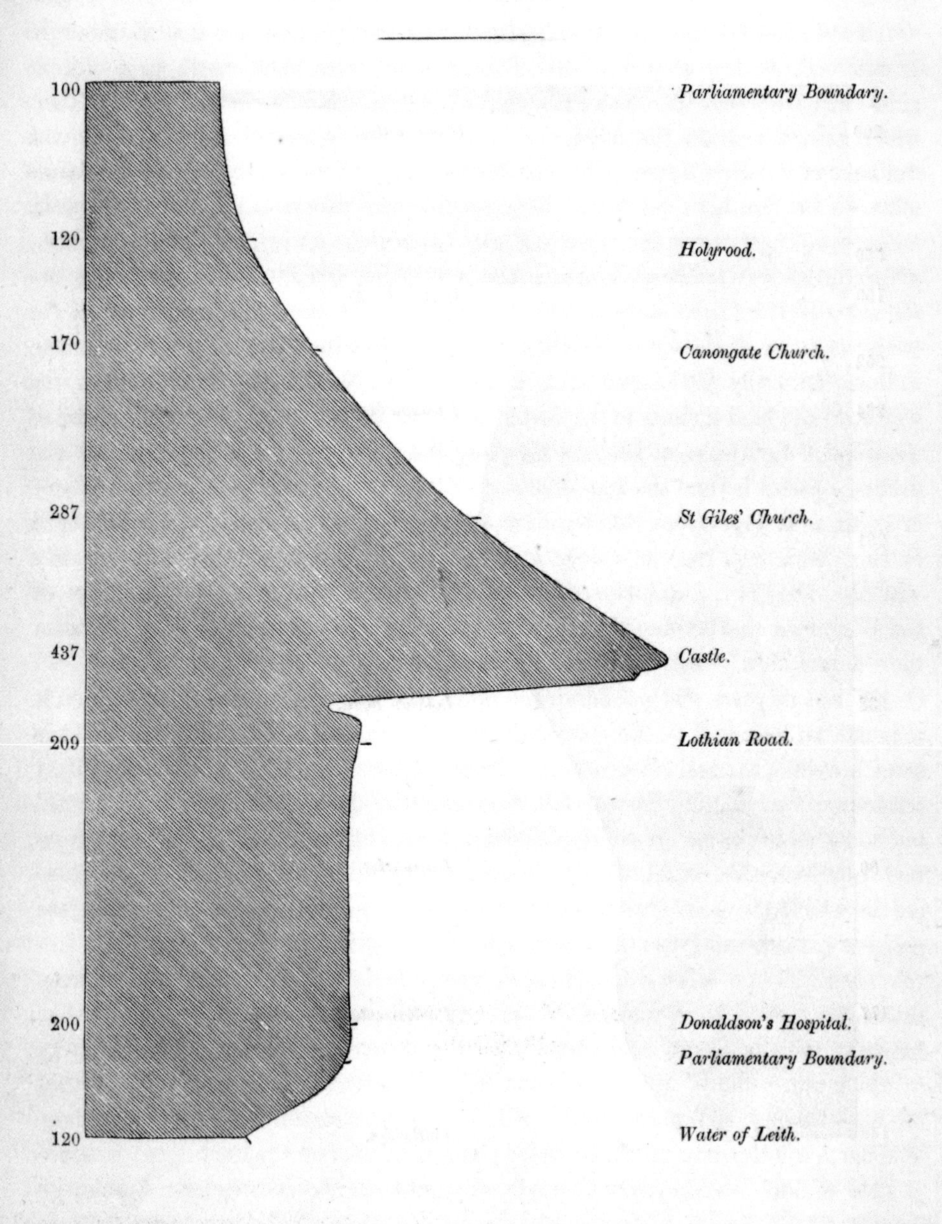

SECTION of the CITY along the ridge of Lauriston, westwards to the Water of Leith at Coltbridge.

The figures denote the height above the sea; and the Vertical is nearly thirteen times greater than the Horizontal Scale.

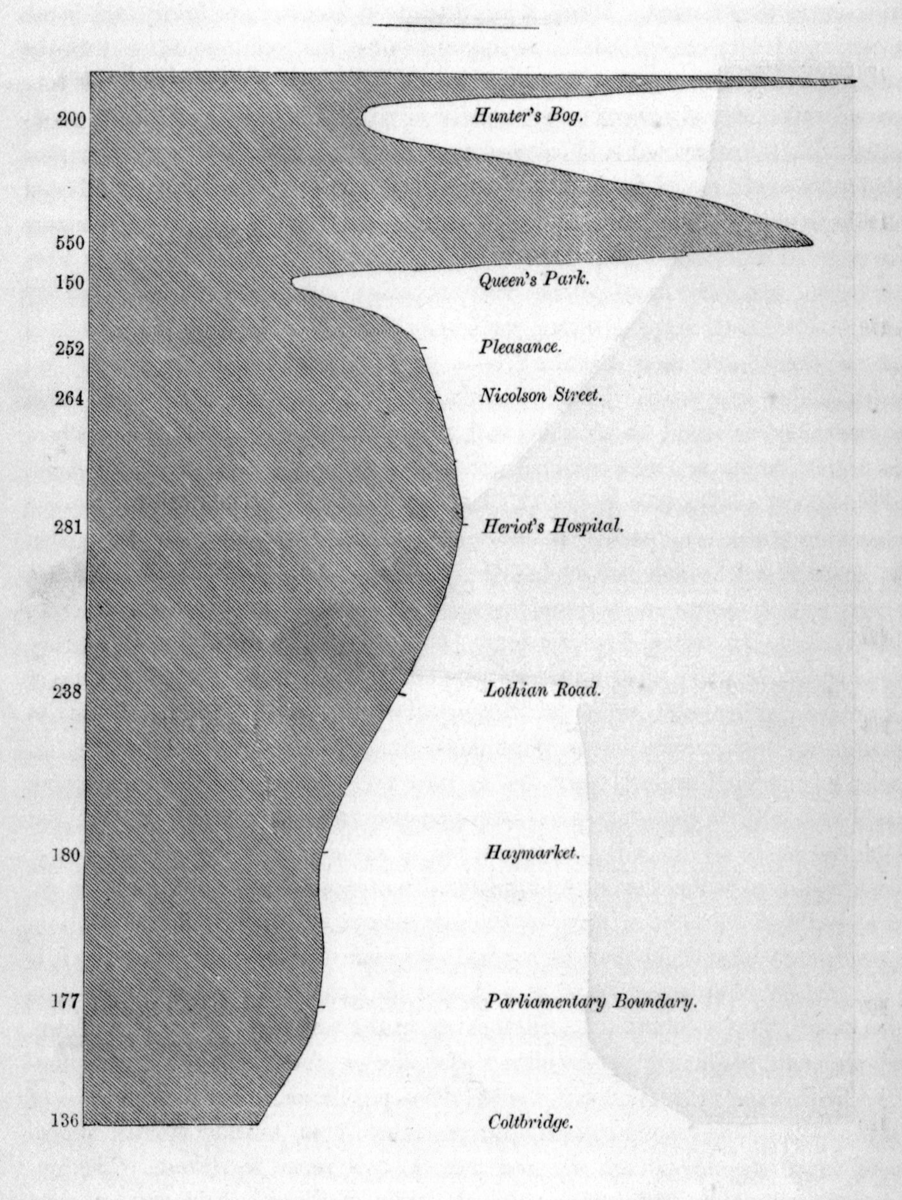

England, which the successive epidemics of cholera were so instrumental in stimulating, was intimately connected with the perfecting of the drainage systems of large towns. This consisted in placing each dwelling-house in communication with the public sewers, and thus permitting the rapid escape of all offensive material. There can be no doubt that this was a sanitary measure of great importance, and as applied to English towns, effected the best results. The necessity of improved drainage was also felt in Scotland, and our chief towns were speedily drained, that is to say, the main sewers were formed. When it was attempted, however, to bring each house in our large tenements or "lands," as they are called, into communication with the sewers, the difficulties arising from our system of house accommodation at once became apparent. A reference to the table at p. 80 will show the difficulties connected with the introduction of conveniences into our crowded houses. Our poor inhabit the dwellings of the wealthy classes of former days, necessarily sub-divided into single rooms, which are occupied by separate families. There the inhabitants live crowded together, without distinction of sex, and in many instances we have the rooms, generally opening one into the other, still further sub-divided by partitions, so as to allow of closer packing. The houses, too, are old, and in a state of decay; and their construction is very imperfect, so far as sanitary requirements are concerned. Under these circumstances, to enforce the introduction of conveniences, would be attended with the worst results. In England, where the poorest houses are self-contained, and necessarily small, with a court behind, in which the convenience is placed, the system works admirably. Any sewage emanations which may escape, at once pass into the atmosphere, and the air in the house is not contaminated; but the houses in the densely peopled districts of our Scottish towns are not supplied with such courts, and were conveniences placed outside the houses, from the large population which would use them, they would closely resemble those which are scattered throughout the City for the use of the public. Where such are largely frequented, it is a matter of great difficulty to preserve any anything like decent cleanliness; the air becomes tainted; what is intended as a public benefit is very apt to become a nuisance to the surrounding neighbourhood. If, however, as has been proposed, they were placed on each flat of our tall lands, all the evils already referred to would exist in a confined atmosphere, and close to the sleeping apartments of our crowded poor. It must be remembered that the simplest form of the convenience, as supplied for houses, is a piece of mechanism which must be handled with some degree of care, otherwise it is apt to get out of order—it becomes no longer air tight, and a leakage of foul gas takes place. This occurs to a notorious extent in the best parts of the New Town, and although productive of discomfort and disease, these evils are greatly modified by the freer ventilation, and the less dense population. But in the houses of the poor this leakage would be constantly occurring in an already vitiated atmosphere, where the inhabitants are overcrowded, and prone to disease. The consequences can easily be imagined. Those forms of illness which are generally considered to be intimately connected with effluvia from drains would soon show themselves, and in such localities would quickly spread in an epidemic form; and it must be remembered that such debilitating diseases as fever and dysentery tell heavily upon the labouring population, and entail a large expense upon the community in the shape of increased poor-rates. The experiment has been tried again and again in our city, and always with similar results,—the production of much annoyance, and, ultimately, the removal of what was considered a sanitary improvement. A few months ago, an excellent opportunity was afforded of putting the matter to a practical test, not in an old house, but in one specially built for the purpose, in Dickson's Close, High Street; and the experiment is at present going on. I subjoin a statement of the population of the tenement. Of the two conveniences on each flat, one was intended for males, and the other for females and children. I have given the number of children under twelve years, as those most likely to accompany the females.

	Rooms.	Families.	Children under 12.	Adults.		Total.	Sinks.	Water Closets.
				Females.	Males.			
First Flat	8	7	14	13	8	35	1	2
Second Flat.........	12	6	11	13	7	31	1	2
Third Flat	14	9	13	13	13	39	1	2
Fourth Flat.........	15	8	15	13	7	35	1	2
Total............	49	30	53	52	35	140	4	8

No sooner were the rooms tenanted, than a large pool of sewage, both solid and liquid, collected at the foot of the main passage, in consequence of the choking of the pipes. Day after day was this sewage removed, but as constantly was it renewed. At length, after the authorities had repeatedly interfered, several of the conveniences were closed, and the number of parties frequenting the remainder curtailed; but in spite of these precautions, a state of matters is produced, by overflow and leakage, of the most nauseous description. No doubt the tenants were for the most part Irish, paying rents from £2, 8s. to £7, 10s., but it must be remembered that this is precisely the class who were supposed to receive most benefit from this sanitary measure. My experience of the poor of this city, and of their house accommodation, has led me to the conclusion that they are not as yet prepared to make a proper use of conveniences. The poor require preliminary education in keeping their houses and stairs clean, before they can be trusted in the manner proposed. Of this they themselves are well aware; and I have been informed that, in some instances, apprehensive of their neighbours, they have requested their landlord to withhold from the tenement the benefit of the so-called boon. One dirty neighbour disgusts another, and the sequel can easily be pictured. The houses, too, in the great majority of cases, were never intended for this sanitary improvement. They are of great age, many of them as strong as fortresses, and others so old as already to be falling to pieces, with walls hardly able to maintain themselves erect, much less to stand the operations of the sanitary engineer. With a population inhabiting such tenements innumerable difficulties must arise. There can be no hesitation in the case of the respectable artisan, who can afford to pay a suitable rent, and secure a house furnished with modern comforts. The great movement to which we have already alluded, in speaking of the density of population—viz., that of supplying suitable houses for the working-classes—has practically determined this. To provide a suitable house for an artisan and his family, with a separate convenience, a rent of at least £6 is required, and this, be it remembered, has only been accomplished with the assistance rendered by philanthropic societies. Of course the class thus benefited is far above that of the ordinary labourer, who, in the time of sickness, becomes chargeable, with his family, upon the parish, and who, in the time of his greatest vigour and best wages, cannot be expected to pay such a rent. Up to the present time, no houses have been built for his requirements, and to this fact the attention of philanthropists and architects is invited. The kind of tenement required is one so constructed that on each landing there should not be more than two families, who shall be provided with a mutual convenience. With such a limited population, there is less risk of derangement of the mechanism, and a greater certainty of fixing upon the offender. If a state of matters be produced which can be described as a nuisance, then, by our local Act the offender is liable to punishment, which exercises a most salutary influence upon the habits of the poor. It is only by constant supervision that such can be taught the important lessons of cleanliness, and the process is a slow one. But where, as in the tenement in Dickson's Close already referred to, we have a large population, it becomes difficult in the extreme to decide upon the culprits; and there is no resource but to charge all the inhabitants in the stair as concerned in the production of the nuisance, which may in reality be the work of some indolent sloven. But, putting our closes out of the question, there is abundant scope for the compulsory introduction of conveniences. We have, first of all, those streets in the New Town which are destitute of them. I refer particularly to the side streets, such as Rose Street, Thistle Street, Jamaica Street, and Cumberland Street. It has been already shown that, even in the New Town, great overcrowding exists; and where there are large sub-divided tenements, as in St James Street, (see p. 36) and at the same time imperfect sewers, it would be most injudicious to enforce the regulation. Then, there is the large and populous district of Nicolson Street, in which the houses are generally of low altitude, and well suited for modern improvements. Of course there are exceptions, as in certain tenements in East Richmond Street; but these demand special consideration. The districts, too, of Broughton, Calton, and Water of Leith afford ample scope for improvement in this respect. Let such localities be attended to at once, where the change can be effected to the manifest improvement of the dwellings, and the health of the inhabitants; and, in the meantime, enforce greater cleanliness in the closes, and supply them with a greater number of public conveniences. At p. 60 of the Appendix I have given the number of these, with their accommodation, and it will be seen that where the destitution is greatest, the wants of the poor are more fully supplied. But there can be no doubt that, were these erections multiplied, the comfort of the poor would be greatly increased, and the salubrity of the poorest districts of the city markedly improved. The same remark applies to the Urinals, the number of which might be doubled, without fully supplying the wants of the public. The present number of these, and their distribution throughout the city, are stated in the same table.

HOUSE CESSPOOLS.

Where house drains exist, it is customary to connect them with a cesspool, the over-flow of which escapes into the nearest sewer. Where there are no main sewers, as in country districts, or as in our own southern suburbs, where villa residences were built before the general drainage was begun, the least offensive method of getting rid of waste water, &c., is by constructing a receptacle at some little distance from the house which shall receive such matters, until it is so full of the sediment deposited that it requires to be emptied. The cesspool is then cleaned out, and the process of filling goes on as before. Of course, where the cesspool is carelessly built, and not properly cemented, it will leak and infiltrate the neighbouring soil; and when, as often happens in towns where there is a divided responsibility, the cesspool is not regularly emptied, and the overflow-drain becomes choked, the sewage escapes either into the soil, or is forced upwards into the foundations of the house. The evil effects of this upon the health are comparatively rarely seen in the country districts, owing to the freedom of the surrounding ventilation, and the out-door life of the inhabitants. But in towns it is otherwise, and this cesspool nuisance in Edinburgh has become so clamant as to demand a thorough remedy. From one of its worst effects—viz., the contamination of water for domestic use, from the soaking of the soil—we are luckily preserved. We have no private wells into which the drainage from our defective cesspools can escape, to contaminate, in the most insidious manner, the water,—even communicating to it an attractive sparkle, but at the same time poisoning the system, which never becomes habituated to its use. This, in a great measure, explains the unusual mortality at times observable in epidemics in our country districts and small towns.

Builders and architects, however, still uphold the necessity of cesspools, even in crowded cities; but their reasoning is, in my opinion, fallacious. That the system should find favour among smaller tradesmen is not to be wondered at. The cesspool demands planning and material, in addition to the skilled labour required for its construction. The laying of a few tubular drains, with a *direct* communication with the main sewer, is comparatively a cheap operation. Indeed, I was so impressed with the importance of the subject, and with the necessity of meeting the arguments of practical men with stronger facts than I could urge, that I requested my colleague, Mr Macpherson, Superintendent of Streets and Buildings, to give me a short description of a cesspool and its connections, with a statement of the disadvantages of the system, and he has kindly furnished the following :—

The greater number of houses of the better class in the City of Edinburgh have each a Cesspool in connection with the branch drain leading from the house to the sewer. It may be taken for granted that all the houses built before the year 1854, as well as many built since that time, have each a Cesspool ; and consequently, to all these houses the following remarks will apply in a greater or less degree.

The form of Cesspool which is usually employed is that shown upon the plan.

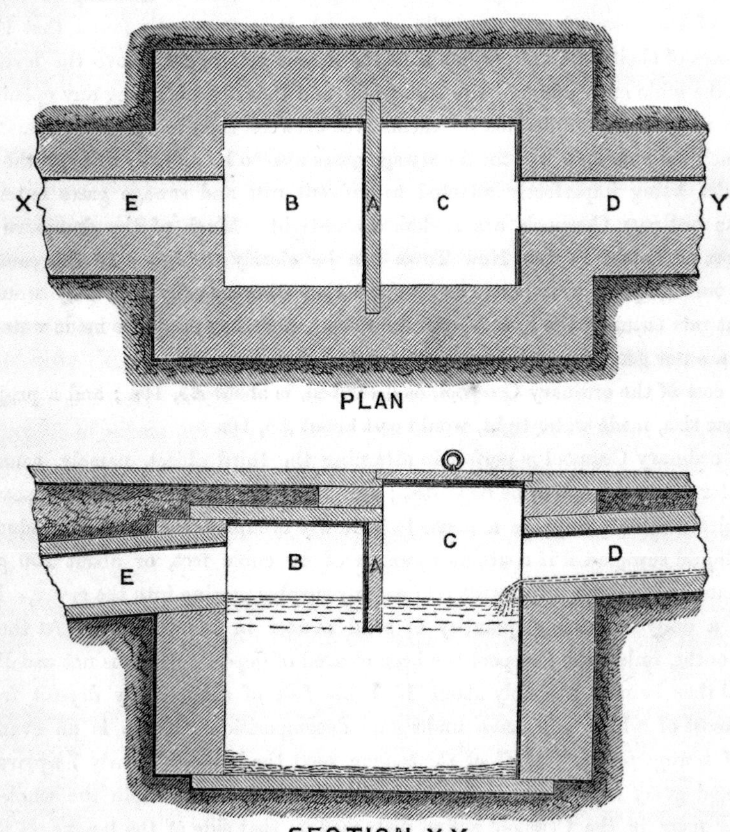

A pit, about 5 feet deep by 5 feet wide, and 7 feet 4 inches long, is dug in the course of the branch drain—generally in the front area of the house. The bottom of this pit is laid with pavement, and a wall of common rough masonry about 14 inches thick is built round its sides. Across the line of the drain a piece of pavement, or tongue A, is set on edge, resting on the side walls, and leaving a space of about 2 feet 5 inches from the lower edge to the surface of the pavement at the bottom of the Cesspool. The Cesspool is then completed by having an opening carried up at C, by which it can be inspected. When the Cesspool thus finished becomes full of water, the air on the side B of the tongue, which is next the main sewer in the street, is separated from the air on the side C, which is next the house.

The objects proposed to be attained by having these Cesspools are—

1*st*, To prevent rats passing from the sewers to the houses;

2*d*, To provide against any foul air from the sewers entering the houses; and

3*d*, To cause the solid matter contained in the sewage to be deposited, with the view of providing against the sewers being silted up by it.

There can only be one opinion as to the desirableness of attaining, in a perfect way, the first two of these objects; but owing to the kind of building of which the side walls of the Cesspools are generally composed, it is frequently found that they are rather places of shelter for rats, which contrive to pass the tongue above the level of the water by the wide open joints of the side walls, and then, by enlarging any opening they find, they make a communication for themselves between the drain and the house,—thus at the same time making a way for the sewage gases also to be diffused through the house.

Besides being imperfectly adapted to prevent rats and sewage gases entering the house, the ordinary Cesspools are seldom water-tight. Much of the dampness in the lower floors of houses in the New Town can be clearly attributed to this cause. No doubt, if the Cesspools were better constructed than they usually are, they would tend to prevent rats entering the houses from the sewers, and they might be made water-tight; but they are not generally either well constructed or water-tight.

The cost of the ordinary Cesspool, as described, is about £3, 10s.; and a proper one, of the same size, made water-tight, would cost about £5, 10s.

The ordinary Cesspool is perfect in attaining the third object, namely, causing the solid matter in the sewage to be deposited; and this object, when attained, appears to be highly objectionable. Suppose a house to be newly occupied, the Cesspool gradually fills up with liquid sewage till it contains upwards of 40 cubic feet, or about 250 gallons: which quantity it always afterwards retains, any surplus passing into the sewer,—leaving, however, a daily increasing quantity of solid matter in the Cesspool. At the end of twelve months, unless the Cesspool has been cleared of deposit, which is not usually done, there will then be most probably about 15 cubic feet of sedimentary deposit from the sewage, most of which will have undergone decomposition. There is an evaporating surface of sewage on the side C of the tongue, next the house, of nearly 7 square feet in extent; and every time water passes from the house into the drain the whole of the putrifying mass in the Cesspool is first disturbed on that side of the tongue, so that any noxious gases contained in it are most likely to be evolved on the side of the tongue nearest the house. By this operation, frequently repeated, the drain becomes charged with noxious gases; and the more air-tight the drain is, the more highly will it be charged with them.

It thus appears that the present Cesspool is imperfect for the attainment of desirable objects, and perfect in fulfilling the objectionable one.

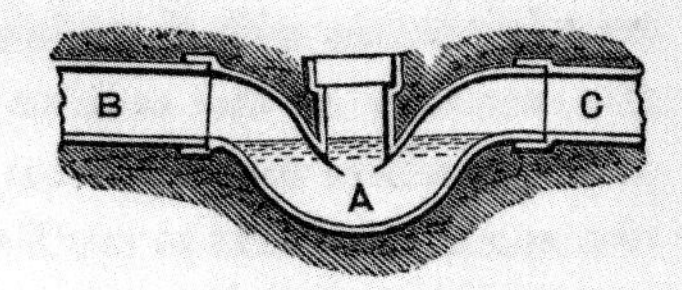

Fortunately there is a very simple substitute, namely, a Syphon Pipe, of glazed stoneware, as shown on the sketch, which costs only about 4s. Suppose the case of a newly occupied house, with a pipe drain of 6 inches in diameter, and having one of these syphon pipes in connection with it. The water gradually fills up the space A until it reaches the level of the outlet at C, which is usually about 2 or 3 inches lower than the inlet B. The quantity of water retained will be rather less than 3 cubic feet, instead of 37, as in the present Cesspool, but there is sufficient, however, to form a perfectly secure trap for gases or rats passing to the house from the sewer.

The advantages of such a trap are, that the whole water can be renewed by allowing a flow for but a few minutes,—thus thoroughly preventing smell; its being perfectly water-tight; its preventing rats passing into the house; and its non-retention of the sedimentary deposit of the sewage, from which, while undergoing the process of decomposition, it is believed that the most deadly sewage emanations are evolved.

The foregoing statement supports entirely the views I have long held as to the disadvantage, in a sanitary point of view, under which the New Town of Edinburgh labours, owing to the prevalence of cesspools. As the main drainage lines are now completed, cesspools are useless, inasmuch as communication can be directly made with the street sewer, and they should, in my opinion, be disused or entirely removed.

STREET CESSPOOLS.

Along the sides of our streets are to be seen gratings for the reception of rain water, &c. These, under the names of street cesspools, and street gullies, are well-known sources of nuisance. Communicating directly with the main sewer, the foul gases generated along its course are, on a change of wind, forced upwards, and taint the air for some distance around. To remedy this, these openings require to be properly trapped. The necessity for this precaution was not recognised when the streets were originally formed, and as the expense attending the alteration is considerable, there has been great delay in carrying out this simple, but very important, sanitary measure. My attention was early called to the subject, and a pretty correct list of these gratings is appended under the head of each street, in Table VI. of the Appendix, specifying their condition, whether trapped or untrapped. Unfortunately, our streets are under a variety of separate management. There is the City Road Trust, the County Road Trust, and also a number of private streets, some of which have been placed under the care of the City Road Trust, while others are managed by the house proprietors in the street. On the other hand, the municipal authorities, wherever they have been effecting improvements in the closes and poorer districts, attend to the surface drainage. In this way, a large number of fully trapped cesspools have been placed in the worst parts of the town, which thus contrast favourably with those inhabited by the wealthier classes. This is well seen in the summary of the number of these cesspools in the various sanitary districts, at p. 56, where the proportion in each district of untrapped to trapped cesspools is also specified. Next to our Town Council, who have allowed no untrapped cesspools within their jurisdiction, during the last 15 or 20 years, the City Road Trust deserves most honourable mention. Fully convinced of the necessity of having every cesspool trapped, they have energetically set themselves to the work, and during the past year they have altered no fewer than 107 cesspools, 83 of which are situated in the New Town north of Princes Street, and 24 in the Old Town to the south. In an improvement like this, contributing so much to the amenity and health of the town, they deserve every encouragement. The changes entail considerable expense, and it is to be hoped that the inhabitants will cheerfully submit to increased rates for a short time, until every street belonging to the Trust is put in a satisfactory state. Many of the streets in the suburbs are under the care of the County Trust, who, as might be expected, display some apathy on the subject. The avenues to the city are often rendered unwholesome, from the amount of sewage emanations which taint the air; and nothing can be more annoying than for the citizen, on leaving the city for a walk in the country to find himself, as he reaches the green fields, assailed by the most forbidding odours. A familiar example of this may be experienced any summer day along Inverleith Row, and the intensity of the nuisance diminishes and increases as you approach or pass one of these street cesspools. Again and again, in my experience, such offensive smells have been attributed most erroneously to the neighbouring water of Leith. The agitation connected with its purification tended to throw into the shade what appeared to be a minor form of nuisance, but now that the stream bids fair to be greatly deodorized, it is to be hoped that the County Trust will render all their streets and roads near to the city as wholesome as possible.

WATER OF LEITH.

We have already seen that the Water of Leith not only drains the whole of the New Town north of George Street, but also receives the sewage of a large district of the City lying to the west, which joins it at Coltbridge. The stream thus polluted enters the Parliamentary area, and in its passage through the city is still further contaminated by the drainage of the New Town. It was to remedy this anomalous state of matters that the bill of last session was passed, which provided for the prevention of further contamination of the river by the construction of large pipes, to collect the sewage and pass it directly to the sea. There can be no doubt that this will be a sanitary improvement. At present the Water of Leith, in its passage through Edinburgh, is a great open sewer, subject to considerable fluctuation in the volume of its waters; and in hot weather, during the prevalence of certain winds, it emits offensive odours. These have, of late years, been much complained of, especially since the formation of the Caledonian Distillery, which, as already stated, has been most unfortunately situated. It was impossible to pass the refuse of this large establishment into any of the large built sewers draining directly to the east. All the strongly offensive material was discharged into the Lochrin Burn, an open drain running westward, and conveying a large amount of sewage into the Water of Leith, which in its turn entered the City, and passed through the village of the Water of Leith, Stockbridge, and Canonmills, on its way to the sea. The inhabitants were thus subjected to a double annoyance. During westerly winds, the odour of the refuse before it reached Coltbridge was carried over the town, and in its further progress infested all the districts along both banks of the Water of Leith. What added to the nuisance was the great diminution effected in the Water of Leith itself by the supply granted to mills along its course. In summer these mill-lades left the main stream dry, and conveyed not pure water, but sewage through densely-peopled localities. This state of matters was not to be tolerated in these days of sanitary progress, more especially when it was found that the rental of the district was being lowered, and when it was believed that the most disastrous results were produced on the health of the inhabitants. My attention was early directed to the subject, and to my surprise I found that the district was a healthy one, and presented no unusual percentage of cases of preventible disease. The two districts of Upper and Lower Water of Leith were mapped out; their area, and their population at the census in 1861, were determined, and all deaths occurring during 1863 were allocated to the various streets. In such an enquiry, it is not only necessary to determine the gross mortality, but as the question at issue was the effect of a nuisance (which, in the scientific language of chemists, assumed a most formidable character), the nature of the diseases producing the mortality was also of importance, and was specially noted. The test thus applied was a fair one. The population was clustered along the banks of a stream, proved by analysis to be fraught with the most noxious compounds; and were the views commonly held by sanitary reformers correct, we should not only have had the presence of this pestiferous stream indicated by a largely increased death-rate, but also by a mortality depending upon the presence of such diseases as fevers, diarrhœa, and dysentery, generally allowed to be the product of sewage exhalations. The death-rates of the districts of Upper and Lower Water of Leith for 1863 were, as we have seen, respectively 19 and 17 per 1000. Now, when we remember the large number of inhabitants in these districts belonging to the working-classes, and also that since the census in 1861 the population has been increased by the addition of several new streets, these figures must be regarded as highly satisfactory. In summer, when the condition of the stream was much worse than in winter, there was no corresponding increase in the number of deaths; and, if we turn to the tables of special mortality, we find that neither fever of any kind, nor such diseases as diarrhœa and dysentery are at all prevalent. One locality in the district of the Upper Water of Leith presents a very dense population, and has a correspondingly high mortality. I refer to that triangular area bounded by India Place, Saunders Street, and Kerr Street. One of the sides is bounded by the stream of the water of Leith, while it is intersected by an open mill lade, notorious for its impurities. The distance of the nearest houses in this locality from the Water of Leith is only 12 yards, while that of the most distant is 93 yards. Here the inhabitants are densely crowded in the proportion of 516·7 to the acre, the death-rate is 26·86, while that of children under 5 years rises to 106·67. But on examining the nature of the mortality, we find such diseases as are the product of a dense population, and not those generally attributed to sewage exhalations. To the north we have another densely-peopled district, of a triangular shape, bounded by Dean Street on the one hand, and Mary Place on the other, and containing such streets as Allan Street, Cheyne Street, Bedford Street, and Hermitage Street, &c., &c. The nearest point of this district to the Water of Leith is 120 yards, and the most distant 283 yards. The density of the population is, however, considerably less, being only 336·9 to the acre, and the total death-rate is 25·02, while that of children under 5 years is as high as 69·07. But here again, we fail to find any indication in the nature of the mortality that the high death-rate is due to any other cause than overcrowding. In the district of the Lower Water of Leith, at only one point, viz., at Canonmills, have we a poor population collected in any number. The death-rate for 1863 is 24·88, while that of children above 5 years is 108.34. There, however, we have a large poor population, and, in many instances, wretchedly housed.

With reference, however, to one disease which has of late years attracted much public attention, viz., Diphtheria, the Upper Water of Leith showed a very marked mortality. This is well seen in the tabular statement of the district mortality from Diphtheria, Appendix, p. 57. The sanitary condition of any district could not be accounted satisfactory with such a mortality; and although, in examining into the mortality of the other city districts from this disease, no marked connection could be proved between it and sewage emanations, yet, where uncertainty prevails as to the precise cause of any unusual sickness, it is clearly the duty of a community to remove all possible sources of disease, and among these must be reckoned the existence of open drains in crowded town districts. In this light, the measure for the purification of the Water of Leith must be looked upon as an important sanitary measure, to be followed, at no late period, it is to be hoped, by the removal or improvement of the mills, which at present divert the run of the water, leaving the channel of the stream for the most part dry, and which are a source of nuisance, besides necessitating the continued preservation of the mill lades. The latter were perfectly innocuous, when the district was a strictly rural one and some miles from the city, but they are now quite an anomaly in the midst of a large population, and ought, sooner or later, to be removed. My object in alluding to this subject, has been to warn the public against supposing, that the sanitary measure in question will have any material influence in diminishing the rate of mortality, although it may render the district more agreeable as a place of residence. Lower than it is at present, we can hardly expect it to be. More reliance is to be placed in the general introduction of conveniences, for which the houses in the district are admirably suited, and in the enforcement of greater cleanliness in stairs and courts.

IRRIGATED MEADOWS.

The volume of the water of Leith, and its peculiar course and termination at a sea-port, led to its being largely employed as a motive power, and it has been stated that there is no stream of equal length in the empire upon which so many mills are situated. At several points, it might have been employed in irrigation, but for other uses it was more valuable. With the other drainage outlets of Edinburgh the case was different. The Foul Burn, draining eastwards to the sea, between Leith and Portobello, irrigated 250 acres of meadow-land, which have acquired a wide celebrity. To the south, the Jordan Burn has been put to similar uses, though to a smaller extent; at present there being only 11 acres under irrigation. To the west, the Lochrin Burn irrigates 90 acres; and close to the Parliamentary Boundary in the district of Broughton, 5 acres are irrigated with the sewage of the Broughton Burn, which is a tributary of the Water of Leith; while a few years ago an attempt was made to irrigate some fields in front of Claremont Crescent. Edinburgh may thus be said to be surrounded by these artificial swamps, which at all times emit odours of not the most agreeable description. Under the influence of the improved agriculture of the present century, extensive swampy tracts which existed to the west of Edinburgh, in the neighbourhood of Corstorphine, have been reclaimed; and it is to be regretted that the sewage of the inhabitants should now be employed to create an evil from which we have so recently been delivered. It cannot but be regarded as an unfortunate circumstance for the sanitary condition of Edinburgh and its neighbourhood, that proprietors have vested rights in the fluids that give value to these irrigated lands, and can compel the inhabitants to send the sewage of the city in a particular direction. Were it ever expedient to intercept the drainage of the city which passes westwards, and direct it either by a more expeditious course into the Water of Leith, or into some of the large conduits which pursue an easterly course, such a measure could at once be put a stop to by proprietors who are directly benefited by the sewage, and yet pay none of the civic burdens. The irrigated meadows have increased the value of the estates ten-fold, and enormous compensation would now be demanded for depriving the land of such rich material for manure. Indeed, whatever interferes with the quality of the sewage, becomes a subject of complaint, and the inhabitants are actually deprived of one of the most obvious uses of a sewer, viz., to pass into it the products of manufactures which ought at once to be removed from the sight and smell. Thus lately at Fountainbridge a paraffin manufactory poured its refuse into the public drains, and this, on being allowed to flow over the surface of the grass of the Roseburn Meadows, adhered to it, and rendered it unfit for food. At once the tenant of the meadows was up in arms, and the paraffin works had to be removed. A similar occurrence took place many years ago with regard to the City Gas Works, the refuse from which destroyed the value of the well-known Craigentinny Meadows to the east of the city. In the litigation which ensued, the Town Council joined with the proprietor of the Craigentinny estate in compelling the Gas Works to adopt some other method of getting rid of the noxious compounds, and the result was the erection of the hideous chimney-stalk to carry them off in a state of vapour. The gas company was thus put to great expense, and the principle was established that the proprietor of the irrigated meadows can prescribe the nature of the sewage which is furnished to him by the town. It would, I think, have been sounder policy on the part of the Corporation to have refused to acknowledge this principle, and rather to have insisted upon the removal of the gas works from their objectionable site in one of our poorest localities to some distance in the country, where neither the smoke nor the emanations could give any annoyance. Such a site would have been obtained at a comparatively small cost, and the gas could have been conveyed into the gasometers for the city in large pipes. At present there is no control over this irrigation. No one can inspect it in operation, without seeing that it is carried on in the cheapest and most slovenly way, and that the smells complained of arise chiefly from the foul state of the larger canals. Their sides are kept in a decaying condition from the alterations in the fall and rise of the stream, as the irrigation is increased or diminished. No attempt is made by proper edging with wood to confine the sewage within proper limits, and to prevent the vegetable decay along the sides of the principal channels. When spread over the land, the sewage quickly disappears; and this part of the process, unless the weather be warm, is attended with little inconvenience. But if the privilege be claimed of monopolising the sewage of a city like Edinburgh, it is surely incumbent upon proprietors to diminish, by every means in their power, the evils attendant upon irrigation, especially when carried on in the immediate neighbourhood of a dense population; for Edinburgh, from its situation, is peculiarly exposed to suffer from the effects of the emanations from these meadows. The easterly are our most prevailing winds, which pass across these meadows before they sweep over the New and the more elevated portions of the Old Town. And it has been plausibly conjectured that the insalubrity of these winds depend largely on this contamination. But, at any rate, a city surrounded by swamps cannot be regarded as in a sound sanitary condition; and it is highly probable that a great part of the mortality of the Abbey, and some of the poorer districts of the Old Town is in a great measure owing to the unhealthy character of these breezes which blow so continuously during many months. It is difficult otherwise to account for the high death-rate of the district of the Abbey, in which there is little overcrowding, and where only a small proportion of the population can be said to belong to the poorest class.

WATER SUPPLY.

One of the most satisfactory circumstances connected with the sanitary condition of Edinburgh is undoubtedly its water supply. At one time the inhabitants had to rely entirely on private wells; but the supply from this source was small and precarious, and so early as 1681, the Magistrates, to meet the necessities of an increasing population, began to introduce supplies from without, and various springs in the immediate neighbourhood were from time to time brought into the city. The amount thus provided for the inhabitants was never large. The supply could in no sense be called abundant, and in dry seasons the poor suffered greatly from the want of water. Indeed, considering the great importance of water as a sanitary agent, and the scarcity that prevailed in the early part of the century, the marvel is that the mortality did not reach an unusually high standard. It must be remembered, however, that the water, scanty though it was in quantity, was comparatively pure, was much more wholesome than that obtained from sunk wells, which, had they been continued to be used, would have been contaminated by the sewage of the adjoining heights, and must have proved a fruitful source of disease. Luckily, before the approach of Cholera, the necessities of the inhabitants became so clamant that, in 1819, the present Water Company was formed, and, the large supply of water afforded by the Crawley springs relieved, for a series of years, the city of all apprehensions. As the population increased, powers have been obtained from Parliament to introduce larger quantities; and so lately as 1863 a new Act was passed, by which the Company was empowered to acquire new springs. It has been calculated that when these have been added to our present resources, a daily supply will be afforded of 39 gallons for each inhabitant. During 1863 it amounted to 31·12 gallons per day. It will be observed, by reference to Table XII. in the Appendix (page 61), that throughout the poorer districts of the city, there are a number of public wells. These at one time were the only sources of supply for the inhabitants; but as water began to be introduced into private houses, and their cisterns had to be maintained, these wells became the property (so to speak) of the poorer classes. In the various Acts of Parliament regulating the introduction of water into Edinburgh, the rights of the poor have always been reserved; these public wells being expressly mentioned as to be maintained and increased in number. The importance of this can hardly be over-estimated, when we consider the very dense population of our Old Town. The houses of our poor are totally unprovided with water, and it was not till the General Police and Improvement (Scotland) Act was passed in 1862, that powers were granted, compelling proprietors to introduce water into houses. These clauses also referred to the providing of conveniences, and, of course, where these are introduced a full supply of water must be obtained. But we have endeavoured to show that, among a certain population, and in a limited class of houses, conveniences can only be introduced to the great risk of the inhabitants. To the supply of water to each house no such objection applies. Not only would

68
69

the comfort of the poor be increased, but their time would be economized. In certain tenements the water could be placed on each landing, while, in the older and more dilapidated, a convenient situation would be at the foot of each stair. In addition to the greater cleanliness in the dwellings of the poor that would follow the free use of water, it would then be possible to enforce the clause in our Local Act referring to the cleansing of the common stairs, and the surface drains in these crowded closes would be in a more wholesome state than they are at present, from the waste attending the drawing of the water, and also from the discharge of water which had been put to use. Mr Ramsay, the manager of the Water Company, has drawn attention to the enormous waste of water that takes place in consequence of the faulty construction of the ordinary water-cocks. Since the publication of his pamphlet, my attention has been drawn to this subject, and I can corroborate his statement that the waste in Edinburgh from leakage and faulty apparatus is enormous. In almost every house and court in the poorer districts supplied with water, this leakage is to be found; and as, from the constant service maintained by the Water Company, it is continuous, the amount of water thus lost to the public is very great. The officers of the Company undertake the task of examining the apparatus in each house; but the evil is so general and widespread, that the present staff of the Company is quite inadequate to keep the waste in check. To Mr Ramsay we are also indebted for a very forcible description of the nuisances caused by the faulty construction of water cisterns, and their connection with the drains. Such receptacles require the utmost cleanliness, but it is no uncommon state of matters to find a house occupied by a succession of families, and the cistern to remain uncleaned during a series of years. It is now well known that there is no more certain method of inducing ill health than by the habitual use of tainted water. The water of a cistern can be rendered unwholesome by its dirty condition, and also by its being impregnated with emanations from the sewers. These reach the water from the overflow pipe, which directly communicates with the drain, and which therefore requires to be carefully trapped to prevent the contamination. The air in the house finally becomes tainted, and, in a short time, the inmates suffer from illness. No more frequent cause of nuisance than this has come under my notice in the upper stories of large tenements, which, from their elevation, appeared to be far removed from all possible effluvia from drainage.

In Table XII., at p. 61 of the Appendix, there is also a list of the drinking fountains throughout the city. These have been erected during the last few years. None appear in the poorer districts of the city, with the exception of St Giles, which has two fountains; but these are situated at the Railway Station, on the very outskirts of the district. It must be remembered, however, with regard to the Abbey, Canongate, Tron, St Giles, and Grassmarket, that the public wells, the greater number of which are to be found in these localities, also serve as drinking fountains. A reference to the distribution of the drinking fountains throughout the city shows that they might be largely increased to the manifest comfort of the inhabitants.

INTRAMURAL INTERMENT.

AMONG other lessons taught us by the Cholera was the danger arising from Intramural Interment, and the necessity of providing, where the Churchyards were overcrowded, suitable Cemeteries at some distance from human habitations. When the first epidemic had passed away, and with it the alarm caused by the pestilence, our crowded Churchyards were allowed to remain in *statu quo*. Here and there, throughout the country, slight additions were made to existing burial-grounds; but no decided movement was made in the formation of public cemeteries. An exception, however, must be noticed in the case of the Metropolis, which was provided, in 1832, with the well-known Cemetery of Kensal Green, extending to 53 acres; while in the course of a few years, six more Cemeteries were opened to the public. Even in London, however, little was done in the way of shutting up existing grave-yards and church-vaults until the second visitation of Cholera in 1848 came to remind us of our sanitary shortcomings. The Metropolis now set to work in earnest. Commissioners were appointed to inspect and report to Parliament on the subject; and, as the result of these inquiries, most of the existing City Churchyards were closed under a special Act of Parliament—the Metropolitan Interment Act, which was passed in 1850, and received various amendments in 1852-55 and -57. In 1853, the attention of the Legislature was directed to the condition of the Churchyards beyond the Metropolis, and a special Act was framed to meet their requirements. Scotland was not dealt with till 1855, when the "Burial Grounds (Scotland) Act" was issued, giving power to Parochial Boards to shut up overcrowded Churchyards, and to acquire land to form Cemeteries. It is to be regretted that we had not the benefit of such a measure long before, and that our Parishes had not combined with one accord to shut the existing City Churchyards, and establish suitable Cemeteries. In this way our Parochial Boards would have been amply remunerated for any pecuniary sacrifice they made to the public health and convenience.

As it was, public enterprise opened the Warriston Cemetery to the inhabitants in 1843; and during the next few years, the state of the money-market was such as to favour enterprises of the kind. In 1846, no fewer than five Cemeteries, with an area of 38 acres, were formed. These varied in extent from 5 to 10 acres, and were placed around the City in various directions. One only, viz., that at Echo Bank, was situated outside the Parliamentary boundary, the area of which was fixed in 1832. It is unfortunate that so many Cemeteries were laid out within the municipal limits. Several of them are already encroached upon by habitations, and if the City continue to extend, as it has been doing for the last few years, our Cemeteries will become similar to the City Churchyards, by being surrounded on all sides.

The accompanying table clearly shows, however, the amount of good which these Cemeteries must have conferred upon the inhabitants, by relieving our crowded burial-grounds. They were hardly formed, when the second epidemic of Cholera came, and found us, so to speak, prepared; and little was said as to intramural interment. Had there been no Cemeteries in existence, when this visitation of the pestilence came upon us, I have no doubt that, through the overwhelming force of public opinion, every one of our City Churchyards would have been closed. The Cholera, however, passed away, and they remain to this day. I have no hesitation in saying that every one of them should be closed. Many of them, as may be gathered from the accompanying table, are of great age. They are all small and overcrowded. The rivalry excited by the various Cemeteries has no doubt led to the Churchyards being more decently kept. But so far as amenity is concerned, in Scotland we are far behind our southern neighbours. Our country Churchyards are generally in a slovenly state, and the same might have been said, a few years ago, as to those in our towns. Much of this, was owing to the age of the tombs, and the manner in which even recent graves were encased in iron rods to prevent any attempt at desecration. This was specially to be feared in and around any town which was the seat of a medical school. But, with the passing of the Anatomy Act in 1832, the graves have remained undisturbed; and I do not know of any case occurring in Edinburgh, since that date, in which bodies have been removed for the purpose of dissection. Graves so covered in could not be kept tidy; they became receptacles for dirt and weeds. As families, too, became extinct, their resting-places were forgotten, and left to decay. My attention was particularly called to this point when examining the Greyfriars Churchyard. This is the largest of our city Churchyards, and was formed in 1561. From its position, it was much used by the inhabitants, and for a long series of years must have been overcrowded. I drew the attention of the Kirk-Session and Town Council to its state, and the Municipality, as superiors, at once, on my representation, gave instructions that no interments should be permitted except in the case of persons possessing private tombs. These were comparatively few in number, and are rapidly diminishing. All burials in the common ground were thus stopped, and there was the prospect that in the course of a few years the Churchyard would be entirely closed. This was a sanitary measure of no small importance. The surrounding district was a most necessitous one, densely peopled, and inhabited by persons of the poorest class. The interments, which had averaged, since the Cemeteries were established, 240 per annum (the Town Council having previously discouraged burials in this ground) have fallen, as will be observed from the table, to 73.

CHURCHYARDS.

No.	NAME.	Date of Formation.	Present Area in Acres.	Total Number of Interments in 1863.	Number of Interments from within the Parliamentary Boundary.	Number of Interments from without the Parliamentary Boundary.	Number of Interments at Lowest Rate.	Number of Interments at Higher Rates.	Sanitary District where situated.	Population in 1861.	Proportion of Population to each Inhabited Acre.
1	West Church or St Cuthbert's	?	4·4	822	795	27	673	122	St Giles,	15,967	234·8
2	Greyfriars	1561	5·	73	73	...	28	45	Do.	15,967	234·8
3	Pleasance (Quakers)	1665	·125	...	...	...	...	...	Pleasance and St Leonard,	11,104	150·
4	Canongate	1688	1·8	152	152	...	140	12	Canongate,	12,200	219·8
5	Calton, Old	1718	1·	119	119	...	98	21	Calton and Greenside,	10,984	120·7
6	Buccleuch	1763	0·5	17	17	...	...	17	Nicolson Street,	18,307	286·
7	Calton, New	1817	3·	866	866	...	825	41	Calton and Greenside,	10,984	120·7
8	Newington	1820	2·4	536	522	14	478	44	Newington,	4,955	39·9
9	Causewayside (Jews)	1820	·41	2	2	...	...	2	Do.	4,955	39·9
10	St John's	1820	1·8	8	6	2	...	6	Upper New Town,	10,930	94·8
11	Trinity, Dean Bridge	1838	0·2	1	...	1	...	...	Upper Water of Leith,	12,332	88·
	Total,		20·635	2,596	2,552	44	2,242	310			

CEMETERIES.

No.	NAME.	Date of Formation.	Present Area in Acres.	Total Number of Interments in 1863.	Number of Interments from within the Parliamentary Boundary.	Number of Interments from without the Parliamentary Boundary.	Number of Interments at Lowest Rate.	Number of Interments at Higher Rates.	Sanitary District where situated.	Population in 1861.	Proportion of Population to each Inhabited Acre.
1	Warriston	1843	15·	583	474	109	108	366	Lower Water of Leith,	3,866	31·1
2	Dalry	1846	5·	276	242	34	79	163	West End,	7,748	44·2
3	Echo Bank	1846	8·	542	513	29	388	125	Landward,	2,323	·7
4	Dean	1846	8·	300	290	10	120	170	Upper Water of Leith,	12,332	88·
5	Grange	1846	10·	443	426	17	236	190	Grange,	1,886	15·9
6	Rosebank	1846	7·	680	155	525	104	51	Broughton,	5,672	48·9
	Total,		53·	2,824	2,100	724	1,035	1,065			

This number should, however, have been only 45, as 28 of those interred at the lowest rate should not have been permitted. The sanctioning of these was quite against the spirit of the resolution of the Town Council, and it is to be hoped that the church authorities will see it to be their duty to resist all such interments.

I was proceeding to deal with the other Churchyards, when a difficulty presented itself for which I was not prepared. The Greyfriars being virtually closed to the poorer classes by whom it was much used, these had to go elsewhere to bury their dead, and naturally betook themselves to the nearest place of interment. The rest of the Churchyards, in order to prevent this influx of the poorest burials, raised their charges. The public Cemeteries, which were intended to supply the wants of the wealthier classes, followed the example; and I found that, while I benefited the immediate neighbourhood by the shutting up of Greyfriars, I had increased the funeral expenses of the poor. In a few months, the charges in and around Edinburgh would have become prohibitory, and the greatest difficulty would have been experienced in the disposal of the dead. No greater sanitary evil could have been experienced. I therefore determined to consider the subject carefully, and ascertain where the burials took place during one year, selecting 1863 as a year of average mortality, in which there had been no epidemic. The results are recorded in the preceding table.

The oldest of our City Churchyards is believed to be that of the West Church, or St Cuthbert's. Its antiquity is such that no precise date can be given for the period of its formation; the earliest reliable date is 1487, but it is evident, that at that time, the church had been long in existence. Indeed, it is stated in the "History of the West Church," published in 1829, that the old Church of St Cuthbert, which was taken down in 1774, had stood for 1000 years. The early parochial records, too, have unfortunately been destroyed. The parish for which the burial-ground served as the only place of interment, was the largest and the most populous in Scotland, comprising as it did nearly the whole of Edinburgh and a large portion of the county. And it is not to be wondered at that, as the population increased, additions were from time to time made to it. At present, however, it has only an area of 4½ acres. We read of its being enlarged in 1701, "the Cemetery having been found to be too small for the increasing population, and the consequent number of interments." Additions were again made to it in 1787; and in 1809, "the Cemetery around the West Church becoming too small for the number of interments," efforts were made, and sucessfully, to obtain from the City of Edinburgh a piece of ground lying immediately to the north. This was of small extent, measuring only 1 rood, 17 ells. "It was enclosed in 1814, and in a few years afterwards, it was completely filled with tombs." Another small portion of ground to the south was added in 1824. The present extent of this burial-ground was completed in 1831 by its being enlarged to the south. This addition was just made in time, as the epidemic of Cholera came and proved very destructive in the parish. Small in extent as this Churchyard is, it has now for many years back gone on filling and enlarging till it reached its present dimensions 34 years ago. And yet, notwithstanding the relief afforded by the Cemeteries, no fewer than 822 interments took place in 1863. Of these 795 belonged to Edinburgh, *i.e.*, came from within the Parliamentary Boundary, which is now co-extensive with the muncipal limits; and 27 are supposed to have come from the landward part of the parish. It would appear that 149 have taken place at the highest rates, and presumably therefore in ground already purchased; but the large number 673 remains as representing those interred at the lowest rates. More complaints have reached me with reference to this burying-ground than to any other, probably for the reason that it is only lately that houses have been built so as to overlook it. That the inhabitants have sufficient ground for remonstrance there cannot be any doubt, and no one can read its previous history in the light of its present statistics without being convinced that its condition is that of an overcrowded Churchyard.

In order to relieve the West Church Burying-Ground, a small piece of land, in 1763, was opened in the southern district of the city, adjoining Buccleuch Church. This was of small extent, measuring only half an acre; and it soon became "so excessively crowded, that it was dangerous to dig a grave in any part of the open ground." It was accordingly shut by orders of the Session in 1819, having been in use for 56 years. The situation and soil of this burying-ground were very faulty, and in my opinion it should never have been formed. It is certainly surprising to find that in 1863, 17 burials were allowed in this over-crowded ground. It was closed, as we have seen, in 1819, and, to supply the urgent necessities of the parish, the Newington Burying-Ground was acquired in 1820. This, too, was of small extent, and, as will be observed from the table, is still largely used, and for a poor class of interments. Indeed, it is well known that the West Church Parish inter their paupers in this ground. It is not to be wondered at that it has become over-crowded, more especially in that portion which is allotted as common ground.

The next in point of age is the Greyfriars, of which we have already spoken.

The Canongate was formed in 1688, in the midst of a crowded population. It was of small size, being only about 2 acres in extent, and it rapidly filled. The inhabitants became alarmed in 1848, and applied to the Sheriff, during the epidemic of cholera, to have it shut up. The attempt was unsuccessful, on account of the conflicting nature of the evidence. The Churchyard was however levelled, relaid with earth, and the interments went on as before. Considerable relief had been afforded to it by the formation of the Old Calton Burying-Ground in 1718. The situation on a rocky eminence was, however, most unsuitable; its size, too, was small, and the new city approach to the east cut it in two. Houses, including public offices and prisons, sprang up in its immediate neighbourhood, and years ago it ought to have been entirely closed. Yet, in 1863, 119 interments took place in this over-crowded spot. So inadequate was the accommodation at an early period, that in 1817, just 100 years after it had been in constant requisition, a larger piece of ground to the east, amounting to 3 acres, was set apart as the New Calton Burying-Ground. The table shows that this continues to the present day to be largely frequented. Indeed, more interments take place in it than in any other Churchyard, or in any of our large Cemeteries. It presents an over-crowded appearance, and its position, favourable in some respects as that was, is now unsuitable, and the interments should, in my opinion, be strictly limited.

In all Acts of Parliament relating to burials, we find special provision made for the burial-grounds of the Quakers and the Jews. That of the Quakers in the Pleasance is supposed to have existed from 1665. It is of very limited extent, and from the small number of the community in question, it is not likely to be over-crowded, though it must now be pretty well filled, having been in use for the last 200 years. At the date of its formation, the locality was not unobjectionable, but now it is overlooked by houses nearly on all sides, and a large and a daily-increasing population is found clustering around it. The Jews were permitted for some-time to inter their dead in a cave or grotto on the Calton Hill, but in 1820 they acquired, in Causewayside, a portion of a field amounting to the 1/24th of an acre. This, in the course of years, has become over-crowded. The position is most unfavourable, being confined and surrounded by a poor population.

In 1863, no fewer than 5420 interments took place in our Churchyards and Cemeteries, and of that number 4878 were buried within the municipal limits. In the table the area of the various Churchyards and Cemeteries is given, and it appears that during 1863, while there were 53 interments to the acre in the Cemeteries, 125 took place in each acre of the overcrowded city Churchyards, although the Greyfriars is now comparatively disused. It would naturally be supposed that the Cemeteries would have relieved the town entirely of what was felt to be an increasing burden, viz., the poorer burials. But we find that the poor have to a large extent continued to use our crowded City Churchyards, while the wealthier classes have betaken themselves to the Cemeteries. Thus, of the 4878 burials, 2596 were interred in the Churchyards, and 2282 in our Cemeteries,—the interments in Echo Bank Cemetery, situated beyond the Parliamentary boundary, being deducted. Of the 2552 in the Churchyards from within the Parliamentary boundary, 2242 were at the lowest rates, and only 310 at the higher; while, in the Cemeteries, of the 2100 from within the same area, there were 1035 at the lowest rates, and 1065 at the highest.

In the City Churchyards, 44 persons were interred from without the municipal limits. It will be observed that 41 of these burials took place in the ground belonging to the West Church, which, as we have seen, is a parish of large extent, and yet its burial-grounds are all situated *within* the city. In the Cemeteries within the municipality, in which that of Echo Bank is not included, a reference to the table will show that there were 695 interments from without. Of these 525 came from Leith and its neighbourhood.

Looking to the position of our City Churchyards, their age, and limited size, and also taking into consideration the increase of the population, it is impossible to resist the conclusion that they are overcrowded, and that they should be closed. The immediate effect of such a measure, would undoubtedly be to place ourselves at the mercy of the various Cemetery companies, whose sole object being to secure a handsome dividend for their shareholders, a rapid rise would take place in the rate of interments. This would seriously affect the poor, who, quite unable to pay the increased expenses, would be compelled to apply for aid to the parishes, and thus the public would, in the long run, be heavily taxed in the shape of poor-rates. Year by year, the Cemetery tariff would be raised for this class of burials, and our poor would only be buried with the greatest difficulty.

84

85

It is high time that this subject should be carefully considered, and that the Town-Council, as acting for the public, should advise with the Parochial Boards as to the best course to be pursued. Sooner or later we will be forced to come to a decision, and possibly under circumstances not admitting of the deliberation that the present juncture affords. The health of the city is satisfactory, and no epidemic is in our midst. Should we be threatened with any pestilence, I feel convinced that Government would not hesitate for a moment in peremptorily preventing all intramural interment.

As the remedy can hardly be supplied by private or joint stock enterprise, I would propose that our City Parishes should combine to provide—which by the Burial Act they are empowered to do—a public Cemetery of large extent at some distance in the country, and of easy access, where the land would be cheap, and in which the rate of interment could be made as reasonable as possible, so as to meet the necessities of the poorest inhabitants. This is, in my opinion, a more crying want than a public park for any district of the city, and it is to be hoped that the scheme will meet with ready approval in these enlightened days of sanitary improvement, when even our Poorhouses are removed outside the city boundary.

If this were determined upon, then our various city burying-grounds could be closed. A similar measure should be extended to them as has been so advantageously employed in the case of the Greyfriars. All interments in the common ground, at the low rates, should be completely stopped; and only for a limited period, say for ten years, should the public be allowed to make use of private enclosures.

Since these remarks were penned, the estate of Craiglockhart has been purchased by the City Parish for the purpose of erecting a suitable Workhouse, to which will be attached such an amount of farm land as the paupers will be able to cultivate. A large portion of the estate is left untouched, and several admirable situations for a public cemetery are to be found on it. Among the advantages that these sites present, may be mentioned proximity to Edinburgh and great seclusion. They will never be encroached upon in any extension of the city. It is rare that such an opportunity as the present occurs, and as the difficulty of securing land in the immediate neighbourhood is daily increasing, the importance of taking advantage of the present opportunity need not be insisted upon.

SANITARY REQUIREMENTS OF THE CITY.

EDINBURGH has never been regarded as an unhealthy city. Its death-rate, although subject to considerable annual variations, will bear favourable comparison with that of other large towns, which do not labour under its special disadvantages. It is, however, peculiarly exposed to the ravages of epidemic disease of all kinds, on account of its dense and badly-housed population; and whether the epidemic be cholera or fever, the poorer inhabitants living in the crowded districts of the Old Town suffer in a marked degree. During the last five years, the health of the community has been good, and among the working-classes food and work have been unusually plentiful. The following table shows that the average death-rate for that period has been only 24 per 1000. It will be observed that the population has been calculated for each year, and that certain deductions have been made from the number of deaths—viz., those of persons who died in the Royal Infirmary, and who belonged to the neighbouring sea-port (which since 1837 has not formed a part of the city), or to various counties of Scotland. By this means a correct estimate can be formed of the death-rate of the city, which would otherwise be burdened with a large amount of mortality, for which it is solely indebted to the celebrity of its Hospital and Medical School.

Year.	Population within the Parliamentary Boundary.	Total Deaths Registered within the Parliamentary Boundary.	Deduct Deaths belonging to		Remaining Mortality.	Births.	Death-Rate per 1000.	Birth-Rate per 1000.	Excess of Birth-Rate over Death-Rate.
			Leith.	County					
1859	166,380	3,619	23	86	3,510	5,446	21·09	32·73	11·64
1860	167,248	4,149	22	97	4,030	5,380	24·09	32·16	8·07
1861	168,121	4,077	23	108	3,946	5,694	23·47	33·87	10·4
1862	168,989	4,661	19	137	4,505	5,722	26·65	33·86	7·21
1863	169,857	4,496	31	149	4,316	6,123	25·4	36·05	10·65
Average							24·15	33·74	9·59

In inquiring into the sanitary requirements of the city, and in attempting to point out how the death-rate may be lowered, it may be useful to generalize our remarks. A glance at the map of Edinburgh shows that the city naturally divides itself into three great divisions, viz., an Old and a New Town, separated by the railway valley, or that of Princes Street Gardens; while, to the south, the Meadows constitute a distinct line of demarcation between the older portions of the city and the suburbs of Newington, Grange, and Morningside. In our inquiry into the sanitary requirements of the city, we shall consider the most urgent necessities of these three divisions, embracing as they do various of the sanitary districts, which naturally group themselves together. In the table below are given the population of the three divisions as at the census of 1861—their respective mortality during 1863—their acreage, and the density of the population.

	Population 1861.			Mortality 1863.			Death-Rate p. 1000.			Area in Imperial Acres.	Proportion of Population to each Acre.
	Above 5 years.	Under 5 years.	Total.	Above 5 years.	Under 5 years.	Total.	Above 5 years.	Under 5 years.	Total.		
NEW TOWN	55,084	5,519	60,603	741	368	1,109	13·27	66·67	18·3	1,765·5	34·3
OLD TOWN	85,187	12,901	98,088	1,618	1,397	3,015	18·99	108·29	30·73	1,078·5	90·9
SOUTHERN SUBURBS	8,513	917	9,430	146	46	192	17·15	50·16	20·36	1,104·	8·5
Total for Parliamentary Area,	148,784	19,337	168,121	2,505	1,811	4,316	16·83	93·65	25·67	3,948·	42·5
LANDWARD	2,130	193	2,323	85	11	96	39·9	57·	41·32	3,127·	·7
Total	150,914	19,530	170,444	2,590	1,822	4,412	17·16	93·29	25·88	7,075·	24·1

NEW TOWN.

THE New Town was laid down on a regular plan. When the extension of the city to the south did not meet the requirements of a rapidly-increasing population, the heights to the north, separated from the Old Town by the North Loch, and now by the railway valley, were surveyed, and streets were mapped out, possessing a width and a regularity which at the time could not be equalled in Europe. The New Town was built, therefore, under the best sanitary notions prevalent at the time. The houses first built were situated at the east end of Princes Street and its immediate neighbourhood, and the three leading streets of the Upper New Town were gradually finished. A great impetus was given to the extension of this part of the city by the building mania of 1825. At that time the Lower New Town may be said to have been entirely built; new streets sprang up with great rapidity; the plans of city extension were felt to be inadequate for the extravagant dreams of speculating builders, and the districts of Calton and Broughton to the eastward were covered with proposed streets and squares. The commercial crisis which ensued not only stopped the building that was going on, but arrested for the long period of thirty years the extension of the city. Many of the streets exhibited unsightly gaps of stances partially built-on, and as a general rule, the corner of the street, the most prominent, and possibly the most expensive tenement to build, was left unoccupied. Within the last few years, however, these have been finished, and the city has extended to the west; but the plans for the enlargement of the city to the north and east still remain unused.

At the time of the building of the New Town, both at its commencement and at its subsequent rapid enlargement in 1825, imperfect notions prevailed as to the internal and external drainage of houses. The domestic use of baths was apparently unknown, and the conveniences were few in number and awkwardly placed, either so as to deprive a principal room of its amenity, or in such a confined space as to be entirely without ventilation. Princes Street, George Street, Queen Street, York Place, and Heriot Row, can still furnish specimens of such faulty arrangement. When unhealthy competition prevails in the building trade, and houses are erected with undue haste, many points of essential importance to their sanitary condition are very apt to be overlooked, while others which bulk largely on the eye of intending purchasers, such as external decoration, receive an undue amount of attention. This, I have no doubt, was the case during our building mania in 1825. Stately houses were erected of the finest freestone, with rooms of excellent ventilating proportions, but the sanitary arrangements were invariably defective. Besides this, no definite drainage plan for such a large town had been prepared, and where street drains were constructed they were imperfectly built, and their communicating branches with the houses, being hastily put together with the chips coming from the stones in the process of being shaped, were of the most faulty description. These, under the name of "shivers," formed an irregular passage for the waste water from the house, and being loosely put together, and coarsely cemented, instead of affording an easy discharge for their contents, presented an uneven surface, full of crevices, and as porous as a sieve. The drainage escaped in all directions, infiltrating the neighbouring soil, undermining it everywhere, and aiding the operations of those persevering tunnellers, the rats. Such drains have become notorious for their instability, and their expense in the shape of repairs: they are fast disappearing before the tubular or pipe drains.

I have witnessed the devastations caused in houses by such imperfect drains, and where a similar principle of construction has been followed in the public sewer, the street, gradually undermined by the constant leakage and the armies of rats, has given way, to the great risk of passers-by. That such a system is detrimental to the health of the inhabitants need not be insisted on; and there can be no doubt that a town would be healthier without drains, than with such apologies for them. Even where greater care was exercised in their construction, and where the stones in the bed and sides of the drain, were more accurately cemented, the surface over which the drainage passed was uneven, and arrested the onward flow; in process of time it became imperfect, gave way, and allowed of escape on all sides. In many parts of the New Town, such drains are to be seen, especially wherever we have a joint-proprietary, as in houses with successive flats or storeys. The main communications with the sewer in the street, being common property, and the parties chiefly suffering being the inhabitants of the ground-floor, complaints leading to repairs involving outlay are not attended to. The proper remedy is, the substitution of the tubular drains, with a smooth interior, allowing of an easy discharge, and presenting-joints at the distance of every three feet, which, if properly cemented, are impervious to water. The progress of sanitary improvement in Edinburgh has always been slow, and even in the present day I have heard experienced builders insisting on the superiority of the old-fashioned built drain, and declaiming against the use of the glazed pipes. We generally find such persons advocates of another arrangement, which has been in use in the New Town from its commencement, and which, as already shown, are equally faulty, and utterly unsuited for the requirements of the present day: I refer to the cesspools in connection with the houses.

Where the house is self-contained, and the proprietor is aware of the necessity of the measure, the cesspool is cleaned out from time to time, with marked benefit to the sanitary condition of the house. In the case of a tenement with several proprietors, and as many separate houses, the drainage of which passes into a common cesspool, there is generally long delay. It is well known that in Edinburgh tenants are peculiarly restless, and frequently change their places of abode. Hence houses may be tenanted for many years before the common cesspool is cleaned out. Even then, this is not accomplished without unusual difficulty. In a tenement in the New Town, consisting of three stories and a main-door flat, there are generally 12 proprietors, each of whom, either personally or through a factor, who is usually chary of responsibility, must give his consent. A thorough cleansing is at last effected; but not until a numerous body of tenants have been subjected to great inconvenience. Each house has been filled with emanations from the sewers. The windows have been kept open in order to dilute the nauseous smell; and although this object is partially effected, the sewage gases are sucked into the house in greater volume, on account of the draught which has been occasioned. It is not to be wondered at, if, under such circumstances, ill-health, in varying degrees of intensity, should be the result,—requiring, it may be, little medical attendance, but causing great discomfort. Should epidemic disease of any kind affect the inmates, the illness is intensified, and the ailment may assume a character of malignancy, which can only be accounted for by the faulty sanitary state of the house. But it must be remembered that the air in the street also becomes tainted. A cesspool filled to overflowing, and leaking, can be recognised in the street by its odour. It is placed in the area, and of course the emanations escape in all directions. The simple remedy for such a nuisance, is to have a survey made of all the cesspools in the city. Let a register be kept of them, and let the City Engineer be instructed to have them inspected from time to time. When their state is once ascertained, it will be easy to enforce the wholesome regulation that every cesspool within the municipal boundary be cleaned out at least once a-year. Not only will the sanitary condition of the better parts of the city be greatly improved, but the inhabitants will have a guarantee that they are secured from one great source of discomfort and ill-health.*

In the plan of the New Town, provision was made for streets of houses of humble pretensions and moderate rent, suitable for the better class of artisans. Such streets had no drain, and the houses of course had no sanitary convenience. This state of matters will appear highly dangerous to persons who are not acquainted with our mode of cleansing the city, and with the stringent regulations in force prohibiting the accumulation of refuse of all kinds in the shape of middens, &c., compelling the inhabitants to bring such to the street, to be collected by the dust-carts. Looking to the imperfect nature of the drains used at the time of the building of the New Town, and the prevalence of cesspools, it will not be denied that such streets as Rose Street, Clyde Street, and Thistle Street, in the Upper, and Jamaica Street and Cumberland Street in the Lower New Town, being destitute of such appliances, were, in respect of drainage, in a healthier condition than those which were inhabited by the rich. In the advance, however, of sanitary improvement, main drains of the best construction have, at great expense, been carried along these streets, so as to permit of the introduction of conveniences into each dwelling-house; and under the compulsory clauses adopted by the Town-Council, water-closets can now be ordered at the instance of the Superintendent of Streets and Buildings. The streets in question loudly call for the change. The sewer is ready for the reception of the discharge, and the houses, from their size and the character of the tenants, are well suited for the enforcement of the measure. But, in addition, these streets, lying between the lines of thoroughfare occupied by the wealthier inhabitants, upon whom the burden of municipal taxation chiefly falls, are, from their dense population and other causes, the seat of great mortality, and in the case of epidemics always afford a large proportion of those inmates of our hospital who come from the New Town. Such hot-beds of infection, inserted like a wedge between the dwellings of the rich, demand from the Sanitary Officer constant surveillance. Epidemic diseases spread with great facility; and in the event of their breaking out in these localities, the inhabitants of the adjoining streets are apt to suffer. Ratepayers, in my opinion, are entitled to protection under such circumstances, and the introduction of conveniences should at once be enforced in the streets I have mentioned. I know of no more clamant cases, and a reference to the tabular statement of the mortality of these streets will show the amount of benefit that may be expected to follow in their case, while, as a necessary consequence, the general mortality of the whole district will undergo a marked diminution.

Among other points to which my attention has been directed in the course of

* These cesspools must not be confounded with the cesspool common in England, *i.e.*, a covered receptacle for sewage, without any connection with a drain; or an uncovered receptacle for ashes, having a privy in connection with it.

my sanitary inspection, was the dampness of the ground-floors of all the houses in this quarter, which are built against the slope either to the north or south of the ridge on the summit of the New Town. This arises from the back-green not being properly drained. It is generally supposed that such a step is not necessary; but where earth, whether covered with grass or not, is freely exposed to the rainfall, the soil becomes a perfect sponge, relieving itself by draining towards the lowest level, which is the foundation of the adjoining house. A constant state of dampness exists, which lowers the salubrity of the residence, besides directly rendering the apartments of the servants unhealthy in a marked degree. Cases have come under my notice of domestics being crippled for life with inveterate rheumatism contracted under such circumstances. And when we remember that to the present hour these under-flats are employed by lawyers—a numerous class of the inhabitants—for the accommodation of their clerks, who are universally acknowledged to be the hardest worked (so far as mere time is concerned) of the labouring class—it is not to be wondered at that these young men suffer in health, and labour under the special diseases incident to long continued work in a damp and close atmosphere. The houses, too, have often a well-marked musty smell, the result of the decay of the joists and flooring, together with the putrefaction of the shavings and other debris which have remained among the foundation since it was laid. Instances of this have come under my notice in Princes Street, on the one hand, and Queen Street, Heriot Row, Northumberland Street, Great King Street, Cumberland Street, and Brunswick Street, on the other. The remedy consists in the laying down of tile drains, similar to what we see used in any farm, or the paving of the whole area. By such means the rainfall is collected, and may be advantageously utilised by conducting it into the leading drain of the house, and thus securing, by an almost continuous flow of pure water, a wholesome condition of the drains, and the perfect dryness of the house.

All street-cesspools, and gullies, as already explained (see p. 85), should at once be properly trapped so as to secure the air of our streets from constant contamination.

I have already adverted to the faulty planning of the better class of houses, so far as the situation of the convenience was concerned. In those houses, however, with rentals varying from £15 to £60, according to the locality, and arranged in our Scotch system of flats or storeys, piled one above another, the plan of the internal arrangements was still more objectionable. The water-closets ventilated into the common stair. The effect of this was, that the air in this, the common entrance to possibly six houses, was seriously contaminated, and whenever a draught was occasioned by the front or street door being opened, this fetid air was forced backwards into the dwellings. The upper flats suffered most, and I have been applied to in instances where parties could not inhale the air at their house door without nausea and sickness. That architects should have been allowed to plan such houses manifests the want of some controlling authority to protect the inhabitants from so flagrant an infringement of the most ordinary sanitary laws. To this hour the evil exists in every part of the New Town, and is perpetrated in the most recently-built houses of the class in question. Few common stairs, I regret to say, are properly ventilated—each proprietor acting on the well known principle that what is everybody's business is nobody's. The natural course of the offensive air is towards the skylight, which in all cases should be fitted with a proper air-hole, and the windows should be regularly opened, so as to secure the free passage of fresh air.

Indeed, I have been impressed with the contrast presented by a street in the best parts of Edinburgh with one in any of our English towns. Owing, I suppose, to the greater uncertainty of our climate, and the rigour and continuance of our biting easterly winds, to which, from its elevated position, Edinburgh is so much exposed, we apparently dread the effects of free ventilation, and as a rule the windows of our houses are rarely opened so freely and frequently as to permit of this taking place. In an English town, on the other hand, even in winter weather, the windows are generally opened. Pass along our principal streets, at any time of the day, and as a general rule the windows will be found obstinately closed. This helps to explain the disagreeable odour perceptible in so many of our lodging-houses; in which, from the occasional stay of invalids, who demand a warm atmosphere, and also no doubt from the ignorance of the masters and servants, the air, from its being seldom renewed, is never sweet and wholesome. The fact does not appear to be known, that thorough ventilation secures the person against cold, and that the invalid requires a wholesome atmosphere, as much as the strongest man. In some parts of the New Town one excuse for this apparent dread of ventilation can be fairly pled. It is only by shutting the windows that the interior of the houses can be protected from the smoke which, in utter defiance of the Act of Parliament, is permitted to be discharged from such establishments as printing-offices, coach manufactories, and others, where furnaces are employed.

Notwithstanding the unusual capacity of the houses, I am convinced that, in the dwellings of the wealthier classes, overcrowding frequently exists; and this helps to explain the otherwise anomalous occurrence of cases of fever, &c., in the airiest districts of the New Town. Our largest houses are too small for the demands of an ordinary family, when we find the dining and drawing-room floors devoted to purposes of social meals and receptions. The remaining flats are barely sufficient for the bedroom, nursery, and bath-room accommodation of the family, to say nothing of the entertainment of guests. The ground-floors are amply occupied with the kitchen, laundry, and store-rooms, while the servants (in such houses by no means few in number) are crowded together in small rooms and closets, and the man-servant may be found huddled under the staircase. Should the under-flat be damp, or in an unhealthy state from imperfect drainage, fever breaks out, and this may spread to the members of the family. Again, this unhealthy mode of living predisposes the servants to fall an easy prey to the contagion of fever and other disorders in their visits to friends in the Old Town, where fever may be said to be endemic.

91

It is remarkable how very little restores the equilibrium in house accommodation. A single room taken from reception uses on the drawing-room floor, sets free another room on every flat, and the domestics are placed in circumstances of comfort; or, as I have had occasion to notice, an apartment of proper dimensions is set apart for the uses of the laundry—a point of some importance, although it is frequently neglected, that the linen of the establishment should be cleaned and dressed in an airy room.

92

In the course of the many calls for assistance and advice, I have been struck at once with the numerous avenues by which disease may enter the best built houses, and how a very slight cause may operate most prejudicially on the health of a household. The comforts by which an inhabitant of the present day are surrounded, can be enjoyed only under the penalty of unceasing watchfulness and care. Are we no longer annoyed by the constant eavesdrop from our roofs, the rhones and pipes conveying the rainfall at once to the drain? The delivery pipe must be carefully trapped, else it acts as an admirably contrived shaft for the conveyance of the sewage gases to the top storeys of the house. Cases of typhoid fever have occurred under circumstances in which at first sight it appeared impossible to trace the connection with bad drains. Such cases have been quoted to me as indubitable instances of typhoid fever, having no connection with drainage effluvia, and I have been asked to explain the immunity enjoyed by those living in the ground-floors, immediately above the sewers. An intermittent odour, however, suggestive of offensive matters, and apparent whenever the windows are open to air the apartment, will lead any one to the true cause of the insalubrity of the house. Again, have we water conveyed to every flat? If this be done through the medium of cisterns, these must be carefully covered so as to protect them from the dust and the inroads of the mice and rats, and in addition, they must be regularly cleaned out at stated intervals, otherwise the water in daily use for domestic purposes may become so contaminated as to induce a constant tendency to illness in the household. Have we in our bedrooms discharge pipes from the bason stands? They too, as well as the conveniences, must be carefully trapped, else the sewage gases quickly pollute the air of our sleeping apartments. Have we on every landing pipes for the purpose of enabling the domestics to get rid of the water that has been used for cleansing? These too must be trapped, else the complicated and expensive system of pipes is but an ingenious and effectual method of vitiating the air of the house. Lastly, not to dwell on the obvious dangers resulting from an escape of ordinary lighting gas, the larder may be so placed within the house, that the apartment is rendered unwholesome from the escape of sewage gases, in which the meat and other viands hang suspended. In one or two instances of deadly sickness in the young, I could ascribe the fatality of the illness to no other cause than that to which I have just alluded. It can easily be understood that, in the case of children, the continued use of such tainted meat must act most prejudicially, lowering the general vitality, and inducing languor and a feebleness of constitution, which must render them an easy prey to disease.

OLD TOWN.

It might have been expected that when the citizens availed themselves of the advantages presented by the New Town, the faulty sanitary condition of the older part of the city, which they had left, should have engaged public attention. But this was not the case. The exodus took place gradually, the relief afforded to the more densely-peopled districts of the Old Town was partial and scarcely felt, and at the period in question the subject of sanitary reform was unknown. The population, instead of diminishing, actually increased in density; and the houses, which had been raised to a great height, to afford an increasing population the protection of a fortified town, under the influence of the times fell in value, and were sub-divided into smaller houses consisting of single apartments. The population was thus quadrupled by a class notorious for its neglect of the most ordinary sanitary precautions; and Edinburgh, at the present hour, is placed in more disadvantageous circumstances, so far as the health of its inhabitants is concerned, than it could possibly have been 200 or 300 years ago, were it to have stood a siege, after the inhabitants of the surrounding districts had been swept into it, and absorbed in its population. Now, districts, the seat of a dense population, if only approached by narrow lanes such as our closes, present great difficulties in the way of sanitary improvement, and if those very closes, by their faulty construction, offer fresh obstacles, the case becomes almost hopeless. As the feus in Scotland are perpetual, there is no hope of the closes being removed, unless by such a calamity as a general conflagration. Looking upon them, therefore, as a permanent evil, our endeavours should be directed to remove from them those disadvantages which their faulty construction has entailed. The first circumstance which attracts the notice of any one who visits our closes and wynds is the imperfect condition of the paving. Now, as the system of cleansing pursued in Edinburgh (which I am prepared to prove is not only the best adapted for Edinburgh, but for other large towns) consists in the removal of all refuse and filth, which, if not passed into water-closets, is ordered to be laid upon the streets, it necessarily follows that where the surface of a close is imperfect and uneven, the filth cannot be satisfactorily removed; and thus the efforts of our cleansing staff are frustrated, and the poorer districts of the city, where the ventilation is most imperfect, and where there exists the greatest demand for pure air, suffer from the effluvia which contaminate the atmosphere. The broom of the scavenger requires to be assisted in its operations; and it stands to reason that the smoother and less uneven the surface to be cleansed, the more thorough will the cleansing be. The closes, therefore, should, one and all of them, be suitably repaved with flat stones or flags. Some of the closes—such as Borthwick's Close—are so already, and contrast most favourably with others—such as Bailie Fyfe's Close, where the paving is most imperfect. All causewaying and hornising should be removed, and the flat pavement substituted. This is an expensive operation, but it is, in my opinion, the first step in the sanitary improvement of what has long been a reproach to Edinburgh. I am well aware that this subject has again and again engaged the attention of the Council, and that the delay which has occurred is attributable, in the first instance, to the desire of the Council to avail themselves of the 210th clause of Provost Lindsay's Act, which gives power to enforce the introduction of water-closets into the houses of the poor, which clause was finally adopted by the Council on the 28th October 1864. Since then, I find that only a few closes have been ordered to be proceeded with, and I must express my gratification that more has not been attempted; for I cannot imagine a more disastrous condition of matters for the poorer districts of our city than the general introduction of water-closets, so long as the present system of house accommodation obtains.

It is to be hoped that this evil will, in course of time, be remedied, and that any new buildings in the poorer districts will be so arranged as to admit of conveniences being provided for every two families. The closes, therefore, ought to be thoroughly drained. This can be satisfactorily accomplished, as the main drainage lines have been completed; and it is easy, under these circumstances, to run a communication into each close, so as to provide for the due discharge of offensive matters. Meanwhile, the public conveniences ought to be increased in number, to supply the necessities of those closes which, in their present condition, are unsuitable for the introduction of conveniences into the densely-crowded tenements.

Of the older houses in the districts of Abbey, Canongate, Tron, St Giles, and Grassmarket, a thorough survey should be made. In the first place, all wooden additions to the fronts or sides of these houses should be peremptorily removed. These not only in many instances narrow the closes, but also interfere with the light and ventilation of the houses to the back. They no longer serve the purpose for which they were permitted to be erected; and whenever the extension of the city beyond the old walls took place, these temporary structures should have been removed. Secondly, all ruinous houses should be taken down, and care should be taken that the new structures are built in accordance with the sanitary requirements of the present day.

We have powers in our Police Act to compel the daily cleansing of common stairs. Now, where the common entrance to houses is kept in a filthy condition, we cannot expect to find clean interiors. I have personally examined the stairs in the High Street and Old Town generally, and found them almost universally in a disgraceful state. A single family wanting in habits of propriety interferes with the cleanliness of a whole stair by thwarting the efforts of their tidier neighbours. The remedy for this state of matters is the enforcement of the clauses referring to the cleansing of common stairs. But, without lighting such stairs, it will be found impossible to enforce cleanliness—a few jets of gas would give the people pleasure in keeping their stairs in good order, and would prevent the nightly deposits of filth which paralyse the efforts of the industrious householder. I submit that were these three measures—viz., the paving and drainage of our closes, the erection of a greater number of public conveniences, and the cleaning and lighting of the common stairs—thoroughly carried out, which require no special enactments, and for enforcing which we already possess ample powers, the sanitary condition of the Old Town of Edinburgh would be greatly improved.

Another evil of great magnitude remains, viz., overcrowding of the population—a necessary result of the size of the houses and the sub-division they have undergone. Over this the authorities have no control, except in the case of common lodging-houses, which are under the surveillance of the police. The Glasgow Police Act, at present on trial in that city, contains the following clauses, which permit the authorities, under certain circumstances, to regulate the number of inhabitants in the poorer tenements:—

"387. It shall be lawful for any person appointed by the Board from time to time to enter any dwelling-house which consists of not more than three apartments for the purpose of measuring in cubic feet the space contained therein, exclusive of lobbies, closets, or presses, and to mark on or over the outside of the door of any such dwelling-house, if the cubic contents thereof do not exceed two thousand feet, or to affix thereto a ticket, on which are marked, in such position and style as the Board see fit, the number of such cubic feet and the number of persons exceeding the age of eight years who, without a breach of the provision next herein contained, may sleep therein; and any person who obliterates, defaces, removes or alters such marking or ticket shall be liable to a penalty not exceeding ten shillings.

"388. If after the 28th day of May 1863 any dwelling-house which consists of not more than three apartments is used for the purpose of sleeping in by a greater number of persons than in the proportion of one person of the age of eight years or upwards for every three hundred cubic feet of space, or of one person of an age less than eight years for every one hundred and fifty cubic feet of space contained therein, exclusive of lobbies, closets, and presses, or by a greater number of persons than is marked therein, in pursuance of the provisions herein-before contained, every person so using, or suffering it to be used, shall be liable to a penalty not exceeding five shillings for every day, or part of a day, during which it is so used, or suffered to be used, by him."

Were such powers available in Edinburgh, a check would be provided to the increasing density of the population, and a large amount of mortality would be prevented. The rapid spread of infectious disorders in our closes is at once accounted for by the manner in which our poor live huddled together, and whenever disease spreads thus rapidly by contagion amid poverty and want, the rate of mortality is always high. Great benefit would also result from limiting the height of the houses. The necessity no longer exists for such castles as form the most picturesque portion of our Old Town. What was permitted centuries ago, in consequence of the contracted area of the city, should not be tolerated in the present day, when the condition of our Old Town is a by-word and reproach. All houses above a certain age, whose condition is not such as to demand instant demolition, should be lowered in height, as was done with so much advantage in the case of Purves' Land in the Canongate, to which allusion has already been made, *see* p. 34. No houses should be allowed to be built of more than four storeys in height. If they are higher than this, they become so unwieldy, and the population so large, that ordinary sanitary rules cannot be enforced. The tenement resembles a rabbit warren in the number of its inhabitants, and it becomes impossible to trace the offenders against police regulations. A similar rule as to height should apply to all old tenements which stand in need of repair. No higher standard should be permitted in the Old Town than the height of the new tenement which replaced the house which fell in the High Street some years ago. This consists of four storeys, three being for dwelling-houses above the range of the shops. No doubt such a limitation would interfere somewhat with the noble outline of the High Street, but this may willingly be sacrificed to improve the sanitary condition of the poor and their dwellings. We have already seen how little that portion of the town, whose necessities we are considering, has been benefited by those philanthropic associations which have done so much to improve the condition of the working-classes by providing them with suitable habitations. Respectable workmen have left the better class of houses in the most densely-peopled parts of the Old Town, and have been succeeded by a poorer and a more ignorant class, which, in its turn, may, through the kindness of charitable persons, be rooted out, and transplanted to the outskirts, only, however, to be followed by the more degraded population of the district.

The peculiar structure of the ridge of the Old Town, consisting of a central street of great length—with narrow closes or passages between elevated dwellings passing off from it in great numbers—helps to account for many peculiarities which have excited the astonishment of strangers. The appearance presented by our chief street has been the favourite subject of comment by travellers; and the shortcomings of Edinburgh, as presented in the Old Town, are almost better known than those of any other capital. At this we have no reason to complain, although some measure of injustice attends the vivid descriptions of travellers. A city cannot have its social and sanitary disadvantages too narrowly exposed; for the greater the amount of public attention that is directed to them, the more likely are the citizens to be roused to remedy or remove them. It must be remembered, however, that there are few cities in the empire which are subjected to a more searching examination by tourists, and there are still fewer in which the objects of chief interest lie in the dirtiest and most squalid districts. Our closes are objects of historical interest, and every year are closely inspected by thousands of strangers; but, wherever you have a dense population of the poorest class, it is impossible, under the best sanitary regulations, to effect a great amount of cleanliness. Squalor and filth meet you at every step. This is as true of London, Dublin, and Glasgow as of the rest of the large towns in the empire. No one can visit the poorest districts of these cities without becoming convinced that were they as regularly visited as Edinburgh by holiday tourists, equally salutary lessons might be taught to the inhabitants. But the track of the tourist in these places does not lie in the direction of poverty and wretchedness. The sights of London and Paris are daily witnessed without the pauperism and misery of these capitals obtruding themselves, as in Edinburgh, on the attention of the visitor. The same remark applies to ports like Liverpool and Glasgow. The spacious streets and docks are carefully inspected, but the poorer districts are never seen. Our closes are narrow, and their poor inhabitants naturally ventilate themselves in the High Street, which, for its proportions and width, contrasts remarkably with the contracted streets of the same period in other capitals. Those places of refreshment, which are too frequently the resort of the poor, are all situated in the chief street. Hence it is not to be wondered at that the visitor, after inspecting Holyrood, when he walks to the Castle, sees Edinburgh poverty and Edinburgh vice in its most repulsive form. Our principal educational institution, the University, and our busy Law Courts, in which the judicial business of the kingdom is transacted, cannot be reached but by crossing this great thoroughfare. Besides this, the traditional and historical associations of our city are to be found in the meanest localities. At every step, therefore, poverty is met, and is justly made the subject of remark. A parallel might be found in London, were Fleet Street and Charing Cross the only breathing-room for the pauperism of the metropolis, and the favourite site for the gin-palaces of the poor. The poverty of other great towns lies hid in obscure districts, and the scenes there presented, which have been described and delineated by the draughtsman, have not the same apology that the worst parts of Edinburgh can plead. The houses of the poor in England are of small size, self-contained, and built of a material and in a manner which permit of easy alteration and repair. They are built, too, for a limited period, and in their very structure afford evidence of a speedy removal. In Edinburgh, the houses are the highest in the world, and the most densely peopled. The stairs leading to the various flats have been aptly likened to upright streets, so numerous are the inhabitants that are met with on every landing. The building feus are perpetual, and the houses are made as if they were intended to last as long.

Many years ago the City Improvement Commission, by forming Victoria Street, and more recently the Railway Access Company, by the construction of Lord Cockburn Street, have supplied the community with valuable hints as to the method of improving our closes and wynds. By simply piercing the closes best with an airy street, you let in light, ventilation, and also the scavenger. At present one of our closes, from its very length, cannot be satisfactorily cleansed; but once divide it into two, and it can be attacked, so to speak, from two ends in addition to its outlets. Let any one compare the condition of the closes which have been cut in two by Lord Cockburn Street with what they were prior to that great sanitary improvement, and he will bear me out in my remarks. In the case of the earlier experiment, the closes which emerge into Victoria Street, and are used as thoroughfares, are kept clean and wholesome, while those which possess no such communication are mere *cul de sacs*, have become receptacles of filth, and severely tax the energy of the scavenger. Of course, I do not contemplate

PROPOSED STREET TO OPEN UP THE CLOSES IN THE TRON AND CANONGATE DISTRICTS.

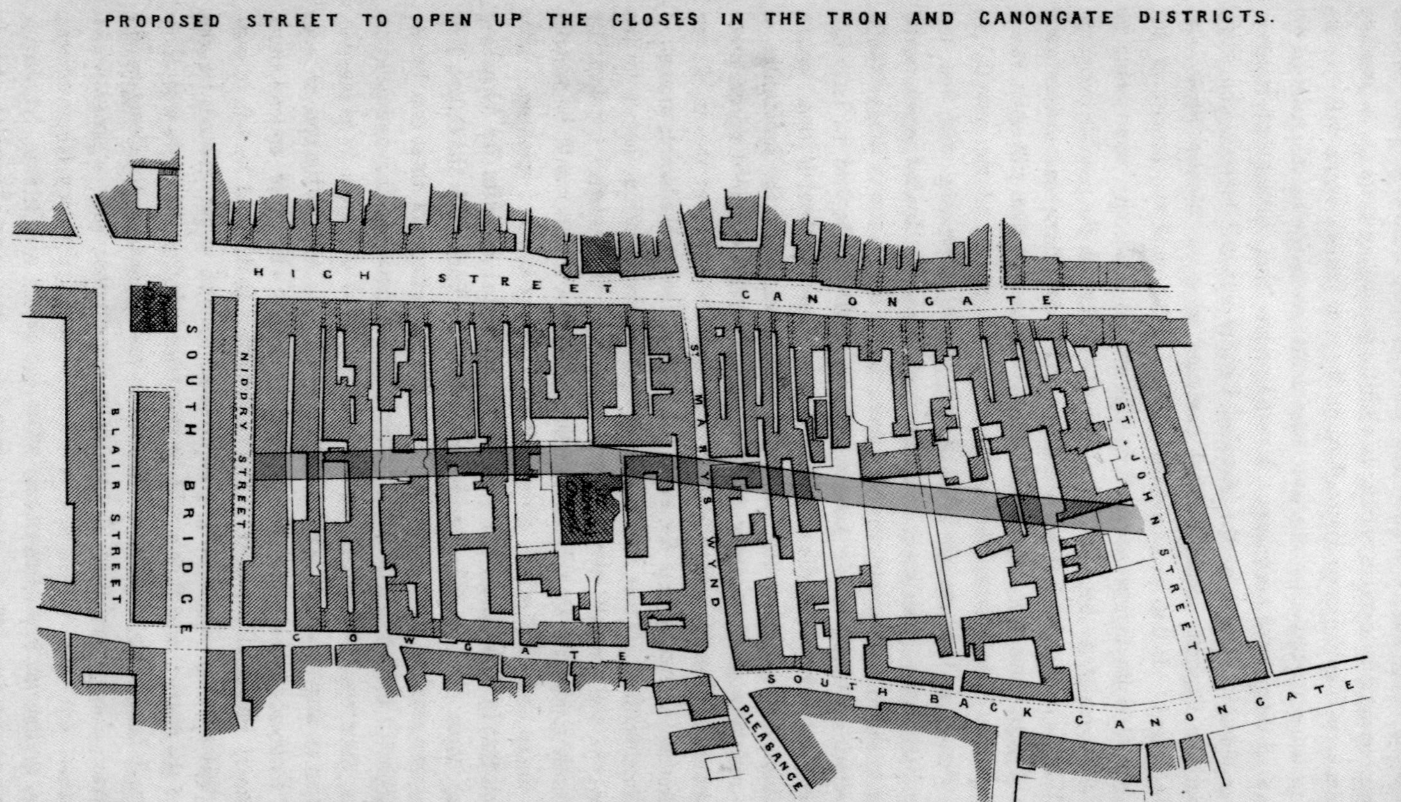

the formation of expensive streets, or the erection of houses with any architectural display. All that is required is, that our most densely-peopled districts should be penetrated by a street, which, in addition to opening them up to sanitary improvements, will at the same time afford, in the new houses which will line its sides, house accommodation for the poor, who must necessarily be dispossessed by the removal of dilapidated tenements. I would propose that, in the first instance, the scheme should be tried in the crowded locality situated between the High Street and the Cowgate, and bounded east and west by Niddry Street and St Mary's Wynd. It has been already shown, p. 30, that the density of the population reaches its highest standard in this portion of the city, there being no less than 646 persons to the acre. It is believed that, with the possible exception of some districts of Liverpool, in no part of the world does there exist greater overcrowding of population. A reference to the accompanying plan will show that a street might be formed from the centre of Niddry Street, to run parallel to the High Street, and to emerge in St Mary's Wynd, interfering with but few houses in its progress. No fewer than 14 closes would be divided, which would contribute to their great sanitary improvement; and a double row of houses might line the street, affording ample accommodation for those who had to leave the condemned tenements in the district. The internal arrangement of these houses might exhibit a specimen of the best method of constructing the habitations of the poor with the latest sanitary reforms. The experience gained might prove useful not only in directing philanthropic efforts in Edinburgh, but also in all our Scottish towns. On one side of the street, there would be a considerable amount of cellar accommodation. These cellars would prove excellent washing-houses for the district, where, for a small sum, the poor could have their clothes satisfactorily and frequently cleansed. By this means their small apartments would be relieved from the damp and smell which always attend the operation of washing. It is well known that in Edinburgh the poor enjoy unrivalled facilities for bleaching and drying their clothes. The Meadows, the Queen's Park, and the Calton Hill are within easy reach of the poorest districts. The advantages of these can hardly be over-estimated in such a city as Edinburgh. With overcrowding and deficient ventilation, the necessity of having the body-linen washed as frequently as possible, and dried in an airy situation, need not be insisted upon; and in the case of sickness, any assistance rendered in procuring more speedy change of underclothing must prove of inestimable service. The vacant space that would be left in constructing this approach might be put to excellent account as playgrounds for the children of the district, who thus would be prevented infesting the closes with their presence, and interfering with the traffic in the main streets of the Cowgate and High Street. As a speculation, I have been assured that such a street would be a success; but even if it should not, I feel certain that my fellow-citizens would not grudge an improvement-tax when the object was not to beautify a superbly-situated town, but to remove from us a stain and a reproach, which we have allowed to rest upon us too long, arising from the misery and wretchedness of the dwellings of our poor. I purposely selected the locality in question for illustration, not only because its wants are clamant and its inhabitants among the most indigent of the city, but also because the engineering difficulties are slight, and the levels are of the most satisfactory description. In the plan, the street proposed has been extended to St John Street, and passes through a necessitous district. The density of the population is, however, not so great as in the Tron Sub-district, there being only 331 persons to the acre; but the closes at the top of the Canongate, and St Mary's Wynd itself, stand much in need of sanitary improvement. It can easily be seen that similar streets, conferring similar advantages, could be constructed between Leith Wynd and New Street, and also between Blair Street and the Old Fishmarket Close.

It may be urged that greater advantages would be gained by the formation of a street which should run diagonally from the corner of the South Bridge, and emerge at the Pleasance, and thus divert more completely the traffic from the north to that point. There can be no doubt that the greater thoroughfare there is in a street, the greater chance is there of its being thoroughly inspected and cleansed;—side streets, where there is little traffic, being proverbial for their dullness and dirt. But I fear the expense attending the opening into the High Street of the new street, and its formation along a downward slope, would be so great as effectually to put a stop to a great sanitary improvement. It must be remembered, too, that the traffic by the Pleasance is of very limited extent. The question, however, of the site of the street, can be safely left to architects to determine. I am convinced that the only method of permanently benefiting these poor localities is by some such measure. The removal of such sanitary evils as are to be met with in them strongly resembles the operations of actual warfare. Before a country can be thoroughly conquered, military roads must be made in all directions, to permit of the operations of the soldier and engineer. In like manner, before such densely-peopled districts as are figured on the plan can be brought satisfactorily and permanently under proper sanitary control, they must be opened up, so as to admit of ready access to every nook and cranny. The services of the cleansing staff would at once become doubly valuable. At present they are paralysed by the very length and tortuosity of the closes and their off-shoots; and when it is known that from some of the closes upwards of a ton of refuse is daily removed, some idea may be formed of the more thorough cleansing that could be effected under more advantageous circumstances. The general introduction of water and gas would speedily follow, and with such a street as is proposed near at hand, the poor would not encumber the High Street and Canongate as they do at present. Provided with better houses, and a freer ventilation, the temptation to drunkenness would also be lessened.

SOUTHERN SUBURBS.

THIS portion of the city includes the three sanitary districts of Newington, Grange, and Morningside, each of which may be said to contain localities inhabited by the poorer classes, and demanding sanitary improvement. These are Causewayside, in Newington; Sciennes, in Grange; and Morningside Village and Wrightshouses, in Morningside. Undoubtedly the most necessitous is Causewayside, the courts of which should receive a similar treatment to that proposed for the closes and courts of the Old Town. The Byres should also be removed, and public conveniences erected. The houses of the poor are for the most part of little elevation, and are therefore more amenable to sanitary improvement than the high "lands" of the High Street and Cowgate. Morningside Village and Wrightshouses are in much better condition, and with more efficient drainage, and the introduction of conveniences, would exhibit a marked improvement—rendering them still more acceptable as resorts for the invalid sick of the middle classes.

The rest of the Southern Suburbs consists of a town of villa residences admirably placed, so far as exposure and general amenity are concerned, but labouring under certain disadvantages. The drainage is only now being completed after a considerable population has flocked to the district. This has led to the general formation of cesspools, the only method of partial drainage available under the circumstances. The dangers attending these structures have already been insisted upon, but it is to be feared that they will be allowed to remain after the main drains are completed, and communications led into the houses. They ought to be removed or shut up, thus preventing the accumulation of offensive matters in close proximity to the houses; or, if allowed to remain, they should be cleaned out regularly at least once a-year—an expensive and annoying process. Until the general drainage is completed, and the cesspool nuisance abated, the district cannot be regarded as in a satisfactory state. No doubt, portions of it, as the Grange, with its rapidly-increasing population, exhibit a low rate of mortality, and the high rate of other parts may admit of explanation by the number of invalids who come to it for change of air; but, at the same time, it must be remembered that the death-rate of the Southern Suburbs, after deducting the mortality of such inhabitants in the east division of Morningside Asylum and Gillespie's Hospital, is 19·68 per 1000, which is higher than it ought to be, and necessitates careful superintendence, and the removal of all causes likely to affect the health of the inhabitants. I would urge that full advantage be taken of the system of drainage; and it is to be hoped that the mortality will, in future years, more closely resemble that of a rural locality—more especially when the character of the population is taken into account, which is far superior to that of ordinary country districts.

CONCLUSION.

Such are the suggestions which I venture to offer for the sanitary improvement of Edinburgh. It will be observed that they range themselves under two great divisions, viz., those which it is the duty of the authorities to carry into execution; and *2dly*, those which should be adopted by the inhabitants themselves. The measures proposed differ much as to their relative urgency; but I have no hesitation in stating, that the sanitary condition of the Old Town, and particularly that portion of it comprising the districts covering the central ridge, with the Abbey and Grassmarket at either extremity, is a subject that can only be properly dealt with by the municipality, and should be taken up without delay. It includes the following points:—

1st, The satisfactory paving and draining of the closes.

2d, The improvement of the house accommodation of the poor, by insisting on the introduction of water and gas, the cleansing of common stairs, and the performance of necessary repairs.

3d, The diminution of overcrowding of the population, by limiting the number of persons in each apartment, by lowering the houses in height, and by removing all tenements in a ruinous condition.

4th, The opening up of the worst localities by the widening of such contracted thoroughfares as the Cowgate and St Mary's Wynd, and by the formation of new streets, which should pass at right angles to the long and unwieldy closes, and give increased facilities for their thorough cleansing. Such new communications would also afford sites for improved dwellings for the poor where they are most required, and would form an era in the sanitary history of Edinburgh.

In the modern part of the City, there is less call for interference on the part of the authorities. Their duty is limited to the general introduction of conveniences, to the improvement of the surface drainage, and to the enforcement of the Smoke Prevention Act. To the inhabitants we look for the removal of cesspools connected with houses. These measures can hardly be expected to improve the very satisfactory death-rate of the New Town, but they will add greatly to the comfort of the inhabitants.

In the Old Town, more may be looked for. Its mortality, though high, might have been expected to have attained an unusual magnitude, considering the density of the population, and the peculiar house accommodation of the poorer classes. It must be remembered, however, that several important sanitary agencies have for many years been in operation, and have powerfully contributed to the improvement of the health of this portion of the city. Among these may be mentioned, 1st, the quality of the water supplied, and the disuse of private wells; 2d, the perfecting of the system of cleansing, by which all accumulations of filth and refuse in houses and courts are prevented; 3d, the periodical lime-washing of our closes, and the thorough cleansing of their surface drains; 4th, the establishment of a public abbattoir of such an extent as to enable the Magistrates to abolish all private killing-booths throughout the city; and 5th, the unusual facilities for immediate medical attendance which are afforded by our Hospital and numerous Public Dispensaries.

It would be very desirable that the death-rate of the following districts should be at least reduced to 25 per 1000:—

District	Death-rate	District	Death-rate
Abbey,	37·1	Grassmarket,	32·52
Tron,	34·46	Canongate,	31·15
St Giles,	28·8.		

The effect of this would be the annual saving of 312 lives—the lowering of the death-rate of the Old Town from 30·73 to 25·28 per 1000, and that of the City generally from 25·4 to 23·82. I believe the suggestions offered will materially tend to this result. In the present day, there are two hopeful signs that its accomplishment may be looked upon as certain. *First*, the evident desire for sanitary improvement manifested by such a measure as the purification of the Water of Leith, costing the city upwards of £40,000, and which will doubtless improve the amenity of the district through which the stream flows. The death-rate of this locality of the city, even after the allocation of the deaths in our public hospitals, is only 19 per 1000; and for the last 30 years, during which, of course, the stream has been becoming daily more polluted, successive epidemics of fever and cholera have visited the city, only to leave the district apparently unscathed. The whole force of these pestilences was spent on those portions of the Old Town whose cause we are pleading. The subject of the Water of Leith excited much discussion among the inhabitants in the view of more pressing questions, but now that that is settled, the condition of the Old Town, and the necessity of remedying it, about which there cannot be any diversity of opinion, should be taken up in earnest. The prospect held out in its improvement is of the most tangible character; and it is a trite remark that, in improving the sanitary condition of the poorer localities of great towns, and lowering their death-rate, every district benefits, and that, in a pecuniary point of view, a saving is effected annually in the taxation for the poor. The *second* point of encouragement is the unexpected but very important determination of the City Parochial Board to remove the Poorhouse to the country, and to employ their paupers in rural occupation. One of the great obstacles to the improvement of the Old Town has undoubtedly been the large pauper population it contains. Wherever you have pauperism, you have its attendant depression, bodily and mental—its apathy and its misery: And where you have these rooted firmly, in the midst of a dense population, and imperfect house accommodation, all the elements are present to ensure a high rate of mortality in ordinary years; and when epidemics are abroad, an amount of sickness and death that is appalling. The greater proportion of the worst class of paupers will now be drafted to the country, and employed there in healthful occupation. This great sanitary measure comes, too, at a most opportune time. One of the obvious difficulties attendant on any measure for diminishing the population in a district is as to how the expelled tenants are to find shelter; and this may be urged where the depopulation is carried on in the most favourable circumstances during the summer weather. The difficulty is, however, greatly lessened, when such assistance is afforded by the Parochial authorities, and a strenuous effort should be made to take advantage of the movement. The citizens should insist that it be extended to the other two parishes of St Cuthbert and Canongate, and that the city should be wholly relieved of their paupers. The present favourable juncture should not be allowed to pass. These three Boards should amalgamate, and thus, not only contribute materially to the sanitary improvement of the city, but also to the interests of all the inhabitants by the diminution of the local rates. The boards in question may be jealous of each other, and possibly hampered by their large staff of officials; but it is for the citizens to speak out decidedly on this question, the solution of which by the City Parish is fraught with so many advantages to the pauper, as well as to the city at large. A better example of the benefit to be derived from centralization and union can hardly be given. The principle has been admirably urged by the *Scotsman* newspaper, in reference to the subject of our Poorhouses, as well as our local charities. The sanitary reformer observes in Edinburgh several instances in which it could be beneficially applied. I need do no more than allude to the City and County Road Trusts, and the proprietary of private streets, all with separate interests, in the struggle for which, the general good is not subserved. I would extend the principle still further, and hold that, in many matters, private rights should succumb to the efficient control of a central authority. This admits of illustration by reference to drainage and house accommodation. The communications with the main sewers may be of the most faulty description, no one can interfere *in limine*, and it is not until the house becomes uninhabitable that the authorities can interfere. But whole districts may be drained without any reference to the drainage plans of other parts of the city, which have been adopted by the Magistrates and Council. Thus the Grange has only been lately drained, but on inquiry I find that over this drainage, although situated within the municipal boundary, the city has no control, and the official who has the superintendence of the rest of the sewers—the City Engineer—was not consulted as to the size or direction of the drains which are made, and his services will not be put into requisition until some defect is ascertained, and an appeal is made to him as the special drainage officer of the city. No district should be built upon, and no house should be erected, until a drainage plan has been prepared and submitted for approval to the Magistrates, in whom all sewers should be vested. Again, in the case of houses intended to be let below a certain rent, there should be some supervision of the general arrangements. Cases have come under my notice where, to avoid the expense of conducting the drain along the outside of the house, they have been carried under sleeping apartments, and where the convenience was so arranged, as to ventilate into a bedroom. These instances have occurred even in newly-built tenements. The city officials could not interfere until the houses became tenanted, when the inhabitants made a special complaint. The ultimate remedy lies in the law courts, a tedious and exasperating process, which might be entirely avoided were the common-sense regulation adopted, that such matters should be determined by the officer appointed by the authorities. It would be for the benefit of the inhabitants were the principle even further extended, and all feuing plans submitted to the Magistrates. Such anomalies as have been perpetrated in Macnab Street, for example, would never be tolerated—where, from the formation of a *cul de sac*, the ventilation of future tenements must be seriously interfered with, not to speak of the disfigurement of the locality. *Lastly*, the leading thoroughfares should be carefully watched over, so that, whenever circumstances permit, they may be widened, or altered to accommodate the traffic of the City. No one can pass Earl Grey Street without seeing how inadequate it is as a means of communication between the wide thoroughfares of Home Street on the one hand, and Lothian Road on the other. The district is a populous one; the traffic is daily increasing; and the passage of vehicles along this part of the route is attended with no little danger. Advantage should also have been taken of the erection of new buildings in the Cowgate, at the east of Geo. IV. Bridge, to have widened that very contracted thoroughfare. A few feet have been added to it at the point in question; but, when we take the height of the new buildings on either side into consideration, we cannot fail to see that, had the Cowgate been doubled in width, such an addition would not have been beyond the necessities of that low-lying locality. The Crown superintends the erection of the new buildings to the north, and it would have been easy for the Magistrates, on the representation of the proper officer, to have claimed the assistance of Government in commencing an important sanitary improvement. Not to multiply instances, the lane which connects Doune Terrace with Heriot Row, and is so much frequented as a means of communication with Stockbridge, should, long ere this, have been improved, so as to make it an agreeable approach to the best districts of the New Town.

The object of this Report has been to deal with those obstacles to the well-being of society which lie on the surface, and which are connected with the manner of living of the inhabitants. We have determined the unhealthiness of the city, and of its various districts. We have made inquiry into the influence exercised on the rate of mortality by various agencies, which have been considered in detail—such as, overcrowding of the population, trades and occupation, drainage and water supply, &c., &c. No one, however, can visit the poorer districts of the city without being impressed with the close connection which exists between outward filth and inward depravity, and with the facilities presented for the germination and rapid growth of vice in all its forms, by the wretched habitations and confined alleys of the Old Town. The division of the city adopted in this Report, and the determination of the area and population of the Sanitary Districts, will, it is conceived, aid philanthropists with their enquiries into the social condition of our poor. In Table No. XIII., p. 62 of the Appendix, an attempt has been made to show the manner in which the arrangement might be made serviceable. It is cheering to reflect, that all measures which have for their object the improvement of the sanitary state of communities, have a corresponding influence in raising their moral and social condition. On all sides, in the most degraded localities, physically and morally, we find ourselves surrounded by religious agencies busying themselves in attending to the higher interests of the masses in the most devoted manner, and at great outlay. Bitter complaints have been made as to the poverty of the results obtained by such multifarious and strenuous endeavours. This need be no wonder, when we reflect on the overwhelming disadvantages against which the missionary and philanthropist have to contend. Our poor are so lodged, that to inhale the atmosphere in their houses is enough to produce a lethargic depression, to escape from which is but to be exposed to the temptations of the High Street and Cowgate. With no comfort at home, the poor labourer is forced to go elsewhere for enjoyment. To his sleeping-place he returns, to find himself in a crowded apartment, where there is no attempt to maintain the ordinary decencies of life. With so many and varied proclivities to vice in all its forms, it is a heartless task to talk to such an one of righteousness, temperance, and judgment to come. The agencies employed ought, in my opinion, to be more varied; and Woman might be enlisted in the cause with great advantage. I have found the Missionaries of all denominations nobly discharging duties to the poor of Edinburgh, which would be more fitly rendered by the other sex. By means of Female assistance, the houses of the poor would be rendered more comfortable, and the food of the working-classes would be more economically and better prepared. There would be less temptation to seek the pleasures of the alehouse, and lessons of thrift would be imparted in the management of the household, that would pave the way for the higher ministrations of the minister of religion. In attempting to raise the poor in our towns from their degraded position, we must attack that which lies on the surface. Until the dwellings of the poor are rendered more habitable, and the poor themselves are taught the wholesome lesson of outward cleanliness, it is not to be expected that their deeper nature can be effectually stirred.

Reported by,

HENRY D. LITTLEJOHN, M.D.,

Medical Officer of Health.

APPENDIX.

TABLE No. I.—CAUSES of DEATH in the CITY of EDINBURGH, at different Periods of Life, in 1863.—Both Sexes.

	DISEASES.	All Ages.	Age under											
			Months.											
			3	6	12	2	3	4	5	10	15	20	25	30
	All Causes	4412	433	154	295	465	224	157	94	188	68	101	150	144
	Specified Causes	4397	429	153	293	465	224	157	94	188	68	100	149	143
	1 Zymotic Diseases	1059	58	44	96	224	141	98	59	97	20	22	29	23
Sporadic Diseases.	2 Diseases of Uncertain Seat	177	3	2	1	1	1	1	2	4	2	...	1	2
	3 Tubercular Diseases	735	18	25	70	84	39	26	12	39	27	54	73	56
	4 Diseases of the Brain, &c.	485	31	8	24	16	2	1	1	7	3	6	7	10
	5 Diseases of the Heart, &c.	253	1	...	...	1	2	1	1	8	3	4	4	12
	6 Diseases of the Lungs, &c.	650	38	43	76	98	29	21	13	14	2	3	14	3
	7 Diseases of the Stomach, &c.	226	28	8	11	16	2	4	1	8	3	2	4	10
	8 Diseases of the Kidney	63	...	...	...	2	...	2	1	4	1	4	1	2
	9 Diseases of the Uterus, &c.	38	...	...	...	...	...	...	...	...	...	1	3	11
	10 Diseases of the Joints, &c.	22	1	1	1	...	...	...	1	1	2	...	2	1
	11 Diseases of the Skin, &c.	10	1	1	...	1	...	...	...	...	...	...	...	...
	12 Malformation	8	5	1	...	1	...	...	...	...	...	...	...	...
	13 Premature Debility	195	189	5	1	...	...	...	...	...	...	...	...	...
	14 Atrophy	69	23	11	7	15	5	...	...	2	...	...	2	...
	15 Age	227	...	...	...	...	...	...	...	...	...	...	...	...
	16 Sudden	12	2	...	...	1	...	...	...	...	...	...	1	...
	17 External Causes	168	31	4	6	5	3	3	3	4	5	4	8	13
	I.													
	Small Pox	48	6	1	2	7	8	4	1	6	1	...	1	4
	Measles	220	3	4	26	102	41	22	7	11	...	2	1	...
	Scarlatina	121	1	...	5	17	22	14	18	34	4	1	2	1
	Diphtheria	134	7	3	12	20	23	24	13	20	3	2	...	2
	Hooping-Cough	53	1	7	12	15	8	5	2	3	...	...	...	...
	Croup	114	3	1	15	35	32	13	8	7	...	...	...	...
	Pyæmia	16	...	1	...	...	...	...	...	...	1	...	4	4
	Diarrhœa	97	23	11	14	14	...	...	1	1	1	...	...	1
	Dysentery	11	...	...	...	1	1	...	...	...	...	...	...	1
	Cholera	11	1	2	1	3	...	...	...	1	...	...	...	...
	Influenza	5	...	1	...	...	...	...	...	...	...	...	...	...
	Purpura	2	1	...	...	...	...	...	...	1	...	...	...	...
	Cancrum Oris	1	...	...	...	...	...	...	...	1	...	...	...	...
	Worms	5	1	...	1	3	...	...	...	...	...	...	...	...
	Typhus Fever	57	...	...	...	1	...	...	...	1	1	5	9	5
	Typhoid ,,	46	...	...	...	...	1	5	3	4	4	9	7	1
	Gastric ,,	41	...	1	1	...	5	2	3	2	5	2	2	3
	Infantile ,,	22	...	2	1	3	...	9	2	5	...	...	...	...
	Metria	12	...	...	...	...	...	...	...	...	...	1	3	1
	Rheumatic Fever	2	...	...	...	...	...	...	1	...	...	...	...	...
	Erysipelas	18	5	4	2	...	...	...	...	...	...	...	...	...
	Syphilis	23	6	6	4	3	...	...	...	...	...	...	...	...
		1059	58	44	96	224	141	98	59	97	20	22	29	23

TABLE No. I.—CAUSES OF DEATH IN THE CITY OF EDINBURGH, at different Periods of Life, in 1863.—BOTH SEXES.—*Continued.*

DISEASES.	Age under														
	35	40	45	50	55	60	65	70	75	80	85	90	95	100	105
All Causes	155	155	132	157	172	179	236	168	244	175	114	39	10	2	1
Specified Causes	155	154	132	157	172	177	236	167	244	174	114	39	10	2	1
Zymotic Diseases	22	24	9	9	18	12	16	11	14	9	2	1	1	...	...
Diseases of Uncertain Seat	6	9	10	12	26	18	27	14	17	13	3	2	...	...	...
Tubercular Diseases	52	39	30	39	25	15	10	2	...	...	...	...	...	...	...
Diseases of the Brain, &c.	16	20	20	24	31	38	51	39	71	35	18	6	...	...	...
Diseases of the Heart, &c.	13	14	24	20	16	22	36	28	18	17	6	1	1	...	...
Diseases of the Lungs, &c.	12	11	12	22	25	36	44	38	48	24	15	5	3	1	...
Diseases of the Stomach, &c.	11	11	11	13	9	19	18	8	18	7	3	...	1	...	...
Diseases of the Kidneys	4	5	3	2	4	4	9	3	4	6	2	...	...	...	...
Diseases of the Uterus, &c.	6	3	4	3	3	1	2	...	...	1	...	...	...	...	...
Diseases of the Joints, &c.	4	1	1	...	2	1	1	2	...	...	...	...	...	...	...
Diseases of the Skin, &c.	...	2	...	1	...	...	...	1	2	...	...	1	...	...	...
Malformation	...	...	...	1	...	...	...	...	...	...	...	...	...	...	...
Premature Debility	...	...	...	...	...	...	...	...	...	...	...	...	...	...	...
Atrophy	...	1	...	...	2	1	...	...	...	...	...	...	...	...	...
Age	...	...	...	...	1	2	14	14	47	58	63	22	4	1	1
Sudden	1	2	1	2	1	1	...	...	...	...	...	...	...	...	...
External Causes	8	12	7	9	9	7	8	7	5	4	2	1	...	...	...
I.															
Small Pox	2	1	1	...	1	1	...	..	1	...	...	...	...	...	...
Measles	1	...	...	...	...	...	...	...	...	...	...	...	...	...	...
Scarlatina	1	1	...	...	...	..	...	...	...	...	...	...	...	..	...
Diphtheria	...	1	1	1	...	...	1	...	1	...	...	...	...	...	...
Hooping-Cough	...	...	...	...	...	...	...	...	...	...	...	...	...	...	...
Croup	...	...	...	...	...	...	...	...	...	...	...	...	...	...	...
Pyæmia	1	3	...	1	...	1	...	...	...	...	...	...	...	...	...
Diarrhœa	1	1	1	1	6	1	3	4	5	5	1	1	1	...	...
Dysentery	...	1	2	...	...	...	3	...	1	1	...	...	...	...	...
Cholera	...	...	...	...	1	...	1	...	1	...	...	...	...	...	...
Influenza	...	...	...	...	...	...	...	...	1	2	1	...	...	...	...
Purpura	...	...	...	...	...	...	...	...	...	...	...	...	...	...	...
Ague	...	...	...	..	...	...	...	...	...	...	...	...	...	...	...
Worms	...	...	...	...	...	...	...	...	...	...	...	...	...	...	...
Typhus Fever	9	4	2	4	6	3	4	2	...	1	...	...	...	...	...
Typhoid ,,	...	2	1	...	3	1	2	2	1	...	...	...	...	...	...
Gastric ,,	2	2	1	1	1	4	2	1	1	...	...	..	..	...	...
Infantile ,,	...	...	...	...	...	...	...	...	...	...	...	...	...	...	...
Metria	3	4	...	...	...	...	...	...	...	...	...	...	...	...	...
Rheumatic Fever	...	...	...	1	...	...	...	...	...	...	...	...	...	...	...
Erysipelas	2	1	...	...	...	...	...	2	2	...	...	...	...	...	...
Syphilis	...	3	...	...	...	1	...	...	...	...	...	...	...	...	...
	22	24	9	9	18	12	16	11	14	9	2	1	1	...	...

TABLE No. I.—CAUSES OF DEATH IN THE CITY OF EDINBURGH, at different Periods of Life, in 1863.—BOTH SEXES.—*Continued.*

DISEASES.	ALL AGES.	AGE UNDER											
		MONTHS. 3	6	12	2	3	4	5	10	15	20	25	30
II.													
Hæmorrhage	9	2	...	...	...	...	1	...	...	...	...	1	...
Dropsy	24	...	...	...	...	...	...	1	3	2	...	...	...
Abscess	15	1	1	1	...	1	...	...	...	...	...	...	...
Ulcer	7	...	1	...	...	...	...	...	1	...	...	...	1
Fistula	...	...	...	...	...	...	...	...	...	...	...	...	...
Mortification	11	...	...	...	1	...	...	...	...	...	...	...	...
Cancer	111	...	...	...	...	...	...	1	...	...	...	...	1
Gout	...	...	...	...	...	...	...	...	...	...	...	...	...
	177	3	2	1	1	1	1	2	4	2	...	1	2
III.													
Scrofula	34	1	3	2	6	8	3	...	4	3	1	1	...
Tabes Mesenterica	77	6	8	18	21	9	5	...	5	1	2	1	...
Phthisis	433	...	1	1	4	4	1	2	15	18	51	71	56
Hydrocephalus	191	11	13	49	53	18	17	10	15	5	...	...	...
	735	18	25	70	84	39	26	12	39	27	54	73	56
IV.													
Cephalitis	18	...	...	...	...	...	...	...	...	...	3	3	1
Apoplexy	73	...	...	1	...	...	...	...	...	...	...	...	1
Paralysis	151	...	...	...	...	...	...	...	...	...	...	...	2
Delirium Tremens	11	...	...	...	...	...	...	...	...	...	...	...	...
Trismus Nascentium	1	1	...	...	...	...	...	...	...	...	...	...	...
Epilepsy	16	...	...	...	...	...	...	...	2	1	1	2	...
Tetanus	2	...	...	...	...	...	...	...	...	...	...	...	...
Insanity	67	...	...	...	...	...	...	...	...	...	...	1	3
Convulsions	75	29	8	19	14	1	1	...	2	...	...	...	...
Brain	71	1	...	4	2	1	...	1	3	2	2	1	3
	485	31	8	24	16	2	1	1	7	3	6	7	10
V.													
Pericarditis	9	...	...	...	1	...	...	...	2	...	1	...	2
Aneurism	8	...	...	...	...	...	...	...	...	...	...	...	...
Heart	236	1	...	...	...	2	1	1	6	3	3	4	10
	253	1	...	...	1	2	1	1	8	3	4	4	12
VI.													
Laryngitis	12	...	1	2	6	...	1	1	...	...	...	...	...
Bronchitis	461	34	34	65	77	23	16	10	10	...	1	6	2
Pleurisy	18	...	...	1	...	...	...	...	...	...	1	2	1
Pneumonia	77	3	8	6	12	3	3	1	2	...	...	3	...
Asthma	41	...	...	...	...	...	...	...	...	...	...	...	...
Lungs	41	1	...	2	3	3	1	1	2	2	1	3	...
	650	38	43	76	98	29	21	13	14	2	3	14	3
VII.													
Teething	18	...	2	6	10	...	...	...	...	...	...	...	...
Quinsey	8	2	...	...	1	2	1	...	1	...	...	...	...
Gastritis	2	...	...	...	...	...	...	...	1	...	...	...	...
Enteritis	40	14	2	4	5	...	2	1	3	...	...	...	...
Peritonitis	24	3	2	...	...	...	...	...	1	1	2	2	...
Ascites	4	...	...	...	...	...	...	...	...	...	...	...	...
Ulceration of Intestines	9	...	...	...	...	...	...	...	...	...	...	1	2
Hernia	6	...	...	...	...	...	...	...	...	...	...	...	...
Ileus	8	1	1	...	...	...	...	...	...	...	...	...	1
Intussusception	2	...	1	...	...	...	...	...	...	...	...	...	...
Stricture of Intestines	...	...	...	...	...	...	...	...	...	...	...	...	...
Stomach	39	...	...	...	...	...	...	...	...	...	...	...	3
Pancreas	...	...	...	...	...	...	...	...	...	...	...	...	...
Hepatitis	5	...	...	...	...	...	...	...	...	...	...	...	...
Jaundice	12	7	...	...	...	...	1	...	...	...	...	...	...
Liver	46	1	...	1	...	...	...	...	2	2	...	...	4
Spleen	3	...	...	...	...	...	...	...	...	...	...	1	...
	226	28	8	11	16	2	4	1	8	3	2	4	10

TABLE No. I.—CAUSES OF DEATH IN THE CITY OF EDINBURGH, at different Periods of Life, in 1863.—Both Sexes.—*Continued.*

DISEASES.	Age under														
	35	40	45	50	55	60	65	70	75	80	85	90	95	100	105
II.															
Hæmorrhage	...	...	1	1	1	...	...	...	1	1	...	...	...	...	...
Dropsy	...	2	1	...	1	1	5	1	4	2	1	...	...	...	..
Abscess	1	...	2	1	...	4	1	...	2	...	...	...	...	...	...
Ulcer	1	...	...	...	...	...	...	...	1	2	...	...	...	...	...
Fistula	...	...	...	...	...	...	...	...	...	...	...	...	...	...	...
Mortification	...	...	...	1	...	...	1	1	2	2	2	1	...	...	...
Cancer	4	7	6	9	24	13	20	12	7	6	...	1	...	...	...
Gout	...	...	...	...	...	...	...	...	...	...	...	...	...	...	...
	6	9	10	12	26	18	27	14	17	13	3	2	...	...	...
III.															
Scrofula	...	1	...	1	...	...	...	...	...	...	...	...	...	...	...
Tabes Mesenterica	...	...	...	...	1	...	...	...	...	...	...	...	...	...	...
Phthisis	52	38	30	38	24	15	10	2	...	...	...	...	...	...	...
Hydrocephalus	...	...	...	...	...	...	...	...	...	...	...	...	...	...	...
	52	39	30	39	25	15	10	2	...	...	...	...	...	...	...
IV.															
Cephalitis	3	2	2	...	...	2	...	1	1	...	...	...	...	...	...
Apoplexy	2	3	3	6	4	10	12	13	9	5	4	...	...	...	...
Paralysis	...	1	3	6	10	13	21	13	46	21	11	4	...	...	...
Delirium Tremens	1	6	1	1	...	1	...	...	...	...	...	...	...	...	...
Chorea	...	...	...	...	...	...	...	...	...	...	...	...	...	...	...
Epilepsy	...	1	3	2	1	...	...	1	2	...	...	...	...	...	...
Tetanus	...	...	...	1	...	1	...	...	...	...	...	...	...	...	...
Insanity	8	4	5	8	8	4	9	8	5	2	2	1	...	...	...
Convulsions	1	...	...	...	...	...	...	...	...	...	...	...	...	...	...
Brain	1	3	3	...	8	7	9	3	8	7	1	1	...	...	...
	16	20	20	24	31	38	51	39	71	35	18	6	...	...	...
V.															
Pericarditis	...	...	...	...	...	1	2	...	...	...	...	...	...	...	...
Aneurism	...	3	2	1	...	1	...	1	...	...	...	...	...	...	...
Heart	13	11	22	19	16	20	34	27	18	17	6	1	1	...	...
	13	14	24	20	16	22	36	28	18	17	6	1	1	...	...
VI.															
Laryngitis	...	...	1	...	...	...	...	...	...	...	...	...	...	...	..
Bronchitis	5	5	8	11	13	19	28	26	34	14	14	3	2	1	..
Pleurisy	2	...	1	...	1	1	1	2	2	3	...	...	...	...	...
Pneumonia	2	2	1	3	6	10	...	3	5	2	1	1	...	...	...
Asthma	1	1	1	5	1	5	11	5	5	4	...	1	1	...	...
Lungs	2	3	...	3	4	1	4	2	2	1	...	...	...	...	...
	12	11	12	22	25	36	44	38	48	24	15	5	3	1	...
VII.															
Teething	...	...	...	...	...	...	...	...	...	...	...	...	...	...	...
Quinsey	...	1	...	...	...	...	...	...	...	...	...	...	...	...	...
Gastritis	...	...	...	...	...	...	...	...	1	...	...	...	...	...	...
Enteritis	...	1	2	2	1	...	1	1	1	...	...	...	...	...	...
Peritonitis	4	3	...	...	1	2	1	...	2	...	...	...	...	...	...
Ascites	...	...	...	...	1	...	1	...	...	1	1	...	...	...	...
Ulceration of Intestines	1	...	...	1	1	2	...	...	1	...	...	...	...	...	...
Hernia	...	...	...	2	1	...	2	...	...	1	...	...	...	...	...
Ileus	1	...	...	1	...	...	...	...	1	1	1	...	...	...	...
Intussusception	...	...	...	...	...	...	1	...	...	...	...	...	...	...	...
Stricture of Intestines	...	...	...	...	...	...	...	...	...	...	...	...	...	...	...
Stomach	2	3	3	3	3	6	8	4	3	1	...	...	...	...	...
Pancreas	...	...	...	...	...	...	...	...	...	...	...	...	...	...	...
Hepatitis	...	...	...	2	...	1	...	1	...	...	...	...	1	...	...
Jaundice	...	...	2	...	...	...	...	...	1	...	1	...	...	...	...
Liver	3	3	3	1	1	8	4	2	8	3	...	...	...	...	...
Spleen	...	...	1	1	...	...	...	...	...	...	...	...	...	...	...
	11	11	11	13	9	19	18	8	18	7	3	...	1	...	...

TABLE No. I.—CAUSES OF DEATH IN THE CITY OF EDINBURGH, at different Periods of Life, in 1863.—BOTH SEXES.—*Continued.*

DISEASES.	ALL AGES.	AGE UNDER											
		MONTHS.											
		3	6	12	2	3	4	5	10	15	20	25	30
VIII.													
Nephritis	4	...	...	...	...	...	...	...	1	...	1	...	...
Nephria	...	...	...	...	...	...	...	...	...	...	...	...	...
Ischuria	1	...	...	...	...	...	...	...	...	...	...	...	...
Diabetes	4	...	...	...	1	...	...	...	...	...	1	...	...
Stone	1	...	...	...	...	...	...	...	...	...	...	...	...
Cystitis	8	...	...	...	...	...	...	...	...	1	...	1	...
Stricture of Urethra	4	...	...	...	...	...	...	...	...	...	...	...	...
Kidneys	41	...	...	...	1	...	2	1	3	...	2	...	2
	63	...	...	...	2	...	2	1	4	1	4	1	2
IX.													
Paramenia	1	...	...	...	...	...	...	...	...	...	...	...	...
Ovarian Dropsy	10	...	...	...	...	...	...	...	...	...	...	...	1
Childbirth	21	...	...	...	...	...	...	...	...	...	1	3	9
Uterus	6	...	...	...	...	...	...	...	...	...	...	...	1
	38	...	...	...	...	...	...	...	...	...	1	3	11
X.													
Arthritis	...	...	...	...	...	...	...	...	...	...	...	...	...
Rheumatism	3	...	...	...	...	...	...	...	...	...	...	...	...
Joints	19	1	1	1	...	...	...	1	1	2	...	2	1
	22	1	1	1	...	...	...	1	1	2	...	2	1
XI.													
Carbuncle	5	...	...	...	...	...	...	...	...	...	...	...	...
Phlegmon	...	...	...	...	...	...	...	...	...	...	...	...	...
Skin	5	1	1	...	1	...	...	...	...	...	...	...	...
	10	1	1	...	1	...	...	...	...	...	...	...	...
XII.													
Cyanosis	4	2	1	...	...	...	...	...	...	...	...	...	...
Spina Bifida	1	1	...	...	...	...	...	...	...	...	...	...	...
Other Malformations	3	2	...	...	1	...	...	...	...	...	...	...	...
	8	5	1	...	1	...	...	...	...	...	...	...	...
XIII.—XVI. See above.	503	214	16	8	16	5	...	...	2	...	...	3	...
XVII.													
Intemperance	13	...	...	...	...	...	...	...	...	...	1	2	1
Privation	1	...	...	...	...	...	...	...	...	...	...	...	...
Want of Milk	9	8	...	1	...	...	...	...	...	...	...	...	...
Neglect	7	7	...	...	...	...	...	...	...	...	...	...	...
Cold	...	...	...	...	...	...	...	...	...	...	...	...	...
Poison	5	1	...	...	...	...	...	...	...	...	1	...	1
Burns, &c.	20	...	...	2	3	1	2	1	...	2	...	...	...
Hanging, &c.	3	...	...	...	...	...	...	...	...	...	...	...	1
Suffocation	21	11	3	1	1	...	...	...	...	...	...	...	2
Drowning	10	...	...	...	1	...	...	...	1	...	...	...	...
Fractures and Contusions	41	2	...	1	...	2	1	1	...	1	1	5	3
Wounds	10	1	...	...	...	...	...	1	...	...	...	...	2
Other Violent Causes	28	1	1	1	...	...	...	...	3	2	1	1	3
	168	31	4	6	5	3	3	3	4	5	4	8	13
Not Specified	15	4	1	2	...	...	...	...	...	...	1	1	1

TABLE No. I.—CAUSES OF DEATH IN THE CITY OF EDINBURGH, at different Periods of Life, in 1863.—BOTH SEXES.—*Continued.*

DISEASES.	AGE UNDER														
	35	40	45	50	55	60	65	70	75	80	85	90	95	100	105
VIII.															
Nephritis	...	...	...	...	...	...	...	1	...	1	...	...	...	...	...
Nephria	...	...	...	...	...	...	...	...	...	...	...	...	...	...	...
Ischuria	...	...	...	...	...	...	...	...	...	...	1	...	...	...	...
Diabetes	...	...	1	1	...	...	...	...	...	...	...	...	...	...	...
Stone	...	...	...	...	...	1	...	...	...	...	...	...	...	...	...
Cystitis	...	...	...	...	...	1	1	...	1	2	1	...	...	...	...
Stricture of Urethra	...	...	1	...	1	1	1	...	...	...	...	...	...	...	...
Kidneys	4	5	1	1	3	1	7	2	3	3	...	...	...	...	...
	4	5	3	2	4	4	9	3	4	6	2	...	...	...	...
IX.															
Paramenia	1	...	...	...	...	...	...	...	...	...	...	...	...	...	...
Ovarian Dropsy	1	...	1	2	2	...	2	...	...	1	...	...	...	...	...
Childbirth	4	2	2	...	...	...	...	...	...	...	...	...	...	...	...
Uterus	...	1	1	1	1	1	...	...	...	...	...	...	...	...	...
	6	3	4	3	3	1	2	...	...	1	...	...	...	...	...
X.															
Arthritis	...	...	...	...	...	...	...	...	...	...	...	...	...	...	...
Rheumatism	...	...	...	...	2	...	...	1	...	...	...	...	...	...	...
Joints	4	1	1	...	...	1	1	1	...	...	...	...	...	...	...
	4	1	1	...	2	1	1	2	...	...	...	...	...	...	...
XI.															
Carbuncle	...	2	...	...	...	...	...	1	2	...	...	...	...	...	...
Phlegmon	...	...	...	...	...	...	...	...	...	...	...	...	...	...	...
Skin	...	...	...	1	...	...	...	...	...	...	...	1	...	...	...
	...	2	...	1	...	...	...	1	2	...	...	1	...	...	...
XII.															
Cyanosis	...	...	...	1	...	...	...	...	...	...	...	...	...	...	...
Spina Bifida	...	...	...	...	...	...	...	...	...	...	...	...	...	...	...
Other Malformations	...	...	...	...	...	...	...	...	...	...	...	...	...	...	...
	...	...	...	1	...	...	...	...	...	...	...	...	...	...	...
XIII.—XVI. See above.	1	3	1	2	4	4	14	14	47	58	63	22	4	1	1
XVII.															
Intemperance	1	2	2	...	2	1	...	...	...	...	1	...	...	...	...
Privation	...	...	1	...	...	...	...	...	...	...	...	...	...	...	...
Want of Milk	...	...	...	...	...	...	...	...	...	...	...	...	...	...	...
Neglect	...	...	...	...	...	...	...	...	...	...	...	...	...	...	...
Cold	...	...	...	...	...	...	...	...	...	...	...	...	...	...	...
Poison	...	...	...	...	1	...	1	...	...	...	...	...	...	...	...
Burns, &c.	1	1	...	...	2	1	2	1	...	...	...	1	...	...	...
Hanging, &c.	...	...	...	2	...	...	...	...	...	...	...	...	...	...	...
Suffocation	...	2	...	...	...	...	...	...	1	...	...	...	...	...	...
Drowning	2	3	...	1	...	1	...	1	...	...	...	...	...	...	...
Fractures & Contusions	2	...	3	2	3	3	4	1	4	1	1	...	...	...	...
Wounds	...	1	1	1	...	1	...	2	...	...	...	...	...	...	...
Other Violent Causes	2	3	...	3	1	...	1	2	...	3	...	...	...	...	...
	8	12	7	9	9	7	8	7	5	4	2	1	...	...	...
Not Specified	...	1	...	...	...	2	...	1	...	1	...	...	...	...	...

TABLE No. II.—CAUSES OF DEATH IN THE CITY OF EDINBURGH, for each Month in 1863, arranged according to Sex.

Only the Monthly Totals of the various Classes of Disease in the Sexes as arranged in Table I. are here given, as it was not considered necessary to give the Tables at full length.

Month.	Temperature.			Mortality.		
	Highest.	Lowest.	Mean.	Total.	Males.	Females.
January	53·0	25·5	38·7	392	199	193
February	59·0	26·5	41·2	402	188	214
March	58·5	25·0	43·0	415	215	200
April	57·0	30·0	44·6	420	205	215
May	64·5	36·5	49·5	372	182	190
June	68·0	42·0	55·6	392	200	192
July	75·2	39·5	58·0	275	139	136
August	69·0	39·0	56·0	326	161	165
September	60·0	41·0	50·0	289	145	144
October	58·0	31·5	46·8	360	180	180
November	57·0	26·5	44·1	371	186	185
December	56·0	24·5	41·4	398	221	177
Total				4412	2221	2191

Month.	Temperature.			I. Zymotic Diseases			II. Uncertain Seat.			III. Tubercular Class.			IV. Brain, &c.		
	Highest.	Lowest.	Mean.	Total.	M.	F.	Total.	M.	F.	Total.	M.	F.	Total.	M.	F.
January	53·0	25·5	38·7	112	65	47	12	3	9	55	32	23	36	22	14
February	59·0	26·5	41·2	97	42	55	13	3	10	62	34	28	40	20	20
March	58·5	25·0	43·0	99	51	48	13	4	9	64	33	31	48	27	21
April	57·0	30·0	44·6	122	53	69	12	6	6	69	36	33	43	27	16
May	64·5	36·5	49·5	81	38	43	14	6	8	69	35	33	41	26	15
June	68·0	42·0	55·6	78	38	39	14	6	8	75	35	40	58	29	29
July	75·2	39·5	58·0	69	39	30	14	7	7	57	29	28	28	14	14
August	69·0	39·0	56·0	75	39	36	16	7	9	58	31	27	38	23	15
September	60·0	41·0	50·0	68	31	37	21	6	15	43	29	14	43	18	25
October	58·0	31·5	46·8	82	39	43	15	4	11	58	29	29	37	21	16
November	57·0	26·5	44·1	92	40	52	17	7	10	63	34	29	35	16	19
December	56·0	24·5	41·4	85	43	42	16	8	8	63	37	26	38	28	10
Total				1059	518	541	177	67	110	735	394	341	485	271	214

Month.	Temperature.			V. Heart, &c.			VI. Lungs, &c.			VII. Stomach, &c.			VIII. Kidney.		
	Highest.	Lowest.	Mean.	Total.	M.	F.	Total.	M.	F.	Total.	M.	F.	Total.	M.	F.
January	53·0	25·5	38·7	17	7	10	66	30	36	23	10	13	2	...	2
February	59·0	26·5	41·2	28	11	17	64	31	33	22	10	12	4	3	1
March	58·5	25·0	43·0	26	13	13	70	38	32	20	10	10	8	8	...
April	57·0	30·0	44·6	23	17	6	70	28	42	16	5	11	3	2	1
May	64·5	36·5	49·5	18	11	7	65	32	33	16	5	11	9	6	3
June	68·0	42·0	55·6	18	10	8	46	27	19	24	12	12	4	4	...
July	75·2	39·5	58·0	12	7	5	34	16	18	10	5	5	4	2	2
August	69·0	39·0	56·0	20	8	12	25	14	11	18	8	10	5	2	3
September	60·0	41·0	50·0	16	8	8	33	19	14	11	9	2	8	6	2
October	58·0	31·5	46·8	31	16	15	50	22	28	23	12	11	5	3	2
November	57·0	26·5	44·1	18	11	7	67	39	28	14	6	8	5	2	3
December	56·0	24·5	41·4	26	12	14	60	34	26	29	15	14	6	5	1
Total				253	131	122	650	330	320	226	107	119	63	43	20

TABLE No. II.—CAUSES OF DEATH IN THE CITY OF EDINBURGH, for each Month in 1863, arranged according to Sex.—*Continued.*

Month.	Temperature.			IX. Uterus, &c.			X. Joints, &c.			XI. Skin, &c.			XII. Malformation.		
	Highest.	Lowest.	Mean.	Total.	M.	F.	Total.	M.	F.	Total.	M.	F.	Total.	M.	F.
January...	53·0	25·5	38·7	...	...	...	...	...	...	...	...	...	...	...	...
February	59·0	26·5	41·2	5	...	5	3	2	1	...	...	...	...	...	...
March ...	58·5	25·0	43·0	4	...	4	1	...	1	3	...	3	...	...	...
April	57·0	30·0	44·6	...	...	...	2	1	1	...	...	...	2	1	1
May	64·5	36·5	49·5	...	...	...	3	1	2	...	...	...	2	2	...
June	68·0	42·0	55·6	6	...	6	3	2	1	1	...	1	2	2	...
July	75·2	39·5	58·0	4	...	4	2	1	1	...	...	...	...	...	...
August ...	69·0	39·0	56·0	3	...	3	2	1	1	2	1	1	1	...	1
September	60·0	41·0	50·0	3	...	3	...	...	...	...	...	...	...	...	...
October ...	58·0	31·5	46·8	5	...	5	2	2	...	1	1	...	...	...	...
November	57·0	26·5	44·1	5	...	5	...	...	...	1	...	1	...	...	...
December	56·0	24·5	41·4	3	...	3	4	2	2	2	1	1	1	1	...
Total......				38	...	38	22	12	10	10	3	7	8	6	2

Month.	Temperature.			XIII. Prem. Debility.			XIV. Atrophy.			XV. Age.			XVI. Sudden.		
	Highest.	Lowest.	Mean.	Total.	M.	F.	Total.	M.	F.	Total.	M.	F.	Total.	M.	F.
January...	53·0	25·5	38·7	15	7	8	3	1	2	26	9	17	...	...	...
February	59·0	26·5	41·2	19	11	8	7	3	4	22	8	14	2	1	1
March ...	58·5	25·0	43·0	19	13	6	5	4	1	15	5	10	2	2	...
April	57·0	30·0	44·6	19	9	10	7	6	1	19	7	12	2	1	1
May	64·5	36·5	49·5	14	6	8	10	5	5	18	5	13	3	...	3
June	68·0	42·0	55·6	17	13	4	5	...	5	23	8	15	1	...	1
July	75·2	39·5	58·0	9	5	4	5	2	3	16	6	10	...	...	...
August ...	69·0	39·0	56·0	23	11	12	4	1	3	21	6	15	...	...	...
September	60·0	41·0	50·0	10	6	4	5	3	2	17	5	12	...	...	...
October ...	58·0	31·5	46·8	18	13	5	5	3	2	13	7	6	1	...	1
November	57·0	26·5	44·1	16	10	6	8	3	5	14	8	6	...	...	...
December	56·0	24·5	41·4	16	13	3	5	1	4	23	9	14	1	1	...
Total......				195	117	78	69	32	37	227	83	144	12	5	7

Month.	Temperature.			XVII. External Causes.			Not Specified.		
	Highest.	Lowest.	Mean.	Total.	M.	F.	Total.	M.	F.
January...	53·0	25·5	38·7	21	12	9	4	1	3
February	59·0	26·5	41·2	14	9	5	...	...	...
March ...	58·5	25·0	43·0	16	6	10	2	1	1
April	57·0	30·0	44·6	11	6	5	...	...	...
May	64·5	36·5	49·5	9	4	5	1	...	1
June	68·0	42·0	55·6	18	14	4	...	...	...
July	75·2	39·5	58·0	10	6	4	1	...	1
August ...	69·0	39·0	56·0	14	8	6	1	1	...
September	60·0	41·0	50·0	11	5	6	...	...	...
October ...	58·0	31·5	46·8	13	7	6	1	1	...
November	57·0	26·5	44·1	15	10	5	1	...	1
December	56·0	24·5	41·4	16	9	7	4	2	2
Total......				168	96	72	15	6	9

	Total	M.	F.
Class I.	1059	518	541
II.	177	67	110
III.	735	394	341
IV.	485	271	214
V.	253	131	122
VI.	650	330	320
VII.	226	107	119
VIII.	63	43	20
IX.	38	...	38
X.	22	12	10
XI.	10	3	7
XII.	8	6	2
XIII.	195	117	78
XIV.	69	32	37
XV.	227	83	144
XVI.	12	5	7
XVII.	168	96	72
Not specified	15	6	9
Total...	4412	2221	2191

TABLE No. III.—DEATHS at different AGES in EDINBURGH,

Month.	Temperature.			All Ages.	Age					
					Months.					
	Highest.	Lowest.	Mean.		3	6	12	2	3	4
January	53·0	25·5	38·7	392	35	14	21	46	23	20
February	59·0	26·5	41·2	402	32	11	20	53	19	19
March	58·5	25·0	43·0	415	45	8	38	44	24	20
April	57·0	30·0	44·6	420	39	16	36	74	18	19
May	64·5	36·5	49·5	372	27	14	22	49	21	15
June	68·0	42·0	55·6	392	39	15	26	27	20	14
July	75·2	39·5	58·0	275	19	12	23	28	17	4
August	69·0	39·0	56·0	326	51	11	15	29	17	10
September	60·0	41·0	50·0	289	27	8	16	17	9	8
October	58·0	31·5	46·8	360	43	16	25	30	17	10
November	57·0	26·5	44·1	371	34	16	26	32	15	11
December	56·0	24·5	41·4	398	42	13	27	36	24	7
Total				4412	433	154	295	465	224	157

TABLE No. IV.—DEATHS at different AGES in EDINBURGH,

Month.	Temperature.			All Ages.	Age					
					Months.					
	Highest.	Lowest.	Mean.		3	6	12	2	3	4
January	53·0	25·5	38·7	199	18	7	14	24	13	14
February	59·0	26·5	41·2	188	19	7	12	28	8	6
March	58·5	25·0	43·0	215	26	4	25	20	18	8
April	57·0	30·0	44·6	205	26	6	21	29	6	11
May	64·5	36·5	49·5	182	17	5	15	24	8	7
June	68·0	42·0	55·6	200	29	10	10	14	12	6
July	75·2	39·5	58·0	139	12	7	12	12	9	2
August	69·0	39·0	56·0	161	26	4	8	14	7	6
September	60·0	41·0	50·0	145	15	5	7	11	6	5
October	58·0	31·5	46·8	180	27	9	16	15	9	4
November	57·0	26·5	44·1	186	22	10	16	14	6	7
December	56·0	24·5	41·4	221	28	9	17	22	13	1
Total				2221	265	83	173	227	115	77

TABLE No. V.—DEATHS at different AGES in EDINBURGH,

Month.	Temperature.			All Ages.	Age					
					Months.					
	Highest.	Lowest.	Mean.		3	6	12	2	3	4
January	53·0	25·5	38·7	193	17	7	7	22	10	6
February	59·0	26·5	41·2	214	13	4	8	25	11	13
March	58·5	25·0	43·0	200	19	4	13	24	6	12
April	57·0	30·0	44·6	215	13	10	15	45	12	8
May	64·5	36·5	49·5	190	10	9	7	25	13	8
June	68·0	42·0	55·6	192	10	5	16	13	8	8
July	75·2	39·5	58·0	136	7	5	11	16	8	2
August	69·0	39·0	56·0	165	25	7	7	15	10	4
September	60·0	41·0	50·0	144	12	3	9	6	3	3
October	58·0	31·5	46·8	180	16	7	9	15	8	6
November	57·0	26·5	44·1	185	12	6	10	18	9	4
December	56·0	24·5	41·4	177	14	4	10	14	11	6
Total				2191	168	71	122	238	109	80

During each Month in 1863.—Both Sexes.

UNDER																				
5	10	15	20	25	30	35	40	45	50	55	60	65	70	75	80	85	90	95	100	105
5	19	6	7	10	12	9	20	8	13	10	16	20	14	29	16	13	4	2	...	...
11	21	7	5	15	12	18	15	11	17	22	9	15	13	27	15	10	3	1	1	...
9	14	4	6	17	13	13	12	15	12	12	16	21	19	18	17	9	7	1	1	...
9	20	6	11	10	14	12	11	11	13	10	14	21	14	18	15	6	2	1	...	...
7	15	4	5	15	9	12	17	7	17	13	14	18	15	27	17	12	...	...	...	...
9	14	8	12	12	13	17	24	12	9	17	19	24	8	26	13	9	4	1	...	...
9	12	5	10	12	7	8	8	7	5	16	13	14	10	11	11	12	1	...	...	1
3	15	6	8	5	6	14	10	11	15	16	14	22	17	5	13	9	4	...	...	...
8	15	7	5	11	12	7	6	7	15	13	18	13	12	26	16	7	5	1	...	...
6	12	5	14	21	16	11	12	14	10	12	20	16	15	16	14	3	1	1	...	...
10	15	8	9	14	17	14	12	12	15	16	13	26	13	18	11	9	3	2	...	...
8	16	2	9	8	13	20	8	17	16	15	13	26	18	23	17	15	5	...	...	...
94	188	68	101	150	144	155	155	132	157	172	179	236	168	244	175	114	39	10	2	1

During each Month in 1863.—Males.

UNDER																				
5	10	15	20	25	30	35	40	45	50	55	60	65	70	75	80	85	90	95	100	105
2	11	1	5	5	7	4	8	4	9	2	8	10	4	13	4	8	2	2	...	...
7	8	4	2	9	3	10	8	7	9	7	3	6	4	8	5	6	1	...	1	...
5	9	...	4	10	10	5	9	8	4	5	7	9	10	7	5	5	1	...	1	...
2	6	4	9	5	11	3	4	5	8	6	11	7	9	6	6	3	1	...	...	...
2	7	2	4	5	3	8	6	5	13	8	6	6	9	16	5	1	...	...	...	...
4	5	5	4	9	4	8	12	7	5	8	11	12	4	12	7	2	...	...	...	...
6	8	...	4	7	4	4	7	3	4	10	5	6	5	3	4	5	...	...	...	1
2	5	3	5	1	4	7	7	6	11	8	10	11	6	3	3	3	1	...	...	...
4	12	3	2	6	7	3	2	2	10	4	10	5	5	10	8	2	1	...	...	...
2	5	4	5	11	5	6	4	7	4	3	9	10	7	7	8	2	...	1	...	...
5	5	5	4	10	7	7	7	7	5	11	5	10	6	7	4	4	2	1	..	...
4	7	1	7	2	5	10	5	14	12	4	8	12	8	16	6	9	1	...	...	...
45	88	32	55	80	70	75	79	75	94	76	93	104	77	108	65	50	10	4	2	1

During each Month in 1863.—Females.

UNDER																				
5	10	15	20	25	30	35	40	45	50	55	60	65	70	75	80	85	90	95	100	105
3	8	5	2	5	5	5	12	4	4	8	8	10	10	16	12	5	2	...	...	...
4	13	3	3	6	9	8	7	4	8	15	6	9	9	19	10	4	2	1	...	...
4	5	4	2	7	3	8	3	7	8	7	9	12	9	11	12	4	6	1	...	...
7	14	2	2	5	3	9	7	6	5	4	3	14	5	12	9	3	1	1	...	...
5	8	2	1	10	6	4	11	2	4	5	8	12	6	11	12	11	...	...	...	...
5	9	3	8	3	9	9	12	5	4	9	8	12	4	14	6	7	4	1	...	...
3	4	5	6	5	3	4	1	4	1	6	8	8	5	8	7	7	1	...	...	...
1	10	3	3	4	2	7	3	5	4	8	4	11	11	2	10	6	3	...	...	...
4	3	4	3	5	5	4	4	5	5	9	8	8	7	16	8	5	4	1	...	...
4	7	1	9	10	11	5	8	7	6	9	11	6	8	9	6	1	1	...	...	...
5	10	3	5	4	10	7	5	5	10	5	8	16	7	11	7	5	1	1	...	...
4	9	1	2	6	8	10	3	3	4	11	5	14	10	7	11	6	4	...	...	...
49	100	36	46	70	74	80	76	57	63	96	86	132	91	136	110	64	29	6	...	...

TABLE No. VI.—New Sanitary Districts,

1. District of Upper New Town.

No.	Name of Street.	Height in feet above the sea.	Population 1861.			Mortality 1863.			Diseases in							
			Above 5.	Under 5.	Total.	Above 5.	Under 5.	Total.	Brain.	Heart.	Chest.	Abdomen.	Phthisis.	Croup.	Diphtheria.	Small-Pox.
1	Canal street	162—190	94	15	109	4	3	7	1	...	2	...	1	...	...	...
2	Castle street	203—221	637	23	660	6	3	9	4	...	2	3	...	...	...	...
3	Charlotte place	201	117	11	128	2	1	3	...	1	...	...	1	...	...	...
4	Charlotte square	212	500	20	520	4	3	7	...	...	1	1	2	...	...	...
5	Charlotte street, North	185—205	143	7	150	...	...	...	...	...	...	...	...	...	...	...
6	Do. do. South	207—211	98	...	98	1	...	1	...	...	...	...	...	...	...	...
7	Do. do. lane	203	33	9	42	...	...	...	...	...	...	...	...	...	...	...
8	Clyde street	214														
9	Do. do. lane, North	...	278	23	301	3	1	4	...	1	...	...	...	...	...	...
10	Do. do. do. South	...														
11	Frederick street	201—224	614	30	644	6	1	7	2	1	...	1	...	...	...	...
12	George street	217—226	1091	72	1163	23	3	26	4	10	2	5	1	...	...	...
13	Glenfinlas street	187—207	36	1	37	...	...	...	...	...	...	...	...	...	...	...
14	Hanover street	208—226	332	37	369	5	2	7	2	...	1	1	1	...	...	...
15	Hill street	211														
16	Do. lane, North	206	88	8	96	...	...	...	...	...	...	...	...	...	...	...
17	Do. do. South	...														
18	Hope street	211	176	14	190	4	1	5	...	...	1	1	1	...	...	...
19	Do. lane	210														
20	New Buildings, N. Bridge	220	48	3	51	...	...	...	...	...	...	...	...	...	...	...
21	Princes street	201—218	806	42	848	10	4	14	1	2	3	1	2	...	2	...
22	Queen street	187—197	603	30	633	6	3	9	...	...	3	1	1	...	1	...
23	Register place	230	31	1	32	...	...	0	...	...	...	...	...	...	...	...
24	Register street, West	228	115	8	123	...	...	0	...	...	...	...	...	...	...	...
25	Rose street	212—227														
26	Do. lanes, south side	...	2325	269	2594	31	20	51	5	3	2	3	7	3	1	1
27	Do. do. north side	...														
28	St Andrew square	231	251	6	257	1	1	2	...	...	...	...	...	...	...	...
29	St Andrew street, North	202—218	57	6	63	...	...	...	...	...	...	...	...	...	...	...
30	Do. do. lane	206	24	1	25	...	...	...	...	...	...	...	...	...	...	...
31	St Andrew street, South	213—228	39	...	39	2	1	3	2	...	...	...	...	...	...	...
32	Do. Meuse lane	222	20	1	21	1	...	1	...	...	...	1	...	...	...	...
33	St David street, North	209	95	8	103	2	3	5	...	...	2	...	1	...	...	...
34	St David street, South	213—228	67	7	74	2	...	2	...	1	...	...	1	...	...	...
35	Thistle court	215	13	2	15	...	...	...	...	...	...	...	...	...	...	...
36	Thistle street	214														
37	Do. lane, north side	208	767	83	850	15	2	17	1	2	1	2	4	...	1	...
38	Young street	209														
39	Do. do. lane	...	149	15	164	2	...	2	...	...	...	1	...	...	...	...
40	York place	188	519	12	531	8	...	8	2	1	...	...	...	...	...	...
	Totals,		10,166	764	10,930	138	52	190	24	22	20	21	23	3	5	1

2. District of Lower New Town.

No.	Name of Street.	Height in feet above the sea.	Population 1861.			Mortality 1863.			Diseases in							
			Above 5.	Under 5.	Total.	Above 5.	Under 5.	Total.	Brain.	Heart.	Chest.	Abdomen.	Phthisis.	Croup.	Diphtheria.	Small-Pox.
1	Abercromby place	161	328	13	341	4	1	5	...	...	1	2	1	...	1	...
2	Albany lane	131—151	15	2	17	...	...	...	...	...	...	...	...	...	...	...
3	Albany street	150—163	530	42	572	3	1	4	...	1	...	1	...	...	...	...
4	Albert place	86	5	...	5	...	...	...	...	...	...	...	...	...	...	...
5	Albyn place	187	116	2	118	1	...	1	...	1	...	...	...	...	...	...
6	Barony street and lane	129	404	40	444	8	5	13	4	...	2	...	2	...	3	...
7	Bellevue crescent	92	118	1	119	1	...	1	...	...	...	...	1	...	...	...
8	Bellevue, south side	92	36	2	38	...	...	...	...	...	...	...	...	...	...	...
	Carry forward,		1552	102	1654	17	7	24	4	2	3	3	4	...	4	...

1. District of Upper New Town.

	1863.													No. of Paupers.	Street Cesspools.			Epidemics.		
					Fevers.													Cholera.	Fever.	
	Scarlatina.	Measles.	Hooping-Cough.	Erysipelas.	Total.	Typhus.	Typhoid.	Gastric.	Infantile.	Diarrhœa and Dysentery.	Scrofula.	Old Age.	Premature Debility.		Trapped.	Untrapped.	Total.	1848.	1847-8.	1857-8.
1	...	...	...	...	1	...	1	...	...	...	1	...	1	...	2	...	2	1	3	...
2	...	...	...	...	...	...	...	...	...	...	...	...	...	2	5	2	7	...	3	...
3	...	1	...	...	...	...	...	...	...	...	...	...	...	...	...	6	6	...	...	...
4	...	...	...	...	...	...	...	...	...	1	2	...	...	...	...	5	5	...	1	...
5	...	...	...	...	...	...	...	...	...	...	...	...	...	...	...	...	...	...	2	...
6	...	...	...	...	...	...	...	...	...	...	...	...	...	4	1	1	2	...	...	...
7	...	...	...	...	...	...	...	...	...	...	...	...	...	...	...	...	...	...	...	...
8																				
9	...	...	...	...	...	...	...	...	...	...	1	...	...	...	1	5	6	4	5	...
10																				
11	...	...	...	...	...	...	...	...	...	1	...	...	...	...	3	7	10	...	2	2
12	...	...	...	...	1	...	...	1	...	...	1	...	...	1	4	2	6	1	5	2
13	...	...	1	...	...	...	...	...	...	...	...	...	...	...	1	1	2	...	...	...
14	...	...	...	...	...	...	...	...	...	1	...	...	...	...	5	5	10	2	1	1
15																				
16	...	...	...	...	...	...	...	...	...	...	...	...	...	...	4	...	4	...	...	...
17																				
18																				
19	...	...	...	...	1	...	1	...	...	...	...	...	...	...	...	1	...	...	...	...
20	...	...	...	...	...	...	...	...	...	...	...	...	...	...	...	1	1	...	...	...
21	...	...	...	...	...	...	...	...	...	...	...	1	...	...	7	20	27	...	6	4
22	...	...	...	...	...	...	...	...	...	2	...	...	1	...	6	6	12	...	...	...
23	...	...	...	...	...	...	...	...	...	...	...	...	...	...	1	1	2	...	...	...
24	...	...	...	...	...	...	...	...	...	...	...	...	...	...	2	...	2	...	2	...
25																				
26	2	...	...	...	3	1	1	1	...	1	4	2	5	66	6	9	15	6	32	4
27																				
28	...	...	...	...	...	...	...	...	...	...	...	1	...	1	3	3	6	1	2	...
29	...	...	...	...	...	...	...	...	...	...	...	...	...	...	...	2	2	...	...	...
30	...	...	...	...	...	...	...	...	...	...	...	...	...	...	...	...	...	...	4	...
31	...	...	...	...	...	...	...	...	...	...	...	...	...	...	1	1	2	1	4	...
32	...	...	...	...	...	...	...	...	...	...	...	...	...	...	...	...	...	...	...	...
33	...	...	...	...	...	...	...	...	...	...	1	...	...	1	2	...	2	1	...	...
34	...	...	...	...	...	...	...	...	...	...	...	...	...	...	1	...	1	...	3	...
35	...	...	...	...	...	...	...	...	...	..	...	...	...	...	...	...	...	...	...	...
36																				
37	...	1	...	...	...	...	...	...	...	...	...	2	...	11	12	3	15	3	11	...
38																				
39	...	...	...	...	...	...	...	...	...	...	...	1	...	...	5	...	5	...	...	...
40	1	1	...	...	...	...	...	...	...	...	...	...	...	...	2	1	3	...	1	1
	3	3	1	...	6	1	3	2	...	6	10	7	7	86	74	81	155	20	87	14

2. District of Lower New Town.

	Scarlatina.	Measles.	Hooping-Cough.	Erysipelas.	Fevers: Total.	Typhus.	Typhoid.	Gastric.	Infantile.	Diarrhœa and Dysentery.	Scrofula.	Old Age.	Premature Debility.	No. of Paupers.	Trapped.	Untrapped.	Total.	Cholera 1848.	Fever 1847-8.	Fever 1857-8.
1	...	...	...	...	...	...	...	...	...	...	...	...	...	...	1	1	2	...	1	1
2	...	...	...	...	...	...	...	...	...	...	...	...	...	...	...	2	2	...	...	...
3	...	...	...	...	...	...	...	...	...	...	...	1	1	2	2	1	3	...	1	...
4	...	...	...	...	...	...	...	...	...	...	...	...	...	...	1	...	1	...	...	...
5	...	...	...	...	...	...	...	...	...	...	...	...	...	...	1	...	1	...	...	...
6	...	...	...	...	...	...	...	...	...	...	...	1	...	...	2	3	5	...	1	...
7	...	...	...	...	...	...	...	...	...	...	...	...	...	...	1	...	1	...	...	...
8	...	...	...	...	...	...	...	...	...	...	...	...	...	...	...	5	5	...	...	...
	...	...	...	...	...	...	...	...	...	...	...	2	1	2	8	12	20	...	3	1

TABLE No. VI.—New Sanitary Districts,

2. District of Lower New Town—*Continued.*

Name of Street.	Height in feet above the sea.	Population 1861. Above 5.	Population 1861. Under 5.	Population 1861. Total.	Mortality 1863. Above 5.	Mortality 1863. Under 5.	Mortality 1863. Total.	Diseases in Brain.	Heart.	Chest.	Abdomen.	Phthisis.	Croup.	Diphtheria.	Small-Pox.
Brought forward,		1552	102	1654	17	7	24	4	2	3	3	4	...	4	...
9 Broughton :—	114—162	...	...	...	...	...	...	...	...	...	...	...	...	...	...
1 Anderson's court......	...	61	9	70	...	...	...	...	...	...	...	...	...	...	...
2 Market	134	25	7	32	...	...	...	...	...	...	...	...	...	...	...
3 New Broughton	...	278	58	336	4	...	4	1	...	2	...	...	...	...	...
4 Old Broughton	...	115	9	124	...	1	1	...	...	...	1	...	...	...	...
5 Paterson's court	...	59	6	65	1	2	3	...	...	...	...	1	...	...	...
10 Church lane..............	118—159	53	11	64	1	1	2	1	...	...	...	...	...	...	...
11 Do. court	...	20	4	24	...	...	...	...	...	...	...	...	...	...	...
12 Circus place, North-East	106	29	4	33	...	...	...	...	...	...	...	...	...	...	...
13 Do. North-West	62--99	206	16	222	4	2	6	...	...	1	2	1	...	1	...
14 Do. South-East	...	55	1	56	...	1	1	...	...	...	...	...	...	...	...
15 Do. South-West	119	54	10	64	1	...	1	...	...	...	1	...	...	...	...
16 Circus lane	87	33	12	45	1	...	1	1	...	...	...	...	...	...	...
17 Cumberland street	93	1061	95	1156											
18 Do. lane, North	75	223	42	265	21	6	27	5	2	2	5	4	...	...	1
19 Do. do. South	92	19	1	20											
20 Darnaway street.........	157	125	7	132	2	...	2	...	1	...	1	...	...	...	...
21 Drummond place	109—120	369	10	379	3	1	4	...	...	...	...	1	...	...	...
22 Dublin street	120—163	381	26	407	6	...	6	...	...	1	1	3	...	...	...
23 Do. do. lane, East	138	41	...	14											
24 Duke street...............	163—202	217	11	228	2	1	3	...	...	...	1	...	...	...	...
25 Duncan street............	82—105	237	32	269	2	4	6	1	...	...	...	...	...	...	...
26 Dundas street	116—163	485	41	526	6	3	9	1	...	...	...	2	...	...	...
27 Fettes row	80	251	19	270	5	2	7	2	...	...	1	...	...	...	...
28 Forres street	161—180	110	10	120	2	...	2	...	...	...	...	...	...	1	...
29 Heriot row	165	355	15	370	4	...	4	...	...	...	1	...	...	...	...
30 Howe street	116—162	481	50	531	10	4	14	...	1	3	1	1	...	...	...
31 Gloucester place.........	117	139	2	141	1	...	1	1	...	...	...	...	...	...	...
32 India street...............	107—150	532	38	570	10	2	12	1	1	1	4	2	...	...	...
33 Jamaica street...........	143	1060	151	1211	20	14	34	1	1	4	4	7	...	1	..
34 Do. lane, South	140	2	2	4											
35 King street, Great	116	733	43	776	4	1	5	...	1	1	...	1	...	...	...
36 London street	114	648	30	678	2	3	5	1	...	2	...	1	...	...	...
37 Mansfield place	108	106	10	116	...	...	...	...	...	...	...	...	...	...	...
38 Nelson place	136	10	2	12	...	...	...	...	...	...	...	...	...	...	...
39 Nelson street, N. and S.	120—159	333	14	347	2	1	3	...	...	...	...	...	...	1	1
40 Northumberland place	136	153	21	174	2	...	2	...	...	...	1	...	...	...	...
41 Northumberland street	140	502	34	536											
42 Do. lane, East	...	9	3	12											
43 Do. do. N.-W.	...	5	1	6	3	3	6	...	...	1	...	...	2	1	...
44 Do. do. S.-W.	...	21	5	26											
45 Pitt street	80—115	481	30	511	5	0	5	...	...	...	...	...	...	1	...
46 Do. North	65—80	24	4	28	...	...	...	...	...	...	...	...	...	...	...
47 Royal circus	100—122	328	13	341	4	...	4	...	...	1	...	...	...	...	...
48 Royal crescent	83	67	4	71	1	1	2	...	...	...	1	...	...	...	...
49 St Colme street	186	58	2	60	...	...	...	...	...	...	...	...	...	...	...
50 St Vincent street	94—116	216	17	233	...	...	...	...	...	...	...	...	...	...	...
51 Scotland street	84—110	474	37	511	8	1	9	2	...	...	2	...	1	...	...
52 Do. do. lane ...	96	22	...	22											
53 Summer bank	75	62	11	73	...	...	...	...	...	...	...	...	...	...	...
54 Wemyss place and lane	170	61	4	65	1	1	2	...	...	...	...	...	...	...	...
55 York lane	154—183	22	2	24	...	...	...	...	...	...	...	...	...	...	...
Totals,....................		12,963	1088	14,024	155	62	217	22	9	22	30	28	3	10	2

AND THEIR VITAL STATISTICS.—*Continued.*

2. District of Lower New Town—*Continued.*

	1863.													No. of Paupers.	Street Cesspools.			Epidemics.		
	Scarlatina.	Measles.	Hooping-Cough.	Erysipelas.	Fevers.					Diarrhœa and Dysentery.	Scrofula.	Old Age.	Premature Debility.		Trapped.	Untrapped.	Total.	Cholera.	Fever.	
					Total.	Typhus.	Typhoid.	Gastric.	Infantile.									1848.	1847-8.	1857-8.
	...	...	...	...	...	...	...	...	...	...	...	2	1	2	8	12	20	...	3	1
9	...	...	...	...	...	...	...	...	...	...	...	...	...	...	...	...	...	...	...	...
1	...	...	...	...	...	...	...	...	...	...	...	...	...	...	...	...	...	...	...	...
2	...	...	...	...	...	...	...	...	...	...	...	...	...	...	...	...	...	...	...	...
3	...	...	...	...	...	...	...	...	...	...	...	...	...	3	3	...	3	...	...	...
4	...	...	...	...	...	...	...	...	...	...	...	...	...	...	1	1	2	...	...	...
5	...	...	...	...	...	...	...	...	...	...	2	...	...	...	...	...	...	...	...	...
10	...	...	...	1	...	...	...	...	...	...	...	...	...	1	...	...	...	...	2	...
11	...	...	...	...	...	...	...	...	...	...	...	...	...	...	...	...	...	...	...	...
12	...	...	...	...	...	...	...	...	...	...	...	...	...	...	...	...	...	...	...	...
13	...	...	...	...	...	...	...	...	...	...	...	...	...	6						
14	...	...	...	...	...	...	...	...	...	1	...	...	...	...	6	3	9	...	...	...
15	...	...	...	...	...	...	...	...	...	...	...	...	...	...						
16	...	...	...	...	...	...	...	...	...	...	...	...	...	...	1	2	3	...	...	...
17																				
18	...	2	...	...	1	1	...	...	...	1	1	...	...	19	3	6	9	4	3	...
19																				
20	...	...	...	...	...	...	...	...	...	...	...	...	...	...	2	...	2	...	...	...
21	...	...	...	...	...	...	...	...	...	...	1	2	...	...	8	1	9	...	1	...
22, 23	...	...	...	...	1	1	...	...	...	...	...	...	...	...	6	...	6	...	...	...
24	...	...	...	...	1	...	1	...	...	...	1	...	...	...	...	...	...	...	...	...
25	...	...	...	...	...	...	...	...	...	1	2	...	1	1	...	...	...	...	1	...
26	1	...	...	...	2	2	...	...	...	...	1	...	2	1	...	0	1	...	1	...
27	...	...	...	...	1	...	...	1	...	...	...	...	...	4	1	2	3	...	1	...
28	...	...	...	...	...	...	...	...	...	1	...	...	...	...	2	...	2	...	...	1
29	3	...	...	...	...	...	...	...	...	...	1	...	...	...	1	2	3	...	...	...
30	...	...	...	...	2	...	...	2	...	1	...	...	...	...	3	1	4	...	2	...
31	...	...	...	...	...	...	...	...	...	...	...	...	...	...	...	2	2	...	...	...
32	...	...	...	...	...	...	...	...	...	...	...	2	...	...	...	3	3	...	1	...
33, 34	...	4	...	...	1	...	...	1	...	2	4	3	...	52	4	...	4	1	9	...
35	...	...	...	...	1	...	...	1	...	...	...	1	...	...	...	5	5	...	1	1
36	1	...	...	...	...	...	...	...	...	...	...	...	...	6	2	...	2	...	3	...
37	...	...	...	...	...	...	...	...	...	...	...	...	...	...	1	...	1	...	...	...
38	...	...	...	1	...	...	...	...	...	...	...	...	...	...	1	...	1	...	...	...
39	...	...	...	...	...	...	...	...	...	...	...	...	...	...	1	1	2	...	3	1
40	...	...	...	...	...	...	...	...	...	...	...	1	...	2	1	...	...	...	...	...
41															2	2	4			
42																...	...			
43	...	...	...	...	...	...	...	..	...	...	...	1	...	5	...	...	...	...	1	...
44															...	...	...			
45	...	...	...	...	...	...	...	...	...	...	...	...	...	8	...	4	4	...	4	...
46	...	...	...	...	...	...	...	...	...	...	...	...	...	...	...	4	4	1	...	...
47	2	...	...	...	...	...	...	...	...	...	...	...	...	...	1	...	1	...	...	...
48	...	...	...	...	...	...	...	...	...	...	...	...	...	...	...	3	3	...	...	...
49	...	...	...	...	...	...	...	...	...	...	...	...	...	...	...	...	...	...	...	...
50	...	...	...	...	...	...	...	...	...	...	...	...	...	...	2	...	2	...	2	...
51, 52	...	...	...	...	1	...	...	1	...	...	1	1	...	8	...	2	2	...	4	...
53	...	...	...	...	...	...	...	...	...	...	...	...	...	2	...	...	...	...	...	...
54	...	...	...	...	1	...	...	1	...	...	...	1	...	1	1	1	2	...	...	...
55	...	...	...	...	...	...	...	...	...	...	...	...	...	...	...	...	...	...	...	...
	7	6	...	2	12	4	1	7	...	7	14	14	4	121	61	57	118	6	42	4

TABLE No. VI.—New Sanitary Districts,

3. District of West End.

	Name of Street.	Height in feet above the sea.	Population 1861.			Mortality 1863.			Diseases in							
			Above 5.	Under 5.	Total.	Above 5.	Under 5.	Total.	Brain.	Heart.	Chest.	Abdomen.	Phthisis.	Croup.	Diphtheria	Small-Pox.
1	Alva street	203	320	13	333	5	2	7	...	...	1	2	1	...	1	...
2	Atholl crescent	202	205	10	215	3	...	3	...	...	...	1	...	...	...	...
3	Do. lane	...	8	1	9	1	1	2	...	...	...	...	...	...	...	...
4	Atholl lane	198	58	15	73	1	1	2	1	...	...	...	...	...	...	...
5	Atholl place	199	142	2	144	...	1	1	...	...	1	...	...	...	...	...
6	Bainfield	206	19	7	26	2	...	2	1	1	...	...	...	...	...	...
7	Cambridge street	210	25	4	29	2	...	2	...	...	1	...	...	...	...	...
8	Castle terrace	209	76	4	80	3	...	3	1	...	1	...	...	...	...	1
9	Wharton buildings	219	40	13	53	1	1	2	...	...	1	...	...	...	...	...
10	Chester street	192	...	...	...	1	...	1	...	...	...	...	1	...	...	...
11	Coates crescent	201	168	2	170	1	...	1	...	...	...	...	...	...	...	...
12	Coates hall	180	69	11	80	...	...	...	...	...	...	...	...	...	...	...
13	Do. lane	...	35	5	40	...	1	1	...	...	...	...	...	...	...	...
14	Coates, West	...	...	...	...	2	1	3	1	...	1	...	...	...	1	...
15	Coates place	192	27	4	31	...	1	1	...	...	1	...	...	...	...	...
16	Dalry lane	184	163	26	189	2	1	3	...	...	2	1	...	...	...	...
17	Dewar place	204—215	44	2	46	2	...	2	...	...	...	1	...	...	...	...
18	Drumsheugh lane	195	18	1	19	...	...	...	...	...	...	...	...	...	...	...
19	Erskine place	207	28	1	29	1	...	1	...	...	...	...	1	...	...	...
20	Gardner's crescent	237	300	34	334	8	1	9	1	...	1	3	...	...	...	...
21	Grove place	207	34	2	36	...	...	...	...	...	...	...	...	...	...	...
22	Grove street	208—228	194	27	221	4	...	4	1	...	1	...	1	...	...	...
23	Haymarket	180	94	8	102	2	3	5	1	...	...	...	1	...	3	...
24	Lothian road	194—234	253	34	287	2	2	4	...	1	...	...	1	...	...	1
25	Maitland street, East	206	151	...	151	3	...	3	...	...	...	1	...	...	...	...
26	Do. do. West.	192	88	5	93	1	...	1	...	...	...	...	...	...	...	...
27	Manor place	198	138	6	144	1	1	2	...	...	...	1	...	...	...	...
28	Merchiston, North	227	...	...	...	...	...	...	...	...	...	...	...	...	...	...
29	Melville place, North	199	82	6	88	...	...	3 }	...	...	...	...	...	...	1	...
30	Do. do. South	205	16	1	17	...	3	... }								
31	Melville crescent	195	45	2	47	...	...	...	...	...	...	...	...	...	...	...
32	Melville street	196	437	24	461	5	1	6	...	1	3	...	...	...	...	...
33	Morrison street	191—217	156	30	186	...	2	2	...	...	...	...	...	...	...	...
34	Osborne terrace	188	...	...	...	...	...	...	...	...	...	...	...	...	...	...
35	Queensferry street	207	112	13	125	2	...	2	...	...	1	...	1	...	...	...
36	Rosebank	226	129	30	159	3	1	4	1	...	...	...	...	...	...	...
37	Rosemount buildings	...	390	64	454	5	6	11	...	...	1	1	2	...	1	...
38	Rutland court	208	19	3	22	...	...	...	...	...	...	...	...	...	...	...
39	Rutland place	...	11	3	14	2	...	2	1	...	...	...	...	...	...	...
40	Rutland street	207	189	12	201	1	...	1	...	...	...	...	...	...	...	1
41	Rutland square	208	306	13	319	2	...	2	1	...	...	1	...	...	...	...
42	St Cuthbert's glebe	204	100	6	106	1	...	1	...	...	...	...	...	...	...	...
43	Do. lane	186—198	71	15	86	1	...	1	...	...	1	...	...	...	...	...
44	St Cuthbert's poorhouse	196	469	34	503	81	28	109	16	3	22	12	9	2	...	1
45	St Cuthbert's street	215	108	10	118	2	1	3	...	1	1	...	1	...	...	...
46	Shandwick place	206	138	9	147	3	...	3	1	1	...	1	...	...	...	...
47	Spittal street	227—236	113	13	126	1	2	3	...	...	1	...	...	...	...	...
48	Stafford street	201	201	17	218	3	2	5	...	1	...	...	1	...	...	...
49	Thomas street	197	11	2	13	...	...	...	...	...	...	...	...	...	...	...
50	Tobago place	209	10	4	14	...	1	1	...	...	...	...	...	...	...	...
51	Tobago street	231	188	37	225	1	2	3	...	...	...	1	...	...	...	...
52	Torphichen street	203	190	18	208	4	...	4	...	1	1	1	1	...	...	...
53	Wallace place	210	46	1	47	...	...	...	...	...	...	...	...	...	...	...
54	Walker street	196	168	15	183	2	...	2	...	...	...	...	1	...	...	...
55	William street	196	619	92	711	6	8	14	3	...	...	1	1	2	1	1
	Totals,		7021	711	7732	173	74	247	30	10	42	28	23	4	8	5

AND THEIR VITAL STATISTICS.—*Continued.*

3. District of West End.

	1863.													No. of Paupers.	Street Cesspools.			Epidemics.		
	Scarlatina.	Measles.	Hooping-Cough	Erysipelas.	Fevers.					Diarrhœa and Dysentery.	Scrofula.	Old Age.	Premature Debility.		Trapped.	Untrapped.	Total.	Cholera.	Fever.	
					Total.	Typhus.	Typhoid.	Gastric.	Infantile.									1848.	1847-8.	1857.
1	...	...	...	...	2	...	2	...	...	...	...	...	...	...	2	...	2	...	1	...
2	...	...	...	...	1	...	1	...	...	...	...	...	...	...	...	1	1	...	...	...
3	2	...	...	...	...	...	...	...	...	...	...	...	...	...	...	1	1	...	..	...
4	...	...	...	...	...	...	...	...	...	...	...	...	1	1	...	...	...	...	...	...
5	...	...	...	...	...	...	...	...	...	...	...	...	...	4	1	...	1	...	...	...
6	...	...	...	...	...	...	...	...	...	...	...	...	...	1	...	...	...	...	...	...
7	...	...	...	...	...	...	...	...	...	...	...	...	...	...	2	...	2	...	...	...
8	...	...	...	...	...	...	...	...	...	...	...	...	...	...	...	6	6	...	...	...
9	1	...	...	...	...	...	...	...	...	...	...	...	...	...	...	...	...	...	...	...
10	...	...	...	...	...	...	...	...	...	...	...	...	...	...	3	...	3	...	...	...
11	...	...	...	...	...	...	...	...	...	...	...	1	...	...	1	1	2	...	...	...
12	...	...	...	...	...	...	...	...	...	...	...	...	...	...	...	...	...	...	...	...
13	...	...	...	...	...	...	..	...	...	...	...	...	1	...	...	...	...	...	...	...
14	...	...	...	...	...	...	...	...	...	...	...	...	...	...	...	...	...	...	...	...
15	...	...	...	...	...	...	...	...	...	...	...	...	...	...	...	...	...	...	...	...
16	...	...	...	...	...	...	...	...	...	...	...	...	...	1	...	2	2	...	...	...
17	...	...	...	...	...	...	...	...	...	...	...	...	...	...	...	3	3	...	...	...
18	...	...	...	...	...	...	...	...	...	...	...	...	...	...	...	...	...	...	...	...
19	...	...	...	...	1	1	...	...	...	...	...	...	...	...	...	...	...	...	...	...
20	...	...	...	...	1	1	...	...	...	...	...	1	...	...	1	1	2	...	2	...
21	...	...	...	...	...	...	...	...	...	...	...	...	...	...	2	...	2	...	...	...
22	1	...	...	...	...	...	...	...	...	...	...	1	...	4	5	...	5	...	1	...
23	...	...	...	...	...	...	...	...	...	...	...	...	...	...	...	12	12	...	4	...
24	...	...	...	...	...	...	...	...	...	...	...	...	...	3	1	9	10	1	9	...
25	...	...	...	...	...	...	...	...	...	...	...	...	...	1	2	...	2	...	...	...
26	...	...	...	...	..	...	...	...	...	1	...	...	...	...	1	5	6	...	1	...
27	...	...	...	...	...	...	...	...	...	...	...	...	1	...	...	3	3	...	...	...
28	...	...	...	...	...	...	...	...	...	...	...	...	...	...	...	...	...	...	...	...
29	...	...	...	...	...	...	...	...	...	...	...	...	1	...	1	2	3	...	...	...
30	...	...	...	...	...	...	...	...	...	...	...	...	...	...						...
31	...	...	...	...	...	...	...	...	...	...	...	...	...	... }	6	3	9	1	2	...
32	...	...	...	...	1	...	...	1	...	...	...	1	...	... }						...
33	...	...	...	...	...	...	...	...	...	...	...	...	1	1	...	5	5	...	2	...
34	...	...	...	...	...	...	...	...	...	...	...	...	...	1	...	...	..	...	...	...
35	...	...	...	...	...	...	...	...	...	...	...	...	...	...	...	1	1	...	...	...
36	2	...	...	...	...	...	...	...	...	1	...	...	...	...	10	...	10	...	...	...
37	1	...	...	...	...	...	...	...	...	...	4	...	..	4	...	...	...	...	...	...
38	...	...	...	...	...	...	...	...	...	...	...	...	...	...	...	...	...	...	...	...
39	...	...	...	...	...	...	...	...	...	...	...	...	...	. .	1	...	1	...	...	...
40	...	...	...	...	...	...	...	...	...	...	...	...	...	...	6	...	6	...	...	...
41	...	...	...	...	...	...	...	...	...	...	...	...	...	...	8	...	8	...	...	...
42	...	...	...	...	...	...	...	...	...	...	...	...	...	...	...	...	...	...	...	...
43	...	...	...	...	...	...	...	...	...	...	.·.	...	...	2	1	5	6	...	1	...
44	1	2	...	1	3	2	...	1	...	4	1	15	1	490	...	...	...	...	26	1
45	...	...	...	...	...	...	...	...	...	...	...	...	...	...	...	...	...	...	1	...
46	...	..	...	...	...	...	...	...	...	...	...	...	...	...	1	...	1	1	..	...
47	...	...	...	...	...	...	...	...	...	...	1	...	1	1	3	...	3	...	...	...
48	...	...	...	...	...	...	...	...	...	...	1	1	...	...	4	...	4	...	1	...
49	...	...	...	...	...	...	.	...	...	...	...	...	...	...	...	...	...	...	...	...
50	...	...	...	...	...	...	...	...	...	...	1	...	...	2	1	1	2	...	1	...
51	...	...	...	...	...	...	...	...	...	..	...	...	...	...	...	...	...	...	1	...
52	...	...	...	...	...	...	...	...	...	...	...	...	...	...	...	...	...	...	...	...
53	...	...	...	...	...	...	...	...	...	...	...	...	...	...	1	1	2	...	...	...
54	...	...	...	...	...	...	...	...	...	1	...	...	...	...	...	4	4	...	...	...
55	...	1	...	...	...	...	...	...	...	...	1	1	1	12	2	3	5	...	1	...
	8	3	...	1	9	4	3	2	...	7	9	21	8	528	66	69	135	3	45	1

TABLE No. VI.—New Sanitary Districts,

4. District of Upper Water of Leith.

Name of Street.	Height in feet above the sea.	Population 1861.			Mortality 1863.			Diseases in							
		Above 5.	Under 5.	Total.	Above 5.	Under 5.	Total.	Brain.	Heart.	Chest.	Abdomen.	Phthisis.	Croup.	Diphtheria.	Small-Pox.
1 Ainslie place	170—183	291	4	295	1	...	1	...	1	...	...	...	...	...	...
2 Allan street	57	354	65	419	5	7	12	1	1	2	1	...	2	1	1
3 Ann street	92—112	237	7	244	4	1	5	...	...	...	2	...	...	1	...
4 Baker's place	75	54	4	58	2	...	2	1	...	1	...	...	...	...	...
5 Bedford street	65	483	107	590	7	7	14	2	...	...	...	2	3	2	...
6 Brunswick street	76	555	67	622	7	5	12	2	1	2	1	1	...	...	1
7 Buckingham terrace	143—165	...	...	...	2	...	2	1	...	...	...	1	...	...	...
8 Carlton street	66	99	4	103	...	...	...	...	...	...	...	...	...	...	...
9 Cheyne street	56	260	31	291	3	2	5	2	1	...	...	...	...	...	...
10 Church street	70—114	102	16	118	2	4	6	...	...	1	...	...	...	...	...
11 Clarendon crescent	143—165	189	10	199	2	...	2	...	...	...	...	...	...	2	...
12 Comely bank	52	107	10	117	2	...	2	...	1	...	1	...	...	...	...
13 Danube street	76	181	8	189	4	...	4	...	1	...	...	...	...	...	...
14 Darling's buildings	57	99	10	109	...	4	4	...	...	...	...	...	...	3	...
15 Deanhaugh street	52—61	100	19	119	1	3	4	...	...	...	...	...	...	1	...
16 Dean bank houses	70	26	3	29	...	...	...	...	...	...	...	...	...	...	...
17 Dean bank institution	71	22	...	22	...	...	...	...	...	...	...	...	...	...	...
18 Dean terrace	61—74	107	6	113	...	1	1	...	...	...	...	...	...	1	...
19 Do. do. upper	76—102	30	...	30	1	...	1	1	...	...	...	...	...	...	...
20 Dean street	52—73	449	62	511	11	4	15	2	2	...	1	2	...	3	...
21 Dean bridge	173	...	...	...	...	...	...	...	...	...	...	...	...	...	...
22 Dean road	73—142	11	2	13	...	1	1	...	...	...	...	...	...	...	...
23 Donaldson's hospital	200	206	1	207	...	...	...	...	...	...	...	...	...	...	...
24 Doune terrace	118—147	87	...	87	...	...	...	...	...	...	...	...	...	...	...
25 Eton terrace	165	118	7	125	...	...	...	...	...	...	...	...	...	...	...
26 Fairnington place	57	26	5	31	...	...	...	...	...	...	...	...	...	...	...
27 Glanville place	65	52	6	58	...	...	...	...	...	...	...	...	...	...	...
28 Great Stuart street	166	249	15	264	...	1	1	...	...	...	...	...	...	...	...
29 Hamilton place	66	244	32	276	6	3	9	...	1	1	3	...	1	1	...
30 Haugh street, north and south	54	271	56	327	3	1	4	1	...	...	...	1	...	...	...
31 Hermitage place	54	96	13	109	2	3	5	1	...	...	...	2	...	...	...
32 Horn lane	70	155	30	185	...	3	3	...	...	...	...	...	...	2	...
33 India place	82	1096	173	1269	15	15	30	1	2	2	5	4	...	2	...
34 Johnstone place	52	56	9	65	...	...	...	...	...	...	...	...	...	...	...
35 Kerr street	66	140	22	162	2	1	3	...	...	1	...	1	...	1	...
36 Lennox street	155	10	...	10	1	...	1	...	...	...	1	...	...	...	...
37 Leslie place	57	24	4	28	...	...	...	...	...	...	...	...	...	...	...
38 Lynedoch place	168—190	124	3	127	1	...	1	...	...	...	...	...	...	...	...
39 Legget's land	57	26	2	28	1	2	3	...	...	...	...	...	1	...	...
40 Mackenzie place	77	138	20	158	1	2	3	1	...	...	...	...	...	2	...
41 Malta green	47	...	...	...	...	...	...	...	...	...	...	...	...	...	...
42 Malta place	...	20	2	22	...	...	...	...	...	...	...	...	...	...	...
43 Malta terrace	49	44	7	51	...	...	...	...	...	...	...	...	...	...	...
44 Market court	70	21	1	22	...	...	...	...	...	...	...	...	...	...	...
45 Market place	73	187	28	215	3	2	5	1	...	1	...	1	...	1	...
46 Mary place	53	90	9	99	2	...	2	1	...	...	1	...	...	...	...
47 Moray place	147—165	468	14	482	1	...	1	...	...	...	...	...	...	...	...
48 Oxford terrace	143	75	9	84	2	...	2	...	...	...	1	...	...	1	...
49 Orphan hospital	185	139	...	139	...	...	...	...	...	...	...	...	...	...	...
50 Patriot hall buildings	55	81	20	101	3	1	4	1	...	1	...	...	...	...	...
51 Raeburn place	51	249	31	280	6	...	6	1	1	1	...	...	...	...	...
52 Randolph cliff	180	64	2	66	...	...	...	...	...	...	...	...	...	...	...
53 Randolph crescent	187—199	152	7	159	1	...	1	...	...	...	...	...	...	...	...
54 Randolph place	201	92	7	99	1	1	2	...	...	1	...	...	...	...	...
55 Spring gardens	75	25	4	29	...	...	...	...	...	...	...	...	...	...	...
Carry forward,		8581	974	9555	105	74	179	20	12	14	17	15	7	24	2

4. District of Upper Water of Leith.

	1863.														Street Cesspools.			Epidemics.		
					Fevers.													Cholera.	Fever.	
	Scarlatina.	Measles.	Hooping-Cough.	Erysipelas.	Total.	Typhus.	Typhoid.	Gastric.	Infantile.	Diarrhœa and Dysentery.	Scrofula.	Old Age.	Premature Debility.	No. of Paupers.	Trapped.	Untrapped.	Total.	1848.	1847-8.	1857-8.
1	...	...	...	...	...	...	...	...	...	...	...	...	...	...	...	2	2	...	...	...
2	...	...	...	...	...	...	...	...	...	...	2	...	...	9	1	1	2	1	1	...
3	1	...	...	...	...	...	...	...	...	1	...	...	...	...	2	2	4	...	...	...
4	...	...	...	...	...	...	...	...	...	...	...	...	...	...	2	...	2	1	...	...
5	...	1	...	...	...	...	...	...	...	...	...	1	1	11	...	6	6	...	...	...
6	...	1	...	...	1	...	...	1	...	...	1	...	...	21	5	1	6	1	...	...
7	...	...	...	...	...	...	...	...	...	...	...	...	...	...	1	...	1	...	...	...
8	...	...	...	...	...	...	...	...	...	...	...	...	...	...	2	...	2	...	...	...
9	...	...	...	...	...	...	...	...	...	1	...	...	...	...	...	...	...	...	...	...
10	...	...	...	...	1	...	...	1	...	1	...	2	1	...	4	4	8	...	...	...
11	...	...	...	...	...	...	...	...	...	...	...	...	...	...	...	1	1	...	...	...
12	...	...	...	...	...	...	...	...	...	...	...	...	...	...	...	1	1	...	2	...
13	...	...	...	...	2	...	2	...	...	...	...	1	...	1	...	2	2	1	...	...
14	1	...	...	...	...	...	...	...	...	...	...	...	...	1	...	2	2	...	...	...
15	1	1	...	1	...	...	...	...	...	...	...	...	...	4	...	2	2	...	...	...
16	...	...	...	...	...	...	...	...	...	...	...	...	...	...	...	2	2	...	...	...
17	...	...	...	...	...	...	...	...	...	...	...	...	...	1	...	...	...	...	...	...
18	...	...	...	...	...	...	...	...	...	...	...	...	...	...	2	...	2	...	...	...
19	...	...	...	...	...	...	...	...	...	...	...	...	...	...	...	...	...	...	...	...
20	...	...	...	...	1	1	...	...	...	...	...	...	1	5	5	3	8	...	...	...
21	...	...	...	...	...	...	...	...	...	...	...	...	...	1	...	6	6	...	...	...
22	...	...	...	...	...	...	...	...	...	...	...	...	...	...	...	...	...	...	...	...
23	...	...	...	...	...	...	...	...	...	...	...	...	...	...	...	...	...	...	...	...
24	...	...	...	...	...	...	...	...	...	...	...	...	...	...	1	1	2	...	...	...
25	...	...	...	...	...	...	...	...	...	...	...	...	...	...	...	1	1	...	...	...
26	...	...	...	...	...	...	...	...	...	...	...	...	...	1	...	...	...	...	...	...
27	...	...	...	...	...	...	...	...	...	...	...	...	...	...	...	...	...	...	...	...
28	...	...	...	...	...	...	...	...	...	...	1	...	...	...	2	...	2	...	...	...
29	...	...	...	...	...	...	...	...	...	...	...	1	...	2	...	12	12	...	...	...
30	...	...	...	...	...	...	...	...	...	...	1	1	...	11	...	1	1	1	...	...
31	...	...	...	...	...	...	...	...	...	...	1	...	...	3	1	...	1	...	...	...
32	...	...	...	...	...	...	...	...	...	...	...	...	1	2	...	1	1	...	...	...
33	1	2	...	1	1	...	...	1	...	3	1	...	1	49	3	3	6	2	5	1
34	...	...	...	...	...	...	...	...	...	...	...	...	...	1	...	...	...	...	...	...
35	...	...	...	...	...	...	...	...	...	...	...	...	...	1	1	...	1	...	...	...
36	...	...	...	...	...	...	...	...	...	...	...	...	...	...	...	...	...	...	...	...
37	...	...	...	...	...	...	...	...	...	...	...	...	...	...	...	...	...	...	...	...
38	...	...	...	...	...	...	...	...	...	...	...	...	...	...	...	...	...	...	...	...
39	2	...	...	...	...	...	...	...	...	...	...	...	...	1	...	...	...	...	...	...
40	...	...	...	...	...	...	...	...	...	...	...	...	...	3	...	1	1	...	...	...
41	...	...	...	...	...	...	...	...	...	...	...	...	...	...	...	...	...	...	...	...
42	...	...	...	...	...	...	...	...	...	...	...	...	...	...	...	...	...	...	...	...
43	...	...	...	...	...	...	...	...	...	...	...	...	...	...	2	...	2	...	...	...
44	...	...	...	...	...	...	...	...	...	...	...	...	...	...	...	9	9	...	...	...
45	...	...	...	...	...	...	...	...	...	...	...	...	1	3	...	1	1	...	...	...
46	...	...	...	...	...	...	...	...	...	...	...	...	...	...	...	...	...	...	...	...
47	...	...	...	...	...	...	...	...	...	...	...	...	...	...	5	1	6	...	...	...
48	...	...	...	...	...	...	...	...	...	...	...	...	...	...	...	1	1	...	...	...
49	...	...	...	...	...	...	...	...	...	...	...	...	...	...	...	...	...	...	...	...
50	1	...	...	...	...	...	...	...	...	...	...	...	...	...	...	...	...	...	...	...
51	...	...	...	...	2	1	1	...	...	...	...	...	...	1	1	2	3	...	...	...
52	...	...	...	...	...	...	...	...	...	...	...	...	...	...	...	1	1	...	...	...
53	...	...	...	...	...	...	...	...	...	...	...	1	...	...	...	2	2	...	...	...
54	...	...	...	...	...	...	...	...	...	...	...	...	1	...	...	...	...	...	...	...
55	...	...	...	...	...	...	...	...	...	...	...	...	...	...	...	...	...	...	...	...
	7	5		2	8	2	3	3		6	7	7	7	132	40	72	112	7	8	1

TABLE No. VI.—New Sanitary Districts,

4. District of Upper Water of Leith—*Continued.*

Name of Street.	Height in feet above the sea.	Population 1861.			Mortality 1863.			Diseases in							
		Above 5.	Under 5.	Total.	Above 5.	Under 5.	Total.	Brain.	Heart.	Chest.	Abdomen.	Phthisis.	Croup.	Diphtheria.	Small-Pox.
Brought forward,		8581	974	9555	105	74	179	20	12	14	17	15	7	24	2
56 St Bernard's court......	70	44	15	59	...	...	...	...	...	...	...	...	...	...	...
57 St Bernard's crescent...	70	156	4	160	3	...	3	...	...	2	...	...	...	...	...
58 St Bernard's place......	57	174	36	210	2	7	9	...	...	2	2	...	...	...	...
59 St Bernard's row	49	98	20	118	1	...	1	...	...	...	...	...	...	...	...
60 Saunder's street	60	348	50	398	6	2	8	1	...	...	1	2	...	1	...
61 Stewart's hospital	162	83	...	83	1	...	1	1	...	...	...	...	...	...	...
62 Stockbridge...............	...	...	...	...	...	...	...	...	...	...	...	...	...	...	...
63 Veitch's place............	52	28	5	33	1	...	1	1	...	...	...	...	...	...	...
64 Veitch's square	50	76	6	82	...	2	2	...	...	...	...	...	...	...	...
65 Water of Leith	...	...:	...	...	9	7	16	...	1	4	1	...	1	...	1
1 Archibald's land ...	111	31	10	41	...	...	...	...	...	...	...	...	...	...	...
2 Bell's brae	127	19	...	19	...	...	...	...	...	...	...	...	...	...	...
3 Bell's mills	130	82	11	93	1	...	1	...	...	...	1	...	...	...	...
4 Brown's close	101	81	18	99	...	1	1	1	...	...	...	...	...	...	...
5 Broken stairs	120	49	6	55	...	...	...	...	...	...	...	...	...	...	...
6 Crombie's close	102—132	...	...	...	...	...	...	...	...	...	...	...	...	...	...
7 Damside	101	185	26	211	...	1	1	...	...	...	...	...	...	...	...
8 Dean and Dean path	103—167	437	80	517	7	5	12	2	1	1	2	1	2	1	...
9 Dean park	162	19	5	24	...	...	...	...	...	...	...	...	...	...	...
10 Hawthorn bank	139	200	40	240	4	1	5	1	1	...	1	...	...	...	...
11 Hay's land	130	4	...	4	...	...	...	...	...	...	...	...	...	...	...
12 Miller's row and Miller's land	89	30	8	38	...	...	...	...	...	...	...	...	...	...	...
13 Mill dam..............	82	113	27	140	...	...	...	...	...	...	...	...	...	...	...
14 Sunbury	130	28	9	37	...	...	...	...	...	...	...	...	...	...	...
66 Watson's (J.) hospital	264	115	1	116	...	...	...	...	...	...	...	...	...	...	...
Totals,....................		10,981	1351	12,332	140	100	240	27	15	23	25	18	10	26	3

5. District of Lower Water of Leith.

Name of Street.	Height in feet above the sea.	Population 1861.			Mortality 1863.			Diseases in							
		Above 5.	Under 5.	Total.	Above 5.	Under 5.	Total.	Brain.	Heart.	Chest.	Abdomen.	Phthisis.	Croup.	Diphtheria.	Small-Pox.
1 Bonnington and Bonnington road	...	246	38	284	6	...	6	2	...	...	...	1	...	...	...
1 Beaver hall...........	38	...	...	...	...	...	...	...	...	...	...	...	...	...	...
2 Blandfield row	60	...	...	...	...	...	...	...	...	...	...	...	...	...	...
3 Heriot hill	57	...	...	...	2	1	3	...	1	1	...	1	...	...	...
4 Heriot terrace.........	57	...	...	...	...	...	...	...	...	...	...	...	...	...	...
5 Logie green...........	33	...	...	...	...	...	...	...	...	...	...	...	...	...	...
6 Powder hall	70	...	...	...	..	...	...	...	...	...	...	...	...	...	...
2 Brandon street	61	143	9	152	...	...	...	...	...	...	...	...	...	...	...
3 Canonmills	36—57	215	31	246	6	5	11	2	...	..	...	1	2	1	...
1 Ann's court...........	46	56	9	65	...	...	...	...	...	..	...	...	...	...	...
2 Baker's land	46	160	22	182	...	2	2	...	...	1	...	...	...	...	...
3 Canon street	53	170	39	209	2	4	6	...	...	1	...	1	...	...	...
4 Huntly street	39	119	12	131	1	2	3	1	...	...	...	...	...	...	...
5 Perth street	65	10	1	11	..	...	...	...	...	...	...	...	...	...	...
6 Water lane	40	34	6	40	...	...	...	...	...	...	...	...	...	...	...
4 Claremont street, west	73	86	3	89	1	...	1	...	...	..	...	...	...	...	...
5 Claremont place.........	67	75	6	81	...	1	1	...	...	...	...	...	...	...	...
6 Clarence street	70	403	45	448	3	3	6	2	...	1	...	1	...	...	...
7 Eyre place	63	51	5	56	1	...	1	...	...	...	1	...	...	...	...
8 Henderson row	65	204	24	228	2	1	3	...	...	...	...	1	...	...	...
9 ... Deaf & Dumb inst....	73	59	...	59	...	...	..	...	...	...	...	...	...	...	...
10 Howard place............ / 11 Do. do. south ...	40—55 / 40	182	15	197	2	...	2	1	...	...	1	...	...	...	...
Carry forward,.................		2213	265	2478	26	19	45	8	1	4	2	6	2	1	...

AND THEIR VITAL STATISTICS.—*Continued.*

4. District of Upper Water of Leith—*Continued.*

	1863. Scarlatina.	Measles.	Hooping-Cough	Erysipelas.	Fevers. Total.	Typhus.	Typhoid.	Gastric.	Infantile.	Diarrhœa and Dysentery.	Scrofula.	Old Age.	Premature Debility.	No. of Paupers.	Street Cesspools. Trapped.	Untrapped.	Total.	Epidemics. Cholera. 1848.	Fever. 1847-8.	1857-8.
	7	5	...	2	8	2	3	3	...	6	7	7	7	132	40	72	112	7	8	1
56	...	...	...	...	...	...	...	...	...	...	...	...	...	1	...	2	2	...	...	...
57	...	...	...	...	...	...	...	...	...	...	...	...	...	...	...	2	2	...	...	...
58	...	1	...	...	...	...	...	...	...	...	1	...	1	16	...	1	1	...	...	...
59	...	...	...	...	...	...	...	...	...	...	...	...	...	1	1	1	2	...	...	...
60	...	...	...	...	...	...	...	...	...	...	2	...	1	10	...	6	6	2	...	...
61	...	...	...	...	...	...	...	...	...	...	...	...	...	...	...	...	...	...	...	...
62	...	...	...	...	...	...	...	...	...	...	...	...	...	...	...	...	...	...	46	1
63	...	...	...	...	...	...	...	...	...	...	...	...	...	1	...	1	1	...	...	...
64	...	...	...	...	...	...	...	...	...	...	1	...	1	4	1	6	7	...	...	...
65	...	2	...	...	...	...	...	...	...	...	1	3	1	1	...	...	...	...	6	...
1	...	...	...	...	...	...	...	...	...	...	...	...	...	2	...	...	...	...	...	...
2	...	...	...	...	...	...	...	...	...	...	...	...	...	...	...	...	...	...	...	...
3	...	...	...	...	...	...	...	...	...	...	...	...	...	2	...	...	...	...	...	...
4	...	...	...	...	...	...	...	...	...	...	...	...	...	4	...	...	...	...	...	...
5	...	...	...	...	...	...	...	...	...	...	...	...	...	...	...	...	...	...	...	...
6	...	...	...	...	...	...	...	...	...	...	...	...	...	1	...	...	...	...	...	...
7	...	1	...	...	...	...	...	...	...	...	...	...	...	10	...	...	...	1	...	...
8	...	...	...	...	...	...	...	...	...	...	...	1	1	13	...	...	...	1	2	...
9	...	...	...	...	...	...	...	...	...	...	...	...	...	...	...	...	...	...	...	...
10	...	...	...	1	...	...	...	...	...	...	...	1	...	17	...	...	...	...	...	...
11	...	...	...	...	...	...	...	...	...	...	...	...	...	...	...	...	...	...	...	...
12	...	...	...	...	...	...	...	...	...	...	...	...	...	...	...	...	...	...	...	...
13	...	...	...	...	...	...	...	...	...	...	...	...	...	...	...	...	...	...	...	...
14	...	...	...	...	...	...	...	...	...	...	...	...	...	...	...	5	5	...	...	...
66	...	...	...	...	...	...	...	...	...	...	...	...	...	...	...	...	...	...	...	...
	7	9	...	3	8	2	3	3	...	6	12	12	12	215	37	98	135	11	62	2

5. District of Lower Water of Leith.

	Scarlatina.	Measles.	Hooping-Cough	Erysipelas.	Fevers. Total.	Typhus.	Typhoid.	Gastric.	Infantile.	Diarrhœa and Dysentery.	Scrofula.	Old Age.	Premature Debility.	No. of Paupers.	Trapped.	Untrapped.	Total.	Cholera. 1848.	Fever. 1847-8.	1857-8.
1	1	...	...	...	...	...	...	...	...	...	...	1	...	3	...	7	7	1	3	...
1	...	...	...	...	...	...	...	...	...	...	...	...	...	...	...	...	...	...	...	...
2	...	...	...	...	...	...	...	...	...	...	...	...	...	...	...	...	...	...	...	...
3	...	...	...	...	...	...	...	...	...	...	...	...	...	...	...	...	...	...	...	...
4	...	...	...	...	...	...	...	...	...	...	...	...	...	...	...	...	...	...	...	...
5	...	...	...	...	...	...	...	...	...	...	...	...	...	...	...	...	...	...	...	...
6	...	...	...	...	...	...	...	...	...	...	...	...	...	...	...	...	...	...	...	...
2	...	...	...	...	...	...	...	...	...	...	...	...	...	...	...	1	1	...	...	...
3	...	1	...	...	...	...	...	...	...	...	2	...	2	9	...	12	12	2	12	1
1	...	...	...	...	...	...	...	...	...	...	...	...	...	2	...	...	...	1	...	...
2	...	...	...	...	...	...	...	...	...	...	...	...	...	2	...	...	...	...	...	...
3	...	1	...	1	...	...	...	...	...	...	1	...	1	2	...	...	...	...	...	...
4	...	1	...	...	...	...	...	...	...	1	...	...	...	...	...	2	2	...	...	...
5	...	...	...	...	...	...	...	...	...	...	...	...	...	...	...	...	...	...	...	...
6	...	...	...	...	...	...	...	...	...	...	...	...	...	...	...	2	2	...	...	...
4	...	...	...	...	...	...	...	...	...	...	...	1	...	...	...	...	...	...	...	...
5	...	...	...	...	...	...	...	...	...	...	...	...	1	...	...	2	2	...	...	...
6	...	2	...	...	...	...	...	...	...	...	...	...	...	11	...	...	...	...	1	...
7	...	...	...	...	...	...	...	...	...	...	...	...	...	1	...	1	1	...	...	...
8	...	...	...	...	...	...	...	...	...	...	...	1	1	...	1	3	4	...	...	...
9	...	...	...	...	...	...	...	...	...	...	...	...	...	...	...	...	...	...	...	...
10	...	...	...	...	...	...	...	...	...	...	...	...	...	...	...	6	6	...	...	...
11																				
	1	5	...	1	...	...	...	...	...	1	3	3	5	30	1	36	37	4	16	1

TABLE No. VI.—New Sanitary Districts,

5. District of Lower Water of Leith—*Continued.*

Name of Street.	Height in feet above the sea.	Population 1861.			Mortality 1863.			Diseases in							
		Above 5.	Under 5.	Total.	Above 5.	Under 5.	Total.	Brain.	Heart.	Chest.	Abdomen.	Phthisis.	Croup.	Diphtheria.	Small-Pox.
Brought forward,		2213	265	2478	26	19	45	8	1	4	2	6	2	1	...
12 Howard street	44	1	...	1	...	...	...	...	...	...	...	...	...	...	...
13 Hugh Miller place	45	...	...	...	...	...	...	...	...	...	...	...	...	...	...
14 Inverleith field	105														
15 Inverleith house	100	26	6	32	...	1	1	...	...	...	1	...	...	...	...
16 Inverleith mains	114														
17 Inverleith place	81	55	2	57	...	1	1	...	...	...	...	...	...	...	...
18 Inverleith row	49—97	381	19	400	3	1	4	1	...	1	...	...	...	...	...
19 Inverleith terrace	49	22	1	23	...	...	...	...	...	...	...	...	...	...	...
20 Queensferry road	106	152	14	166	...	...	...	...	...	...	...	...	...	...	...
21 Reid terrace	45	...	...	...	2	1	3	...	...	...	...	1	...	...	...
22 Rintoul place	45	...	...	...	...	...	...	...	...	...	...	...	...	...	...
23 St Mark's place	34	...	...	...	...	...	...	...	...	...	...	...	...	...	...
24 St Stephen street	76—91	15	1	16	...	...	...	...	...	...	...	...	...	...	...
25 Saxe-Coburg place	76	161	8	169	2	...	2	1	...	...	1	...	...	...	...
26 Silvermills	52	148	25	173	5	1	6	2	...	...	...	...	1	...	...
27 Summer place	40	50	6	56	1	...	1	...	...	...	...	1	...	...	...
28 Tanfield	40	29	1	30	...	...	...	...	...	...	...	...	...	...	...
29 Warriston crescent	38	191	7	198	1	2	3	...	...	...	..	...	...	...	...
30 Warriston cemetery	50	10	3	13	...	...	...	...	...	...	...	...	...	...	...
31 Warriston house	63	...	...	...	1	...	1	...	...	...	1	...	...	...	...
32 Warriston place	44	50	4	54	1	...	1	...	...	1	...	...	...	...	...
Totals,		3504	362	3866	42	26	68	12	1	6	5	8	3	1	...

6. District of Broughton.

Name of Street.	Height in feet above the sea.	Pop. Above 5.	Pop. Under 5.	Pop. Total.	Mort. Above 5.	Mort. Under 5.	Mort. Total.	Brain.	Heart.	Chest.	Abdomen.	Phthisis.	Croup.	Diphtheria.	Small-Pox.
1 Annandale street	90—114	164	24	188	1	1	2	...	...	...	...	...	...	...	...
2 Do. do. lane	103	5	...	5											
3 Antigua street	144	138	7	145	2	...	2	2	...	...	...	...	...	...	...
4 Bellevue terrace	97	126	3	129	...	...	...	...	...	...	...	...	...	...	...
5 Broughton court	106	73	15	88	...	2	2	...	...	...	...	...	...	...	...
6 Broughton place	123	348	23	371	3	...	3	1	...	...	...	1	...	..	...
7 Broughton place, East	120	100	5	105	1	2	3	...	...	1	...	...	...	...	...
8 Broughton road, Low	89—114	33	3	36	...	...	...	...	...	...	...	...	...	...	...
9 Broughton street	114—162	847	71	918	19	4	23	3	2	1	4	5	...	...	...
10 Do. do. lane	160	5	1	6	...	...	...	...	...	...	...	...	...	...	...
11 Do. do. lane, low	109	10	3	13	...	...	..	...	...	...	...	...	...	...	...
12 Claremont crescent	93	123	13	136	1	...	1	...	...	...	...	...	...	...	...
1 Ferniehill,	75	...	...	...	1	...	1	...	...	...	1	...	...	...	...
2 Zoological Gardens	97	...	...	...	1	...	1	...	...	...	...	...	...	...	...
13 Claremont street, East	97	213	15	228	2	...	2	1	...	1	...	...	...	...	...
14 Forth street	150	210	9	219	2	...	2	...	...	...	...	...	...	...	...
15 Gayfield lane	...	46	10	56	1	1	2	...	...	...	...	1	...	...	...
16 Gayfield place	124	93	6	99	1	2	3	...	...	1	...	...	1	...	...
17 Gayfield square	103—131	465	39	504	7	1	8	...	...	1	...	3	...	...	...
18 Gayfield street	116	18	4	22	...	...	...	...	...	...	...	...	...	...	...
19 George place	72	74	...	74	...	...	...	...	...	...	...	...	...	...	...
20 Haddington place	106—121	331	26	357	5	1	6	...	...	1	2	...	...	...	...
21 Hart street	129—144	113	2	115	3	...	3	...	...	1	1	...	...	...	...
22 Hope crescent	94	37	4	41	...	...	...	...	...	...	...	...	...	...	...
23 James street	81	31	11	42	1	...	1	...	...	...	...	...	...	...	...
24 Middlefield	78	74	8	82	1	1	2	...	1	1	..	...	...	...	...
25 Moray street	71—80	270	41	311	3	...	3	...	...	1	1	...	...	...	...
Carry forward,		3947	343	4290	55	15	70	7	3	9	9	10	1	...	...

AND THEIR VITAL STATISTICS.—*Continued.*

5. District of Lower Water of Leith—*Continued.*

	1863.														Street Cesspool.			Epidemics.		
					Fevers.													Cholera.	Fever.	
	Scarlatina.	Measles.	Hooping-Cough	Erysipelas.	Total.	Typhus.	Typhoid.	Gastric.	Infantile.	Diarrhœa and Dysentery.	Scrofula.	Old Age.	Premature Debility.	No. of Paupers.	Trapped.	Untrapped.	Total.	1848.	1847-8.	1857-8.
	1	5	...	1	...	...	...	...	...	1	3	3	5	30	1	36	37	4	16	1
12	...	...	...	...	...	...	...	...	...	...	...	...	...	...	...	...	...	...	...	...
13	...	...	...	...	...	...	...	...	...	...	...	...	...	...	...	...	...	...	...	...
14																			...	...
15	...	...	...	...	...	...	...	...	...	...	...	...	...	...	...	...	...	...	...	...
16																				
17	...	...	...	...	1	...	...	...	1	...	...	...	...	...	...	1	1	...	1	...
18	...	...	...	...	1	...	1	...	...	...	1	...	...	...	1	4	5	...	2	...
19	...	...	...	...	...	...	...	...	...	...	...	...	...	...	...	...	...	...	...	...
20	...	...	...	...	...	...	...	...	...	...	...	...	...	...	...	...	...	...	...	...
21	...	...	...	...	...	...	...	...	...	...	...	...	1	...	...	...	...	...	...	...
22	...	...	...	...	...	...	...	...	...	...	...	...	...	...	...	...	...	...	...	...
23	...	...	...	...	...	...	...	...	...	...	...	...	...	...	...	...	...	...	...	...
24	...	...	...	...	...	...	...	...	...	...	...	...	...	...	...	...	...	...	...	...
25	...	...	...	...	...	...	...	...	...	...	...	...	...	...	...	6	6	...	1	...
26	...	...	...	...	...	...	...	...	...	1	...	1	...	4	...	...	...	1	1	...
27	...	...	...	...	...	...	...	...	...	...	...	...	...	4	...	1	1	...	...	...
28	...	...	...	...	...	...	...	...	...	...	...	...	...	...	...	...	...	...	...	...
29	...	...	...	...	...	...	...	...	...	...	1	...	1	...	3	...	3	...	2	...
30	...	...	...	...	...	...	...	...	...	...	...	...	...	...	...	...	...	...	...	...
31	...	...	...	...	...	...	...	...	...	...	...	...	...	...	...	...	...	...	...	...
32	...	...	...	...	...	...	...	...	...	...	...	...	...	1	...	2	2	...	1	...
	1	5	...	1	2	...	1	...	1	2	5	4	7	39	5	50	55	5	24	1

6. District of Broughton.

	Scarlatina.	Measles.	Hooping-Cough	Erysipelas.	Total.	Typhus.	Typhoid.	Gastric.	Infantile.	Diarrhœa and Dysentery.	Scrofula.	Old Age.	Premature Debility.	No. of Paupers.	Trapped.	Untrapped.	Total.	Cholera 1848.	Fever 1847-8.	Fever 1857-8.
1																				
2	...	...	...	...	...	...	...	...	...	...	1	1	...	...	...	2	2	...	...	...
3	...	...	...	...	...	...	...	...	...	...	...	...	...	...	...	...	...	...	...	...
4	...	...	...	...	...	...	...	...	...	...	...	...	...	...	...	1	1	...	...	...
5	...	...	...	...	...	...	...	...	...	...	1	...	1	...	...	...	...	...	...	...
6	...	...	...	...	...	...	...	...	...	...	...	1	...	...				...	...	...
7	1	...	...	...	...	...	...	...	...	...	1	...	...	1	3	...	3	...	2	...
8	...	...	...	...	...	...	...	...	...	...	...	...	...	...				...	...	...
9	1	...	...	...	2	1	...	...	1	...	...	2	2	10	5	3	8	2	7	...
10	...	...	...	...	...	...	...	...	...	...	...	...	...	...	...	...	...	...	...	...
11	...	...	...	...	...	...	...	...	...	...	...	...	...	...	...	...	...	...	...	...
12	...	...	...	...	1	...	1	...	...	...	...	...	...	...	1	3	4	...	...	...
1	...	...	...	...	...	...	...	...	...	...	...	...	...	...	...	...	...	...	...	...
2	...	...	...	...	1	...	...	1	...	...	...	...	...	...	...	...	...	...	...	...
13	...	...	...	...	...	...	...	...	...	...	...	...	...	...	...	...	...	...	...	...
14	...	...	...	...	...	...	...	...	...	...	...	...	...	...	1	4	5	...	2	...
15	...	1	...	...	...	...	...	...	...	...	...	...	...	...	...	...	...	...	...	...
16	1	...	...	...	...	...	...	...	...	...	...	...	...	...	...	...	...	...	...	...
17	...	...	...	...	...	...	...	...	...	2	...	1	1	5	2	1	3	3	1	...
18	...	...	...	...	...	...	...	...	...	...	...	...	...	...	...	...	...	...	...	...
19	...	...	...	...	...	...	...	...	...	...	...	...	...	...	...	...	...	...	...	...
20	1	...	...	...	...	...	...	...	...	...	...	1	...	3	...	...	...	...	1	...
21	...	...	...	...	...	...	...	...	...	...	...	...	...	...	...	...	...	...	...	...
22	...	...	...	...	...	...	...	...	...	...	...	...	...	...	...	4	4	...	...	...
23	...	...	...	...	...	...	...	...	...	...	...	...	...	...	...	...	...	...	...	...
24	...	...	...	...	...	...	...	...	...	...	...	...	...	...	...	...	...	...	...	...
25	...	...	...	...	...	...	...	...	...	...	...	1	...	3	5	...	5	...	...	...
	4	1	...	...	4	1	1	1	1	2	3	7	4	22	17	18	35	5	13	...

TABLE No. VI.—New Sanitary Districts,

6. District of Broughton—*Continued.*

Name of Street.	Height in feet above the sea.	Population 1861.			Mortality 1863.			Diseases in							
		Above 5.	Under 5.	Total.	Above 5.	Under 5.	Total.	Brain.	Heart.	Chest.	Abdomen.	Phthisis.	Croup.	Diphtheria.	Small-Pox.
Brought forward,		3947	343	4290	55	15	70	7	3	9	9	10	1	...	...
26 Picardy place...........	161—173	199	10	209	2	...	2	...	...	...	...	1	...	...	...
27 Pilrig Model buildings	76	169	34	203	4	...	4	1	...	...	...	2	...	...	...
28 Pilrig place..............	67	19	...	19	...	...	...	...	...	...	...	...	...	...	...
29 Pilrig street	34—61	112	9	121	2	...	2	...	1	...	...	...	...	...	...
30 Rosebank	54	...	...	...	1	...	1	...	...	...	...	...	...	...	...
31 Shrub place..............	86	231	39	270	7	2	9	...	1	2	1	1	...	...	...
32 Shrub hill	86	60	18	78	1	1	2	...	...	...	...	...	...	...	...
33 Union place, N. and S.	155—170	192	13	205	3	...	3	...	...	1	1	1	...	...	...
34 Union street	150	244	22	266	4	3	7	1	1	2	...	1	...	...	...
35 Do. do. lane	160	10	1	11	...	...	...	...	...	...	...	...	...	...	...
Totals,....................		5183	489	5672	79	21	100	9	6	14	11	16	1	...	...

7. District of Calton and Greenside.

Name of Street.	Height in feet above the sea.	Pop. Above 5.	Pop. Under 5.	Pop. Total.	Mort. Above 5.	Mort. Under 5.	Mort. Total.	Brain.	Heart.	Chest.	Abdomen.	Phthisis.	Croup.	Diphtheria.	Small-Pox.
1 Baxter's place...........	152	63	2	65	1	...	1	...	...	...	...	...	...	...	...
2 Blenheim place	139	73	14	87	3	...	3	1	...	1	...	...	...	...	...
3 Brunswick street	112	47	3	50	1	...	1	...	...	...	1	...	...	...	...
4 Do. do. lane...	...	10	1	11	...	...	...	...	...	...	...	...	...	...	...
5 Brunton place	117	53	1	54	1	...	1	1	...	...	...	...	...	...	...
6 Calton hill	350	...	...	...	...	...	...	...	...	...	...	...	...	...	...
7 Calton hill street	194—235	421	57	478	5	2	7	...	1	3	...	1	...	...	...
8 Calton street	191	157	12	169	1	1	2	..	...	2	...	...	...	...	...
9 Carlton terrace	183	140	5	145	1	...	1	1	...	...	...	...	...	...	...
10 Do. do. lane......	178—191	3	2	5	...	...	...	...	...	...	...	...	...	...	...
11 Catherine street.........	181	278	59	337	1	2	3	...	1	...	...	...	...	...	...
12 Easter road..............	90—115	103	16	119	...	...	...	...	...	...	...	...	..	...	...
13 Elder street	197—225	356	22	378	9	1	10	2	...	...	1	3	...	...	...
14 Elm row	132	211	28	239	3	...	3	1	...	...	1	...	...	...	...
15 Greenside	110—147	...	...	...	...	...	...	...	...	...	...	...	...	...	...
1 Cuddie lane...........	131	39	3	42	...	1	1	1	...	...	...	...	...	...	...
2 Gilchrist's entry	149	148	34	182	1	...	1	...	...	...	...	...	...	...	...
3 Glenorchy place	121	107	21	128	5	5	10	1	...	2	...	3	...	2	...
4 Greenside court	134	134	25	159	2	...	2	...	...	1	...	1	...	...	...
5 Greenside end.........	110	53	8	61	3	...	3	...	...	...	2	...	...	...	...
6 Greenside lane, upper	117	136	28	164	5	4	9	...	1	1	...	1	...	1	...
7 Do. do., lower	117	30	8	38	...	...	...	...	...	...	...	...	...	...	...
8 Greenside place	170	484	71	555	9	6	15	...	1	2	1	6	...	1	...
9 Greenside row, lower	112	} 491	100	591	5	8	13	1	...	5	1	1	1	...	...
10 Do. do., upper	116—143														
11 Greenside street......	181	380	60	440	8	6	14	4	...	...	...	2	...	1	...
12 Marshall's court.......	117	81	20	101	...	...	...	...	...	...	...	...	...	...	...
13 Nottingham place ...	143—183	20	1	21	...	...	...	...	...	...	...	...	...	...	...
14 Nottingham terrace	177	95	9	104	1	3	4	...	...	...	...	...	...	...	...
15 Queen's place	147	303	55	358	8	2	10	2	1	1	1	1	...	...	...
16 Simpson's court	134	235	49	284	3	1	4	...	...	4	...	...	...	...	...
16 Hillside crescent.........	117	59	3	62	1	...	1	...	...	1	...	...	...	...	...
17 Leith street..............	188—216	143	15	158	4	3	7	1	1	2	1	...	...	1	...
18 Leith street terrace ...	203—222	369	38	407	3	2	5	...	...	1	1	...	...	1	...
19 Leith walk, East side...	72—119	198	30	228	4	1	5	...	1	...	...	2	...	...	...
20 Leopold place...........	119—136	220	13	233	5	...	5	1	...	...	3	...	...	...	...
21 Little King street	179—207	165	36	201	4	2	6	...	2	...	1	...	...	...	...
22 London road	...	...	...	...	...	...	...	...	...	...	...	...	...	...	...
Carry forward,....................		5805	849	6654	97	50	147	17	9	26	14	21	1	7	...

AND THEIR VITAL STATISTICS.—*Continued.*

6. District of Broughton—*Continued.*

	1863.														Street Cesspools.			Epidemics.		
					Fevers.													Cholera.	Fever.	
	Scarlatina.	Measles.	Hooping-Cough	Erysipelas.	Total.	Typhus.	Typhoid.	Gastric.	Infantile.	Diarrhœa and Dysentery.	Scrofula.	Old Age.	Premature Debility.	No. of Paupers.	Trapped.	Untrapped.	Total.	1848.	1847-8.	1857-8.
	4	1	...	...	4	1	1	1	1	2	3	7	4	22	17	18	35	5	13	...
26	...	...	...	...	1	...	1	...	...	...	...	...	...	...	...	...	...	...	2	...
27	...	...	...	...	...	...	...	...	...	...	...	1	...	...	2	4	6	...	...	...
28	...	...	...	...	...	...	...	...	...	...	...	...	...	...	...	...	...	...	...	...
29	...	...	...	...	1	...	...	1	...	...	...	...	...	2	...	1	1	...	...	1
30	...	...	...	...	...	...	...	...	...	...	...	1	...	...	...	...	...	...	...	...
31	...	...	...	...	...	...	...	...	...	...	...	1	...	3	...	...	...	...	...	...
32	...	...	...	...	1	...	...	...	1	...	...	1	...	...	...	...	...	...	...	...
33	...	...	...	...	...	...	...	...	...	...	...	...	...	...	2	1	3	...	3	...
34	1	...	...	...	...	...	...	...	...	...	...	...	1	...	...	...	...	...	3	...
35	...	...	...	...	...	...	...	...	...	...	...	...	...	...	...	...	...	...	...	...
	5	1	...	...	7	1	2	2	2	2	3	11	5	27	21	24	45	5	21	1
7. District of Calton and Greenside.																				
1	...	...	...	...	...	...	...	...	...	...	...	...	...	...	...	...	...	...	...	...
2	...	...	...	...	...	...	...	...	...	...	...	1	...	...	1	...	1	...	...	...
3	...	...	...	...	...	...	...	...	...	...	...	...	...	...	...	2	2	...	...	...
4	...	...	...	...	...	...	...	...	...	...	...	...	...	...	...	...	...	...	...	...
5	...	...	...	...	...	...	...	...	...	...	...	...	...	...	...	1	1	...	...	...
6	...	...	...	...	...	...	...	...	...	...	...	...	...	...	4	...	4	...	...	...
7	1	...	...	...	...	...	...	...	...	...	1	...	...	2	7	...	7	...	1	...
8	...	...	...	...	...	...	...	...	...	...	...	...	...	1	...	...	...	2	3	...
9	...	...	...	...	...	...	...	...	...	...	...	...	...	...	2	...	2	...	...	...
10	...	...	...	...	...	...	...	...	...	...	...	...	...	...	...	...	...	...	...	...
11	...	1	...	...	...	...	...	...	...	...	...	...	...	3	2	...	2	...	7	...
12	...	...	...	...	...	...	...	...	...	...	1	...	...	...	1	12	13	...	...	...
13	1	...	...	...	...	...	...	...	...	...	...	...	...	1	1	2	3	...	2	...
14	...	...	...	...	...	...	...	...	...	1	...	1	...	...	...	...	...	...	...	...
15	...	...	...	...	1	...	...	1	...	...	...	...	...	...	...	...	...	...	...	...
1	...	...	...	...	...	...	...	...	...	...	...	...	...	1	...	...	...	...	...	...
2	...	...	...	...	...	...	...	...	...	...	...	...	...	15	...	...	...	...	...	...
3	...	1	...	...	...	...	...	...	...	...	...	...	...	2	...	...	...	...	...	...
4	...	...	...	...	...	...	...	...	...	...	...	...	...	5				1	3	...
5	1	...	...	...	...	...	...	...	...	...	...	...	...	1	3	9	12	...	...	...
6	2	...	...	...	...	...	...	...	...	...	2	...	...	12				...	...	...
7	...	...	...	...	...	...	...	...	...	...	...	...	...	4				...	...	...
8	...	1	...	...	...	...	...	...	...	...	...	...	2	12	...	...	...	1	1	...
9	...	1	...	...	...	...	...	...	...	...	2	...	1	20	...	...	...	1	28	...
10	...	...	...	...	...	...	...	...	...	...	...	...	...	...	...	...	...	...	...	...
11	...	...	...	...	...	...	...	...	...	...	3	1	...	11	...	...	...	1	39	...
12	...	...	...	...	...	...	...	...	...	...	...	...	...	3	...	...	...	...	...	...
13	...	...	...	...	...	...	...	...	...	...	...	...	...	...	...	...	...	...	...	...
14	...	...	...	...	...	...	...	...	...	...	1	...	2	...	...	...	...	...	1	...
15	...	...	...	...	3	1	1	...	1	...	1	...	...	8	...	...	...	...	1	...
16	...	...	...	...	...	...	...	...	...	...	...	...	...	16	...	...	...	1	...	...
16	...	...	...	...	...	...	...	...	...	...	...	...	...	...	...	1	1	...	...	...
17	1	...	...	...	...	...	...	...	...	...	...	...	...	3	1	...	1	...	7	...
18	...	...	...	...	1	1	...	...	...	...	1	...	...	...	...	...	...	1	...	...
19	...	...	...	...	...	...	...	...	...	...	...	1	...	1	1	10	11	1	23	...
20	...	...	...	...	...	...	...	...	...	...	1	...	...	2	...	...	...	...	4	...
21	...	...	...	...	...	...	...	...	...	1	2	...	...	3	...	...	...	...	...	...
22	...	...	...	...	...	...	...	...	...	...	...	...	...	...	...	16	16	...	...	...
	6	4	...	...	5	2	1	1	1	2	15	4	5	126	23	53	76	9	120	...

TABLE No. VI.—New Sanitary Districts,

7. District of Calton and Greenside—*Continued.*

Name of Street.	Height in feet above the sea.	Population 1861.			Mortality 1863.			Diseases in							
		Above 5.	Under 5.	Total.	Above 5.	Under 5.	Total.	Brain.	Heart.	Chest.	Abdomen.	Phthisis.	Croup.	Diphtheria.	Small-Pox.
Brought forward,		5805	849	6654	97	50	147	17	9	26	14	21	1	7	...
23 Lover's lane	92—112	28	3	31	...	1	1	...	...	...	...	...	...	...	...
24 Maryfield	100	46	1	47	...	...	...	...	...	...	...	...	...	...	...
25 Montgomery street and lane	123	93	14	107	4	...	4	...	2	...	...	1	...	...	...
26 Norton place	120—128	163	13	176	2	4	6	...	...	2	...	...	...	1	...
27 Norton place, West ...	115—136	165	32	197	4	2	6	...	1	...	...	...	...	...	...
28 Regent Arch place... ..	167	32	7	39	3	2	5	...	...	...	...	...	...	1	...
29 St Ninian's row	181	7	...	7	...	...	...	...	...	...	...	...	...	...	...
30 Regent road	160—236	9	1	10	1	1	2	...	...	...	...	...	...	...	...
31 Prison, Calton hill	239	343	5	348	4	3	7	1	1	1	...	...	...	...	...
32 Regent terrace	191—215	258	14	272	3	...	3	1	1	...	...	...	...	...	...
33 Do. do. lane ...	...	47	11	58	...	...	...	...	...	...	...	...	...	...	...
34 Register street, East...	222—238	88	5	93	...	1	1	1	...	...	...	...	...	...	...
35 Royal terrace............	170—180	329	15	344	3	1	4	...	1	1	...	...	...	2	...
36 St James' place	212	257	36	293	4	1	5	1	...	1	...	...	...	...	...
37 St James' square	236	667	73	740	9	5	14	...	...	5	...	2	...	...	2
38 St James' street, East	216	124	17	141	1	2	3	...	...	...	...	...	...	1	...
39 St James' street, North	218	271	25	296	4	6	10	1	...	1	1	1	1	...	...
40 St James' street, South	207—236	679	105	784	14	7	21	5	3	4	1	3	...	...	...
41 Shakspeare square	...	...	...	...	...	...	...	...	...	...	...	...	...	...	...
42 Swinton row	209	...	...	...	...	...	...	...	...	...	...	...	...	...	...
43 Waterloo place	218—232	121	8	129	2	...	2	...	...	1	...	...	...	...	...
44 Windsor street	125	202	11	213	1	1	2	1	...	1	...	...	...	...	...
45 Do. do. lane ...	115	5	...	5	...	...	...	...	...	...	...	...	...	...	..
Totals,....................		9739	1245	10,984	156	87	243	28	18	43	16	28	2	12	2

8. District of Abbey.

Name of Street.	Height in feet above the sea.	Above 5.	Under 5.	Total.	Above 5.	Under 5.	Total.	Brain.	Heart.	Chest.	Abdomen.	Phthisis.	Croup.	Diphtheria.	Small-Pox.
1 Abbey hill	102—116	486	75	561	18	13	31	2	3	5	2	4	...	...	...
1 Begg's (Dr) Buildings	130	184	41	225	1	2	3	...	...	1	...	...	...	...	...
2 Croall's buildings ...	113	...	...	...	1	...	1	...	...	...	...	1	...	...	...
3 Currie's close (86) ...	115	33	9	42	...	3	3	...	...	...	...	...	...	2	...
4 Duncan's court (25)	112	28	6	34	...	...	...	...	...	...	...	...	...	...	...
5 Fullerton's close (6)	109	...	...	...	...	...	...	...	...	...	...	...	...	...	...
6 Hogg's place (49) ...	112	36	10	46	...	...	...	...	...	...	...	...	...	...	...
7 Holyrood terrace ...	130	...	...	...	2	...	2	...	...	...	...	1	...	...	...
8 Ironside court.........	114	21	5	26	1	...	1	...	...	1	...	...	...	...	...
9 Ironside place.........	113	121	9	130	...	...	...	...	...	...	...	...	...	...	...
10 Megget's court (46)	112	35	3	38	...	1	1	...	...	...	...	...	...	...	...
2 Abbey lane..............	106	20	2	22	...	...	...	...	...	...	...	...	...	...	...
3 Abbey mount...........	119—145	41	6	47	...	2	2	...	...	...	...	1	...	...	...
4 Abbey strand...........	118	39	5	44	2	2	4	1	...	1	...	...	...	...	...
5 Thomson's court (13)...	...	93	11	104	2	1	3	...	...	...	...	1	1	...	...
6 Brand place	106	144	31	175	6	3	9	1	...	1	2	...	...	...	...
7 Comely Green crescent	102	43	6	49	...	...	...	...	...	...	...	...	...	...	...
8 Comely Green place ...	102	112	23	135	2	...	2	...	...	2	...	...	...	...	...
1 Jane terrace	95	...	...	...	...	...	...	...	...	...	...	...	...	...	...
2 Rose lane	102—106	15	3	18	...	...	...	...	...	...	...	...	...	...	...
9 Croft-an-Righ	106	202	43	245	6	4	10	...	...	2	2	...	1	...	...
1 Rowley's court	112	33	5	38	...	...	...	...	...	...	...	...	...	...	...
10 Holyrood palace.........	119	21	2	23	...	...	...	...	...	...	...	...	...	...	...
11 Horse wynd	118	72	11	83	2	2	4	...	1	1	...	...	...	...	...
Carry forward,..................		1779	306	2085	43	33	76	4	4	14	6	8	2	2	...

7. District of Calton and Greenside—*Continued.*

	1863.													No. of Paupers.	Street Cesspools.			Epidemics.		
	Scarlatina.	Measles.	Hooping-Cough.	Erysipelas.	Fevers. Total.	Fevers. Typhus.	Fevers. Typhoid.	Fevers. Gastric.	Fevers. Infantile.	Diarrhœa and Dysentery.	Scrofula.	Old Age.	Premature Debility.		Trapped.	Untrapped.	Total.	Cholera. 1848.	Fever. 1847-8.	Fever. 1857-8.
	6	4	...	...	5	2	1	1	1	2	15	4	5	126	23	53	76	9	120	...
23	...	...	...	...	...	...	...	...	...	...	...	...	...	...	...	...	...	...	...	...
24	...	...	...	...	...	...	...	...	...	...	...	...	...	...	...	...	...	...	...	...
25	...	...	...	...	...	...	...	...	...	...	...	...	...	...	1	...	1	...	...	...
26	...	...	...	...	...	...	...	...	...	...	1	...	2	...	...	4	4	2	1	...
27	...	2	...	...	...	...	...	...	...	...	...	...	...	...	3	1	4	...	...	...
28	...	...	...	...	2	2	...	...	...	...	...	...	1	1	...	...	...	...	...	...
29	...	...	...	...	...	...	...	...	...	...	...	...	...	...	...	...	...	...	...	...
30	...	...	...	...	...	...	...	...	...	...	...	...	...	...	...	6	6	...	1	...
31	...	...	...	...	...	...	...	...	...	1	...	...	1	...	...	...	...	1	11	...
32	...	...	...	...	...	...	...	...	...	...	...	...	...	...	1	...	1	...	...	...
33	...	...	...	...	1	...	1	...	...	...	...	...	...	...	...	...	...	...	...	...
34	...	...	...	...	...	...	...	...	...	...	...	...	...	...	...	...	...	...	...	...
35	...	...	...	...	...	...	...	...	...	...	...	...	...	...	11	1	12	...	...	...
36	...	...	...	...	1	1	...	...	...	...	1	1	...	13	2	1	3	...	2	...
37	...	...	...	...	...	...	...	...	...	2	1	...	...	5	...	3	3	2	3	...
38	1	...	...	...	1	...	1	...	...	...	...	...	...	1	...	...	...	...	...	...
39	...	...	...	...	...	...	...	...	...	1	2	2	...	2	2	3	5	...	4	...
40	...	1	...	...	1	...	1	...	...	1	1	1	...	15	...	...	...	2	11	1
41	...	...	...	...	...	...	...	...	...	...	...	...	...	...	...	...	...	2	7	...
42	...	...	...	...	...	...	...	...	...	...	...	...	...	...	...	...	...	...	...	...
43	...	...	...	...	1	...	1	...	...	...	...	...	...	...	...	3	3	...	1	1
44	...	...	...	...	...	...	...	...	...	...	...	...	...	...	...	2	2	...	...	...
45	...	...	...	...	...	...	...	...	...	...	...	...	...	...	...	...	...	...	...	...
	7	7	...	...	12	5	5	1	1	7	21	8	9	163	43	77	120	18	161	2

8. District of Abbey.

	Scarlatina.	Measles.	Hooping-Cough.	Erysipelas.	Fevers. Total.	Fevers. Typhus.	Fevers. Typhoid.	Fevers. Gastric.	Fevers. Infantile.	Diarrhœa and Dysentery.	Scrofula.	Old Age.	Premature Debility.	No. of Paupers.	Trapped.	Untrapped.	Total.	Cholera. 1848.	Fever. 1847-8.	Fever. 1857-8.
1	...	3	...	...	4	2	..	1	1	...	5	...	2	13	11	...	11	2	7	...
1	...	...	...	...	...	...	...	...	...	...	1	...	...	3	...	...	...	...	...	...
2	...	...	...	...	...	...	...	...	...	...	...	...	...	1	...	...	...	...	...	...
3	...	...	...	...	...	...	...	...	...	...	...	...	1	1	...	...	...	...	...	...
4	...	...	...	...	...	...	...	...	...	...	...	...	...	...	...	...	...	...	...	...
5	...	...	...	...	...	...	...	...	...	...	...	...	...	...	...	...	...	...	...	...
6	...	...	...	...	...	...	...	...	...	...	...	...	...	...	...	...	...	...	...	...
7	...	...	...	...	...	...	...	...	...	...	1	...	...	...	...	...	...	...	...	...
8	...	..	...	...	...	...	...	...	...	...	...	...	...	1	...	...	. .	...	...	...
9	...	...	...	...	...	...	...	...	...	...	...	...	...	3	...	...	...	...	...	...
10	...	1	...	...	...	...	...	...	...	...	...	...	...	1	...	...	...	...	...	...
2	...	...	...	...	...	...	...	...	...	...	...	...	...	...	...	...	...	...	1	...
3	...	1	...	...	...	...	...	...	...	...	...	...	...	...	...	2	2	...	1	...
4	...	1	...	...	...	...	...	...	...	...	...	...	...	...	3	...	3	...	...	...
5	...	...	...	...	...	...	...	...	...	...	...	...	...	3	2	...	2	1	2	...
6	...	1	...	...	...	...	...	...	...	2	...	...	...	1	...	...	...	...	...	...
7	...	...	...	...	...	...	...	...	...	...	...	...	...	...	1	1	2	...	...	...
8	...	...	...	...	...	...	...	...	...	...	...	...	...	...	...	1	1	...	...	...
1	...	...	...	...	...	...	...	...	...	...	...	...	...	...	...	...	...	...	...	...
2	...	...	...	...	...	...	...	...	...	...	...	...	...	...	...	...	...	...	...	...
9	...	...	...	...	1	1	...	...	...	...	...	...	2	4	1	1	2	...	2	...
1	...	...	...	...	...	...	...	...	...	...	...	...	...	...	...	...	...	...	...	...
10	...	...	...	...	...	...	...	...	...	...	...	...	...	...	...	...	...	...	...	...
11	...	...	...	...	...	...	...	...	...	...	1	...	...	5	4	...	4	...	...	...
	...	7	...	...	5	3	...	1	1	2	8	...	5	36	22	5	27	3	13	...

TABLE No. VI.—New Sanitary Districts,

8. District of Abbey—*Continued.*

Name of Street.	Height in feet above the sea.	Population 1861.			Mortality 1863.			Diseases in							
		Above 5.	Under 5.	Total.	Above 5.	Under 5.	Total.	Brain.	Heart.	Chest.	Abdomen.	Phthisis.	Croup.	Diphtheria.	Small-Pox.
Brought forward,		1779	306	2085	43	33	76	4	4	14	6	8	2	2	...
12 Queen's park	113—118	...	...	...	...	...	...	...	...	...	...	...	...	...	...
1 St Margaret's loch ...	120	...	...	...	3	...	3	...	...	...	...	...	...	...	...
2 Dunsappie loch	371	...	...	...	1	...	1	...	...	...	...	...	...	...	...
13 Spring gardens	106	95	12	107	...	...	...	...	...	...	...	...	...	...	...
1 Brown's place.........	106	42	3	45	2	...	2	...	...	...	...	...	...	...	...
Totals, ...		1916	321	2237	49	33	82	4	4	14	6	8	2	2	...
9. District of Canongate.															
1 Canongate	118—214	1995	287	2282	57	34	91	6	8	13	4	9	1	2	1
1 Bakehouse close (146)	160	227	33	260	3	2	5	...	...	1	...	1	...	...	...
2 Bell's close (272) ...	210	53	8	61	1	...	1	...	...	...	1	...	...	...	...
3 Boyd's close (276) ...	210	300	36	336	1	6	7	1	...	...	...	...	...	...	...
4 Brown's close (79) ...	210	135	24	159	1	4	5	...	...	...	1	...	...	...	...
5 Brown's court (125)	126	78	19	97	...	...	...	...	...	...	...	...	...	...	...
6 Bull's close (106) ...	157	132	27	159	...	2	2	...	...	...	...	...	...	...	...
7 Callender's entry (67)	140	32	8	40	...	1	1	...	...	...	...	...	...	...	...
8 Campbell's close (87)	147	378	64	442	5	10	15	...	...	5	...	1	1	...	...
9 Canongate workhouse	138	67	4	71	13	1	14	3	...	2	...	2	...	...	...
10 Carfrae's entry (112)	160	57	7	64	...	...	...	...	...	...	...	...	...	...	...
11 Chessel's court (240)	203	209	34	243	3	4	7	...	1	1	...	3	1	...	...
12 Cooper's entry (130)	168	86	12	98	2	1	3	1	...	...	...	...	1	...	...
13 Coull's close (317) ...	208	127	22	149	1	3	4	1	...	...	...	...	2	...	...
14 Dunbar's close (137	161	216	43	259	2	6	8	...	...	1	1	1	1	1	...
15 Duncan's close (35)	125	50	8	58	1	1	2	...	...	1	1	...	...	...	...
16 Galloway's entry (53)	132	40	5	45	...	...	...	...	...	...	...	...	...	...	...
17 Gentle's close (122)	163	38	4	42	1	...	1	...	...	1	...	...	...	...	...
18 Gibb's close (250) ...	206	27	6	33	...	1	1	...	...	...	...	...	...	...	...
19 Gilmore street	152	65	4	69	...	...	...	...	...	...	...	...	...	...	...
20 Gladstone's ct. (181)	174	...	...	...	...	...	...	...	...	...	...	...	...	...	...
21 Gullan's close (264)...	206	209	38	247	...	9	9	...	...	1	...	...	2	1	...
22 Haddington's en. (80)	145	79	10	89	1	...	1	...	...	...	...	...	...	...	...
23 High School cl. (307)	207	27	2	29	...	1	1	...	...	...	...	...	...	...	...
24 House of Refuge (64)	138	405	10	415	14	1	15	4	2	2	...	1	...	...	...
25 Hume's close (307)	211	170	30	200	5	1	6	...	...	2	2	...	...	...	...
26 Jack's close, Big (225)	181	191	43	234	4	4	8	...	1	1	...	1	...	1	...
27 Do. do. Little (223)	184	169	31	200	2	6	8	...	...	3	...	...	...	1	...
28 Lochend's close (107)	152	298	51	349	4	9	13	...	...	3	1	...	2	1	...
29 Do. do. Little (115)	153	115	22	137	2	2	4	...	...	...	1	...	...	...	...
30 Logan's close (287)...	207	29	5	34	...	2	2	...	...	...	...	...	...	...	...
31 Macdowell street ...	149	207	31	238	3	8	11	...	...	1	1	1	1	1	...
32 Magdalene asylum ...	174	66	...	66	...	...	...	...	...	...	...	...	...	...	...
33 Malloch's close (75)	144	83	23	106	...	2	2	...	...	...	...	...	...	...	...
34 Midcommon cl. (295)	207	130	23	153	1	7	8	1	...	1	1	...	...	...	1
35 Miller's close (171)...	173	69	17	86	1	...	1	...	...	...	...	1	...	...	...
36 Milne's close (212) ...	195	120	24	144	1	2	3	...	...	...	...	...	...	...	...
37 Morocco close (273)	202	133	25	158	5	1	6	...	...	...	...	...	...	...	..
38 Morocco court.........	202	17	...	17				1	...	...	...	3	...	...	...
39 Munro's close (119)	154	34	7	41	...	...	...	...	...	...	...	...	...	...	...
40 New street	139—190	358	64	422	6	8	14	2	1	...	...	...	2	...	3
41 ...Riddle's entry (35)	176	95	19	114	3	2	5	...	1	1	...	2	...	...	...
42 ...Walker's place (25)	188	47	6	53	...	1	1	...	...	...	...	...	...	...	...
Carry forward, ...		7363	1136	8499	143	142	285	20	14	40	14	26	14	8	5

8. District of Abbey—*Continued.*

	1863.													No. of Paupers.	Street Cesspools.			Epidemics.		
	Scarlatina.	Measles.	Hooping-Cough.	Erysipelas.	Fevers. Total.	Fevers. Typhus.	Fevers. Typhoid.	Fevers. Gastric.	Fevers. Infantile.	Diarrhœa and Dysentery.	Scrofula.	Old Age.	Premature Debility.		Trapped.	Untrapped.	Total.	Cholera. 1848.	Fever. 1847-8.	Fever. 1857-8.
	...	7	...	...	5	3	...	1	1	2	8	...	5	36	22	5	27	3	13	...
12	...	...	...	...	...	...	...	...	...	...	...	...	...	...	...	...	...	...	1	...
1	...	...	...	...	...	...	...	...	...	...	...	...	...	...	...	...	...	...	...	...
2	...	...	...	...	...	...	...	...	...	...	...	...	...	...	...	...	...	...	...	...
13	...	...	...	...	...	...	...	...	...	...	...	...	...	...	...	5	5	1	2	...
1	...	...	...	...	...	...	...	...	...	...	...	1	...	...	...	...	...	...	...	...
	...	7	...	...	5	3	...	1	1	2	8	1	5	36	22	10	32	4	16	...

9. District of Canongate.

	Scarlatina.	Measles.	Hooping-Cough.	Erysipelas.	Fevers. Total.	Fevers. Typhus.	Fevers. Typhoid.	Fevers. Gastric.	Fevers. Infantile.	Diarrhœa and Dysentery.	Scrofula.	Old Age.	Premature Debility.	No. of Paupers.	Trapped.	Untrapped.	Total.	Cholera. 1848.	Fever. 1847-8.	Fever. 1857-8.
1	4	4	1	...	6	6	...	...	...	4	4	3	2	92	19	...	19	18	568	9
1	...	...	...	...	...	...	...	...	...	...	1	...	...	9	2	...	2	2	2	...
2	...	...	...	...	...	...	...	...	...	...	...	...	...	2	3	...	3	...	...	...
3	...	3	...	...	2	...	...	1	1	...	...	...	...	3	6	...	6	1	...	...
4	1	1	...	...	1	...	...	1	...	...	1	...	...	16	...	1	1	...	4	...
5	...	...	...	...	...	...	...	...	...	...	...	...	...	...	2	...	2	...	...	...
6	...	...	...	...	...	...	...	...	...	...	...	...	2	3	4	...	4	...	...	...
7	...	...	...	...	...	...	...	...	...	1	...	...	...	...	2	...	2	...	...	...
8	...	1	...	...	2	1	...	...	1	...	...	1	2	23	4	...	4	4	14	1
9	...	1	...	...	1	1	...	...	...	...	...	4	...	69	...	...	...	...	...	...
10	...	...	...	...	...	...	...	...	...	...	...	...	...	...	...	...	...	...	1	...
11	...	...	...	...	...	...	...	...	...	...	...	...	1	9	1	...	1	1	...	...
12	...	...	...	...	...	...	...	...	...	...	...	1	...	3	1	...	1	...	...	...
13	...	...	...	...	...	...	...	...	...	...	1	...	...	13	4	...	4	1	1	...
14	...	1	...	...	1	...	...	1	...	...	...	...	1	3	4	1	5	5	1	...
15	...	...	...	...	...	...	...	...	...	...	...	...	...	5	1	...	1	3	...	...
16	...	...	...	...	...	...	...	...	...	...	...	...	...	...	2	...	2	...	...	...
17	...	...	...	...	...	...	...	...	...	...	...	...	...	2	1	...	1	1	...	...
18	...	...	...	...	...	...	...	...	...	...	1	...	...	...	2	...	2	...	...	...
19	...	...	...	...	...	...	...	...	...	...	...	...	...	7	...	...	...	...	...	...
20	...	...	...	...	...	...	...	...	...	...	...	...	...	1	...	...	...	...	...	...
21	...	3	...	...	...	...	...	...	...	...	1	...	1	12	6	...	6	1	7	...
22	...	...	...	...	...	...	...	...	...	1	...	...	...	4	2	...	2	...	...	...
23	...	...	...	...	...	...	...	...	...	...	...	...	...	3	...	...	...	...	...	...
24	...	...	...	...	...	...	...	...	...	1	1	2	...	1	...	...	...	8	58	..
25	...	...	...	...	...	...	...	...	...	...	...	1	...	18	...	...	...	3	...	...
26	2	...	...	...	...	...	...	...	...	...	2	...	...	15	...	...	...	...	1	...
27	...	...	...	...	1	...	1	...	...	...	1	...	1	11	3	1	4	...	...	...
28	1	1	...	...	...	...	...	...	...	...	...	1	2	18	2	...	2	1	1	...
29	1	...	...	...	...	...	...	...	...	...	...	...	1	1	1	...	1	...	...	...
30	...	1	...	...	...	...	...	...	...	...	1	...	...	...	3	...	3	...	...	...
31	...	2	...	...	...	...	...	...	...	...	2	1	1	...	2	2	4	...	2	...
32	...	...	...	...	...	...	...	...	...	...	...	...	...	...	...	...	...	...	...	...
33	1	1	...	...	...	...	...	...	...	...	...	...	...	3	...	1	1	...	2	...
34	...	2	...	...	...	...	...	...	...	1	1	...	...	1	1	...	1	...	...	...
35	...	...	...	...	...	...	...	...	...	...	...	...	...	1	2	...	2	2	1	...
36	...	...	...	...	...	...	...	...	...	...	1	...	1	11	1	...	1	3	...	...
37	...	...	1	...	...	...	...	...	...	...	...	...	...	16	3	...	3	3	...	...
38																				
39	...	...	...	...	...	...	...	...	...	...	...	...	...	...	1	...	1	...	...	...
40	...	...	...	...	1	1	...	...	...	...	1	...	2	18	6	...	6	5	2	...
41	...	...	...	...	...	...	...	...	...	...	1	...	...	1	...	...	...	...	...	...
42	...	...	1	...	...	...	...	...	...	...	...	...	...	...	...	...	...	...	3	...
	10	21	3	...	15	9	1	3	2	8	20	14	17	394	91	6	97	62	668	10

TABLE No. VI.—NEW SANITARY DISTRICTS,

9. District of Canongate—*Continued.*

Name of Street.	Height in feet above the sea.	Population 1861. Above 5.	Population 1861. Under 5.	Population 1861. Total.	Mortality 1863. Above 5.	Mortality 1863. Under 5.	Mortality 1863. Total.	Diseases in Brain.	Heart.	Chest.	Abdomen.	Phthisis.	Croup.	Diphtheria.	Small-Pox.
Brought forward,		7363	1136	8499	143	142	285	20	14	40	14	26	14	8	5
43 Old Fleshmarket cl. (333)	212	182	25	207	2	2	4	...	...	...	1	...	...	...	...
44 ... Ramsay's court...	212	59	10	69	...	1	1	...	...	...	...	...	...	...	...
45 Playhouse close (200)	189	35	6	41	2	...	2	1	...	...	...	1	...	...	...
46 Do. do., Old (196)	188	54	8	62	...	...	...	...	...	...	...	...	...	...	...
47 Panmure close (129)	160	70	18	88	1	...	1	...	...	...	...	1	...	...	...
48 Pirrie's close (246)...	204	120	25	145	1	3	4	...	...	2	...	...	...	...	...
49 Plainstone close (232)	200	119	20	139	...	...	...	...	...	...	...	...	...	...	...
50 Rae's close (281)......	204	54	8	62	...	...	...	...	...	...	...	...	...	...	...
51 Ramsay's close (41)	126	17	2	19	2	...	2	...	...	...	...	...	...	...	...
52 Reid's close (80)......	145	125	23	148	...	...	...	...	...	...	...	...	...	...	...
53 Reid's court (95)......	150	29	1	30	...	...	...	...	...	...	...	...	...	...	...
54 St John's close (188)	184	78	9	87	1	...	1	...	1	...	...	...	...	...	...
55 St John's street	164—180	355	42	397	7	2	9	2	...	1	...	2	...	...	...
56 Seton's close (265) ...	202	41	15	56	...	...	...	...	...	...	...	...	...	...	...
57 Shoemaker's cl. (215)	180	241	48	289	9	5	14	...	2	2	...	1	...	...	...
58 Strathie's close (86)	147	30	3	33	1	2	3	1	...	...	...	1	...	1	...
59 Tolbooth wynd (165)	172	81	20	101	...	1	1	...	...	...	...	...	1	...	...
60 Vallance's entry (72)	141	32	3	35	...	...	...	...	...	...	...	...	...	...	...
61 Weir's close (206) ...	192	55	7	62	1	2	3	1	1	...	...	...	...	...	...
62 Wilson's court (134)	167	61	8	69	1	...	1	1	...	...	...	...	...	...	...
63 Whitehorse close (31)	124	189	23	212	4	12	16	1	1	3	1	...	...	...	...
2 Canongate, N. Back ...	117—147	294	47	341	3	2	5	...	...	...	2	...	...	...	...
1 Amphion place	140	186	33	219	...	...	...	...	...	...	...	...	...	...	...
2 Burns' land............	133	...	...	...	...	1	1	...	...	...	...	...	1	...	...
3 Calton, High	147—167	149	24	173	1	3	4	...	...	...	1	...	...	...	...
4 Calton, Low	151	14	3	17	...	...	...	...	...	...	...	...	...	...	...
5 Miller's entry (92) ...	146	63	10	73	...	...	...	...	...	...	...	...	...	...	...
3 Canongate, S. Back ...	118—190	299	59	358	12	7	19	5	2	4	...	1	...	...	1
1 Chalmers' court (81)	167	2	...	2	...	...	...	...	...	...	...	...	...	...	...
2 Clermiston buildings	140	...	...	...	...	1	1	...	...	1	...	...	...	...	...
3 Holyrood street	132	140	27	167	4	...	4	2	1	...	...	1	...	...	...
Totals,....................		10,537	1663	12,200	195	186	381	34	22	53	19	34	16	9	6

10. District of Tron.

Name of Street.	Height in feet above the sea.	Population 1861. Above 5.	Population 1861. Under 5.	Population 1861. Total.	Mortality 1863. Above 5.	Mortality 1863. Under 5.	Mortality 1863. Total.	Diseases in Brain.	Heart.	Chest.	Abdomen.	Phthisis.	Croup.	Diphtheria.	Small-Pox.
1 Adam square	243	15	2	17	...	...	...	...	...	...	...	...	...	...	...
2 Bridge street, North ...	220—253	106	18	124	2	...	2	...	1	...	1	...	...	...	...
3 Bridge street, South ...	243—256	305	41	346	2	6	8	1	2	...	...	...	...	...	...
4 Cowgate, from South Bridge eastwards ...	189—211	910	160	1070	19	26	45	5	1	5	2	5	1	1	...
1 Bull's close (307) ...	196	45	13	58	...	1	1	...	...	...	...	...	...	...	...
2 Hall's court (230) ...	204	54	8	62	...	2	2	...	...	1	...	...	1	...	...
3 High School wd.(387)	200—213	110	18	128	1	3	4	...	1	1	...	...	...	...	...
4 Robertson's cl. (263)	205—239	117	12	129	1	1	2	...	...	...	...	...	...	...	...
5 High School yards......	218	191	28	219	6	6	12	...	1	1	1	1	1	1	...
6 Surgeon's square.........	226	6	2	8	...	...	...	...	...	...	...	...	...	...	...
7 High street, from South Bridge eastwards ...	256—226	370	60	430	23	14	37	1	5	5	1	3	2	1	1
1 Bailie Fyfe's cl. (101)	238	126	15	141	4	1	5	...	...	2	1	1	...	...	...
2 Barringer's close (91)	235	80	16	96	...	2	2	...	...	...	...	...	...	...	...
3 Bishop's close (129)	248	109	11	120	1	1	2	...	...	1	...	...	1	...	...
Carry forward,....................		2544	404	2948	59	63	122	7	11	16	6	10	6	3	1

9. District of Canongate—*Continued.*

	1863. Scarlatina.	Measles.	Hooping-Cough.	Erysipelas.	Fevers. Total.	Typhus.	Typhoid.	Gastric.	Infantile.	Diarrhœa and Dysentery.	Scrofula.	Old Age.	Premature Debility.	No. of Paupers.	Street Cesspools. Trapped.	Untrapped.	Total.	Epidemics. Cholera. 1848.	Fever. 1847-8.	Fever. 1857-8.
	10	21	3	...	15	9	1	3	2	8	20	14	17	394	91	6	97	62	668	10
43	...	...	...	...	1	...	1	...	...	...	...	...	1	4	2	1	3	2	...	...
44	...	...	...	...	...	...	...	...	...	...	...	...	...	...	...	...	...	...	...	...
45	...	...	...	...	...	...	...	...	...	...	...	...	...	4	...	...	...	...	1	...
46	...	...	...	...	...	...	...	...	...	...	...	...	...	...	2	...	2	...	...	...
47	...	...	...	...	...	...	...	...	...	...	...	...	...	...	5	...	5	3	...	...
48	...	...	...	...	...	...	...	...	...	...	1	...	1	12	2	...	2	...	...	...
49	...	...	...	...	...	...	...	...	...	...	...	...	...	12	2	...	2	...	...	...
50	...	...	...	...	...	...	...	...	...	...	...	...	...	5	3	...	3	...	...	...
51	...	...	...	...	...	...	...	...	...	...	...	...	...	...	1	...	1	...	...	...
52	...	...	...	...	...	...	...	...	...	...	...	...	...	6	3	...	3	...	1	1
53	...	...	...	...	...	...	...	...	...	...	...	...	...	...	1	...	1	...	...	...
54	...	...	...	...	...	...	...	...	...	...	...	...	...	4	1	...	1	...	...	...
55	...	...	...	...	...	...	...	...	...	...	2	2	...	...	...	2	2	...	4	...
56	...	...	...	...	...	...	...	...	...	...	...	...	...	1	2	...	2	1	4	...
57	1	...	...	...	2	1	...	...	1	...	1	3	1	11	3	1	4	1	2	...
58	...	...	...	...	...	...	...	...	...	...	...	...	...	4	2	...	2	...	1	...
59	...	...	...	...	...	...	...	...	...	...	...	...	...	9	4	2	6	1	...	...
60	...	...	...	...	...	...	...	...	...	...	...	...	...	1	1	...	1	...	...	...
61	...	...	...	...	...	...	...	...	...	...	1	...	...	1	2	...	2	2	...	...
62	...	...	...	...	...	...	...	...	...	...	...	...	...	...	2	...	2	1	...	...
63	...	4	...	...	1	...	1	...	...	...	2	...	1	44	3	...	3	15	1	1
2	...	...	...	...	...	...	...	...	...	...	...	...	1	...	9	11	20	...	...	...
1	...	...	...	...	...	...	...	...	...	...	...	...	...	1	...	...	...	...	1	...
2	...	...	...	...	...	...	...	...	...	...	...	...	...	...	...	...	...	...	...	...
3	...	...	...	...	...	...	...	...	...	...	...	1	...	1	...	...	...	...	4	...
4	...	...	...	...	...	...	...	...	...	...	...	...	...	...	...	...	...	...	4	...
5	...	...	...	...	...	...	...	...	...	...	...	...	...	...	...	...	...	...	...	...
3	...	...	...	...	1	...	1	...	...	...	...	...	2	5	11	4	15	...	...	...
1	...	...	...	...	...	...	...	...	...	...	...	...	...	...	...	...	...	...	...	...
2	...	...	...	...	...	...	...	...	...	...	...	...	...	...	...	...	...	...	...	...
3	...	...	...	...	...	...	...	...	...	...	...	...	...	1	...	...	...	...	1	...
	11	25	3	...	20	10	4	3	3	8	27	20	24	520	152	27	179	88	692	12

10. District of Tron.

	Scarlatina.	Measles.	Hooping-Cough.	Erysipelas.	Fevers. Total.	Typhus.	Typhoid.	Gastric.	Infantile.	Diarrhœa and Dysentery.	Scrofula.	Old Age.	Premature Debility.	No. of Paupers.	Trapped.	Untrapped.	Total.	Cholera. 1848.	Fever. 1847-8.	Fever. 1857-8.
1	...	...	...	...	...	...	...	...	...	...	...	...	...	...	...	...	...	...	...	...
2	...	...	...	...	...	...	...	...	...	...	...	...	...	...	3	1	4	...	1	...
3	1	2	...	...	...	...	...	...	...	...	1	...	...	1	6	2	8	1	9	...
4	...	6	2	...	1	1	...	...	...	2	2	...	3	62	4	...	4	11	566	2
1	...	1	...	...	...	...	...	...	...	...	...	...	...	4	1	...	1	8	2	...
2	...	...	...	...	...	...	...	...	...	...	...	...	...	1	...	...	...	3	2	1
3	...	1	...	...	...	...	...	...	...	...	...	...	...	15	1	1	2	2	8	...
4	...	...	...	...	...	...	...	...	...	...	...	1	1	8	1	...	1	3	3	1
5	1	...	...	...	...	...	...	...	...	1	...	...	1	12	...	1	1	...	7	...
6	...	...	...	...	...	...	...	...	...	...	...	...	...	...	...	...	...	2	4	...
7	2	4	...	...	6	2	2	...	2	1	...	...	2	15	3	2	5	3	256	2
1	...	...	...	...	...	...	...	...	...	...	...	...	...	27	4	...	4	8	7	1
2	...	...	...	...	...	...	...	...	...	...	2	...	...	4	2	...	2	1	...	...
3	...	...	...	...	...	...	...	...	...	...	...	...	...	3	...	...	...	...	...	...
	4	14	2	...	7	3	2	...	2	4	5	1	7	152	25	7	32	42	865	7

TABLE No. VI.—New Sanitary Districts,

10. District of Tron—*Continued.*

Name of Street.	Height in feet above the sea.	Population 1861.			Mortality 1863.			Diseases in							
		Above 5.	Under 5.	Total.	Above 5.	Under 5.	Total.	Brain.	Heart.	Chest.	Abdomen.	Phthisis.	Croup.	Diphtheria.	Small-Pox.
Brought forward,		2544	404	2948	59	63	122	7	11	16	6	10	6	3	1
4 Blackfriars' wynd (96)	200—243	785	123	908	16	25	41	3	1	9	2	2	2	...	1
5 ... Hodge's court ...	200	85	12	97	...	2	2	...	...	...	...	...	...	...	...
6 Cant's close (108) ...	248	226	33	259	3	4	7	...	...	2	...	...	...	1	...
7 Carrubber's cl. (135)	250	557	85	642	16	9	25	1	1	6	2	4	2	...	...
8 Chalmers' close (81)	232	337	59	396	1	3	4	...	...	1	...	...	1	1	...
9 ... Milne's buildings	194	[61	11	72]	...	1	1	...	...	1	...	...	...	...	...
10 Dickson's close (118)	250	276	44	320	4	14	18	1	...	6	1	1	...	...	...
11 Foulis' cl., South (42)	227	324	43	367	4	8	12	2	...	5	...	...	...	...	...
12 Gray's cl., North (125)	246	131	24	155	...	4	4	...	...	2	...	...	...	...	...
13 Do. do. South (56)	232	143	20	163	2	1	3	...	...	...	...	...	...	...	...
14 ... Elphinstone court	200	86	11	97	...	...	...	...	...	...	...	...	...	...	...
15 ... Mint	196	136	24	160	3	1	4	...	...	...	1	...	...	...	...
16 Halkerston's wd. (163)	254	8	1	9	...	1	1	...	...	...	...	...	...	...	...
17 Hyndford's close (50)	230	194	31	225	4	9	13	1	...	3	...	1	...	...	...
18 Kinloch's close (149)	253	2	...	2	...	...	...	...	...	...	...	...	...	...	...
19 Monteith's close (61)	230	198	27	225	6	4	10	2	...	5	1	...	...	...	...
20 ... Ironside court ...	190	24	2	26	1	...	1	1	...	...	...	...	...	...	...
21 Morrison's close (117)	243	132	29	161	2	4	6	1	...	2	...	1	...	...	...
22 Murdoch's close (68)	236	74	8	82	...	1	1	1	...	...	...	...	...	...	...
23 Paisley close (101) ...	238	240	35	275	2	2	4	...	...	2	...	...	...	...	...
24 Sandiland's close (71)	231	37	10	47	...	2	2	...	...	...	...	...	...	...	...
25 Skinner's close (64)	235	223	30	253	6	8	14	1	...	8	...	...	...	1	...
26 Strichen's close (104)	246	57	7	64	...	2	2	1	...	...	...	...	...	...	...
27 Toddrick's wynd (80)	238	396	62	458	4	8	12	2	1	5	...	1	...	...	...
28 Trunk's close (55) ...	228	155	22	177	...	7	7	1	...	2	...	...	...	...	...
29 ... Chapel Court......	198	68	13	81	...	...	...	...	...	...	...	...	...	...	...
8 Netherbow	215—226	...	...	...	...	...	...	...	...	...	...	...	...	...	...
1 Baron Grant's cl. (15)	220	60	12	72	...	...	...	...	...	...	...	...	...	...	...
2 Fountain close (28)	225	249	44	293	1	9	10	1	...	1	...	1	1	...	...
3 Society close (21) ...	221	15	2	17	...	...	...	...	...	...	...	...	...	...	...
4 ... Ashley buildings	215	145	33	178	2	...	2	1	...	...	...	...	...	...	...
5 ... Ashley court......	215	51	11	62	...	1	1	...	...	...	...	...	...	...	...
6 Tweeddale court (16)	221	65	14	79	1	4	5	1	...	2	...	1	2	...	...
7 World's End cl. (10)	221	83	5	88	...	...	...	...	...	...	...	...	...	...	...
9 Leith wynd...............	152—210	403	63	466	5	5	10	...	...	2	...	...	...	...	...
1 Canal court (33)	160	91	26	117	1	5	6	...	...	...	1	...	...	...	...
2 Douglas' court (63)	158	90	11	101	...	...	...	...	...	...	...	...	...	...	...
3 Shepherd's court (47)	166	38	7	45	1	...	1	...	1	...	...	...	...	...	...
4 Well close (33)	178	...	...	...	...	2	2	1	...	1	...	...	...	...	...
10 St Mary's wynd.........	189—215	589	91	680	10	19	29	4	...	6	3	2	1	...	...
1 Boyd's entry	201	60	18	78	...	1	1	...	...	...	...	...	...	...	...
11 Royal Infirmary.........	226—239	470	8	478	4	1	5	1	...	1	1	1	...	...	...
12 Infirmary street.........	227—247	57	1	58	3	...	3	...	1	1	...	...	...	...	...
13 Niddry street............	252	107	12	119	4	2	6	...	...	3	1	1	...	...	...
14 Do. do. South ...	208	33	5	38	2	1	3	...	1	...	...	...	...	...	...
15 Physic gardens	147—164	61	9	70	2	...	2	...	...	...	...	2	...	...	...
Totals..........................		10,105	1531	11,636	169	233	402	34	17	92	19	28	15	6	2

10. District of Tron—*Continued.*

	1863.													No. of Paupers.	Street Cesspools.			Epidemics.		
	Scarlatina.	Measles.	Hooping-Cough.	Erysipelas.	Fevers.					Diarrhœa and Dysentery.	Scrofula.	Old Age.	Premature Debility.		Trapped.	Untrapped.	Total.	Cholera.	Fever.	
					Total.	Typhus.	Typhoid.	Gastric.	Infantile.									1848.	1847-8.	1857-8.
	4	14	2	...	7	3	2	...	2	4	5	1	7	152	25	7	32	42	865	7
4	...	6	1	...	1	...	...	...	1	...	3	...	5	39	1	...	1	15	71	7
5	...	2	...	...	...	...	...	...	...	...	...	...	...	...	...	...	...	...	...	...
6	...	1	...	...	1	1	...	...	...	1	...	...	...	12	5	...	5	6	8	...
7	...	1	1	...	...	...	...	...	...	...	2	2	2	33	7	...	7	2	2	...
8	...	...	...	...	1	...	...	1	...	...	...	...	...	13	4	...	4	1	7	...
9	...	...	...	...	...	...	...	...	...	...	...	...	...	2	...	...	...	...	...	...
10	...	4	2	...	...	...	...	...	...	...	2	...	1	39	5	...	5	2	9	3
11	...	1	1	...	...	...	...	...	...	...	1	...	1	36	2	...	2	8	...	...
12	1	...	...	...	...	...	...	...	...	...	...	...	...	9	5	...	5	5	5	...
13	...	...	1	...	1	...	1	...	...	1	...	...	...	14	3	...	3	2	7	1
14	...	...	...	...	...	...	...	...	...	...	...	...	...	5	...	...	...	1	...	...
15	...	...	...	...	1	1	...	...	...	...	1	...	...	4	...	...	...	1	...	...
16	...	...	...	...	...	...	...	...	...	...	...	...	...	1	2	...	2	...	...	...
17	...	2	...	...	...	...	...	...	...	2	1	...	1	15	2	...	2	4	5	...
18	...	...	...	...	...	...	...	...	...	...	...	...	...	...	...	...	...	...	1	...
19	...	...	...	...	...	...	...	...	...	1	...	...	1	19	4	...	4	1	1	...
20	...	...	...	...	...	...	...	...	...	...	...	...	...	...	...	...	...	...	...	...
21	...	...	...	...	...	...	...	...	...	1	1	...	...	6	2	...	2	2	...	...
22	...	...	...	...	...	...	...	...	...	...	...	...	...	12	2	...	2	...	...	...
23	...	...	...	...	...	...	...	...	...	...	1	...	...	11	...	...	...	...	...	...
24	...	1	...	...	...	...	...	...	...	...	...	...	1	6	1	...	1	...	2	...
25	...	1	1	...	...	...	...	...	...	..	1	...	1	23	2	...	2	2	21	...
26	...	1	...	...	...	...	...	...	...	...	...	...	...	...	...	...	...	...	1	...
27	...	1	...	...	...	...	...	...	...	1	...	...	...	56	5	...	5	15	56	...
28	...	2	...	...	...	...	...	...	...	...	...	...	...	11	3	...	3	1	...	...
29	...	...	...	...	...	...	...	...	...	...	...	...	...	...	...	...	...	...	...	...
8	...	...	...	...	...	...	...	...	...	...	...	...	...	...	...	...	...	...	34	...
1	...	...	...	...	...	...	...	...	...	...	...	...	...	8	1	1	2	2	...	...
2	...	4	...	...	...	...	...	...	...	1	1	...	...	14	3	...	3	3	2	...
3	...	...	...	...	...	...	...	...	...	...	...	...	...	...	3	...	3	2	...	...
4	...	...	...	...	...	...	...	...	...	...	...	...	...	8	...	...	...	...	...	...
5	1	...	...	...	...	...	...	...	...	...	...	...	...	...	...	...	...	...	...	...
6	...	...	2	...	...	...	...	...	...	...	...	...	...	2	3	...	3	1	...	...
7	...	...	...	...	...	...	...	...	...	...	...	...	...	1	...	...	...	...	...	...
9	...	...	...	...	1	...	1	..	...	1	...	...	...	19	5	4	9	10	71	1
1	...	2	...	...	...	...	...	...	...	...	1	...	1	6	...	...	...	...	3	...
2	...	...	...	...	...	...	...	...	...	...	...	...	...	2	...	...	...	...	...	...
3	...	...	...	...	...	...	...	...	...	...	...	...	...	...	...	...	...	1	...	...
4	...	...	...	...	...	...	...	...	...	...	...	...	...	4	...	...	...	3	2	...
10	...	4	...	...	1	...	1	...	...	...	2	1	1	35	4	...	4	15	34	3
1	...	1	...	...	...	...	...	...	...	...	...	...	...	5	2	...	2	...	2	...
11	...	...	...	...	1	1	...	...	...	...	...	...	...	...	...	...	...	18	102	2
12	...	...	...	...	1	1	...	...	...	...	...	...	..	...	1	1	2	...	5	1
13	...	...	...	...	...	...	...	...	...	...	...	...	...	13	1	2	3	...	2	...
14	...	...	...	...	...	...	...	...	...	...	1	1	...	5	2	...	2	...	...	...
15	...	...	...	...	...	...	...	...	...	...	...	...	...	...	4	5	9	...	2	...
	6	48	11	...	16	7	5	1	3	13	23	5	22	640	109	20	129	165	1320	25

TABLE No. VI.—New Sanitary Districts,

11. District of St Giles.

Name of Street.	Height in feet above the sea.	Population 1861.			Mortality 1863.			Diseases in							
		Above 5.	Under 5.	Total.	Above 5.	Under 5.	Total.	Brain.	Heart.	Chest.	Abdomen.	Phthisis.	Croup.	Diphtheria	Small-Pox.
1 Argyle square	264—272	160	14	174	2	...	2	1	...	...	...	...	...	...	...
2 Bank street	281—290	155	17	172	1	2	3	...	...	...	...	...	...	...	...
3 Bank street, North	260—281	25	6	31	...	...	...	...	...	...	...	...	...	...	...
4 Blair street	211—254	256	54	310	1	4	5	...	...	...	...	...	2	...	...
5 Brown square	271	84	4	88	1	...	1	1	...	...	...	...	...	...	...
6 Candlemaker row	233—270	407	59	466	6	4	10	...	1	2	2	1	1	...	...
7 Castle	437	816	38	854	11	4	15	2	...	4	...	1	2	...	...
8 Castlebank	260	...	...	...	1	...	1	...	...	...	...	1	...	...	...
9 Castlehill	332	232	41	273	1	8	9	1	...	3	...	...	1	...	...
1 Blair's close (400)	330	114	16	130	...	1	1	...	...	1	...	...	...	...	...
2 Boswell's court (392)	320	65	7	72	1	1	2	...	1	...	...	...	...	...	...
3 Brown's close (385)	330	10	1	11	...	...	...	...	...	...	...	...	...	...	...
4 Brown's court (396)	328	...	...	...	...	...	...	...	...	...	...	...	...	...	...
5 Castle wynd (386)	291—332	...	...	...	...	...	...	...	...	...	...	...	...	...	...
6 Jollie's close (595)	...	...	...	...	...	...	...	...	...	...	...	...	...	...	...
7 Ramsay gardens	309	36	3	39	1	...	1	...	...	1	...	...	...	...	...
8 Do. lane	330	...	...	...	2	...	2	...	...	...	1	1	...	...	...
9 Do. lodge	307	...	...	...	2	...	2	...	...	...	1	...	...	...	...
10 ... Orig. Ragged Sch.	320	85	...	85	...	...	...	...	...	...	...	...	...	...	...
11 Rockville close (388)	318	24	3	27	...	...	...	...	...	...	...	...	...	...	...
12 Semple close (541)	316	...	...	...	...	...	...	...	...	...	...	...	...	...	...
10 Lawnmarket	287—304	352	47	399	13	13	26	...	1	6	1	6	...	...	1
1 Baxter's close (469)	297	139	13	152	1	3	4	...	...	1	...	...	...	...	2
2 Brodie's close (304)	296	...	...	...	...	...	...	...	...	...	...	...	...	...	...
3 Brown's close (385)	290	11	2	13	...	...	...	...	...	...	...	...	...	...	...
4 Buchanan's court (300)	296	16	2	18	...	...	...	...	...	...	...	...	...	...	...
5 Cranston's close (517)	302	12	...	12	...	...	...	...	...	...	...	...	...	...	...
6 Dunbar's close (413)	291	44	7	51	...	1	1	...	...	1	...	...	...	...	...
7 Fisher's close (312)	299	64	7	71	1	1	2	...	...	...	...	...	1	...	...
8 Galloway's close (425)	292	4	1	5	...	...	...	...	...	...	...	...	...	...	...
9 James' court (501)	302	330	50	380	4	...	4	...	...	1	2	1	...	...	...
10 Johnston's close (332)	302	61	8	69	...	...	...	...	...	...	...	...	...	...	...
11 Lady Stair's cl. (477)	300	64	1	65	2	...	2	...	...	...	...	...	...	...	...
12 Milne's court (517)	303	350	74	424	} 6	3	9	1	1	2	...	1	...	...	...
13 Milne's entry (527)	304	68	10	78											
14 Paterson's court (441)	294	45	6	51	...	...	...	...	...	...	...	...	...	...	...
15 Riddle's close (322)	301	153	30	183	1	7	8	1	...	...	...	...	...	...	...
16 Seller's close	290	49	8	57	...	...	...	...	...	...	...	...	...	...	...
17 Wardrop's court (459)	295	115	17	132	2	3	5	1	...	...	...	...	...	...	...
11 High street (east to Bridges)	287—260	413	41	454	17	7	24	...	...	2	3	5	...	...	1
1 Advocate's cl. (357)	288	351	73	424	3	4	7	1	...	...	1	...	...	1	...
2 Allan's close (269)	277	8	1	9	1	...	1	...	...	...	...	...	...	...	...
3 Do. court (269)	215	...	...	...	...	...	...	...	...	...	...	...	...	...	...
4 Anchor close (243)	271	58	5	63	...	...	...	...	...	...	...	...	...	...	...
5 Bell's wynd (146)	268	236	41	277	5	2	7	1	1	3	...	...	...	...	...
6 Borthwick's cl. (190)	276	184	40	224	2	4	6	...	1	1	1	...	...	...	...
7 Burnet's close (156)	269	131	23	154	1	2	3	...	1	...	...	...	1	...	...
8 Byre's close (373)	290	40	11	51	...	...	...	...	...	...	...	...	...	...	...
9 Conn's close (162)	271	69	19	88	...	3	3	...	...	3	...	...	...	...	...
10 Covenant close (162)	270	198	27	225	1	5	6	1	...	1	...	...	...	...	...
11 Craig's close (265)	277	104	21	125	3	6	9	...	1	2	...	...	...	1	...
12 Fishmarket	189	27	5	32	1	3	4	...	...	1	...	...	...	...	...
13 Fleshmarket cl. (199)	260	142	17	159	...	4	4	...	...	...	...	...	...	...	...
14 Foulis cl., North (229)	268	32	4	36	1	...	1	...	...	...	...	...	...	...	...
15 Geddes' close (233)	267	46	7	53	1	...	1	...	...	...	1	...	...	...	...
Carry forward,		6385	881	7266	96	95	191	11	8	35	13	17	8	2	4

11. District of St Giles.

	1863.														Street Cesspools.			Epidemics.		
					Fevers.													Cholera.	Fever.	
	Scarlatina.	Measles.	Hooping-Cough.	Erysipelas.	Total.	Typhus.	Typhoid.	Gastric.	Infantile.	Diarrhœa and Dysentery.	Scrofula.	Old Age.	Premature Debility.	No. of Paupers.	Trapped.	Untrapped.	Total.	1848.	1847-8.	1857-8
1	...	...	...	...	...	...	...	...	...	...	...	1	...	...	...	...	...	...	...	...
2	...	...	1	...	1	...	...	...	1	...	1	...	...	7	...	...	...	...	8	...
3	...	...	...	...	...	...	...	...	...	...	...	...	...	...	...	...	...	...	...	...
4	...	1	...	...	...	...	...	...	...	...	1	...	...	4	...	2	2	...	2	3
5	...	...	...	...	...	...	...	...	...	...	...	...	...	6	2	...	2	...	...	1
6	...	...	1	...	...	...	...	...	...	...	...	...	...	8	1	4	5	...	25	...
7	1	...	...	...	1	1	...	...	...	...	...	...	1	...	...	...	...	...	...	1
8	...	...	...	...	...	...	...	...	...	...	...	...	...	...	...	...	...	1	3	...
9	...	1	...	...	...	...	...	...	...	...	1	...	2	5	...	3	3	3	18	6
1	...	...	...	...	...	...	...	...	...	...	...	...	...	...	...	...	...	1	...	...
2	...	...	...	...	...	...	...	...	...	...	...	...	1	...	...	...	...	...	...	...
3	...	...	...	...	...	...	...	...	...	...	...	...	...	1	...	...	...	...	...	...
4	...	...	...	...	...	...	...	...	...	...	...	...	...	...	...	...	...	...	...	...
5	...	...	...	...	...	...	...	...	...	...	...	...	...	...	...	...	...	...	...	...
6	...	...	...	...	...	...	...	...	...	...	...	...	...	...	...	...	...	2	1	...
7	...	...	...	...	...	...	...	...	...	...	...	...	...	...	...	...	...	...	...	...
8	...	...	...	...	...	...	...	...	...	...	...	...	...	...	...	2	2	...	...	...
9	...	...	...	...	...	...	...	...	...	...	1	...	...	...	...	...	...	...	...	...
10	...	...	...	...	...	...	...	...	...	...	...	...	...	...	...	...	...	...	...	3
11	...	...	...	...	...	...	...	...	...	...	...	...	...	...	...	...	...	...	...	...
12	...	...	...	...	...	...	...	...	...	...	...	...	...	...	...	1	1	...	...	...
10	1	2	...	...	1	...	1	...	...	...	1	...	2	37	...	...	...	2	81	2
1	...	...	...	...	1	...	1	...	...	...	...	...	...	8	2	...	2	2	2	...
2	...	...	...	...	...	...	...	...	...	...	...	...	...	...	...	...	...	...	...	...
3	...	...	...	...	...	...	...	...	...	...	...	...	...	...	...	...	...	...	...	...
4	...	...	...	...	...	...	...	...	...	...	...	...	...	1	...	...	...	...	...	...
5	...	...	...	...	...	...	...	...	...	...	...	...	...	...	...	...	...	...	...	...
6	...	...	...	...	...	...	...	...	...	...	...	...	...	...	1	...	1	...	...	...
7	...	1	...	...	...	...	...	...	...	...	...	...	...	6	...	...	...	...	...	...
8	...	...	...	...	...	...	...	...	...	...	...	...	...	...	1	...	1	...	...	...
9	...	...	...	...	...	...	...	...	...	...	...	...	...	7	6	...	6	1	2	...
10	...	...	...	...	...	...	...	...	...	...	...	...	...	3	2	...	2	2	...	...
11	...	...	...	...	...	...	...	...	...	1	...	1	...	5	1	..	1	1	1	...
12 13	...	...	1	...	1	...	...	1	...	...	...	1	...	48	3	...	3	3	9	...
14	...	...	...	...	...	...	...	...	...	...	...	...	...	...	...	...	...	...	...	...
15	1	1	...	...	...	...	...	...	...	...	1	...	2	11	..	...	...	...	1	1
16	...	...	...	...	...	...	...	...	...	...	...	...	...	...	..	...	...	...	...	...
17	1	...	...	...	...	...	...	...	...	...	1	...	1	9	2	...	2	...	...	...
11	...	...	2	1	1	...	...	...	1	2	...	...	1	1	...	...	...	4	450	3
1	1	...	2	...	...	...	...	...	...	...	...	1	...	21	2	...	2	4	4	...
2	...	...	...	...	...	...	...	...	...	...	...	...	...	...	2	...	2	...	1	...
3	...	...	...	...	...	...	...	...	...	...	...	...	...	...	...	...	...	...	...	...
4	...	...	...	...	...	...	...	...	...	...	...	...	...	2	4	...	4	5	1	2
5	...	...	...	...	...	...	...	...	...	...	...	...	...	43	4	...	4	8	10	1
6	...	1	...	...	...	...	...	...	...	1	...	...	...	8	...	...	...	1	6	...
7	...	...	...	...	...	...	...	...	...	...	...	...	...	10	7	...	7	1	2	...
8	...	...	...	...	...	...	...	...	...	...	...	...	...	2	...	...	...	...	1	...
9	...	...	...	...	...	...	...	...	...	...	...	...	...	14	5	...	5	...	3	1
10	...	...	...	...	...	...	...	...	...	...	3	...	...	28	2	...	2	12	1	...
11	3	...	...	...	...	...	...	...	...	1	...	...	1	8	2	...	2	3	2	...
12	...	...	...	...	...	...	...	...	...	...	...	...	1	...	...	...	...	...	...	...
13	...	...	...	...	...	...	...	...	...	...	2	...	2	9	2	...	2	7	5	...
14	...	...	...	...	...	...	...	...	...	...	...	1	...	6	...	1	1	1	9	...
15	...	...	...	...	...	...	...	...	...	...	...	...	...	6	...	...	...	1	...	...
	8	7	7	1	6	1	2	1	2	5	12	5	14	324	51	13	64	65	648	24

TABLE No. VI.—New Sanitary Districts,

11. District of St Giles—*Continued.*

Name of Street.	Height in feet above the sea.	Population 1861.			Mortality 1863.			Diseases in							
		Above 5.	Under 5.	Total.	Above 5.	Under 5.	Total.	Brain.	Heart.	Chest.	Abdomen.	Phthisis.	Croup.	Diphtheria.	Small-Pox.
Brought forward,		6385	881	7266	96	95	191	11	8	35	13	17	8	2	4
16 Jackson's close (209)	260	63	7	70	2	1	3	1	...	...	...	...	...	...	...
17 Lyon's close (215) ...	261	17	2	19	1	...	1	...	...	...	...	1	...	...	...
18 Mary King's close ...	280	...	...	...	...	...	...	...	...	...	...	...	...	...	...
19 Milne's square (173)	259	197	25	222	1	4	5	...	...	1	...	...	1	...	...
20 Old Assembly close (170)	219—271	286	41	327	8	4	12	1	...	1	1	5	...	...	...
21 Old Fishmarket close (196)	223—274	295	75	370	6	5	11	...	...	4	1	1	...	1	...
22 ... Night Asylum ...	...	36	3	39	...	...	...	...	...	...	...	...	...	...	...
23 Old Post Office close (253)	270	...	...	...	...	...	...	...	...	...	...	...	...	...	...
24 Old Stamp Office close (221)	267	17	3	20	...	...	...	...	...	...	...	...	...	...	...
25 Roxburgh close (341)	287	37	2	39	...	...	...	...	...	...	...	...	...	...	...
26 Stevenlaw's cl. (134)	264	360	64	424	3	5	8	...	1	3	...	...	1	...	...
27 Writer's court (315)	284	120	28	148	...	3	3	...	1	...	...	...	...	...	1
28 Warriston close (332)	285	...	...	..	...	...	...	...	...	...	...	...	...	...	...
12 Cowgate, east to South Bridge	211—233	1438	263	1701	30	36	66	5	1	13	4	7	2	...	2
1 Allison's close (34) ...	232	216	32	248	4	8	12	...	...	3	...	...	1	...	...
2 Anderson's close (14)	233	25	9	34	1	...	1	...	...	...	...	1	...	...	...
3 Back close (138) ...	220	58	5	63	...	...	...	...	...	...	...	...	...	...	...
4 Baillie's court (50) ...	232	116	20	136	3	4	7	...	1	1	1	1	...	...	...
5 Barker's land (108)...	227	39	8	47	...	...	...	...	...	...	...	...	...	...	...
6 Brodie's close (52) ...	232	92	14	106	2	2	4	...	...	...	...	...	...	...	...
7 Campbell's cl. (109)	228	...	...	...	...	1	1	...	...	...	...	...	...	...	...
8 College wynd (205)...	212—252	459	87	546	17	15	32	2	2	7	...	2	2	1	...
9 ... Boswell's ct. (22)	...	59	19	78	...	...	...	...	...	...	...	...	...	...	...
10 ... Dick's court (17)	...	66	15	81	...	...	...	...	...	...	...	...	...	...	...
11 ... Good's entry (23)	...	...	...	...	...	...	...	...	...	...	...	...	...	...	...
12 Commercial ct. (247)	211	46	4	50	...	1	1	...	...	1	...	...	...	...	...
13 Cowan's close (95) ...	229	23	...	23	2	...	2	1	...	...	1	...	...	...	...
14 Cowgate head.........	233	66	13	79	5	...	5	2	1	...	...	1	...	...	...
15 Dick's close (195) ...	214	17	5	22	...	...	...	...	...	...	...	...	...	...	...
16 Forrester's wynd (98)	228	159	21	180	...	1	1	...	...	...	...	...	1	...	...
17 Hammerman's cl. (55)	231	61	5	66	1	1	2	2	...	..	...	...	...	...	...
18 Hastie's close (225)...	212	150	21	171	3	2	5	2	1	...	...	...	...	2	...
19 Heron's court (184)	222	49	10	59	1	1	2	...	...	...	...	1	...	...	...
20 Horse wynd (179) ...	216—254	339	46	385	8	4	12	...	2	2	...	1	...	...	...
21 Hume's or Dyer's cl. (101)	228	66	16	82	...	3	3	...	...	...	...	1	...	...	...
22 Kincaid's court (159)	222	...	...	...	...	...	...	...	...	...	...	...	...	...	...
23 Kitchen's court (175)	218	134	21	155	1	3	4	...	...	1	...	1	...	...	...
24 Maconochie's cl. (44)	232	87	22	109	2	3	5	1	...	...	...	...	...	...	...
25 Mealmarket (122) ...	222	[295	65	360]	1	1	2	1	...	...	...	...	...	...	...
26 Peter's close (187) ...	215	...	...	...	...	...	...	...	...	...	...	...	...	...	...
27 Pollock's close (28)...	233	...	...	...	...	...	...	...	...	...	...	...	...	...	...
28 Rattray's close or entry (115)	227	76	...	76	1	...	1	...	...	...	...	1	...	...	...
29 Scott's close (123) ...	224	264	37	301	...	2	2	...	...	1	...	...	...	...	...
30 Scott's entry (123) ...	270	15	3	18	1	...	1	1	...	...	...	...	...	...	...
13 College street, West ...	256—275	9	1	10	...	...	...	...	...	...	...	...	...	...	...
14 College street, North ...	248—256	15	2	17	...	...	...	...	...	...	...	...	...	...	...
15 Geo. IV. bridge	279	53	2	55	1	...	1	...	...	...	1	...	...	...	...
16 Greyfriar's place.........	278	55	14	69	...	1	1	...	...	...	1	...	...	...	...
Carry forward, ...		12,065	1846	13,911	201	206	407	30	18	73	23	41	16	6	7

11. District of St Giles—*Continued.*

	1863.													No. of Paupers.	Street Cesspools.			Epidemics.		
					Fevers.													Cholera.	Fever.	
	Scarlatina.	Measles.	Hooping-Cough.	Erysipelas.	Total.	Typhus.	Typhoid.	Gastric.	Infantile.	Diarrhoea and Dysentery.	Scrofula.	Old Age.	Premature Debility.		Trapped.	Untrapped.	Total.	1848.	1847-8.	1857-8.
	8	7	7	1	6	1	2	1	2	5	12	5	14	324	51	13	64	65	648	24
16	...	...	...	...	...	...	...	...	...	...	1	1	...	1	3	...	3	...	2	...
17	...	...	...	...	...	...	...	...	...	...	...	...	...	1	1	...	1	...	...	...
18	...	...	...	...	...	...	...	...	...	...	...	...	...	...	...	...	...	...	...	...
19	...	...	...	...	...	...	...	...	...	1	...	1	...	19	1	1	2	1	5	...
20	...	...	...	...	...	...	...	...	...	...	1	1	2	6	1	...	1	7	29	...
21	...	...	1	...	1	...	...	1	...	...	1	...	...	26	2	...	2	11	21	...
22	...	...	...	...	...	...	...	...	...	...	...	...	...	...	...	...	...	...	47	...
23	...	...	...	...	...	...	...	...	...	...	...	...	...	...	...	1	1	...	...	...
24	...	...	...	...	...	...	...	...	...	...	...	...	...	3	...	1	1	...	...	...
25	...	...	...	...	...	...	...	...	...	...	...	...	...	2	1	...	1	...	...	...
26	...	...	...	...	...	...	...	...	...	...	...	1	1	22	1	...	1	11	4	2
27	...	...	...	...	...	...	...	...	...	...	...	...	1	10	1	...	1	2	...	...
28	...	...	...	...	...	...	...	...	...	...	...	...	...	...	2	...	2	3	1	...
12	...	4	6	...	5	4	...	1	...	2	2	...	6	60	6	16	22	16	826	2
1	...	1	4	...	...	...	...	...	...	...	1	1	...	15	2	...	2	1	3	...
2	...	...	...	...	...	...	...	...	...	...	...	...	...	1	...	...	...	1	...	...
3	...	...	...	...	...	...	...	...	...	...	...	...	...	9	1	...	1	...	...	...
4	...	...	...	...	...	...	...	...	...	...	1	...	1	1	...	...	...	3	...	...
5	...	...	...	...	...	...	...	...	...	...	...	...	...	...	...	...	...	...	...	...
6	...	...	...	...	...	...	...	...	...	...	1	...	1	11	...	...	...	11	5	...
7	...	...	...	...	...	...	...	...	...	...	...	...	1	8	1	...	1	...	3	...
8	...	4	2	...	1	1	...	...	...	1	3	1	...	28	...	...	...	18	85	6
9	...	...	...	...	...	...	...	...	...	...	...	...	...	10	2	...	2	...	...	...
10	...	...	...	...	...	...	...	...	...	...	...	...	...	4	...	...	...	...	...	...
11	...	...	...	...	...	...	...	...	...	...	...	...	...	8	...	...	...	...	...	...
12	...	...	...	...	...	...	...	...	...	...	...	...	...	1	...	...	...	...	...	...
13	...	...	...	...	...	...	...	...	...	...	...	...	...	...	...	...	...	...	1	...
14	...	...	...	...	...	...	...	...	...	...	...	...	...	41	...	...	...	5	...	...
15	...	...	...	...	...	...	...	...	...	...	...	...	...	...	1	...	1	...	...	...
16	...	...	...	...	...	...	...	...	...	...	...	...	...	5	...	...	...	2	4	1
17	...	...	...	...	...	...	...	...	...	...	...	...	...	4	...	...	...	2	...	...
18	...	...	...	...	...	...	...	...	...	...	...	...	...	27	...	...	...	13	3	...
19	...	...	...	...	...	...	...	...	...	...	1	...	...	...	...	...	...	...	...	...
20	...	...	...	...	2	2	...	...	...	...	2	1	...	38	...	...	...	7	44	1
21	...	1	...	...	...	...	...	...	...	...	...	...	...	8	3	...	3	...	4	...
22	...	...	...	...	...	...	...	...	...	...	...	...	...	...	...	...	...	...	...	...
23	1	...	...	...	...	...	...	...	...	...	...	...	...	20	...	...	...	5	2	...
24	...	1	2	...	...	...	...	...	...	...	...	...	...	1	2	...	2	...	2	...
25	...	1	...	...	...	...	...	...	...	...	...	...	...	25	...	...	...	13	12	...
26	...	...	...	...	...	...	...	...	...	...	...	...	...	...	1	...	1	...	...	...
27	...	...	...	...	...	...	...	...	...	...	...	...	...	...	1	...	1	...	1	...
28	...	...	...	...	...	...	...	...	...	...	...	...	...	...	1	...	1	...	...	...
29	...	...	...	...	...	...	...	...	...	...	1	...	...	15	3	...	3	4	8	...
30	...	...	...	...	...	...	...	...	...	...	...	...	...	...	...	...	...	...	...	...
13	...	...	...	...	...	...	...	...	...	...	...	...	...	...	1	...	1	...	...	...
14	...	...	...	...	...	...	...	...	...	...	...	...	...	...	...	2	2	...	...	...
15	...	...	...	...	...	...	...	...	...	...	...	...	...	...	1	2	3	...	1	...
16	...	...	...	...	...	...	...	...	...	...	...	...	...	...	...	...	...	...	...	...
	9	19	22	1	15	8	2	3	2	9	27	12	27	754	90	36	126	201	1761	36

TABLE No. VI.—New Sanitary Districts,

11. District of St Giles—*Continued.*

Name of Street.	Height in feet above the sea.	Population 1861. Above 5.	Population 1861. Under 5.	Population 1861. Total.	Mortality 1863. Above 5.	Mortality 1863. Under 5.	Mortality 1863. Total.	Diseases in Brain.	Heart.	Chest.	Abdomen.	Phthisis.	Croup.	Diphtheria.	Small-Pox.
Brought forward,		12,065	1846	13,911	201	206	407	30	18	73	23	41	16	6	7
17 Hunter square............	254	23	2	25	...	...	...	...	...	...	...	...	...	...	...
18 Lindsay place	278	13	2	15	1	...	1	...	...	1	...	...	...	...	...
19 Lothian street	278	547	58	605	13	6	19	3	1	5	1	3	...	...	...
20 Lord Cockburn street...	204—260	[114	19	133]	1	2	3	1	...	...	...	1	...	...	...
21 Market street	182—204	164	21	185	3	3	6	...	1	...	...	2	1	...	...
22 Melbourne place	288	82	7	89	...	...	...	...	...	...	...	...	...	...	...
23 Merchant street	250	100	14	114	2	6	8	...	...	2	1	...	1	...	...
24 Mound	215	12	1	13	...	...	...	...	...	...	...	...	...	...	...
25 Mound place	290	62	7	69	...	...	...	...	...	...	...	...	...	...	...
26 Parliament square	284	15	1	16	...	...	...	...	...	...	...	...	...	...	...
1 Police Office, Head...	278	63	7	70	...	...	...	...	...	...	...	...	...	...	...
27 Royal Exchange.........	282	103	11	114	3	1	4	...	1	...	...	...	...	1	1
28 Society	280	219	49	268	3	2	5	...	...	2	...	...	...	1	...
29 Victoria street...........	250—280	85	17	102	1	1	2	...	...	...	...	...	...	...	...
30 Victoria terrace	285	2	...	2	...	...	...	...	...	...	...	...	...	...	...
31 Waverley bridge	194	...	...	...	...	...	...	...	...	...	...	...	...	...	...
32 West bow	236—300	321	48	369	4	1	5	1	1	...	...	1	...	...	...
Totals,....................		13,876	2091	15,967	232	228	460	35	22	83	25	48	18	8	8

12. District of Grassmarket.

Name of Street.	Height in feet above the sea.	Population 1861. Above 5.	Population 1861. Under 5.	Population 1861. Total.	Mortality 1863. Above 5.	Mortality 1863. Under 5.	Mortality 1863. Total.	Diseases in Brain.	Heart.	Chest.	Abdomen.	Phthisis.	Croup.	Diphtheria.	Small-Pox.
1 Grassmarket	211—233	806	99	905	20	16	36	...	1	10	5	4	...	...	3
1 Aird's close (135) ...	231	52	11	63	1	4	5	1	1	...	1	...	...	...	...
2 Brown's close (14) ...	211	121	27	148	2	2	4	...	...	...	1	...	...	...	...
3 Castle wynd (46) ...	216	145	27	172	3	6	9	2	...	3	...	...	...	...	...
4 Cowie's close (107)...	227	53	14	67	...	1	1	...	...	...	...	...	...	...	...
5 Crawford's close (8)	210	114	25	139	1	3	4	...	...	3	1	...	...	...	...
6 Currie's close (94) ...	229	163	27	190	4	4	8	...	1	1	...	1	1	...	...
7 Dewar's close (102)...	230	64	7	71	1	...	1	1	...	...	...	...	...	...	...
8 Dunlop's court (36)...	215	[25	2	27]	1	...	1	...	...	...	...	...	...	...	...
9 Gilmour's close (99)	226	61	5	66	1	2	3	1	...	2	...	...	...	...	...
10 Gladstone's close (20)	...	...	...	...	...	...	...	...	...	...	...	...	...	...	...
11 Hunter's close (129)	230	76	15	91	1	2	3	...	...	1	...	...	...	...	...
12 Jamieson's close (68)	227	115	16	131	...	1	1	...	...	...	...	...	...	...	...
13 Lamond's close (23)	211	51	16	67	...	...	...	...	...	...	...	...	...	...	...
14 Marshall's close (3)...	210	...	...	...	...	...	...	...	...	...	...	...	...	...	...
15 Plainstones close (78)	227	60	16	76	1	2	3	1	...	...	...	...	...	...	...
16 Smith's close, East (125)	230	77	20	97	2	4	6	1	...	...	1	...	1	...	...
17 Smith's close, West (119)	230	56	8	64	1	3	4	...	...	...	1	1	1	...	...
18 Temple's close (145)	232	41	9	50	...	...	...	...	...	...	...	...	...	...	...
19 Thomson's court (54)	222	109	25	134	2	2	4	...	...	...	...	...	...	1	...
20 Warden's close (139)	229	112	10	122	...	...	...	...	...	...	...	...	...	...	...
2 Heriot bridge	218	130	27	157	1	3	4	1	...	1	...	...	1	...	...
3 Johnston terrace	232—300	5	...	5	...	...	...	...	...	...	...	...	...	...	...
4 King's stables............	201	111	18	129	2	2	4	...	...	...	...	2	...	...	...
5 West port	210—249	1008	160	1168	17	20	37	2	3	6	5	1	1	1	2
1 Aitchison's close (58)	227	119	26	145	4	3	7	...	1	1	1	2	1	...	...
2 Baird's close (135) ...	239	44	8	52	1	...	1	...	...	...	...	...	...	...	...
3 Brown's land (29) ...	...	57	19	76	1	2	3	1	1	...	...	...	...	...	...
4 Chapel wynd (51) ...	221	4	1	5	...	...	...	...	...	...	...	...	...	...	...
Carry forward,................		3754	636	4390	67	82	149	11	8	28	16	11	6	2	5

11. District of St Giles—*Continued.*

	1863.														Street Cesspools.			Epidemics.		
					Fevers.													Cholera.	Fever.	
	Scarlatina.	Measles.	Hooping-Cough.	Erysipelas.	Total.	Typhus.	Typhoid.	Gastric.	Infantile.	Diarrhœa and Dysentery.	Scrofula.	Old Age.	Premature Debility.	No. of Paupers.	Trapped.	Untrapped.	Total.	1848.	1847-8.	1857-8.
	9	19	22	1	15	8	2	3	2	9	27	12	27	754	90	36	126	201	1761	36
17	...	...	...	...	...	...	...	..	...	...	...	...	...	...	...	...	...	...	...	...
18	...	...	...	...	...	...	...	...	...	...	...	...	...	...	1	...	1	...	...	...
19	...	...	...	...	...	...	...	...	...	1	1	1	1	2	...	3	3	1	3	...
20	...	...	1	...	...	...	...	...	...	...	...	...	...	1	...	...	...	...	...	...
21	...	...	...	...	...	..	...	...	...	...	1	...	...	...	4	...	4	1	1	2
22	...	...	...	...	...	...	...	...	...	...	...	...	...	...	...	1	1	...	...	...
23	1	1	...	...	...	...	...	...	...	1	...	...	1	9	1	1	2	...	...	1
24	...	...	...	...	...	...	...	...	...	...	...	...	...	...	2	7	9	...	...	...
25	...	...	...	...	...	...	...	...	...	...	...	...	...	...	...	...	...	...	...	...
26	...	...	...	...	...	...	...	...	...	...	...	...	...	...	...	8	8	...	...	...
1	...	...	...	...	...	...	...	...	...	...	...	...	...	...	...	...	...	..	5	...
27	...	1	...	...	...	...	...	...	...	...	...	...	...	2	...	...	...	...	...	...
28	...	...	...	...	...	...	...	...	...	...	...	1	...	5	...	...	...	1	...	...
29	...	...	...	...	...	...	...	...	...	...	2	...	...	...	1	2	3	...	...	...
30	...	...	...	...	...	...	...	...	...	...	...	...	...	...	...	...	...	...	...	...
31	...	...	...	...	...	...	...	...	...	...	...	...	...	...	4	...	4	...	...	...
32	...	...	...	...	...	...	...	...	...	...	...	...	...	4	...	...	...	2	5	...
	10	21	23	1	15	8	2	3	2	11	31	14	29	777	103	58	161	206	1775	39

12. District of Grassmarket.

	Scarlatina.	Measles.	Hooping-Cough.	Erysipelas.	Fevers: Total.	Typhus.	Typhoid.	Gastric.	Infantile.	Diarrhœa and Dysentery.	Scrofula.	Old Age.	Premature Debility.	No. of Paupers.	Trapped.	Untrapped.	Total.	Cholera 1848.	Fever 1847-8.	Fever 1857-8.
1	...	5	...	...	1	...	1	...	...	2	2	...	3	53	15	...	15	48	825	5
1	...	1	...	...	...	...	...	...	...	1	...	...	...	6	2	...	2	6	...	...
2	...	1	...	...	1	...	1	...	...	...	...	...	...	13	2	...	2	...	...	...
3	...	...	...	...	1	1	...	...	...	...	1	...	1	3	...	...	...	...	1	...
4	...	...	...	...	...	...	...	...	...	...	...	...	...	2	1	...	1	2	...	...
5	...	...	..	...	...	...	...	...	...	...	...	...	...	8	1	...	1	5	2	...
6	...	...	1	...	...	...	...	...	...	...	1	...	1	8	1	...	1	5	20	1
7	...	...	...	...	...	...	...	...	...	...	...	...	...	7	1	...	1	...	...	...
8	...	...	...	...	...	...	...	...	...	...	...	...	...	1	...	...	...	...	...	...
9	...	...	...	...	...	...	...	...	...	...	...	...	...	...	1	...	1	...	...	...
10	...	...	...	...	...	...	...	...	...	...	...	...	...	...	1	...	1	3	...	...
11	...	...	...	...	...	...	...	...	...	...	...	...	1	...	2	...	2	...	8	...
12	...	1	...	...	...	...	...	...	...	...	...	...	...	1	1	...	1	7	4	...
13	...	...	...	...	...	...	...	...	...	...	...	...	...	6	...	...	...	...	...	...
14	...	...	...	...	...	...	...	...	...	...	...	...	...	...	...	...	...	...	...	...
15	...	2	...	...	...	...	...	...	...	...	...	...	...	10	1	...	1	5	3	...
16	...	2	...	...	...	...	...	...	...	...	...	...	1	13	2	...	2	...	...	...
17	...	1	...	...	...	...	...	...	...	...	...	...	...	16	1	...	1	2	...	...
18	...	...	...	...	...	...	...	...	...	...	...	...	...	...	1	...	1	...	...	...
19	1	...	...	...	...	...	...	...	...	...	...	...	...	...	2	...	2	...	...	...
20	...	...	...	...	...	...	...	...	...	...	...	...	...	...	2	...	2	...	...	...
2	...	1	...	...	...	...	...	...	...	...	...	...	...	1	...	...	...	...	...	...
3	...	...	...	...	...	...	...	...	...	...	...	...	...	...	...	4	4	...	...	...
4	...	...	...	...	...	...	...	...	...	...	...	...	2	11	6	9	15	3	7	...
5	1	4	1	...	...	...	...	...	...	2	4	2	1	46	10	...	10	14	373	1
1	...	...	...	...	...	...	...	...	...	...	...	...	1	1	2	...	2	...	...	...
2	...	...	...	...	..	...	...	...	...	...	...	...	...	1	1	...	1	...	...	...
3	...	1	...	...	...	...	...	...	...	...	...	...	...	...	...	...	...	...	...	...
4	...	...	...	...	...	...	...	...	...	...	...	...	...	...	...	...	...	...	...	...
	2	19	2	...	3	1	2	...	...	5	8	2	11	207	56	13	69	100	1243	7

TABLE No. VI.—New Sanitary Districts,

12. District of Grassmarket—*Continued.*

Name of Street.	Height in feet above the sea.	Population 1861.			Mortality 1863.			Diseases in							
		Above 5.	Under 5.	Total.	Above 5.	Under 5.	Total.	Brain.	Heart.	Chest.	Abdomen.	Phthisis.	Croup.	Diphtheria.	Small-Pox.
Brought forward,		3754	636	4390	67	82	149	11	8	28	16	11	6	2	5
5 Crombie's land (49)	227	39	7	46	1	2	3	...	1	...	...	...	...	...	1
6 Inglis' court (17) ...	208	117	26	143	2	1	3	1	...	1	...	...	...	...	...
7 Ink's close (6)	210	87	8	95	...	...	...	...	...	...	...	...	...	...	...
8 Killibrae (26)	216	114	22	136	1	3	4	...	...	...	...	...	1	...	...
9 Lady wynd (25)	212	12	3	15	...	...	...	...	...	...	...	...	...	...	...
10 St. Cuthbert's cl.(167)	247	67	13	80	1	...	1	...	...	1	...	...	...	...	...
11 Stevenson's close(153)	245	106	19	125	1	3	4	...	...	...	1	...	...	...	...
12 Tanner's close (123)	237	95	28	123	...	3	3	...	...	2	...	...	...	...	...
13 Well close (86)	237	41	9	50	1	1	2	1	...	...	...	...	...	...	...
14 Weaver's close (65)	225	23	1	24	...	1	1	...	...	...	...	..	1	...	...
Totals,....................		4455	772	5227	74	96	170	13	9	32	17	11	8	2	6

13. District of Fountainbridge.

Name of Street.	Height in feet above the sea.	Population 1861.			Mortality 1863.			Diseases in							
		Above 5.	Under 5.	Total.	Above 5.	Under 5.	Total.	Brain.	Heart.	Chest.	Abdomen.	Phthisis.	Croup.	Diphtheria.	Small-Pox.
1 Brandfield place	217	44	4	48	1	...	1	...	...	...	1	...	...	...	...
2 Bread street	238	294	33	327	7	...	7	2	1	...	1	2	...	...	...
3 Castle barns	238	117	23	140	2	1	3	...	1	...	1	...	...	...	...
1 Robb's court	238	26	2	28	...	...	...	...	...	...	...	...	...	...	...
4 Cowfeeder row	250	214	47	261	4	...	4	...	...	1	...	...	...	...	...
1 Belfrage lane	245	77	18	95	3	1	4	1	...	...	...	1	...	...	...
2 Fleming's close (1) ...	249	24	5	29	...	...	...	...	...	...	...	...	...	...	...
5 Downie place	238	254	15	269	...	...	...	...	...	...	...	...	...	...	...
6 Drumdryan..............	241	45	5	50	...	...	...	...	...	...	...	...	...	...	...
7 Dunbar street...........	236	279	43	322	3	4	7	1	1	1	...	...	...	1	...
8 Earl Grey street	239	481	58	539	5	7	12	...	...	...	1	2	...	1	1
9 Fountainbridge street...	...	1531	224	1755	30	21	51	4	2	5	3	5	...	...	3
1 Chalmers' buildings (136)..................	234	110	25	135	1	2	3	1	...	...	...	...	...	...	...
2 Fountain court (81)...	222	74	18	92	...	...	...	...	...	...	...	...	...	...	...
3 Hamilton's court(133)	236	[9	56	65]	1	...	1	...	...	1	...	...	...	...	...
4 Hopetoun court (39)	238	78	11	89	...	1	1	...	...	...	...	...	...	1	...
5 Inglis' entry (8)	245	78	12	90	3	...	3	...	1	2	...	...	...	...	...
6 Knowles' pend (63)...	225	...	...	...	...	...	...	...	...	...	...	...	...	...	...
7 Strachan's court (12)	244	78	30	108	1	1	2	...	...	1	...	...	...	...	...
8 Walker's pend (18)...	244	111	17	128	3	2	5	...	1	1	...	...	1	...	...
9 Viewforth park	222	...	...	...	2	4	6	1	...	1	...	1	...	...	...
10 Freer street	236	...	...	...	...	...	...	...	...	...	...	...	...	...	...
11 Gillespie street	245	21	...	21	...	...	...	...	...	...	...	...	...	...	...
12 Gilmore park	...	11	3	14	...	1	1	...	...	...	...	...	...	...	...
13 Gilmore place	246	392	33	425	3	1	4	2	...	1	...	1	...	...	...
14 Gilmore place, Lower...	240	30	5	35	...	...	...	...	...	...	...	...	...	...	...
15 Gilmore place, Upper...	247	44	1	45	...	...	...	...	...	...	...	...	...	...	...
16 Grove road	223	124	19	143	1	1	2	...	...	...	...	1	...	...	...
17 Hailes street	250	64	9	73	...	...	...	...	...	...	...	...	...	...	...
18 High riggs	240	236	38	274	5	6	11	...	1	2	3	...	...	...	1
1 Hamilton place	240	116	18	134	3	3	6	...	2	1	...	1	...	...	...
2 Robb's court (12) ...	250	27	4	31	...	1	1	...	...	1	...	...	...	...	...
3 Watson's court (9) ...	246	23	4	27	1	2	3	...	...	...	...	1	...	...	...
19 Home street	236	819	159	978	12	10	22	3	...	3	1	1	...	1	...
20 Ladyfield place	231	18	...	18	1	...	1	...	...	1	...	...	...	...	...
21 Leven street	245	306	41	347	4	5	9	...	...	3	...	...	...	...	...
22 Lochrin	235	9	3	12	...	...	...	...	...	...	...	...	...	...	...
Carry forward,.................		6155	927	7082	96	74	170	15	10	25	11	16	1	4	5

12. District of Grassmarket—*Continued.*

	1863.													No. of Paupers.	Street Cesspools.			Epidemics.		
	Scarlatina.	Measles.	Hooping-Cough	Erysipelas.	Fevers.					Diarrhœa and Dysentery.	Scrofula.	Old Age.	Premature Debility.		Trapped.	Untrapped.	Total.	Cholera.	Fever.	
					Total.	Typhus.	Typhoid.	Gastric.	Infantile.									1848.	1847-8.	1857-8.
	2	19	2	...	3	1	2	...	...	5	8	2	11	207	56	13	69	100	1243	7
5	...	...	...	...	...	...	...	...	...	...	...	...	...	...	...	...	...	...	...	...
6	...	...	...	...	...	...	...	...	...	...	...	...	1	3	4	...	4	...	...	...
7	...	...	...	...	...	...	...	...	...	...	...	...	...	14	1	...	1	1	1	...
8	...	1	...	...	1	...	1	...	...	...	...	...	...	15	2	...	2	...	...	...
9	...	...	...	...	...	...	...	...	...	...	...	...	...	...	...	...	...	...	...	...
10	...	...	...	...	...	...	...	...	...	...	...	...	...	1	...	...	...	...	2	...
11	1	...	...	...	...	...	...	...	...	...	...	...	1	1	1	...	1	1	3	...
12	...	...	...	...	...	...	...	...	...	1	...	...	...	...	...	1	1	...	...	...
13	...	1	...	...	...	...	...	...	...	...	...	...	...	9	1	...	1	...	1	...
14	...	...	...	...	...	...	...	...	...	...	...	...	...	...	...	...	...	...	...	...
	3	21	2	...	4	1	3	...	...	6	8	2	13	250	65	14	79	102	1250	7

13. District of Fountainbridge.

	Scarlatina.	Measles.	Hooping-Cough	Erysipelas.	Fevers Total.	Typhus.	Typhoid.	Gastric.	Infantile.	Diarrhœa and Dysentery.	Scrofula.	Old Age.	Premature Debility.	No. of Paupers.	Trapped.	Untrapped.	Total.	Cholera 1848.	Fever 1847-8.	Fever 1857-8.
1	...	...	...	...	...	...	...	...	...	...	...	...	...	1	...	...	...	...	...	...
2	...	...	...	...	1	...	...	1	...	...	...	...	...	5	3	2	5	...	...	1
3	...	...	...	...	...	...	...	...	...	...	...	...	1	...	...	...	...	...	1	...
1	...	...	...	...	...	...	...	...	...	...	...	...	...	5	...	...	...	...	...	...
4	...	...	...	...	...	...	...	...	...	...	...	2	...	8	1	2	3	...	10	...
1	...	...	...	...	...	...	...	...	...	...	...	1	1	3	1	...	1	...	...	...
2	...	...	...	...	...	...	...	...	...	...	...	...	...	1	...	...	...	...	...	...
5	...	...	...	...	...	...	...	...	...	...	...	...	...	3	2	...	2	...	2	...
6	...	...	...	...	...	...	...	...	...	...	...	...	...	...	...	...	...	...	...	...
7	...	...	...	...	...	...	...	...	...	...	...	...	...	5	1	...	1	...	9	...
8	...	1	...	...	...	...	...	...	...	...	2	1	1	2	2	1	3	...	4	...
9	3	4	...	2	3	...	1	2	...	3	4	1	2	64	15	3	18	...	63	2
1	1	...	...	...	...	...	...	...	...	...	...	...	1	...	...	...	...	...	...	...
2	...	...	...	...	...	...	...	...	...	...	...	...	...	...	...	...	...	...	...	...
3	...	...	...	...	...	...	...	...	...	...	...	...	...	...	1	1	2	...	...	...
4	...	...	...	...	...	...	...	...	...	...	...	...	...	3	1	...	1	...	...	...
5	...	...	...	...	...	...	...	...	...	...	...	...	...	8	...	...	...	...	...	...
6	...	...	...	...	...	...	...	...	...	...	...	...	...	...	...	...	...	...	...	...
7	...	...	...	...	...	...	...	...	...	...	...	1	...	6	...	...	...	...	...	...
8	...	...	1	...	...	...	...	...	...	...	...	...	...	1	...	...	...	...	...	...
9	1	...	...	...	...	...	...	...	...	...	...	...	2	...	...	...	...	...	...	...
10	...	...	...	...	...	...	...	...	...	...	...	...	...	2	...	...	...	...	...	...
11	...	...	...	...	...	...	...	...	...	...	...	...	...	...	...	...	...	...	...	...
12	...	...	...	...	...	...	...	...	...	...	...	...	...	...	...	...	...	...	...	...
13	...	...	...	...	...	...	...	...	...	...	...	...	...	...				...	...	...
14	...	...	...	...	...	...	...	...	...	...	...	...	...	...	1	7	8	...	...	...
15	...	...	...	...	...	...	...	...	...	...	...	...	...	...				...	...	...
16	...	...	...	...	...	...	...	...	...	1	...	...	...	...	...	2	2	...	...	...
17	...	...	...	...	...	...	...	...	...	...	...	...	...	...	...	...	...	...	...	...
18	...	1	...	...	1	...	...	1	...	...	...	...	2	7	...	...	...	1	...	...
1	1	...	...	...	...	...	...	...	...	...	1	...	...	1	...	...	...	...	1	...
2	...	...	...	...	...	...	...	...	...	...	...	...	...	...	2	...	2	...	...	...
3	...	1	...	...	...	...	...	...	...	1	...	...	...	...	...	...	...	...	...	...
19	3	1	1	...	1	...	1	...	...	...	1	1	...	13	...	5	5	...	8	1
20	...	...	...	...	...	...	...	...	...	...	...	...	...	...	1	...	1	...	...	...
21	...	...	...	...	...	...	...	...	...	2	...	1	2	1	1	2	3	...	...	...
22	...	...	...	...	...	...	...	...	...	...	...	...	...	...	...	...	...	...	...	...
	9	8	2	2	6	...	2	4	...	7	8	8	12	139	32	25	57	1	98	4

TABLE No. VI.—New Sanitary Districts,

13. District of Fountainbridge—*Continued.*

Name of Street.	Height in feet above the sea.	Population 1861. Above 5.	Population 1861. Under 5.	Population 1861. Total.	Mortality 1863. Above 5.	Mortality 1863. Under 5.	Mortality 1863. Total.	Diseases in Brain.	Diseases in Heart.	Diseases in Chest.	Diseases in Abdomen.	Diseases in Phthisis.	Diseases in Croup.	Diseases in Diphtheria.	Diseases in Small-Pox.
Brought forward,		6155	927	7082	96	74	170	15	10	25	11	16	1	4	5
23 Main point	234	53	15	68	1	2	3	...	...	2	...	...	...	...	...
1 Hay's court	245	23	1	24	...	...	...	...	...	...	...	...	...	...	...
24 Newport street	238	219	41	260	6	1	7	...	...	2	...	3	...	...	...
25 Orchardfield court	237	...	...	...	...	...	...	...	...	...	...	...	...	...	...
26 Orchardfield place	238	29	4	33	1 (26 and 27 bracketed)	...	1	1	...	...	...	...	...	...	...
27 Orchardfield street	239	69	14	83											
28 Ponton street	239	447	87	534	5	14	19	1	1	2	2	1	...	...	...
29 Public Slaughterhouses	237	...	...	...	...	...	...	...	...	...	...	...	...	...	...
30 Riego street	246	285	59	344	5	2	7	...	1	1	1	2	...	...	...
31 Romilly place	231	291	37	328	1	3	4	2	...	...	...	...	...	...	1
32 St Anthony place	237	188	21	209	3	1	4	2	...	1	...	...	...	...	...
33 Semple street	236	151	27	178	3	2	5	...	...	2	...	...	...	...	...
1 Weaver's land (6)	236	76	8	84	...	1	1	...	...	...	...	...	...	...	...
34 Spence's place	238	244	63	307	3	6	9	1	1	1	1	...	...	...	...
35 Tarvit street	241	25	2	27	1	...	1	...	1	...	..	...	...	...	...
36 Thornybauk	235	202	40	242	5	4	9	1	2	1	...	1	...	1	...
37 Tollcross	236	67	10	77	3	1	4	1	...	1	...	1	...	...	...
38 Union Canal basin	238	...	...	...	3	2	5	...	...	...	...	...	...	...	...
Totals,		8524	1356	9880	136	113	249	24	16	38	15	24	1	5	6

14. District of George Square and Lauriston.

Name of Street.	Height in feet above the sea.	Population 1861. Above 5.	Population 1861. Under 5.	Population 1861. Total.	Mortality 1863. Above 5.	Mortality 1863. Under 5.	Mortality 1863. Total.	Diseases in Brain.	Diseases in Heart.	Diseases in Chest.	Diseases in Abdomen.	Diseases in Phthisis.	Diseases in Croup.	Diseases in Diphtheria.	Diseases in Small-Pox.
1 Archibald place	253—278	214	28	242	5	3	8	...	1	...	2	2	...	1	...
2 Brougham place	237	...	...	...	...	...	...	...	...	...	...	...	...	...	...
3 Brougham street	237	60	8	68	1	...	1	...	...	...	...	...	...	...	...
4 Buccleuch place and lane	249	588	46	634	10	2	12	2	...	1	1	...	...	2	...
5 Chalmers' hospital	278	...	...	...	...	...	...	...	...	...	...	...	...	...	...
6 Chalmers' street	237—278	39	1	40	1	1	2	...	...	...	...	1	...	1	...
7 Charles street and lane	269	287	32	319	5	...	5	2	...	...	...	...	...	...	...
8 Crichton street	267	151	21	172	...	3	3	...	...	...	...	...	1	...	...
9 Forrest road	282	7	...	7	...	...	...	...	...	...	...	...	...	...	...
1 City Poorhouse	281	569	52	621	111	19	130	20	8	26	10	9	...	...	...
10 George square	252—270	477	19	496	4	1	5	1	1	...	1	1	...	...	...
11 Do. do. lanes	...	...	...	...	...	...	...	...	...	...	...	...	...	...	...
12 Graham street	279	143	13	156	2	2	4	1	...	1	1	...	...	...	...
13 Heriot's hospital	290	203	1	204	...	...	...	...	...	...	...	...	...	...	...
14 Heriot place	290	149	18	167	1	1	2	1	...	...	...	...	...	...	...
15 Hope park square	239	63	15	78	1	...	1	...	1	...	...	..	...	...	...
16 Keir street	284	269	23	292	5	1	6	...	1	1	...	2	...	...	...
17 Lady Lawson's wynd	244—276	367	70	437	5	8	13	...	1	1	1	2	...	...	...
18 Lauriston gardens	248	16	...	16	...	...	...	...	...	...	...	...	...	...	...
19 Lauriston lane	243	107	8	115	2	1	3	...	...	...	2	...	1	...	...
1 Sick Children's hosp.	246	22	5	27	...	1	1	...	...	...	...	...	1	...	...
20 Lauriston park and terrace	245	35	5	40	...	1	1	...	...	...	...	...	...	...	...
21 Lauriston place	278	365	37	402	1	2	3	...	1	...	...	...	2	...	...
22 Lauriston place, West	253	97	7	104	3	2	5	...	...	1	2	...	...	...	...
23 Lauriston street	262	644	117	761	11	10	21	2	3	4	...	4	...	1	...
24 Meadows	237	...	...	...	...	...	...	...	...	...	...	...	...	...	...
25 Merchant Maiden hosp.	250	101	...	101	...	...	...	...	...	...	...	...	...	...	...
26 Portland place	245	84	5	89	3	1	4	...	1	...	...	1	...	...	...
Carry forward,		5057	531	5588	171	59	230	29	18	35	20	22	5	5	...

13. District of Fountainbridge—*Continued.*

	1863.													No. of Paupers.	Street Cesspools.			Epidemics.		
	Scarlatina.	Measles.	Hooping-Cough.	Erysipelas.	Fevers.					Diarrhœa and Dysentery.	Scrofula.	Old Age.	Premature Debility.		Trapped.	Untrapped.	Total.	Cholera.	Fever.	
					Total.	Typhus.	Typhoid.	Gastric.	Infantile.									1848.	1847-8.	1857-8.
	9	8	2	2	6	...	2	4	...	7	8	8	12	139	32	25	57	1	98	4
23	...	...	...	...	...	...	...	...	...	...	...	...	...	1	...	1	1	...	...	...
1	...	...	...	...	...	...	...	...	...	...	...	...	...	3	...	...	...	...	...	...
24	...	...	...	...	...	...	...	...	...	...	...	1	...	3	1	...	1	...	1	...
25	...	...	...	...	...	...	...	...	...	...	...	...	...	...	...	...	...	...	...	...
26																				
27	...	...	..	...	...	...	...	...	...	...	...	...	...	3	...	...	...	...	...	...
28	1	1	...	1	1	...	...	...	1	...	3	1	1	17	2	...	2	...	6	...
29	...	...	...	...	...	...	...	...	...	...	...	...	...	...	11	...	11	...	...	...
30	...	...	...	...	...	...	...	...	...	...	1	1	...	4	...	...	...	...	...	...
31	...	...	...	...	...	...	...	...	...	...	1	...	...	2	1	1	2	...	1	...
32	...	...	...	...	...	...	...	...	...	1	...	...	...	2	...	2	2	...	3	...
33	...	...	...	...	...	...	...	...	...	...	1	...	...	2	...	1	1	1	3	...
1	...	...	...	...	...	...	...	...	...	...	...	...	1	...	...	...	...	...	...	...
34	1	...	...	...	2	...	...	...	2	...	1	...	1	3	...	...	...	...	1	...
35	...	...	...	...	...	...	...	...	...	...	...	1	...	...	...	...	...	...	...	...
36	...	...	...	...	...	...	...	...	...	1	1	...	1	6	3	3	6	...	4	2
37	...	...	...	...	...	...	...	...	...	...	...	1	...	4	...	...	...	...	2	...
38	...	...	...	...	...	...	...	...	...	...	...	...	...	...	...	...	...	...	...	...
	11	9	2	3	9	...	2	4	3	9	16	13	16	189	50	33	83	2	119	6

14. District of George Square and Lauriston.

	Scarlatina.	Measles.	Hooping-Cough.	Erysipelas.	Fevers. Total.	Typhus.	Typhoid.	Gastric.	Infantile.	Diarrhœa and Dysentery.	Scrofula.	Old Age.	Premature Debility.	No. of Paupers.	Cesspools Trapped.	Untrapped.	Total.	Cholera 1848.	Fever 1847-8.	Fever 1857-8.
1	...	...	...	...	...	...	...	..	...	...	...	...	...	...	...	2	2	...	1	...
2	...	...	...	...	...	...	...	...	...	...	...	...	...	...	...	...	...	...	...	...
3	...	...	...	...	...	...	...	...	...	...	1	...	...	2	...	...	...	...	...	...
4	...	...	...	...	1	...	1	...	...	...	2	2	...	...	2	8	10	...	2	2
5	...	...	...	...	...	...	...	...	...	...	...	...	...	...	...	...	...	...	...	...
6	...	...	...	...	...	...	...	...	...	...	...	...	...	...	...	...	...	...	...	...
7	...	...	...	...	...	...	...	...	...	...	...	2	...	7	...	...	...	...	...	...
8	1	...	...	...	...	...	...	...	..	...	1	...	...	3	1	...	1	...	1	1
9	...	...	...	...	...	...	...	...	...	...	...	...	...	...	...	1	1	2	...	...
1	...	...	...	...	...	...	...	...	...	4	4	29	8	606	...	...	...	1	48	2
10	...	...	...	...	...	...	...	..	...	...	...	..	1	...	2	...	2	...	3	2
11	...	...	...	...	...	...	...	...	...	...	...	...	...	...	1	7	8	...	...	...
12	...	...	...	...	...	...	...	...	...	1	...	...	...	...	1	...	1	...	...	...
13	...	...	...	...	...	...	...	...	...	...	...	...	...	...	...	...	...	...	...	...
14	...	...	...	...	...	...	...	...	...	..	1	...	...	1	...	...	...	2	1	...
15	...	...	...	...	...	...	...	...	...	...	...	...	...	1	...	...	...	...	...	...
16	...	...	...	...	...	...	...	...	...	...	1	1	...	...	3	...	3	...	2	...
17	1	2	...	...	...	...	...	...	...	...	1	1	3	25	6	...	6	2	1	...
18	...	...	...	...	...	...	...	...	...	...	...	...	..	...				...	...	...
19	...	...	...	...	...	...	...	...	...	...	...	...	...	1				...	...	...
1	...	...	...	...	...	...	...	...	...	...	..	...	...	...				...	...	...
20	...	...	...	...	...	...	...	...	...	...	1	...	...	...	7	13	20	...	...	...
21	...	...	...	...	...	...	...	...	...	...	...	1	...	...				1	...	...
22	...	...	1	...	...	...	...	...	...	...	...	1	...	...				...	...	...
23	3	1	...	...	1	1	...	...	...	...	2	...	...	8	3	1	4	...	6	...
24	...	...	...	...	...	...	...	...	...	...	...	...	...	...	...	...	...	...	...	...
25	...	...	...	...	...	...	...	...	...	...	...	...	...	...	...	...	...	...	...	...
26	...	...	...	...	...	...	...	...	...	...	...	...	...	...	...	...	...	...	...	...
	5	3	1	...	2	1	1	...	...	5	14	37	12	654	26	32	58	8	65	7

TABLE No. VI.—New Sanitary Districts,

14. District of George Square and Lauriston—*Continued.*

Name of Street.	Height in feet above the sea.	Population 1861. Above 5.	Population 1861. Under 5.	Population 1861. Total.	Mortality 1863. Above 5.	Mortality 1863. Under 5.	Mortality 1863. Total.	Diseases in Brain.	Heart.	Chest.	Abdomen.	Phthisis.	Croup.	Diphtheria.	Small-Pox.
Brought forward,		5057	531	5588	171	59	230	29	18	35	20	22	5	5	...
27 Park place and lane ...	277	55	4	59	1	...	1	...	...	1	...	...	...	...	...
28 Park street ...	274	148	18	166	...	3	3	...	...	...	...	...	1	...	...
29 Teviot row ...	280	58	4	62	1	2	3	...	...	...	1	...	2	...	...
30 Vennel ...	210—284	110	25	135	2	...	2	...	...	...	...	2	...	...	...
1 Brown's place ...	...	71	10	81	1	1	2	...	...	...	...	1	...	...	...
2 Wemyss terrace ...	229	43	7	50	...	...	...	...	...	...	...	...	...	...	...
31 Watson's hospital ...	260	110	4	114	...	...	...	...	...	...	...	...	...	...	...
32 Windmill lane ...	249—267	48	6	54	1	...	1	...	...	...	...	...	...	...	...
1 Wilkie's court ...	249	40	9	49	...	1	1	...	...	...	...	...	...	...	...
2 Wilson's court ...	255	22	4	26	...	...	...	...	...	...	...	...	...	...	...
33 Windmill street ...	...	105	5	110	1	...	1	...	...	...	1	...	...	...	...
34 Wharton lane ...	238—280	32	4	36	...	...	...	...	...	...	...	...	...	...	...
35 Wharton place ...	278	60	3	63	2	1	3	...	...	...	2	...	...	1	...
Totals, ...		5959	634	6593	180	67	247	29	18	36	24	25	8	6	...

15. District of Nicolson Street.

Name of Street.	Height in feet above the sea.	Population 1861. Above 5.	Population 1861. Under 5.	Population 1861. Total.	Mortality 1863. Above 5.	Mortality 1863. Under 5.	Mortality 1863. Total.	Diseases in Brain.	Heart.	Chest.	Abdomen.	Phthisis.	Croup.	Diphtheria.	Small-Pox.
1 Adam street, East ...	244—256	332	22	354	4	6	10	...	...	2	1	...	1	...	...
2 Adam street, West ...	256—265	247	38	285	3	1	4	1	...	...	...	...	...	...	...
3 Allison square ...	269	116	12	128	2	...	2	...	1	...	...	...	...	...	...
4 Brighton street ...	280	247	23	270	4	1	5	1	1	1	...	...	1	...	...
5 Bristo place ...	280	73	17	90	...	1	1	...	...	1	...	...	...	...	...
6 Bristo port ...	278	25	5	30	...	1	1	...	...	...	...	...	...	...	...
7 Bristo street ...	263—277	623	81	704	10	10	20	3	2	4	1	1	1	...	...
1 Dickson's court (18)	...	32	5	37	...	...	...	...	...	...	...	...	...	...	...
2 General's entry (58)	...	12	2	14	1	...	1	...	...	1	...	...	...	...	...
3 Hamilton's entry (36)	...	136	23	159	1	...	1	1	...	...	...	...	...	...	...
4 Middleton's entry (32)	...	275	59	334	5	12	17	2	...	2	...	3	...	1	...
8 Buccleuch pend ...	249	66	7	73	1	2	3	...	...	...	...	1	..	1	...
9 Buccleuch street ...	243—249	957	143	1100	32	22	54	4	3	8	2	4	1	3	...
10 Chapel street ...	255—264	154	22	176	2	...	2	...	...	...	...	1	...	...	...
11 Clerk street ...	250	507	67	574	13	2	15	2	2	2	2	2	...	...	...
12 College street, South ...	259—274	267	32	299	3	2	5	...	1	...	...	1	...	2	...
13 Crosscauseway, East ...	246—253	417	71	488	12	11	23	3	1	3	1	3	1	...	...
1 Brown's court (27) ...	251	42	4	46	...	...	...	...	...	...	...	...	...	...	...
2 Cowan's close (43) ...	251	414	76	490	3	9	12	...	...	1	...	2	1	...	...
3 Kay's court (76) ...	251	155	28	183	2	7	9	1	...	...	...	1	...	...	...
4 Kennedy's close (62)	252	33	3	36	1	...	1	...	...	...	...	...	...	...	...
5 Lamb's close (84) ...	249	70	16	86	1	...	1	...	...	...	...	...	...	...	...
6 Manual's court (92)	248	3	1	4	...	...	...	...	...	...	...	...	...	...	...
7 Murray street (52) ...	253	55	8	63	2	1	3	...	...	...	...	2	...	...	...
8 Smith's court (70) ...	251	13	2	15	...	...	...	...	...	...	...	...	...	...	...
14 Crosscauseway, West ...	253—258	166	19	185	4	3	7	...	...	3	1	1	...	...	...
1 Quarry close (26) ...	254	40	9	49	2	1	3	...	...	3	...	...	...	...	...
15 Davie street ...	259	197	33	230	7	2	9	1	...	...	...	...	...	...	...
16 Drummond street ...	251—260	439	63	502	8	6	14	1	...	4	...	2	...	...	...
17 Do. do., East ...	227—251	104	13	117	1	2	3	...	...	...	...	1	1	...	...
18 Gifford park ...	247	424	100	524	10	5	15	3	2	2	1	1	1	...	...
19 Gilmour street ...	256	170	27	197	3	1	4	...	...	...	1	1	...	...	...
20 Hay street ...	267	108	12	120	3	2	5	1	...	...	...	...	...	...	...
21 Hill place ...	264	363	42	405	8	3	11	1	...	...	1	1	...	3	...
22 Hill square ...	264	190	16	206	4	1	5	...	1	...	1	1	1	...	...
Carry forward, ...		7472	1101	8573	152	114	266	25	14	37	12	29	9	10	...

14. District of George Square and Lauriston—*Continued.*

	1863.													No. of Paupers.	Street Cesspools.			Epidemics.		
	Scarlatina.	Measles.	Hooping-Cough.	Erysipelas.	Fevers. Total.	Typhus.	Typhoid.	Gastric.	Infantile.	Diarrhœa and Dysentery.	Scrofula.	Old Age.	Premature Debility.		Trapped.	Untrapped.	Total.	Cholera. 1848.	Fever. 1847-8.	Fever. 1857-8.
	5	3	1	...	2	1	1	...	...	5	14	37	12	654	26	32	58	8	65	7
27	...	...	...	...	...	...	...	...	...	...	...	...	...	...	...	2	2	...	...	...
28	...	...	...	...	...	...	...	...	...	1	1	...	...	1	...	1	1	...	...	...
29	...	...	...	...	...	...	...	...	...	...	...	...	...	...	...	1	1	...	...	...
30	...	...	...	...	...	...	...	...	...	...	...	...	...	...	1	1	2	...	1	...
1	...	...	...	...	...	...	...	...	...	1	...	...	...	...	...	...	...	...	...	...
2	...	...	...	...	...	...	...	...	...	...	...	...	...	...	...	...	...	...	...	...
31	...	...	...	...	...	...	...	...	...	...	...	...	...	...	...	...	...	...	...	...
32	1	...	...	...	...	...	...	...	...	...	...	...	...	3				1	...	...
1	1	...	...	...	...	...	...	...	...	...	...	...	...	...	2	1	3	...	...	...
2	...	...	...	...	...	...	...	...	...	...	...	...	...	...				...	...	...
33	...	...	...	...	...	...	...	...	...	...	...	...	...	1				...	...	1
34	...	...	...	...	...	...	...	...	...	...	...	...	...	...	...	...	...	...	...	...
35	...	...	...	...	...	...	...	...	...	...	...	...	...	...	...	...	...	...	...	1
	7	3	1	...	2	1	1	...	...	7	15	37	12	659	29	38	67	9	66	9

15. District of Nicolson Street.

	Scarlatina.	Measles.	Hooping-Cough.	Erysipelas.	Fevers. Total.	Typhus.	Typhoid.	Gastric.	Infantile.	Diarrhœa and Dysentery.	Scrofula.	Old Age.	Premature Debility.	No. of Paupers.	Trapped.	Untrapped.	Total.	Cholera. 1848.	Fever. 1847-8.	Fever. 1857-8.
1	1	...	1	...	...	...	...	...	...	...	1	1	1	3	...	...	...	...	1	...
2	...	...	...	...	1	1	...	...	...	...	2	...	...	7	1	1	2	...	1	...
3	...	...	...	...	...	...	...	...	...	...	...	1	...	3	1	...	1	...	3	...
4	...	...	...	...	...	...	...	...	...	...	...	...	...	...	...	...	...	...	...	...
5	...	...	...	...	...	...	...	...	...	...	...	...	...	1				...	...	...
6	...	...	...	...	1	...	1	...	...	...	...	...	...	...	5	4	9	...	...	...
7	...	1	1	...	2	...	1	1	...	1	...	...	2	25				1	11	1
1	...	...	...	...	...	...	...	...	...	...	...	...	...	...	2	...	2	...	...	...
2	...	...	...	...	...	...	...	...	...	...	...	...	...	...	1	...	1	...	...	...
3	...	...	...	...	...	...	...	...	...	...	...	...	...	3	3	1	4	...	...	1
4	...	4	...	...	...	...	...	...	...	...	3	...	2	14	2	1	3	1	3	1
8	...	...	...	...	...	...	...	...	...	...	...	...	1	2	...	...	...	...	1	...
9	1	2	...	...	5	2	...	2	1	1	4	7	4	24	2	...	2	2	5	...
10	...	...	...	...	...	...	...	...	...	...	...	...	...	2	1	2	3	...	...	...
11	1	...	...	...	...	...	...	...	...	...	...	1	1	2	2	2	4	2	1	...
12	...	...	...	...	...	...	...	...	...	...	...	...	...	2	...	2	2	...	7	...
13	...	2	...	...	...	...	...	...	...	1	3	1	...	35	10	...	10	1	27	1
1	...	...	...	...	...	...	...	...	...	...	...	...	...	...	1	...	1	...	...	...
2	...	...	1	...	1	...	...	...	1	1	2	...	2	16	6	...	6	...	...	...
3	1	1	...	...	1	...	...	1	...	...	2	...	...	12	4	1	5	2	3	...
4	...	...	...	...	...	...	...	...	...	...	...	1	...	3	3	...	3	...	...	...
5	...	...	...	...	...	...	...	...	...	...	1	...	...	...	2	...	2	...	...	...
6	...	...	...	...	...	...	...	...	...	...	...	...	...	...	1	...	1	...	...	...
7	1	...	...	...	...	...	...	...	...	...	...	...	...	3	2	...	2	...	...	...
8	...	...	...	...	...	...	...	...	...	...	...	...	...	1	2	...	2	...	...	...
14	...	..	...	...	2	...	1	...	1	..	...	...	...	2	4	...	4	...	10	...
1	...	...	...	...	...	...	...	...	...	...	...	...	...	7	...	...	...	...	...	...
15	5	...	...	...	1	1	...	...	...	...	...	1	...	3	2	...	2	...	...	...
16	...	...	...	1	1	...	...	1	...	...	2	1	1	10	...	...	...	1	13	...
17	...	...	1	...	...	...	...	...	...	...	...	...	...	1	...	...	...	...	...	...
18	...	...	...	...	...	...	...	...	...	...	2	2	...	15	5	...	5	...	2	...
19	...	...	...	...	...	...	...	...	...	...	...	1	1	11	3	...	3	...	4	...
20	...	1	...	...	...	...	...	...	...	...	...	...	1	1	1	1	2	...	2	...
21	...	...	...	...	...	...	...	...	...	...	2	..	...	10	2	...	2	...	2	1
22	1	...	...	...	...	...	...	...	...	...	1	...	...	3	...	...	...	...	1	...
	11	11	4	1	15	4	3	5	3	4	25	17	16	221	68	15	83	10	97	5

TABLE No. VI.—New Sanitary Districts,

15. District of Nicolson Street—*Continued.*

Name of Street.	Height in feet above the sea.	Population 1861. Above 5.	Population 1861. Under 5.	Population 1861. Total.	Mortality 1863. Above 5.	Mortality 1863. Under 5.	Mortality 1863. Total.	Diseases in Brain.	Diseases in Heart.	Diseases in Chest.	Diseases in Abdomen.	Diseases in Phthisis.	Diseases in Croup.	Diseases in Diphtheria.	Diseases in Small-Pox.
Brought forward,		7472	1101	8573	152	114	266	25	14	37	12	29	9	10	...
23 Hope park	...	90	10	100	1	1	2	1	...	...	...	...	...	...	...
24 Hope park end	240	86	12	98	3	...	3	...	1	...	1	...	...	...	...
1 Roy's court (82)	240	63	14	77	...	2	2	...	...	1	...	...	...	...	...
25 Ingliston street	240	56	8	64	1	3	4	1	...	1	...	...	...	...	...
26 Montague street.........	249	294	30	324	3	1	4	1	...	...	...	1	...	...	...
27 Nicolson street	255—264	820	108	928	21	6	27	3	3	5	3	3	...	...	...
1 Gibb's entry (104) ...	259	212	38	250	3	3	6	...	...	...	1	...	1	...	...
2 Gray's court (95) ...	260	35	9	44	...	...	...	...	...	...	...	...	...	...	...
3 Haddow's court (112)	259	106	12	118	...	...	...	...	...	...	...	...	...	...	...
4 Law's court (127) ...	257	41	8	49	...	1	1	...	...	1	...	...	...	...	...
5 Reikie's court (65) ...	264	47	14	61	...	1	1	...	...	...	...	...	...	...	...
28 Nicolson square	270	211	13	224	9	2	11	1	...	2	3	1	...	...	...
29 Nicolson street, West	263	354	37	391	5	3	8	...	1	1	...	...	1	...	...
30 Paul street	257	112	21	133	2	5	7	...	...	1	...	...	...	1	...
31 Potterow	265—277	896	162	1058	12	15	27	3	...	6	1	5	...	1	...
1 Clerk's close (64)......	266	15	2	17	...	...	...	...	...	...	...	...	...	...	...
2 Graham's buildings and court (23)	276	29	2	31	...	...	...	...	...	...	...	...	...	...	...
3 Hall court (48)	274	20	5	25	...	...	...	...	...	...	...	...	...	...	...
4 Haxton's court (11)	276	14	...	14	...	...	...	...	...	...	...	...	...	...	...
5 Simpson's court (56)	...	151	25	176	5	2	7	...	1	1	1	...	...	...	...
6 Turnbull's entry (25)	276	73	12	85	2	1	3	...	...	...	...	1	...	...	...
32 Rankeillor place	245	41	9	50	...	...	...	...	...	...	...	...	...	...	...
33 Rankeillor street.........	245—251	395	48	443	5	4	9	2	...	1	...	1	...	1	...
34 Richmond court	264	100	19	119	3	3	6	1	...	...	...	...	1	...	...
35 Richmond lane	255	91	13	104	1	2	3	...	...	1	...	...	...	...	...
36 Richmond pend	257	53	5	58	...	...	...	...	...	...	...	...	...	...	...
37 Richmond place	257—264	393	78	471	4	11	15	...	2	1	1	1	...	1	1
1 Union court (16) ..	258	63	11	74	...	3	3	...	...	1	...	...	...	...	...
2 Williamson's ct. (6)	258	55	9	64	1	...	1	...	...	...	...	...	...	...	...
38 Richmond street, East	253	323	57	380	4	3	7	...	...	1	2	1	...	...	...
39 Richmond street, North	255	735	110	845	13	15	28	2	2	1	2	3	...	1	...
40 Richmond street, South	257	510	109	619	14	16	30	1	3	4	1	3	1	1	...
41 Richmond street, West	254—262	549	85	634	5	6	11	...	1	2	1	2	1	...	1
42 Roxburgh place	262	190	21	211	2	...	2	...	...	...	...	1	...	...	...
43 Roxburgh street.........	254	192	20	212	2	1	3	...	...	...	...	...	...	...	...
44 Roxburgh terrace	251	121	20	141	1	2	3	2	1	1	...	...	...	...	...
45 Royal Maternity hosp.	264	24	6	30	1	15	16	...	...	...	2	1	...	...	...
46 St Patrick street.........	254	25	4	29	...	...	...	...	...	...	...	...	...	...	...
47 St Patrick square	252	476	51	527	8	2	10	2	1	1	1	1	...	...	...
48 Sibbald place	251	34	6	40	1	...	1	...	...	...	...	1	...	...	...
49 Simon square	259	357	59	416	2	3	5	1	...	...	...	1	...	...	...
Totals, ...		15,924	2383	18,307	286	246	532	46	30	70	32	56	14	16	2

16. District of Pleasance and St Leonard.

Name of Street.	Height in feet above the sea.	Population 1861. Above 5.	Population 1861. Under 5.	Population 1861. Total.	Mortality 1863. Above 5.	Mortality 1863. Under 5.	Mortality 1863. Total.	Diseases in Brain.	Diseases in Heart.	Diseases in Chest.	Diseases in Abdomen.	Diseases in Phthisis.	Diseases in Croup.	Diseases in Diphtheria.	Diseases in Small-Pox.
1 Arthur place, East......	193	131	24	155	2	5	7	...	1	...	...	...	...	2	...
2 Arthur place, Middle...	219	361	66	427	3	6	9	...	...	1	2	...	...	...	1
3 Arthur place, West ...	237	91	14	105	...	1	1	...	...	...	...	...	...	...	...
4 Arthur street	170—245	849	166	1015	11	12	23	2	2	6	...	2	...	...	...
5 Beaumont place	240—248	218	45	263	3	6	9	1	1	1	1	...	...	...	...
6 Brown street and lane	242	466	88	554	7	8	15	...	1	3	1	2	...	...	...
Carry forward, ...		2116	403	2519	26	38	64	3	5	11	4	4	...	2	1

AND THEIR VITAL STATISTICS.—*Continued.*

15. District of Nicolson Street—*Continued.*

	1863.														Street Cesspools.			Epidemics.		
					Fevers.													Cholera.	Fever.	
	Scarlatina.	Measles.	Hooping-Cough.	Erysipelas.	Total.	Typhus.	Typhoid.	Gastric.	Infantile.	Diarrhœa and Dysentery.	Scrofula.	Old Age.	Premature Debility.	No. of Paupers.	Trapped.	Untrapped.	Total.	1848.	1847-8.	1857-8.
	11	11	4	1	15	4	3	5	3	4	25	17	16	221	68	15	83	10	97	5
23	...	...	...	...	...	...	...	...	...	...	1	...	...	...	...	...	...	...	2	...
24	...	...	...	...	...	...	...	...	...	...	...	...	...	1	2	...	2	...	3	...
1	...	...	1	...	...	...	...	...	...	...	...	...	...	2	...	...	...	...	...	...
25	1	1	...	...	...	...	...	...	...	...	...	...	...	...	...	...	...	...	...	...
26	...	...	...	...	...	...	...	...	...	1	...	...	...	1	...	3	3	...	...	...
27	...	...	1	...	2	...	1	1	...	1	2	1	...	12	8	2	10	...	21	1
1	...	...	...	...	...	...	...	...	...	...	2	...	1	19	3	...	3	2	8	...
2	...	...	...	...	...	...	...	...	...	...	...	...	...	...	2	...	2	...	...	...
3	...	...	...	...	...	...	...	...	...	...	...	...	...	2	2	...	2	...	...	...
4	...	...	...	...	...	...	...	...	...	...	...	...	...	2	2	...	2	...	1	...
5	...	...	...	...	...	...	...	...	...	...	1	...	...	...	1	1	2	...	...	...
28	1	...	...	...	...	...	...	...	...	...	1	1	...	...	...	...	...	1	...	...
29	1	...	...	...	1	1	...	...	...	1	1	...	...	3	3	...	3	...	...	...
30	...	...	...	...	...	...	...	...	...	...	2	...	...	6	3	...	3	...	5	...
31	1	2	...	...	...	...	...	...	...	1	1	...	4	42	9	3	12	2	49	...
1	...	...	...	...	...	...	...	...	...	...	...	...	...	...	...	1	1	...	...	...
2	...	...	...	...	...	...	...	...	...	...	...	...	...	...	2	...	2	...	...	..
3	...	...	...	...	...	...	...	...	...	...	...	...	...	...	1	...	1	...	...	...
4	...	...	...	...	...	...	...	...	...	...	...	...	...	...	...	...	...	...	...	...
5	...	...	...	...	...	...	...	...	...	...	2	...	...	11	3	...	3	1	1	...
6	...	...	...	...	...	...	...	...	...	...	1	...	...	...	...	...	...	...	...	...
32	...	...	...	...	...	...	...	...	...	...	...	...	...	...	...	...	...	...	...	...
33	...	...	...	...	...	...	...	...	...	1	...	...	2	2	2	...	2	...	...	...
34	...	...	...	...	...	...	...	...	...	1	2	...	..	5	..	1	1	1	1	...
35	...	1	...	...	...	...	...	...	...	...	...	1	...	7	2	...	2	1	1	...
36	...	...	...	...	...	...	...	...	...	...	...	...	...	...	...	...	...	1	1	...
37	...	2	...	...	...	...	...	...	...	...	2	1	1	16	5	...	5	...	3	...
1	...	1	...	...	...	...	...	...	...	...	1	...	...	...	1	2	3	...	...	...
2	...	...	...	...	...	...	...	...	...	...	...	1	...	...	1	...	1	...	...	...
38	...	...	...	...	...	...	...	...	...	...	2	...	...	15	1	...	1	5		
39	...	1	...	...	...	...	...	...	...	1	5	1	5	11	6	...	6	2		
40	2	4	...	...	1	1	...	...	...	...	4	1	...	22	4	...	4	2	36	1
41	...	2	...	...	...	...	...	...	...	...	...	1	...	31	5	...	5	...		
42	..	...	...	..	...	...	...	...	...	...	...	...	...	1	3	...	3	1	...	...
43	...	1	...	...	...	...	...	...	...	...	...	...	...	...	...	1	1	...	3	...
44	...	...	...	...	1	...	...	...	1	...	...	...	...	...	...	...	...	...	...	...
45	...	...	...	1	...	...	...	...	...	...	1	...	8	...	...	...	...	...	...	...
46	...	...	...	...	...	...	...	...	...	...	...	...	...	...	...	2	2	...	...	...
47	...	...	...	...	1	...	1	...	...	1	...	...	1	7	1	1	2	...	2	...
48	...	...	...	...	...	...	...	...	...	...	...	...	...	...	...	2	2	...	...	...
49	...	1	...	...	...	...	...	...	...	...	2	...	...	17	4	...	4	...	7	...
	17	27	6	2	21	6	5	6	4	12	58	25	38	456	144	34	178	29	241	7

16. District of Pleasance and St Leonard.

	Scarlatina.	Measles.	Hooping-Cough.	Erysipelas.	Fevers Total.	Typhus.	Typhoid.	Gastric.	Infantile.	Diarrhœa and Dysentery.	Scrofula.	Old Age.	Premature Debility.	No. of Paupers.	Trapped.	Untrapped.	Total.	Cholera 1848.	Fever 1847-8.	Fever 1857-8.
1	1	1	...	...	...	...	...	...	...	...	1	...	...	...				...		
2	1	1	...	...	1	...	1	...	...	...	...	1	...	4				...	2	...
3	...	...	...	...	...	...	...	...	...	...	1	...	...	...	14	...	14	...		
4	...	3	...	...	...	...	...	...	...	1	3	...	2	14				1	8	2
5	...	...	...	...	1	...	...	1	...	...	3	...	...	4	4	...	4	...	2	...
6	1	2	...	...	...	...	...	...	...	...	...	...	3	11	6	...	6	...	1	...
	3	7	...	...	2	...	1	1	...	1	8	1	5	33	24	...	24	1	13	2

TABLE No. VI.—New Sanitary Districts,

16. District of Pleasance and St Leonard—*Continued.*

Name of Street.	Height in feet above the sea.	Population 1861.			Mortality 1863.			Diseases in							
		Above 5.	Under 5.	Total.	Above 5.	Under 5.	Total.	Brain.	Heart.	Chest.	Abdomen.	Phthisis.	Croup.	Diphtheria.	Small-Pox.
Carry forward,		2116	403	2519	26	38	64	3	5	11	4	4	...	2	1
7 Carnegie street	237—250	823	159	982	11	8	19	1	1	3	2	4	...	...	...
8 Castle o' Clouts	270	42	4	46	...	...	...	...	...	...	...	...	...	...	...
9 Craigside house	158	24	4	28	...	...	...	...	...	...	...	...	...	...	...
10 Craigside place	166—204	155	32	187	2	1	3	...	...	...	...	1	...	...	...
11 Dalrymple place	246	441	103	544	13	5	18	1	1	2	3	4	...	2	...
12 Dumbiedykes	136—149	72	10	82	2	...	2	...	...	1	...	1	...	...	...
1 Prince Albert buildings	150	...	...	...	5	4	9	...	1	1	...	2	...	...	...
2 View Craig row	175	...	...	...	1	...	1	...	...	...	...	1	...	...	...
13 Forbes place	241	...	...	...	...	...	...	...	...	...	...	...	...	...	...
14 Forbes street	241	44	13	57	...	...	...	...	...	...	...	...	...	...	...
15 Henry place	258	78	10	88	2	1	3	...	...	...	...	2	...	...	...
16 Henry street	259	191	22	213	2	1	3	1	...	...	...	...	...	1	...
17 Hercles street	210—236	265	43	308	2	4	6	1	...	1	...	...	...	...	...
1 Hill mount	...	...	...	...	...	1	1	...	...	...	...	...	1	...	...
2 Holyrood cottages	...	...	...	...	...	...	...	...	...	...	...	...	...	...	...
18 Heriot mount	237	114	33	147	2	2	4	...	...	2	...	...	...	...	...
19 Holyrood and St Leonard's lodges	113—240	10	...	10	...	1	1	...	...	...	...	...	...	1	...
20 Jeanie Deans' cottage	267	6	2	8	...	...	...	...	...	...	...	...	...	...	...
21 Parkside street	256	272	35	307	3	2	5	...	...	...	...	1	...	...	...
22 Pleasance	190—253	1887	305	2192	34	31	65	5	3	6	12	5	1	2	2
1 Hardwell close (193)	249	151	22	173	2	...	2	1	...	1	...	...	...	...	...
2 Hatter's close (154)	253	113	17	130	1	4	5	...	...	...	...	...	...	1	...
3 Innes' court (93)	250	62	14	76	...	...	...	...	...	...	...	...	...	...	...
4 Long close (26)	206	89	23	112	...	...	...	...	...	...	...	...	...	...	...
5 Oakfield court (108)	250	115	15	130	3	1	4	...	...	...	...	...	...	...	...
6 Pleasance court (90)	249	23	7	30	...	...	...	...	...	...	...	...	...	...	...
23 Prospect street	170	...	...	...	3	1	4	1	...	...	...	...	...	...	...
24 Ritchie place	236	9	2	11	...	...	...	...	...	...	...	...	...	...	...
25 Salisbury square	220	64	17	81	...	2	2	...	...	...	...	...	...	...	...
26 Salisbury street	194—251	514	51	565	11	2	13	3	1	2	1	2	...	...	...
27 St John's hill, Upper	200	268	62	330	8	6	14	2	2	2	1	1	1	...	...
28 Do. do. Lower	...	...	...	...	...	...	...	...	...	...	...	...	...	...	...
1 Robb's entry	185	69	14	83	1	...	1	...	...	...	1	...	...	...	...
29 St Leonard's hill	240—265	282	62	344	6	5	11	1	1	...	1	...	...	2	...
1 Holyrood street	239	72	4	76	...	...	...	...	...	...	...	...	...	...	...
2 Victoria place	239	67	8	75	1	...	1	...	...	...	...	...	...	...	...
30 St Leonard's lane	243	83	6	89	...	1	1	...	...	...	...	...	1	...	...
31 St Leonard's street	244—279	675	114	789	11	15	26	...	6	6	1	3	1	...	...
1 Begrie's entry (69)	259	...	...	...	1	...	1	...	...	1	...	...	...	...	...
2 Bell's entry (17)	245	37	10	47	...	...	...	...	...	...	...	...	...	...	...
3 Brown's entry (81)	264	...	...	...	...	...	...	...	...	...	...	...	...	...	...
4 Christie's entry (77)	262	59	11	70	1	3	4	...	...	...	1	...	...	...	...
5 Gray's place (29)	244	18	3	21	...	...	...	...	...	...	...	...	...	...	...
6 John's place (19)	245	30	5	35	1	...	1	...	...	1	...	...	...	...	...
7 Mino park	244	53	7	60	...	2	2	...	...	...	...	...	...	...	...
8 Rockville place	271	...	...	...	...	...	...	...	...	...	...	...	...	...	...
9 St Leonard's court (9)	245	35	5	40	...	...	...	...	...	...	...	...	...	...	...
10 Victoria grove	239	17	2	19	...	...	...	...	...	...	...	...	...	...	...
Totals,		9445	1659	11,104	155	141	296	20	21	40	27	31	5	11	3

16. District of Pleasance and St Leonard—*Continued.*

	1863.													No. of Paupers.	Street Cesspools.			Epidemics.		
	Scarlatina.	Measles.	Hooping-Cough	Erysipelas.	Fevers.					Diarrhoea and Dysentery.	Scrofula.	Old Age.	Premature Debility.		Trapped.	Untrapped.	Total.	Cholera.	Fever.	
					Total.	Typhus.	Typhoid.	Gastric.	Infantile.									1848.	1847-8.	1857-8.
	3	7	...	...	2	...	1	1	...	1	8	1	5	33	24	...	24	1	13	2
7	...	2	...	...	...	...	...	...	...	...	1	2	1	17	4	...	4	2	11	...
8	...	...	...	...	...	...	...	...	...	...	...	...	...	1	...	...	...	...	...	...
9	...	...	...	...	...	...	...	...	...	...	...	...	...	...	...	1	1	...	...	...
10	...	1	...	...	...	...	...	...	...	...	...	...	...	1	...	...	...	...	...	...
11	1	...	...	...	1	1	...	...	...	...	...	1	...	9	2	...	2	...	8	...
12	...	...	...	...	...	...	...	...	...	...	1	...	1	2	1	2	3	...	...	...
1	1	1	..	...	1	1	...	...	...	...	1	...	1	...	2	...	2	...	...	...
2	...	...	...	...	...	...	...	...	...	...	...	...	...	1	...	1	1	...	...	...
13	...	...	...	...	...	...	...	...	...	...	...	...	...	...	...	...	...	...	...	...
14	...	...	...	...	...	...	...	...	...	...	...	...	...	2	1	...	1	...	...	...
15	...	...	...	...	...	...	...	...	...	...	1	...	...	...	...	...	...	...	...	...
16	...	...	...	...	1	...	...	1	...	...	...	...	...	2	...	1	1	...	...	..
17	...	1	...	...	...	...	...	...	...	...	...	...	1	6	2	2	4	...	1	...
1	...	...	...	...	...	...	...	...	...	...	...	...	...	...	...	...	...	...	...	...
2	...	...	...	...	...	...	...	...	...	...	...	...	...	...	...	...	...	...	...	...
18	...	...	...	...	...	...	...	...	...	...	...	1	...	1	...	...	...	...	2	...
19	...	...	...	...	...	...	...	...	...	...	...	...	...	...	...	...	...	...	...	...
20	...	...	...	...	...	...	...	...	...	...	...	...	...	...	...	...	...	...	...	..
21	...	1	...	...	...	...	...	...	...	...	...	2	...	5	...	1	1	...	...	...
22	2	4	3	...	1	...	...	...	1	1	5	5	3	97	16	3	19	14	132	3
1	...	...	...	...	...	...	...	...	...	...	...	...	...	8	...	...	...	...	4	...
2	...	1	...	...	...	...	...	...	...	...	2	1	...	9	4	...	4	...	3	...
3	...	...	...	...	...	...	...	...	...	...	...	...	...	4	...	...	...	...	...	...
4	...	...	...	...	...	...	...	...	...	...	...	...	...	7	...	...	...	1	...	1
5	...	1	...	...	...	...	...	...	...	...	...	1	1	3	1	...	1	...	...	...
6	...	...	...	...	...	...	...	...	...	...	...	...	...	1	2	...	2	...	...	...
23	...	...	...	...	...	...	...	...	...	1	...	...	...	1	...	...	...	...	...	...
24	...	...	...	...	...	...	...	...	..	...	...	...	...	...	...	...	...	...	1	...
25	1	1	...	...	...	...	...	...	...	...	...	...	...	4	...	...	...	...	...	...
26	...	...	...	...	...	...	...	...	...	1	1	2	...	4	...	...	...	...	3	...
27	...	1	...	...	...	...	...	...	...	1	2	...	...	13	...	...	...	...	8	...
28	...	...	...	...	...	...	...	...	...	...	...	...	...	...	...	...	...	...	...	...
1	...	...	...	...	...	...	...	...	...	...	...	...	...	...	...	...	...	...	...	...
29	1	...	...	...	...	...	...	...	...	...	2	...	1	12	...	...	...	...	...	...
1	...	...	...	...	...	...	...	...	...	...	...	...	...	1	...	...	...	...	...	...
2	...	...	...	...	...	...	...	...	...	...	...	1	...	1	...	...	...	...	...	...
30	...	...	...	...	...	...	...	...	...	...	...	...	...	2	...	2	2	...	1	...
31	...	2	...	...	1	...	...	...	1	1	2	...	1	24	...	7	7	2	15	...
1	...	...	...	...	..	...	...	...	...	...	...	...	...	1	...	...	...	...	...	...
2	...	...	...	...	...	...	...	...	...	..	...	...	...	...	...	...	...	...	...	...
3	...	...	...	...	...	...	...	...	...	...	...	...	...	2	...	...	...	...	...	...
4	1	...	...	...	...	...	...	...	...	...	1	...	1	...	...	...	...	...	...	...
5	...	...	...	...	...	...	...	...	...	...	...	...	...	...	...	...	...	...	...	...
6	...	...	...	...	...	...	...	...	...	...	...	...	...	1	...	...	...	...	...	...
7	2	...	...	...	...	...	...	...	...	...	...	...	...	3	...	2	2	...	...	...
8	...	...	...	...	...	...	...	...	...	...	...	...	...	...	...	...	...	...	...	...
9	...	...	...	...	...	...	...	...	...	...	...	...	...	2	2	...	2	...	...	...
10	...	...	...	...	...	...	...	...	...	...	...	...	...	...	...	...	...	...	...	...
	12	23	3	...	7	2	1	2	2	6	27	17	16	280	61	22	83	20	202	7

TABLE No. VI.—New Sanitary Districts,

17. District of Newington.

Name of Street.	Height in feet above the sea.	Population 1861.			Mortality 1863.			Diseases in							
		Above 5.	Under 5.	Total.	Above 5.	Under 5.	Total.	Brain.	Heart.	Chest.	Abdomen.	Phthisis.	Croup.	Diphtheria.	Small-Pox.
1 Arniston place	262	102	5	107	2	...	2	...	...	...	...	...	...	...	...
2 Blacket place	239—260	223	21	244	2	...	2	...	...	...	...	...	...	...	...
3 Blacket place, South	236—250	...	...	...	...	...	...	...	...	...	...	...	...	...	...
4 Causewayside	205—255	934	124	1058	23	7	30	4	3	5	2	3	...	2	1
1 Amos' close (22)	255	73	19	92	...	2	2	...	...	...	...	...	...	1	...
2 Gow's close (14)	254	62	10	72	1	2	3	...	...	...	...	1	...	...	...
3 Grange court (68)	250	113	28	141	4	2	6	1	1	1	...	...	...	...	...
4 Jew's close (44)	255	8	2	10	...	...	...	...	...	...	...	...	...	...	...
5 Wallace's close (28)	255	38	6	44	...	...	...	...	...	...	...	...	...	...	...
6 Canning place	255	175	24	199	3	1	4	1	1	...	...	...	...	...	...
7 Grange place	245	95	9	104	1	1	2	...	1	...	...	...	...	...	...
8 Ratcliffe terrace	215	25	4	29	...	1	1	...	...	...	...	...	...	...	...
9 Ratcliffe place	215	47	10	57	...	...	...	...	...	...	...	...	...	...	...
10 Sciennes street, East	252	82	11	93	3	...	3	...	...	1	...	...	...	...	...
5 Clerk street, South	250—260	215	31	246	4	...	4	...	...	...	1	1	...	...	...
6 Craigie terrace	249	16	2	18	...	...	...	...	...	...	...	...	...	...	...
7 Dalkeith road	207—281	95	9	104	1	1	2	...	1	...	...	...	...	...	...
8 Duncan street	235	90	7	97	1	...	1	...	...	...	...	1	...	...	...
9 Gibbet toll, Old	280	16	3	19	...	...	...	...	...	...	...	...	...	...	...
10 Gray street, North	236—250	117	4	121	2	1	3	...	...	1	1	1	...	...	...
11 Gray street, South	207—235	69	3	72	...	...	...	...	...	...	...	...	...	...	...
12 Hamilton place	208	41	1	42	1	...	1	...	...	...	...	...	...	...	...
13 Hope park crescent	240	...	...	...	1	...	1	...	...	...	...	...	...	...	...
14 Hope park terrace	240—254	...	...	...	...	1	1	...	...	...	...	...	...	...	...
15 Lord Russell place	246	133	11	144	2	1	3	1	...	...	...	...	...	...	...
16 Lutton place	257	135	14	149	2	...	2	...	...	...	1	...	...	...	...
17 Mayfield loan, East	208—214	36	5	41	3	...	3	1	...	...	1	...	...	...	...
18 Mayfield loan, West	207	22	...	22	...	...	...	...	...	...	...	...	...	...	...
19 Mayfield street	211	...	...	...	...	...	...	...	...	...	...	...	...	...	...
20 Mayfield terrace	225	58	3	61	1	...	1	...	...	...	...	...	...	...	...
21 Macnab street	246	...	...	...	...	...	...	...	...	...	...	...	...	...	...
22 Middleby street	222	70	5	75	2	...	2	...	...	1	...	...	...	...	...
23 Minto street	211—260	284	27	311	4	...	4	2	...	...	1	...	...	...	...
24 Newington, West	263	40	...	40	2	...	2	...	...	...	...	1	...	...	...
25 Newington place, North	264	96	15	111	2	2	4	...	...	1	1	1	...	...	...
26 Newington place, East	273	16	3	19	...	...	...	...	...	...	...	...	...	...	...
27 Newington place, West	264	47	4	51	...	...	...	...	...	...	...	...	...	...	...
28 Newington terrace	264	53	2	55	...	1	1	...	...	...	...	...	...	...	...
29 Oxford street	274	...	...	...	...	...	...	...	...	...	...	...	...	...	...
30 Peel terrace	194	...	...	...	...	...	...	...	...	...	...	...	...	...	...
31 Powburn	184	22	2	24	...	...	...	...	...	...	...	...	...	...	...
32 Preston street, East	267—280	49	6	55	1	1	2	...	...	...	...	...	...	...	...
1 Preston terrace	267	...	...	...	1	1	2	...	...	1	...	...	...	...	...
2 Talbot place	271	40	3	43	1	...	1	...	...	...	...	...	...	...	...
33 Preston street, West	250—261	237	34	271	3	1	4	...	...	...	...	1	...	...	1
1 Farquharson place	250	26	2	28	...	...	...	...	...	...	...	...	...	...	...
2 ... Francis place	...	...	...	...	...	...	...	...	...	...	...	...	...	...	...
34 Rosehall	230—251	94	18	112	1	...	1	...	...	...	...	1	...	...	...
35 Salisbury place	250—258	64	9	73	1	...	1	...	...	1	...	...	...	...	...
36 Salisbury place, West	251	24	5	29	1	...	1	...	...	...	...	...	...	...	...
1 Thomson's court	251	18	5	23	...	...	...	...	...	...	...	...	...	...	...
37 Salisbury road	260—277	100	7	107	2	...	2	...	...	...	1	...	...	...	...
38 Summerhall	240	45	3	48	...	...	...	...	...	...	...	...	...	...	...
39 Summerhall place	246	83	11	94	2	2	4	...	...	2	...	...	...	...	...
Totals,		4428	527	4955	80	28	108	10	7	14	9	11	...	3	2

17. District of Newington.

	1863.														Street Cesspools.			Epidemics.		
					Fevers.													Cholera.	Fever.	
	Scarlatina.	Measles.	Hooping-Cough	Erysipelas.	Total.	Typhus.	Typhoid.	Gastric.	Infantile.	Diarrhoea and Dysentery.	Scrofula.	Old Age.	Premature Debility.	No. of Paupers.	Trapped.	Untrapped.	Total.	1848.	1847-8.	1857-8.
1	...	...	...	...	1	...	...	1	...	...	...	...	...	...	...	1	1	...	...	...
2	...	...	...	...	...	...	...	...	...	...	...	1	...	...	3	4	7	...	...	...
3	...	...	...	...	...	...	...	...	...	...	...	...	...	...	...	...	...	...	...	...
4	1	...	...	1	...	...	...	...	...	...	...	4	1	35	20	2	22	...	10	...
1	...	1	...	...	...	...	...	...	...	...	...	...	...	4	...	...	...	...	...	...
2	...	...	...	1	...	...	...	...	...	1	...	...	...	1	1	...	1	...	...	...
3	...	...	1	...	...	...	...	...	...	...	1	...	...	5	3	...	3	...	1	...
4	...	...	...	...	...	...	...	...	...	...	...	...	...	...	...	...	...	...	...	...
5	...	...	...	...	...	...	...	...	...	...	...	...	...	1	1	...	1	...	...	...
6	...	...	...	...	...	...	...	...	...	...	2	...	...	...	...	...	...	...	...	...
7	...	1	...	...	...	...	...	...	...	...	...	...	...	...	...	...	...	...	...	...
8	...	...	...	...	...	...	...	...	...	...	1	...	...	...	...	...	...	...	...	...
9	...	...	...	...	...	...	...	...	...	...	...	...	...	...	...	...	...	...	...	...
10	...	...	...	...	...	...	...	...	...	1	...	1	...	3	...	...	...	...	...	...
5	...	...	...	...	1	...	1	...	...	...	...	...	...	...	1	3	4	...	...	...
6	...	...	...	...	...	...	...	...	...	...	...	...	...	...	...	...	...	...	...	...
7	...	...	...	...	...	...	...	...	...	...	...	...	...	1	...	7	7	...	...	...
8	...	...	...	...	...	...	...	...	...	...	...	...	...	...	2	...	2	...	...	...
9	...	...	...	...	...	...	...	...	...	...	...	...	...	...	...	...	...	...	...	...
10 } 11 }	...	...	...	...	...	...	...	...	...	...	...	...	...	...	...	1	1	...	...	...
12	...	...	...	...	...	...	...	...	...	...	...	1	...	...	...	...	...	...	...	...
13	...	...	...	...	...	...	...	...	...	...	...	...	...	...	2	...	2	...	...	...
14	...	...	...	...	...	...	...	...	...	...	1	...	...	...	2	...	2	...	...	...
15	...	...	...	...	...	...	...	...	...	...	1	...	...	1	...	...	...	...	...	...
16	...	...	...	...	...	...	...	...	...	...	...	...	...	...	...	...	...	...	...	...
17	...	...	...	...	...	...	...	...	...	1	...	...	...	...	...	3	3	...	...	...
18	...	...	...	...	...	...	...	...	...	...	...	...	...	...	...	1	1	...	...	...
19	...	...	...	...	...	...	...	...	...	...	...	...	...	...	...	2	2	...	...	...
20	...	...	...	...	...	...	...	...	...	...	...	...	...	...	...	...	...	...	...	...
21	...	...	...	...	...	...	...	...	...	...	...	...	...	...	1	...	1	...	...	...
22	...	...	...	...	...	...	...	...	...	...	...	1	...	...	2	...	2	...	...	1
23	...	...	...	...	...	...	...	...	...	...	...	...	...	...	...	8	8	1	1	...
24	...	...	...	...	...	...	...	...	...	...	...	...	...	...	...	2	2	...	...	...
25	...	...	...	...	...	...	...	...	...	...	...	...	...	2	...	...	...	...	...	...
26	...	...	...	...	...	...	...	...	...	...	...	...	...	...	...	...	...	...	...	...
27	...	...	...	...	...	...	...	...	...	...	...	...	...	...	...	...	...	...	...	...
28	...	...	...	1	...	...	...	...	...	...	...	...	...	...	...	1	1	...	...	...
29	...	...	...	...	...	...	...	...	...	...	...	...	...	...	...	...	...	...	...	...
30	...	...	...	...	...	...	...	...	...	...	...	...	...	...	...	...	...	...	...	...
31	...	...	...	...	...	...	...	...	...	...	...	...	...	...	...	...	...	...	...	...
32	...	...	...	...	...	...	...	...	...	...	...	1	1	...	...	1	1	...	...	...
1	...	...	...	...	...	...	...	...	...	...	...	1	...	...	...	...	...	...	...	...
2	...	...	...	...	...	...	...	...	...	...	1	...	...	...	...	...	...	...	...	...
33	...	...	...	...	...	...	...	...	...	...	...	...	1	...	...	2	2	...	1	1
1	...	...	...	...	...	...	...	...	...	...	...	...	...	2	...	...	...	...	...	...
2	...	...	...	...	...	...	...	...	...	...	...	...	...	...	...	...	...	...	...	...
34	...	...	...	...	...	...	...	...	...	...	...	...	...	5	...	...	...	...	1	...
35	...	...	...	...	...	...	...	...	...	...	...	...	...	...	2	...	2	...	...	...
36	...	...	...	...	...	...	...	...	...	...	...	...	...	1	...	...	...	...	...	...
1	...	...	...	...	...	...	...	...	...	...	...	...	...	1	2	...	2	...	...	...
37	...	...	...	...	...	...	...	...	...	...	...	1	...	...	...	1	1	...	...	...
38	...	...	...	...	...	...	...	...	...	...	...	...	...	...	...	...	...	...	...	...
39	...	...	...	...	...	...	...	...	...	...	1	...	...	...	4	1	5	...	...	...
	1	2	1	3	2	...	1	1	...	3	8	11	3	62	46	40	86	1	14	2

TABLE No. VI.—New Sanitary Districts,

18. District of Grange.

Name of Street.	Height in feet above the sea.	Population 1861.			Mortality 1863.			Diseases in							
		Above 5.	Under 5.	Total.	Above 5.	Under 5.	Total.	Brain.	Heart.	Chest.	Abdomen.	Phthisis.	Croup.	Diphtheria.	Small-Pox.
1 Argyle place	240	26	7	33	...	1	1	...	...	...	...	...	...	1	...
2 Carlung place	260	...	...	...	1	...	1	...	...	1	...	...	...	...	...
3 Cumin place	273	74	8	82	...	1	1	...	...	...	...	...	...	...	...
4 Dalrymple crescent	250	...	...	...	...	2	2	...	...	...	...	...	...	...	...
5 Dick place	245—268	136	12	148	1	2	3	...	...	...	...	...	...	...	...
6 Dick place, West	268—278	...	...	...	...	...	...	...	...	...	...	...	...	...	...
7 Findhorn place	222—252	76	11	87	...	1	1	...	...	...	...	...	...	...	...
8 Fingal place	240	51	2	53	1	...	1	...	...	...	...	...	...	...	...
9 Grange loan	222—268	325	36	361	...	...	...	...	...	...	...	...	...	...	...
1 Hewit's place	222	34	2	36	...	...	...	...	...	...	...	...	...	...	...
10 Grange road	250—288	181	17	198	2	1	3	...	...	...	...	...	...	1	...
11 Lauder road	230—279	58	8	66	...	...	...	...	...	...	...	...	...	...	...
12 Mansionhouse road	276—288	57	3	60	3	...	3	1	...	...	...	...	...	...	...
13 Meadow place	240—260	167	10	177	2	...	2	...	...	...	...	...	...	...	...
14 Rillbank terrace	243	...	...	...	...	...	...	...	...	...	...	...	...	...	...
15 St Catherine's place	255	3	3	6	...	...	...	...	...	...	...	...	...	...	...
16 Sciennes street	245—255	264	46	310	2	2	4	1	...	...	...	...	...	1	...
1 Murray street	253	46	11	57	...	...	...	...	...	...	...	...	...	...	...
17 Sciennes place	247	19	...	19	...	...	...	...	...	...	...	...	...	...	...
18 Sciennes hill	255	36	2	38	3	...	3	2	...	...	...	...	...	...	...
19 Sciennes road	255—260	17	7	24	...	...	...	...	...	...	...	...	...	...	...
20 Seton place	260	27	2	29	...	...	...	...	...	...	...	...	...	...	...
21 Sylvan place	242	42	7	49	...	...	...	...	...	...	...	...	...	...	...
22 Tantallon place	256—270	...	...	...	...	1	1	...	...	...	...	...	...	...	...
23 Trades Maiden hospital	260	53	...	53	...	...	...	...	...	...	...	...	...	...	..
Totals,		1692	194	1886	15	11	26	4	...	1	...	...	...	3	...

19. District of Morningside.

Name of Street.	Height in feet above the sea.	Population 1861.			Mortality 1863.			Diseases in							
		Above 5.	Under 5.	Total.	Above 5.	Under 5.	Total.	Brain.	Heart.	Chest.	Abdomen.	Phthisis.	Croup.	Diphtheria.	Small-Pox.
1 Abbotsford park	323—327	43	5	48	...	...	...	...	...	...	...	...	...	...	...
2 Albert terrace	324	...	...	...	...	...	...	...	...	...	...	...	...	...	...
3 Banner place	310—325	21	5	26	...	...	...	...	..	...	...	...	...	...	...
4 Blackford road	308	64	7	71	1	...	1	...	...	...	...	...	...	...	...
5 Blackford place	...	17	3	20	...	...	...	...	...	...	...	...	...	...	...
6 Boroughmuirhead	310	66	11	77	2	1	3	...	...	...	...	2	...	...	...
7 Bruntsfield place	282—318	120	8	128	1	...	1	...	...	...	1	...	...	...	...
8 Bruntsfield terrace	314	27	...	27	...	...	...	...	...	...	...	...	...	...	...
9 Canaan lane	260—262	210	12	222	5	...	5	1	1	...	...	2	...	...	...
10 Chamberlain road	307—310	8	2	10	...	...	...	...	...	...	...	...	...	...	...
11 Churchhill	320—326	70	3	73	2	...	2	...	...	...	...	...	...	...	1
12 Clinton road	310	38	4	42	...	...	...	...	...	...	...	...	...	...	...
13 Colinton road, with Merchiston castle and bank	302—318	176	5	181	3	...	3	...	3	...	...	...	...	...	...
14 Eden lane	279—292	19	5	24	...	...	...	...	...	...	...	...	...	...	...
15 Esplin place	287	...	...	...	1	...	1	...	...	...	...	1	...	...	...
16 Gillespie's hospital	274	47	...	47	2	...	2	...	...	...	...	...	...	...	...
17 Greenhill bank	309—325	38	3	41	...	1	1	...	...	...	...	...	...	1	...
18 Greenhill gardens	309—320	210	9	219	1	1	2	...	...	...	...	...	...	...	...
19 Greenhill park	318	47	4	51	...	...	...	...	...	...	...	...	...	...	...
20 Hope terrace	318	61	4	65	1	...	1	1	...	...	...	...	...	...	...
21 Jordan lane and bank	256—260	124	10	134	8	3	11	1	...	2	...	3	1	...	...
22 Merchiston park	301—315	41	...	41	...	...	...	...	...	...	...	...	...	...	...
Carry forward,		1447	100	1547	27	6	33	3	4	2	1	8	1	1	1

AND THEIR VITAL STATISTICS.—*Continued.*

18. District of Grange.

	1863.														Street Cesspools.			Epidemics.		
					Fevers.													Cholera.	Fever.	
	Scarlatina.	Measles.	Hooping-Cough	Erysipelas.	Total.	Typhus.	Typhoid.	Gastric.	Infantile.	Diarrhœa and Dysentery.	Scrofula.	Old Age.	Premature Debility.	No. of Paupers.	Trapped.	Untrapped.	Total.	1848.	1847-8.	1857-8.
1	...	...	...	...	...	...	...	...	...	...	...	...	...	...	...	...	...	...	...	...
2	...	...	...	...	...	...	...	...	...	...	...	...	...	...	...	...	...	...	...	...
3	1	...	...	...	...	...	...	...	...	...	...	...	...	...	...	...	...	...	...	...
4	...	...	...	...	...	...	...	...	...	...	...	...	2	...	...	...	...	...	...	...
5	...	...	...	...	1	...	...	1	...	1	...	...	1	...	2	...	2	...	...	...
6	...	...	...	...	...	...	...	...	...	...	...	...	...	...	...	...	...	...	...	...
7	...	...	...	...	...	...	...	...	...	...	...	...	...	...	...	...	...	...	...	...
8	...	...	...	1	...	...	...	...	...	...	...	...	...	...	...	...	...	...	...	...
9	...	...	...	...	...	...	...	...	...	...	...	...	...	...	1	12	13	...	1	...
1	...	...	...	...	...	...	...	...	...	...	...	...	...	...	...	...	...	...	...	...
10	1	...	...	1	...	...	...	...	...	...	...	...	...	...	...	...	...	...	...	...
11	...	...	...	...	...	...	...	...	...	...	...	...	...	...	...	...	...	...	...	...
12	...	...	...	...	...	...	...	...	...	...	1	...	...	...	...	1	1	...	...	...
13	...	...	...	...	1	...	1	...	...	...	...	...	...	...	...	...	...	...	...	...
14	...	...	...	...	...	...	...	...	...	...	...	...	...	...	...	...	...	...	...	...
15	...	...	...	...	...	...	...	...	...	...	...	...	...	...	1	...	1	...	...	...
16	...	...	...	...	1	...	...	1	...	1	...	...	...	6				...	6	...
1	...	...	...	...	...	...	...	...	...	...	...	...	...	...	7	1	8	...	...	...
17	...	...	...	...	...	...	...	...	...	...	...	...	...	...				...	...	...
18	...	...	...	...	...	...	...	...	...	...	...	...	...	...				...	...	...
19	...	...	...	...	...	...	...	...	...	...	...	...	...	...	...	...	...	...	...	...
20	...	...	...	...	...	...	...	...	...	...	...	...	...	...	...	...	...	...	...	...
21	...	...	...	...	...	...	...	...	...	...	...	...	...	...	...	6	6	...	...	...
22	...	...	...	...	...	...	...	...	...	...	...	...	1	...	...	...	...	...	...	...
23	...	...	...	...	...	...	...	...	...	...	...	...	...	...	...	...	...	...	...	...
	2	...	...	2	3	...	1	2	...	2	1	...	4	6	11	20	31	...	7	...

19. District of Morningside.

	Scarlatina.	Measles.	Hooping-Cough	Erysipelas.	Fevers: Total.	Typhus.	Typhoid.	Gastric.	Infantile.	Diarrhœa and Dysentery.	Scrofula.	Old Age.	Premature Debility.	No. of Paupers.	Trapped.	Untrapped.	Total.	Cholera 1848.	Fever 1847-8.	Fever 1857-8.
1	...	...	...	...	...	...	...	...	...	...	...	...	...	...	1	...	1	...	...	...
2	...	...	...	...	...	...	...	...	...	...	...	...	...	...	...	...	...	...	...	...
3	...	...	...	...	...	...	...	...	...	...	...	...	...	...	...	...	...	...	...	...
4	...	...	...	...	...	...	...	...	...	...	...	1	...	...	1	...	1	...	...	...
5	...	...	...	...	...	...	...	...	...	...	...	...	...	...	...	...	...	...	...	...
6	...	...	...	...	...	...	...	...	...	...	...	...	1	1	...	...	...	...	...	...
7	...	...	...	...	...	...	...	...	...	...	...	...	...	...	4	4	8	...	...	...
8	...	...	...	...	...	...	...	...	...	...	...	...	...	...	...	...	...	...	...	...
9	...	...	...	...	...	...	...	...	...	...	...	...	...	...	4	5	9	...	1	...
10	...	...	...	...	...	...	...	...	...	...	...	...	...	...	...	...	...	...	...	...
11	...	...	...	...	...	...	...	...	...	...	...	...	...	...	3	...	3	...	...	...
12	...	...	...	...	...	...	...	...	...	...	...	...	...	...	3	2	5	...	...	...
13	...	...	...	...	...	...	...	...	...	...	...	...	...	...	...	...	...	...	...	...
14	...	...	...	...	...	...	...	...	...	...	...	...	...	...	...	...	...	...	...	...
15	...	...	...	...	...	...	...	...	...	...	...	...	...	...	...	...	...	...	...	...
16	...	...	...	...	...	...	...	...	...	...	...	1	...	...	...	...	...	...	...	...
17	...	...	...	...	...	...	...	...	...	...	...	...	...	...	...	...	...	...	...	...
18	...	...	...	...	...	...	...	...	...	1	1	...	...	...	6	3	9	...	...	...
19	...	...	...	...	...	...	...	...	...	...	...	...	...	...	...	...	...	...	...	...
20	...	...	...	...	...	...	...	...	...	...	...	...	...	...	...	...	...	...	...	...
21	...	...	...	...	2	1	...	1	...	...	1	...	...	1	1	1	2	...	2	...
22	...	...	...	...	...	...	...	...	...	...	...	...	...	...	...	2	2	...	...	...
	...	...	...	...	2	1	...	1	...	1	2	2	1	2	23	17	40	...	3	...

TABLE No. VI.—New Sanitary Districts,

19. District of Morningside—*Continued.*

Name of Street.	Height in feet above the sea.	Population 1861.			Mortality 1863.			Diseases in							
		Above 5.	Under 5.	Total.	Above 5.	Under 5.	Total.	Brain.	Heart.	Chest.	Abdomen.	Phthisis.	Croup.	Diphtheria.	Small-Pox.
Brought forward,		1447	100	1547	27	6	33	3	4	2	1	8	1	1	1
23 Merchiston place, North	301—310	29	9	38	...	...	...	...	...	...	...	...	...	...	...
24 Morningside	259—326	172	16	188	7	1	8	...	1	1	1	2	...	...	...
25 Morningside place	297	46	4	50	1	...	1	...	...	...	...	...	...	...	...
26 Morningside terrace ...	320	31	...	31	...	...	...	...	...	...	...	...	...	...	...
27 Montpelier	311	26	...	26	...	...	...	...	...	...	...	...	...	...	...
28 Napier road	...	...	...	...	...	...	...	...	...	...	...	...	...	...	...
29 Newbattle terrace	294—308	33	5	38	...	...	...	...	...	...	...	...	...	...	...
1 Church lane..............	...	...	...	...	...	...	...	...	...	...	...	...	...	...	...
30 Pitsligo road	293—320	13	3	16	...	...	...	...	...	...	...	...	...	...	...
31 Royal Asylum, East Division	...	87	...	87	7	...	7	5	...	...	2	...	...	...	...
32 Steel's place..............	271	14	1	15	1	...	1	...	...	...	...	...	...	...	...
33 Strathearn road	315	27	2	29	4	...	4	1	...	...	...	1	...	...	...
34 Tipperlin..................	282	21	5	26	...	...	...	...	...	...	...	...	...	...	...
35 Viewforth place	250—317	...	...	...	...	...	...	...	...	...	...	...	...	...	...
36 Viewforth road	250—317	38	4	42	1	...	1	...	...	...	...	...	...	...	...
37 Whitehouse loan.........	291—315	121	8	129	2	...	2	...	1	...	...	...	...	...	...
38 Wright's houses	249—274	273	38	311	1	...	1	...	...	...	...	...	...	...	...
Totals, ...		2378	195	2573	51	7	58	9	6	3	4	11	1	1	1

20. Landward District.

Name of Street.	Height in feet above the sea.	Population 1861.			Mortality 1863.			Diseases in							
		Above 5.	Under 5.	Total.	Above 5.	Under 5.	Total.	Brain.	Heart.	Chest.	Abdomen.	Phthisis.	Croup.	Diphtheria.	Small-Pox.
1 Canongate, Landward portion..................	...	13	1	14	...	...	...	...	...	...	...	...	...	...	...
2 Coltbridge	146	1305	187	1492	1	1	2	...	...	1	...	...	...	...	...
1 Murrayfield............	139—200	...	...	...	2	...	2	...	...	1	1	...	...	...	...
2 Roseburn..............	150	...	...	...	1	1	2	...	...	...	1	...	...	...	...
3 Craigleith	150	...	...	...	2	...	2	...	...	1	...	...	...	...	...
1 Black's entry	100	...	...	...	1	...	1	1	...	...	...	...	...	...	...
2 Porterfield	100	...	...	...	1	...	1	1	...	...	...	...	...	...	...
3 Windlestrawlee	109	...	...	...	1	...	1	...	...	...	1	...	...	...	...
4 Gorgie......................	160	...	...	...	3	4	7	...	...	1	...	2	...	...	...
1 Damhead..............	150	...	...	...	...	1	1	...	...	...	...	...	...	...	...
2 Tynecastle	160	...	...	...	1	1	2	...	...	...	...	...	...	...	...
5 Morningside	...	...	...	...	...	...	...	...	...	...	...	...	...	...	...
1 Asylum (pauper) ...	260	706	..	706	64	...	64	63	...	...	...	...	...	...	...
2 Egypt	250	...	...	...	...	1	1	...	...	...	...	...	...	...	...
3 Myreside...............	250	...	...	...	...	2	2	...	...	...	...	...	...	...	...
6 Saughton..................	150	...	...	...	...	...	...	...	...	...	...	...	...	...	...
1 Asylum	150	106	5	111	4	...	4	3	...	...	...	...	...	...	1
2 Balgreen house	150	...	...	...	3	...	3	3	...	...	...	...	...	...	...
3 Carrickknowe	150	...	...	...	1	...	1	...	...	...	1	...	...	...	...
Totals, ...		2130	193	2323	85	11	96	71	...	4	4	2	...	...	1

Note.—*In the First Column*—The Closes and Courts in Streets are generally arranged alphabetically under the Streets to which they belong, and are distinguished by smaller-sized figures.

Numerals immediately following the names of Closes, &c., refer to the Number in the Street.

In the Second Column—Two Elevations are frequently given: where only one appears, it is taken at the highest level.

AND THEIR VITAL STATISTICS.—*Continued.*

19. District of Morningside—*Continued.*

	1863.													No. of Paupers.	Street Cesspools.			Epidemics.		
	Scarlatina.	Measles.	Hooping-Cough.	Erysipelas.	Fevers. Total.	Typhus.	Typhoid.	Gastric.	Infantile.	Diarrhœa and Dysentery.	Scrofula.	Old Age.	Premature Debility.		Trapped.	Untrapped.	Total.	Cholera. 1848.	Fever. 1847-8.	Fever. 1857-8.
	...	...	...	...	2	1	...	1	...	1	2	2	1	2	23	17	40	...	3	...
23	...	...	...	...	...	...	...	...	...	...	...	...	...	...	...	...	...	...	...	...
24	...	...	...	...	...	...	...	...	...	...	1	1	...	1	10	1	11	...	5	...
25	...	...	...	...	...	...	...	...	...	...	1	...	...	...	...	5	5	...	...	...
26	...	...	...	...	...	...	...	...	...	...	...	...	...	...	...	...	...	...	...	...
27	...	...	...	...	...	...	...	...	...	...	...	...	...	...	...	...	...	...	...	...
28	...	...	...	...	...	...	...	...	...	...	...	...	...	...	2	...	2	...	...	...
29	...	...	...	...	...	...	...	...	...	...	...	...	...	...	...	...	...	...	...	...
1	...	...	...	...	...	...	...	...	...	...	...	...	...	...	4	7	11	...	...	...
30	...	...	...	...	...	...	...	...	...	...	...	...	...	...	...	...	...	...	...	...
31	...	...	...	...	...	...	...	...	...	...	...	...	...	...	...	...	...	...	...	...
32	1	...	...	...	...	...	...	...	...	...	...	...	...	...	1	...	1	...	...	...
33	...	...	...	...	1	...	1	...	...	...	...	...	...	...	...	1	1	...	...	...
34	...	...	...	...	...	...	...	...	...	...	...	...	...	...	...	...	...	...	...	...
35	...	...	...	...	...	...	...	...	...	...	...	...	...	... }	2	3	5	} ...	...	...
36	...	...	...	...	...	...	...	...	...	...	...	1	...	...				...	...	...
37	...	...	...	...	...	...	...	...	...	...	...	...	...	...	...	4	4	...	...	...
38	...	...	...	...	...	...	...	...	...	...	...	...	...	4	...	1	1	...	...	...
	1	...	...	...	3	1	1	1	...	1	4	4	1	7	42	39	81	...	8	...

20. Landward District.

	Scarlatina.	Measles.	Hooping-Cough.	Erysipelas.	Fevers. Total.	Typhus.	Typhoid.	Gastric.	Infantile.	Diarrhœa and Dysentery.	Scrofula.	Old Age.	Premature Debility.	No. of Paupers.	Trapped.	Untrapped.	Total.	Cholera. 1848.	Fever. 1847-8.	Fever. 1857-8.
1	...	...	...	...	...	...	...	...	...	...	...	...	...	...	...	...	...	...	...	...
2	...	...	...	...	...	...	...	...	...	...	1	...	...	1	...	...	...	...	3	...
1	...	...	...	...	...	...	...	...	...	...	...	1	...	2	...	...	...	...	...	...
2	...	...	...	...	...	...	...	...	...	...	...	...	...	...	...	...	...	...	...	...
3	...	...	...	...	...	...	...	...	...	...	...	...	...	...	...	...	...	...	1	...
1	...	...	...	...	...	...	...	...	...	...	...	...	...	1	...	...	...	...	...	...
2	...	...	...	...	...	...	...	...	...	...	...	...	...	...	...	...	...	...	...	...
3	...	...	...	...	...	...	...	...	...	...	...	...	...	...	...	...	...	...	...	...
4	...	...	...	...	...	...	...	...	...	1	1	...	...	5	...	...	...	...	5	...
1	...	...	...	...	1	...	1	...	...	...	...	...	...	...	...	...	...	...	...	...
2	...	...	...	...	1	1	...	...	...	1	...	...	...	3	...	...	...	...	...	...
5	...	...	...	...	...	...	...	...	...	...	...	...	...	...	...	...	...	...	...	...
1	...	...	...	...	1	...	1	...	...	...	...	...	...	483	...	...	...	...	8	...
2	1	...	...	...	...	...	...	...	...	...	...	...	...	1	...	...	...	...	...	...
3	1	...	...	...	...	...	...	...	...	...	...	...	1	...	...	...	...	...	...	...
6	...	...	...	...	...	...	...	...	...	...	...	...	...	...	...	...	...	...	1	...
1	...	...	...	...	...	...	...	...	...	...	...	...	...	...	...	...	...	...	...	...
2	...	...	...	...	...	...	...	...	...	...	...	...	...	...	...	...	...	...	...	...
3	...	...	...	...	...	...	...	...	...	...	...	...	...	...	...	...	...	...	...	...
	2	...	...	...	3	1	2	...	...	2	2	1	1	496	...	...	...	...	18	...

At page 16 the population of North Merchiston has been omitted. The mistake has been rectified in all the Tabular Abstracts.

In the Third Column—Where no Population is appended, the place was not built or inhabited at the Census in 1861. In some few cases, as in Cockburn Street, the Population has been specially taken during 1864, but is printed within brackets. Where deaths are recorded, and no Population, it has been found impossible to separate the Population of the Close or Court from that of the main street.

16.72

TABLE No. VII.—Abstract of Table vi., including District Birth and Death Rates, Density of Population, &c.

No.	Names of the Districts.	Population in 1861.			Mortality in 1863.			Births 1863.	Death-Rate per 1000.			Birth-Rate per 1000.	Birth-Rate in excess of Death-Rate.	Death-Rate in excess of Birth-Rate.	Area in Imperial Acres.	Inhabited Area in Imperial Acres.	Proportion of Population to each Acre.	Proportion of Population to each Inhabited Acre.
		5 years and upwards.	Under 5 years.	Total.	5 years and upwards.	Under 5 years.	Total.		5 years and upwards.	Under 5 years.	Total.							
1	Upper New Town	10,166	764	10,930	138	52	190	225	13·57	68·	17·38	20·58	3·2	...	121	115¼	90·3	94·8
2	Lower New Town	12,936	1,088	14,024	155	62	217	326	11·98	56·98	15·47	23·24	7·77	...	147	111	95·4	126·3
3	West End	7,036	712	7,748	173	74	247†	199	24·58	103·93	31·88	25·68	...	6·2	350	175	22·1	44·2
4	Upper Water of Leith	10,981	1,351	12,332	140	100	240	417	12·74	74·	19·46	33·81	14·35	...	416	140	29·6	88·
5	Lower Water of Leith	3,504	362	3,866	42	26	68	100	11·98	71·82	17·58	25·86	8·28	...	539	124	7·2	31·1
6	Broughton	5,183	489	5,672	79	21	100	141	15·24	42·94	17·63	24·85	7·22	...	197	116	28·8	48·9
7	Calton and Greenside	9,739	1,245	10,984	156	87	243	337	16·	69·87	22·12	30·68	8·56	...	281	91	39·	120·7
8	Abbey	1,916	321	2,237	49	33	82	121	25·57	102·8	36·65	54·09	17·44	...	110	48	20·3	46·6
9	Canongate	10,537	1,663	12,200	195	186	381†	537	18·5	111·84	31·23	44·01	12·78	...	59	55½	206·7	219·8
10	Tron	10,105	1,531	11,636	169	233	402	490	~~48·64~~	152·18	34·55	42·11	7·56	...	37	33	314·5	352·6
11	St Giles	13,876	2,091	15,967	232	228	460	600	16·71	109·	28·8	37·57	8·77	...	131	68	121·8	234·8
12	Grassmarket	4,455	772	5,227	74	96	170	247	16·61	124·35	32·52	47·25	14·73	...	22	22	237·6	237·6
13	Fountainbridge	8,524	1,356	9,880	136	113	249	450	15·95	83·33	25·2	45·54	20·34	...	104	86	95·	114·8
14	George Square and Lauriston	5,959	634	6,593	180	67	247†	170	30·2	105·67	37·46	25·78	...	11·68	182	89	36·2	74·
15	Nicolson Street	15,924	2,383	18,307	286	246	532	1,017	17·9	103·23	29·	55·55	26·55‡	...	64	64	286·	286·
16	Pleasance and St Leonard	9,445	1,659	11,104	155	141	296	518	16·41	84·99	26·65	46·64	19·99	...	84	74	132·2	150·
17	Newington	4,428	527	4,955	80	28	108	144	18·	53·13	21·79	29·06	7·27	...	233	124	21·2	39·9
18	Grange	1,692	194	1,886	15	11	26	54	8·86	56·7	13·78	28·63	14·85	...	251	118	7·5	15·9
19	Morningside	2,378	195	2,573	51	7	58	39	21·44	35·89	22·54	15·15	...	7·39	620	315	4·1	8·1
	Total for Parliamentary Area,	148,784	19,337	168,121	2,505	1,811	4,316	6,132	16·83	93·65	25·67	36·47	10·8	...	3,948*	1,968¾	42·5	85·4
20	Landward	2,130	193	2,323	85	11	96	46	39·9	57·	41·32	19·8	...	21·52	3,127	...	·7	...
	Total,	150,914	19,530	170,444	2,590	1,822	4,412	6,178	17·16	93·29	25·88	36·24	10·36	...	7,075	1,968¾	24·1	86·5

* This does not include portion of Arthur's Seat within Parliamentary Boundary, amounting to 243 acres. By adding this, Parliamentary Area is 4191 acres. † Poorhouse. ‡ Maternity Hospital.

110

TABLE No. VIII.—Abstract of Table vi., including District Mortality, arranged according to Disease.

No.	Names of the Districts.	Brain.	Heart.	Chest.	Abdomen.	Phthisis.	Croup.	Diphtheria.	Small-Pox.	Scarlatina.	Measles.	Hooping-Cough.	Erysipelas.	Fevers.					Diarrhœa and Dysentery.	Scrofulous Diseases.	Old Age.	Premature Debility.
														Total.	Typhus.	Typhoid.	Gastric.	Infantile.				
1	Upper New Town	24	22	20	21	23	3	5	1	3	3	1	...	6	1	3	2	...	6	10	7	7
2	Lower New Town	22	9	22	30	28	3	10	2	7	6	...	2	12	4	1	7	...	7	14	14	4
3	West End	30	10	42	28	23	4	8	5	8	3	...	1	9	4	3	2	...	7	9	21	8
4	Upper Water of Leith	27	15	23	25	18	10	26	3	7	9	...	3	8	2	3	3	...	6	12	12	12
5	Lower Water of Leith	12	1	6	5	8	3	1	...	1	5	...	1	2	...	1	...	1	2	5	4	7
6	Broughton	9	6	14	11	16	1	...	...	5	1	...	...	7	1	2	2	2	2	3	11	5
7	Calton and Greenside	28	18	43	16	28	2	12	2	7	7	...	...	12	5	5	1	1	7	21	8	9
8	Abbey	4	4	14	6	8	2	2	...	...	7	...	...	5	3	...	1	1	2	8	1	5
9	Canongate	34	22	53	19	34	16	9	6	11	25	3	...	20	10	4	3	3	8	27	20	24
10	Tron	34	17	92	19	28	15	6	2	6	48	11	...	16	7	5	1	3	13	23	5	22
11	St Giles	35	22	83	25	48	18	8	8	10	21	23	1	15	8	2	3	2	11	31	14	29
12	Grassmarket	13	9	32	17	11	8	2	6	3	21	2	...	4	1	3	...	...	6	8	2	13
13	Fountainbridge	24	16	38	15	24	1	5	6	11	9	2	3	9	...	2	4	3	9	16	13	16
14	George Square and Lauriston	29	18	36	24	25	8	6	...	7	3	1	...	2	1	1	...	...	7	15	37	12
15	Nicolson Street	46	30	70	32	56	14	16	2	17	27	6	2	21	6	5	6	4	12	58	25	38
16	Pleasance and St Leonard	20	21	40	27	31	5	11	3	12	23	3	...	7	2	1	2	2	6	27	17	16
17	Newington	10	7	14	9	11	...	3	2	1	2	1	3	2	...	1	1	...	3	8	11	3
18	Grange	4	...	1	...	...	...	3	...	2	...	...	2	3	...	1	2	...	2	1	...	4
19	Morningside	9	6	3	4	11	1	1	1	1	...	...	...	3	1	1	1	...	1	4	4	1
	Total for Parliamentary Area	414	253	646	333	431	114	134	49	119	220	53	18	163	56	44	41	22	117	300	226	235
20	Landward	71	...	4	4	2	...	...	1	2	...	...	...	3	1	2	...	...	2	2	1	1
	Total,	485	253	650	337	433	114	134	50	121	220	53	18	166	57	46	41	22	119	302	227	236

TABLE No. IX.—ABSTRACT OF TABLE VI., including DISTRICT PERCENTAGE OF MORTALITY, arranged according to DISEASE.

No.	NAMES OF THE DISTRICTS.	Population in 1861.	Proportion of Population to each Inhabited Acre.	Brain, per cent.	Heart, per cent.	Chest, per cent.	Abdomen, per cent.	Phthisis, per cent.	Croup, per cent.	Diphtheria per cent.	Small-Pox, per cent.	Scarlatina, per cent.	Measles, per cent.	Hooping-Cough, per cent.	Erysipelas, per cent.	Fevers, per cent.	Diarrhoea and Dysentery, per cent.	Scrofulous Diseases, per cent.	Old Age, per cent.	Premature Debility, per cent.
1	Upper New Town	10,930	94·8	·22	·2	·18	·19	·21	·03	·04	·009	·03	·03	·009	...	·05	·05	·09	·06	·06
2	Lower New Town	14,024	126·3	·15	·06	·15	·21	·19	·02	·07	·01	·05	·04	...	·01	·08	·05	·09	·1	·03
3	West End	7,748	44·2	·38	·12	·54	·36	·29	·05	·1	·06	·1	·04	...	·01	·12	·09	·11	·27	·1
4	Upper Water of Leith	12,332	88·	·21	·12	·18	·2	·14	·08	·21	·02	·06	·07	...	·02	·06	·05	·1	·1	·1
5	Lower Water of Leith	3,866	31·1	·31	·03	·15	·12	·2	·08	·03	...	·03	·13	...	·03	·05	·05	·13	·1	.18
6	Broughton	5,672	48·9	·15	·1	·24	·19	·28	·02	...	...	·09	·02	...	...	·12	·04	·05	·19	·09
7	Calton and Greenside	10,984	120·7	·25	·16	·39	·14	·25	·02	·11	·02	·06	·06	...	...	·11	·06	·19	·07	·08
8	Abbey	2,237	46·6	·18	·18	·62	·27	·36	·09	·09	...	...	·31	...	...	·22	·09	·36	·04	·22
9	Canongate	12,200	219·8	·28	·18	·43	·15	·28	·13	·07	·05	·09	·2	·02	...	·16	·06	·22	·16	·19
10	Tron	11,636	352·6	·29	·14	·79	·16	·24	·13	·05	·02	·05	·41	·08	...	·14	·11	·19	·04	·19
11	St Giles	15,967	234·8	·22	·13	·52	·15	·3	·11	·05	·05	·06	·13	·14	·006	·09	·07	·19	·08	·18
12	Grassmarket	5,227	237·6	·24	·17	·61	·32	·21	·15	·04	·11	·06	·4	·04	...	·08	·11	·15	·04	·24
13	Fountainbridge	9,880	114·8	·24	·16	·38	·15	·24	·01	·05	·06	·11	·09	·02	·03	·09	·09	·16	·13	·16
14	George Square and Lauriston	6,593	74·	·44	·27	·54	·36	·37	·12	·09	...	·1	·05	·02	...	·03	·1	·23	·56	·18
15	Nicolson Street	18,307	286·	·25	·16	·38	·17	·3	·07	·09	·01	·09	·15	·03	·01	·11	·07	·32	·13	·2
16	Pleasance and St Leonard	11,104	150·	·18	·18	·36	·24	·27	·04	·1	·03	·1	·2	·03	...	·06	·05	·24	·15	·14
17	Newington	4,955	39·9	·2	·14	·28	·18	·22	...	·06	·04	·02	·04	·02	·06	·04	·06	·16	·22	·06
18	Grange	1,866	15·9	·21	...	·05	...	...	...	·16	...	·1	...	...	·1	·16	·1	·05	...	·21
19	Morningside	2,573	8·1	·35	·23	·11	·15	·42	·04	·04	·04	·04	...	...	...	·11	·04	·16	·16	·04
	Total for Parliamentary Area	168,121	85·3	·24	·14	·38	·19	·25	·07	·08	·03	·07	·13	·03	·01	·09	·07	·17	·13	·14
20	Landward	2,323	...	·3	...	·17	·17	·08	...	...	·04	·08	...	...	...	·13	·08	·08	·04	·04
	Total,	170,444	86·5	·28	·14	·38	·19	·25	·07	·08	·03	·07	·13	·03	·01	·09	·07	·17	·13	·14

TABLE No. X.—Monthly Distribution of Cases of Diphtheria and Fever in 1863.

No.	Names of the Districts.	Diphtheria.													Fever.												
		January.	February.	March.	April.	May.	June.	July.	August.	September.	October.	November.	December.	Total.	January.	February.	March.	April.	May.	June.	July.	August.	September.	October.	November.	December.	Total.
1	Upper New Town	...	...	...	...	...	2	...	...	...	...	2	1	5	...	...	...	...	...	1	...	1	1	1	1	1	6
2	Lower New Town	...	...	...	1	...	...	1	2	...	1	2	3	10	3	2	...	...	...	...	1	1	...	1	2	2	12
3	West End	...	...	...	...	...	1	2	...	...	2	2	1	8	...	1	2	...	...	...	...	...	2	2	2	...	9
4	Upper Water of Leith	...	1	1	1	3	3	6	5	1	...	4	1	26	...	...	...	1	...	1	...	...	3	1	1	1	8
5	Lower Water of Leith	...	...	...	...	...	...	...	1	...	...	...	...	1	...	1	...	1	...	...	...	...	...	...	...	...	2
6	Broughton	...	...	...	...	...	...	...	...	...	...	...	...	...	...	1	1	...	...	...	1	...	1	1	1	1	7
7	Calton and Greenside	...	...	3	2	...	...	1	1	2	3	...	...	12	1	1	...	...	1	...	3	1	...	1	2	2	12
8	Abbey	...	...	...	...	...	...	...	...	...	...	1	1	2	1	1	...	...	1	...	...	1	...	1	...	...	5
9	Canongate	...	...	1	1	1	1	1	...	...	3	...	1	9	1	2	...	2	1	...	2	2	...	5	3	2	20
10	Tron	...	..	...	1	1	...	1	...	...	1	...	2	6	2	...	1	...	3	2	1	2	2	...	1	2	16
11	St Giles	1	...	...	1	...	1	1	2	...	1	1	...	8	2	1	1	3	1	2	...	...	...	1	3	1	15
12	Grassmarket	...	...	...	1	...	...	1	...	...	...	...	...	2	...	...	...	...	1	1	...	...	...	...	1	...	3
13	Fountainbridge	...	...	...	1	...	2	...	...	...	...	1	1	5	1	...	...	3	...	...	...	...	3	1	...	1	9
14	George Square and Lauriston	...	2	...	1	1	...	1	...	...	...	...	1	6	...	1	...	...	...	...	...	...	1	...	...	...	2
15	Nicolson Street	1	1	1	1	2	1	1	2	...	2	3	1	16	1	1	2	5	2	1	...	2	...	3	3	1	21
16	Pleasance and St Leonard	1	...	...	2	3	1	1	...	...	1	...	2	11	...	1	...	...	1	...	2	...	1	...	1	1	7
17	Newington	...	...	...	...	...	...	1	1	...	...	1	...	3	...	1	...	...	...	...	...	...	...	...	1	...	2
18	Grange	...	...	...	1	...	1	...	...	1	...	...	...	3	...	...	...	...	...	...	...	...	...	2	1	...	3
19	Morningside	...	...	...	...	...	...	...	...	...	...	1	...	1	...	...	...	...	...	...	...	...	1	2	...	...	3
	Total,	3	4	6	14	11	13	18	14	4	14	18	15	134	12	14	7	15	11	8	10	10	15	22	23	16	163

TABLE No. XI.—Abstract of Table vi., including District Distribution of Paupers, Epidemic Diseases, &c., &c.

No.	Names of the Districts.	Population 1861.	Proportion of Population to each Inhabited Acre.	Number of Paupers.*	Street Cesspools.			Cholera Epidemic 1848.	Fever.		Percentage of Paupers to Population.	Percentage of Untrapped Cesspools.	Percentage of Cholera Cases to Population.	Percentage of Fever Cases to Population.	
					Trapped.	Untrapped.	Total.		1847-8.	1857-8.				1847-8.	1857-8.
1	Upper New Town	10,930	94·8	91	74	81	155	20	87	14	·83	52·3	·18	·8	·13
2	Lower New Town	14,024	126·3	138	61	57	118	6	42	4	·98	48·3	·04	·3	·03
3	West End	7,748	44·2	535	66	69	135	3	54	1	6·9	51·1	·04	·7	·01
4	Upper Water of Leith	12,332	88·	309	37	98	135	11	62	2	2·5	72·6	·09	·5	·02
5	Lower Water of Leith	3,866	31·1	49	5	50	55	5	24	1	1·27	90·9	·13	·62	·03
6	Broughton	5,672	48·9	38	21	24	45	5	21	1	·67	53·3	·09	·37	·02
7	Calton and Greenside	10,984	120·7	187	43	77	120	18	161	2	1·7	64·2	·16	1·46	·02
8	Abbey	2,237	46·6	41	22	10	32	4	16	...	1·83	31·2	·18	·72	...
9	Canongate	12,200	219·8	566	152	27	179	88	692	12	4·64	15·1	·72	5·67	·01
10	Tron	11,636	352·6	676	109	20	129	165	1,320	25	5·81	15·5	1·16	11·34	·21
11	St Giles	15,967	234·8	820	103	58	161	206	1,775	39	5·13	36·	1·29	11·12	·24
12	Grassmarket	5,227	237·6	304	65	14	79	102	1,250	7	5·81	17·7	1·95	23·91	·13
13	Fountainbridge	9,880	114·8	293	50	33	83	2	119	6	2·96	39·7	·02	1·2	·06
14	George Square and Lauriston	6,593	74·	680	29	38	67	9	66	9	10·31	56·7	·14	1·	·14
15	Nicolson Street	18,307	286·	673	144	34	178	29	241	7	3·67	19·1	·16	1·32	·04
16	Pleasance and St Leonard	11,104	150·	396	61	22	83	20	202	7	3·56	26·5	·18	1·82	·06
17	Newington	4,955	39·9	95	46	40	86	1	14	2	1·91	46·5	·02	·28	·04
18	Grange	1,886	15·9	9	11	20	31	...	7	...	·47	64·5	...	·37	...
19	Morningside	2,573	8·1	8	42	39	81	...	8	...	·31	48·1	...	·31	...
	Total for Parliamentary Area	168,121	85·4	5,908	1,141	811	1,952	694	6,161	139	3·51	41·5	·39	3·66	.08
20	Landward	2,323	...	502	...	...	...	...	18	...	21·61	...	...	·78	...
	Total,	170,444	86·5	6,410	1,141	811	1,952	694	6,179	139	3·76	41·5	·39	3·62	·08

* These figures include the dependants of Paupers belonging to St Cuthberts, and which could not be inserted in the detailed Statement.

TABLE No. XII.—District Distribution of Lodging-Houses, Public Wells, &c., &c.

No.	Names of the Districts.	Population 1861.	Lodging-Houses.			Number of Public Wells.	Number of Drinking Fountains.	Public Conveniences.		Number of Urinals.
			Total Number of Licenses.	Number of Apartments.	Number of Lodgers.			Number.	Accommodation.	
1	Upper New Town	10,930	1	1	5	...	4	1	8	3
2	Lower New Town	14,024	...	...	...	...	...	...	...	...
3	West End	7,748	...	...	...	...	1	...	...	1
4	Upper Water of Leith	12,332	...	...	...	1	3	4	19	...
5	Lower Water of Leith	3,866	...	...	...	...	1	...	...	...
6	Broughton	5,672	...	...	...	...	1	...	...	1
7	Calton and Greenside	10,984	...	...	...	1	2	3	30	6
8	Abbey	2,237	...	...	...	...	...	1	9	1
9	Canongate	12,200	33	84	138	12	...	3	37	2
10	Tron	11,636	87	211	556	6	...	2	54	3
11	St Giles	15,967	142	473	1,049	14	2	4	81	7
12	Grassmarket	5,227	131	362	813	4	...	3	47	3
13	Fountainbridge	9,880	...	...	...	...	3	2	28	3
14	George Square and Lauriston	6,593	...	...	...	...	2	1	4	4
15	Nicolson Street	18,307	...	...	...	7	1	1	10	2
16	Pleasance and St Leonard	11,104	1	1	3	3	...	1	8	1
17	Newington	4,955	...	...	...	1	...	3	12	1
18	Grange	1,886	...	...	...	...	...	...	...	...
19	Morningside	2,573	...	...	...	...	...	1	4	1
	Total,	168,121	395	1,132	2,564	49	20	30	351	39

TABLE No. XIII.—District Distribution of Births (Legitimate and Illegitimate) in 1863, and of Licences in 1864.

No.	Names of the Districts.	Proportion of Population to each Inhabited Acre.	Births in 1863.					Percentage of Illegitimate to Total Births.	Percentage of Illegitimate Births to Population.	Licences Granted in 1864.					Proportion of Population to each Public House.	Percentage of Public Houses to Total Licences.
			Males.	Females.	Total.	Legitimate.	Illegitimate			Total Number issued.	For Public Houses.	For Grocers.	For Hotels.	For Spirit Dealers.		
1	Upper New Town	94·8	120	105	225	214	11	4·9	·1	120	46	42	26	6	237·6	38·3
2	Lower New Town	126·3	169	157	326	313	13	4·	·09	49	17	32	...	...	825·	34·7
3	West End	44·2	95	104	199	196	3	1·5	·04	32	12	18	2	...	645·7	37·5
4	Upper Water of Leith	88·	222	195	417	385	32	7·7	·26	38	11	26	1	...	1,121·	29·
5	Lower Water of Leith	31·1	48	52	100	96	4	4·	·1	11	4	7	...	...	966·5	36·4
6	Broughton	48·9	80	61	141	130	11	7·8	·19	24	9	14	1	...	630·	37.5
7	Calton and Greenside	120·7	164	173	337	318	19	5·6	·17	54	23	22	7	2	477·6	42·6
8	Abbey	46·6	52	69	121	111	10	8·3	·45	10	5	5	...	...	447·4	50·
9	Canongate	219·8	286	251	537	484	53	9·9	·44	54	28	25	1	...	435·7	51·8
10	Tron	352·6	250	240	490	436	54	11·	·46	46	24	19	1	2	484·8	52·1
11	St Giles	234·8	326	274	600	564	36	6·	·22	85	54	28	2	1	295·7	63·5
12	Grassmarket	237·6	111	136	247	228	19	7·7	·36	38	15	20	2	1	348·5	39·5
13	Fountainbridge	114·8	227	223	450	430	20	4·4	·2	49	20	29	...	...	494·	40·8
14	George Square and Lauriston	74·	76	94	170	167	3	1·8	·05	10	4	6	...	...	1,648·	40·
15	Nicolson Street	286·	512	505	1,017	729	288*	28·3	1·57	107	48	58	...	1	381·4	44·9
16	Pleasance and St Leonard	150·	290	228	518	492	26	5·	·23	41	15	25	1	...	740·3	36·6
17	Newington	39·9	68	76	144	142	2	1·4	·04	20	7	13	...	...	708·	35·
18	Grange	15·9	28	26	54	53	1	1·8	·05	...	...	...	...	...	...	...
19	Morningside	8·1	22	17	39	37	2	5·1	·08	5	2	3	...	...	1,286·5	40·
	Total for Parliamentary Area	85·4	3,146	2,986	6,132	5,525	607	9·9	·36	793	344	392	44	13	488·7	43·4
20	Landward	...	25	21	46	44	2	4·3	·08	...	...	...	...	...	...	...
	Total,	...	3,171	3,007	6,178	5,569	609	9·8	·35	793	344	392	44	13	495·5	43·4

* Including Royal Maternity Hospital, *vide* Report, page 17.

APPENDIX No. II.

TABLE No. I.

CLASSIFIED LIST OF BYRES

WITHIN THE

PARLIAMENTARY BOUNDARY.

1. District of Upper New Town.

No.	Locality.	Name.	No. of Cows.	Under Dwellings.	Cleanliness.	Ventilation.	Condition of Court.
1	Rose Street Lane,	Campbell	9	Apart	dirty	imperfect	dirty
2	... ...	Robertson	16	...	...	...	...
3	... ...	Houston*	5	...	...	...	...
4	... ...	Wilson*	9	...	...	...	...
		Total	39				

2. District of Lower New Town.

No.	Locality.	Name.	No. of Cows.	Under Dwellings.	Cleanliness.	Ventilation.	Condition of Court.
1	Duke Street Lane,	Wilson	7	Apart	dirty	imperfect	pretty clean
2	Northumberland Place,	Doughtie	8	...	...	...	dirty
3	Jamaica Street Lane,	Orr	24	...	...	...	pretty clean
		Total	39				

* Have been shut and empty during the autumn.

3. District of West End.

No.	Locality.	Name.	No. of Cows.	Under Dwellings.	Cleanliness.	Ventilation.	Condition of Court.
1	Melville Street Lane,	Harley	8	Apart	pretty clean	imperfect	clean
2	Lothian Road,	White	2	...	dirty	...	dirty
3	...	Anderson	14	...	...	...	...
4	St Cuthbert's Lane,	Wilson	2	...	removed this autumn.		
5	Morison Street,	Gibson	42	...	clean	good	...
6	...	Waldie	10	...	pretty clean	pretty good	...
7	Grove Place,	Bell	10	...	dirty	imperfect	...
8	... Cottage,	Hodge	1	...	clean	good	clean
9	Rosemount,	Simpson	17	...	...	...	dirty
10	Bainfield,	M'Culloch	18	...	dirty	imperfect	...
11	Dalry Lane,	Honeyman	35	...	clean	excellent	clean
12	...	M'Farlane	5	...	dirty	imperfect	dirty
13	...	Begbie	9	...	clean	...	pretty clean
		Total	173				

4. District of Upper Water of Leith.

No.	Locality.	Name.	No. of Cows.	Under Dwellings.	Cleanliness.	Ventilation.	Condition of Court.
1	The Dean,	Lockhart	7	Apart	clean	pretty good	clean
2	Bell's Mills,	Finnie	3	...	pretty clean	imperfect	dirty
3	...	Crombie	22	...	...	...	very dirty
4	Dean Brae,	Veitch	6	...	dirty	...	dirty
5	... Street,	Watson	16	...	clean	good	clean
6	...	Robertson	24	...	...	...	...
7	Allan Street Lane,	Orr	7	...	...	imperfect	dirty
8	... Court,	Dick	11	...	...	...	...
9	Veitch's Place,	Boa	19	...	dirty	...	...
10	Dean Bank Lane,	Gray	4	...	...	...	very dirty
11	Patriot Hall,	Pinkerton	7	...	clean	...	clean
12	Hamilton Place,	Fleming	17	...	dirty	...	dirty
13	Saunders Street Lane	Jack	18	...	clean	good	...
14	Circus Lane,	Wilson	9	...	clean	imperfect	...
		Total	170				

5. District of Lower Water of Leith.

No.	Locality.	Name.	No. of Cows.	Under Dwellings.	Cleanliness.	Ventilation.	Condition of Court.
1	Silver Mills,	Waterston	19	Apart	rather dirty	good	dirty
2	...	Henderson	17	...	clean	...	...
3	...	Scott	22	...	...	...	pretty clean
4	...	Mitchell	3	...	...	...	...
5	...	Niven	15	...	clean	imperfect	clean
6	...	Smith	9	...	...	...	...
7	...	Morton	39	...	...	good	...
8	...	Wilson	10	...	...	imperfect	...
9	...	Muir	3	...	...	...	...
10	...	Robertson	1	...	...	...	...
11	Water Lane,	Haddow	27	...	...	good	...
12	...	Brooks	3	...	} removed during the summer.		
13	...	White	6	...			
	Carry	forward,	174				

District of Lower Water of Leith, *Continued.*

No.	Locality.	Name.	No. of Cows	Under Dwellings.	Cleanliness.	Ventilation.	Condition of Court.
	Brought	forward,	174				
14	Canonmills,	Arnold	8	Apart	clean	good	clean
15	...	Cameron	3	...	dirty	...	...
16	...	M'Farlane	4	...	...	imperfect	dirty
17	...	Coltherd	19	...	clean	good	clean
18	...	Munro	26	...	dirty	imperfect	dirty
19	Heriot Hill,	Craw	11	...	clean	good	clean
20	Logie Green,	M'Ewen	17	...	...	...	...
21	Beaver Hall,	Niven	34	...	...	...	pretty clean
22	Powder Hall,	Inglis	1	...	...	...	clean
23	Bonnington Mills,	Smith	8	...	...	...	...
		Total	305				

6. District of Broughton.

No.	Locality.	Name.	No. of Cows	Under Dwellings.	Cleanliness.	Ventilation.	Condition of Court.
1	Broughton Lane (low)	Christie	37	Apart	clean	good	pretty clean
2	... ...	Cooper	24	...	dirty	imperfect	...
3	... ...	Gardiner	49	...	...	...	...
4	... ...	Robertson	21	...	clean	good	clean
5	Cuddie Park	Jack	21	...	dirty	imperfect	dirty
6	Blandfield Cottage,	Wilson	29	...	clean	good	clean
		Total	181				

7. District of Calton and Greenside.

No.	Locality.	Name.	No. of Cows	Under Dwellings.	Cleanliness.	Ventilation.	Condition of Court.
1	Greenside,	M'Morran	13	Apart	dirty	imperfect	dirty
2	...	Mackintosh	45	...	pretty clean	...	...
3	Swinton Row,	M'Dougal	21	...	dirty	...	...
4	London Road,	Macfarlane	6	...	clean	pretty good	...
5	Easter Road,	Jackson	13	...	...	...	...
		Total	98				

8. District of Abbey.

No.	Locality.	Name.	No. of Cows	Under Dwellings.	Cleanliness.	Ventilation.	Condition of Court.
1	Abbeyhill,	White	7	Apart	dirty	imperfect	dirty
2	...	Wilkie	2	Under	...	...	...
3	...	Davidson	12	Apart	...	...	...
4	Croft-an-Righ,	Thom	4	...	pretty clean	...	clean
5	Spring Gardens,	Brown	6	...	dirty	good	dirty
6	...	Brown	3	...	clean	...	clean
		Total	34				

9. District of Canongate.

No.	Locality.	Name.	No. of Cows.	Under Dwellings.	Cleanliness.	Ventilation.	Condition of Court.
1	Brown's Close,	Findlay	9	Apart	dirty	imperfect	dirty
2	Campbell's ...	Ross	5	Under	...	...	...
3	Gullan's ...	Smith	7	...	...	...	...
4	Logan's ...	Thompson	16	Apart	pretty clean	good	pretty clean
5	... ...	Somerville	10	...	dirty	imperfect	dirty
6	Reid's ...	White	11	...	...	...	...
7	Tolbooth Wynd,	Gibson	18	...	pretty clean	...	pretty clean
8	North Back	M'Bean	6	...	dirty	good	dirty
9	...	Fraser	1	...	...	imperfect	...
10	South Back	Brotherston	15	Apart & under	pretty clean	...	...
11	...	Carroll	2	Under	dirty	...	...
12	...	Kelloch	6	...	...	...	...
13	...	Cameron	10	Apart	pretty clean	...	...
14	M'Dowal Street,	Thompson	5	...	...	...	pretty clean
15	New Street,	M'Morran	14	...	...	...	...
		Total	135				

10. District of Tron.

No.	Locality.	Name.	No. of Cows.	Under Dwellings.	Cleanliness.	Ventilation.	Condition of Court.
1	Blackfriars Wynd,	Weir	6	Apart	pretty clean	imperfect	dirty
2	Leith Wynd,	Pringle	19	...	...	...	...
3	South Niddry Street,	Ramage	28	...	...	...	...
		Total	53				

11. District of St Giles.

No.	Locality.	Name.	No. of Cows.	Under Dwellings.	Cleanliness.	Ventilation.	Condition of Court.
1	Cowgate—Rattray's Close,	Laidlaw	13	Apart	pretty clean	imperfect	dirty
2	... Peter's Close,	Smith	7	...	dirty	...	...
3	Candlemaker Row,	Brown	24	...	...	...	...
		Total	44				

12. District of Grassmarket.

No.	Locality.	Name.	No. of Cows.	Under Dwellings.	Cleanliness.	Ventilation.	Condition of Court.
1	Cowie's Close,	Lyons	5	Under	dirty	imperfect	dirty
2	Inglis' Court, West Port,	Ramsay	14	Apart	...	...	...
3	King's Stables,	Smith	8	...	...	...	...
4	...	Croan	1	...	clean	good	clean
		Total	28				

13. District of Fountainbridge.

No.	Locality.	Name.	No. of Cows.	Under Dwellings.	Cleanliness.	Ventilation.	Condition of Court.
1	Main Point.	Shaw	15	Apart	dirty	imperfect	dirty
2	High Riggs, Fleming's Cl.	M'Pherson	3	...	clean	good	...
3	... No. 5,	Laidlaw	10	...	...	imperfect	...
4	... Robb's Entry,	Stevenson	17	...	dirty	...	...
5	... ...	Bell	2	...	clean	...	...
6	Hamilton Place,	Wardrop	5	...	dirty	...	...
7	...	Hamilton	3	...	clean	...	pretty clean
8	Toll Cross,	Alexander	12	...	...	good	clean
9	Lochrin,	Goodwell	9	...	...	...	...
10	Leven Lodge,	Porteous	23	...	pretty clean	...	dirty
11	Valleyfield,	Thomson	14	...	dirty	...	...
12	...	Hannah	9	...	pretty clean	...	...
13	Dunbar Street,	Prentice	8	...	excellent	excellent	excellent
14	Thornybauk,	Spence	48	Apart & under	pretty clean	good	dirty
15	...	Ogg	17	Apart	...	...	...
16	...	Aitken	2	Under	dirty	imperfect	...
17	...	Scott	1	Apart	...	...	...
18	Fountainbridge,	Brown	9	...	...	...	...
19	...	Cairns	10	...	clean	good	...
20	...	Goodwin	2		...	...	...
21	Castlebarns,	White	17	...	dirty	imperfect	...
22	...	Telford	2	...	...	...	...
		Total	238				

14. District of George Square and Lauriston.

No.	Locality.	Name.	No. of Cows.	Under Dwellings.	Cleanliness.	Ventilation.	Condition of Court.
1	Buccleuch Place Lane,	Main	6	Apart	pretty clean	imperfect	pretty clean
2	... ...	Burton	7	...	...	...	...
3	George Square Lane,	Forrest	13	...	...	...	...
4	Windmill Lane,	Chisholm	14	...	dirty	...	dirty
5	...	Learmonth	30	...	...	...	...
6	Lauriston Street,	Hardie	2	...	pretty clean	...	pretty clean
		Total	72				

15. District of Nicolson Street.

No.	Locality.	Name.	No. of Cows.	Under Dwellings.	Cleanliness.	Ventilation.	Condition of Court.
1	Potterrow,	Dickson	17	Apart	dirty	imperfect	dirty
2	North Richmond Street,	Cockburn	8	...	...	...	...
3	Buccleuch Street,	Learmonth	23	...	...	...	...
4	...	Walker	5	...	...	...	...
5	Sibbald Place,	Chisholm	21	...	pretty clean	...	pretty clean
6	Crosscauseway, East,	Begbie	53	Under	...	...	...
7	... Cowan's Close,	Traquair	10	Apart	...	good	...
8	... ...	Leadbetter	4	..	...	imperfect	...
9	... Murray Street,	Sanderson	25	...	...	...	...
10	Crosscauseway, West,	Shaw	6	.	...	...	...
		Total	172				

16. District of Pleasance and St Leonard.

No.	Locality.	Name.	No. of Cows	Under Dwellings.	Cleanliness.	Ventilation.	Condition of Court.
1	Pleasance, St John's Hill,	Drysdale	6	Apart	pretty clean	good	dirty
2	... James' Court,	Edgar	17	...	dirty	imperfect	...
3	... Thomson's Park,	Wood	21	...	...	good	...
4	... Hatter's Court,	Waldie	10	...	...	imperfect	...
5	... Hardwell Close,	Aitken	11	...	...	...	...
6	... No. 192,	Walker	15	...	...	...	...
7	Forbes Street,	Graham	17	...	pretty clean	...	pretty clean
8	Hercles Street,	Burnet	10	...	dirty	...	dirty
9	St Leonard's Street,	Purdie	1	...	removed this summer.		
10	... ...	Aitchison	11	...	pretty clean	good	dirty
11	... ...	Stobie	31	Apart & under	...	imperfect	...
12	... ...	Gilroy	3	Apart	...	...	...
13	... Hill,	Wright	19	...	dirty	...	...
14	... Lane,	Finlay	2	...	removed this summer.		
		Total	174				

17. District of Newington.

No.	Locality.	Name.	No. of Cows	Under Dwellings.	Cleanliness.	Ventilation.	Condition of Court.
1	Causewayside,	Currie	8	Apart	clean	good	clean
2	... 58,	Clapperton	16	...	dirty	imperfect	dirty
3	... 68,	Chisholm	12	...	pretty clean	...	...
4	... 115,	Galloway	3	...	...	...	...
5	... 127,	Guthrie	3	...	...	...	pretty clean
6	... 183,	Gibb	7	...	...	...	...
7	West Salisbury Place,	Middlemas	13	...	dirty	...	dirty
8	Old Gibbet Toll,	Finlay	3	...	pretty clean	good	pretty clean
9	...	Thomson	2	...	...	...	...
10	Dalkeith Road,	Souter	13	...	clean	...	...
		Total	80				

18. District of Grange.

No.	Locality.	Name.	No. of Cows	Under Dwellings.	Cleanliness.	Ventilation.	Condition of Court.
1	Grange Loan,	Rae	4	Apart	pretty clean	good	dirty
2	...	Girdwood	5	...	...	...	pretty clean
3	Lover's Lane,	Stewart	17	...	dirty	imperfect	very dirty
		Total	26				

19. District of Morningside.

No.	Locality.	Name.	No. of Cows	Under Dwellings.	Cleanliness.	Ventilation.	Condition of Court.
1	Merchiston,	Porteous	15	Apart	pretty clean	imperfect	pretty clean
2	Morningside,	Miller	4	...	...	good	...
3	Canaan Lane,	M'Gregor	1	...	...	...	...
4	...	Utterson	1	...	...	...	...
5	...	Bremner	1	...	...	...	...
6	...	Oswald	1	...	...	...	...
7	... Lodge,	Cassels	1	...	...	...	...
		Total	24				

TABLE No. II.—SUMMARY of the preceding TABLE, along with the POPULATION of the Sanitary Districts.

No.	NAMES OF THE DISTRICTS.	Population 1861.	Proportion of Population to each Inhabited Acre.	Number of Byres.	Number of Cows.	Under Dwellings.		Cleanliness.		Ventilation.		Condition of Court.	
						Under.	Apart.	Clean.	Dirty.	Good.	Imperfect.	Clean.	Dirty.
1	Upper New Town	10,930	94·8	4	39	4	...	...	4	...	4	...	4
2	Lower New Town	14,024	126·3	3	39	3	...	...	3	...	3	2	1
3	West End	7,748	44·2	13	173	13	...	8	5	5	8	4	9
4	Upper Water of Leith	12,332	88·	14	170	14	...	10	4	4	10	4	10
5	Lower Water of Leith	3,866	31·1	23	305	23	...	17	6	14	9	19	4
6	Broughton	5,672	48·9	6	181	6	...	3	3	3	3	5	1
7	Calton and Greenside	10,984	120·7	5	98	5	...	3	2	2	3	...	5
8	Abbey	2,237	46·6	6	34	5	1	2	4	2	4	2	4
9	Canongate	12,200	219·8	15	135	10	5	6	9	2	13	4	11
10	Tron	11,636	352·6	3	53	3	...	3	...	...	3	...	3
11	St Giles	15,967	234·8	3	44	3	...	2	1	...	3	...	3
12	Grassmarket	5,227	237·6	4	28	3	1	1	3	1	3	1	3
13	Fountainbridge	9,880	114·8	22	238	20	2	13	9	11	11	4	18
14	George Square and Lauriston	6,593	74·	6	72	6	...	4	2	...	6	4	2
15	Nicolson Street	18,307	286·	10	172	9	1	6	4	1	9	6	4
16	Pleasance and St Leonard	11,104	150·	14	174	13	1	6	8	4	10	2	12
17	Newington	4,955	39·9	10	80	10	...	8	2	4	6	6	4
18	Grange	1,886	15·9	3	26	3	...	2	1	2	1	1	2
19	Morningside	2,573	8·1	7	24	7	...	7	...	6	1	7	...
	Total for Parliamentary Area,	168,121	85·4	171	2,085	160	11	101	70	61	110	71	100

No. III.

COPY OF CLAUSE 93 of the METROPOLIS LOCAL MANAGEMENT ACTS AMENDMENT, relative to Licensing Cow-houses, 25 and 26 Vict., Cap. 102.

93. From and after the first day of November One thousand eight hundred and sixty-two, no place within any Parish or Place mentioned in the Schedules to the firstly-recited Act shall be used by any person carrying on the business of a Slaughterer of Cattle, or Cow Keeper, or Dairyman, as a Slaughterhouse for the purpose of slaughtering cattle, or a Cow-house or Place for the keeping of cows, without a Licence had for such purpose respectively from the Justices of the Peace, assembled at a Special Sessions, held in the Division or District where such Slaughterhouse, Cow-house, or Place is situate, and such Licence shall continue in force for the period of one year from the granting thereof, and thenceforth until the Special Sessions to be held next after the expiration of such period; and no fee or reward exceeding Five Shillings shall be taken for any such Licence; and if any person carrying on such business of a Slaughterer of Cattle, Cow-keeper, or Dairyman, use as a Slaughterhouse or Cow-house any place within any Parish or Place mentioned in the Schedules of the firstly recited Act which is not so licensed, every person so offending shall, for each offence, be liable to a Penalty not exceeding Five Pounds, of which offence the fact that cattle have been taken into such a place shall be deemed sufficient *prima facie* evidence: Provided always that before any Licence for the use of any place as a Slaughterhouse or Cow-house is granted as aforesaid, Fourteen Days' Notice of the intention to apply for such Licence shall be given to the Vestry or District Board of the Parish or District in which any such place is situate, to the intent that such Vestry or District Board, if they think fit, may show cause against the granting of any such Licence, and also Seven Days' Notice previous to such Special Sessions being held of the intention to apply for such Licence shall be given to the Clerk of the Justices for such Division: Provided, that nothing in this Act contained shall extend to Slaughterhouses erected, or to be erected, in the Metropolitan Cattle Market, under the authority of the Metropolitan Market Act 1851, or the Metropolitan Market Act 1857.

COPY OF CLAUSE 95.

VESTRIES and BOARDS to Contract for REMOVAL of MANURE from Stables and Cow-houses.

95. It shall be lawful for every Vestry and District Board, if they in their discretion think fit, to appoint and employ a sufficient number of persons, or to contract with any company or persons for collecting and removing the manure and refuse straw from such Stables and Cow-houses within their Parish or District, the occupiers of which may signify their consent in writing to such removal: Provided that such consent shall not be with-

drawn or revoked without one month's previous notice to the Vestry or District Board, and that no person shall be hereby relieved from any penalty or penalties to which they may be subject for placing Dung or Manure upon the foot-ways or carriage ways of any Parish or District, or for having any Accumulation or Deposit of Manure, so as to be a nuisance, or injurious to health.

No. IV.

LAWS Regulating Cow-Houses in Paris, passed and confirmed 1838.

To obviate as completely as possible the serious inconveniencies resulting from Cow-houses, the Council of the Seine decided that it would only authorize the establishment of Cow-houses in very open and spacious localities, at the same time fixing, in an invariable manner, the number of cows permitted to be kept in them.

The following are the conditions imposed upon the trade:—

1*st.* The stables for cows not to be less than 13 feet 2 inches in height.

2*d.* The stables for one row of cows not to be less than 13 feet 2 inches in breadth from the manger to the opposite wall.

3*d.* The stables for two rows of cows not to be less than 23 feet in width from one manger to another, if the mangers are placed against the walls; and not less than 26 feet if the mangers are placed in the centre of the stables.

4*th.* The space reserved for each cow not to be less than 6 feet 6 inches in breadth.

Lastly, the Council decided that it was necessary to determine positively, that no cow establishment situated lower than the surrounding soil should be authorised, and that authorization should always be refused when it is sought for in a locality where the drainage from the Cow-house is received into a cesspool.

Regulations confirmed by the Ordinance of Police of 27th February 1838.—*Dictionnaire d'Hygiène Publique, art. Vacheries, by Dr Tardieu.*

No. V.

CLAUSES in GENERAL POLICE ACT [SCOTLAND], passed 1862, referring to Cow-Houses, 25 and 26 Vict., Cap. 101.

141. All Stables and Byres, and areas therewith connected, shall be constantly kept in a clean condition to the satisfaction of the Inspector of Cleansing, under a penalty not exceeding twenty shillings for each offence; and it shall be the duty of the Inspector from time to time to examine the state of all such places with a view to the enforcement of this enactment.

143. It shall be lawful for the Commissioners, or any of them, after inspection and report by the Superintendent of Police, or Inspector of Cleansing, to regulate and limit the time within which all common necessaries and dungsteads shall be emptied and cleaned out; and if any other person under obligation by contract or otherwise to empty or clean out such places shall fail so to do within the time so limited, such other person shall be liable in a penalty not exceeding twenty shillings, besides forfeiture of any Stable or Byre dung in such place, which dung the Inspector of Cleansing, or any other officer authorized by the Commissioners, may remove or dispose of, or cause to be removed and disposed of, and the proceeds, under deduction of the expenses of removal, shall be applied to the police purposes under this Act.

No. VI.

RELATIVE PROPORTION OF COWS, and their Increase, in the OLD and NEW TOWN.

	1857.	1864.	Increase.
North of Princes Street,	729	840	111
South of Princes Street,	1068	1245	177
Total,	1797	2085	288

No. VII.

The average annual quantity of Milk brought by the Railways into Edinburgh is 132,000 Gallons.

By the North British Railway, (including the Peebles, and the Edinburgh, Perth, & Dundee lines), . 11,206 Gallons.
... Edinburgh and Glasgow Railway, . . 915 ...
... Caledonian Railway, . . . 120,000 ...
132,121 ...

This represents but the $\frac{1}{17}$th part of the Milk furnished by the Dairies within the Parliamentary Boundary; for, allowing the low average of three gallons a-day for each cow, we have 2,283,075 gallons as the yearly supply, which gives to each inhabitant 13½ gallons per annum.

INDEX.

COLSTON & SON, PRINTERS, EDINBURGH.

Explanatory notes on the facsimile

1 For the 1866 edition 'WITH RELATIVE APPENDICES, &c.' was removed and the imprint changed to the following: EDINBURGH: | PRINTED FOR THE RIGHT HONOURABLE THE LORD PROVOST, | MAGISTRATES, AND TOWN COUNCIL, | BY | COLSTON & SON, 80 ROSE STREET. | – – – – | MDCCCLXVI.

2 In the 1866 edition the word APPENDIX was printed with wider letter spacing. The list of tables was entirely replaced with a list of tables I to VIII on pages 121–128. Details of the changes to the appendices are given below following page 120 of the *Report*.

3 In the 1866 edition the content of this page was replaced entirely with the list of diagrams transferred from the following page which was left blank. The two coloured maps (the fold-out map of sanitary districts and the proposed street) were omitted from the 1866 edition; diagrams 2–6 were renumbered 1–5.

4 In the 1866 edition the words 'for the first time' were inserted after 'it became possible'.

5 Because the 1866 edition contained no map Littlejohn changed this sentence to 'This division is, however, very faulty.'

6 In the 1866 edition the preceding two sentences were altered to the following: 'Again, from the peculiar division adopted, it is a matter of difficulty to determine the exact registration district of a locality; and as tabular guides have had to be provided for the use of the medical profession and the Registrars themselves, the difficulties experienced by the public can easily be imagined. We have, for example, Princes Street and the Cowgate respectively in three registration districts.'

7 In the 1866 edition the last line ends 'A portion of Canonmills is in St George's, and the'.

8 In the 1866 edition 'for that parish' was added after 'Registrar's office'.

9 In the 1866 edition 'while another is' was replaced with 'while another portion is'.

10 In the 1866 edition 'mortality of the various portions of the city' was replaced with 'district mortality'.

11 In the 1866 edition 'the mortality' was replaced with 'deaths'.

12 In the 1866 edition 'well-founded one, that, in the case' was replaced with 'well-founded one. In the case'.

13 In the 1866 edition 'must' was replaced with 'required to'.

14 In the 1866 edition 'a new division of the city' was replaced with 'dividing the city anew'.

15 In the 1866 edition 'sanitary districts' was replaced with 'Sanitary Districts'.

16 In the 1866 edition 'the accompanying map of the city, which' was replaced with 'a map of the city which I have prepared, and which'.

17 In the 1866 edition the first line begins 'Leith was marked out'.

18 In the 1866 edition the words 'upper' and 'lower' were changed to 'Upper' and 'Lower'.

19 This improbably small area was only corrected to "3127 acres" in the 1866 popular edition.

20 The first printing read 'containing at this portion of its course but little sewage, along with a large amount of refuse'.

21 The first printing the page break came after the word 'various'.

22 In the first printing after 'attendant mortality,' the sentence finished 'are generally included under that of Edinburgh'.

23 The first printing read 'if we except what was occasioned by Small-pox'.

24 The first printing had 'rigorous'. Littlejohn's handwriting was not always easy to read.

25 In the first printing there was no paragraph break at this point.

26 In the first printing the paragraph ended 'Perth 24 per cent' not 'Perth ·24 per cent'. In the 1866 edition the type was re-spaced but unaltered in content.

27 In the 1866 edition 'In the Appendix, Tables No. VI., and VIII.,' was replaced with 'In the Appendix it will be found that'.

28 In the 1866 edition 'special column in Table VII., p. 56 of' was replaced with 'special Table in'.

29 In the 1866 edition 'In Table XII. of the Appendix, p. 61,' was replaced with 'In the Appendix'.

30 In the 1866 edition 'At p. 60 of Appendix, Table XI.' was replaced with 'In the Appendix'.

31 In the 1866 edition 'in epidemic of cholera and fever, as shown in' was replaced by 'in epidemics of Cholera and Fever, as shown by'.

32 In the 1866 edition there were five corrections: in the eighth column 29·73 and 26·12 were changed to 29·77 and 26·13 respectively; in the bottom row 25·67, ·74 and 37·24 were changed to 25·67, ·79 and 36·64.

33 In the first printing there was an erroneous comma at the end of this sentence.

34 Chimney-stalk was current usage for chimney-stack. The phrase 'what quarter soever' would now be rendered 'whatsoever quarter'.

35 In the first printing 'were there divided' read 'were divided'.

36 In the 1866 edition 11 lines of type were re-spaced but with no alteration to the text.

37 In the 1866 edition 69 was changed to 128.

38 In the 1866 edition '110' was changed to '101'.

39 In the 1866 edition 'appended to this report (p. 69), with the accompanying map' was replaced with 'appended to this report)p. 128), with the map', with an erroneous opening parenthesis.

40 In the 1866 edition '(see Appendix, No. 6),' was deleted.

41 In the 1866 edition 'It will be seen, however, (see Appendix, No. 7), to what a small extent' was replaced by 'It is remarkable, however, to what a small extent'.

42 In the 1866 edition, ', a copy of which is given in the Appendix to this Report (page 71)' was deleted.

43 In the 1866 edition, the semi-colon after 'obtained' was replaced with a comma and the line ends 'Act were en-'.

44 In the 1866 edition, 'organized' was replaced with 'organised'. There was also some re-spacing of type in the first two paragraphs with no other changes to the text.

45 In the 1866 edition 'localized' was replaced with 'localised'.

46 In the 1866 edition 'Dairymen' was replaced with 'dairymen'.

47 In the 1866 edition 'Dairies' was replaced with 'dairies'.

48 In the 1866 edition 'Slaughter-houses' was replaced with 'Slaughterhouses'.

49 In the 1866 edition 'City' was replaced with 'city'.

50 In the 1866 edition there was some re-spacing of type in the third paragraph with no changes to the text.

51 In the 1866 edition 'tubular one' was replaced with 'pipe'.

52 In the 1866 edition 'had been' was replaced with 'was'.

53 In the 1866 edition '67' was replaced with '69'.

54 Littlejohn, uncharacteristically, presented the raw numbers as percentages. In the 1866 edition he corrected the figures as follows. '96', '117', '89' and '19' were replaced with '·54', '·58', '·52' and '·1'. 'In the New Town the same percentage occurs, viz., 19.' and 'rises to 21 per cent.' were replaced with 'In the New Town the percentage was ·09 per cent.' and 'rises to ·1 per cent.' respectively.

55 In the last column on the right the figure for Coppersmiths is printed 3·54. This is an error, possibly a printer's error, for 3·45. It was corrected in the 1866 edition.

56 In the 1866 edition, which did not contain the statistical appendix, the comment 'but will be found noticed in the Appendix, St Giles' district, pp. 36, 37.' was removed.

57 This should have read 'At p. 61 of the Appendix'. In the 1866 edition 'At p. 60 of the Appendix' was replaced by 'In the Appendix,'.

58 In the 1866 edition 'each street, in Table VI. of the Appendix' was replaced with 'each street in the Appendix'.

59 In the 1866 edition 'at p. 56' was replaced with 'in the Appendix'.

60 The lower case w in water of Leith is found in all editions of the *Report*.

61 In the first printing 'which, as already' read 'which was most'.

62 In the 1866 edition 'unfortunately situated' was replaced with 'stated, has been most unfortunately situated'.

63 In the 1866 edition 'Diphtheria, Appendix, p. 57' was replaced with 'Diphtheria in the Appendix'.

64 In the first printing 'divert the run of the water' read 'absorb the water'.

65 In the 1866 edition 'and are' was changed to 'and which are'.

66 In this second printing Littlejohn added clarity and emphasis by replacing 'These, which were perfectly innocuous, when the district was a strictly rural one and some miles from the city, are quite an anomaly in the midst of a large population, and must sooner or later be removed.' with 'The latter were perfectly innocuous, when the district was a strictly rural one and some miles from the city, but they are now quite an anomaly in the midst of a large population, and ought, sooner or later, be removed.'

67 In the first printing the first two lines were at the bottom of page 89 and the heading of that page was moved higher.

68 In the first printing the heading and first two lines were on page 90.

69 In the 1866 edition this sentence begins 'It will be observed, by reference to the Appendix, that'.

70 In the first printing page 92 starts 'the free use of water ...'.

71 In the 1866 edition 'In Table XII., at p. 61 of the Appendix' was replaced with 'In the Appendix'.

72 In the 1866 edition Littlejohn added a comma after 'largely increased'.

73 In the first printing 'One only, viz., that at Echo Bank, was situated' read 'One only was situated'. The page break was after 'Several'.

74 In the first printing the first line starts 'of then are already encroached upon'.

75 In the first printing 'Cholera' was printed 'cholera'.

76 In the first printing 'Cholera' was printed 'cholera'.

77 In the first printing, under churchyards, 'Trinity, Dean Bridge' was 'Trinity, Deanbridge' and the figures '6', '...', and '310' under the number of interments at the higher rates were '2', '1' and '304'. Under Cemeteries figures for Rosebank were changed from '676', '4', '461' and '215', to '155', '525', '104' and '51', and the totals from '2,621', '203', '1,392' and '1,229' to '2,100', '724', '1,035' and '1,065'.

78 In the first printing the page break was here, a line being moved back a page to accommodate new material on page 98.

79 In the first printing the two figures were respectively 5411 and 4869.

80 The sentence 'In the table ... comparatively disused' was inserted in the second printing.

81 In the first printing these last two sentences read as follows: 'Thus, of the 4869 burials, 2587 were interred in the Churchyards, and 2282 in our Cemeteries. And of the 2587 in the Churchyards, 2242 were at the lowest rates, and only 307 at the higher; while, in the Cemeteries, of the 2282 already referred to, there were 1004 at the lowest rates, and 1104 at the highest.' In the 1866 edition the last part of that passage reads 'while, in the Cemeteries, of the 1587 from within the same area, there were 647 at the lowest rates, and 940 at the highest.'

82 In the first printing the number buried in the City Churchyards was given as 41. The following sentence began, 'It will be observed that these burials took place'.

83 The last two sentences replaced the following in the first printing: 'In the Cemeteries within the municipality there were 174 interments from without.'

84 In the first printing a new paragraph began after 'should be closed.'

85 In the first printing the page break came after the word 'poor'.

86 In the first printing 'and which, as already shown, are equally faulty, and utterly unsuited' reads 'and which is, in my opinion, equally faulty and utterly unsuited'.

87 In the 1866 edition 'the tabular statement of' was removed.

88 In the first printing ', so to speak,' followed 'which are built'.

89 In the first printing this sentence reads 'A constant state of dampness exists, which lowers the healthiness of the residence, not to speak of directly rendering the apartments of the servants unhealthy in a marked degree.

90 In the first printing 'to say nothing' read 'not to speak'.

91 In the first printing ', so to speak,' followed 'equilibrium'.

92 In the first printing this paragraph begins 'Indeed, in'.

93 The sentence 'Besides this ... meanest localities' was inserted in the second printing.

94 In the first printing this passage read 'The poverty of other great towns lies huddled away in districts, and the scenes thus presented,'.

95 In the first printing the word 'best' was in the preceding line – 'as to the best method of improving' – and appeared at the end of the line. In the second printing the metal type appears to have been misplaced, introducing an obvious error. Littlejohn corrected this error when sending complimentary copies and it is corrected in the 1866 edition. Five of the nine copies of the second printing that have been examined have this manuscript correction; three of these are inscribed with a salutation to the recipient. In the first printing the full point at the end of the sentence was omitted.

96 In the 1866 edition '*cul de sacs*' was replaced with '*culs de sac*'.

97 In the second printing there is an imprint below the name BACK CANONGATE: 'W. & A. K. Johnston, Edinburgh'.

98 The words 'even if it should not,' were inserted in the second printing.

99 Comma added in second printing.

100 In the first printing page 114 started after the word 'long'.

101 In the first printing Littlejohn had 'the poorest in the city'.

102 Littlejohn missed this misspelling of abattoir.

103 The double d in attendance is an obvious printer's error.

104 In the first printing the remainder of this paragraph read 'Such anomalies as have been perpetrated in Macnab Street, for example, – where the ventilation of future tenements must be seriously interfered with, not to speak of the appearance of the locality, by the eccentricity of the builder or proprietor, – would never be tolerated.' In altering this and adding 314 extra words, Littlejohn substantially amplified his conclusion with these ideas on town planning improvements and their potential benefits.

105 In the 1866 edition 'Table No. XIII., p. 62 of the Appendix' should have been changed to 'Table No. VII., p. 127' but Littlejohn failed to make the correction.

106 In the first printing the last page of the *Report* (120) began 'no comfort at home'.

107 Littlejohn presumably meant 'such a one'.

108 In the 1866 edition – referred to as a 'People's Edition' – The three appendices were reduced to eight tables. The following pages were removed: 1–55 (containing tables I–VI), 63–68 (the 'Classified List of Byres') and 70–72 (laws and further details relating to cow keeping). The remaining tables were re-numbered I to VIII and the pages numbered 121–128.

109 The totals for Population 1861 do not agree with those given elsewhere in the *Report* (page 10 and Appendix pages 56, 58, 60, 61 and 69) where they are 7036, 712 and 7048.

110 The death rate for those aged 5 years and upwards in Tron district is printed as 43·64 and was corrected by hand in the copy used for this facsimile to 16·72. There is no discernible explanation for this major error; it was corrected in the 1866 edition. Three other mistakes in the death-rate columns are not due to rounding error: 17·90 in Nicolson Street should be 17·96; 18·00 in Newington should read 18·07; 29· should be 29·06. Only the first of these was corrected in the 1866 edition. The first printing lacked the footnotes to the Poorhouse and the Maternity Hospital.

111 In the 1866 edition 'ABSTRACT OF TABLE VI.' was removed from the title.

112 In the 1866 edition 'ABSTRACT OF TABLE VI.' was removed from the title and there were six small changes to the percentages: District 2, Scrofulous ·09 changed to ·1; District 19, Abdomen ·15 changed to ·16; Total Parliamentary Area, Heart ·14 changed to ·15; Total, Heart ·14 changed to ·15; Total Parliamentary Area, Scrofulous ·17 changed to ·18; Total, Scrofulous ·17 changed to ·18.

113 In the 1866 edition the totals in the third column from the right were corrected from ·39 to ·41.

114 The footnote was added at the second printing.

115 In the first printing this was the last page; there was no index. The bottom of the page contained the imprint under a narrow rule: 'COLSTON AND SON, PRINTERS, EDINBURGH.' In this second printing the imprint was moved to page iii of the index.

116 The index was added at the second printing. The bottom of the page contained the imprint under a narrow rule: 'COLSTON AND SON, PRINTERS, EDINBURGH.' In this second printing the imprint was moved to page iii of the index. For the 1866 edition the index was substantially revised with consequent repagination. Seven headword entries were removed; three sub-heads were added. Sixty-four Appendix page numbers were changed; one was added to an entry where the number was omitted. Under 'Elevation' the word 'Diphtheria' was changed to 'Diptheria'. Under 'House Accommodation' the hyphen in 'Working-Classes' was removed. Under 'Licenses [*sic*] granted in 1864' the hyphen in 'Per-centage' was removed.

Bibliography and sources

Primary sources

Edinburgh City Archives

The archival sources are presented in two elements: archive call numbers (ECA ED9/23/1–2); and a description of item or volume (ECA Council Minutes, vol. 284).

ECA 9/25/2/13, Half Yearly Report and Return of Crimes since the year 1841 (1848)

ECA ACC 378, Edinburgh Exhibition Trust, Minutes, 1888

ECA ACC 657, Littlejohn Family Papers

ECA Bailie Court Processes, Box 412, 11–17, 1783, Procurator Fiscal v. W. Thomson

ECA Box 00/01/20/E74, Annual Accounts of the Police Establishment, 1834–37

ECA Box 00/01/20 (formerly DRT17 Box 4 A1/9) Murrayburn 261 B, miscellaneous bundles A–E

ECA Box 00/01/20/A14, Regulations on Lodging Houses drawn up by the Surgeon

ECA Box 00/01/21, Lord Provost's Committee, Reports, 1862

ECA Council Minutes, vols 283–5 and Scroll Index to Council Minutes, vols 289–300

ECA ED006/1/19, *Report and Returns as to Crimes, Offences, and Contraventions and to Cases of Drunkenness, within the Police Bounds of the City of Edinburgh, during the Six Years ended with 1860. Prepared for the Magistrates and Council, by Thomas Linton, Superintendent of Police. 1861*, 17

ECA ED006/1/1a, Annual Reports and Returns from the Superintendent of Police, 1865 to 1881

ECA ED9/1/1–23, Edinburgh Police Commissioners Minutes, 1805–56

ECA ED9/1/3, Streets and Buildings and Sanitary and Drainage Committee Report, Report on Smoke Pollution, 1855

ECA ED9/1/10, General Police Commissioners Minutes, 1846

ECA ED9/1/12, Special Meeting of the General Commissioners of Police, 1854, and Transcript of Notes by Dr Glover, 21 March 1854; letter, Gavin to Board of Health, 1 May 1854

ECA ED9/1/12–13, Police Commissioners General Minutes, 1850–54

ECA ED9/1/12/74, Police Commissioners, letters, 1850

ECA ED9/1/5, General Commissioners, Minutes, 1823

ECA ED9/2/1–5, Minutes of the Watching Committee, 1820–56

ECA ED9/3/5, Cleaning Committee Minutes, Letters, 1844–49 [subsequent minutes in Joint Cleaning and Sanitary Committee ED9/3/6 (1849–53) and ED9/3/7 (1853–56)]

ECA ED9/3/5, Sanitary and Drainage Committee Minutes, 1854

ECA ED9/3/5, Minutes, Special Meeting of the General Commissioners of Police, Minutes, 1854

ECA ED9/3/5, General Commissioners Minutes, 1848–49

ECA ED9/3/5, Report by the Sub-Committee on Dr Glover's Cholera Accounts, 1849

ECA ED9/3/5, Joint Finance and Sanitary Committee Minutes, February–March 1849

ECA ED9/3/5, Sanitary Committee Minutes, 1849

ECA ED9/3/1–7, Minutes of Cleaning Committee, 1819–56

ECA ED9/5/4, Law Committee Minutes, 1847–50

ECA ED9/7/3–4, Law and Finance Committee Minutes, 1846–56

ECA ED9/9/1–2, Minutes of Drainage Committee, 1853–56

ECA ED9/22/3, Letter Books, 1822–26

ECA ED9/22/11, Police Commissioners Letter Book, 1852–55

ECA ED9/23/1–2, Indexes to Minutes, 1842–45
ECA ED9/24/6, Edinburgh Police Commissioners, Accounts, 1848–49
ECA ED9/25/1, Lodging House regulations, 1848
ECA ED9/25/2, Sanitary Committee Minutes, 1849 and Cleaning Committee and Sub-Sanitary Committee letters to and from Glover, 1849
ECA ED9/25/2/2, Proposed byelaws as to Lodging-houses, prepared by the Surgeon
ECA ED9/25/2/4, Report of the Special Committee appointed by the Police Commissioners
ECA ED9/25/3, Annual Statistics on Crime and Drunkenness
ECA ED9/25/3, Cleansing and Lighting Committee, Report XVII, account of Police Manure 1840–59
ECA EDP25/1–26, Edinburgh Police Commissioners, Reports, 1822–54
ECA EDP25/1/XXII, *Report of the Lord Provost's Committee regarding Proposed Bills for extending the Municipal Boundaries and for Improving the Sanitary Condition of the City* (Edinburgh, 1847)
ECA MYBN 322B, Police Establishment Accounts (unlisted) 1805–11; 1819–21; 1832–58
ECA Edinburgh Police Accounts, 1848–49; 1862–65
ECA SL1/1/282–3, 290–1, 293, 300–2, Minutes of the Town Council
ECA SL12/287(2), Reports and Minutes concerning the office … of the Town Clerk, 1873
ECA SL2/187(1), Report to the Council on the Sanitary Condition of the Closes, 1864
ECA SL8/1/4–5, Minutes of the Parochial Board, Volume E
ECA SL8/6/2, Parochial Board Index
ECA SL25/1/1–2, Agenda Books and Scroll Minutes of the Lord Provost's Committee, 1862–66
ECA SL26/1/1, Minutes of the Public Health Committee, 1872
ECA SL26/4/14; /82; /88; /105; /120 Remits to Committee, including letters and reports from Littlejohn
ECA SL26/4/557, Duties of Medical Officer of Health, 1890
ECA SL26/4/1105 Printed Conditions for Appointment of Medical Officer of Health, 1908
ECA SL44/1, Scroll Minutes of the Plans and Works Committee, 1861–68
ECA SL45/1, Slaughter-houses Investigation Committee, 1864
ECA SL46/1, Minutes of the Cleaning Committee, 1857
ECA SL56/1416, Register of Voters, 1867–71
ECA SL64/1/1, Improvement Trustees' Minute Books, 1870
ECA SL64/3/6, Accounts of the Improvements Trustees
ECA SL80/2/1, Leith Town Council Minutes, 1767–84
ECA SL123, Cleansing and Lighting Sub-Committee, 1877–1921
ECA SL137/5/1 and SL137/15/6, Royal High School Matriculation Book 1827/28–1842/43, and Library Register 1838/39–1864/65
ECA SL158/1, Lord Provost's Explanatory Statement, 13 February 1866
ECA SL158/1, Minutes of the Lord Provost's Committee relative to the Sanitary Improvement of the City, 1866
ECA SL158/1, Scroll Minutes of the Sanitary Improvement Committee, 1865
ECA SL158/1, Minutes of the Town Council, 1866
ECA SL158/1, Report by the Sub-Committee of the Lord Provost's Committee, Appendix, 1866
ECA SL158/1, Report of the Sanitary Sub-Committee, 23 March 1866
ECA SL158/1, The Lord Provost's Statement to the Town Council Respecting Sanitary Improvements, 1865. NLS copy, 3.1919 (6).
ECA SL1/1/288/118, Report of Sub-Committee of the Lord Provost's Committee on application of registrars for increase of salary, 1864
ECA U 332 B Bundle 5 E9 Re-arrangement of Wards, 1869

Edinburgh Central Library: publications by Henry Littlejohn

Edinburgh Corporation, *Suggestions as to a vaccination act for Scotland by J.D. Marwick and Sir Henry Littlejohn* (1863) [B16944] YRM 784
Littlejohn, Sir Henry Duncan, *Report on the Sanitary Condition of the City of Edinburgh; with relative appendices etc.* (1865) [G80822] [D5226] [5953N] YRA 244
[Littlejohn, Sir Henry Duncan] Edinburgh Corporation, Medical Officer of Health *Report … on Broughton Burn* (1872) [B18984] yTD 584

Littlejohn, Henry Duncan, *Return as to the public houses in the city of Edinburgh referred to in report by Dr. Littlejohn, medical officer of health, to the magistrates of the city, April 5, 1875* (1875) [B17870] YHV5080

Littlejohn, [Sir] Henry Duncan, *On the compulsory intimation on infectious diseases* (*c*.1876) [B18057] qYRA 643

Littlejohn, Sir Henry Duncan, *What are the advantages of a system of notification of infectious diseases and what are the best means of carrying the same into execution* (1882) [G20204] YRA643

Littlejohn, Sir Henry Duncan, *Report on the city cemeteries* (1883). [B16457] qYRA 630

Edinburgh Corporation, *Report by the town clerk and medical officer of health as to the present and prospective arrangements for the treatment of infectious diseases in the city ...* (1884) [B17863] qYRA 643

Littlejohn, Sir Henry Duncan, *Report as to the seizure and condemnation of diseased carcases at the slaughter-houses* (1888) [B18035] qYHD 9421.8

[Littlejohn, Sir Henry Duncan] Edinburgh Corporation, Medical Officer of Health, *Report ... on petition as to sanitary condition of ground at the gymnasium, and minute of the Lord Provost's committee thereon* (1888). [B18034] YTD

Littlejohn, Sir Henry Duncan, *Report on pulmonary consumption in the city for the year 1899* (1900?) [A5445] YRC 316

Edinburgh water supply: a sketch of its history past and present. With an introduction by Sir Henry Littlejohn (1908) [33426, G80721] YTD 262

Edinburgh Central Library pamphlets and publications

These are too numerous to list but include:

Book of reference for improvement scheme 1866 [44466] qYHT 165

Town Council minutes from 1875 [4167] YJS 4245 A2 and qYJS 4245 A2

Edinburgh Corporation Public Health Department, Duties of the MOH 1873, [42067.14] YRA 415

Glasgow City Archives

LP1/13 Sanitary Department, Glasgow. Annual Report on the Health of the City, for the year 1871. By W.T. Gairdner, M.D., Medical Officer; and on the Operations of the Sanitary Department, for the year ending 30th April, 1872. By Kenneth M MacLeod, Sanitary Inspector (Glasgow 1872), 15–30.

House of Lords Library

HL/PO/JO/10/9/627, House of Lords, Report from the Committee on the Edinburgh Improvement Bill, 13 May 1867

Images

Edinburgh Central Library and Edinburgh City Art Centre: Capital Collections: J. Balmain, T. Begbie, J. Blair, A. Burns, W.D. Clark, D.A. Hill, A.A. Inglis, T. Keith, G. Morham, G.W. Wilson

Royal Commission for Ancient and Historical Monuments of Scotland: Canmore and SCRAN Digital Images databases

Liverpool Record Office (LRO)

LRO 352 HEA 1/1, folios 289–92, Medical Officer of Health, Letter Books, vol. 1, Duncan to Shattuck, 14 December 1849; Duncan to Stark, 9 November 1849

LRO 352 HEA 3, Medical Officer of Health Letter Books, vol. 3, folios 216–17, 280 and 331–2

LRO Health Committee Minutes, vol. 1, 239, 294, 307–8, 316, 349, 374, 412–13 and 423

Lothian Heath Archive

LHB1/1/22 Royal Infirmary of Edinburgh, Managers' Minutes, November 1862 to February 1865

LHB1/1/100 Index to volume 22 of Royal Infirmary of Edinburgh Minutes.

LHB1/126/30–31 General Register of Patients October 1842 to September 1848

National Registers of Scotland

HO45/1824, Testimonial for Dr W.H. Duncan by Edwin Chadwick

National Library of Scotland (NLS)

NLS APS 1.77.122, Letter from Henry Johnston to the Lord Provost, 15 May 1856

NLS K77.a.11(5), R.A.F.A. Coyne, Estimate and Prospectus of the Annexed Plan of Sanitary and City Improvements, 25 January 1866.

NLS l.c.2243, *Precognition of Witnesses examined at the instance of the Procurator-Fiscal for the City of Edinburgh, regarding the falling of the Tenement, nos. 99–103 High Street, on November 24, 1861*, 5.

NLS SNPG MS583/581, Watson Autographs, Alison to the Lord Advocate, 10 December 1838

NLS Map Library, Town Maps, Edinburgh, 1817–1920. See also http://maps.nls.uk/towns/#edinburgh-city

National Registers of Scotland (NRS)

GRO1/473/149–50; 1/473/188; 1/473/724–5; GRO1/474/192; 1/474/273, Letters to and from Registrar-General to Littlejohn, 1862–63

NRS CH2/718, Records of St Cuthbert's Church

NRS CH3/1152/1–32, Records of Lauriston Place United Presbyterian Church

NRS GD1/895/6, Personal papers of the Littlejohn family

NRS JC7/41, Justiciary Court, 13 March 1781, 9 April 1783

NRS SC70, Sheriff Court Inventories: SC70/1/37, /60, /99; /111; /253; /256; SC70/4//66; /182/ 223

Royal College of Physicians, Edinburgh

RCPEd Aesculapian Club Collection

RCPEd General Minutes, 1843–51, 3732–50; Minutes 1846–65, 25 September 1854, 737

RCPEd A.D.7.2, Cholera Returns, 1847–48

Registrar-General for Scotland, Annual Reports of Births, Deaths, and Marriage, 1855–75

Royal College of Surgeons, Edinburgh

RCSEd GD/23, Henry Duncan Littlejohn papers

RCSEd Minutes, 1846–54; 1854–59; 1859–68

RCSEd 5/1–2, Archives of the Extra-Mural Medical School

University of Edinburgh Special Collections

Da43 1847, Henry Littlejohn's university record

Q.d7/18, D. Cousin and J. Lessels, *Plan of Sanitary Improvements of the City of Edinburgh* (Edinburgh 1866)

Minutes of Senatus [College Minutes] Volume X (28 March 1891 to 19 October 1895), award of Honorary Doctorate to Henry Littlejohn

Wellcome Institute

WA/BSR/BA/Pub/A1/11, memorandum on Sir Henry Littlejohn, 12 October 1914 by Andrew Balfour, CMG, MD

Parliamentary Papers

All finding aids for Parliamentary Papers, including the official indexes, use abbreviated titles which vary in their consistency and accuracy. To avoid confusion, here we give the session, volume number, first page of the paper (which is not necessarily the portion referred to in our footnotes), and the number of the command paper [in brackets] or sessional paper (in parentheses); the last is the sure way of identifying these items on-line. All those listed are House of Commons papers.

PP 1819 II, 449, Select Committee to consider Validity of Doctrine of Contagion in Plague, Minutes of Evidence
PP 1833 XXXVII, 1 (149), Abstract of the Population Returns of Great Britain, Volume 2
PP 1837 XXI, 19 (31), Royal Commission on Religious Instruction in Scotland, First Report
PP 1839 XX, 163 (177), Report by a Committee of the General Assembly on the Management of the Poor in Scotland, Appendix
PP 1842 XXVIII, 1 (8), Poor Law Commissioners. Reports on the Sanitary Condition of the Labouring Population of Scotland
PP 1843 XXII, 1 [496], Census of Great Britain 1841, Enumeration Abstract
PP 1843 XII, 395 (509), Report on the Sanitary Condition of the Labouring Population of Great Britain. A Supplementary Report on the ... Practice of Interment in Towns made by Edwin Chadwick
PP 1844 XVII, 1 [572], 572 Royal Commission for Inquiring into the State of Large Towns and Populous Districts. First Report
PP 1844 XX, 1 [557], Royal Commission on the Administration and Practical Operation of the Poor Laws in Scotland, Minutes of Evidence and Appendices
PP 1844 XXI, 1 [544], Royal Commission on the Administration and Practical Operation of the Poor Laws in Scotland, Appendix, part VII and Analytical Index
PP 1844 XX, 81 [563], Royal Commission on the Administration and Practical Operation of the Poor Laws in Scotland, Appendix, part I
PP 1844 XXIII, 1 [597], Royal Commission on the Administration and Practical Operation of the Poor Laws in Scotland, Appendix, part IV
PP 1852–53 LXXXVI, 1 [1632], Census of Great Britain, 1851. Population tables. Volume 2.
PP 1852–53 XXXVI, 161 (715), Select Committee on Police, Second Report
PP 1854 XL, 417–56 (172–IV), Civil Service Estimates, etc., for the year ending March 1855.
PP 1854 XLV, 259 [1892], Report on Common and Model Lodging Houses in the Metropolis
PP 1857 XX, 447 [2262], Report on Means of Deodorizing and Utilizing Sewage of Towns, by H. Austin
PP 1857–58 XXXII, 347 [2372], Royal Commission to inquire into Best Mode of Distributing Sewage of Towns. Preliminary Report
PP 1861 XXVIII, 543 [2760], Board of Supervision for the Relief of the Poor in Scotland, 15th Annual Report, 1860
PP 1862 IV, 199 (57), Police and Improvement (Scotland) Bill
PP 1862 IV, 357 (133), Police and Improvement (Scotland) Bill, as amended in committee
PP 1862 IV, 535 (236), Police and Improvement (Scotland) Bill, Lords Amendments
PP 1862 L, 945 [3013], Census of Scotland, 1861. Population Tables and Report
PP 1864 VIII, 1 (431), Select Committee on Cattle Disease Prevention, and Cattle, &c. Importation Bills, Report and Evidence
PP 1865 XXVII, 303 [3472], Royal Commission on Sewage of Towns, 3rd Report, Appendix 5, Report by Stevenson Macadam on the Contamination of the Water Supply of Leith by the Sewage of Edinburgh and Leith
PP 1866 XXII, 1 [3591], Royal Commission into Origin and Nature of the Cattle Plague, 1st Report
PP 1866 XXXIII, 421 [3645], Eighth Report of the Medical Officer of the Privy Council, 1865
PP 1866 LXVI 373 (394), Reports to Secretary of State by Mr. Tremenheere on Operation of Bakehouses Regulation Act
PP 1867–68 XXXIII 625 [3957], Board of Supervision for the Relief of the Poor in Scotland, 22nd Annual Report. Appendix (A) No. 11, Report by Dr H.D. Littlejohn on the Sanitary State of the Parish of Wemyss
PP 1867–68 XXXIII 625 [3957], Board of Supervision for the Relief of the Poor in Scotland, 22nd Annual Report. Appendix (A) No. 16, Report by Dr H.D. Littlejohn on the Sanitary State of the Parish of Lochgelly
PP 1868–69 XI, 1 (301) Report from the Select Committee on the Poor Law (Scotland)
PP 1870 XI, 1 (357) Report from the Select Committee on Poor Law (Scotland)
PP 1870 XXXVIII, [C. 208], 'Report by Dr. Buchanan and Mr. J. Netten Radcliffe on the Systems in Use in Various Northern Towns for Dealing with Excrement', Twelfth Report of the Medical Officer of the Privy Council, 1870
PP 1872 LXVIII, 305 [C.592], Census of the Population of Scotland

PP 1872 XXXIV, 1 [C.603-I], Royal Commission into Prevention of Pollution in Rivers, 4th Report
PP 1873 X, 431 (284), Select Committee on Noxious Businesses, Report
PP 1873 XXIX, 613 [C.681], Board of Supervision for the Relief of the Poor in Scotland, 27th Annual Report
PP 1873 XXVII, 1 [C.775], Royal Commission into Endowed Schools and Hospitals (Scotland), First Report
PP 1874 XXXI, 33 [C. 1066], Report by Mr. J. Netten Radcliffe on Certain Means of Preventing Excrement Nuisances in Towns and Villages. Reports of the Medical Officer of the Privy Council and Local Government Board, new series 2, supplementary reports
PP 1875 LXIV, 249 [C.1143] Information furnished … by the authorities of the cities of Edinburgh and Glasgow, and of the borough of Liverpool, with regard to the operation of their respective improvements and sanitary acts
PP 1876 XXXII, 1 [C.1382], Board of Supervision for the Relief of the Poor and of Public Health in Scotland, 30th Annual Report 1874–75, Appendix (A) No. 14, Report by Dr Littlejohn as to the Outbreak of Typhoid Fever at Crosshill, Parish of Cathcart
PP 1876 XXXVIII, 117 [C.1410], Local Government Board Committee Inquiring into Treating Town Sewage
PP 1882 XXIX, 1 [C.334], Hospital Commission. Report on Small-pox and Fever Hospitals
PP 1882 LXXVI, 285 [C.3320], Ninth Decenniel Census of the Population of Scotland 1881, vol. 1
PP 1883 LXXXI, [C.3657], Ninth Decenniel Census of the Population of Scotland 1881, vol. 2
PP 1884–56 XXX, [C.4409], Royal Commission on the Housing of the Working Classes, Scotland. Vol. 5, Minutes of Evidence and Appendices
PP 1888 XXXII, 295 [C.5461-I], Report of the Departmental Committee appointed to inquire into Pleuro-pneumonia and Tuberculosis in the United Kingdom
PP 1889 CCCVI, 907 [C.5815], Board of Supervision for Relief of the Poor and of Public Health in Scotland, 44th Annual Report, Appendix (A) No. 12, Report on the Notification of Infectious Diseases, by Dr H. D. Littlejohn
PP 1892 XCIV, 217 [C.6755], Tenth Decenniel Census of the Population of Scotland 1891, vol. 1
PP 1893–94 XL, 195 (373) (402), Select Committee on Death Certification, Evidence, and Digest of Evidence
PP 1893–94 XLIV, 425 [C.7078], Board of Supervision for Relief of the Poor and of Public Health in Scotland, 48th Annual Report, 1892, Appendix (A) No. 11, Circular and Memoranda on Diarhoea and Cholera from Dr H.D. Littlejohn
PP 1896 XLVI, [C.7992], 88–98 Royal Commission on Tuberculosis, Report
PP 1917–18 XIV, 345 [Cd.8731], Royal Commission on the Housing of the Industrial Population of Scotland, Report

Parliamentary Journals

House of Commons Journal, 103, session 1847–48
House of Commons Journal, 11, session 1856
House of Lords Journal, 11, session 1854

Other works cited

Report on Measures Adopted for Sanitary Improvements in India from June 1869 to June 1870, together with Abstracts of Reports for 1868 forwarded from Bengal, Madras and Bombay. India Office Paper 6017, 1870

Newspapers

Over 400 individual citations are given in the footnotes based on almost 2,000 items consulted in the following titles:

Aberdeen Journal
Caledonian Mercury
Dundee Courier and Argus
Edinburgh Evening Courant
Edinburgh Evening Dispatch

Edinburgh Evening News
Edinburgh Evening Post and Scottish Record
Edinburgh Evening Post
Glasgow Herald
Liverpool Mercury
Scottish Jurist
Student
The Scotsman
The Times
The Witness

Other periodicals

British and Foreign Medical Review
British Medical Journal
Edinburgh Almanac or Universal Scots and Imperial Register
Edinburgh Annual Register
Edinburgh and Leith Post-Office Annual Directory
Edinburgh Medical and Surgical Journal
Edinburgh Review
Gambolier (Edinburgh University house journal)
Journal of Public Health and Monthly Record of Sanitary Improvement
Liverpool Health of Towns Advocate
London Medical Gazette
Medical Directory for Scotland
New Edinburgh Almanac
Public Health
Quarterly Review
Sanitary Journal for Scotland
The Lancet

Selected secondary works

Ackerknecht, E.H., 'Hygiene in France, 1815–1848', *Bulletin of the History of Medicine*, 22 (1948), 117–55

Alison, A., *The Principles of Population and their Connection with Human Happiness*, 2 vols (Edinburgh, 1840)

Alison, W.P., 'Observations on the epidemic fever now prevalent among the lower orders in Edinburgh', *Edinburgh Medical and Surgical Journal*, 23 (1827), 233–62

Alison, W.P., *Illustrations of the Practical Operations of the Scottish System of Management of the Poor* (Edinburgh, 1840)

Alison, W.P., *Observations on the Management of the Poor in Scotland and its Effects on the Health of the Great Towns* (Edinburgh, 1840)

Alison, W.P., 'On the destitution and mortality in some of the large towns in Scotland', *Journal of the Royal Statistical Society of London*, 5:3 (1842), 289–92

Alison, W.P., *On the Epidemic Fever of 1843 in Scotland and its Connection with the Destitute Condition of the Poor* (Edinburgh, 1844)

Allan, C.M., 'The genesis of British urban development with special reference to Glasgow', *Economic History Review*, 18 (1965), 598–613

Anderson, W., *The Poor of Edinburgh and their Homes* (Edinburgh, 1867)

Anderson, M. and Morse, D.J., 'The people', in W.H. Fraser and R.J. Morris (eds), *People and Society in Scotland, vol. II, 1830–1914* (Edinburgh, 1990), 13–45

Anon., *House of Refuge for the Destitute, and Asylum for their Children: Origin, Progress and Nature of the Institution* (Edinburgh, 1855)

Anon., *The Aged Poor: Centenary of the House of Reform (Queensberry House), 1832–1932* (Edinburgh, 1932)

Anon., *The Lord Provosts of Edinburgh, 1296 to 1932* (Edinburgh, 1932)
Atkinson, M., *Local Government in Scotland* (Edinburgh, 1904)
Baker, R., 'On the industrial and sanitary economy of the borough of Leeds in 1858', *Journal of the Statistical Society of London*, 21 (1858), 427–43
Barrie, D.G., '"Epoch-Making" beginnings to lingering death: the struggle for control of the Glasgow Police Commission, 1833–46', *Scottish Historical Review*, 86 (2007), 253–77
Barrie, D.G., *Police in the Age of Improvement: Police Development and the Civic Tradition in Scotland, 1775–1865* (Cullompton, 2008)
Becker, H.P., *Outsiders: Studies in the Sociology of Deviance* (New York, 1963)
Bell, G., *Day and Night in the Wynds of Edinburgh* (Edinburgh, 1849)
Bell, G., *Blackfriars' Wynd Analyzed* (Edinburgh, 1850)
Bell, J. and Paton, J., *Glasgow: Its Municipal Organization and Administration* (Glasgow, 1896)
Best, G.F.A., 'The Scottish Victorian city', *Victorian Studies*, 11 (1968), 329–58
Best, G.F.A., 'Another part of the island', in H.J. Dyos and M.J. Wolff (eds), *The Victorian City: Images and Realities*, vol. 2 (London, 1973 edn), 389–412
Blackden, S., 'The Board of Supervision and the Scottish Parochial Medical Service, 1845–95', *Medical History*, 30 (1986), 145–72
Blackden, S., 'The parochial medical service in nineteenth-century Scotland', *Social Science History Medical Bulletin*, 38 (1986), 21–4
Blackden, S., 'The development of the Scottish Poor Law medical service, 1845–1914', *Proceedings of the Royal Physicians of Edinburgh*, 20 (1990), 349–54
Brockington, C.F., 'The cholera 1831', *Medical Officer*, 96 (1956), 75
Brotherstone, J.H.F., *Observations on the Early Public Health Movement in Scotland* (London, 1952)
Brown, C., *The Social History of Religion in Scotland since 1730* (London, 1987)
Brown, C., 'Did urbanization secularize Britain', *Urban History Yearbook, 1988*, 1–14
Brown, C., 'Religion, class and church growth', in W.H. Fraser and R.J. Morris (eds), *People and Society in Scotland* (Edinburgh, 1990), 310–35
Brown, S.J., 'The Disruption and urban poverty: Thomas Chalmers and the West Port Operation in Edinburgh, 1844–47', *Scottish Church History Society*, 20 (1978), 65–89
Brown, S.J., *Thomas Chalmers and the Godly Commonwealth in Scotland* (Oxford, 1982)
Brown, S.J., *The National Churches of England, Ireland and Scotland, 1801–46* (Oxford, 2001)
Bruce, J., *Letters on Destitution and Vice in Edinburgh* (Edinburgh, 1850)
Buchan, W., *Domestic Medicine: A Treatise on the Prevention and Cure of Diseases by Regimen and Simple Medicines* (London, 1772)
Burke, J.G., 'Kirk and causality in Edinburgh, 1805', *Isis*, 61 (1970), 341
Cage, R.A., *The Scottish Poor Law, 1745–1845* (Edinburgh, 1981)
Cage, R.A. and Checkland, E.O.A., 'Thomas Chalmers and urban poverty: the St John's experiment in Glasgow, 1819–37', *Philosophical Journal*, 13 (1976), 39–52
Cameron, A., 'The establishment of civil registration in Scotland', *Historical Journal*, 50 (2007), 377–95
Campbell, J.W., *Trembling for the Ark of God: James Begg and the Free Church of Scotland* (Edinburgh, 2011)
Campbell, R.H. and Skinner, A.S. (eds), *The Origins and Nature of the Scottish Enlightenment* (Edinburgh, 1982)
Carroll, P.E., 'Medical police and the history of public health', *Medical History*, 46 (2002), 461–94
Carson, K. and Idzikowska, H., 'The social production of Scottish policing, 1795–1900', in D. Hay and F. Snyder (eds), *Policing and Prosecution in Britain* (Oxford, 1983)
Chadwick, E., *A Supplementary Report on the Results of a Special Inquiry into the Practice of Interment in Towns* (London, 1843), Parliamentary Papers 1843 [509] XII. See also M.W. Flinn (ed.), 'Introduction' (1965)
Chalmers, A.K., 'The development of sanitary science in Britain during the nineteenth century', *Proceedings of the Royal Philosophical Society of Glasgow*, 36 (1904–05), 250–65
Chambers, R., *Notices of the Most Remarkable Fires in Edinburgh: from 1385 to 1824* (Edinburgh, 1824)
Chambers, W., *Report on the Sanitary State of the Residences of the Poorer Classes in the Old Town* (Edinburgh, 1840)
Checkland, E.O.A., *Philanthropy in Victorian Scotland: Social Welfare and the Voluntary Principle* (Edinburgh, 1980)

Checkland, E.O.A. and Lamb, M. (eds), *Health Care as Social History: the Glasgow Case* (Aberdeen, 1982)

Cheyne, A.C., *Studies in Scottish Church History* (Edinburgh, 1999)

Chisholm, R., 'The history and results of the Glasgow City Improvement Trust', *Proceedings of the Royal Philosophical Society of Glasgow*, 27 (1895–96), 39–56

Chitnis, A., *The Scottish Enlightenment and Early Victorian English Society* (London, 1986)

Christison, R., 'Account of the arrangements made by the Edinburgh Board of Health', *Edinburgh Medical and Surgical Journal*, 37 (1832), cclv–cclvi

Christison, R., *The Medico-Legal Examination of Dead Bodies* (1839)

Cleland, J., *The Annals of Glasgow* (Glasgow 1816)

Cleland, J., *The Rise and Progress of the City of Glasgow* (Glasgow, 1820)

Cockburn, H., *Memorials of His Time* (New York, 1856 edn)

Cohen, S., *Folk Devils and Moral Panics: the Creation of Mods and Rockers* (London, 1972)

Colston, J., *The Edinburgh and District Water Supply: a Historical Sketch* (Edinburgh, 1890)

Comrie, J.D., *History of Scottish Medicine* (London, 1932)

Cousin, D. and Lessels, J., *Plan of Sanitary Improvements of the City of Edinburgh* (Edinburgh, 1866), 20–1

Couper, W.J., *The Edinburgh Periodical Press* (Stirling, 1908) vol. 2

Creighton, C., *A History of Epidemics in Britain* (London, 1965, 2nd edn)

Crellin, J.K., 'The dawn of the germ theory: particles, infection and biology', in F.N.L. Poynter (ed.), *Medicine and Science in the 1860s* (London, 1968), 57–76

Crew, F.A.E., 'Centenary of appointment of the first Medical Officer of Health for the City of Edinburgh', *Scottish Medical Journal*, 8 (1963), 53–62

Crowther, M.A., review of C. Hamlin, *Public Health and Social Justice in the Age of Chadwick: Britain, 1800–54*, *American Historical Review*, 105 (2000), 280–1

Crowther, M.A. and White, B., 'Medicine, property and the law in Britain, 1800–1914', *Historical Journal*, 31 (1988), 853–70

Crowther, M.A. and White, B., *On Soul and Conscience: the Medical Expert and Crime* (Aberdeen, 1988)

Cunningham, A. and Thorpe, B.A., 'The milk supply of the city of Edinburgh', *Journal of Hygiene*, 19 (1920), 107–14

Damer, S., *From Moorepark to 'Wine alley': the Rise and Fall of a Glasgow Housing Scheme* (Edinburgh, 1989)

Daunton, M.J., 'Introduction', in M.J. Daunton (ed.), *The Cambridge Urban History of Britain*, vol. 3, *1820–1950* (Cambridge, 2000), 14–29

Daunton, M.J., *Trusting Leviathan: The Politics of Taxation in Britain, 1799–1914* (Cambridge, 2001)

Defoe, D., *A Tour Thro' the whole Island of Great Britain, Divided into Circuits or Journies*, vol. III (London, 1727)

Devine, T.M., *The Scottish Nation, 1700–2000* (Harmondsworth, 1999)

Dingwall, H.M., *A History of Scottish Medicine* (Edinburgh, 2003)

Dinsmor, A. and Urquhart, R., 'The origins of modern policing in Scotland', *Scottish Archives: The Journal of the Scottish Records Association*, 7 (2001), 39–42

Dinsmor, A., and Goldsmith, A., 'Scottish policing – a historical perspective', in D. Donnelly and K. Scott (eds), *Policing Scotland* (Cullompton, 2005), 40–56

Donnelly, D., *Municipal Policing in Scotland* (Dundee, 2008)

Douglas, M., 'Environments at risk', in B. Barnes and D. Edge (eds), *Science in Context* (Cambridge, 1982)

Driver, F., 'Moral geographies: social science and the urban environment in nineteenth century England', *Transactions British Institute of British Geographers*, 13 (1988), 275–87

Duncan, A., *A Short View of the Extent and Importance of Medical Jurisprudence, Considered as Branch of Education* (Edinburgh, 1798)

Duncan, W. H., *Report to the Health Committee of the Borough of Liverpool, on the Health of the Town during the years 1847–48–49–50, and on Other Matters within his Department* (Liverpool, 1851)

Eason, C., 'The tenement homes of Dublin: their condition and regulation', *Journal of the Statistical and Social Inquiry Society of Ireland*, 10 (1898/99), 383–98

Edwards, B., 'Thomson – pioneer of sustainable architecture', *The Architectural Review*, 205, no. 1228 (1999), 80–4

Engels, F., *The Condition of the Working Class in England in 1844* (London, 1936 edn)

Ewen, S., 'Professional elites and urban governance: chief fire officers in late Victorian British municipalities', in S. Couperas, C. Smit and D.J. Wolffram (eds), *In Control of the City: Local Elites and the Dynamics of Urban Politics, 1800–1960* (Leuven, 2007), 147–57

Ewen, S., *Fighting Fires: Creating the British Fire Service, 1800–1978* (Basingstoke, 2010), 30–50

Ewing, W. (ed.), *Annals of the Free Church of Scotland, 1843–1900*, vol. 1 (Edinburgh, 1914)

Flinn, M.W., 'Introduction' to the *Report on the Sanitary Condition of the Labouring Population of Gt Britain by Edwin Chadwick, 1842* (Edinburgh, repr. edn, 1965)

Flinn, M.W., 'Introduction', in A.P. Stewart and E. Jenkins, *Medical and Legal Aspects of Sanitary Reform* (Leicester repr., 1969)

Forsythe, R., *Foul Burn Agitation* (Edinburgh, 1840)

Frank, J.P., *System einer vollständigen medicinischen Polizey* (1789–1827) [*A Complete System of Medical Police*, E. Lesky (ed.) (Baltimore, 1976)]

Fraser, W.H., 'Municipal socialism and social policy', in R.J. Morris and R. Rodger (eds), *The Victorian City, 1820–1914: A Reader in Urban History* (Harlow, 1993), 258–80

Fry, M., *The Scottish Empire* (Edinburgh, 2001)

Gairdner, W.T., *Public Health in Relation to Air and Water* (Edinburgh, 1862)

Gairdner, W.T., *Memorandum for the Chairman of the Sanitary Committee to Accompany a Map of the Sanitary Districts of Glasgow by the Medical Officer of Health* (Glasgow, 1865)

Gairdner, W.T. and Begbie, J.W., *First Report of the Medico-Statistical Association* (Edinburgh, 1852)

Gamgee, J., 'The Scope and Objects of the Veterinary Profession ... Introductory Lecture delivered in the New Veterinary College', *Edinburgh Veterinary Review and Annals of Comparative Pathology*, 6 (1864), 709

Gibson, G.A., *Life of Sir William Tennant Gairdner: With a selection of papers on general and medical subjects* (Glasgow, 1912)

Glen, W.C., *The Nuisances Removal and Diseases Prevention Acts, 1848 & 1849* (3rd edn, London, 1849)

Gifford, J. *et al.*, *The Buildings of Scotland: Edinburgh* (Harmondsworth, 1988 edn)

Goldman, L., *Science, Reform, and Politics in Victorian Britain: the Social Science Association, 1857–1886* (Cambridge, 2007)

Gray, R.Q., *The Labour Aristocracy in Victorian Edinburgh* (Oxford, 1976)

Griffiths, T. and Morton, G. (eds), *A History of Everyday Life in Scotland, 1800–1900* (Edinburgh, 2010)

Gulland, J.W., *How Edinburgh is Governed. A Handbook for Citizens* (Edinburgh, 1891)

Guthrie, D., *Scottish Influence on the Evolution of British Medicine* (London, 1960)

Guthrie, D., *The Royal Edinburgh Hospital for Sick Children, 1860–1960* (Edinburgh, 1960)

Hamlin, C., 'Muddling in Bumbledom: on the enormity of large sanitary improvements in four British towns, 1855–1885', *Victorian Studies*, 32 (1988), 55–84

Hamlin, C., 'Predisposing causes and public health in early nineteenth-century medical thought', *Social History of Medicine*, 5 (1992), 43–70

Hamlin, C., 'Environmental sensibility in Edinburgh, 1839–40: the "fetid irrigation" controversy', *Journal of Urban History*, 20 (1994), 311–39

Hamlin, C., 'Could you starve to death in England in 1839? The Chadwick–Farr controversy and the loss of the "social" in public health', *American Journal of Public Health*, 85:6 (1995), 856–66

Hamlin, C., *Public Health and Social Justice in the Age of Chadwick, Britain, 1800–1854* (Cambridge, 1998)

Hamlin, C., 'William Pulteney Alison, the Scottish philosophy, and the making of a political medicine', *Journal of the History of Medicine and Allied Sciences*, 61 (2006), 144–86

Handley, J.E., *The Irish in Scotland* (Cork, 1943)

Harvey, D., 'The geography of capitalist accumulation: a reconstruction of the Marxian theory', in R. Peet (ed.), *Radical Geography* (Chicago, 1977), 263–92

Heiton, J., *The Castes of Edinburgh* (Edinburgh, 1861)

Hennock, E.P., 'Central/local government relations in England, 1835–1900', *Urban History Yearbook*, 9 (1982), 38–49

Heysham, J., *An Account of the Jail Fever or* Typhus Carcerum *as it appeared in Carlisle in the year 1781* (Carlisle, 1782)

Hope, E.W., *Report on the Health of the City of Liverpool during 1900* (Liverpool, 1901)

Houston, R., *Social Change in the Age of Enlightenment: Edinburgh, 1660–1760* (Oxford, 1994)

Ireland, J., *Hogarth Illustrated* (London, 1791)

Jacyna, L. S., *Philosophic Whigs: Medicine, Science and Citizenship in Edinburgh, 1789–1848* (London, 1994)

Jenkinson, J., *Scottish Medical Societies, 1731–1939: Their History and Records* (Edinburgh, 1993)

Johnson, J. and Rosenburg, L., *Renewing Old Edinburgh: the Enduring Legacy of Patrick Geddes* (Argyll, 2010)

Jordanova, L., 'Medical police and public health: problems of practice and ideology', *Society for the Social History of Medicine*, 27 (1980), 15–19

Jordanova, L., 'Policing public health in France, 1780–1815', in T. Ogawa (ed.), *Public Health: Proceedings of the 5th International Symposium on the Comparative History of Medicine* (Tokyo, 1981), 12–32

Joyce, P., *The Rule of Freedom: Liberalism and the Modern City* (London, 2003), 20–97

Keir, D. (ed.), *The Third Statistical Account of Scotland: The City of Edinburgh* (Glasgow, 1966)

Kames, Lord, *Sketches of the History of Man* Book II (repr. Indianapolis, 2007)

Kaplan, S., *Bread, Politics and Political Economy in the Reign of Louis XV*, vol. 1 (The Hague, 1976)

Knox, W.W., 'The attack of the "Half-Formed Persons": the 1811–12 Tron Riot in Edinburgh revisited', *Scottish Historical Review*, 91:2 (2012), 287–310

La Berge, A.F., 'The Paris health council, 1801–1848', *Bulletin of the History of Medicine*, 49 (1975), 339–52

La Berge, A.F., 'The early nineteenth-century French public health movement: the disciplinary development and institutionalization of hygiene publique', *Bulletin of the History of Medicine*, 58 (1984), 363–79

La Berge, A.F., *Mission and Method: the Early Nineteenth-century French Public Health Movement* (Cambridge, 1992)

Laxton, P., 'Fighting for public health: Dr Duncan and his adversaries, 1847–63', in S. Sheard and H. Power (eds), *Body and City: Histories of Urban Public Health* (Aldershot, 2000), 59–88

Laxton, P., 'This nefarious traffic: livestock and public health in mid-Victorian Edinburgh', in P. Atkins (ed.), *Animal Cities: Beastly Urban Histories* (Farnham, 2012), 107–71

Lesky, E. (ed.), *A System of Complete Medical Police: Selections from Johann Peter Frank* (Baltimore, 1976)

Levitt, I., *Poverty and Welfare in Scotland, 1890–1948* (Edinburgh, 1988)

Levitt, I., 'Henry Littlejohn and Scottish health policy, 1859–1908', *Scottish Archives*, 2 (1996), 63–77

Levitt, I. and Smout, T.C., *The State of the Scottish Working Class in 1842* (Edinburgh, 1979)

Lewis, A., 'The builders of Edinburgh's New Town, 1767–1795', University of Edinburgh, Ph.D. thesis, 2006

Lieberman, D., 'The legal needs of a commercial society: the jurisprudence of Lord Kames', in I. Hont and M. Ignatieff (eds), *Wealth and Virtue: the Shaping of Political Economy in the Scottish Enlightenment* (Cambridge, 1983)

Lindsay, J. (ed.), *Municipal Glasgow: its Evolution and Enterprises* (Glasgow, 1914)

Littlejohn, H.D., *On the Cleansing Operations of Edinburgh, as Compared with Other Towns* (Edinburgh, 1865)

Littlejohn, H.D., 'Valedictory address to the Edinburgh Medico-chirurgical Society', *Edinburgh Medical Journal*, XXXI (1885–86), 601–12

Livingstone, E. and S., *The Royal Edinburgh Hospital for Sick Children, 1860–1960* (Edinburgh, 1960)

Lloyd, C.F., 'The search for legitimacy: universities, medical licensing bodies, and governance in Glasgow and Edinburgh from the late eighteenth to the late nineteenth centuries', in R.J. Morris and R.H. Trainor (eds), *Urban Governance: Britain and Beyond since 1750* (Aldershot, 2000), 198–210

Lynch, M., *Scotland: A New History* (London, 1991)

Macadam, S., *On the contamination of the Water of Leith by the sewage of Edinburgh and Leith* (London, 1865)

MacCormick, D.N., 'Adam Smith on law', in K. Haakonssen (ed.), *Adam Smith* (Aldershot, 1998)

Macdonald, H., 'Public health legislation and problems in Victorian Edinburgh, with special reference to the work of Dr Littlejohn as Medical Officer of Health', University of Edinburgh, Ph.D. thesis, 1971

Macdonald, A.A., Warwick, C.M. and W.T. Johnston, 'Locating veterinary education in Edinburgh in the nineteenth century', *Book of the Old Edinburgh Club*, N.S. 6 (2005), 41–71

MacDougall, I. (ed.), *The Minutes of the Edinburgh Trades Council, 1859–1873* (Edinburgh, 1968)

MacGillivray, N., 'Food, poverty and epidemic disease, Edinburgh, 1840–1850', University of Edinburgh Ph.D. thesis, 2003
Macintyre, I. and MacLaren, I. (eds), *Surgeons' Lives* (Edinburgh, 2005)
MacKelvie, W., *Annals and Statistics of the United Presbyterian Church* (Edinburgh, 1873)
MacLaren, A.A., *Religion and Social Class: The Disruption Years in Aberdeen* (London, 1974)
MacLeod, R., 'The anatomy of state medicine: concept and application', in F.N.L. Poynter (ed.), *Medicine and State in the 1860s* (London, 1968), 199–227
MacPherson, C., *Report to the Sub-Committee of the Lord Provost's Committee on the Water of Leith Improvement* (Edinburgh, 1863)
McCrie, B.T., *Life of John Knox*, 5th edn, vol. 2 (Edinburgh, 1831)
McGowan, J., *Policing the Metropolis of Scotland: A History of the Police and Systems of Police in Edinburgh & Edinburghshire, 1770–1833* (Musselburgh, 2011)
McLeod, H., 'Religion', in J. Langton and R.J. Morris (eds), *Atlas of Industrialising Britain, 1780–1914* (London, 1986), 212–17
Madgin, R. and Rodger, R., 'Inspiring capital? Deconstructing myths and reconstructing urban environments, Edinburgh, 1860–2010', *Urban History*, 40:3 (2013), 507–29
Malthus, T., *An Essay on the Principle of Population, as it Affects the Future Improvement of Society* (London, 1798)
Mapother, E.D., *Lectures on Public Health, delivered at the Royal College of Surgeons* (Dublin, 1867)
Martin, S.M.K., 'William Pulteney Alison: activist, philanthropist and pioneer of social medicine', University of St Andrews Ph.D. thesis, 1997
Marwick, J., *A Retrospect* (Glasgow, privately published, [1905])
Massard-Guilbaud, G., 'French local authorities and the challenge of industrial pollution *c.*1810–1917', in R.J. Morris and R.H. Trainor (eds), *Urban Governance: Britain and Beyond since 1750* (Tokyo, 2000), 150–64
Maver, I., 'The Scottish provost since 1800: tradition, continuity, and change in the leadership of local self government', in J. Garrard (ed.), *Heads of the Local State: Mayors, Provosts and Burgomaster since 1800* (Aldershot, 2007), 29–46
Meller, H.E., *Patrick Geddes: Social Evolutionist and City Planner* (London, 1990)
Miller, M., *The Representation of Place Urban Planning and Protest in France and Great Britain, 1950–1980* (Aldershot, 2003)
Millward, R., 'The political economy of urban utilities', in M.J. Daunton (ed.), *Cambridge Urban History of Britain*, vol. 3, *1840–1950* (Cambridge, 2000), 315–50
Miskell, L., 'From conflict to co-operation: urban improvement and the case of Dundee', *Urban History*, 29 (2002), 369–70
Mitchison, R., 'The creation of the Disablement Rule in the Scottish Poor Law', in T.C. Smout (ed.), *The Search for Wealth and Stability: Essays in Economic and Social History Presented to M.W. Flinn* (London, 1979), 199–217
Mitchison, R., 'The Poor Law', in T.M. Devine and R. Mitchison (eds), *People and Society in Scotland*, vol. I, *1760–1830* (Edinburgh, 1988), 252–67
Mooney, G., 'Public health versus private practice: the contested development of compulsory infectious disease notification in late nineteenth-century Britain', *Bulletin of the History of Medicine*, 73:2 (1999), 238–67
Moore, J. and Rodger, R., 'Who really ran the cities? Municipal knowledge and policy networks in British local government, 1832–1914', in R. Roth and R. Beachy (eds), *Who Ran the Cities? City Elites and Urban Power in Europe and North America* (Aldershot, 2007), 37–69
Morrell, J.B. and Thackray, A. (eds), *Gentlemen of Science*, Camden Fourth Series, vol. 30 (London, 1984)
Morris, R.J., 'Civil society and the nature of urbanism: Britain, 1750–1850', *Urban History*, 25 (1988), 289–301
Morris, R.J., 'Urbanisation in Scotland', in W.H. Fraser and R.J. Morris (eds), *People and Society in Scotland*, vol. II, *1830–1914* (Edinburgh, 1990), 73–102
Morris, R.J., 'Philanthropy and poor relief in nineteenth-century Edinburgh. The example of a capital city without a national State government', *Mélanges de l'Ecole française de Rome. Italie et Méditerranée*, 111:1 (1999), 367–79
Morris, R.J., 'The capitalist, the professor and the soldier: the re-making of Edinburgh Castle, 1850–1900', *Planning Perspectives*, 22 (2007), 55–78

Morton, G., *Unionist Nationalism: Governing Urban Scotland, 1830–1860* (Edinburgh, 1999)
Morton, G., 'Identity within the Union state, 1800–1900', in T.M. Devine and J. Wormald (eds), *Oxford Handbook of Modern Scottish History* (Oxford, 2012), 474–90
Morton, G. and Morris, R.J., 'Civil society, governance and nation, 1832–1914', in R.A. Houston and W.W. Knox (eds), *The New Penguin History of Scotland* (London, 2001), 355–416
Mosley, S., *The Chimney of the World: A History of Smoke Pollution in Victorian and Edwardian Manchester* (London, 2008)
Murray, A., *Nuisances in Edinburgh with Suggestions for the Removal Thereof Addressed to the General Commissioners of Police* (Edinburgh, 1847)
Niemi, M., *Public Health and Municipal Policy Making: Britain and Sweden, 1900–40* (Aldershot, 2007), 1–24
Nisbet, W., *First Lines of the Theory and Practice in Venereal Disease* (Edinburgh, 1787)
Ogborn, M., 'Local power and state regulation in nineteenth-century Britain', *Transactions of the Institute of British Geographers*, 17:2 (1992), 215–26
Parry, J., *The Rise and Fall of Liberal Government in Victorian Britain* (Yale, 1993)
Paterson, R., 'The Health of Towns Association, 1844–1849', *Bulletin of the History of Medicine*, 22 (1948), 373–402
Patterson, A., 'The poor law in nineteenth-century Scotland', in D. Fraser (ed.), *The New Poor Law in the Nineteenth Century* (London, 1976), 171–93
Pentland, G., *Radicalism, Reform and National Identity in Scotland, 1820–1833* (Woodbridge, 2008)
Phillipson, N.T., 'The Scottish Enlightenment', in R. Porter and M. Teich (eds), *The Enlightenment in National Context* (Cambridge, 1981), 19–40
Pickstone, J.V., 'Dearth, dirt and fever epidemics: rewriting the history of British "public health", 1780–1850', in T.O. Ranger and P. Slack (eds), *Epidemics and Ideas: Essays on the Historical Perception of Pestilence* (Cambridge, 1992), 125–48
Porter, D., *Health, Civilization and the State: A History of Public Health from Ancient to Modern Times* (London, 1999)
Pryde, G.S., *Central and Local Government in Scotland since 1707* (London, 1960)
Richardson, R., *Death, Dissection and the Destitute* (London, 1988)
Roberton, J., *A Treatise on Medical Police*, 2 vols (Edinburgh, 1809), vol. II, 223–93
Rodger, R., 'The evolution of Scottish town planning', in G. Gordon and B. Dicks (eds), *Scottish Urban History* (Aberdeen, 1983), 71–91
Rodger, R., 'Wages, employment and poverty in the Scottish cities, 1841–1914', in G. Gordon (ed.), *Perspectives of the Scottish City* (Aberdeen, 1985), 25–63
Rodger, R., 'The Victorian building industry and the housing of the Scottish working class', in M. Doughty (ed.), *Building the Industrial City* (Leicester, 1986), 151–206
Rodger, R., *Housing in Urban Britain, 1780–1914* (Cambridge, 1995)
Rodger, R., *The Transformation of Edinburgh: Land, Property and Trust in the Nineteenth Century* (Cambridge, 2001; pbk edn, 2004)
Rodger, R., 'The "Common Good" and civic promotion: Edinburgh, 1860–1914', in R. Colls and R. Rodger (eds), *Cities of Ideas: Civil Society and Urban Governance in Britain, 1800–2000* (Aldershot, 2004), 144–77
Rodger, R., *Edinburgh's Colonies: Housing the Workers* (Argyll, 2011)
Rosen, G., 'Cameralism and the concept of medical police', *Bulletin of the History of Medicine*, 27 (1952), 21–42
Rosen, G., *From Medical Police to Social Medicine* (New York, 1974)
Rosner, L., *Medical Education in the Age of Improvement: Edinburgh Students and Apprentices, 1760–1826* (Edinburgh, 1991)
Rugg, J., 'The rise of cemetery companies in Britain, 1820–53', Stirling University Ph.D. thesis, 1992
Russell, J.B., 'On the "Ticketed Houses" of Glasgow', *Proceedings of the Royal Philosophical Society of Glasgow* (1888)
Schuyler, D., *The New Urban Landscape: the Redefinition of City Form in Nineteenth-century America* (Baltimore, 1986)
Serneri, S.N., 'Water pollution in Italy: the failure of the hygienic approach, 1890s–1960s', in C. Bernhardt and G. Massard-Guilbaud (eds), *The Modern Demon: Pollution in Urban and Industrial European Societies* (Clermont Ferrand, 2002), 157–78

Sheail, J., 'Town wastes, agricultural sustainability and Victorian sewage', *Urban History*, 23 (1996), 189–210

Sher, R.B., *Church and University in the Scottish Enlightenment: the Moderate Literati of Edinburgh* (Edinburgh, 1985)

Simpson, J., *Brief Reports of Lectures Delivered to the Working Classes of Edinburgh: on the means in their own power of improving their character & condition* (Edinburgh, 1844)

Sinclair, J., *Case for the Extension of the Municipal Boundary of Edinburgh and the Transference of Powers of the Police and Paving Boards to the Town Council* (Edinburgh, 1855)

Smith, A., *Lectures on Jurisprudence* [1762] (Oxford, 1978)

Smith, A., *Wealth of Nations*, Book V.i.b, 711 (R.H. Campbell and A. Skinner edn, Indianapolis, 1981)

Smith, F., *Life of Sir James Kay-Shuttleworth* (London, 1974 edn)

Smith, P.J., 'Pollution abatement in the nineteenth century: the purification of the Water of Leith', *Environment and Behavior*, 6 (1974), 3–36

Smith, P.J., 'The foul burns of Edinburgh: public health attitudes and environmental change', *Scottish Geographical Magazine*, 91 (1975), 25–37

Smith, P.J., 'The rehousing/relocation issue in an early slum clearance scheme: Edinburgh, 1865–1885', *Urban Studies*, 26 (1989), 100–14

Smith, P.J., 'Slum clearance as an instrument of sanitary reform: the flawed vision of Edinburgh's first slum clearance scheme', *Planning Perspectives*, 9 (1994), 1–27

Smout, T.C., 'The strange intervention of Edward Twistleton: Paisley in depression', in T.C. Smout (ed.), *The Search for Wealth and Stability* (London, 1979), 218–42

Stark, J., 'Report on the Mortality of Edinburgh and Leith, for the months of January and February 1846', *Edinburgh Medical and Surgical Journal*, 65 (1846), 523–8

Stark, J., *Inquiry into some points of the sanatory state of Edinburgh; the rate of mortality of its inhabitants since 1780; their average duration of life; the differences in the rate of mortality among its different classes, and among the married and single; and its comparative eligibility as a place of residence, and for the education of children* (Edinburgh, 1847)

Stark, J., 'Report on the Mortality of Edinburgh and Leith, for the months of January to May 1848', *Edinburgh Medical and Surgical Journal*, 70 (1848), 247–52

Stark, J., 'The Sanitary Condition of the Old Town of Edinburgh', *Journal of Public Health and Monthly Record of Sanitary Improvement*, 1 (1848), 268–9

Stark, J., 'Contribution to the vital statistics of Scotland', *Journal of the Statistical Society*, 14 (1851), 48–87

Stevenson, D., and MacPherson, C., *Report … Relative to the Drainage of the Water of Leith* (Edinburgh, 1861)

Stevenson, D. and A., *Report to the Police Commission of the City of Edinburgh* (Edinburgh, 1853)

Stewart, D., *Elements of the Philosophy of the Human Mind*, 3 vols (Edinburgh, 1792, 1814, 1827)

Sutcliffe, A., *The Autumn of Central Paris: the Defeat of Town Planning, 1850–1970* (London, 1970)

Sutherland, H., *A Time to Keep* (London, 1934)

Swinney, G.N., '"I am utterly disgusted …" – the Edinburgh Museum of Science and Art effecting moral decline?', *Review of Scottish Culture*, 16 (2004), 78–9

Swinney, G.N., 'Reconstructed visions: the philosophies that shaped part of the Scottish national collection', *Museum Management and Curatorship*, 21 (2006), 128–42

Swinney, G.N. and Heppell, D., 'Public and privileged access: a historical survey of admission charges and visitor figures for part of the Scottish National Collections', *Book of the Old Edinburgh Club*, 4 (1997), 69–84

Symonds, D.A., *Notorious Murders, Black Lanterns, & Moveable Goods: The Transformation of Edinburgh's Underworld in the Early Nineteenth Century* (Akron, 2006), 52–73

Szreter, S., 'The importance of social intervention in Britain's mortality decline *c.*1850–1914: a reinterpretation of the role of public health', *Social History of Medicine*, 1 (1988), 1–38

Szreter, S., 'Economic growth, disruption, deprivation, disease and death: on the importance of the politics of public health for development', *Population Development Review*, 23 (1997), 693–728

Szreter, S., 'Rethinking McKeown: the relationship between public health and social change', *American Journal of Public Health*, 92:5 (2002), 722–5

Tait, H.P., 'The Cholera Board of Health, 1831–34', *Medical Officer*, 98 (1957), 235

Taylor, A.S., *The Principles and Practice of Medical Jurisprudence* (London, 1865)

Thomson, M., *Report as to the Cause or Causes of the Offensive Smells in the West Side of the City, and from the Water of Leith* (Edinburgh, 1863)

Tyzack, R., '"No mean city"? The growth of civic consciousness in Aberdeen with particular reference to the work of the Police Commissioners', in T. Brotherstone and D.J. Withrington (eds), '*The City and its Worlds: Aspects of Aberdeen's History since 1794* (Glasgow, 1996), 150–67

Urquhart, R.M., *The Burghs of Scotland and the Burgh Police (Scotland) Act, 1833* (Motherwell, 1989)

Urquhart, R.M., *The Burghs of Scotland and the Police of Towns (Scotland) Act, 1850* (Motherwell, 1989)

Warren, A., 'Sir Robert Baden-Powell, the Scout movement and citizen training in Great Britain, 1900–1920', *English Historical Review*, 101 (1986), 376–98

White, B.M., 'Medical police. Politics and police: the fate of John Roberton', *Medical History*, 27 (1983), 407–22

Williams, C.A., 'The Sheffield Democrats' critique of criminal justice in the 1850s', in R. Colls and R. Rodger (eds), *Cities of Ideas: Civil Society and Urban Governance in Britain, 1800–2000* (Aldershot, 2004), 96–120

Williams, J.D., 'Edinburgh politics, 1832–1852', University of Edinburgh Ph.D. thesis, 1972, 50–2

Withrington, D.J., 'The Disruption: a century and a half of historical interpretation', *Records of the Scottish Church History Society*, 25 (1993), 118–53

Withers, C.W.J., *Urban Highlanders: Highland–Lowland Migration and Urban Gaelic Culture, 1700–1900* (East Linton, 1998)

Wohl, A., *Endangered Lives: Public Health in Victorian Britain* (London, 1983)

Womersley, J., 'The evolution of health information service', in G. McLachlan (ed.), *Improving the Common Weal: Aspects of Scottish Health Services, 1900–1984* (Edinburgh, 1987), 541–94

Worboys, M., 'Germ theories of disease and British veterinary medicine, 1860–1890', *Medical History*, 35 (1991), 308–27

Wood, A., *Report on the Condition of the Poorer Classes of Edinburgh* (Edinburgh, 1840)

Young, M. and Willmott, P., *Family and Kinship in East London* (London, 1957)

Youngson, A.J., *The Making of Classical Edinburgh* (Edinburgh, 1966)

Index

References to images are in italics. References to footnotes are indicated by 'n'. All streets and thoroughfares are listed under 'street'. Individual physicians and surgeons are listed under 'doctors' with cross references only where they are mentioned in the text in a role other than medicine. Dates and professions have been added where they are known and where they may aid identification or provide context to the narrative.

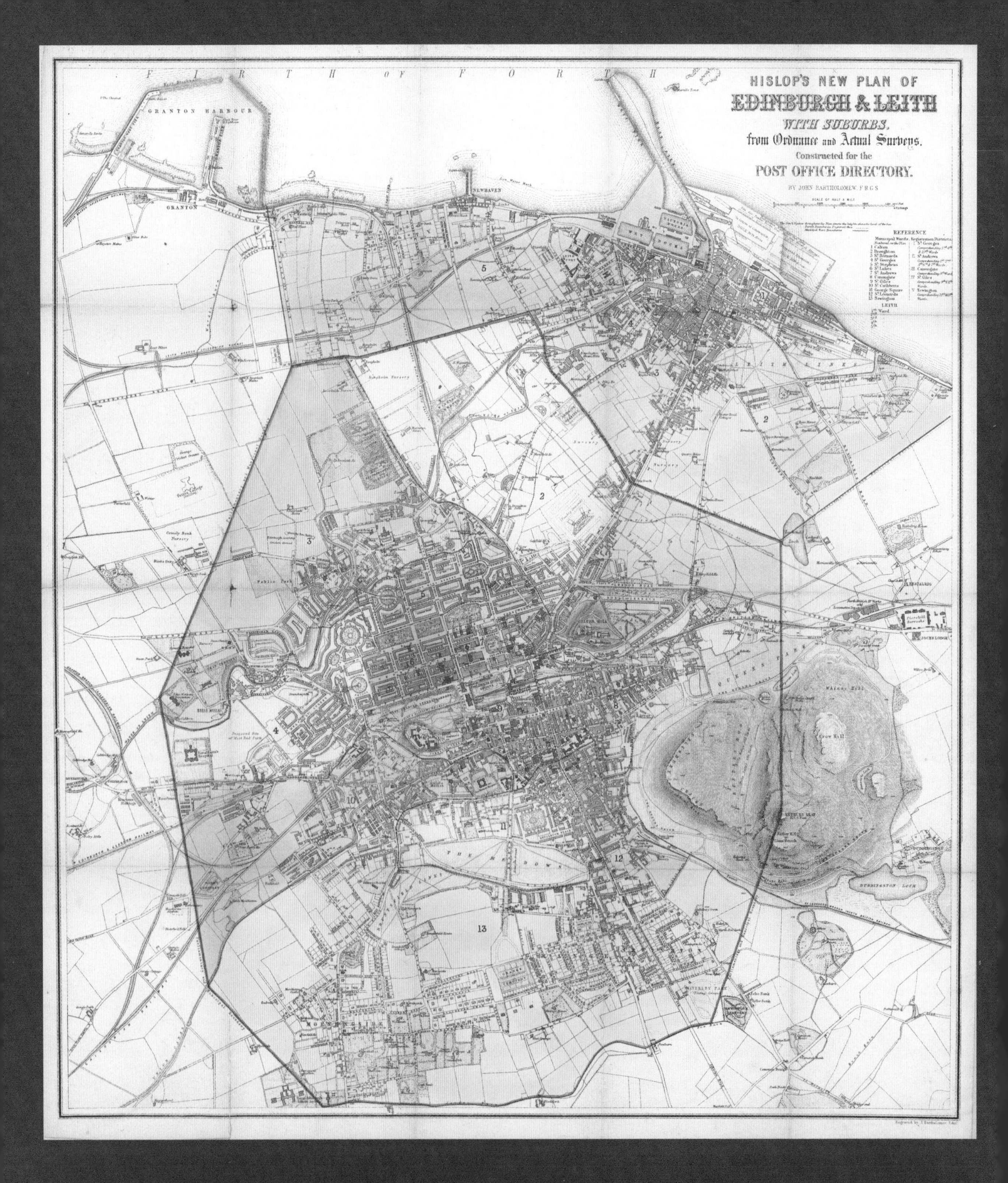

***Hislop's New Plan of Edinburgh & Leith … for the Post-Office Directory* (1865) showing municipal wards.**
Scale of original 6.0 inches to one mile.